Praise for *Success*

"Growing old may be the only event in lif
Daniel Levitin alleviates the fear with sc
ance so that we have more healthy years a
of this book is that Levitin not only tells us what to do and what not to do—he gracefully and eloquently shares the science behind how we can change our minds and brains, and how even small changes can reap large benefits. Share this book—especially with anyone you hope to grow old with."**—Diane Halpern, former president of the American Psychological Association and professor at Claremont McKenna College**

"We are living longer than past humans, and with this comes undeniable challenges to our physical and mental well-being. Building on the psychology of personality types and developmental neuroscience, Daniel Levitin will enthrall you with this fascinating story of how the human brain ages, as he reveals just how rewarding our later years can be."**—Joseph LeDoux, professor of neural science at New York University, director of the Emotional Brain Institute at the Nathan S. Kline Institute for Psychiatric Research, and author of *Anxious* and *The Deep History of Ourselves***

"A tour through a huge scientific literature, full of potentially life-changing nuggets, and laced with compelling personal experiences. The good news is that aging need not be dreaded but can be a time of health and creativity in the decades beyond seventy—and Levitin's got the science to back it up. Read this book. At any age."**—Michael S. Gazzaniga, director of the SAGE Center at UC Santa Barbara and author of *The Consciousness Instinct***

"An excellent perspective on aging and aging well. Dan's ability to combine science with personal insights, and reflections on various experiences of aging, captures the complexity of the subject, while still being easy to read. This fascinating book is especially important for young adults to understand all the aspects that go into healthy aging and to know that they can influence the outcome, starting at any time."**—Concetta Tomaino, executive director of the Institute for Music and Neurologic Function and an associate at the Albert Einstein College of Medicine**

"This book's breadth is impressive. Excellent popular science in the service of fending off aging."—***Kirkus Reviews***

"Dan is a long-time collaborator with us here at Salk, and in *Successful Aging*, he offers a compelling new look at the promise and effects of neuroplasticity. He's at his best here, communicating difficult scientific concepts in a way that anyone can understand. This is why his research talks at the Salk Institute are enormously popular, and everyone is abuzz about them for many months afterward."—**Ursula Bellugi, PhD, director of the Laboratory for Cognitive Neuroscience at the Salk Institute for Biological Studies**

"Levitin's book is quite extraordinary, literally. I rarely, if ever, have seen such a rigorous treatment of a health subject."—**David B. Teplow, professor of neurology at the David Geffen School of Medicine at UCLA and editor of *Progress in Molecular Biology and Translational Science***

"Here is a 'how-to' book for everyone's favorite alternative to death—aging. Bringing together the fields of developmental psychology and personality theory, Dr. Levitin shows us how to reach old age as the best version of ourselves: engaged, wise, and creative; emotionally resilient, cognitively flexible, and happy. *Successful Aging* is the fountain of youth, although you don't drink it, you read it."—**Eric Kaplan, Emmy-winning comedy writer of *The Simpsons*, *Late Show with David Letterman*, *The Big Bang Theory*, and *Young Sheldon***

"Dan Levitin's latest is an inspiring, hopeful, and useful message—expounding on the best lessons science and art can teach us about how to expand your potential as you age."—**Ben Folds, recording artist and *New York Times* bestselling author of *A Dream About Lightning Bugs***

"Society for too long has underestimated the value of people in their seventies, eighties, and nineties. Working in tandem with younger colleagues, the political, economic, and creative power we can contribute together could well trigger solutions to our biggest global problems. Daniel Levitin superbly defines the new longevity in a book that will change the way you think about aging."—**Vicente Fox, fifty-fifth president of Mexico**

"This evolving narrative builds as new topics are introduced in reaction to the previous topic, like chord changes in a great piece of music. Levitin's not just offering a compelling narrative but guiding the reader's imagination to a larger view of things—and that feels masterful."—**Mike Lankford, author of *Becoming Leonardo***

"*Successful Aging* is an ambitious and much-needed call for a 'new truth' about aging in the twenty-first century. Daniel Levitin uses what we know about brain science to make a powerful case for positively transforming how we think about aging. This is a fascinating and vital contribution to doing just that."—**George Vradenburg, chairman and cofounder of UsAgainstAlzheimer's**

"An eloquent spokesperson for our field, Levitin writes about the brain with an ease and familiarity that is captivating."—**the late David Hubel, Nobel Laureate for work in neuroplasticity**

ALSO BY DANIEL J. LEVITIN

This Is Your Brain on Music: The Science of a Human Obsession

The World in Six Songs: How the Musical Brain Created Human Nature

The Organized Mind: Thinking Straight in the Age of Information Overload

A Field Guide to Lies: Critical Thinking with Statistics and the Scientific Method

SUCCESSFUL AGING

A Neuroscientist Explores
the Power and Potential of Our Lives

Daniel J. Levitin

DUTTON

DUTTON

An imprint of Penguin Random House LLC
penguinrandomhouse.com

LIBRARY OF CONGRESS CATALOGING-IN-PUBLICATION DATA
Names: Levitin, Daniel J., author.
Title: Successful aging : a neuroscientist explores the power and potential of our lives / Daniel J. Levitin.
Description: First. | New York : Dutton, [2020] | Includes bibliographical references and index.
Identifiers: LCCN 2019026873 (print) | LCCN 2019026874 (ebook) | ISBN 9781524744182 (hardcover) | ISBN 9781524744199 (ebook) | ISBN 9781524746414 (international edition)
Subjects: LCSH: Brain—Aging. | Brain—Aging—Health aspects.
Classification: LCC QP376 .L43 2020 (print) | LCC QP376 (ebook) | DDC 612.8/2—dc23
LC record available at https://lccn.loc.gov/2019026873
LC ebook record available at https://lccn.loc.gov/2019026874

Printed in the United States of America
1 3 5 7 9 10 8 6 4 2

To my sweet wife, Heather, who never gets old

CONTENTS

INTRODUCTION xi

PART ONE
The Continually Developing Brain 1

1. INDIVIDUAL DIFFERENCES AND PERSONALITY 3
The search for the magic number

2. MEMORY AND YOUR SENSE OF "YOU" 31
The myth of failing memory

2.5. INTERLUDE 62
A brief biography of the brain

3. PERCEPTION 88
What our bodies tell us about the world

4. INTELLIGENCE 115
The problem-solving brain

5. FROM EMOTIONS TO MOTIVATION 146
Snakes, rickety bridges, *Mad Men,* and stress

6. SOCIAL FACTORS 179
Life with people

7. PAIN 205
It hurts when I do this

PART TWO

The Choices We Make 233

8. THE INTERNAL CLOCK 235

It's two A.M. Why am I hungry?

9. DIET 251

Brain food, probiotics, and free radicals

10. EXERCISE 280

Movement matters

11. SLEEP 295

Memory consolidation, DNA repair, and sleepy hormones

PART THREE

The New Longevity 311

12. LIVING LONGER 313

Telomeres, tardigrades, insulin, and zombie cells

13. LIVING SMARTER 344

Cognitive enhancement

14. LIVING BETTER 367

The greatest days of our lives

APPENDIX: REJUVENATING YOUR BRAIN 401

NOTES 403

ACKNOWLEDGMENTS 475

ART CREDITS 477

INDEX 479

INTRODUCTION

The poet Dylan Thomas wrote that one should not go gently into that good night, that old age should burn and rage at close of day. As a younger man reading that poem, I saw futility in those words. I saw aging only as a failing: a failing of the body, of the mind, and even of the spirit. I saw my grandfather suffer aches and pains. Once agile and proudly self-sufficient, by his sixties he struggled to swing a hammer and was unable to read the label on a box of Triscuit crackers without his glasses. I listened as my grandmother forgot words, and I cried when eventually she forgot what year it was.

At work, I watched as people neared retirement age, the spark gone from their eyes, the hope from their smiles, counting the days until they could walk away from it all, yet with only the vaguest plans about what they would do once they had so much free time, all day, every day.

But as I've grown older myself, and have spent more time with people who are in the last quarter of their lives, I've seen a different side of aging. My parents are now in their mideighties and are as engaged with life as they have ever been, immersed in social interactions, spiritual pursuits, hiking, and nature, and even starting new professional projects. They look old, but they feel like the same people they were fifty years ago, and this amazes them. Where certain faculties have slowed, they find that extraordinary compensatory mechanisms have kicked in—positive changes in mood and outlook, punctuated by the exceptional benefits of experience. Yes, older minds might process information more slowly than younger ones, but they can intuitively synthesize a lifetime of information and make smarter decisions based on decades of learning from their mistakes. Among the many advantages of being old, they are less fearful of calamities because they've been dealt a few in the past and managed to work through them. Resilience—both their own and each other's—is something they know they can count on. At the same time, they are comfortable with the idea that they may die soon. That's not the same as saying they want to die, but they no longer fear it. They've lived full lives and treat each new day as an opportunity for new experiences.

Brain researchers speculate that old age brings chemical changes in the brain that make it easier to accept death—to feel at ease with it rather than be frightened by it. As a neuroscientist, I've wondered why some people seem to age better than others. Is it genetics, personality, socioeconomic status, or just plain dumb luck? What is going on in the brain that drives these changes? What can we do to stem the cognitive and physical slowdown that accompanies aging? Many people thrive well into their eighties and nineties, while others seem to retreat from life, prisoners of their own infirmities, socially isolated and unhappy. How much control do we have over our outcomes, and how much is predetermined?

Marrying recent research in developmental neuroscience with the psychology of individual differences, *Successful Aging* sets out a new approach to how we think about our final decades. Drawing from diverse disciplines, this book demonstrates that aging is not simply a period of decay, but a unique developmental stage that—like infancy or adolescence—brings with it its own demands and its own advantages.

The book will show that how well we age depends on two parallel streams:

1. the confluence of a number of factors reaching back into our childhoods; and
2. our responses to stimuli in our environments, and shifts in our individual habits.

This provocative argument can revolutionize the way we plan for old age as individuals, family members, and citizens in industrial societies where the average life expectancy continues to rise. It offers choices we can make that will keep us mentally agile well into our eighties, nineties, and perhaps beyond. We need not stumble, stooped and passive, into that good night; we can live it up.

❖

Two of the teachers I had in college are now in their eighties and another is in his nineties. All are still active and whip-smart. One of them, Lewis R. Goldberg, now eighty-seven, is considered the father of modern-day scientific conceptions of personality—the unique compendium of traits and features that set us apart from one another and that can profoundly influence the course of our lives. He has found that personalities can change: You can improve yourself at any stage of life, becoming more conscientious, agreeable, humble—any number of things. This is surprising, and it upends decades of casual speculation. We tend to think of personality traits as being durable, persisting forever. (Think of the curmudgeon Larry David in TV's *Curb Your Enthusiasm.*) But personality traits are also malleable. And the degree to which habitual traits drive our behavior is influenced by the situations we find ourselves in and by our own striving to improve ourselves, to become better people.

The darker side of this, unfortunately, is that some encounters and environments can cause our personalities to change for the worse. Learning how to avoid certain environments, habits, and stimuli that influence our personalities in negative ways is a crucial part of aging well. This potential malleability of personality as we age is essential to understand. Dark shifts in personality are, regrettably, all too common in our world. We all know of people who have grown bitter, isolated, or depressed as they got older.

Much of this is culturally driven. In the 1960s, when I grew up, many young people couldn't wait to push old people out of the way. For all the tolerance, peace, and love that our Woodstock generation espoused, we were quick to try to sideline our parents' generation. We chanted, "Don't trust anyone over thirty," and we might as well have chanted, "Don't even *pay attention* to anyone over seventy." Roger Daltrey of the Who summed up a pervasive sense of derision toward the elderly when he sang, "I hope I die before I get old." My friends who were born in the 1930s and 1940s have shared with me stories of indignities, prejudices, and disrespect shown toward them by people of my generation.

Aging, as it has been depicted in the media and our collective consciousness for centuries, implies both physical and emotional pain and, in many cases, social isolation. As the body became more frail, intellectual faculties weakened, and diminished vision and hearing prevented the elderly from engaging with their communities as they once did. Retirement spelled the end of life's purpose and, sadly, seemed to accelerate the end of one's life.

My grandfather, a first-generation college student who worked his way through medical school to become one of the first radiologists in California, was pushed out of the very department he founded at his hospital, just because he turned sixty-five. From what we know today about diagnostic radiology, he was probably better at his job at sixty-five than when he was younger, because so much of it depends on pattern-matching circuits in the brain that improve with experience. The sense of marginalization and uselessness my grandfather experienced in the workplace was opposite what he had with us at home in the family—we loved and venerated him, and we were devastated when he died at sixty-seven. In a letter he wrote to the family before the surgery that ultimately cost him his life, he expressed deep sadness about the "loss of respect" for him at the hospital. I always suspected that this loss of respect had an impact on his stamina, resilience, and mood to such a degree that a minor surgical complication cost him his life.

I want to draw out explicitly what happens in the brain when we feel rejected or underappreciated. Our bodies react to insults, both psychological and physical, by releasing cortisol, the stress hormone. Cortisol is very useful if you need to invoke the fight-or-flight response—say, when you're confronted by an attacking tiger—but it is not so useful when you're dealing with longer-term psychological challenges such as loss of respect. The cortisol-induced stress reaction reduces immune-system function, libido, and digestion. This is why, when you're stressed, you might have an upset stomach. It makes sense for the fight-or-flight response to do this: It needs to direct all your resources to the temporary state of physically dealing with an imminent threat. But the psychological stresses that can come from interpersonal conflicts, left unresolved, can leave us in a physiologically stressed state for months or years. In contrast, when we're actively engaged and excited about life, our levels of mood-enhancing hormones such as serotonin and dopamine increase, and the production of NK (natural killer) and T cells (lymphocytes) also increases, strengthening our immune systems and cellular repair mechanisms. My grandmother, my family, and I might have enjoyed my grandfather's company a lot longer if social stressors hadn't come into play.

Fast-forward twenty-five years. My own father, a businessman, was strongly encouraged to retire when he was sixty-two, to make way for someone younger. Like his father before him, he felt pushed out and began to question his self-worth. His social world shrank, he began to suffer physical ailments, and he became depressed. But by then, in 1995, the tide was already turning. Society and employers were awakening to the Eastern idea that the elderly may be not only of some value, but of superior value. My father put out feelers and was offered a job teaching a course at the USC Marshall School of Business. Soon he was teaching a full load of four courses per semester. That was twenty-five years ago. My father just signed a four-year renewal to teach until he's eighty-nine. The students love him because he is able to pass on his real-world experience to them in a way that younger professors can't. And by the way, that depression and those physical ailments were dramatically reduced once he found meaningful work.

❖

Of course, finding ways to stay active and engaged is not always easy in old age, and it doesn't completely compensate for biological decline. But new medical advances and positive lifestyle changes can help us to find enhanced fulfillment in life where previous generations may not have been able to do so.

When I was in college, one of my favorite professors was John R. Pierce, a former director of the Jet Propulsion Laboratory, the inventor of satellite telecommunication, a prolific sci-fi writer, and the person who named the transistor when a team under his supervision invented it. I met him when he was eighty, in the second iteration of his "retirement," giving classes on sound and vibration. He invited me to dinner at his house once; we became friends and went out to dinner regularly. Around the time John turned eighty-seven, he grew depressed. One of the pastimes he enjoyed most was reading, but now his eyesight was failing. I bought him some large-type books and that perked him up for a few weeks, but much of what he wanted to read—technical books, science fiction—was not available in large type. I'd go over and read to him when I could, and I arranged for some Stanford students to do the same. But he still kept slipping. Then he was diagnosed with Parkinson's. His shaking bothered him. His memory was failing. He no longer found pleasure in things that he used to enjoy. And he was growing increasingly disoriented.

I suggested that he ask his doctor about taking Prozac, which was new at the time, and just being prescribed for the kinds of age-related problems he was facing. (Prozac helps to boost levels of serotonin in the brain—one of those mood-enhancing hormones I mentioned previously.) It was transformative. Although it didn't help the Parkinson's specifically, his attitude changed. He felt younger. He started holding dinner parties again, and lecturing to students, something he had given up doing just a year earlier. A simple chemical change in his brain gave him a second wind. John lived to ninety-two, and much of those last five years were filled with joy and satisfaction for him. And for me, too—it felt like getting a second chance with my grandfather who had died too soon.

I saw John two weeks before he passed at age ninety-two, and he was excitedly planning some new experiments he wanted to do. That's the way to go out.

At the time I knew John, I was young and not thinking about my own inevitable aging. But in the decades since then, in experiencing my own gradual mood shifts and in talking to a great many research colleagues and doctors, I've come to see a future in which we can plan ahead to fend off some of the adverse effects of aging; a future in which we can harness what we know about neuroplasticity to write our own next chapters the way we want them to come out; a future in which healthy lifestyle choices and a broader use of antidepressants and other medications can temper or reverse the effects of depression and other changes in mood that we have for too long assumed were an irreversible part of the aging process. In addition, new innovations in medical science and treatment protocols are sure to become available.

For example, recent discoveries about changes in sleep chemistry and neuronal waveforms suggest a different approach to this most basic of human activities. Sleep deprivation at any age is bad for you. It has been tied to diabetes in pregnancy, postpartum depression in new fathers, and bipolar disorder at all ages. You may have read that "old people" don't need as much sleep as young people and can get by on four or five hours a night. This myth has recently been exposed by Matthew Walker at UC Berkeley. It's not that we need less sleep as we get older—it's that changes in the aging brain make it difficult for older adults to get the sleep they need. And the consequences are serious. Sleep deprivation in the aged is directly responsible for cognitive decline, not to mention increased risk of cancer and heart disease. Grandma didn't forget where she put her glasses because she's senile—it's because she's sleep-deprived. Walker has found evidence that sleep deprivation increases the risk of Alzheimer's.

Alzheimer's disease (AD) is now the third leading cause of death in the United States. This doesn't mean we should jump to the conclusion that there is an epidemic in the making, or that environmental toxins are causing it. They might be, but AD is primarily an old person's disease; medical advances have made it so that we are living longer, and that means we are living long enough to *get* Alzheimer's. Now, for reasons we don't yet understand, AD is selective with regard to sex. Sixty-five percent of patients are women, and a woman's chances of getting AD now exceed her chances of getting breast cancer.

Approximately two-thirds of the overall risk that you'll get Alzheimer's comes from your genes, with the remaining one-third associated with environmental factors such as whether or not you have a history of depression or head injuries. In this way, events of childhood can have an effect many, many decades later. Recent science demonstrates that environmental stimuli, behavior, and luck all play a role, as I will show throughout the book. On the biological side, a brain with Alzheimer's is easily recognized by the shrinkage of the hippocampus—the seat of memory—and of the outer layers of the cerebral cortex (the part of the brain associated with complex thought and movements). You may have heard of amyloids, aggregates of proteins that have been found in the brains of Alzheimer's patients. One particular protein, beta-amyloid, begins destroying synapses (connections between the brain's neurons) before it clumps into plaques that cause the death of neurons themselves.

Dale Bredesen, a neurologist who studied under my colleague Stan Prusiner at UCSF, has studied these interacting factors for thirty years. His Bredesen Protocol is the topic of a *New York Times* bestseller. Fending off Alzheimer's, he says, involves five key components: a diet rich in vegetables and good fats, oxygenating the blood through moderate exercise, brain training exercises, good sleep hygiene, and a regimen of supplements individually tailored to each person's own needs, based on blood and genetic testing. The Bredesen Protocol is still in its early stages of validation—the primary proof of concept was based on only ten patients. The patients have to be in very early stages of Alzheimer's. And since the protocol is new, they haven't had anyone on it for more than five years. The protocol may or may not help, but at least the first four parts won't cause any harm—we don't know enough about the supplements—and to many it makes sense to start following these healthy lifestyle practices on the chance that they will end up being scientifically validated.

Prusiner won the Nobel Prize for discovering prions, proteins that can accumulate and cause neurogenerative diseases like Creutzfeldt-Jakob disease, a fatal condition that is characterized by memory loss and behavioral changes. Sound familiar? These are the markers of Alzheimer's, of course, and Prusiner now believes that prions, because they can assemble into amyloid fibrils, are responsible for Alzheimer's and Parkinson's disease. At the cutting edge of this research is the idea of neuroinflammation as a precursor to Alzheimer's, appearing long before clinical signs and symptoms. This is because the visible symptoms appear only during the actual destruction of brain regions—the cognitive effects we notice, such as memory loss and mood change, reflect relatively late stages of the underlying disease process. Depressive-like symptoms, such as loss of interest and energy, often appear long before other, more serious manifestations.

Several teams of scientists have found that a chronic inflammatory process precedes the onset of Alzheimer's, and this strongly suggests a potential health-care strategy involving anti-inflammatory drugs, one that we might see in widespread use in the next few years. Current research is focused on whether anti-inflammatories (such as ibuprofen) can ease symptoms once they've arrived, or whether the drugs must be given before the onset of symptoms and thus act as a preventative (which is appearing to be the case). Another cutting-edge treatment being investigated involves immunization with antibodies that can prevent the formation of amyloid fibrils in the first place.

We talk about life span as the length of time that one is alive. Except for cases of death by accident, most of us will die of some kind of disease, or our parts will just wear out. You can think of the time line of your life span as being divided into two parts: the period of time that you're generally healthy (the health span) and the period of time that you're sick (the disease span). Obviously, it is important to minimize the disease span.

Consider two friends who die at one hundred, both with identical life spans but very different disease spans. Grace begins a gradual health decline at fifty and by eighty requires twenty-four-hour care. Eloise begins to decline at seventy but the real health problems don't kick in until ninety-five. All of us would prefer to have that extra twenty years of smooth sailing, followed by an extra fifteen years of happy life before disease limits our activities. I wrote this book on the premise that it is never too late to tilt the balance in our favor, to increase our health span by making important changes to how we approach aging.

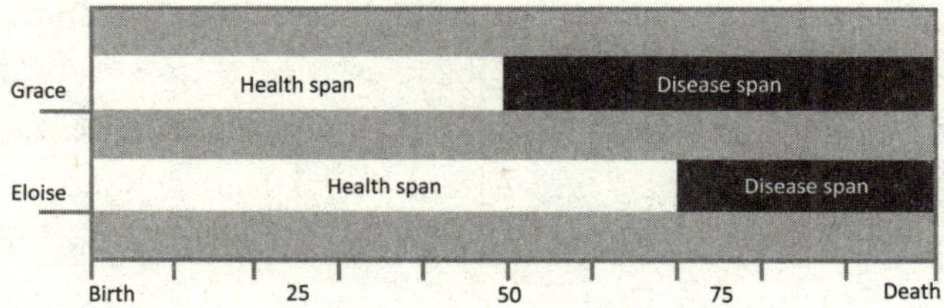

The environmental factors I've described here can have either a positive or negative impact on the way we experience old age—our engagement with the world, our habits, our will to live, and medicine. A second strand of the narrative for *Successful Aging* is the developmental side, a story that begins, ironically, in childhood.

I mentioned earlier that social stress can lead to a compromised immune system. That happens at any age. Michael Meaney at McGill University showed that the kind of care a mother gives to her offspring alters the chemistry of the DNA in certain genes involved in physiological stress responses. Rat pups who are licked more in the first six days of life grow into adult rats who are far more secure and less likely to be afflicted with stress. In particular, those baby rats that received a great deal of licking and grooming produced fewer stress hormones when dealing with a challenging or stressful situation than the rats who received less care, and here's the kicker: The effects held well into adulthood.

Meaney has gone on to show comparable effects in humans, and the opposite set of outcomes for children who are neglected or abused as infants. In the stress story, early experience interacts with genetics and brain structure. "Women's health is critical," Meaney says. "The single most important factor determining the quality of mother-offspring interactions is the mental and physical health of the mother. This is equally true for rats, monkeys and humans." Parents living in poverty, suffering from mental illness, or facing great stress are much more likely to be fatigued, irritable, and anxious. "These states clearly compromise the interactions between parents and their children," he says. And, subsequently, they compromise their children's brain chemistry and resilience in the face of setbacks—even future ones.

Meaney emphasizes that "human brain development occurs within a socioeconomic context, and childhood socioeconomic status (SES) influences neural development—particularly of the systems that subserve language and executive function" (deciding what to do next and then doing it). Research has shown the importance of prenatal factors, parent-child interactions, and cognitive stimulation in the home environment in promoting healthy, lifelong neural development. These findings should direct us toward improving the programs and policies that are designed to alleviate SES-related disparities in mental health and academic achievement.

Nurture (or lack thereof) early in life affects the development of a number of brain systems selectively, such as glucocorticoid (GLUE-co CORT-ick-oid) receptors in the hippocampus, which are a primary component of the stress response, part of the feedback mechanism in the immune system that reduces inflammation. Meaney also showed that parenting affects the function of the pituitary and adrenal glands, which regulate growth, sexual function, and the production of cortisol and adrenaline. Early traumas can last a lifetime. They can be overcome with the right behavioral and pharmacological interventions, but it takes some work. More cuddles and hugs go a long way, particularly in the vulnerable first year of life. As parents (and grandparents and teachers), our choices about how we raise our children in their first years will have a far greater impact on what their last years look like than we might previously have recognized.

A third strand of *Successful Aging*, along with environmental influences and neural development, is that I've come to see old age as a unique period of growth, a life stage with its own distinct character, rather than a period of decline or a gradual turning down of the dials and knobs one by one.

When many of us think of aging, what first comes to mind might be a panoply of age-related problems that we're all familiar with: loss of vision, loss of hearing, aches and pains. What exactly happens when the brain and body age—what physiological changes affect our experience of ourselves and others? I'll delve into these questions in this book, including brain cell atrophy, DNA sequence damage, compromised cellular repair functions, and neurochemical and hormonal changes.

I'll also explore some effects that are just as common but less talked about. For example, most of us experience metabolic changes that mean you can't just continue eating the same things you've always eaten and maintain your weight or your figure. We may become lactose intolerant. (Evolutionary forces were mainly concerned with digesting mother's milk when we're young, not eating ice cream when we're fifty.) Our digestive system experiences changes that, along with causing lactose intolerance, may make us gassier as we age. Our skin becomes drier. Our eyes become drier. Caffeine may affect us differently or stop providing its beneficial effects entirely. Processing refined sugar becomes more difficult as our pancreas ages. *Successful Aging* will tell you what to expect, or perhaps explain some of the things you're already experiencing. But this is not a book about problems. My goal is to provide some solutions, guidelines, and helpful tips from the cutting edge of scientific medicine about how to live fully and happily, in a way that pushes these infirmities and indignities to the background and allows us to fully experience the meaningful things in the third act of our lives.

❖

Now that the Woodstock generation is entering our sixties and seventies, we have a chance to change the status quo about the role older people play in daily life. Of course, this satisfies our own self-interest, but, more important, it can help to rekindle our generation's ideal of improving society, ideals like respecting the planet and all the living beings who call it home, helping those less fortunate than ourselves, promoting tolerance and inclusiveness, and allowing people who are different from us to embrace, not be embarrassed by, those differences.

The cost of sidelining the elderly is enormous in lost economic and artistic productivity, severed family connections, and diminished opportunities. We can begin to model better behavior by embracing those who are a generation ahead of us—our parents' generation. And we can adopt practices that will keep us, as older beings, relevant and engaged with others well into our eighties and nineties . . . and perhaps beyond. I argue here for a very different vision of old age, one that sees our final decades as a period of blossoming, a resurgence of life that does not chase after our younger years, but instead embraces the gifts that time can bring.

What would it mean for all of us to think of the elderly as resource rather than burden and of aging as culmination rather than denouement? It would mean harnessing a human resource that is being wasted or, at best, underutilized. It would promote stronger family bonds and stronger bonds of friendship among us all. It would mean that important decisions at all scales, from personal matters to international agreements, would be informed by experience and reason, along with the perspective that old age brings. And it might even mean a more compassionate world. Among the chemical changes we see in the aging brain are a tendency toward understanding, forgiveness, tolerance, and acceptance. While older adults may become more set in their ways, and there is a tendency toward conservatism, they can at the same time become more accepting of individual differences and appreciative of the struggles that others have had to face. Older adults can bring a much-needed compassion to a world being rent by impatience, intolerance, and lack of empathy.

❖

We have a silo problem in my field of cognitive neuroscience. There's a tendency for researchers to talk to people in their own area, and not to talk across areas. In the last thirty years we've seen big, transformative advances in the understanding of many core ideas about personality, emotions, and brain development. But few people in one area talk to people in another, and so we're left with a situation where neither medical professionals nor the public are able to leverage these advances for our individual and common good.

I was extraordinarily fortunate when I started out, to have mentors who were working in diverse areas, and all of them are still active—personality psychologists (like Lew Goldberg and Sarah Hampson, now eighty-seven and sixty-eight, respectively), cognitive psychologists (Michael Posner and Roger Shepard, now eighty-three and ninety, respectively), and developmental neuroscientists (Ursula Bellugi, now eighty-eight, and Susan Carey, now seventy-seven). This led me to bridge two areas that have maintained separate intellectual traditions—developmental neuroscience and individual differences (personality) psychology. The more I study the intersection of these two, the more intrigued I am at how they can help us to understand the aging brain and the choices all of us can make to maximize our chances of living long, happy, and productive lives. The intersection of these two scientific fields, and how they apply to aging, is the core theme that runs throughout *Successful Aging,* and something that no one else has written about for a popular audience.

The developmental neuroscience view I will present here is that it is the interactions among genes, culture, and opportunity that are the biggest determinants of

- the trajectory our lives take;
- how our brains will change; and
- whether or not we'll be healthy, engaged, and happy throughout our life span.

No matter what age we are, our brains are always changing in response to pressures from genes, culture, and opportunity. The choices we make dictate much of the lives we lead. But we are also affected by random things that happen to us, and the choices that others make. Opportunity, or lack thereof, is often a matter of luck, governed by large historical forces, such as wealth, plagues, access to clean water, education, and good laws. In ways both large and small your brain has been changed by your life's experiences, whatever they are—by disappointment, love, interactions with key people, successes, illnesses, accidental injuries, pain, environmental toxins. In short, your brain is continually being changed by life itself.

I add to this perspective the rich body of work on individual differences. The story of traits—the ways in which we understand our individual differences—is one of the most fascinating stories in modern science. It traces its roots back to Aristotle, who explained differences in personalities among individuals as differences in their "matter." The eighteenth-century scientist Franz Joseph Gall and the nineteenth-century scientist Sir Francis Galton launched the modern study of individual differences, with Gall even anticipating the modern neuroscientific idea that specific mental functions can be localized to different parts of the brain. (Gall invented phrenology, the study of bumps on the head; this has now been shown to be ridiculous, but his primary hypothesis of localization of brain function still stands today.) Gordon Allport, Hans Eysenck, Amos Tversky, and Lew

Goldberg, among many talented others, established individual differences as a science and a rigorous field.

Individual differences psychology seeks to both characterize and quantify the thousands of ways that we humans differ from one another. It uses relatively sophisticated mathematical-statistical tools, such as principal components analysis, and seeks to understand not just the ways we differ from one another, but also the roots of these differences. The goal of this work has always been to predict others' future behaviors—if I know that you're conscientious, for example, will I have a better chance of knowing how you'll react to a certain situation than if I didn't know that about you?

❖

So what can we do to maintain strength of body, mind, and spirit while coming to terms with the limitations that aging can bring? What can we learn from those who age joyously, remaining vital and engaged well into their eighties, nineties, and even beyond? How do we adapt our culture to service the needs of aging generations while also taking greater advantage of their wisdom, experience, and motivation to contribute to society?

Throughout this book, I'll be reinforcing the lifestyle concept that we *can* change our personalities and our responses to the environment, while continually adapting to the random and unpredictable things life throws at us. This concept has five parts: Curiosity, Openness, Associations, Conscientiousness, and Healthy practices, what I call the COACH principle. This is not another book telling you to do sudoku. *Successful Aging* will explain what is going on in our brains as we age, and what we can do about it, based on a rigorous analysis of neuroscientific evidence.

Successful Aging has three aims: first, to harness our knowledge so that we can anticipate changes—both positive and negative—and put systems in place that will ease our transitions and minimize the possibility of unwanted outcomes. These can be as simple as establishing a good relationship with your doctor, taking supplements to improve myelination of the nervous system, and hiding a key in a lockbox in case you forget yours in the house (as I once did in subzero temperatures—*before* I had a lockbox). There are definite things we can do to dampen the ill effects of memory loss, perceptual loss, and the shrinking social circles that often accompany aging. We can fight to reverse the tendency to narrow our interests, to become set in our ways, and to fear even moderate risk taking. We can learn to exploit the wisdom and skills that we have attained, becoming much-sought-after friends, rather than forgotten old people.

Second, this book aims to stimulate all of us to think about what ingredients presage a feeling of life well-lived when we look back from the end of life. What decisions can we make, both ahead of time and in the present moment, that will maximize our life satisfaction and infuse our lives with meaning? In previous books, I've been vocal about the overuse of social media, including Facebook. Don't get me wrong—I use them, and I think that they are a fantastic way of staying in touch with our friends and family who are scattered across great distances. But when you're at the end of your life, lying on your deathbed, the research literature strongly predicts you won't be saying, "I wish I had spent more time on Facebook." Instead, you'll probably be saying, "I wish I had spent more time with loved ones," or, "I wish I had done more to make a difference in the world."

Ultimately, this book aims to help us think completely differently about aging, as individuals, as community members, as a society; it aspires to advance the evolution of a culture that embraces the gifts of the elderly, weaving cross-generational interactions into the fabric of everyday experience. By looking at the science of the brain—specifically the insights from developmental neuroscience and individual differences psychology—this book seeks to induce a transformative understanding of the aging process, the final chapter of our human story.

When older people look back on their lives and are asked to pinpoint the age at which they were happiest, what do you suppose they say? Maybe age eight, when they had few cares? Maybe their teenage years because of all the activity and the discovery of sex? Maybe their college years, or the first years of starting a family? Wrong. The age that comes up most often as the happiest time of one's life is eighty-two! The goal of this book is to help raise that number by ten or twenty years. Science says it can be done. And I'm with science.

PART ONE

THE CONTINUALLY DEVELOPING BRAIN

What are the determinants in how we age? The different systems in our brains age at different rates. Some systems decline as others actually increase in efficiency and effectiveness. The basic message we hear in popular culture, that aging is a time of unmitigated decline, is not accurate. Yes, some things do slow down, but our health, happiness, and mental sparkle need not. The latest neuroscientific research suggests an entirely new way of thinking about aging—about memory, our perceptual systems, intelligence, even about motivation, pain, and our social lives. You might think, as I used to, that the story of why some of us age better than others has to do with all of these cognitive and emotional factors. In fact, the biggest single determinant of living a productive and happy life is something that you're born with (partly) and something that you can decide to change: your personality.

1

INDIVIDUAL DIFFERENCES AND PERSONALITY

The search for the magic number

I visited a day care center for preschoolers recently and was struck by how early the differences in children's traits and individual dispositions show up. Some children are more outgoing, while others are shy; some like to explore the environment and take risks, while others are more fearful; some get along well with others and some are bullies—even by age four. Young parents who have more than one child see immediate differences in the dispositions of siblings, as well as differences between their offspring and themselves.

At the other end of life, there are clear differences in how people age—some people simply seem to fare better than others. Even setting aside differences in physical health, and the various diseases that might overcome us late in life, some older adults live more dynamic, engaged, active, and fulfilling lives than others. Can you look at a five-year-old and tell whether they will be a successful eighty-five-year-old? Yes, you can.

The discovery that aging and health are related to personality was the result of a lot of work. First, scientists had to figure out how to measure and define personality. What is it? How do you observe it accurately and quantitatively? Here, they may have taken inspiration from Galileo, who said, "The job of the scientist is to measure what is measurable and to render measurable that which is not." And so they did.

Among the most solid findings is that a child's personality affects adult health outcomes later in life. Take, for example, a child who was always getting into trouble in elementary school and continued to do so as a preteen. As a teenager, they might have smoked cigarettes, drunk alcohol, and used marijuana. In personality terms, we might say that this teenager was sensation- and adventure-seeking, high on the quality of extraversion, low on conscientiousness and emotional stability. The kid would have been at increased risk for hard drug use, or being killed in a motor vehicle accident while driving drunk. If they survived these increased risks in young adulthood but didn't change their habits, they'd enter middle age with a highly inflated risk of lung cancer from smoking or liver damage from drinking. Even more subtle behaviors can influence outcomes many decades later: Early and compulsive exposure to the sun and sun tanning; poor dental hygiene; poor exercise habits; and obesity all take their toll.

One of the pioneers in the relationship between personality and aging is Sarah Hampson, a research scientist at the Oregon Research Institute. As Hampson notes, "Lack of self-control may result in behaviors that increase the probability of exposure to dangerous or traumatic situations and adversely affect health through long-lasting biological consequences of stress." She has found that childhood is a critical period for laying down patterns of behavior with biological effects that endure into adulthood. If you want to live a long and healthy life, it helps to have had the right upbringing. Childhood personality traits, assessed in elementary school, predict a person's lipid levels, blood glucose, and waist size forty years later. These three markers, in turn, predict risk for cardiovascular disease and diabetes. The same childhood traits even predict life span.

Although these correlations between early childhood and late adulthood personality are robust, they tell only a part of the story. People age differently, and part of that story has to do with the interaction of genetics, environment, and opportunity (or luck). Scientists developed a mathematical way of tracking personality, comparing traits as they differ across individuals or change within a person over time. With it, we can talk about age-related, culture-related, and medically induced changes in personality, such as occur with Alzheimer's disease. Often one of the first indications of a problem with your brain is a change in personality.

And in the past few years, developmental science has shown that people, even older adults, can meaningfully change—we do not have to live out a life that was paved for us by genetics, environment, and opportunity. The great psychologist William James wrote that personality was "set in plaster" by early adulthood, but fortunately he was wrong.

The idea that people retain the capacity to change throughout their life span didn't take hold until the midseventies, when an idea first put forward by psychologist Nancy Bayley was popularized by the German developmental psychologist Paul Baltes:

> Most developmental researchers do accept the notion that developmental change is not restricted to any specific stage of the life-span and that, depending upon the function and the environmental context, behavior change can be pervasive and rapid at all ages. In fact . . . the rate of change is greatest in infancy and old age.

Not everyone takes advantage of this capacity, but it is there, like the ability to adjust your diet or your wardrobe. The events of your childhood can be overcome and transformed based on experiences you have later in life. Bayley and Baltes' big idea was that no single period of life holds supremacy over another.

Of course, the idea that people can change is the entire basis of modern psychotherapy. People seek psychiatrists and psychologists because they want to change, and modern psychiatry and psychology are largely effective in treating or curing a great number of mental disorders and stressors, especially phobias, anxiety, stress disorders, relationship problems, and mild to moderate depression. Some of these volitional changes revolve around improved lifestyle choices, while others entail changing our personalities, sometimes only slightly, to give us the best chance of aging well. To implement the changes that will be most effective, each of us might think about the fundamental components of how we are now, how we used to be, and how we'd like to be.

The collection of dispositions and traits that we have in any given period comprise our personalities. All cultures tend to describe people using trait-based labels, such as *generous*, *interesting*, and *reliable* (on the positive side) or *stingy*, *boring*, and *erratic* (on the negative side), along with more or less neutral or context-dependent terms such as *boyish* and *breezy*. This "trait" approach, however, can obscure two important facts: (1) we often display different traits as situations change, and (2) we can change our traits.

Few people are generous, interesting, or reliable all the time—opportunity and the fluidly evolving situations in which we find ourselves can exert a strong pull on what may be genetic predispositions toward certain behaviors and certain habitual ways of presenting ourselves to the world. Traits are probabilistic descriptions of behavior. Someone who is described as high on one trait (having a lot of it) will display that trait more often and more intensely than someone low on that trait. Someone who is agreeable has a greater probability of displaying agreeableness than someone who is disagreeable, but disagreeable people are still agreeable some of the time, just as introverts are extraverted some of the time.

Culture plays a role as well, both macro- and microculture. What is considered shy, reserved behavior in the United States (macrolevel culture) might be regarded as perfectly normal in Japan. And staying within the United States for the moment (microlevel culture), behavior that is considered acceptable in a hockey game might not be acceptable in the boardroom.

Booker T. Washington wrote that "character, not circumstance," makes the person. Ralph Waldo Emerson wrote, "No change of circumstances can repair a defect of character." While character makes for a good story or poem, in reality we are less shaped by character traits than we think, and more than we realize by the circumstances that life deals us—and our responses to those circumstances. It would be nice to be able to grade these circumstances from severely deleterious to benign, but what makes that impossible to do is individual differences in the way we respond to things. Some children who were (or felt) abandoned by their parents grow up to be well-adjusted, do-gooding members of society; others become axe murderers. Resilience, grit, and gratitude for the small things in life ("at least I still have food to eat") are personality traits that are unevenly distributed in the population.

We think of our genes as influencing physical traits, like hair color, skin color, and height. But genes also influence mental and personality traits, such as self-assuredness, a tendency toward compassion, and how emotionally variable we are. Look at a room full of one-year-olds and it is apparent that some are more calm than others, some more independent, some loud, some quiet. Parents with more than one child marvel at how different their personalities were from the start. I carefully referred to genes *influencing* traits because the effect of genes is not chiseled in stone. Your genes don't *dictate* how you'll be, but they do provide a set of constraints, limits on how your personality will be shaped. Genetics is not an edict—the traits that our genes contribute to still need to navigate the twisty and unpredictable roads of culture and opportunity. Complex traits are best described as emergent properties that you cannot read in any one gene, nor even in a large set of genes, because how the genes express themselves over time is critical to the development of the trait as a social reality.

Genes can be present in your body but in a dormant state, waiting for the right environmental trigger to activate them—what is called gene expression. A traumatic experience, a good or bad diet, how and when you sleep, or contact with an inspiring role model can cause chemical modifications to your genes that in turn cause them to wake up and become activated, or to go to sleep and turn off. The way the brain wires itself up, both in the womb and throughout the life span, is a complex tango between genetic possibilities and environmental factors. Neurons become connected whenever you learn something, but this is subject to genetic constraints. If you've inherited genes that contribute to making you five feet tall, no amount of learning is likely to get you into the NBA (although Spud Webb is five foot seven and Muggsy Bogues is five foot three). More subtly, if your genes constrain the auditory memory circuits in your brain—perhaps because they favor visual-spatial cognition—you're unlikely to become a superstar musician no matter how many lessons you take, because musicianship relies on auditory memory.

One way to think about gene expression is to think of your life as a film or multiyear TV series. Think of your DNA as the script: the set of instructions, dialogue, and stage directions for all the participants in the film. Your cells are the actors. Gene expression is the way that the actors decide to express that script. The actors may bring a certain interpretation to those words, based on their experience, and might surprise even the writers.

And, of course, the actors interact with and play off one another, for better or for worse. Jason Alexander, the actor who played George Costanza on *Seinfeld,* complained about how difficult it was to work with Heidi Swedberg (who played George's fiancée, Susan). "I couldn't figure out how to play off of her. . . . Her instincts for doing a scene, where the comedy was, and mine were always misfiring." Julia Louis-Dreyfus and Jerry Seinfeld had similar complaints and reportedly said that doing scenes with her was "impossible." But the chemistry between Alexander, Louis-Dreyfus, Seinfeld, and Michael Richards (Cosmo Kramer) was palpable, making *Seinfeld* the most successful comedy series in history.

Your genes, then, give you a kind of life script with only the most general things sketched out. And from there, you can improvise. Culture affects the ways you interpret that script, as do opportunity and circumstance. And then, once you interpret the script, it influences the way others respond to you. Those responses in your social world can change your brain's wiring and chemistry, in turn affecting how you'll respond to future events and which genes turn on and off—over and over again, cascading in complexity.

The second feature in the triad, *culture,* plays an important role in our understanding of traits. Humility is more valued in Mexico than in the United States, and more valued in rural Wisconsin than on Wall Street. Polite in Tel Aviv might be thought of as rude in Ottawa. The terms we use to describe others are not absolutes; they are culturally relative—when we describe differences in personality traits, we're necessarily talking about how an individual compares to their society and to their societal norms.

Family is a microculture, and traditions, outlook, political and social views differ widely, especially within large industrialized countries. Go door to door in any town or city and you'll find a wide range of attitudes about things as mundane as whether friends can just drop by or need to schedule in advance; how often teeth should be flossed (if at all); or whether TV and device time are regulated. And these unique family cultural values map onto particular personality traits: spontaneity, conscientiousness, and willingness (or at least ability) to follow rules. Culture is a potent factor in who we become.

The third part of the developmental triad is *opportunity.* Opportunity and circumstance play a larger part in behavior than most of us appreciate, and they do this in two different ways: how the world treats us, and the situations we find (or put) ourselves in.

Fair-skinned children burn more quickly in the sun than dark-skinned children and so may spend less time outdoors; skinny children can explore the insides of drainage pipes and the tops of trees more easily than heavy children. You may start out with an adventure-seeking personality, but if your body won't let you realize it, you may seek other experiences, or adventure in less physical ways (like video games—or math).

Apart from these physical features, we all play roles, in our families and in society. The eldest child in a multichild household tends to take on some of the parenting and instruction of the younger ones; the youngest child may be relatively coddled or ignored, depending on the parents; the middle child may find herself thrust into the role of peacemaker. These factors influence our development, but again, as with genes, they are not deterministic—we can break free of them to improvise, to create our own futures, but it takes some effort (and for some, a lot of false starts, failures, and therapy).

How the World Treats Us

You might assume that identical twins end up with similar personalities just because they share identical (or near-identical) genes. But it might also be due to the fact that, to some extent, the world treats people who look alike in similar ways. People generally react with certain biases to the way you look, and by the time you were twelve or so, you probably recognized a pattern in how others reacted to you. Skin color, weight, and attractiveness are key determinants of how people are treated by teachers, strangers, and, unfortunately, the police. In one study of St. Petersburg, Florida, police department operations, male, nonwhite, poor, and younger suspects were all treated with more physical force, irrespective of their behavior.

Suppose there is something about your face and physique that makes you look mean—a certain way that your eyebrows curl downward toward your eyes, a squinty look to your eyelids, deep creases around your mouth—what is colloquially known as "resting bitch face." According to *The Washington Post,* actress Kristen Stewart is the poster child for it, and Anna Kendrick is a self-described sufferer. (It applies to males as well, including Kanye West.) You may find that people are wary around you and even fear you. You may be kind and gentle on the inside, but after a lifetime of being misjudged, of people treating you suspiciously, you could turn cold in your social interactions, a real-life Shrek—the ogre who looks mean and frightens people but has a heart of gold.

One way this has been studied experimentally is to look at inter-rater agreement. Participants in an experiment meet strangers, or view photographs or videos of strangers, and then have to describe those strangers using a range of personality terms. The assumption is that, if you don't know someone, your judgments of them will be based on their physical appearance—the particulars of their face, body type, dress, and body language. Studies like these go back to the early work in the sixties of Lew Goldberg at the University of Oregon and the Oregon Research Institute. These studies found consistent agreement across a variety of personality traits, such as *sociable, extraverted, good-natured, responsible, calm, conscientious,* and *intellectual* just based on what someone looked like. There is far less consistency in judgments for other terms such as *agreeable, neurotic,* and *emotionally stable.*

Of course, a bunch of strangers agreeing that someone is *responsible* doesn't make them so. All that these experiments show is that when we interact with strangers, we bring some social-psychological baggage. The consensus about that baggage suggests that people within a culture share beliefs about how personality traits are linked to physical characteristics. When participants' ratings of themselves were compared to the strangers' ratings, some terms show high agreement, especially *sociable* and *responsible.* And although our self-perceptions are often flat-out wrong or distorted by ego needs, sometimes they are accurate—the problem is, we don't know which times.

The culture we live in has a great deal of influence on how we categorize and evaluate traits. A body type that one culture finds threatening another might find nurturing; a face that one culture finds honest another may view as mocking.

The Search for the Magic Number

How do scientists study such a personal and seemingly subjective thing as personality? I wondered this for many years, until as fate would have it—*opportunity,* you might say—I met someone who was in the thick of figuring this out.

In 1980, I was looking to rent a cabin on the Oregon coast for a short while. I picked up the local newspaper, found an ad for one, and called the landlord on a pay phone. We met later that day. The landlord turned out to be Lew Goldberg—the psychology professor who had done much of the seminal work on measuring personality. He was leaving on sabbatical and wanted to rent out his weekend house. Although he ended up not renting to me—he chose an older, more financially stable renter—we ended up becoming friends. He introduced me to Sarah Hampson, who was his research colleague at the Oregon Research Institute. The mere fact that I got to know Sarah and Lew speaks to their gregariousness and their openness to meeting new people, even a young, ignorant student like me.

Lew doesn't usually like talking about himself. He is outgoing and enthusiastic, but modest. After we had known each other for a while, I got him to talk about his work in measuring personality. Lew began by asking, "How would *you* study personality?" (You might stop for a moment and think about this before reading further.)

I thought: Maybe you could put somebody in a brain scanner and show them pictures of homeless people asking for money. If the part of the brain that's responsible for feelings of generosity becomes excited, you might infer the person is generous, and if that same part of the brain is repulsed, you might infer they're stingy. But how do we know which part of the brain is the "generosity" region? The truth is we don't, and if we were to set about discovering *that,* we'd have to *start out* with generous people in order to locate that brain part. So we're left back where we started: How do you know if someone is generous?

Maybe you could put them in a situation where they have an opportunity to demonstrate generosity. For example, on their way to your office, they pass by a homeless person and you secretly watch what they do.

There are three problems here, though. First, a person could be generous in a whole lot of situations but not the one you're observing. Imagine someone philanthropically minded who prefers to donate to established charities. That person may have given a thousand dollars to a homeless shelter just yesterday, and another thousand dollars to a soup kitchen, and more money to the Red Cross, Oxfam, Habitat for Humanity, and United Way. Yet that person might fail your test. Or maybe the person just had their wallet stolen and doesn't *have* any money to hand out today, although on any other day they would have given.

Second problem: How do you distinguish personality traits that might be triggered by the same scenario but are different? A person might *not* be generous but the scenario triggers something that looks like it: compassion—maybe this particular homeless person reminds her of her dear, departed sister, causing her to reach into her wallet for a few loose dollars. Or maybe due to a brain injury, a man lacks impulse control and simply can't say no to any request of any kind—again, he's not what you might conventionally consider *generous;* he simply appears that way in the particular circumstance you're viewing.

Third problem: The sheer number of possible traits that a person can have would mean that we'd have to experiment on thousands of behaviors, making the research unwieldy and impractical. There must be an easier way.

I was not able to figure out this problem myself, but Lew had an elegant answer. He starts with an assumption, first popularized by Sir Francis Galton in the 1800s. Here's Lew:

> Let's assume that those individual differences that are of the most significance in the daily transactions of persons with each other will eventually become encoded into their language. This is the lexical hypothesis. The more important such a difference is, the more will people notice it and wish to talk about it, with the result that eventually they will invent a word for it, such as those nouns (e.g., *bigot, bully, fool, grouch, hick, loafer, miser, sucker*) and adjectives (e.g., *assertive, brave, energetic, honest, intelligent, responsible, sociable, sophisticated*) that are used to describe persons.

Is Lew's assumption true? Maybe not. But it's a good starting point. Maybe there are some personality traits not captured in words, either because they are relatively rare (in which case we don't need to worry about them now) or because they represent things that we're uncomfortable talking about (in which case we need to create different assessment instruments). Let's assume that the lexical hypothesis doesn't mean we'll identify every single personality trait possible, only that we'll get most of the really important ones.

If you're thinking that such terms might be culturally dependent—consistent with the triad of the developmental approach—you get a gold star (and, at least based on this example, you are *clever, intelligent,* and *sophisticated*). The cultural dependence might be obvious with a term such as *hick.* In a remote, closed community that doesn't interact with outsiders, it would be difficult to imagine calling someone a *hick* or a *bigot.* Those seemingly depend on living in a more urbanized culture with opportunities to contrast city folk with country bumpkins, and tolerant, open-minded people with bigots. Similarly, a strictly monogamous society might not need a word for *bigamy,* and a society that stresses communal ownership of all property might not need a word for *thief.*

The possibility that personality traits are influenced by culture doesn't doom the enterprise of measuring them—it all depends on what you want to use the information for. If you want to understand the personality traits that people exhibit in your own culture, or how they might change across the life span for you and your friends, there's no problem. If, like some cross-cultural psychologists, you want to understand how personality varies from one culture to another, or if there are personality universals that show up in all cultures, then you take whatever tests you've come up with and administer them to as diverse a range of humans as possible. As Lew says:

> The more important an individual difference is in human transactions, the more languages will have a term for it.

And so intrepid researchers, explorers of the personality domain, have gone off and studied the languages of diverse cultures from around the globe. Consider one type of individual difference, mental illness. It seems rather important to know whether a person you're interacting with is *sane, rational,* and *emotionally stable,* or *hears voices in their head.* It turns out that peoples as diverse as the Inuit, in northwest Alaska; the Yoruba tribes of rural Nigeria; and the Pintupi aborigines of central Australia, who until a generation or two ago lived like Paleolithic hunter-gatherers, have words in their languages for these important personality descriptors. Furthermore, there is very little that is distinctive culturally in these societies' attitudes and actions toward the mentally ill. Even words for more common and minor forms of mental illness, such as anxiety and depression, are found throughout the world.

Once scientists figured out *how* to measure personality, and how to describe people, another problem arose. There are thousands and thousands of different words used to describe personality traits—in English, there are 4,500 of them in *Webster's Unabridged Dictionary,* and more than 450 in current and common use. The sheer number can make a science of trait descriptions unwieldy—difficult to summarize, talk about, or make predictions with. This was one of the first "big data" problems, decades before there was Facebook or climate change data to analyze.

What scientists typically do with such mounds of data is to use mathematical techniques for data reduction, merging similar items into the same category or dimension. Doing so can allow us to discuss the data using a shorthand. We don't discard the original data, so we can always go back to it.

Consider by analogy the shorthand we use to talk about spatial location—where people and things are in the world. We could use a three-dimensional coordinate system, such as latitude, longitude, and height above sea level, and for some things we do. But it is a cumbersome system that provides more information than we usually need. Instead, we divide the world into continents, countries, cities, neighborhoods, and so on, and this is usually enough.

Suppose you're trying to schedule a meeting with people in your Houston-based organization and you haven't been able to reach Terry. Briana says, "Oh, Terry is in Europe for the next couple of weeks." That's really all you need to know—you don't need to know if he's in Portugal or Macedonia, or if he's staying on rue des Capuchins in Lyon, but presumably you could find out his exact location if you wanted to FedEx him some meeting notes—or maybe you only need his email address. And just because we've described Terry's location simply as *Europe* doesn't mean we'll confuse Terry's location with that of other people or things in Europe. If Doug says, "Oh—my cousin's suitcase was just sent to Europe by mistake; maybe Terry will run into it there," we see the folly: Europe is big. And so it goes with personality descriptions.

Even if we could find a way to summarize personality descriptions, to give us a shorthand for talking about them, it wouldn't mean that everyone who is included in a personality description category is alike. But there may exist broad and meaningful trends we can talk about that, in general, distinguish a North American temperament or outlook from, say, an Asian or African one, without losing sight of individual differences and variability. And personality traits fall along a continuum: We can use modifiers to say that a person is more or less charming, more or less grouchy, more or less European.

Dozens of researchers spanning several countries set about trying to understand the best way to organize personality terms, to create a useful taxonomy. Ideally, whatever system we come up with would work across languages and cultures, which would greatly facilitate comparisons. It took more than fifty years for scientists to come to a consensus about this.

One prominent scientist argued for twenty to thirty dimensions; several others for two. Some argued for five or thirteen. Our friend Lew Goldberg initially gravitated toward a three-factor (three-dimensional) model proposed by psychologist Dean Peabody, rejecting the five-factor model, now known as the Big Five. "To my scientific tastes," Lew said, "the Peabody model was elegant and beautiful, whereas the five-factor structure was a nightmare: All of the Big-Five factors but the first, extraversion, were highly related to evaluation [good-bad], meaning that they weren't truly independent dimensions." From roughly 1975 to 1985, he worked on collecting and analyzing data from a variety of sources to support the Peabody three-factor model, but no matter what he did, a five-factor model emerged from the analyses. Lew appealed to Dean Peabody to set up an experiment that would help them choose between three and five dimensions, something they designed together. When the data came in, they published a paper together showing that five dimensions comprised a more useful system (and it incorporated the original Peabody three). Goldberg became a reluctant convert, as did Peabody himself.

This never would have happened if Goldberg and Peabody had not been *collaborative, open to new experience, agreeable,* and at least slightly *extraverted.*

Collaborating with someone you disagree with represents a scientific ideal. When two or more researchers who are pursuing different theories, and who disagree with one another, decide to work together, the results can transform a field. Today many consider Lew the father of the Big Five personality categories. There have been cross-cultural replications in dozens of languages and cultures, including Chinese, German, Hebrew, Japanese, Korean, Portuguese, and Turkish. As you might expect, some minor differences emerge in disparate cultures, but the Big Five remain the best description.

The Big Five dimensions are:

I. Extraversion
II. Agreeableness

III. Conscientiousness
IV. Emotional Stability versus Neuroticism
V. Openness to Experience + Intellect (also called Imagination)

Each of these categories includes many dozens of individual traits. As you can see, there has been some controversy around what to call the last one, but don't let that bother you—it is a well-defined dimension that includes a number of traits that cohere in real life.

EXTRAVERSION includes *talkative, bold, energetic,* and their opposites, *quiet, timid,* and *lethargic.* People who score high on the Extraversion dimension tend to be comfortable around other people, start conversations, and don't mind being the center of attention.

AGREEABLENESS includes *warm, cooperative, generous,* and the opposites *cold, adversarial,* and *stingy.* People who score high on this dimension tend to be interested in other people, sympathize with others' feelings, and make people feel at ease.

CONSCIENTIOUSNESS includes *organized, responsible, careful,* and *practical,* and the opposites *disorganized, irresponsible, sloppy,* and *impractical.* People who score high on this dimension tend to be prepared, be diligent, pay attention to details, and do what they say they will do.

EMOTIONAL STABILITY includes *stable, contented,* and *at ease,* and *unstable, discontented,* and *nervous.* People who score high on this dimension are not easily bothered by things, are relaxed, and don't change their moods a lot.

OPENNESS (also called INTELLECT and IMAGINATION) includes *curious, intelligent,* and *creative,* as well as *uninquisitive, dumb,* and *uncreative.* It includes cognitive and behavioral flexibility. People who score high on this dimension are quick to understand things, have a vivid imagination, and like trying new things, new restaurants, and going to new places. It is separate from intellectual ability but speaks to a propensity to enjoy intellectual, cultural, aesthetic, and artistic experiences.

If you want to sound like a personality researcher, you can use the shorthand of the factor numbers, such as, "Oh, that Nancy is very low on Factor II," or, "I think you should promote Stan in accounting—he's high on Factors II and III."

The drive to organize people's traits into categories is ancient; astrology is one such attempt to assign personalities to people systematically, depending on when they were born. While it is still popular throughout the world, it has no scientific basis. Sure, you may know a Capricorn who is stubborn, but statistically, you're just as likely to find stubborn Leos, Libras, and Sagittarians.

One point that often gets confused is that people tend to think of the Big Five as a typology (the extraverted type, the neurotic type, etc.). That's not the case—it's the configuration (or profile) of the five factors that represents someone's personality. Just as we can describe physical objects in terms of length, width, and height, the Big Five framework allows us to describe human personality in terms of the five factors. Proponents of the Big Five never intended to reduce the rich tapestry of personality to a mere five traits. Rather, they seek to provide a framework in which to organize the myriad individual differences that characterize human beings. This organization reveals a great deal about things that have historically been important for humans to know about one another.

Factor I. Is Jason *active* and *dominant* or *passive* and *submissive*? (Can I bully Jason or will Jason try to bully me?)

Factor II. Is Mari *agreeable* or *disagreeable*? (Will my interactions with Mari be warm and pleasant or cold and distant?)

Factor III. Is Letitia *responsible* and *conscientious* or *negligent* and *erratic*? (Can I count on Letitia?)

Factor IV. Is Hannah *crazy* or *sane*? (Can I predict what Hannah will do, and will her actions make sense to me?)

Factor V. Is Felix *smart* or *dumb*? (How easy will it be for me to teach Felix? Is there anything I can learn from him?)

So What?

What does all this mean for us, people who are interested in the science of aging? The Big Five gives us a universally recognized structure for organizing what would otherwise be an unwieldy number of traits.

Whenever genes, situations, or therapy changes our personalities, they must do so by changing the brain. In that sense, all personality differences are biological, regardless of whether they are influenced by genetics or not, because they must go through the brain. These neurobiological changes are accompanied by chemical changes in the brain. As an example, assertiveness, competitiveness, dominance, and belligerence all are influenced by testosterone across genders. Higher levels lead us toward aggressive behaviors; lower levels lead us toward politeness. Testosterone levels are affected by the triad of factors—genes, culture, and opportunity. Situations such as a successful hunt, driving a fast car, being in the public eye, or being in charge of a large number of people can increase testosterone levels. The normal process of aging tends to lower them. A typical professional career trajectory finds one gaining more power as one gets older—this can compensate for biologically lowered levels of testosterone in some individuals.

Conscientiousness, Agreeableness, and Emotional Stability can be thought of as reflecting a tendency toward reducing unwanted drama in our lives, and evidence is mounting that these are influenced by serotonin. Openness and Extraversion reflect a general tendency to explore and engage with possibilities, and these appear to be influenced by dopamine. Drugs that increase dopamine can cause us to want to explore more and engage in riskier behaviors. Low levels of serotonin are associated with aggression, poor impulse control, and depression, and drugs that improve serotonergic function are often prescribed to treat these.

The structure of genes has also been shown to influence personality. Alterations to the gene known as *SLC6A4* are associated with neuroticism-related traits including anxiety, depression, hopelessness, guilt, hostility, and aggression. Other genes with hard-to-pronounce names are associated with self-determination and self-transcendence and with novelty seeking. The novelty-seeking genes are involved in dopamine regulation. An active area of research is dedicated to mapping these kinds of interactions between genes, brain, neurochemicals, and personality.

Temperament versus Personality

Babies are born with certain predispositions—a pattern of individual differences in how they react to different situations, as well as the regulation of those patterns. In babies and children, these patterns are usually called temperament, whereas in adults these patterns are called personality. Temperament and the young child's early life experiences contribute to growing a personality. That personality will be based on the child's developing views of self and others as they are shaped by experience. A child who grows up in an environment with many dangers and hazards will surely view the world differently than one who is nurtured and sheltered. The fascinating thing is that personality development doesn't always go the way one might predict.

You might think that a child who grows up in a dangerous environment will learn to be fearful and will develop a fearful, anxious, and perhaps neurotic personality. This can certainly occur. But a different child, with different genetic predispositions, uterine environment, and parenting may become fearless, brave, and challenge seeking. Temperament becomes personality as the child develops its own values, attitudes, and coping strategies. And it is biologically based, linked to, but not completely determined by, an individual's genetic makeup.

Temperament is typically measured in young children along dimensions that parallel temperament in animals. These include surgency (activity level, or Factor I), sociability (Factor II), self-regulation (Factor III), and curiosity (Factor V). These have been found to correlate highly with the Big Five. Factor IV, whether a person is crazy or sane, is more difficult to assess in animals and infants. (Although at times, I think every parent of a two-year-old thinks their child must be crazy. And, of course, they are! Babies are entirely egocentric, true psychopaths, who don't care about anyone but themselves.)

Age-Related Personality Changes

There are a number of ways in which the natural aging process itself tends to cause some personality changes. In a meta-analysis of ninety-two research papers, covering the life course from age 10 to 101, 75 percent of personality traits studied changed significantly after the age of forty and well beyond sixty. (These tendencies will not apply to all people. Some people don't change at all, and some change in ways that contradict statistical trends.) Some changes result from diseases and injuries, such as Alzheimer's, Pick's disease, stroke, or concussion due to falling.

So what are the trends? Older adults tend to be better at controlling impulses; that is, they're better at self-control and self-discipline and tend to be better at rule-following than young adults—traits that have to do with Factor III (Conscientiousness). Self-control increases steadily every decade after the age of twenty. Some of this has to do with the development of the prefrontal cortex, which continues through the early twenties, and yet we see additional age-related dispositional changes in impulse control that we haven't found a cause for yet.

Flexibility—your ability to easily adapt to changes in plans or to your environment—decreases steadily in every decade after twenty. With age, men typically show increased emotional sensitivity, and women experience decreasing emotional vulnerability. As you might expect—and may have experienced yourself—Openness increases around adolescence, but then declines with age.

In addition, older adults are generally more concerned with making a good impression and with cooperating and getting along with others—Agreeableness increases substantially. They show increased Emotional Stability and calm as well. I'm sure you can think of exceptions—remember, these are just averages. One of my favorite pictures in social neuroscience comes from a study of nearly 1 million individuals from sixty-two countries, showing how consistently Emotional Stability, Agreeableness, and Conscientiousness increase with age. The chart for one country, Canada, is shown on the next page.

Conscientiousness, Openness, and Extraversion decreased during old age, whereas Agreeableness and Emotional Stability increased substantially. Similarly, these results suggested that the initially increasing levels of Conscientiousness may in fact start to decrease following the age of fifty. Individuals appear to become more self-content in old age, an aspect of Emotional Stability called the La Dolce Vita effect: the sweet life. Older adults are more content with what they have, more self-contained and laid-back, less driven toward productivity. Mood disorders, anxiety, and behavioral problems decrease past age sixty, and onset of these problems after that age is very rare.

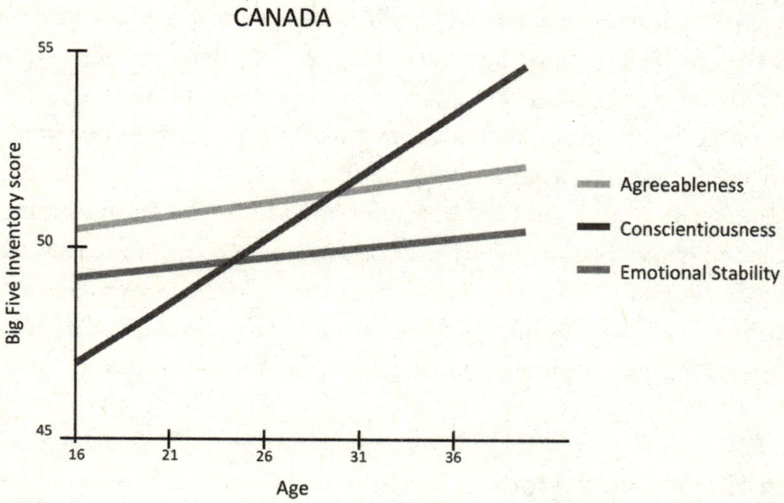

Older adults are less likely to engage in risky or thrill-seeking behaviors and tend to be more morally responsible and less open to new experience. In terms of the Big Five factor model, older people show declines in Extraversion and Openness and increases in Conscientiousness, Emotional Stability, and Agreeableness.

Some of these age-related changes are based on microculture and opportunity—the social roles that we and our cohort of friends invest in during earlier life stages. By late adolescence and early adulthood, people become more independent and begin investing in their education and career. Success in these domains depends very much on being reliable, dependable, and competent. Prior to this period, there is probably less need to behave conscientiously because parents and institutions are in place to guide people through life. For some, Conscientiousness declines after retirement not because the brain has changed but because there is less need to be a hardworking, driven personality—it seems okay to loosen one's grip a bit and enjoy la dolce vita. And many transitions in social roles occur in older adulthood, when we might become grandparents, retire from full-time work, or take up new hobbies. Health challenges present us with a stark choice and an opportunity to mold our personalities: Am I someone who folds up and gives in, or do I double down, embrace resilience and optimism, and try to make the best of the time I have left?

Optimism predicts longevity. But too much optimism can lead to bad health outcomes. If you're unrealistically optimistic, you might not have that dark spot on your forehead checked for cancer; you might ignore the fact that you've been putting on ten pounds every decade since you were forty, figuring it will all work out just fine. Although optimism is a crucial part of disease recovery, tissue repair, and so on, it needs to be tempered with realism and conscientiousness.

Illness often causes us to change our personalities. In Sarah Hampson's work on people with type 2 diabetes, it was not uncommon for people to say that the onset of this disease made them take better care of themselves. Aspiring to a healthier lifestyle may thus lead to personality change—an increase in self-control, methodicalness, and conscientiousness.

The Role of Role Models

Role models show us we can step outside of who we are. We look at them and see the kinds of changes we want to make, the kinds of lives we want to lead—we see that what might have remained a dusty and dark secret aspiration is *possible.* They help us realize that we can become our own autobiographers—we can alter the story of our lives for better or worse. But one person's inspiring role model might just be annoying to another person. That's the reason that so many different voices grace this book. You may not agree with everyone's politics or outlook on life, but these individuals are included to show the wide range of possibilities for staying healthy, engaged, and active in one's later years, for—as Jane Fonda described it to me—aging *gracefully.*

Creating your own future is possible at any age. Julia "Hurricane" Hawkins is a native of Baton Rouge, Louisiana, and a retired schoolteacher. She is a devoted gardener with an affection for bonsai trees. Hawkins took up competitive athletics for the first time at age seventy-five. She competed as a cyclist in the National Senior Games, winning bronze and gold medals. Twenty-five years later, she branched out, taking up running at age one hundred. Hawkins again competed in the National Senior Games at age 101, establishing the record for women one hundred and older in the hundred-yard dash at 39.62 seconds. She also competed in the fifty-yard dash against other runners as "young" as ninety, finishing in 18.31 seconds. Her secret? "Keep in good shape, try not to be overweight, get good sleep, and keep exercising and training." However, she adds, "There is a fine line of pushing yourself and wearing yourself out. You don't want to overdo it. You just want to do the best you can do." In 2017, after winning the hundred-yard dash in the National Senior Games, she said, "I don't feel 101. I feel about 60 or 70. You are not going to be perfect at 101, but nothing stops me." A year later, at age 102, Hawkins set a new world record for running sixty meters in 24.79 seconds. "I just like the feeling of being independent and doing something a little different and testing myself, trying to get better." In June 2019, at age 103, she won gold medals in the 50 and 100 meter races.

Testing oneself and trying to get better are themes that run through the inspirational lives of so many. At age ninety-three, the guitarist Andrés Segovia launched a new tour, and in one of his last interviews before his death at ninety-four he said that he still practiced five hours a day. Why, having accomplished so much in his life and being regarded as the greatest living guitarist, was he still practicing? "There's this one passage that has been giving me a little bit of trouble," he said.

The Netflix series *Grace and Frankie,* in its fifth season airing in 2019, stars Jane Fonda, eighty-two, and Lily Tomlin, eighty. Tomlin's character, Frankie Bergstein, is a textbook case of someone with great openness—she smokes marijuana regularly, is a painter, and once hired a building contractor who lived in the woods behind a neighbor's house. Fonda's character, Grace Hanson, is set in her ways, emotionally cold, and conservative. In the second season, they start their own business, something that is completely new for the hippie-socialist Frankie, and in season four Grace starts dating a younger man, played by Peter Gallagher. What draws so many people to the show is the message that you can change in later life, you can try new things, and you can have fun doing it. "What Lily and I hear very often," Fonda says, "is 'It makes us feel less afraid of getting older. It makes us feel hopeful.' . . . I left the [entertainment] business at age 50, and I came back at age 65. It's been an unusual situation to re-create a career at that age. . . . One of the things that Lily and I are proud of—and want to continue with—is showing that you may be old, you may be in your third act, but you can still be vital and sexual and funny . . . that life isn't over."

Anna Mary Robertson, better known as Grandma Moses, didn't even start painting seriously until she was seventy-five, and continued until she was 101. Today her works are displayed at the Smithsonian and New York's Metropolitan Museum of Art, among others, and have sold for more than a million dollars. One of her paintings hangs in the White House and was turned into a commemorative stamp. She painted it at age ninety-one. Alma Thomas didn't have her first art exhibition until she was seventy-five. She was the first African American woman to have a solo show at the Whitney, and now her works hang in the Smithsonian and the White House.

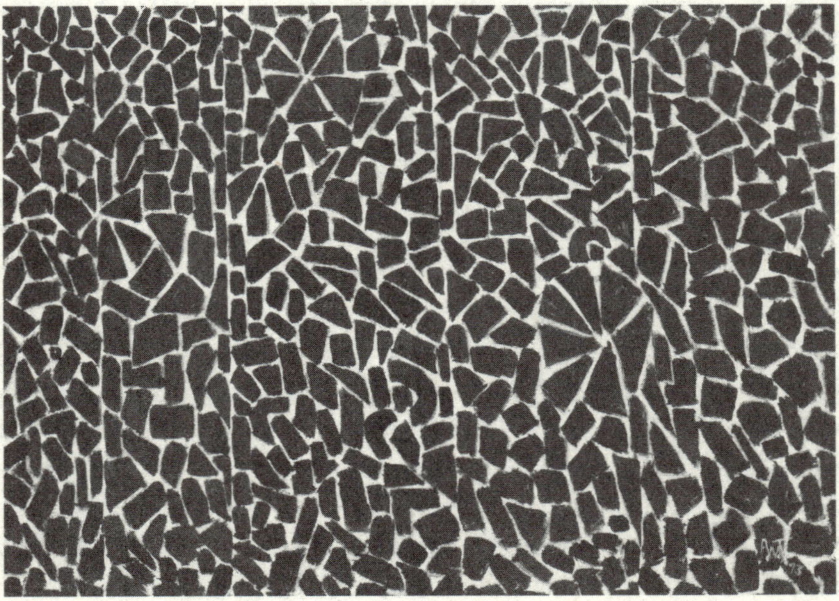

I'm reminded of another story, of a man who was born poor in Indiana in 1890 and whose father died when he was five. An unmotivated child, he dropped out of school in the middle of seventh grade and never went back. By age seventeen, he had already been fired from four jobs. He became a drifter, moving from one unskilled job to another, finding himself broke most of his life. If early childhood and young adult experiences were all there was to a life story, you could predict that his life would be characterized by one disappointment after another. Indeed, he appeared aimless and unfocused. Among other things, he found work as a steam engine stoker, farmhand, blacksmith, soldier, railroad fireman, buggy painter, streetcar conductor, janitor, insurance salesman, and filling station operator, but never managed to hold on to a job or to save any money. At age fifty, he started another doomed job, a roadside eatery in Corbin, Kentucky. The restaurant eked along and then finally gave its last gasp, going out of business when he was sixty-two. There he was, pushing retirement age, broke (again), and living out of his car. How many of us would give up at that point? He had never had a success in his life, and the life expectancy for a sixty-two-year-old in 1952 was just another 3.2 years.

One day he took an old family recipe and, imagining the potential of franchised restaurants, opened one in Utah with borrowed money. That might be the end of the story, except that his name was Harland Sanders, and the restaurant was Kentucky Fried Chicken, now known as KFC and one of the largest suppliers of food in the world. Sanders sold the company at age seventy-four for $2 million, about the equivalent of $32 million in today's dollars. The company he conceived of at age sixty-two now has annual revenues of $23 billion and is known throughout the world. He continued advising the company and working as a brand ambassador into his nineties.

At age eighty-nine, Colonel Sanders was asked, "You don't believe in retirement?" "No," he answered adamantly. "Not a bit in the world. When the Lord put Father Adam here he never told him to quit at 65, did he? He worked into his final years. I think as long as you've got health, and ability, use it . . . to the end."

Trying something new later in life, like competitive sports, business enterprises, or artistic endeavors, can dramatically increase both your quality of life and how long you live. Openness and curiosity correlate highly with good health and long life. People who are curious are more apt to challenge themselves intellectually and socially and reap the rewards of the mental calisthenics that result. They are also more likely to be interested and engaged, which makes them more fun to be around, and interacting with others socially is a good way to stay mentally agile and alert.

Conscientiousness

Perhaps the most important traits to foster and develop throughout the life span are those in Factor III, Conscientiousness. Conscientious people are more likely to have a doctor and to go see one when they're sick. They're more likely to get regular medical checkups and to reliably keep up with their professional, family, and financial commitments. This may sound like a mostly practical matter, but Factor III traits are highly correlated with a panoply of positive life outcomes, including longevity, success, and happiness. Conscientiousness has been linked to lower all-cause mortality. Conversely, lower childhood conscientiousness predicts greater obesity, physiological dysregulation, and worse lipid profiles in adulthood. To become more conscientious, one must change underlying cognitive processes such as self-regulation (controlling impulsive behaviors) and self-monitoring (noticing which circumstances lead to successful self-regulation and which circumstances sabotage self-regulation). If you wish you had more of these, a number of different methods have been shown to work for adults of any age, from cognitive behavioral therapy to David Allen's book *Getting Things Done*.

A recent psychological study, published in the flagship journal of the Association for Psychological Science, corroborated what Charles Koch, CEO of one of the largest companies in the world, says: "I'd rather hire someone who is conscientious, curious, and honest than someone who is highly intelligent but lacks those qualities. Runaway intelligence without conscientiousness, curiosity and honesty, I learned, can lead to dismal outcomes."

IQ, one's intelligence quotient, is a familiar metric. Increasingly, so too is EQ, the emotional intelligence quotient, thanks in part to the popular writings of Daniel Goleman. Cognitive scientists now talk about a third metric, CQ, the curiosity quotient, and it predicts life success as well as, and often better than, IQ or EQ.

As you might imagine, there are limits to both Conscientiousness and Curiosity. Too much of either can cause trouble. Someone who is too conscientious might stray into obsessive compulsive disorder behaviors; it's helpful to distinguish healthy conscientiousness from extreme rigidity or compulsion. Systemic conscientiousness, if it involves blind adherence to faulty rules, is also a problem, such as when the medical community recommends policies that can cause harm. Screening for prostate cancer with the prostate-specific antigen (PSA) biomarker is probably the most notorious case of causing significant harm to patients. Most men with elevated PSA levels will never develop symptoms of prostate cancer, but many have died or suffered serious health problems after receiving unnecessary treatment. The ratio of those helped versus harmed by PSA screening is around one in a hundred. Overdiagnosis is common in other "conscientious" cancer screenings as well.

Openness

Can too much openness lead someone to engage in risky, dangerous behaviors? Yes. John Lennon was famously open to new experiences and at one point considered an untested form of therapy that involved having a hole drilled in his skull. Amy Winehouse, who faced great difficulties with impulse control, died at twenty-seven from alcohol poisoning. Steve Jobs, also famous for his openness, pursued an untested treatment for his pancreatic cancer, and that openness—rather than a reliance on scientifically validated medical treatments—killed him.

Fortunately, our traits and personalities are malleable, like the brain itself. We can change. We can learn from our experiences. All of us have an internal monologue, a narrator in our heads keeping track of things such as "I'm hungry" or "I'm cold." The internal narrator also tells us, "This is what I'm like—these are the things I like to do, these are the ways I respond to certain situations." Knowing this about ourselves is the first step toward change, toward affirming that our past behavior does not necessarily determine our future behavior. Even models we learn about through the media can help us to make aspirational changes. And personal affirmations ("I am generous, I am kind") can help us to become what we're not. A famous old psychology experiment showed that people who *act* as if they're happy end up *being* happy. The zygomatic facial muscle is what you use to smile when you're genuinely happy. In one experiment people who forced a smile actually felt happier than people who forced a frown, just because that muscle was engaged. It turns out that the nervous system is bidirectional. It doesn't matter whether the brain makes the mouth smile or the mouth makes the brain smile. So smile, think positive thoughts, and try new things. If you're not feeling good, act as if you are. A cheerful, positive, optimistic outlook—even if it starts out fake—can end up becoming real.

Compassion

There is an inherent asymmetry in the amount and kind of information we have about ourselves versus what we know about others. You have unique access to your past actions and to your current mental states and motivations, but you do not have this level of access to others' memories and states of mind (except in a good movie or novel). They have the same lack of access when judging you. Imagine you're driving a fancy car and a homeless person walks up and asks for a dollar as you're waiting at a stoplight. Imagine also that you don't give it to him. He may conclude that you're a tightwad. You may have wanted to help but not have had any cash on you. One behavior, two different interpretations.

One tangible thing that we can all do to avoid misjudging others is to exercise compassion, to allow for the possibility that you might be wrong in attributing a trait to someone's behavior. Indeed, this is *the* core principle at the heart of both social psychology and the teachings of the Dalai Lama. "Compassion is the key to happiness," he says. "We are a social species and our happiness is defined by our relationship with others." The Dalai Lama believes this comes from the biology of our species, of the importance of social interactions to all primates. He tries to avoid feeling anger, suspicion, and distrust and instead practices patience, tolerance, and compassion. In addition, he avoids thinking of himself as privileged or special, and this increases his happiness a great deal:

> I never considered myself as something special. If I consider myself to [be] something different from you, like, 'I am Buddhist' or even more [with haughty voice] 'I am His Holiness the Dalai Lama' or even if I consider that 'I am a Nobel laureate,' then actually you create yourself as a prisoner. I forget these things—I simply consider I am one of seven billion human beings.

Buddhism, like most of the world's religions, teaches you how to change your personality. You may feel that your personality is fixed, inflexible, and was determined in childhood, but science has shown otherwise. In particular, studies since Bayley and Baltes have found that volitional (not disease-induced) personality change is possible at least through one's eighties, in the three continents so far studied, North America, Europe, and Asia.

The compassionate attitude and outlook are also related to experiencing less stress. You can choose not to be stressy—or learn how—and this can save your life. The HPA (hypothalamic-pituitary-adrenal) axis is an endocrine system that controls the secretion of stress hormones (glucocorticoids) including cortisol. Exposure to high levels of glucocorticoids can be particularly detrimental for the aging hippocampus and is associated with decrements in learning and memory. Among the things that psychotherapy is best at, stress reduction is one of the most important things you can do for your overall health. And yet, there can be too much of a good thing. Too much stress reduction, like too much optimism, may cause you to ignore important health issues or to become unmotivated to work or seek social contact. Moderate amounts of stress impel us to do things—to exercise, eat well, and nurture our mental health by making friends and spending time with them.

Is a Good Personality Sufficient?

Curiosity, Openness, Associations (as in sociability), Conscientiousness, and Healthy practices are the five lifestyle choices that have the biggest impact on the rest of our lives. The first four are elements of anyone's personality. The acronym they make is COACH, a term I use a few times in these pages and which comes ultimately from reading thousands of pages on aging research. I will return to its many implications in subsequent chapters.

But one infamous aspect of aging does not fit into a personality trait: memory. It's a topic that gets at the core of who we are and how we experience life. Many of us wouldn't mind having someone else's hair, maybe someone else's intellect or emotional composure, but someone else's memories? We'd cease being who we are. So what do we know about the brain basis of memory, and why does memory seem to be the first thing to go?

2

MEMORY AND YOUR SENSE OF "YOU"

The myth of failing memory

I'm standing in front of the hall closet. I was packing my suitcase in the bedroom and came here to find something, and I now can't remember what. I walk back to the bedroom to see if something there will remind me. My mind is blank. I walk to the kitchen thinking maybe I had stopped at the hall closet by accident on my way here, hoping that there will be some object, something in plain view, that will remind me why I'm here. I go back to the bedroom and stare at the suitcase and piles of clothes, but there is no clue there either.

This is not the first time it's happened. In fact, it's nothing new—I used to do this in my thirties, but back then, I just figured I was distracted. If I wasn't a neuroscientist, I'd be worried now, in my sixties, that this was a sure sign that my brain is decaying and that I'll soon be in an assisted living facility waiting for someone to feed me my dinner of smashed peas and pulverized carrots. But the research literature is comforting—these kinds of slips are normal and routine as we age and are not necessarily indicative of any dark, foreboding illness. Part of what explains this is a general neurological turn inward—every decade after our fortieth birthday, our brains spend more time contemplating our own thoughts versus taking in information from the external environment. This is why we find ourselves standing in front of an open closet door with no memory of what we went there for. This is part of the normal developmental trajectory of the aging brain and not always a sign of something more sinister.

The panic that we feel upon forgetting something, particularly when we're older, is visceral and disturbing. It underscores how important and fundamental memory is—not just to getting things done, but to our deep sense of self. Memories tell us who we are in moments of conflict or doubt. Good memories comfort us. Bad ones haunt us. And the feelings they invoke in us are very personal and intimate.

As philosophers and writers have long known, without memory we lack identity. The Christopher Nolan film *Memento* makes a vivid case for this, as does the current Netflix hit *Westworld,* by Christopher's brother Jonathan. (Now, *there's* an argument for the genetic basis of talent. Or is it an argument for shared home environment? Of course, it is the interaction of these two things.) Our very conception of ourselves and who we are is dependent on a continuous thread, a mental narrative of the experiences we've had and the people we've encountered. Without memory, you don't know if you're someone who likes chocolate or not, if clowns amuse or terrify you; you don't know who your friends are or whether you have the skill to prepare chocolate pots de crème for ten people who are going to arrive at your apartment in an hour.

But if it's so important, why isn't memory more reliable? You'd think that eons of evolution would have improved it, but the story of how memory evolved has a few twists and turns, a few counterintuitive features. For one, our memories are less like videotaped recordings of experiences than they are like jigsaw puzzles. That simple fact fuels many jokes about age-related memory loss, such as this one:

> Two elderly gentlemen were sitting next to each other at a dinner party.
>
> "My wife and I had dinner at a new restaurant last week," one of the men said.
>
> "Oh, what's it called?" asked the other.
>
> "Um . . . I . . . I can't remember. [Thinks. Rubs chin.] Hmm . . . What is the name of that flower that you buy on romantic occasions? You know, it usually comes by the dozen, you can get it in different colors, there are thorns on the stem . . . ?"
>
> "Do you mean a rose?"
>
> "Yes, that's it!" (Leans across the table to where his wife is sitting.) "Rose, what was the name of that restaurant we went to last week?"

Memory can indeed seem like a puzzle with many missing pieces. We rarely retrieve all the pieces, and our brains fill in the missing information with creative guesses, based on experience and pattern matching. This leads to many unfortunate misrecollections, often accompanied by the stubborn belief that we are recalling accurately. We cling to these misrememberings, storing them in our memory banks incorrectly, and then retrieving them in a still-incorrect form and with a stronger (misplaced) sense of certainty that they are accurate. George Martin, the Beatles' producer, described his own experience with this:

> There's this nice fellow named Mark Lewisohn. When I made the film "The Making of Sergeant Pepper" we had him come in as a sort of consultant. And I had George and Paul and Ringo come 'round, and I interviewed them about the making of the album. The interesting thing was there were parts of it that all of us remembered differently. When I was interviewing Paul, he would recollect something and it would be wrong. And I had to keep telling Mark Lewisohn not to correct Paul because for Lewisohn to say, "That's not right—according to these documents here and these logs, it was this way," . . . well, for Paul it would be rather humiliating. So Paul tells his story and that's how he remembers it. The thing about Lewisohn's logs is they made me realize that my memory was faulty as well—Paul and I would remember something in two different ways and the documents would prove it was done in a completely different, third way.

Why does this happen?

How Memory Works

Memory is not just one thing. It is a set of different processes that we casually use a single term to describe. We talk about memorizing phone numbers, remembering a particular smell, remembering the best route to school or to work, remembering the capital of California and the meaning of the word *phlebotomist*. We remember that we're allergic to ragweed or that we just had a haircut three weeks ago. Smartphones "remember" phone numbers for us and smart thermostats learn when we're likely to be home and will want to set the temperature to seventy degrees. As with many concepts, we have intuitions about what memory is, but those intuitions are often flat-out wrong.

Like other brain systems, memory wasn't designed; it evolved to solve adaptive problems in the environment. What we think of as memory is actually several biologically and cognitively distinct systems. Only some things that you experience get stored in memory. This is because one of the evolutionary functions of memory is to abstract out regularities from the world, to generalize. That generalization allows us to use objects like toilets and pens—you can use a new toilet, or a new pen, without special training because functionally, it is the same as other toilets or pens you've used. Why and how this generalization learning occurs is one of the oldest topics in experimental psychology and has been a specialty of my postdoctoral supervisor Roger Shepard for more than fifty years. (At age ninety, Roger is still active, working on two different books and collaborating on a paper with me—I'm embarrassed to say that I am the bottleneck for the paper, not he.)

Perhaps the most basic example of generalization is food—you learn as a child that the chicken tenders you're eating today are not identical in size and appearance to ones you ate yesterday but that they are still edible and taste pretty much the same. We see this generalization principle in tool use as well. If you need a knife to cut your food, you might go to the silverware drawer in your kitchen and take whatever knife is there—functionally they are all the same. We generalize like this thousands of times a day without even knowing it. It's related to memory in that your memory's representation of chicken tenders, or a table knife, is usually a somewhat generalized impression, not a mental photograph of a particular chicken tender or particular knife.

Two other professors of mine, Michael Posner and Steve Keele, provided some of the first and most interesting evidence of this back in the 1960s. They wanted to find a way to determine what it was about an assortment of similar items that actually got stored in the brain's memory system—was it the unique features of a specific item or the generalized features of the average item? You can think about this like a family resemblance in your own family—there may be a particular color hair that people in your family tend to have, a particular nose, a particular chin. Not everyone in the family has these, and the hair, nose, and chin have variations from person to person, and yet . . . there is something about them that binds them all together. This is the abstract generalization that Posner and Keele wanted to explore.

Family resemblance includes variability around a prototype—here the prototype, or patriarch, is in the center.

As cognitive psychologists do, Posner and Keele started out with very simple items, much less complex than a human face. They presented computer-generated patterns of dots that they had made by starting with a parent, or prototype, and then shifted some of the dots one millimeter or so in a random direction. This created patterns that all shared a family resemblance with the original—very much like the variation in faces that we see in parents and their children. On the following page is an example of the one they began with (the prototype, upper left) and some of the variations (at the ends of the arrows). The one on the upper right is an unrelated pattern, used as a control in their experiment.

If you look carefully, you'll see a kind of family resemblance across the four related squares—all have a kind of triangular pattern of three dots in

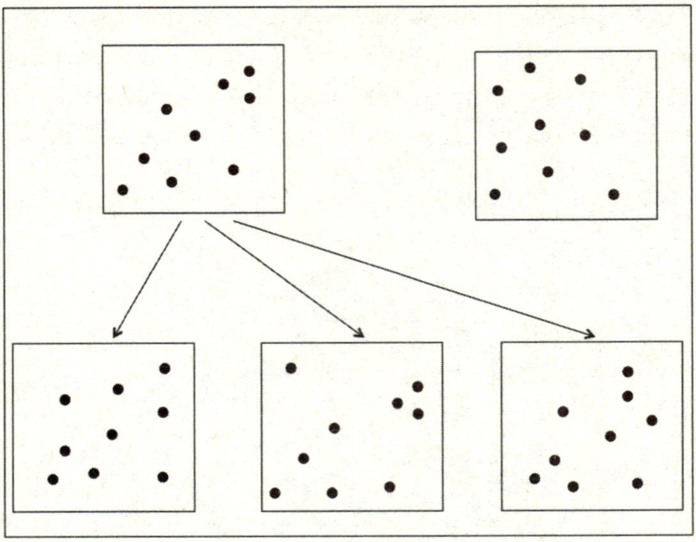

the lower left, although the dots vary in how close together they are. All have a diagonal of three dots running down the center roughly from the upper left to the lower right, and they vary in how stretched out they are and where the first dot begins.

In the experiment, people were shown version after version of squares with dot patterns in them, each of them different. The participants weren't told how these dot patterns had been constructed. Here's the clever part: Posner and Keele showed people the descendants (like the ones on the bottom row) and didn't show them the parents (like the one on the upper left, the parent). A week later the same people came back in and saw a bunch of dot patterns, some old and some new, and simply had to indicate which ones they'd seen before. Although the participants didn't know this, some of the "new" patterns were actually the parents, the prototypes used to generate the other dot patterns. If people are storing the exact details of the figures—if their memories are like video recordings—this task would be easy. On the other hand, if what we store in memory is an abstract, generalized version of objects, people ought to recall seeing the parent even if they hadn't—it constitutes an abstract generalization of the children that were created from it. That's exactly what they found.

As we age, our brains become better and better at this kind of pattern matching and abstraction, and although dot patterns seem pretty far removed from anything of real-world importance, the experiment illuminates that abstraction occurs without our conscious awareness, and it accounts for one of the most widespread traits that oldsters have: wisdom. From a neurocognitive standpoint, wisdom is the ability to see patterns where others don't see them, to extract generalized common points from prior experience and use those to make predictions about what is likely to happen next. Oldsters aren't as fast, perhaps, at mental calculations and retrieving names, but they are much better and faster at seeing the big picture. And that comes down to decades of generalization and abstraction.

Now, you might object and say that you have very precise memories for *particular* objects. You'd recognize if someone switched your wedding ring on you. You know the feel of your favorite pair of shoes. If you have a fancy pen that someone gave you as a gift, you would be sad if you lost it. But if you lost a ten-cent Bic disposable pen, you probably would just reach into your drawer and take out another because they're interchangeable, which is just another way of saying you've generalized them. If you've ever tried to take away the favorite fuzzy blanket from a young child, replacing the frayed, worn, and tattered one with a brand-new one, you know that they freak out—to them a blanket is not just a blanket and they don't generalize: This particular blanket is *their* special blanket.

In most cases of generalization, it's not that we can't *notice* the difference between this pen and that pen if we were asked to study them, nor is it necessarily that we can't remember differences—it's just that we don't need to. Our memory systems strive to be efficient in the service of not cluttering our minds with unnecessary detail.

Again, we see individual differences in how we generalize. To Lew Goldberg, a car is a car is a car. Its only value is in getting you from one place to another. He doesn't understand people who collect cars or who have more than one. "Why would you want to have two cars?" he would ask. "It would be like having two dishwashers." He sees the world of objects transactionally, with little sentimentality or interest in their differences. He does not seem to see the irony that someone whose lifework is studying individual differences in human beings has little interest in the individual differences in human-made objects. He does get excited at the individual differences he finds in nature, between trees, mountains, lakes, rocks, and sunsets. He's just not a manufactured-objects guy.

Some people do have obsessions with objects in their lives—a favorite pair of boots that you wear way beyond the time when they should probably have been replaced; a favorite sofa that long ago needed re-covering. In cases like these, it's not that we fail to generalize; it's that the objects have taken on a special, personal meaning beyond their utility, a sentimentality. And they've activated a privileged circuit in memory.

Generalization promotes cognitive economy, so that we don't focus on particulars that don't matter. The great Russian neuropsychologist Alexander Luria studied a patient, Solomon Shereshevsky, with a memory impairment that was the opposite of what we usually hear about—Solomon didn't have amnesia, the loss of memories; he had what Luria called hypermnesia (we might say that his superpower was superior memory). His supercharged memory allowed him to perform amazing feats, such as repeating speeches word for word that he had heard only once, or complex mathematical formulas, long sequences of numbers, and poems in foreign languages he didn't even speak. Before you think that having such a fantastic memory would be great, it came with a cost: Solomon wasn't able to form abstractions because he remembered every detail as distinct. He had particular trouble recognizing people. From a neurocognitive standpoint, every time you see a face, it is likely that it looks at least slightly different from the last time—you're viewing it at a different angle and distance than before, and you might be encountering a different expression. While you're interacting with a person, their face goes through a parade of expressions. Because your brain can generalize, you see all of these different manifestations of the face as belonging to the same person. Solomon couldn't do that. As he explained to Luria, recognizing his friends and colleagues was nearly impossible because "everyone has so many faces."

Memory Systems

The recognition that memory is not one thing, but many different things, has been one of the most important discoveries in neuroscience. Each is influenced by different variables, governed by different principles, stores different kinds of information, and is supported by different neural circuits. And some of these systems are more robust than others, allowing us to preserve accurate memories for a lifetime, whereas others are more fickle, more affected by emotion, and are inconstant.

Remember that evolution happens in fits and starts; it doesn't start out with a plan or goal. After hundreds of thousands of years of brain evolution, we don't end up with the kind of neat-and-tidy system we would have if everything had been engineered from the start. It's likely that the different human memory systems we have today followed separate evolutionary trajectories, as they addressed distinct adaptive problems. So we end up today with one memory system that keeps track of where you are in the world (spatial memory), another that keeps track of which way you turn a faucet on and off (procedural memory), and another that keeps track of what you were just thinking thirty seconds ago (short-term memory). Those age-related memory lapses start to make sense as we see that they tend to affect one memory system but not another.

Our memory systems form a hierarchy. At the highest level are explicit memory and implicit memory. They contain what they sound like—explicit memory contains your conscious recollections of experiences and facts; implicit memory contains things that you know without your being aware of knowing them.

An example of implicit memory is knowing how to perform a complex sequence of actions, such as touch-typing or playing a memorized song on the piano. Normally, we can't break these down into their subcomponents, the conscious movements of each finger—they are bound together as a bundled sequence in our memories. Even more implicit is conditioning, such as salivating when you open a jar of pickles, or showing aversion to the smell of a food that previously made you sick—you may not be conscious of this, but your body remembers.

Explicit memory comes in two broad types, reflecting two different neurological systems. One of these is general knowledge—your memory of facts and word definitions. The other is episodic knowledge—your memory of specific episodes in your life, often autobiographical. Scientists call the memory for general knowledge *semantic memory* and the memory for the specific episodes in your life *episodic memory.* (I think they got the name right for *episodic memory,* but the term *semantic memory* has always bothered me because I find it less descriptive. I prefer to think of it as generalized memory, but at this point we're stuck with the name.)

Semantic memory, your general knowledge store, is all those things that you know without any memory of when you actually learned them. This would be things like knowing the capital of California, your birthday, even your times tables (3 × 1 = 3; 3 × 2 = 6; 3 × 3 = 9; etc.).

In contrast, episodic memory is all those things you know that involve a particular incident or episode. This would be things like remembering your first kiss, your twenty-first birthday party, or what time you woke up this morning. These events happened to you, and you remember the instance of them and the *you* in them. That's what distinguishes them from semantic memories—they have an autobiographical component. Do you remember when you learned that 4 + 3 = 7, or when you learned your birth date? Probably not. These are things that you *just know,* so they're your semantic memories.

Of course there are variations across people, and exceptions. I was talking about the different types of memory with my friend Felix last year, when he was age nine. By way of demonstration, I asked if he knew what the capital of California was. He said, "Yes, it's Sacramento." I then asked if he remembered when he learned it. He said, "Yes." I slightly skeptically asked if he remembered the actual day that he learned it, assuming he meant that he learned it last year in school or some other general time. He said yes, he remembered the actual day. I asked what day that was. He answered, "Today." So for Felix, the capital of California was an episodic memory, not a semantic one. It might even stay that way for him, since all of us—my wife and I and Felix and his parents—got a laugh out of how suddenly a college professor was bested by a nine-year-old. A detail that would normally fade into obscurity in the annals of Felix's brain might become elevated to a kind of special status because emotions were attached to it. This is one of the rules of memory that is now well established: We tend to remember best the episodic component of those things that were imprinted with an emotional resonance, positive or negative, regardless of whether the learning would have normally become *semantic* or *episodic.*

But for most people, such episodic memories as this—ones that involve information literacy and general knowledge—become semantic memories over time, and the specific moment of learning becomes lost.

Think how overwhelming it would be if you remembered not just the meaning of every word you knew, and your whole treasure trove of basic knowledge about the world (What continent is Portugal in? Who was born first, Beethoven or Mozart? Who wrote *War and Peace*?), *and* you also remembered exactly when and how you learned it. The brain evolved efficiencies to jettison this (normally) unnecessary contextual information, selectively retaining the parts of the knowledge that are likely to come in most handy—the facts. Some people, however, including some with autism spectrum disorders, don't do this jettisoning and retain all of the details, and it can be either a source of comfort and success for them or a source of irritation and debilitation.

There are some gray areas. Memory for things such as an allergy to ragweed, or your favorite cut of steak, may be semantic—just something you know—or they may be episodic, in that it's possible that you recall the specific instances involved, the time and place, and conjure them up in memory; for example, the very moment you realized, after swelling like a puffer fish with an allergic reaction, that you can't brush your bare skin against ragweed on a hike. The biological distinction is that different parts of the brain hold semantic memories versus episodic ones, and this is a critical step toward understanding why memory failure tends to happen to one system rather than the whole of memory—it's because memory is not just one thing, but several.

Two particular brain regions, crucial to some kinds of memory, are the ones that decay and shrink with age and with Alzheimer's disease: They are the hippocampus (Greek for *seahorse,* because its curved shape resembles that sea creature) and the medial temporal lobe (neurology-speak for the middle part of a structure just behind and above your ears). The hippocampus and medial temporal lobe are important for forming some of the kinds of explicit memory, and they're not needed for implicit memory. This is why eighty-eight-year-old Aunt Marge, lost in a fog of amnesia-induced disorientation, cannot remember you, where she is, or what year it is but still knows how to use a fork, adjust the television station, read, and is excited to see appetizing food, all forms of implicit memory. The impaired brain structures affect her explicit memory but not her implicit memory.

The hippocampus is also necessary for storing spatial navigation and memory for places. Damage to this and to associated temporal lobe regions, as often happens with age, can lead to disorientation and getting lost. In most cases, it doesn't shrink or decay all at once, and so patients are left with fragmented spatial memories, wandering around, registering some landmarks and familiar sights but not able to string them all together into a meaningful mental map.

All of what I've been talking about to this point applies to long-term memory—that more-or-less durable storehouse of memories that can last a lifetime. Short-term memory is another animal entirely. It contains the contents of your thoughts right now and maybe for a few seconds after. If you're doing some mental arithmetic, thinking about what you'll say next in a conversation, or walking to the hall closet with the intention of getting a pair of gloves, that is short-term memory.

All of these memory systems—even the healthy ones—are easily disturbed or disrupted. Working backward up this list, short-term memory depends on your actively paying attention to the items that are in the "next thing to do" file. You do this by thinking about them, perhaps repeating them over and over again, or building up a mental image ("I'm going to the closet to get gloves . . ." or "It's time to take my heart pills—they're on the kitchen counter near the phone"). But the fragility of the item becomes clear if you start thinking about something else, even momentarily ("I wonder how the grandchildren are doing in their new school? Now, *why* did I come into the kitchen?"). Any distraction—a new thought, someone asking you a question, the telephone ringing—can disrupt short-term memory. Our ability to automatically restore its contents declines slightly as we age with every decade after thirty.

But the difference between a short-term memory lapse in a seventy-year-old and one in a twenty-year-old isn't what you think. I've been teaching twenty-year-old undergraduates for my entire career and I can attest that they make *all kinds* of short-term memory errors: They walk into the wrong classroom; they show up to exams without a pencil; they forget something I just taught two minutes ago. I've even called on students who were raising their hand and who sheepishly admitted that they forgot what they had to say in the short time it took me to call on them. These are similar to the kinds of things seventy-year-olds do. The difference is how we self-describe these events, the stories we tell ourselves. Twenty-year-olds don't think, "Oh dear, this must be early-onset Alzheimer's." They think, "I've got a lot on my plate right now" or "I really need to get more than four hours of sleep." The seventy-year-old self-observes these same events and worries about brain health. This is not to say that Alzheimer's- and dementia-related memory impairments are fiction—they are very real, and very tragic for all concerned—but every little lapse of short-term memory doesn't necessarily indicate a biological disorder.

Distraction also disrupts procedural memory. In procedural memory, a form of implicit memory, you've typically practiced a set of movements slowly over time to create a kind of performance. If you learned to drive a manual transmission (stick shift) at some point, you may remember that your first attempts behind the wheel were characterized by a lot of lurching and screeching and probably a few engine stalls. (Mine were certainly that way. I learned on the steep hills of San Francisco, so there was a fair amount of rolling backward and bumping into the car behind me while waiting for the clutch to engage.) The coordination of clutch, brake, and accelerator, while taking into account slope and inertia, is a complex set of actions that need to be synchronized, not to mention making sure you're in the right gear (more than once I tried to move forward from a stoplight with the transmission in third gear or in reverse). But with practice, all these things somehow mesh together seamlessly so that you no longer need to think about them.

Learning to touch-type, to play a piece on a musical instrument, to dribble and shoot a basketball, to dance choreographed steps, to knit, and to shuffle cards are all things that are difficult at first. But at some point, if you got good at them, you no longer needed to think about them. When that happens, we say that the action has become automatic. It no longer requires our conscious effort and active monitoring. It no longer requires short-term memory. It becomes stored in your brain as an intact unit, a sequence of knowledge. And *that* is easily disrupted if you try to turn back the clock and once again think about what you're doing while you're in the middle of it. The easiest way to break your automatic muscle memory—to stall an engine, to fall off a bike, or to forget how to play Chopin—is to try to reconstruct the earlier, unintegrated pieces of that constructed sequence. It's when you try to teach someone else to do these things piece by piece that you realize you no longer have piece-by-piece memory, just a holistic, self-governed memory of how to do it.

Long-term memories are also easily disrupted, and when that happens, it can erase, or more often rewrite, your permanent store of information, causing you to believe things that just aren't so—the state that Beatles producer George Martin described earlier in this chapter. By analogy, suppose you have a Microsoft Word or a Pages or other text document on your computer that you wrote after getting home from a particularly interesting party you went to ten years ago. That document contains a contemporaneous recollection of the events. It is probably imperfect in a few ways. First, you didn't write down every possible thing that happened because you were unaware of some of them—you couldn't hear every conversation, or didn't notice what Carlos was wearing, didn't know about the last-minute drama in the kitchen when a whole plate of cheese puffs fell on the floor. Second, you didn't write down every possible thing you *were* aware of because you selected those events that were important or interesting to you, the things that you wanted to remember. Third, your recollections are biased by your subjective perspective. Fourth, some of your recollections could simply be wrong because you misremembered or misperceived—you thought that John said, "There's a bathroom on the right," and what he said was, "There's a bad moon on the rise."

Now, if you open the document ten years later, it's editable. You can change what you wrote, even unintentionally. You might leave the document open while you go get a cup of coffee and the cat steps all over the keyboard, replacing some of the writing with a bunch of gibberish. Someone else might discover the document and edit it. A computer problem could damage the file, obliterating or changing parts of it. Then you (or the cat) hit "save," or the computer autosaves the file, and there you have it: an altered document that replaces the previous one and becomes your new reality of what happened at that party.

If the edits are subtle enough, or enough time has elapsed since you created the document, you might not even notice. If you've forgotten the incident itself and the document is your only record of it, even if it has been changed without your knowledge, it *becomes* the reality.

This is how memory works in the brain—as soon as you retrieve a memory, it becomes editable, just like a text document; it enters a vulnerable state and can get rewritten without your intent, consent, or knowledge. Often, a memory is rewritten by new information that gets colored in during one recollection, and then that new information gets grafted onto and stored with the old, all seamlessly, without your conscious awareness. This process can happen over and over again until the original memory in your brain has been replaced with subsequent interpretations, impressions, and recollections.

Memory is the way that it is because across human developmental history it solved certain adaptive problems, giving our ancestors a survival advantage over their slower-to-adapt neighbors. Twenty thousand years ago, in a preindustrial age, it's easy to imagine how such rewriting could be beneficial to our survival. Suppose the freshwater spring where you and your tribe get your water runs dry. You go exploring and find a new one. But the next time you try to find it you get lost, making a bunch of wrong turns, until eventually you find it and figure out a simpler set of landmarks to guide you there. Which mental map would be best to keep in your brain, the one that retraces all those faulty steps, or a new and improved one that keeps only the simpler, helpful landmarks?

Or imagine that you notice a jackal around your campfire and coax it near. It seems friendly enough, and in fact, it lets you pet it and snuggles by your feet one night. But the next day it turns on you, biting you and your sister and making off with that piece of meat that was roasting on the fire. If your memory dwells on the earlier, more pleasant time, you might make the same mistake. Better for you to rewrite your memory of the jackal as an unpredictable predator, not to be taken lightly. (Dogs won us over, but it was a slow process.)

Autobiographical memory is perhaps the system that is most closely associated with your sense of self, of who you are and what experiences shaped you. The autobiographical memory system informs your life choices in important ways. Without it, you wouldn't know if you are capable of hiking for two hours, if you can eat food with peanuts in it, or whether or not you're married.

And yet, the autobiographical memory system is prone to huge distortions. It's a goal-oriented system. It recalls information that is consistent with your goals or perspective. We all tend to recontextualize our own life stories and the memories that formed them, based on the stories we tell ourselves or others tell us. Our original memories become corrupted, in effect, to conform to the more compelling narrative.

We also do a lot of filling in based on logical inferences. I don't have many specific memories of the last time I visited London, but using my semantic memory, my general knowledge of London travel, I assume I took the Tube, that it was gray-skied, that I was jet-lagged, and that I drank especially good tea. Because I can easily picture myself riding the Tube from all the times that I have over the last forty years, that image can become grafted into my autobiographical memory for the most recent trip to

London, and before I know it, I have a "memory" of riding the Tube last year that isn't really my memory—it's an editorial insertion, and we're usually not aware that we're doing it.

Memories can also be affected and rewritten by the mood you're in. Suppose you're in a grumpy, irritable mood—maybe because you've just arrived in Los Angeles from London (with its great public transit), and you are fed up with the lousy public transit system in LA. To cheer yourself up you recall a time walking in Griffith Park with a friend that ordinarily is a happy memory. But your current mood state can cause a reevaluation of that as a less happy time—instead of focusing on the great walk, you conjure up the memory of all the traffic on the way there, the difficulty you had parking. All this rewrites the extracted memory before it gets put back in the storage locker of your brain, so that the next time you retrieve the memory, it is no longer as happy as it was before.

There is a famous case of mass memory rewriting involving the attacks on the Twin Towers of the World Trade Center in New York City on September 11, 2001. You'll notice that it conceptually parallels the story I described about finding a new freshwater spring.

Eighty percent of Americans say that they remember watching the horrifying television images of an airplane crashing into the first tower (the North Tower), and then, about twenty minutes later, the image of a second plane crashing into the second tower (the South Tower). But it turns out this memory is completely false! The television networks broadcast real-time video of the South Tower collision on September 11, but video of the North Tower collision wasn't discovered until the next day and didn't appear on broadcast television until then, on September 12. Millions of Americans saw the videos out of sequence, seeing the video of the South Tower impact twenty-four hours earlier than the video of the North Tower impact. But the narrative we were told and knew to be true, that the North Tower was hit about twenty minutes *before* the South Tower, causes the memory to stitch together the sequence of events *as they happened,* not as we experienced them. This caused a false memory so compelling that even President George W. Bush falsely recalled seeing the North Tower collapse on September 11, although television archives show this to be impossible.

And so a huge misunderstanding that most of us have about our personal memories is that they are accurate. We think it because some of them *feel* accurate; they *feel* as though they are like video recordings of things that happened to us, and that they haven't been tampered with. And that's because our brains present them to us that way.

Another way that our memories are defective is that we often store only bits and pieces of events or facts, and then our brains fill in the missing pieces based on logical guesses. Again, our brains do this so often that we don't even notice that they're doing it. So much of our mental activity has gaps in it. Speech sounds may be obscured by noise, your view of something may be occluded by other objects, not to mention your momentary view of the world being interrupted, on average, fifteen times a minute by blinking. The brain mixes up—confabulates—what it really knows with what it infers, and doesn't often make a meaningful distinction between the two.

When we age, we begin to confabulate more, as our brains slow down and the millions of memories we hold begin to compete with one another for primacy in our recollection, creating an information bottleneck. We all have, etched in our minds as true, things that never happened, or are combinations of separate things that did.

Confabulation shows up particularly vividly in people who have had a stroke or other brain injury and are having trouble piecing fragmented memories together. Neuroscientist Michael Gazzaniga has written about this as a lesson in lateralization—the idea that the left and right hemispheres perform some distinct functions. (If you're right-handed, confabulation takes place in your left hemisphere. If you're left-handed, the confabulation could be taking place in either hemisphere—lefties have a less predictable lateralization of brain function than righties do.)

Gazzaniga tells the story of a patient who was in the hospital after a right-hemisphere stroke but had no memory of what brought her there—she was convinced that the hospital was her home. When Gazzaniga challenged her by asking about the elevators just outside her room, she said, "Doctor, do you have any idea how much it cost me to have those put in?" That's the left hemisphere confabulating, making things up, in order to keep a coherent story that fits with the rest of our thoughts and memories. She had no memory of being brought to the hospital, and no ability to process this new information, and so, as far as her left hemisphere was concerned, she was still at home.

Think about the last children's birthday party you were at, and try to remember as many details as you can—walk through the sequence of events in your mind. This is what an attorney might ask you to do at a trial if you were a witness. You might remember things like whether the attendees played pin the tail on the donkey, whether there was cake, whether the birthday kid opened all the presents in front of everyone or decided to do that later. But other details may be lost—whether there was a trampoline in the backyard, whether the other kids were given party favors. Other people and photographs might remind you of things, and those help to trigger some memories.

But still there are gaps. How many different kinds of beverages were served? If you were a bartender or ran a catering company you might have noticed; otherwise not. What color temperature was the light bulb in the bathroom? If you were in the lighting business you might have noted whether it was cool white or warm white or daylight or yellowish. But otherwise, probably not. Memory is filtered by your own interests and expertise. Other gaps: Did the lights in the living room flicker at one point? The insurance investigator wants to know because there was an electrical fire the next day. I suppose that they could have flickered, you think. Yes, now that I think about it, they did. I distinctly remember it. I can *picture* it happening. But there *were* no lights on in the living room—the fuse had previously blown. Your memory's not as reliable as you think, is it? Once you've lived awhile, and collected a number of experiences, it's quite easy to *imagine* things happening the way they're described, and these imaginings become grafted on your memories. Trial attorneys know this and use it as a way to make juries doubt a witness's testimony. Human memory makes logical inferences from the available information, and it delivers them to you with a potent mix of fact and confabulatory fiction.

I had surgery a few years ago and spent several days in bed on pain-killing opioids. They left me a bit disoriented, to say the least. I couldn't remember what day of the week it was, or even what month it was. I recall looking out the window and seeing garbage trucks. Ah! It must be Monday, garbage day. My semantic memory of garbage day was intact, even if my awareness of the day of the week was compromised. I saw that lettuce and onions in the vegetable garden outside were just getting started—in Los Angeles, that means it must be February. I could answer the kinds of questions that doctors ask in order to get a read on your cognitive state, without actually knowing the answers, but by inferring them from my surroundings.

A friend suffered a stroke and is now making these kinds of inferences all the time, masking her inabilities and confounding her doctors. She was a woman with great dignity and independence before the stroke, and these kinds of questions make her feel trapped. When the two of us were alone, I asked her what year it was and I saw that she surreptitiously glanced at a magazine on her table and used that date. I asked her the time of day, and seeing the crust of a sandwich on a plate nearby, she guessed "early afternoon." I asked who the president was and she said she didn't know but could probably figure it out. That seemed unlikely to me, and I didn't want to embarrass her, so I dropped it.

So is your autobiographical memory accurate? Are any of our memory systems? Yes and no. Our memory for perceptual details can be strikingly accurate, particularly in domains we care about. I knew a housepainter in Oregon, Matthew Parrott, who could walk into a house and identify the finish (flat, eggshell, satin, semigloss, or high-gloss), the brand (Benjamin Moore, Sherwin-Williams, Pratt and Lambert, Glidden), and often the precise shade of white, just by looking at the walls. And he could study the texture on the drywall and infer how many different "mudders" (drywall texture contractors) had worked on the house. "Look here," he said, "notice these swirls—they were done by a left-handed mudder." This was his business and he was especially good at it. (He told me that his father had been in the business before him. "My fadder was a mudder," he said.) A lighting designer might remember particular colors and intensities of bulbs. A musician might know, just by listening, the brand and model of the instrument being played.

I conducted an experiment in 1991 in which I simply asked random college students to sing their favorite song from memory. I compared what they sang to the CD recordings of those songs to see how accurate their musical memories were. The astonishing finding was that most people hit the exact notes, or very near to them. And these were people without musical training. But, of course, if it's your *favorite* song, you probably know it well. This finding contradicted decades of work on memory that showed the great inaccuracies in recollections. So we are left with a bit of a messy picture—memories are astonishingly accurate, except when they aren't. Paul McCartney and George Martin have completely different memories of who played what instrument on something as important as a Beatles album. But fans can sing near-perfect versions of those same Beatles songs.

The way that memories are organized in the brain is mediated by memory tags. No one has ever seen a memory tag in the brain, so at the moment, they are just a theory that helps explain how memory works—we may see them in the near future as brain-imaging technology improves.

Think back to that hypothetical birthday party that I described earlier. There are a multitude of queries that could trigger memory tags for that party:

- When's the last time you were at a party?
- Where were you the last time you ate hors d'oeuvres?
- When's the last time you saw Bob and Kate?
- Do any of your friends have a trampoline in their backyard?
- What did you do last Saturday?

Each of these is a way into the memory for that party, and there are probably hundreds more. If there was a particular smell there that you haven't smelled since, encountering it again, even in another context, is likely to bring back a stream of associated memories. Our memories are therefore associative. The events that constitute them link to one another in an associative network. It's as though you have a giant index in the back of your head that lets you look up any possible thought or experience and then points to where to find it. Some memories are easier to retrieve because the cue we use—the index entry—is so unique that there's only one memory with which it could be associated; think, for example, of your first kiss. Others are difficult to retrieve because the cue taps into hundreds or thousands of similar entries. That's why it's difficult to remember things like what time you woke up two Mondays ago—waking up is such a day-to-day, routine event that unless something extraordinary happened two Mondays ago, you pull up a bunch of similar-sounding awakenings that are hard to distinguish from one another. In other cases, memories are easier to retrieve because you've retrieved them many times before—the act of pulling a memory out can improve its future accessibility (although, as we've seen, pulling it out can also distort it and reduce its accuracy under some circumstances).

A great deal of research on memory over the last century has been concerned with the question of *where* in the brain memories are located. It seems like a logical question, but as with many things in science, the answer is counterintuitive: They are not stored in a particular place. Memory is a process, not a thing; it resides in spatially distributed neural circuits, not in a particular location, and those circuits are different for semantic and episodic memory, procedural and autobiographical memory.

If the idea of something not existing in a particular place makes you uncomfortable, consider government, universities, and corporations—these are real entities, but like memory, they don't really exist in a particular, well-defined place. You could point to a particular building where the government has some offices—the state capitol, say—and argue that this is the location of the government. But if that building becomes condemned, the individuals who work there would just move to another building and we would say that the government is *there* now. Or with the rise in telecommuting, we might find that the employees of the state government are scattered around the state, working from their homes. Where is the government now? A major function of government is enacting traffic rules and regulations. Where are traffic laws located? Actually, they're distributed in the brains of every person with a driver's license. (We hope.)

Some *parts* of the memory process are localized. The temporal lobes and hippocampus are responsible for the consolidation of memories—a variety of neurochemical processes that take experiences, massage them, organize them, and otherwise prepare them for storage. This action is catalyzed by sleep and by the distinctive neurochemistry of dreaming, including the modulation of acetylcholine in the brain (remember this chemical because it plays an important part in aging and memories). But consolidation is merely the preparatory process. If memories aren't stored in a particular place, how do they work? The way I came to learn about this was largely through luck, or—to take the developmental science approach—opportunity.

Like most scientists, I spend a large proportion of my time poring over journal articles written by other scientists about their newest findings. My mother and father are both history buffs, and from an early age, we had dinner table discussions about the American West, classical Greece, and biblical times. When I was eight years old, my parents co-founded a club dedicated to studying the history of the town I grew up in, the Moraga Historical Society.

My grandfather died when I was ten, and he left me his *Encyclopædia Britannica* from 1910. I spent hours on my bedroom floor learning about the world as it appeared to people in 1910. There were no entries for *airplane, automobile, radio,* or *penicillin.* Entries on *food preservation* (with an emphasis on salting and drying), *aeronautics* (filled with photographs of dirigibles and zeppelins), and *Alaska* ("formerly called Russian America") were an intriguing counterpoint to what we know now. And so, not surprisingly, when I studied neuroscience as a student, I gravitated toward the field's history; I started looking backward to what scientists were writing about it in the late 1800s. I was fascinated by many of the things we think we are discovering for the first time but that were either previously discovered or intuited by earlier scientists, often one hundred or more years ago.

Memory is a perfect example of modern scientists forgetting what came before. (How's that for irony?) When I entered graduate school in 1992, memory researchers were focused on understanding two problems: What kinds of things are likely to be remembered versus forgotten, and what were the roles of the temporal lobes and hippocampus? There was confusion, disagreement, and outright ignoring of the basic issue of how a memory gets stored or retrieved. It turns out this is something that a group of researchers had already worked on in the early 1900s, but their discovery held no currency for years until it was resurrected and revived by a large body of evidence that had no other explanation.

I entered the PhD program at the University of Oregon, and Doug Hintzman was my mentor, an expert in human memory. During the spring of my first year, I went down to the Bay Area to visit the Psychology Department at UC Berkeley to give a talk about my research. Two professors there, Erv Hafter and Steve Palmer, had invited me. (After obtaining my PhD, I went on to do a postdoctoral fellowship with Steve, and, years later, Erv officiated at my wedding.)

During that visit, Steve introduced me to a professor who had been an inspiration to him for many years, Irv Rock. (Yes, there are two people with identical-sounding first names in this story, Erv and Irv.) Irv had retired from Rutgers at age sixty-five and moved to Berkeley to work with Steve. Irv Rock had studied under the last of the Gestalt psychologists, an influential group of scientists formed in Germany in the 1890s. If you've ever heard the phrase "the whole is greater than the sum of the parts," that comes from the research of the Gestalt psychologists (indeed, the word *gestalt* has entered the English language to mean a unified whole form). One can think of a suspension bridge as a gestalt—the functions and utility of the bridge are not easily understood by looking at pieces of cable, girders, bolts, and steel beams; it is only when they come together to form a bridge that we can see how a bridge is different from, say, a construction crane that might be made out of the same parts.

Irv was seventy when I met him, and I was thirty-five. He and I bonded over our love of salty pickles and the history of science. More than one hundred years earlier, Gestalt psychologists believed that each time you experience something—a walk around your neighborhood, worrying thoughts about your future, the taste of a pickle—it lays down a trace in the brain and leaves a kind of chemical residue. This trace, or residue, theory was largely ignored for one hundred years, but not by Irv. He introduced me to the richness of the Gestalt psychology writings. It was like reading the 1910 *Britannica* again on the floor of my bedroom. Their papers had a contemporary feel to them and a ring of truth—they simply lacked the rigorous experimental protocols that we apply today.

Meanwhile, back at the University of Oregon, Doug Hintzman was developing a contemporary version of the residue theory—multiple-trace theory. In Doug's conception, extending the work of the gestaltists, every mental experience lays down a trace in memory. Doug is a true scientist. He doesn't jump to conclusions, he is measured and cautious in his approach, and he doesn't really have a pet theory—he just designs clever experiments and waits to see what the data tell him. And they told him that trace theory was the most efficient account for thousands of memory observations.

Here's how Doug explained it to me in one of our first meetings (as recorded in my lab notebook from 1992):

> The number of times an event is repeated affects several aspects of memory performance. By performance, I mean your ability to retrieve the event at some later time. The more times the event has been presented, the more accurate you'll be in recall and recognition, and the shorter will be the time it takes you to retrieve it from memory. These effects may not all be due to the same underlying process, but it's most parsimonious to assume, lacking clearly contradictory evidence, that they are.

That underlying process is multiple-trace theory, or MTT. Every experience lays down a unique trace, and repetitions of an experience don't overwrite earlier traces; they simply lay down more, near-identical but unique traces of their own.

The more traces that there are for a given mental event, the more likely you'll recall it and that you'll recall it accurately and rapidly. This is how you learn things—by repeating them, playing around with them, exploring them—laying down multiple, related traces of the concept, experience, or skill. Interestingly, MTT also accounts for the astonishing findings of Posner and Keele in the 1960s, about abstraction in those random dot patterns. The creation of multiple, related traces facilitates the extraction of information common among them, and this occurs in brain cells without having to involve the hippocampus.

The beauty of MTT is that it unifies explicit and implicit memory, and semantic and episodic memory. There might be many different systems, but they are governed by one process. That one process stores episodic and semantic traces, and then abstract knowledge as such does not have to be stored but can be derived from the pool of traces of specific experiences. The reason you get better after practicing procedures, like scales on the piano, is because you have so many traces to draw on. And you can play those scales on different pianos because your brain, automatically as a part of the biology of memory, forms an abstract representation of the piano keyboard that is independent of any one particular keyboard.

I've come to believe that MTT is the correct way of looking at memory. Each experience we have, even purely mental ones—every thought, desire, question, answer—is preserved as a trace in memory. But these are not stored in a special "memory" location like they would be in a computer. When you experience something—say, looking at the letter *a* typed in this book, or imagining your next beach vacation—a certain network of brain cells becomes active. The same is true when you cry during a sad movie, become fearful while walking on a shaky bridge, or look into your baby's eyes—these experiences are represented uniquely in assemblies of brain cells. The act of storing a memory entails keeping track of what that original activation pattern was and then corralling as many as you can of those original brain cells to fire in the same way they did during the original experience. The part of the brain that does the keeping track is initially the hippocampus and allied parts of the temporal lobes, which act as a kind of index or table of contents. Over time, those indexes are no longer needed and the memories reside entirely in the same cells that were involved in the original experience.

If you're like most people, you probably have a core set of memories that you toss over in your mind regularly and have done so throughout your life—major life events, or funny stories that your parents told you or that you tell your kids.

Many memory theorists are still not convinced of MTT. Some don't even know much about it. But it is the explanation that is most consistent with the data. And in terms of aging, it provides a compelling explanation for why we forget recent events when we age but still remember older ones: The older ones created more memory traces, either through repetition or through multiple recollections of them. Add to that the uniqueness of some memories, or at least the unique memory tags associated with them, and it explains why some memories are easier to retrieve than others—they aren't as easily confused with other memories. They stand out.

Storing and retrieving memories is an active process. One of the great historical figures in memory research, Frederic Bartlett, avoided naming his 1932 book *Memory* because he felt it implied something static. Instead, he called his landmark book *Remembering* to reflect an active, adaptive, and changing process. Think of it this way. The neurons you use to taste chocolate are members of a unique circuit of neurons that convey that experience to you. If you want to enjoy that memory sometime later, you have to gather the members of that neuronal circuit together to form the same circuit. In this way, you make the neurons members of that group once again—you "re-member" them.

The key to remembering things is to get involved in them actively. Passively learning something, such as listening in a lecture, is a sure way to forget it. Actively using information, generating and regenerating it, engages more areas of the brain than merely listening, and this is a sure way to remember it. Many older adults complain of not being able to remember the names of people they're introduced to at parties. Generating the information, being active with it, simply means using the person's name just as you hear it. "Nice to meet you, *Tom*." "Have you read any good books lately, *Tom*?" "Oh, you're from *Grand Forks, Tom*. I've never been there." This can boost your memory by 50 percent with very little effort. Laboratory work by Art Shimamura at UC Berkeley has shown that this kind of generating and regenerating items of information increases brain activity and retention, especially among older adults.

What Does All This Mean?

We need to fight against complacency and passive reception of new information. And we need to fight these with increasing vigilance every decade after sixty. Fortunately, there are things we can do, strategies we can employ, to increase the durability and accuracy of memory. For short-term memory problems, training our attentional networks helps us to focus on what is going on right now and to store with clarity and increased precision the most important things we are thinking and sensing. This can be done by slowing down and practicing mindfulness; trying to mono-task instead of multitasking; and trying to follow the Zen master's advice of *be here now.*

Next, we can externalize our fallible memories to objects in the world that don't change as readily as brain cells. We can do this by writing things down and list making. There also exist computer and cell phone applications for building memory, and those are an integral part of the program of healthy brain practices, such as Neurotrack, the memory baseline measurement and enhancement tool developed by a team of scientists at Stanford, the Karolinska Institute, and Cornell.

We tend to remember best those things that we pay the most attention to. And the deeper we pay attention, the more likely those things are to form robust memories in our brains. If you see a bird outside your window and notice the yellow feathers under its chin, that's deeper and more elaborate processing than simply noticing the bird. If you start to turn over in your mind the difference between this bird and others you've seen before, noticing differences in the tail and beak shape, for example, you're processing more deeply still. This depth of processing is now well established to be one of the key features that aids deep memory. When a musician can play a thousand songs from memory, they haven't learned the songs from paying only superficial attention to them, but by elaborating deep processing on them, by registering the differences and similarities among other songs they know. Along these lines, there's a growing body of research suggesting that if we need to remember something, we should draw it—drawing something forces you into the kind of deep processing that is required.

Attention is regulated by structures in the prefrontal cortex and by dopamine-sensitive and GABA-sensitive neurons there. GABA stands for gamma-aminobutyric acid, and it is an inhibitory neurochemical in the brain. Earlier I noted that the prefrontal cortex doesn't mature until the twenties. And it is our human prefrontal cortex that has increased in size, massively, compared to monkeys—in fact, it's the only brain area to show much of a difference between us and our primate cousins. Knowing that the prefrontal cortex is responsible for cognitive control, planning, and generally being alert and conscientious, you might think that the species-related and age-related changes are to pack it full of "intelligence" neurons or something like that. But in fact, the biggest difference in the human versus monkey prefrontal cortex, and between the teenage and adult prefrontal cortex, is the presence of neurons that are GABA receptors—lots of them. That's right, the inhibition neurochemical. Much of what it means to be human, and to be an adult, involves inhibiting responses that we might naturally make. Think about it: not punching someone because you're mad at them; delaying gratification and continuing to work on that important project when you know there is something good on TV; saying no to that third alcoholic beverage; eating healthy foods even though the unhealthy ones are tempting.

Those GABA and dopamine neurons, in combination, help us to focus on what we choose to, without giving in to distraction. Yet with aging, the prefrontal cortex loses some of its pizazz and zing, and we do find ourselves more distracted. We need to make more of an effort to focus.

Federal judge Jack Weinstein (age ninety-eight) says, "I keep thinking of Dr. Spock who wrote all of the child-rearing books that we followed when I was a young parent and [laughs] I remember him saying on the radio—I heard this program maybe seventy years ago—you have to try to have little tricks to deal with your memory loss and he gave this example which has stayed with me. He said if you're listening to the radio or watching TV and it says it's going to rain outside, at that moment—before you forget it—you get your umbrella and hang it on your door so that you pick it up on the way out." Your visible environment is reminding you. Cognitive neuroscientist Stephen Kosslyn calls these cognitive prostheses.

Joni Mitchell (age seventy-six) also uses the environment of her house. "I remember in *Dr. Zhivago,* that as soon as Julie Christie walks in the door she puts her keys on the counter right by the door. *Brilliant,* I thought—that way she always knows where they'll be. I've done that ever since. When I built my new house in British Columbia about ten years ago, I had a whole extra set of small drawers built into the kitchen to hold things that I'm always losing track of, one drawer for each: batteries, matches, chopsticks, Scotch tape, and those kinds of things. I can't stand not being able to find things. I wish I had done this years ago."

Lots of people have different tricks for remembering things when they leave the house. George Shultz, former US secretary of state (age ninety-nine), explains, "You have a routine. I have my hearing aid in my right jacket pocket. Always the same pocket. My keys to my house in another pocket and my wallet in another." Filmmaker Jeffrey Kimball (age sixty-three) has a mental checklist of five things he always has when he leaves the house, repeating it like a mantra: reading glasses, wallet, keys, cell phone, binoculars (he's an avid bird-watcher). And he leaves the wallet and keys inside his shoes by the door when he gets home.

I have two friends who had to undergo chemotherapy for cancer. They were warned that they might experience cognitive lapses, or "chemo-head." They both put systems in place using the technology they had available. Just fifteen years ago they might have had to buy multiple timers and label them for different things they needed to do during the day. Now they do it on their smartphones by programming "appointments" into their cloud-based calendar. They programmed an appointment for each time they needed to take a pill, see a doctor, or fill out a health status report. They'd program little things like "Take a shower" or "Get dressed for grandkids coming over." They might enter "Call doctor fifteen minutes from now," which gave them time to sit and reflect on what they wanted to talk about.

They both recovered completely and have kept using their electronic calendars as a combination to-do list and sticky-paper reminder system. They love the freedom of being able to relax their minds, to let go of worrying about what they might be forgetting. They live more in the moment. And just the act of writing things down, of paying close attention to what they want to schedule, has improved their memories.

Does Memory Really Decline with Age?

I mentioned earlier that the hippocampus and the medial temporal lobes tend to shrink with age, and that the prefrontal cortex changes in ways that may make us more distractible. Distractibility is the enemy of memory encoding. I also suggested that every little memory lapse we experience after a certain age doesn't necessarily mean decline is imminent. And yet, it is commonly said that memory loss with age is to be expected. Neuroscientist Sonia Lupien, an expert on stress, has studied the detrimental effects that stress has on memory and the way it can raise cortisol levels. She had a hunch that the particular way in which older adults are given memory tests stressed them out, thereby causing them to perform more poorly than they otherwise would.

"I don't believe in age-related memory impairment," Lupien says. "If it exists at all, it's much less than people think. I studied the methodology in the experiments that claim age-related memory loss. The older people who came in had cortisol levels that were through the roof before we even started testing. Think about it: We test them in unfavorable environments. Normally, novelty, unpredictability, lack of control, and threat to ego are the four big stressors in humans. And when we test older adults' memory, we're subjecting them to all four!"

Almost every study of older adults' memory is conducted in a university lab. This is a familiar environment to the young people who serve as controls in these studies—they're all students at the university. But the older adults don't find it familiar at all. They're looking around for parking. They don't know where the elevators are in the building. They finally show up, stressed out that they're late, and they are greeted by a cheerful young research assistant who they *know* is looking for possible memory defects. That is stressful.

There are also time-of-day effects. Testing often takes place in the late morning or early afternoon. The twenty-one-year-old controls have just woken up and are at their peak mental ability, but an older adult has probably been awake since five A.M. "We use a favorable environment and a favorable time for the college-age control participants," Lupien says. "But not for the older adults."

Lupien turned the traditional form of memory testing on its head to remove any advantages experienced by the control group of college students. She had her older adult participants come into the laboratory for a get-acquainted visit before the testing day, so that when they came in for a second visit, they'd be less stressed about how to get there and find the right room. On both occasions, instead of being greeted by a young student with whom they had little in common (and by whom they might have felt intimidated), they were met by Betsy, a seventy-two-year-old research assistant. On the day of testing, Betsy shared some refreshments with them to allow them time to get over any residual stress they experienced in traveling to and even being in the lab. After an appropriate "cool-down" time, Betsy brought out a photo album and went through it with them. She might show them a picture of a woman named Laura who keeps a cat as a pet. Or a picture of a backyard with a nice elm tree in it. In reality, Betsy was showing them the stimuli for the memory test. Later, when shown the picture of Laura, the participants answered, "Oh. She's the one with the cat." When asked about the tree in the backyard, they correctly recalled it was an elm. Relieved of all these stressors, including the pressure of actually being evaluated, and fears that they might come up short, the older adults performed as well as younger controls.

There's another explanation for the sometimes poor performance of older adults on memory tests: sensory decline. Uncorrected losses to vision and hearing could account for 93 percent of the variability in cognitive performance. When put in a quiet environment, hearing-impaired older adults performed as well as younger adults; they also performed better when given more time.

Deborah Burke, who directs the Pomona College Project on Cognition and Aging, found that retrieval of words, and in particular proper names, can decline with age among older adults, and that it is a by-product of atrophy in the left insula, a region associated with retrieving the phonological form of the word. That is, we don't actually forget the word itself, just the sound of it—that's why we feel as though we still know the word, why it feels like it's on the tip of our tongues, and why if someone volunteers it we recognize it as the right word. None of those things happen when we truly forget something.

What It Feels Like to Be You

Your memory is an indispensible part of who you are. What does it feel like to be you? When you step outside into the sun on the first warm spring day, do you focus on the way the heat feels on your skin, or on the blue sky, the smells, the colors of the trees? Some of us have an internal focus—when experiencing new situations we turn inward; the first thing we notice is how our bodies feel: warm, cold, itchy, pressure on the skin, the way our clothes fit either loosely or tightly. Others of us have an external focus—being alive involves experiencing the outside world and focusing on it and other people in it.

There are lots of other ways in which being *you* feels different from being someone else—the memories you associate with current experiences, both good and bad, or the activities you like doing. When Alzheimer's and dementia set in, we can lose access to these idiosyncratic and very personal ways of being in the world. Our personalities change; our memories become lost or, worse, confabulated. Simple things like eating fresh berries don't feel familiar. People may feel that they are in someone else's body. This can lead to a great deal of anxiety. Individuals with dementia are often agitated, uncomfortable, angry, and confused. And for good reason—they don't feel at home in their own bodies, their own surroundings.

Part of compassionate care is giving them back a sense of self. Touch can do this—the simple act of a kiss on the cheek or rubbing the back. Music can do it too—listening to songs that you know well that stretch back into childhood can wake up and reactivate the neural circuits that give you that strong sense of "I am me."

2.5

INTERLUDE

A brief biography of the brain

All of us started out life as a single cell, a fertilized egg that then divided into two cells. Those two divided into four, and so on, exponentially. Early in this cell-division stage of life, cells begin to differentiate and specialize, eventually to become skin, toes, veins, tendons, pancreas cells, brain cells—all the different parts and components of your body. At around four weeks of gestation, you can see the brain emerging in ultrasound images. What is this young developing brain thinking about? Or is it devoid of thought, waiting for birth to begin its mental life?

The Greek physicians Herophilus and Erasistratus discovered the nervous system in 322 BC, placing the seat of thought in the brain. It might be fair to say that they were the first neuroscientists. Previously, Aristotle and others thought the brain's function was simply to cool the blood, due to its many folds and creases. It's been said that the Bible taught us the centrality of ethics and that the ancient Greeks taught us the centrality of knowledge and rationality. Just FYI, the Bible did speak of the brain, in Job 12:3 (Iyov, responding to Tzofar, "But I too have a brain, as much as you"), and in Jeremiah 5:21 ("Hear this, stupid, brainless people, who have eyes but do not see, who have ears but do not hear"). These passages were written three hundred years or so before Herophilus and Erasistratus took to studying the brain. How the authors of the Old Testament knew this centuries before the Greeks is a topic for theologians, literary historians, and philosophers of science, not a simple country neuroscientist like me.

During week four of gestation, you can recognize the brain's four distinct structures. One of them, the optical vesicle, will grow into the key components of the visual system: the optic nerve, retina, and iris. Within another week, the brain stem and cerebellum start to differentiate—including the neural circuits that will eventually guide movement, sleep-wake cycles, and temperature regulation. Neural growth in the womb will reach a rate of 250,000 neurons per minute. From their humble origins in a single cell, all the different specialized systems find their places in the brain and in the body. These early, undifferentiated cells are called stem cells because they are like the stem of a flower—which will eventually create petals and leaves and pistils and stamens—all the different parts of the flower. Because stem cells have the power to become anything, they are on the frontier of efforts to repair aging and damaged tissue and to cure diseases. In the early days of stem cell research, the only way to get them was to take them from discarded human embryos. This led to an ethical debate during George W. Bush's presidency. The debate became moot in 2017, when scientists discovered a way to create stem cells from adult human skin cells. Stem cells are promising for a range of medical treatments. In the next twenty years, we may well see stem cell therapies taking the place of contact lenses and hearing aids, skin moisturizers and hormone replacement therapies, and treating diabetes and cancer. They may even reverse decaying memory traces.

As the fetus's cells divide and differentiate, the brain gets built in bits and pieces. Among the first pieces to arrive is our visual system, followed quickly by our other senses. By week twenty the auditory system is fully functional. The developing fetus can hear the world, filtered by amniotic fluid, uterine walls, and muscle; it sounds like what you'd hear if you put your head underwater in the bathtub or a pool. The fetus can detect variations in loudness, pitch, and the rhythms and durations of sounds. From this information, the developing brain begins to wire itself up, to form neuronal connections that map out the very nature and structure of the auditory world in preparation for life outside the womb. The bass lines and chord progressions of music are extracted alongside the pitch and rhythmic patterns of speech. One year after birth, the infant will show a preference for, and familiarity with, the specific kinds of sound patterns it encountered in the womb.

At week twenty-eight, the eyes open and even start to blink. The nose started to develop at week seven, and two tiny nostrils formed around week eleven, remaining plugged up until around week thirty. At that point, the soon-to-be baby starts to smell and become familiar with its mother's scent—this is an important part of infant-parent bonding and prepares the infant for nursing, because the smells of the womb are chemically similar to those of the mother's breast milk. In fact, new research suggests that even before the nostrils become unplugged, the baby becomes familiar with its mother's scent as the amniotic fluid flows through its mouth and nasal cavity.

Why are humans at the top of the food chain? We're not the fastest runners—even a cat is faster. We can't lift the most weight. We don't have fangs like a lion, poisonous venom like a rattlesnake, armor like a rhino. We learn in school that it's the opposable thumbs and using tools. But it's not—it's the brain.

All our thoughts and experiences are mediated by our brains, and the building blocks of our brains are their specialized cells, neurons. There are 85 billion of them in an adult brain. The electrical machinery of your brain consumes vast amounts of fuel—around 20 percent of all the energy of the entire body, even though the brain represents only 2 percent of our body weight. It uses up about twenty watts of power, enough to power my car stereo at full bore in 1978.

A baby's brain is a lot like a mass of undeveloped land, and the process of brain development is like bringing in tractors to cut roads through the tall grasses. The neuron is a specialized cell for transmitting information in the form of nerve impulses. Its long transmission line, the axon, is like a highway. Its branching dendrites are like a bustling city of feeder roads, frontage roads, streets, driveways, and alleys. There are constraints in both sides of the analogy. You can't easily build a road in solid granite or through a mountain; not every neuron can synapse (connect to) every other neuron. The topographical constraints of the brain limit certain kinds of connections and promote others. For example, your plot of undeveloped land may have some existing trails where the deer have already trampled down the grasses and softened the dirt—that would be a path of least resistance for building a road. And there are some places where it is more advantageous to have a trail than others—to the water well, for example. The brain gets general instructions about the topography of its land from information coded in DNA, which we might say is the brain equivalent of trail maps that, among other things, show all the deer trails.

Our brains are predisposed to immense neural growth during the first year of life. An explosion of new connections occurs—more than 1 million per minute at birth, and by six months, up to 2 million new connections a minute. The neurons in the baby's brain begin connecting to one another as they learn about the world; each of those connections represents an experience, a memory, or a perception. When the infant learns that early-morning sunlight is followed by a meal, or that crying will bring someone to come change a soiled diaper, an electrochemical reaction begins inside its brain. In the tiny space between two neurons a new connection is formed, called a synapse. Once neurons are synaptically connected, their electrical activity will become synchronized. As neuroscientists say, they will fire together. This neural firing in tandem is the essence of thought, learning, memory, and experience. Connections like this are forged throughout the brain, and any given neuron could have up to ten thousand of them. If you work out the math, you'll find that by adulthood, there will be more connections in a human brain—more possible thoughts and brain states, that is—than there are particles in the known universe. This may be one of the reasons we can have so much trouble predicting one another's behavior.

Starting around six months, the neural pathways that transmit electrical pulses become more efficient through a biologically ingenious evolutionary adaptation that insulates them. A layer of a fatty, nonconducting biological material called myelin (MY-el-linn) coats the transmission lines and increases the transmission speed. Myelin is white in color, and neuron cell bodies are gray. What we call *white matter* in the brain are the bundles of these highly efficient transmission lines connecting the *gray matter* computational hubs.

There are hundreds of different neuronal types. How does a single cell—the fertilized egg—give rise to each of them? Proteins determine how neurons acquire their identities, and the how and where of axons and dendrites growing toward target cells and forming synaptic connections. The protein genes in your DNA contain instructions about how and when to make these proteins. Humans have roughly twenty to twenty-five thousand protein-encoding genes on twenty-three pairs of chromosomes. (The number of non-protein-encoding genes is about twenty-six thousand. Some individuals are missing one chromosome from a pair, leading to monosomic conditions such as Turner syndrome; some individuals have a third chromosome, leading to trisomic conditions such as Down syndrome.)

The growth of the nervous system depends on the expression of particular genes at particular places and particular times during development. Most of the key instructions for the development and formation of the nervous system are found in organisms separated by millions of years of evolution. Humans have 99 percent of our DNA in common with chimps. And that banana that we and our chimp cousins like to eat? We have a whopping 60 percent of our DNA in common with it, as well as with the fruit flies that like to swarm around it. This is because many of the genes that are necessary for cellular housekeeping—basic cellular function, replicating DNA, controlling the life cycle of the cell, and helping cells divide—are shared across plants and animals.

These blueprints are ancient. The common ancestor that gave rise to both humans and chimps lived between 4 and 13 million years ago. And the overlap with bananas is because animals and plants evolved from a common ancestor some 3 or 4 billion years ago, named LUCA (for last universal common ancestor). Because of this similarity, neuroscientists have learned most of what we know from relatively simpler organisms that are easier to study, both logistically and ethically. If you really want to sound in the know, casually mention in a conversation *C. elegans* (a worm) and *Drosophila melanogaster* (the fruit fly)—two organisms that have taught us a great deal about how DNA works.

The Role of Exploration and Input

The job of the infant brain is first to explore the world, and then to create neural circuits that incorporate that understanding of the world. Some understandings appear to be hardwired, such as understanding (at two months) that objects fall down, not up. But whether this is actually innate or learned is still a matter of debate—by two months, babies have had a lot of experience with the world.

These two jobs of the brain—exploration and wiring up the results of that exploration—are robustly supplemented by a third major job that reaches a peak in old age: prediction. Our brains try to find patterns in both the physical world and the world of ideas, and to make predictions about them. This entails forming categories, making inferences, and problem solving—the operations of higher cognition.

Although the brain begins to take in information while still in the womb, it does so in a state that might best be described as semi-awake, or dreamlike. How does the nascent, developing brain get "turned on" to operate more like a postnatal brain? Neurobiologist Evan Balaban describes the fetal brain this way:

> Most of us biologists would expect to see something that looked like adult brain function, maybe just not as much of it. We'd expect to see that start off slowly and grow. And what we see instead, almost until birth, is these multiple, different states that the brain is in, none of them that look like being awake.

Are these states like being asleep, or like being in a coma, or a different state entirely? Balaban, who is good with electronics, developed a small transmitter that can record brain-wave activity from embryos to answer this question. One thing we know already is that in fetal brains that are normally not getting much stimulation from the outside world, giving them external stimulation has an enormous effect on their development. And giving external stimulation to a newborn is essential for normal brain development; without it, there can be terrible consequences.

At birth, the receptors for the five senses (vision, hearing, touch, taste, and smell) are continuing the job they started in utero, branching their way to the appropriate part of the brain to deliver to your consciousness an impression of what is out there in the world. But they need perceptual stimulation to grow. At this point, everything is new to the baby—the feel of milk going down their throat, the sound of voices down the hall, the many colors of the environment around them.

During the first six months or so of life, the infant brain is unable to clearly distinguish the source of sensory inputs; vision, hearing, smell, touch, and taste meld into a unitary perceptual representation—as William James called it, a blooming, buzzing confusion. It's like the Grateful Dead sang, "Trouble with you is the trouble with me / Got two good eyes but you still don't see." The regions of the brain that will eventually become the auditory cortex, the sensory cortex, and the visual cortex are experientially undifferentiated, and inputs from the various sensory receptors have the potential to connect to many different parts of the brain, awaiting the pruning that will occur later in life.

With all this sensory cross talk, the senses are merged, and the newborn experiences a jumbled flood of sensory impressions. The stream of information from the eyes mixes in with those from the ears, nose, mouth, and skin. The young infant lives in a state of psychedelic splendor in which a green light might have a taste, or their mother's voice might elicit a warm and smooth sensation on the skin. Some babies never completely achieve sensory differentiation and then have a condition called synesthesia. There is some evidence that adults who develop certain forms of dementia can revert to this state, and it has been suggested that this may account, in part, for why some older adults develop a new interest in art quite suddenly.

It is only through interacting with the world that our infant selves learn to separate these sensory inputs; we learn that sounds have an internal mental quality distinct from tastes. Once we learn to differentiate the senses, we go through a phase of reintegrating the information from them. We learn that when someone's lips are moving, sound usually comes out; that the sight of something falling to the ground is usually accompanied by a sound and maybe a vibration; that a pungent smell predicts a sharp taste.

While all this is going on, the infant brain overwires, making many more connections than it will need; axons and dendrites extend to more targets than are required for normal function in adulthood. The primary mission of the brain during the first few years of life is to make as many connections as possible based on sensory inputs, because the infant brain doesn't know which ones it will need later on. New neural connections grow exuberantly. Think of it as building a new house—before the walls are put in you might add many more wires and cables than you'll actually need because the cost of putting them in at this early stage is relatively low; you can always ignore the ones you don't need. But the brain, being a biological organism, doesn't simply ignore the ones it doesn't need; it gets rid of them, by retracting them or using cellular housekeeping procedures to dismantle them.

Starting at around age two, the brain begins this two-decade-long pruning process, getting rid of synaptic connections that aren't being used. By age ten, the brain will have pruned out 50 percent of the connections it had at age two, and this pruning continues into your twenties. Some adult, late-onset mental disorders, such as schizophrenia, may result from incomplete pruning of the prefrontal cortex during adolescence. You might ask, "Why don't all neurons connect to every other neuron and just stay that way?" For one thing, the brain would be gigantic if it did this—twenty kilometers across. For another, pruning lets us sculpt an efficient brain in response to our particular environment. The pruning forces the brain to specialize, to create local circuits that can function apart from others and that can automate certain tasks. The end result is thousands of modules, each doing their own thing.

Take language, for example. The infant brain is configured so that it is receptive to learning any of the languages spoken in the world. We're born with circuits that extract the form and structure of individual consonant and vowel sounds, grammar, syntax, and all the other features of language. A baby of Chinese parents is no more predisposed to learning Chinese than it is to learning Spanish—it is what that brain is exposed to that determines the language the child will speak. And there appears to be no limit to the number of languages a very young child can learn. Studies have disproven the old folk wisdom that a multilingual child is only a fraction as good at each of the languages it speaks—the different languages coexist in the brain and don't take away from one another. In other words, it's not like you've got a maximum capacity for a vocabulary of thirty thousand words that needs to be shared among the three or four languages you speak; each language gets its own vocabulary storage space in the brain, and no one has yet found a limit.

Guinness World Records lists Ziad Fazah as being able to speak fifty-nine languages. (He himself claims to be fluent in "only" fifteen at a time and requires a practice period to get up to speed on the others he knows.) The seventeenth-century poet John Milton could speak English, Latin, French, German, Greek, Hebrew, Italian, Spanish, Aramaic, and Syriac. One of the most impressive polyglots I know is the cognitive scientist Douglas Hofstadter, whose hobby is translating poems from one language to another while observing all of the formal and structural constraints of the poetic form. I once heard him take a five-hundred-year-old poem written in Old French and translate it into modern English, Shakespearean English, French, Italian, German, and Russian while trying to preserve the metric features of the original. He even did an English translation in which the first letter of each line spelled out the name of the poem and the poet.

❖

How does pruning fit into all of this? The infant brain has the capacity to learn any of the thousand or so sounds of the world's languages. As it hears a subset of those sounds in its environment, it wires itself up to them. No infant will hear all of these thousand sounds, and many of the sounds it hears it will not need—the passing foreign language speaker in the street, the mispronunciation because a talker's mouth is full. We recognize speech sounds so quickly and effortlessly because there is little competition in our brains from the sounds of other languages that have been pruned out. Even multilinguals enjoy this efficiency because when they are immersed in conversation in a given language, their brain expects that language's sounds to be heard, and so the neurons for that particular set of sounds are primed and on alert, and the neurons representing other sounds remain in the background.

Much of this pruning and synaptic connecting is based on our brains' ability to take in a large amount of data and extract order and structure from it. Think of the world as having statistical structure that shapes the brain from repeated interactions. In that sense, the brain is a giant statistical analysis engine.

We learn based on co-occurrences of things. Babies learn that the /st/ sound at the beginning of the English words *start* or *stop* is a common cluster for starting words in English, but not in Spanish. (This is why Spanish speakers speaking English put a vowel in front of the word *start*, saying *estart*). Babies learn that the combination of /wszczn/ never appears in English (although it does in Polish). Statistical inferencing is the basis for other types of knowledge too. We learn that touching a hot burner, statistically, leads to pain. That statistically, crying tends to bring Mommy to the infant.

The more experience you have with something, the better your database of what is normal, and the more fine-tuned your mental representations become. A baby who has heard thirty instances of the vowel *ă* is not going to be as effective at recognizing it as a teenager who has heard thirty thousand instances of it. This statistical inferencing applies not just to language but to nearly everything we learn. It's how we learn to read, by recognizing letters of the alphabet **even** when **they** *appear* in different **fonts**, and fonts you've never seen before. Your brain knows what an average letter *a* looks like and pulls variations of that form in, like a magnet, toward the average. This is a general principal of perceptual learning. Squares, circles, the color red, dogs, houses, tables, cups, hamburgers . . . our brains form categories for these based on the myriad examples of them that we see. We get to the point where we can see a distorted or geometrically impossible triangle that may not look like any one we've ever seen before, and we still see it as a triangle.

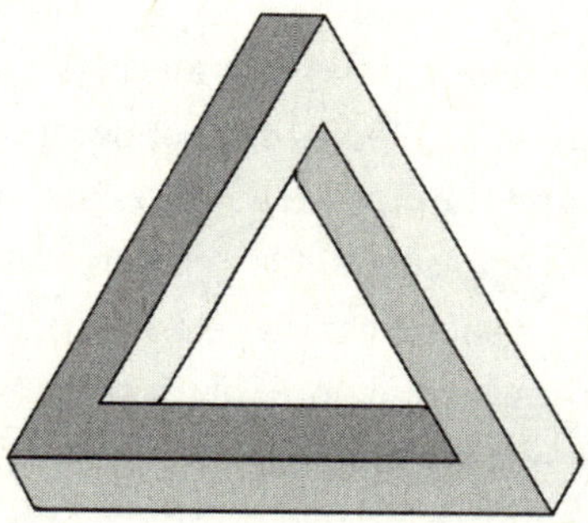

Interacting with the environment through movement and exploration is also important for proper neural growth and development. In infancy, it is the way that we learn to reach and grab, develop depth perception and those important visual-motor circuits. Successfully making contact with a moving target, such as a spinning mobile over the crib, or catching a ball, is so important that it has a special name, *interceptive timing*. This skill is a precursor to mathematical ability: It usually has to develop before a child can represent abstract concepts such as numbers.

Interceptive timing requires that we hone and develop prediction circuits in the brain—we have to predict where a moving object is going to be in the future, based on where it is now, its velocity, and its trajectory. You have to make a similar set of calculations about the movement of your hand in order to calibrate your grasp. Intrinsic in all of this is a sense of quantity and order. It may even be the case that interceptive timing is a prerequisite to language, because successful language use requires temporal order discrimination—in order to understand spoken or written language, sounds that appear quite close together in time have to be put in the proper order. The word *tsar* does not mean the same thing as *star* and it's only because we have refined millisecond timing about whether the /t/ came before or after the /s/ that we can make sense of things.

Interceptive timing is a form of neuroplasticity—the brain accommodating information about the environment into its very wiring, changing itself to develop eye-hand coordination based on experience.

Critical Periods, Infant and Adult Neuroplasticity

The development of mental abilities is an intricate four-way dance of genetic instructions carried by DNA, the topography of the brain, environmental stimulation, and the culture we are raised in. Cortical development is dependent on experience. At birth, the perceptual system is waiting for information to come in that it can assimilate and wire itself up to. Depriving babies of the normal environment, both social and physical, during early critical periods of development can have profound effects much later in life. The term *critical period* is used to describe a time window within which a particular skill or ability needs to be cultivated with the right environmental input, or it can never be acquired. The time course of these windows is a statistical distribution, meaning that after a certain age it becomes extremely unlikely that an ability can be developed at all. Neural development during critical periods involves a multitude of processes in combination, making it difficult to reopen the windows once they've been closed.

You may remember some of these famous examples if you ever took a psychology class. Kittens who are deprived of normal visual input during a critical period never develop normal eyesight. Kittens that wore an eye patch, depriving them of input from one eye, never develop binocular vision or depth perception even after the eye patch is removed. Kittens raised in the dark never learn to see, even though their eyes are fine. (Many scientists today regret that the kitten experiments were considered ethical at the time, in the 1950s.) Although no one has done these experiments with humans, human children who are born without sight in one eye and have it restored after the critical period (by removing a cataract, for example) never develop depth perception either. The key fact here is that signals from the eye tell the visual brain when to grow and how to organize itself. It works this way for the other senses as well.

Similar to vision, the auditory system requires input from the environment in order to develop normally. Infants with peripheral hearing loss (a problem with the ear and not the auditory parts of the brain) are also subject to a critical period. Cochlear implants, which can provide needed input to the cortex, need to be introduced early in life in order to be fully effective. Implantation in the teen years or later never results in normal speech perception, although it does have the survival advantage of allowing the recipient to hear approaching objects that are not visible, such as a car coming up behind them.

The developing brain starts out with some biological biases—for example, that auditory output from the ear will wire up to the auditory cortex. But if experience doesn't yield that, say, because of peripheral ear damage, different things will happen. The brain is thus like a block of clay in its early years and can be molded to its environment, almost any environment, within limits.

For decades we thought that auditory input was necessary for children to acquire any kind of language. Based on a new study just published in 2018, we now know that it's not *sound* that the brain needs to acquire the statistical underpinnings of language; it's *language*—even sign language. If deafness is identified early enough and the young child is exposed to sign language during the critical period for language development, the brain doesn't miss a beat—it acquires sign language as a full-fledged native language just like it would acquire Dutch or Japanese or Swahili. This finding explains why deaf children who receive cochlear implants after ages eighteen to twenty-four months often don't develop as well as deaf children who are exposed to sign language during their first year of life.

Language acquisition and sensory learning in general are possible because of neuroplasticity, the ability of the brain to change itself. It's called neuroplasticity because the neuronal connections are shapeable and flexible, like soft plastic. And the brain is at its most plastic during the first few years of life. Fortunately, some form of neuroplasticity is with us throughout our life spans, even in our older years.

The term *sensitive period* refers to neuroplastic learning that can take place outside a critical period but which tends to be qualitatively different because it is less constrained by biological events. Two examples are playing a musical instrument and speaking a foreign language. These can be learned at any age, but those who take up either late in life may end up less fluent than those who do so early, say, before the ages of eight to twelve.

Although it's not usually called a critical period, the time in the womb is certainly critical. Because the fetus is living within its mother's body and sharing a blood supply and nutrients, things can go terribly wrong if the mother ingests anything that interferes with normal neural development. Steroids, hormones, alcohol, heroin, opiates, and other prescription drugs can all cause developmental defects. A famous case in my era was the prescription drug thalidomide, prescribed for morning sickness in pregnant women starting in 1957. More than ten thousand babies of mothers taking the drug were born with malformed arms and legs—twisted hands, an arm that stopped at the elbow, no thumbs. Taking the antidepressants Paxil and Prozac during pregnancy in rare cases has led to heart and lung defects. The use of Valium or other antianxiety drugs during the first trimester has been associated with facial clefts and malformations. And it's not just mothers' behaviors that contribute to fetal development—having an alcoholic father may increase the risk of having poorly developed organs, lowered ability to deal with anxiety, and motor deficits. A current threat to fetal health is the Zika virus, which causes microencephalopathy, a smaller than normal brain. There are a lot of syndromes with complicated-sounding names, but they all boil down to one thing: interference in the fetus's environment.

Infants who are deprived of physical or emotional contact with their parents or caregivers experience a range of socialization problems that can last the rest of their lives. Infants don't just need food and sleep; they need warmth and they need to be held, and as they develop into toddlers and children, they need adults to interact with them. This applies across species, not just to mammals, and across the life span. A child's social development is a fragile system and good parenting is not a given, particularly among people who themselves may not have had good parenting. Parents who are inconsistent in their affections and attentions can also cause psychological harm. Many children who lacked healthy parental interactions grow into adults who cannot trust other people.

Neuroplasticity and Remapping

The brain has specific regions and circuits devoted to particular mental activities—we refer to the auditory cortex, for example, or the visual cortex or the motor cortex; we refer to the language areas of the brain. When brain development proceeds in a typical fashion, neurons from the eye find their way to the visual cortex. Similarly the sensory receptors in the fetus's developing tongue wind their way through the brain to end up in the gustatory (taste) cortex so that a particular combination of impulses gets interpreted as "sour" or "sweet." Neurons from the inner ear grow until they find the auditory cortex, stopping first at five relay stations that help to prepare the sound for detailed processing. (For those of you keeping track, the relay stations are the cochlear nuclei in the brain stem, the superior olivary complex, the inferior colliculus, the superior colliculus—for control of head turning toward startling sounds—and the medial geniculate body.)

But what about people who are born deaf, who don't get any inputs from their ears to the brain? When this happens, the brain often adapts, rewiring itself to maximize its efficiency. Visual information, particularly that which conveys communicative information like sign language does, routes its way into the so-called auditory cortex, using that plot of neural real estate for communication. Sign languages have syntax and grammar just like spoken language—they are not composed of a bunch of unstructured gestures—and they use many of the same brain regions that spoken languages do. Consistent with the principle of critical periods outlined a moment ago, infants born deaf have to be exposed to sign language or receive cochlear implants during the critical period for language development or they will never achieve language fluency.

Similarly, blind people who read braille are using regions of their so-called visual cortex to do so, remapping their fingers' touch information into areas of the brain that are normally activated by visual input. Neuroplasticity provides this compensatory mechanism for people who are blind from birth, and the altered cerebral organization allows their visual cortex to be activated by braille—tactile reading—as well as by speech.

How this remapping occurs is still unclear. We don't know exactly how "auditory" neurons find the visual cortex, or how "visual" neurons find the auditory cortex. What would happen if the taste receptors from the tongue ended up in the visual cortex instead of the gustatory cortex? Would you see tastes? Would a sour flavor fill your eyes with a particular color or shape? This may be what is going on in infants during their stage of non-differentiation, the psychedelic splendor.

In an extraordinary series of experiments, researchers have begun to understand a little about this. A team led by Mriganka Sur of MIT blocked the path from the retina to the visual cortex in young ferrets. With their usual pathway blocked, where did those retinal neurons connect? They not only found their way to the auditory cortex, but once they got there, they created a kind of topographical map of the ferret's visual world inside of the auditory cortex. In humans, the existence of this sort of cross-modal plasticity may underlie the instances in which some people who are blind or deaf often have superior abilities in their intact senses.

Specific Effects of Aging on the Brain

Infancy is a time of perceptual and mental growth, but before that growth is complete we might say it is also a time of some confusion and lack of control over our bodies. In some respects, then, aging is similar to infancy. We may become incontinent. We may become unable to feed ourselves. We have trouble understanding speech and can't always express ourselves as fluently and seamlessly as we'd like. Although sensory integration can begin to fail as we age, in general, older adults are more apt to use both auditory and visual information when presented together—which can be a good thing. They may need more time than younger adults do to successfully imprint new information.

Most of us will face a range of mental challenges as we age, and they come from multiple sources. Due to plaque buildup and partially blocked arteries (arteriosclerosis), blood flow may not be as smooth as it used to be. A reduction in the ability to produce neurochemicals may cause neurons to fire less efficiently. Dopamine levels fall about 10 percent per decade, and serotonin- and brain-derived neurotrophic factor levels also fall off with increasing age. Years of alcohol consumption can lead to neuronal death and are implicated in brain shrinkage. A decrease in the efficiency of synaptic connections leads to a general slowing of mental processes. There is decay or failure to regenerate the insulating myelin sheath surrounding axons—causing reduced electrical conductivity. Finally, most adults experience a gradual reduction in brain volume after the age of thirty-five of about 5 percent per decade through age sixty, with the decline speeding up after age seventy. All of these factors lead to a general slowing of cognitive function.

Much of this volume and weight reduction comes from shrinkage of the prefrontal cortex and hippocampus. The prefrontal cortex is what we use to set goals, make plans, divide a large project up into smaller pieces, exercise impulse control, and decide what we're going to pay attention to. As I mentioned earlier, the prefrontal cortex is the last region to develop in childhood and doesn't fully mature until well after puberty—into the late twenties. Because of its involvement in impulse control, there have been several cases in which defense attorneys argued that eighteen- to twenty-year-olds shouldn't be held responsible for law-breaking acts because they lack an adult-like, mature prefrontal cortex that would allow them to exercise adult-like impulse control.

The prefrontal cortex is also the first cortical region to show wear and tear as we get older. "That is why one of the most significant problems in older adults is the ability to keep track of thoughts and prevent stray ones from interfering," says Art Shimamura. "Brain fitness as we age depends significantly on maintaining a healthy and active prefrontal cortex. The more we engage this brain region during daily activities, the better we will be able to control our thoughts and think flexibly."

Another important brain region that we need for mental engagement is the medial temporal lobe, above and behind your ears. This brain region includes that seahorse-shaped region called the hippocampus that is crucial for memory storage and retrieval. Imagine you're out with friends seeing a play. It's your prefrontal cortex that makes you want to read the program notes, that helps you to attend to what your companions are saying and to think up coherent things to say in return. Once the play starts, it's your prefrontal cortex that restrains your impulse to talk or shout during the performance. In the meantime, the medial temporal lobe is linking up features of this experience with previous, similar experiences—the previous times you were at a play, the previous times you were in this theater, the previous times you were with these particular friends—and in addition, the medial temporal lobe is helping to store all these thoughts and experiences so that your brain will be able to retrieve them in the future. Without the medial temporal lobe, these links would all be lost and you wouldn't be able to recollect the experience later as an encapsulated event. And without hippocampal function, you wouldn't remember all the fun you had when you woke up the next morning.

Another big factor in mental decline has to do with myelin, that fatty coating around axons that serves as an insulator. White-matter tracts—the transmission lines of the brain, the myelin-coated axons—decay with age starting at age fifty or so, and remyelination slows down to the point where it can no longer keep up. While the gray matter of the human frontal lobe and hippocampus shrinks an average of about 14 percent between the ages of thirty and eighty, shrinkage of white matter is even more drastic, averaging 24 percent. Moreover, unlike gray matter, which shows a more gradual shrinkage over time, the decline in white matter is particularly steep between the ages of seventy and eighty. It's not that the tracts themselves disappear; it's that the loss of insulation causes misfirings and disturbances of the electrical signal and slows down the transmission of thoughts in the brain.

This leads to a generalized slowing in older adults, affecting all of our mental systems, including the transmission of perceptual information, memory, decision making, and motor movements. That in turn may account for memory problems and other cognitive slowing because the white-matter tracts that are most compromised are those in the prefrontal cortex and the hippocampus.

Now, with declining efficacy of the prefrontal cortex and the medial temporal lobe, along with overall shrinking brain volume and white-matter reduction, you can see why older adults can find it more difficult to integrate and act on the information coming in from multiple sources, and why they find multitasking especially difficult. This is why when we age, we can have a harder time both focusing and switching our attention. It's why we get distracted. And it's why we have trouble dealing with new technology, especially new cell phones: The brain has slowed down, it's smaller, and the shaping of our brains by repeated exposure to existing structures in the environment has made it easier to deal with familiar situations but harder to deal with new ones.

You can try out this slowing down yourself. Hold a pen upright, pinched between your thumb and forefinger near the writing end of the instrument. Open your grip and then, as the pen is falling, try to grab it as quickly as you can, and measure how much of the pen passed through your fingers. Compare this to what younger people can do, or make a monthly log to see if you can stay quick or start to slow down.

One of the most important things we can do to promote neural health involves myelin, which is 80 percent lipids. Our bodies' ability to create and maintain myelin relies on dietary fats. Without them, or with a reduced ability to metabolize them, we see even more decay of the myelin sheath than is caused by aging alone. Not every word retrieval problem or lost wallet is due to demyelination, but improving and maintaining myelination does help. Two easy mechanisms are eating fatty fish and getting enough vitamin B_{12}. You may have heard the expression that fish is brain food, and that's true. Fish oil provides the omega-3 fatty acids that the body uses to create myelin, and it can even repair damaged myelin caused by traumatic brain injury.

The cumulative effects of aging include everything from repeated exposure to toxins, illness, and the breakdown of DNA. There are a number of things that can damage DNA—tobacco smoke, ultraviolet rays from suntanning or tanning booths, certain drugs, and even stress. Fortunately, our bodies have sophisticated DNA repair mechanisms that can detect damage and fix it. But the repair mechanisms aren't perfect. The instructions for how the repair mechanisms work are themselves contained within DNA, so if those get damaged . . . well, you can see what the problem would be.

Up to this point I've glossed over the term *attention*, assuming (as William James did) that everyone knows what it is. We experience different modes of attention throughout the day. Two of the most noticeable are what neuroscientists call the central executive mode and the default, or resting-state mode. In the central executive mode we are focused, we direct our thoughts and filter our distractions. In the resting-state mode, our thoughts meander, they are loosely connected, and this has led to its being called the "daydreaming mode" of the brain. The daydreaming mode is restorative after you've been focusing on something intensely for a while, and it is often the mode during which you can effectively solve problems. If you've ever been walking down the breakfast cereal aisle in the grocery store, not thinking about anything in particular, and the solution to a problem you've been struggling with suddenly appears in your head, that's the daydreaming mode. The two modes tend to work in opposition, like a seesaw—when one is up, the other is down. Disruptions of this daydreaming mode have been seen in individuals with autism, and those with Alzheimer's.

Mild Cognitive Impairment, Alzheimer's Disease, and Dementia

Mild cognitive impairment is defined as cognitive decline greater than what would normally be expected for an individual's age and education level but that does not interfere notably with activities of daily life. In about 50 percent of patients it leads to Alzheimer's disease (AD) and can be an early warning sign for it; other times it exists independently. That is, some mild cognitive impairment patients will maintain the same level of impairment for many years (good news), whereas for others it is a transitional stage toward dementia. People with mild cognitive impairment can still perform daily chores and look after themselves, but they have difficulties with memory and misplacing things. (Actually, that's a good description of most of the scientists I know, even ones in their forties!)

We haven't found a single brain correlate for mild cognitive impairment, making its neuroanatomical basis heterogeneous—that is, a number of different brain conditions could lead to it. And just when you observe systematic changes in the brain for people with mild cognitive impairment, brain scans show highly similar lesions in the brains of people who show no symptoms at all! This is similar to dementia—there is no single neurophysiological profile because it arises from a large number of different brain abnormalities.

As I write this, a new paper was just published by a group of neuroscientists in China that decomposed brain imaging signals into distinct frequency bands, and using this new technique, the neuroscientists were able to classify individuals with mild cognitive impairment with 93 percent accuracy. This is only a single paper and further work will need to be done to confirm the accuracy and utility of this, but it is a promising start.

The kinds of redundancies that exist in the brain, and the concept of cognitive reserve, may be just as important as what is actually showing up in those scans. Cognitive reserve is the idea that people with more education and who are more intelligent may be able to withstand biological degradation better than others. Cognitive reserve is like that extra secret gas tank that Volkswagens used to have in the old days (how ingenious was *that*?). It is the capacity of the mature brain to roll with the punches, to sustain the effects of disease or injury that would otherwise impair others.

Think about it in terms of strength or endurance in physical activity. If you can lift two hundred pounds or run for twenty minutes at top speed, it will not exert you to lift fifty pounds or run for five minutes, compared to someone who is out of shape. And even with a cold, something that impairs your muscle tone and lung capacity, you would still likely be able to outperform others. That's the concept of reserve.

Dementia is a catchall term used to describe any brain disorder that causes deficits in more than one cognitive domain, such as attention, memory, and language. Alzheimer's is a form of dementia, and there are many other types.

Alzheimer's is characterized by abnormal protein aggregates (plaques) and neurofibrillary tangles, which disrupt neural transmission. One particular protein, called beta-amyloid, starts out by destroying synapses before it clumps into plaques that cause neuronal death. The disease typically starts in the medial temporal lobe and then spreads throughout much of the brain. Damage is particularly likely to affect regions linked to learning and memory, for reasons we don't yet understand. Early symptoms include memory impairment, particularly for recent events, but then other cognitive disorders begin to appear, such as problems in attention, language, and spatial processing. There is a genetic factor, though as with virtually all disorders, the extent to which you take care of your body influences the degree and extent of the disease.

I'd like to be able to report that after the $1.8 billion the United States spent in 2018 alone, and decades of research, we know what causes Alzheimer's, how to cure it, and how to prevent it. For a while we thought that the accumulation of amyloid was the problem, and if we could reduce it, we'd have a cure. There are now drugs that reduce amyloid buildup, but they don't stop or reverse the disease. No drugs have managed to even improve symptoms modestly. And not everyone with these amyloid plaques and tangles has the disease or the symptoms of it. Many normal, apparently healthy human brains show the buildup of beta-amyloid plaque deposits, the loss of neural connections, and the degradation of myelinated pathways (white matter) and remain symptom-free.

Some early evidence suggests that chronic inflammatory processes feed existing Alzheimer's disease, or perhaps even cause it. Some researchers have suggested that taking NSAIDs (nonsteroidal anti-inflammatory drugs) as much as ten years before the expected onset of Alzheimer's symptoms might be advisable, but a great deal of further work needs to be done—we don't know what other negative effects may accrue from such chronic use of NSAIDs.

If you're one of the millions of people who have sent away saliva samples for commercial genetic testing, you may have received a report on a particular genetic factor that can predict the likelihood of developing dementia. The *APOE* gene is a genetic factor that greatly increases the risk of developing dementia, as well as late-onset Alzheimer's disease (after the age of sixty-five). The problem with such information is that genetic contributions to dementia are complex; interactions with other genes and other biomarkers need to be taken into account in order to get an accurate picture. *APOE* alone does not cause dementia or Alzheimer's. And, of course, an increased risk does not mean you'll develop the disease with perfect certainty, and in some groups, the presence of the gene is protective. I find this information does more harm than good in people who lack advanced training in statistics and risk analysis—that is, most of us. As I described in my book *The Organized Mind,* some things you do can triple your risk of certain rare diseases. That means one thing if your chance of getting the disease was one in three to begin with—you're going from a possibility of getting it to a near certainty. But if your chance of getting the disease was one in 60 million to begin with, and you triple your risk, you still only have one chance in 20 million of getting it—you're more likely to get hit by lightning, win the lottery, and die in a car crash all on the same day.

I want to join John Zeisel, founder of the I'm Still Here Foundation, and say that the biggest challenge faced by dementia is the public narrative of despair, that nothing can be done about it. I do not believe that this is true. I believe we should replace the stigmatization of dementia with hope, and the recognition that people with dementia are still there.

The *Lancet*'s expert panel provides some hope. As they state,

> Dementia is by no means an inevitable consequence of reaching retirement age, or even of entering the ninth decade. There are lifestyle factors that may reduce, or increase, an individual's

> risk of developing dementia. In some populations dementia is already being delayed for years. . . . One-third of dementia cases may be preventable.

Stroke

A stroke is the restriction of blood flow in the brain that causes cell death. Strokes come in three types. When a clot forms in the brain, preventing oxygenated blood from reaching particular regions, it's called an *ischemic stroke.* (*Ischemia* is the word used for restrictions of blood supply.) If the clot is only temporary, the resulting stroke is called a *transient ischemic attack,* or TIA. These are usually warning signs for subsequent strokes. When a weakened blood vessel in the brain bursts and causes internal bleeding, it's called a *hemorrhagic stroke.* (A hemorrhage is the escape of blood from a blood vessel.)

The main risk factor for any type of stroke is high blood pressure. Antihypertensives are prescribed therefore not just to reduce the risk of cardiac disease but to reduce the risk of stroke, especially in people who have other risk factors, such as obesity, poor health, or a family history of stroke. Lifestyle interventions, such as restricting salt intake, learning to cope with stress, and aerobic exercise also lower blood pressure.

For years, doctors advised people over fifty or sixty to take a baby aspirin (around 80 mg) every day as a preventative, to thin the blood, thus reducing the risk of a blood clot or ischemic stroke. The problem with this is that if you have a hemorrhagic stroke, the thin blood won't clot and the damage from internal bleeding will be more severe. It's one of those weird situations in medicine where you effectively have to choose how you want to die or be otherwise damaged: Would I rather have the damage from a clot or from a rupture? On the other hand, if you've already experienced an ischemic stroke—and you know for sure that it was ischemic and not hemorrhagic—taking aspirin or other blood thinners is usually advised to reduce the chance of a second ischemic stroke. As of 2019, there is mounting evidence that taking the low dose aspirin is preventively not worth the risk, and a study of twelve thousand Europeans found that it had no effect on stroke.

The aftermath of stroke is highly variable. Some people experience no aftereffects at all; others are left partially paralyzed, are unable to speak, or experience profound personality changes. In some cases, cognitive and physical therapy can restore function to nearly 100 percent, but we still don't know which patients will recover fully and which will not. Genetics, resilience, determination, and environmental factors all play a role, but we have not yet elucidated the how or the why.

Neuroplasticity across the Life Span

For decades, physicians and scientists assumed that our brains are built from a finite number of "cells," each with its own job to do, and after the brain reaches maturity, we lose cells one by one until we end up in a second infancy. Although we generally believed this, we had inklings that it wasn't true. Neuroscientist Karl Lashley argued eighty years ago that if part of the brain was damaged, other brain areas would take over, but the idea of the brain as an immutable machine held sway. As explained by physician Abigail Zuger, "Every part had a specific purpose, none could be replaced or repaired. . . . Now sophisticated experimental techniques suggest the brain is more like a Disney-esque animated sea creature. Constantly oozing in various directions, it is apparently able to respond to injury with striking functional reorganization, and can at times actually think itself into a new anatomic configuration."

Along these same lines, scientists used to think that the human brain couldn't grow any new neurons after birth. Then, evidence emerged that neurogenesis—the growth of new neurons—occurred in the hippocampus of adults, and some estimates placed the number at seven hundred new neurons per day. That is not a lot considering that the hippocampus is estimated to have around 47 million neurons; it represents the growth of around 1.5 percent of the total number of neurons each year. Then, in 2018, two studies were published in the same month that reached opposite conclusions. One study, published in *Nature*, from the University of California, San Francisco, showed that hippocampal neurogenesis drops to undetectable levels in childhood. Another study, from Columbia University, found preserved neurogenesis in adults.

Two review papers that year attempted to resolve the contradiction. There are a number of complex technical and methodological challenges to measuring neuronal growth, and since neurons can't be physically counted in humans (yet), the estimates rely on a number of inferences, both conceptual and statistical. Both teams used the presence of protein markers (DCX and PSA-NCAM) that typically accompany neuronal growth. These markers can only be measured in autopsies, and variations in how brains are preserved and the delay between time of death and time of examination could yield such wildly contradictory results. In addition, some studies have found that, in animals, the growth of new neurons isn't necessarily accompanied by these protein markers. Confused yet? So am I and other neuroscientists. The field is still working all this out, and so at present, I'd have to say we don't really know if adult humans can grow new hippocampal neurons. But the weight of the evidence, spanning the past twenty years of research, strongly suggests we do. A single study that fails to find growth isn't sufficient to negate a dozen other studies that did, or the dozens of studies in animals that show *they* continue to grow new neurons—there is no reason we know of that humans would be different. But even the lack of neurogenesis doesn't mean we don't form new memories, or that our memory capacity is limited. Memory resides in the *connections* between neurons, and in synaptic plasticity, which *is* a lifelong process.

The Canadian psychiatrist Norman Doidge describes case studies of individuals who experienced this kind of synaptic plasticity, a rewiring of their brains, from a woman with a damaged vestibular (balance) system to a man suffering phantom pain in a limb that had been amputated—all achieved functional reorganizations of their brains as adults.

I had been taught in 1976 that this kind of neuroplasticity peaked in adolescence and young adulthood, that sixty-plus-year-olds could not hope to experience such complete and rapid remodeling of their brains. But research in the past ten years has shown these assumptions to be wrong. Older adults' brains *are* plastic, capable of great feats of rewiring and adaptation; it just takes a little longer because much (but not everything) that older brains do is slowed down.

Neuroplasticity does not seem to slow down nearly as much for older adults who have been making demands on their brains to think differently and rewire for many years. If you're involved in the creative arts—painting, sculpture, architecture, dance, writing, music, and other forms of creativity—you've been exercising your brain, pushing your brain, in interesting ways all along because every project you undertake requires new adaptations, some way of looking at the world differently, and then acting on it. And it's not limited to the creative arts—any job or hobby that requires you to interact with the world and to respond to it differently each time is an activity that helps protect the brain against dementia, rigidity, and neural atrophy. This can apply to housepainters, arborists, athletes, serial entrepreneurs, publicists, professional drivers, crossword puzzle players, bridge players, and so on.

My own experience with musical instruments shows this remodeling can occur at any age. Sometimes at a concert, musician friends call me up onstage to perform a song or two, and I play whatever guitar is already there. Every guitar is different and I typically face parameters I'm not used to—differences in the height of the frets, the distance between the strings, the gauge of the strings, and the thickness of the neck. Or I might be handed an acoustic after having played electric guitar for several months. The adaptation is almost immediate. A musician's brain contains an abstract representation of how their instruments are supposed to work, and how their fingers are supposed to interact with them, and it makes appropriate adjustments. Even more sophisticated is what happened when I broke a nail the other day on the middle finger of my right hand, my fingerpicking hand. I just "told myself" that this finger was out of commission and shifted to the next two fingers down the line everything that this finger used to do. It took all of five minutes to make the adjustment, an example of neuroplasticity. Mari Kodama, the great concert pianist, says that she often has to change well-rehearsed fingerings on the spot during a performance, depending on the piano or the acoustics of the hall. So although we have finger patterns deeply memorized, abstractions of those patterns are apparently memorized as well and are there to be tapped into.

You've probably experienced this yourself in daily activities and not even known that it was something as lofty as neuroplasticity or brain adaptation: driving a rental car, using a pen with a body of a different thickness than you've used before, cooking in someone else's kitchen, buttoning up a new shirt, listening to someone speak in an accent you've never heard before. Even something as simple as drinking coffee out of a new cup that is weighted differently and has a differently sized handle than you're used to. These are all examples of adaptive neuroplasticity.

Neuroplasticity continues until we die, but, like reaction times, it does slow down, and the extent to which brain remodeling can occur is reduced as we age. The good news is that *previously* learned motor skills are well-preserved at least through age sixty and for many well beyond their eighties. The musician Glen Campbell is a prime example. At age seventy-six, deeply affected by Alzheimer's disease, disoriented and unable to take care of himself, he was still performing complex songs that he had known for more than forty-five years, which underscores how certain remarkable motor routines are embedded deep in memory where disease can't touch them. Other motor routines fly off the rails, and Campbell would sometimes lose his place and not know how to get back. One of the most protective things you can do against aging is to learn a manual skill when you're young and keep it up. The next best thing you can do is to start learning something new when you're old.

The efficiency with which we learn new motor skills, however, declines with age—we can learn well into our nineties and beyond, but the learning takes more concentration and more time. In what has become a familiar conversation between grandparents and their grandchildren, older adults can learn how to use computers and cell phones, but they make more errors while they're learning and don't retain the new information as long as younger people. In adapting to new glasses, or shoes, or directions due to roadwork, older adults take longer, and longer as well to readapt to the previous way of doing things. It's not just that older adults are slower at doing many things; it's that they are slower at adjusting to new things. If you are thinking that there might be a correlation between this and the tendency for older adults to become more politically conservative—to want things to stay the way they are—you might be on to something.

Our senses are among the earliest things to emerge in the womb, but unfortunately they can wear out sooner than many of our other faculties, as we've seen in older adults. Half of adults over the age of seventy-five report hearing loss and one in six report vision loss. A whopping 90 percent of people over the age of fifty-five wear glasses; only one in six Americans with hearing loss wears hearing aids, and *not* wearing hearing aids is associated with an increased risk of hospitalization in older adults. Fortunately, neuroplasticity offers the brain a number of ways to compensate for the decline in the quality of sensory information. Neuroplasticity leverages what our bodies can tell us about the world, how and how well our senses perceive it. Understanding how perception works and develops is essential to understanding successful aging.

3

PERCEPTION

What our bodies tell us about the world

The British philosopher John Locke proposed what we now call Locke's challenge: Try to imagine a smell that you've never smelled before. Or try to describe a novel taste to someone who hasn't experienced it. Locke's insight was that everything we know about the world we know through our senses. Locke was not just a one-idea guy, by the way. He was the first to propose that our sense of self comes from the continuity of consciousness. And it was he who first wrote about the importance of the separation between church and state—the same idea that Alexander Hamilton and the founding fathers of the United States later incorporated into the US Constitution.

Locke's challenge put the senses front and center in our understanding of human information processing. His observation changed the way that we think about knowledge—what it is, and how we acquire it. How does the brain go from an apparently undeveloped state to one that is more adult-like? The single most important factor is input from the outside world. The brain learns to become fully functional through its interactions with its environment. Without that, the brain never becomes fully adult-like, never reaches its full potential. This is a lesson that applies equally to animals and humans and to children and adults of all ages. *Interactions with the outside world are crucial.* Roboticists and AI engineers have learned the hard way that no matter how fast their CPUs can process algorithms, the biggest barrier to achieving human-like capabilities is a lack of sensory input and integration of inputs across these artificial senses.

We learn in elementary school that humans have five senses. Less well-known is that some animals use other senses that we lack. Some are rather exotic. Sharks, for example, can detect the neural firings of species they want to eat using an electrical sense. Bees find flowers by detecting electric fields (flowers have a slightly negative electrical charge, which contrasts with the bees' slightly positive charge). Snakes find their prey using an infrared heat detector, and elephants are sensitive to vibrations through special receptors in their feet. Many animals have sharper senses than we do—a dog's sense of smell is a million times more sensitive than ours. (With that much olfactory power, I imagine that sniffing at a fire hydrant might give a smart dog a pretty good idea of who's in the neighborhood, their diet, and possibly even the overall health status of the local canine population.)

Sensory receptors are specialized cells, constantly detecting and collecting information in the world and transmitting it to the brain. Our eardrums, for example, respond to disturbances of molecules in air or liquid—vibrations. Our eyes register the amplitude and frequency of light waves. (Light is a form of electromagnetic energy, and so our visual sense is not that different from sharks' and bees' electrical senses—the difference is in how our brains interpret that information.) Our tactile receptors register temperature, wetness, pressure, and injury; they exist even on some of our internal organs—think back to your last stomachache. Our taste and smell receptors detect the chemical content of objects.

Once our sensory receptors pick up information from the outer world, they send electrical impulses to areas of the brain that are specialized for interpreting those signals. The spike-spike-spike of electrical pulses coming from the various sensory receptors brings us the entire range of sensory experiences: sour, sweet, hot, cold, painful, soothing, loud, soft, bright, dark, red, purple, fragrant, acrid, and dozens more. There is nothing "sour" about the nerve impulse coming off your tongue—"sour" occurs in your gustatory cortex, a part of the brain dedicated to interpreting these impulses. Sir Isaac Newton, a contemporary of Locke's, knew that the rich perceptual experiences we have are created in our brains, not out there in the world. He wrote that the light waves illuminating a blue sky are not themselves blue—they only *appear* blue because our retina and cortex interpret light of a particular frequency, 650 terahertz, as blue. Blueness is an interpretation that we place on the world, not something that is objectively there.

The Logic of Perception

We tend to think that our senses give us an undistorted view of the world—that what we see, hear, or experience through our senses is reality. But nothing could be further from the truth that science pursues. If I shine light waves of different colors on a screen, some will seem brighter than others even if I carefully control the luminance output of the projector. (Our eyes are most sensitive to green light and least sensitive to blue, meaning that even if green, blue, and red colors are presented at equal luminance, the green will appear brighter and the blue dimmer than red.) This might be due to the hundreds of thousands of years, when, even prior to walking on two legs, our eyes scanned green leaves looking for food. Musical instruments or voices that are precisely the same amplitude will not be perceived as having the same loudness because some frequencies simply *sound* louder, to us, to our brains, than others.

Our internal perceptual system constructs a version of reality that is in some ways better for our survival needs than what our sensory receptors detect. For example, the auditory frequencies our brains are most sensitive to are the ones that distinguish one vowel or consonant from another in speech—our brains effectively favor some frequencies over others to help us understand one another better. The lens of the eye is shaped such that straight lines in the world should appear slightly curved, and certain curved lines should appear straight. But they don't—the visual cortex "knows" the distortion of the lens and makes corrections. Then there's chromatic aberration—colors of light coming from the same source do not strike the retina on a common focal point, because of their different wavelengths, but the brain compensates so that we perceive them coming from the same source. These are just a few of the hundreds of brilliant compensatory adjustments performed by the brain, and they occur unconsciously.

My friend and mentor Irv Rock (who was age seventy when we met at Cal) wrote an influential book called *The Logic of Perception* that summarized his life's work. As he noted, the signals hitting our sensory receptors are often incomplete or distorted, and our sensory receptors don't function perfectly. There are other cases in which what our receptors might tell us about the world is wrong and the brain needs to step in. Rock further showed how our perceptual system uses logical inferences to help us perceive the world. Perception doesn't just happen—it entails a string of logical inferences and is the outcome of unconscious inference, problem solving, and outright guesses about the structure of the physical world.

Brightness constancy is a striking example. When you go to a movie theater, the screen is white and the projector shines a bright light on it. But of course, there are dark images on the screen—villains wearing black hats, cats with black fur, George Clooney wearing a black tuxedo. But black is the absence of light, so how does the projector do it? The answer is that it doesn't—your brain has to make some inferences. All that the projector can do is shine light or not shine light on that white screen. Everything on the screen that appears black is in reality just the color of the screen. What's happening is that your brain has evolved to make inferences about colors and brightness as they appear in relation to other colors and brightnesses. (There is a current new rage for black movie screens and some theaters have them because they render truer blacks.)

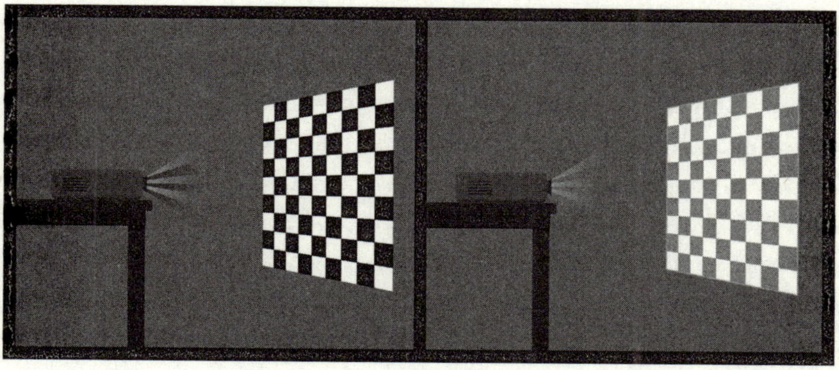

On the left is how you perceive a checkerboard that is projected. On the right is what the projector is actually projecting. Your brain uses the logic of perception to infer that the image on the left is what was intended. Your brain does this unconsciously—knowing that this principle is at work doesn't allow you to shut off the neural circuitry that makes it so. Our brains know that George Clooney's tuxedo is not gray and thus render it the blackest of blacks.

The visual illusion by Edward Adelson on the following page makes the point. Squares A and B are exactly the same shade of gray, but they appear to be different because the brain—through an automatic process of logical inference—distorts the image coming from the eye and corrects it. The

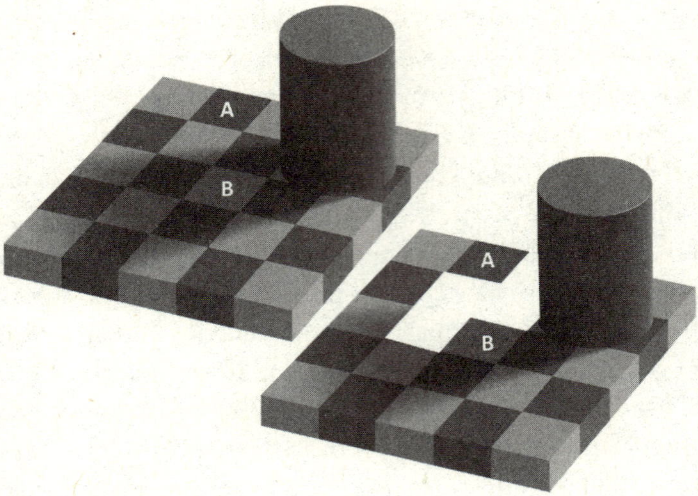

brain assumes that because the square is in a shadow it must *be* lighter than it *appears.* If you cut a piece of paper about the size of this figure, and cut out little squares revealing only A and B, you will see that this is true.

There are dozens and dozens of such principles. Another is color constancy. If you've ever seen a photograph taken indoors, back in the old days of analog photography and actual film, you may have noticed that the entire scene has a kind of yellowish hue, and people's skin tones look unnatural. That's because the camera's lens saw the room as it really was, yellowed by incandescent lights. But your eye doesn't see it that way, because your brain employs color constancy. That red dress looks the same to you indoors and outdoors, but it does not look the same to the camera.

Most of the examples of this we know of come from vision and hearing because those are the two most studied senses. But there are examples of them in the other senses. If I touch your toe and your forehead at the same instant, you will perceive that they were touched at the same time. But it takes a lot longer for the nerve impulse from your toe to reach your brain than the impulse from your forehead. What *really* happens is that your brain gets a message from the forehead touch first, and then the toe touch comes in and the brain has to subtract a delay constant (factoring in how long neural transmission takes) and then come to the logical conclusion that both were touched at the same time.

Irv Rock referred to *the logic of perception* because he believed that the brain did all of this based on probabilities. Given what is hitting the sensory receptors, the brain tries to work out what is the most likely thing that is happening. Perception is the end product of a chain of events that starts with sensory input and includes a cognitive, interpretive component. Have I convinced you that the brain is full of tricks and that the world is not always as it appears? Here's where it gets really interesting. The brain *fills in* missing information without your knowing it. And the older you get, the more it does this. This perceptual completion is also based on the logic of perception. If you're talking to someone in a crowded room, it's likely that some of their words will be masked by other conversations, clinking glasses, or footsteps. But you can still interpret what they're saying. For years I've used a demo in my classes of a person speaking a sentence in which one syllable has been completely removed and replaced by a cough. Students know that the cough is there, but they don't realize that a syllable has been excised, and they have no trouble understanding—their perceptual system simply fills in the missing information. Perception is a constructive process—it builds for us a representation of what is out there in the world, a mental image that allows us to interact with the world as our brain concludes it is, and not as it may merely appear to be.

There are illusions in each of the five senses. A West African berry called miracle fruit can create a taste illusion, removing the sensation of bitterness from foods. Drinking orange juice after brushing your teeth makes it taste sour. There are even motor illusions: As kids, my sister and I would stand in a doorway with our hands by our sides, then press them outward against the frame as hard as we could for about one minute. When we left the doorframe, our hands would oddly float up without our volition—a kind of motor control illusion.

Perceptual completion emerges in infancy between around four and eight months, and adult-like adjustments come at around age five. A more everyday example of perceptual completion involves the blind spot in our visual field. In the part of the retina where the optic nerve passes through, there are no cones and rods, and so no visual image is projected there—and yet our brains fill in the missing information based on what surrounds it.

There is a trend, as we age, to get better and better at this sort of perceptual completion, precisely because we have experienced so much more of the world that our mental database of what is likely and what is unlikely is informed by millions more observations. These observations become data for the (unconscious) statistical processor of our brains. Through neuroplasticity, this changes the wiring of our brains with each new observation. So even though our sensory receptors begin to show wear as we age, and our brains show atrophy, decreased blood flow, and other deficits, our perceptual completion can improve. This is another of the many compensatory mechanisms that bring an advantage to the aging brain. Older people may well be more efficient and accurate at dealing with degraded signals than young people, because their perceptual system has more experience with the world.

The Berlin and Innsbruck Experiments

An astonishing example of neuroplasticity, of the brain rewiring itself, comes from a series of experiments begun in the 1800s by Hermann von Helmholtz. I think of Helmholtz as one of the fathers of modern cognitive neuroscience, and his work deeply inspired Irv Rock. Helmholtz was interested in all the senses and how they worked, and he was a tinkerer. He knew that our visual system could adapt to new experiences, but he wondered what the limits of that neuroplastic adaptation were; he studied this using distorting glasses.

Volunteers in Berlin wore prismatic glasses that shifted their visual field several inches to the left or right. Then Helmholtz asked them to reach for a coffee cup or pen or some other object nearby. Because the visual information was now shifted, their hands would go to the wrong place, several inches away from the object they wanted to grasp. Within an hour, their brains began to adjust, using perceptual adaptation. This was neuroplasticity in action! The brain took in the new information and rewired the motor system to accommodate the change. When the glasses were removed, the participants again made mistakes in the opposite direction for a short time, but the brain readapted quickly.

The prism adaptation experiment showed the degree to which the visual system and the movement (motor) system in our brains are connected and interdependent. It strongly suggests that our brains contain a spatial map of our surroundings. After putting on prism glasses we experience that this internal map is wrong and that it needs to be updated. These adaptations produce changes in the brain, in the sensory cortex, the motor cortex, the intraparietal sulcus, a region associated with error detection and correction, and in the hippocampus, the seat of spatial maps.

You've experienced these spatial maps if you've ever reached for a glass of water on the night table next to your bed in the dark, or found your way to the bathroom in the middle of the night without turning on the lights. The mental maps can be high-resolution, durable, and stable over time. Yet they're also changeable if new information comes in that contradicts them.

Helmholtz thought that the degree of adaptation depended on the length of time the prismatic glasses were worn, but it has been shown recently that the process is instead dependent on the number of interactions between the visual and motor system that you have. In fact, if you just wear distorting glasses and don't interact with the environment actively, no adaptation will occur. If a nurse moves your arm for you, no matter how many times, you won't adapt. It's not the eyes or visual cortex that make the adaptation in cases like this; it's the motor (motion) system and brain circuits that govern the interaction between vision and movement. But as few as three interactions can bootstrap the brain to rewire itself.

Helmholtz's pioneering experiments became a fascination in Innsbruck, Austria, and led to a series of experiments in the 1920s and 1930s. In one, people wore left-right reversing goggles. The adaptation took a lot longer than a simple shift of the visual image to the left or right, but astonishingly, full adaptation did occur. At least one brave soul drove a motorcycle through the streets of Innsbruck while wearing them (then again, perhaps it was the Innsbruck pedestrians witnessing it who were brave).

Pushing the adaptation notion to an extreme, the Innsbruck experiments included a pair of inverting goggles that turned the world upside down. The drive for the brain to adapt to perceptual changes is so powerful that it even corrected for this by eventually turning everything the right way around in the perceiver's brain. For the first three days of wearing them, the participants made many mistakes. One held a cup upside down as it was about to be filled. Another tried to step over a lamppost, thinking that its top was on the ground. For two days there was a gradual adjustment, and by the fifth day, when participants woke up in the morning and viewed the world through their inverting goggles, everything appeared right-side up. They could navigate, go about their daily activities, as though nothing had happened. Various real-life activities, such as watching a movie or a circus performance, going to a tavern, motorcycling, biking, and going on ski tours, were part of the experience of the goggle-wearing participants. When they eventually took the goggles off, the right-side-up world appeared upside down to them. But the readaptation back to normal took only a few minutes. The brain was able to reset itself to the mode of perception it had known for decades with amazing quickness.

Why does the original adaptation take so long and the readaptation, going back, happen so fast? It's the difference in the biology between really well-trodden paths and the changes that happen over a few days. All learning results in synaptic connections. Things that have been learned and practiced many times produce greater synaptic strength, and so it is easier to return to them.

This may all seem merely theoretical, or something that would only interest geeky perception neuroscientists. But it has helpful clinical uses as well. Consider strokes, something that affects one-quarter of people over age seventy.

Following a stroke, nearly one-third of people experience hemispatial neglect, also known as unilateral neglect. This causes the stroke survivor to ignore one side of their body or visual field and to be unaware that they have a deficit. As you can imagine, it is a leading cause of falls and other injuries. A reliable way to treat hemispatial neglect is through the use of prismatic glasses that gradually shift the patient's attention toward the side that is neglected.

The prism adaptation experiments are also relevant for all of us who wear glasses. Ophthalmologists study these experiments to learn about the extent to which the visual system can adapt to distortions. If you find a new pair of strong glasses uncomfortable, your eye doctor may counsel you to just give it a couple of weeks. The stronger the lens, the higher its refractive index, and so the greater the distortions it will cause in the images around you. In really strong prescriptions, you might even see rainbow-like colors appearing around the edges of your visual field. In time, the brain can usually adapt to these (although it can be rough going until it does).

I experienced prism adaptation myself when I was an undergraduate at MIT. After learning about the experiments in my neuropsychology class, I built a pair of prism glasses one Friday afternoon that shifted the entire world about thirty degrees to the left. Before the experiment, my hands knew where things were in the world, and they simply found them. Once I put on the glasses, all bets were off. I tried to pick up the coffee cup on my dorm room desk and I missed it by twelve inches. On my second attempt, I tried to adjust, but I still missed it. I had to extend my hand and move it slowly to the right until it met the cup. Walking was a special challenge. Trying to navigate the long hallway in my dorm, I kept bumping into the wall. I dared not leave the building. But I stayed committed to the project. I walked around, reaching for things. I ate meals and read my textbooks with the glasses on.

That night, my dreams were full of little episodes of me reaching for things, walking around, and in my dreams I managed to grab hold of everything I reached for. When I woke up in the morning, the world and my interactions with it appeared normal. It felt miraculous. I spent the weekend walking around with these weird-looking glasses, studying, eating in the cafeteria, and successfully getting food from the plate into my mouth.

I took the prism glasses off Monday morning, two and half days after the experiment began. The world was completely shifted to the right now by thirty degrees, and I bumped into walls again, spilled eggs on my clean shirt, completely missed doorknobs, and so on. My brain had successfully adapted to the original shift and would have to relearn and readapt to this new one. By noon everything was back to normal—the readaptation took much less than the original adaptation time. This is because the adaptation required me to learn something new; the readaptation simply required that I reactivate those very well-established pathways and synaptic connections that already existed.

The prism adaptation experiments are a compelling story of short-term neuroplasticity—the brain adapting to changing conditions and rewiring itself. These experiments also tell a story about sensory integration—the interactions between the motor system and the visual system—not just about the visual system itself.

We are constantly updating our own representation of our body, where it is in space, and how it relates to us and to others—we do this through a combination of touch and vision. One illustration of this is the "rubber hand illusion." In it, the experimenter hides your hand from you, say, underneath a table, and puts a rubber hand on top of the table oriented in the same way that your own hand would be. The experimenter puts one of his hands on yours, out of sight and underneath the table, and another on the visible rubber hand. Next, the experimenter strokes both hands in synchrony. After just one minute, most people come to believe strongly that the rubber hand is their own. This is because the visual system informs the tactile system, and when there is ambiguity or a conflict, the visual system usually wins. Interestingly, this can happen even if the rubber hand doesn't look especially realistic, or if it has a different skin tone or complexion—your visual system works in tandem with your tactile system to override the knowledge that you have about which one really is your hand. The illusion doesn't occur if you simply watch the rubber hand without having your own hand surreptitiously stroked—the synchronous tactile-visual input is necessary. The illusion can also work with other parts of your body. Astonishingly, it works with your face. In the enfacement illusion, you watch a video of someone else's face being stroked with a Q-tip in synchrony with an experimenter stroking yours, and you come to feel that the other face belongs to you, even if it doesn't really look that much like you! What all this means is that your very sense of self is constructed, that it is built out of perceptual inputs and is malleable.

The power of vision to overcome other senses is captured in a Warner Bros. cartoon short directed by Chuck Jones called "Mouse Wreckers." Two mice, living behind the baseboards of a large human house, feel constrained by the presence of the house cat and plot to drive him crazy so that he'll move out. In one sequence, they nail all of the furniture in the living room to the ceiling and remove the ceiling lamp and attach it to the floor. When the cat wakes up from a nap, he looks around and sees the ceiling lamp next to him. He looks up and sees the couch, the coffee table, the easy chair, and so on and concludes that he must be on the ceiling and that the floor—where he belongs—is where all the furniture is. Panicked, he tries to jump up toward the ceiling, where he thinks he'll be safe. But his claws are unable to hold on as gravity pulls him back down. He keeps making leaps toward the ceiling (which he is certain is the floor) and keeps falling back down. His visual system has turned out to be an unreliable indicator of reality, but he can't override it. The brilliance of the cartoon lies, in part, in the fact that it is based on this well-established neuroscientific principle.

Airplane pilots spend dozens of hours learning not to place too much emphasis on their visual system, or, for that matter, on their vestibular system, and instead to "trust the gauges." Our brains and bodies have not had time to evolve systems for accurately interpreting the sensations that come from being in flight, and so they can be unreliable. Many fatal accidents have occurred from pilots ignoring their gauges and instead relying on their perceptions. This is what happened to John F. Kennedy Jr. Flying at dusk in poor weather, he may have been unable to distinguish the sky from the water he was flying above and he may have had the bodily and visual sensation that he was upside down. His gauges would have told him whether this was true or not, but he may have thought that the gauges were malfunctioning—this happens occasionally, but less often than our senses mislead us. It seems he turned the plane upside down and flew into the water, thinking he was ascending into the sky. This is also believed to be what is responsible for aviation accidents in the Bermuda Triangle—pilots become disoriented with no landmarks, they confuse the air and the sea, and while ignoring their gauges but trusting their (unreliable) senses, they fly their planes right into the deep.

Exploratory behaviors are the key to building sensory experience and neuroplasticity. Children fail to develop normal behavior if they are victims of motor deprivation. This was shown in an experiment with kittens. One young kitten was able to move around its environment more or less freely. A littermate was placed in a cart that replicated the movements of the first kitten. If the first kitten turned left, so did the second kitten's cart. If the first kitty jumped, so did the second kitten, via its cart. The two kittens received essentially the same visual stimulation, but only one was actively exploring its environment. The passive kitten did not develop normal behaviors. It didn't blink at an approaching object. It didn't extend its paws to ward off a collision when carried gently downward toward the floor, and it didn't avoid a visual cliff. (A visual cliff is an apparent drop of several feet underneath a safe piece of thick glass; in other words, there is no actual danger, but higher mammals with an intact sense of motor behaviors will avoid it. This is why glass-bottomed walkways, although popular in some cities, make a lot of people nauseous or cause their hearts to flutter—it's a deeply embedded reaction.) Those toys in the crib for your grandchild are most effective if the child can reach for and grasp them, not just stare at them passively. And if their hands and legs can actually cause something to move, that is even better training for them. Older adults who want to maintain their sense of balance and orientation must not just observe the environment but also move around in it.

Neuroplastic adjustments occur throughout the life span. As babies grow into adulthood, the brain needs to adapt to the way that sensory information changes with increasing separation between the eyes and ears and increased size of the tongue. Your tactile system has to adapt to changes in the distance between parts of your growing body. The growth of bones and muscles requires a gradual modification of the signals your brain sends to initiate smooth, coordinated movements—these are all forms of compensatory neuroplasticity.

Our touch sense can remap very quickly. After pain is experienced in a localized part of the skin, such as from an injection or pinprick, an area around the affected area, up to five-eighths of an inch, can immediately become hypersensitive. This kind of neuroplasticity may protect us from harm if nerve cells are damaged by an injury, by allowing us to be more sensitive to pain surrounding the initial site. That feeling of pain can motivate us to withdraw from a dangerous environment or remove thorns and splinters and other foreign objects from our skin.

When a limb or digit or other body part is amputated, the nerve endings in it are severed. But the other end of the nerve fibers still connects to the brain. As a result, many people report feeling sensations in a body part that is no longer there; indeed, phantom limb pain affects 90 percent of amputees. Using a visual-touch therapeutic approach that is conceptually similar to the rubber hand, therapists can promote neural remapping by touching parts of the patient's body, stump, or surrounding area while the patient watches and experiences touch sensations that were previously associated with the missing limb. The synchronized seeing and feeling speeds up the process. Similar techniques help in treating referred pain, pain that originates in one set of sensory receptors but feels as though it's coming from another.

A different approach to phantom limb pain was pioneered by Vilayanur Ramachandran of UC San Diego. People who suffer from phantom limb pain often experienced paralysis or pain in the limb before it was amputated and complain of their (phantom) limb having a cramp or being in an uncomfortable or clenched position. Ramachandran places a mirror in the center, with one limb on each side of it, and instructs the patient to look at the side of the mirror with the intact limb—the patient now sees two limbs, one a mirror image of the other. The patient is then asked to move both of their limbs symmetrically. Of course, they can't actually move the phantom limb, but as they look into the mirror, they see two limbs moving—their intact limb and its reflection. The brain is fooled into thinking it is seeing the phantom limb in motion, and this causes a welcome remapping of the circuits that were causing the discomfort, cramp, or clenching, and in many cases, their pain is relieved.

Age-Related Dysfunctions

Vision

Perhaps the most well-known and reliable marker of aging is declining vision, specifically, an inability to read. Starting around age forty, people begin showing up at the reading glasses section of the nearby drugstore or make appointments with an optometrist.

My first recollection of adult aging was exactly on my fiftieth birthday. It was late December, and I had awakened early to *carpe* the *diem*. It was still dark outside—a product of the short days of a Montreal winter—and I held the morning newspaper out in front of me at arm's length so that my eyes could focus on the letters, just as I had done hundreds of mornings before. But on *this* morning, my arms seemed to be shorter, the letters too small and blurry for me to read. My first thought was that the *Times* had changed their font. I rooted through the recycling basket to find yesterday's paper and I had just as much trouble with that. I tried holding the newspaper farther away until the letters came into focus, but my arms were about an inch or two too short. It felt like somehow my arms had shrunk during the night because holding the paper at arm's length had been working for me so well for the last year or so.

This change in vision is called presbyopia. It occurs because of age-related changes in proteins in the lens, making the lens harder and less elastic over time. Age-related changes also take place in the muscle fibers surrounding the lens. With less elasticity, the eye has a harder time focusing up close, which takes more muscle tension than focusing far away.

You would think that if it's just a muscle issue you might be able to do exercises to prevent it from happening or to slow down the process, but there is no evidence supporting this, nor for preventing the lens hardening. Because proteins are at the root of this, and DNA encodes for protein synthesis, there may be genetic therapies in our lifetimes that can address these problems. But for now, reading glasses or surgical correction of presbyopia are in the future for most of us.

Most of us will experience something like this change in our visual system. Because of adaptation, we don't notice the soft transition between good eyesight and weakening eyesight. We hold things farther away, we install higher-output light bulbs; we increase the font size for text messages on our phones. Our brain adapts in a continuous fashion using its powerful pattern-recognition systems. The signal our retina sends to our brain is blurred, and from the actual input stream we might not be able to tell a lowercase *c* from a lowercase *o*, but context is everything. One combination of letters forms a word (*look*) and one does not (*lcck*). And sometimes we need a larger context, evaluating not just the single word, but the sentence and semantic context surrounding it: *Please lock the door.* Even if the data reaching the brain for the second word is ambiguous or appears as *lcck*, your brain sorts it out, automatically, and without your conscious awareness.

This automatic correction of the input stream is a form of perceptual completion, and something that the brain has had a chance to practice throughout our entire lives. As we age, the ratio of how much our brains rely on the input signal versus our perceptual inferencing shifts with every decade after forty. Our magnificent pattern-matching brains do more and more filling in, not just because our senses require them to, but because they've had so many more experiences than young brains that it is simply more efficient to make inferences than to try to decode every little perceptual detail. Have you ever read a word and then found out a few moments later you read it wrong? You go back and look at the word and you could've sworn you saw one word, and now you see another. Your pattern-matching brain simply made an error and sent a realistic, vivid representation of the wrong word up to your conscious awareness.

This happened to me just the other day. I was planning a trip to New York and my hotel gave me a bunch of vouchers for free meals and attractions on Coney Island. That day, at lunchtime, a friend served bratwurst and put out several jars of condiments, including one of a new mustard I'd never seen. I looked at the jar and I clearly and assuredly read *Coney Island* and decided to try some. It was delicious, and so I looked at the bottle more carefully to write down the brand, and only then did I realize the words I had seen were in fact *Honey Mustard.* My brain had *Coney Island* on its mind and so *Honey* became *Coney* and then *Mustard* had just enough letters in common with *Island* to fill in and replace what was actually there. Here was pattern matching and perceptual completion run amok: The words *Coney* and *Honey* differ by only a single letter, and both *Island* and *Mustard* have the form *s*-blank-*a*-blank-*d*. (Plus, to my aging visual system, which has come to rely on statistical inferencing, the stylized *r* probably looked like an *n*.)

Perceptual completion is a kind of categorization, a cognitive-driven effect, and is called top-down processing, as opposed to purely stimulus-driven perception, which is called bottom-up. When we're young, or when we're learning something new, we have few preconceptions and so we see things more as they really are. The process of maturing, and of aging, involves categorization of things. We tend to categorize more as we get older because in most cases, it is mentally efficient to do so. A brand-new study shows that this kind of automatic categorization is dependent to a large degree on how prevalent category members are. Like an efficient filing clerk, we tend to combine things, to make larger categories, so that we don't end up with a bunch of mental file folders with only a single item in them.

If you're shown a bunch of blue dots and a bunch of purple dots in equal numbers and asked to label them "blue" or "purple," you'll have no trouble doing this. But if I decrease the total number of blue dots present, you'll begin to classify some of the purple dots as blue—the rarity of blue dots causes you to expand your category.

This doesn't happen just with colors, but with emotional stimuli as well. Asked to categorize faces as threatening or benign, you'll expand your definition of threatening if the proportion of threatening faces decreases below a certain level. The same is true with more abstract judgments, such as judging whether a certain behavior is ethical: In the absence of *clearly* unethical behaviors, behaviors that were seen as acceptable before now loom as unethical. This has large societal implications. As one study's authors explain, "When violent crimes become less prevalent, a police officer's concept of 'assault' should not expand to include jay-walking. What counts as a ripe fruit should depend on the other fruits one can see, but what counts as a felony, a field goal, or a tumor should not, and when these things are absent, police officers, referees, and radiologists should not expand their concepts and find them anyway. . . . Although modern societies have made extraordinary progress in addressing a wide range of social problems, from poverty and illiteracy to violence and infant mortality, the majority of people believe that the world is getting worse. The fact that concepts grow larger when their instances grow smaller may be one source of that pessimism."

It's certainly easy to fall into pessimism if you're losing the sensory systems you've relied on most of your life. Another common visual problem is cataracts, which are a clouding of the lens of one or both eyes. You can get them at any age, but they more often show up after forty, although they tend to be small and therefore don't affect vision much. By age sixty they can begin to cause blurred vision, and by age eighty, more than half of Americans will have them. Normally, light passes through the lens and is projected on the retina in back of the eye. The cataracts cause a blurry image. The lens is mostly made up of water and—you guessed it—proteins. As we age, some of those proteins clump together and cloud a region of the lens.

Remember that evolution is dependent on reproduction to transmit survival advantages across multiple generations. Consequently, evolution does not generate adaptive improvements for conditions that occur outside of normal reproductive age. Hence, there has been no evolutionary pressure to favor people who don't get cataracts or presbyopia, and so they are ever present in aging populations.

There is an emerging but still small body of evidence linking cataracts to smoking and diabetes. Healthy practices going back to your teen years can influence this outcome years later. The best cataract protection comes from wearing sunglasses when you're outdoors starting at a young age. Cataract surgery replaces your cloudy, protein-clumpy lens with an artificial lens. It is one of the most common and safest operations performed if it is done by a qualified doctor at a good facility. Starting at age sixty, you should have your eyes examined every two years for early detection of cataracts, macular degeneration, glaucoma, and other diseases of the eye. Early detection of these can save your ability to see.

Hearing

Perhaps the next most common failing is hearing—presbycusis—and most of us will end up needing hearing aids at some point. Presbyopia and presbycusis come from the Greek root *presby,* which means old. (Presbyterians are so called because their religion follows a system of church governance by the elders of the church.) As with vision, the loss tends to be gradual. There are several causes of hearing loss, and scientists haven't fully worked out the story yet. In part, hair cells in the ear stiffen and no longer conduct the necessary electrical signals up toward the brain.

Like the ultraviolet rays of the sun damaging the lens of the eye, environmental factors can damage the ear: Noise-induced hearing loss, from prolonged exposure to sudden loud sounds in the workplace or at rock concerts, can damage the hair cells of the ear irreversibly. The best preventative is to wear earplugs when you're going to be around loud noises. High blood pressure, diabetes, and chemotherapy can also irreparably damage the hair cells. Another possible cause is age-related deterioration in mitochondrial DNA in the different structures of the cochlea (inner ear). Oxidative stress is thought to be a major cause of mutations in the mitochondrial DNA that cause the deterioration. You've probably heard of antioxidants—oxidative stress occurs when there is a chemical imbalance between antioxidants and chemical free radicals in your body, compromising the body's ability to detoxify. This imbalance can lead to problems with lipids, proteins, and DNA and can trigger a number of diseases. An antioxidant is a molecule that can donate an electron to a free radical, thereby neutralizing it. Foods that are high in antioxidants, such as blueberries, might be a promising way to forestall or correct this, but it's too early to tell; evidence for the effectiveness of antioxidant foods is mixed. Still, the Mayo Clinic and other experts recommend making them a regular part of your diet while the evidence comes in, not just for fending off hearing loss, but for a range of maladies including cancer and Alzheimer's (more on that later).

Hearing loss affects one-third of people in the United States between the ages of sixty-five and seventy-four, and (as I mentioned earlier) nearly half of people over seventy-five. Hearing loss in someone who was born with hearing is far more socially isolating than vision loss, because it gets to the very core of how we communicate with one another. Even when deaf individuals learn sign language, they still experience social isolation from the hearing community, most of whom do not know sign language. From the brain standpoint, once input from the ear has diminished, entire populations of neurons are left without external stimulation. What do you suppose they do? They make up their own stimulation, or resort to random firing, resulting in auditory hallucinations, some of which can be musical. Loss of input to the visual system can result in visual hallucinations. This happens often enough that there's a name for it: Charles Bonnet syndrome.

The auditory hallucinations caused by hearing loss often manifest as tinnitus, a ringing in the ears, which affects one out of five adults, and which can be intermittent or chronic. Most patients with tinnitus do not find it severe, but a great many find it distracting, annoying, or intrusive, interfering with sleep, work, and leisure activities. Many experience emotional distress because of it. Chronic tinnitus almost certainly leads to a reduction in quality of life; it's difficult to experience the peacefulness and serenity of a quiet environment when you've got a constant ringing in your ears. As one researcher said, "The notion of peace and quiet is no longer an option for many tinnitus patients."

Tinnitus does appear to be occurring in the brain, not in the ear, although it is experienced as coming from the ear. It has been compared to phantom limb pain in that it results from a loss of input to a cortical area. The newest hypothesis is that it results from homeostatic neural plasticity: Neurons in the auditory cortex that have grown accustomed to receiving input at a wide range of frequencies, across an entire lifetime, suddenly find themselves with no input due to peripheral, age-related hearing loss. In order to obtain a stable supply of the full range of expected stimuli (homeostasis), these neurons start amplifying spontaneous and random activity, causing the tinnitus—ringing in the ears. An experimental therapy for tinnitus based on this idea shows promise. Neurons in the inner ear fire in response to very specific frequencies. Because the ringing typically occurs at a specific and unchanging frequency, fatiguing those neurons selectively can bring relief. An adjustable noise machine or even a hearing aid can be programmed to provide stimulation at the precise frequency of the tinnitus, thus giving those orphaned neurons some stimulation, which causes them to calm down and, voilà, the tinnitus disappears.

Hearing aid technology has benefited enormously from the digital electronics revolution. As recently as a generation ago, hearing aids were little more than an updated version of those huge ear horns that people used to amplify sound in the 1700s. Modern ones can be programmed by an audiologist to emphasize some frequencies more than others and to focus on sounds coming from a particular direction, which, ironically, was something the old ear horns could do well and the "improved" analog hearing aids could not. (If you wanted to emphasize different frequencies, you'd choose a differently sized and shaped horn; if you wanted to hear sounds from a particular direction you'd get one with tubing turned toward that direction—front, behind, up, down.) There are many different brands of hearing aids, and they vary a great deal in cost, but the most important factor in how helpful one will be is the quality of the audiologist doing the tuning and personal adjustments—a really good audiologist with a mediocre hearing aid is better than the reverse.

For a hearing aid to work, however, you need to still have viable hair cells. Because hair cells are frequency selective—they only fire off an electrical signal to the frequencies they are tuned for—you can have hearing loss that is confined to particular frequencies. This is where the frequency tuning of digital hearing aids is most helpful.

But what if your hair cells are completely shot? A relatively new device, a cochlear implant, can work for many people who become profoundly deaf. A microphone, similar to that in a hearing aid, picks up sounds from the environment and is usually mounted behind your ear. It connects to a device that is surgically implanted into the cochlea, a part of the inner ear. A cochlear implant can allow truly deaf people to hear, but the current technology does not restore hearing anywhere near to normal levels. This is because your cochlea is normally receiving information on thousands of auditory channels, and these provide information across the frequency range of human hearing—providing the low sounds of thunder or a bass violin, the high sounds of cicadas in the summer or cymbals in a drum set, and everything in between. All those channels allow us to have precise resolution of frequencies, giving music, speech, laughter, and environmental noises their distinctive acoustic and psychological colors. In contrast, a cochlear implant typically has only twelve to twenty-two channels of information. If properly configured, it can provide a kind of scratchy, noisy signal that allows you to understand speech, but music and other sounds don't come through well. New bio-nanotechnologies are certain to improve this in the years to come.

Touch

Our sense of touch also declines with age. Decreased blood flow to the extremities—hands and feet—can impair the touch receptors there; older adults may not be able to feel that the shower is slippery or be able to differentiate between hot and cold water. With age, the touch sensors in the pads of the fingers deteriorate, producing a loss of sensitivity. We fumble with things. Arthritis makes it painful to move our fingers and toes. As Atul Gawande writes, "Loss of motor neurons in the cortex leads to losses of dexterity. Handwriting degrades. Hand speed and vibration sense decline. Using a standard mobile phone, with its tiny buttons and touch screen display, becomes increasingly unmanageable."

Patches of skin may become numb as our touch sensors wear out or myelination decreases. There's also a common affliction of old age that is going to sound made-up but is real: a patch of skin on your back, typically just out of reach, that itches intermittently, and sometimes incessantly. And scratching it provides no relief—none at all! Because the condition arises from damage within certain nerve pathways, those same pathways block the relief that scratching usually provides. The condition is called *notalgia paresthetica.* There is no known cure, and few treatments. An anti-inflammatory gel, diclofenac (brand name Voltaren), can provide relief to some patients, and there are promising results with CBD cream and oil, based on cannabinols.

Taste and Smell

We are more familiar with disorders of the visual and auditory systems than with disorders of the other senses, but taste and smell can also be impacted by aging. Olfactory dysfunctions can show up in three different ways: a reduced sense of smell called *hyposmia,* a complete loss of the ability to smell called *anosmia,* and an altered perception in which things smell differently than they should, called *phantosmia.* (If these foreign-sounding words bother you, just look at the prefixes to remember what they mean: *Hypo-* is too little of something, *a-* is without something, and *phantom-*, well, you know that means something that isn't there.) Phantosmia often shows up as the illusory experience of something smelling burned, spoiled, rotten, or otherwise unpleasant.

Decreased sense of smell is very common among older adults, reported by half of those between the ages of sixty-five and eighty and three-quarters of those over eighty. It's not merely an inconvenience. Your sense of smell isn't merely there so that you can smell the pine needles in the forest or the perfume of a loved one. It is critical for our ability to perceive health- and life-threatening situations such as dangerous fumes, polluted environments, and rotten or decayed food, and it serves as an early detection system for fire. Also important is that if you can't smell, you can't really taste anymore, either. Without smell, an onion is easily confused for an apple (with your eyes closed) and you've lost an important mechanism for keeping rotten foods out of your body. A disproportionate number of older adults die in accidental natural gas poisonings and petroleum explosions every year because they cannot detect these odors. The risk of dying of any cause is 36 percent higher for older adults with an olfactory impairment.

Women generally have a more refined sense of smell than men and can detect odors that men can't, thanks to having a larger concentration of olfactory neurons. In order for you to smell something, chemicals from the object you're smelling need to enter the nasal cavity through either the nostrils or the mouth, where they come in contact with a layer of mucus covering a skin-like layer of cells that house our smell receptors. There are more than 350 different receptor proteins in the human system, and in combination with one another, they allow us to detect a trillion different smells.

These cells can become damaged through normal usage, and normally they're repaired, just like damaged skin cells. With aging, however, the repairs become more difficult or impossible, due to cumulative damage from pollution and from viral and bacterial infections. Another factor limiting repair is age-related telomere shortening. Telomeres are protective caps at the end of DNA sequences that become shorter with each replication. The forefront and cutting edge of antiaging research is seeking to find a way to inhibit the shortening of telomeres, and we may see that in our lifetimes.

Another factor in the way the world smells to us is the neurotransmitter acetylcholine. Like all neurotransmitters, acetylcholine is involved in several functions in the brain and body; it is too simplistic to think that each brain chemical controls a single behavior, emotion, or response. Acetylcholine is part of the brain's cholinergic system, and it is necessary for the consolidation of memories during stage 4 sleep. It is also intimately involved in the sense of smell, facilitating attention, learning, and memory for odors. As with many neurochemicals and hormones, acetylcholine production diminishes with old age. In some cases, an olfactory deficit signals an age-related disease, such Alzheimer's, Parkinson's, and Korsakoff's syndrome, as well as the non-age-related diseases of ALS (amyotrophic lateral sclerosis) and Down syndrome; all of these appear to be associated with damage to the cholinergic system. Drugs that enhance cholinergic activity, such as rivastigmine, may be helpful to older adults to relieve symptoms, whether or not the olfactory deficit is related to a disease or is simply an independent disorder.

It's tempting to think of taste only for the pleasure it brings—a good meal, a fine wine, your favorite dessert, your loved one's skin. But taste is an important sense for other reasons. Taste deficits alter food choices and lead to poor nutrition, weight loss, and reductions in immune-system function when we don't ingest the vitamins and minerals we need. In addition, taste helps us prepare the body to digest food by triggering the production of saliva, alongside gastric, pancreatic, and intestinal fluids. The pleasurable feelings from eating tasty food become more important in old age when other sources of sensory gratification—like physical contact—may have become compromised or are less frequent.

You may have learned in school that we can detect four tastes: sour, salty, sweet, and bitter. Taste scientists (yes, there is such a thing) identified a fifth taste, umami, which detects the presence of an amino acid, glutamic acid, that is typically described as a meaty or brothy taste. We encounter it in meats, fish, mushrooms, and soy sauce, and it is also present in breast milk in about the same proportion as in soup broths. Yet even this new, fifth taste doesn't complete the picture. Our taste sense allows us to detect fat content of foods, in particular, emulsified oils; this is what gives ice cream with a high butterfat content its compelling "mouthfeel." We can also detect chalky tastes, such as those found in the calcium salts that are a principal ingredient of antacid tablets, and metallic tastes, such as we encounter in foods rich in iron or magnesium. These varied taste sensations help us to maintain a balanced diet of essential nutrients.

Many older adults complain that food lacks flavor. This is usually due to olfactory deficits—smell works in tandem with taste to convey the flavor of food and drink, and sensors inside the cheeks feed into the brain's olfactory centers. Other causes of taste deficit are a history of upper respiratory infections, head injury, drug use, and an age-related reduction in saliva production. All of these factors can cause loss of appetite, loss of pleasure from eating, malnutrition, and even depression.

The loss of flavor can result from normal age-related declines in the sensory receptors themselves, but in many cases they result from diseases (especially liver disease and cancers) or medications. The list of medications that can alter taste and smell reads like the medicine cabinet of a typical seventy-five-year-old. They include certain lipid-lowering drugs, antihistamines, antibiotics, anti-inflammatories, asthma medication, and antidepressants. Chemotherapy, general anesthesia, and other medical treatments can also cause permanent damage to the chemistry-based senses of taste and smell.

The most noticeable problem in taste perception affecting older adults is an upward change in thresholds—it takes more of a given flavor to be perceived as the same amount as before. For a typical older individual, with one or more medical conditions and taking three prescription medications, the number of flavor molecules required to detect a taste shows marked increases depending on the flavor. If you're typical, you'll need to have a whopping twelve times the amount of salt to detect that salt is even present compared to when you were in your fifties. For bitter tastes, such as quinine, seven times the amount; for the brothy-meaty flavor of umami, five times the amount; and for sweeteners, around three times the normal amount. (Maybe this is why Grandma always has candies around to offer the grandkids.)

Another aspect of taste declines with age—the change threshold, or the amount of a flavor you have to add to an existing one to detect that it has changed. You're probably more familiar with this idea from the auditory or visual domains. Suppose you're at home and you notice your refrigerator making a humming noise. It has to be loud enough for you to notice, and that's called the minimum discrimination threshold. A separate question that concerns sensory neuroscientists is how much louder or softer that refrigerator hum would have to change before you noticed. Of course this depends on factors such as whether you're paying close attention to it or not, but these thresholds can be measured reliably. Some playful psychologists many years ago named this threshold the JND, for *just noticeable difference.*

We study JNDs for all kinds of things. How much would I have to change the intensity, or brightness, of the lighting in a room before you noticed it had increased or decreased? In a room well-lit by one hundred bulbs, each producing fifteen hundred lumens, a single photon change will go unnoticed. But in a completely dark room, with your eyes adapted to the darkness, you will notice a single photon. Or imagine that you're carrying a shopping bag with groceries in it. How much weight do I have to add or take away before you notice? If I add a single grain of rice, you will not notice. If I add a one-pound box of rice you probably will, but it depends on how much was already in the bag—we notice an increase from one pound to two pounds, but not from fifty pounds to fifty-one pounds.

With taste among older individuals, the JNDs change, in just the direction you might predict: It takes a greater change to notice a change at all. That is, JNDs for taste are increased in older individuals. There are also age-related changes in sensitivity across different areas of the tongue and the mouth. A teenager may experience a burst of flavor as soon as they put a SweeTart or Starburst candy in their mouth. An older adult may have to swirl it around in their mouth a bit. All of this leads to a reduced ability of older adults to identify foods just on the basis of taste—the sight, smell, and sound of foods become more important. Aging research scientist Susan Schiffman (age seventy-nine) advises that "switching among different foods on the plate at a meal reduces sensory adaptation or fatigue. . . . Providing meals with a variety of tastes and flavors increases the likelihood that at least one item on the plate will be appealing." Now I understand why my mentor Irv Rock at age seventy-three loved to order variety plates when we went out for lunch. The *thali* at Indian and Nepalese restaurants we frequented in Berkeley, or the *mezze* platter at Middle Eastern restaurants, gave him a way to keep his taste and smell receptors stimulated. Or maybe he was just high on Factor V and liked to try new things.

When I turned sixty, I began to notice that the foods I was eating weren't as flavorful as I remembered them being. Was this a memory trick, were modern commercially farmed foods less flavorful, or had my taste buds changed? In the spring of that year I had the opportunity to go to Mexico to meet with former president Vicente Fox and discuss his strategies and advice for successful aging. While in Centro Fox, near León, in central Mexico, I enjoyed three of the most delicious, flavorful meals of my life. There was nothing wrong with my taste buds; it was the food I was eating! As happens with many people over sixty, my doctor had suggested a diet that was low in calories, salt, and red meat, no bread or pasta, low in carbohydrates, and with zero refined sugar. I had given up my morning breakfast of tasty granola, bacon, and omelets for oatmeal and egg whites—in short, I was eating a bland diet, not by design, but as a by-product of trying to eat healthy. The fix? When I got home, I started putting Cholula and Tabasco sauce on my egg whites, and spicing up my morning oatmeal with cinnamon and nutmeg, and my zest for food came back without my gaining any weight or increasing my cholesterol numbers.

Unfortunately, there are no prosthetics available for olfactory and gustatory deficits, the equivalent of hearing aids and glasses. To be safety conscious, a gas detection device with a visual signal is advised for people with olfactory impairment so that dangerous fumes won't go undetected. The odors of food gone bad can also go overlooked, so some culinary alert system may be needed, perhaps as simple as an understanding caregiver.

Disgust is a complex emotion that arises from thoughts or perceptions that we find repellant—the taste or smell of rotten food can cause disgust, as can a betrayal by a loved one or public figure who violates trust. Because our reactions to certain smells and tastes are so immediate and so visceral, it's tempting to think that there is some molecule or quality in the object that *is* disgusting, but this would be wrong—the brain has to interpret it as disgusting, and not all brains react the same way. Some of this is learned—if you ate a bad cantaloupe that made you sick to your stomach, you may find *all* cantaloupes disgusting for quite some time. But, of course, disgusting is in the brain of the beholder. Dogs, for example, seem to show no disgust—they will eat or roll in practically anything. There is a cultural overlay as well—Americans find it disgusting that people in other cultures eat grasshoppers, ants, dogs, and monkeys, and I'm sure there are a great many who find our diet of cheeseburgers and potato chips unimaginable.

Perception and Complex Environments

We evolved in complex, varied, natural environments. Some scientists have come to appreciate the wisdom that Joni Mitchell offered in her song "Woodstock": "And we've got to get ourselves back to the garden." Plants, dirt, sky, and wildlife offer stimulation to our perceptual systems. Perhaps the visual input is the first thing you think of, but there are sounds and smells as well; the taste of wet air before a rain; the touch of tree bark or rocks underneath our feet. Because everything we know originates with our senses, keeping our senses stimulated is critical to keeping our brains active, alert, and healthy. Neurologist Scott Grafton is a big believer in the healing power of the outdoors. "Take old people out of a complex environment and they age quicker," he notes. "The brain doesn't just need physical activity to remain vital, but complex physical activity—the brain needs it to stay healthy and engaged." Something as simple as walking in a new environment provides this critical brain input. Your feet have to adjust to different surfaces and angles, your ankles need to move in conjunction with your feet. Your eyes are scanning the surroundings for new things as you take in information from all the other senses. Many older adults have an urge to travel, and this may originate in an adaptive, biological drive that will serve to keep them healthy for longer, especially if the travel involves walking tours of new places. Those who lack the mobility or finances for exotic travel can benefit from visiting a local park, forest, or garden, or even a dense city street with all of its bustling activity. These sensory inputs cause otherwise dormant and complacent neurons to perk up, to fire, and to make new connections. Neuroplasticity is what keeps us young, and it is only a walk in the park away.

4

INTELLIGENCE

The problem-solving brain

The most noticeable effect of aging, apart from wrinkles and hair loss, is the decline in intellectual processing that some people undergo. But not all people. Some of us remain happy, healthy, and mentally fit while others start to lose it.

What's going on in the brains of those older adults who remain mentally vital into their eighties and nineties? Are they just barely hanging on to what they had, or are they actually improving in some ways? I've come to believe that life after seventy-five can launch a period of intellectual growth, and not mere maintenance. At the age of eighty, the great cellist Pablo Casals was asked why he continued to practice so much, and his swift reply was, "Because I want to get better!" Casals believed like Segovia, that self-improvement and expertise are possible at any age, whether it's intellectual, physical, emotional, or spiritual.

One of the best examples I've seen of expertise in older adults happened just last year. Like many musicians, I put a home recording studio in a spare bedroom. If the room acoustics aren't just right, you can end up making serious errors because what you're hearing in the room isn't indicative of what is really happening on the recording. Speaker placement is especially crucial. Once all the equipment was hooked up and plugged in, and I attached sound treatment to the walls and ceiling, I knew that I had to bring in a consulting acoustician to "tune" the room—that is, to make critical adjustments. Michael Brook, a film composer and record producer friend, had recommended George Augspurger. George is a legend in the business and has tuned many of the best studios in the world. But I was worried since he was eighty-seven years old, and it is well-known that high-frequency hearing declines precipitously after age sixty-five. My friend said he had had the same concerns but that George performed brilliantly in tuning his home studio. So I hired him.

George came to the house and brought a James Taylor CD with him, and cued up the song "Line 'Em Up" to play on a loop. He walked around the room, listening intently to the song from different positions. He did this for forty minutes. Then he told me to sit in front of the mixing desk and listen for the conga drum at 0:36 (thirty-six seconds into the song).

"Where does it sound like it's coming from?" he asked.

"The center," I told him.

"It's supposed to be coming from the right. You've got some imaging smear in the room. Now," he asked, "do you hear the organ?" He advanced the CD to 1:22.

"No," I answered.

"The organ is being masked by the room reflections." He rubbed his chin, looked around, and then said, "Move the left speaker one inch to the left. Move the right speaker one-half inch to the left and back one-half inch. Then put one of those sound treatment panels on the door behind you."

I did all of these things. He sat down and listened again, and then had me move my desk three inches to the left. He put the CD on and smiled. "Listen now," he said, and motioned for me to take the chair.

It was transformational. I could hear the conga coming clearly from the right speaker and not the center, just as it had been recorded. I could hear an organ part I had never heard before. George's high-frequency hearing may have been diminished, but his experience and exquisite knowledge and memory allowed him to make the adjustments that needed to be made. Only then did he take out a spectrum analyzer, a digital device that measures the sound characteristics of the room. After looking at the readout of the device, he told me to increase the volume of the subwoofer by one-half a decibel. And that was that. Musicians who have come over to the room marvel at how good it sounds, and it is not a specially designed room by any means—it's just a spare bedroom. But it is properly configured, thanks to George's expertise. His fee was three hundred dollars; that was for the special kind of intelligence that only sixty-plus years of professional experience can bring.

I've seen a similar drive toward remaining meaningfully engaged in my own family and in my university colleagues. My mother published more than forty novels in her career but was unable to keep publishers interested in her work after age seventy-five. So she branched out to another art form and began writing plays, which required her to learn a whole new vocabulary and an entirely new set of skills and techniques. She's written four in all now, and two have been staged in well-known theaters in Los Angeles, the first when she was seventy-eight. That part required her to learn about writing and properly formatting a script on her computer, finding a venue, hiring a director, auditioning actors, overseeing rehearsals, costume design, set design, lighting, ticket sales—all things that were completely new to her. "It was more work than I had imagined," she recalled. "I began at seven in the morning and stayed at my desk until evening. During auditions and rehearsals I was often out until midnight. I discovered I had more stamina than I had realized." It was a grueling schedule for someone half her age. And stressful—she wasn't sure anyone would show up to see it, or if they'd like it. "There is no feeling as rapturous as sitting there on opening night and seeing your play come alive before your eyes, hearing the laughter of the audience, seeing tears, applause. Applause!" At seventy-eight, my mother learned that she loves applause. And I learned the power of being willing to try something new—at any age.

George Shultz, the former secretary of state under President Ronald Reagan, published his eleventh book at age ninety-seven and continues to engage in scholarly research. He has become a leading advocate for reducing climate-damaging emissions, is promoting new ideas for international monetary reform, and publishes his views in peer-reviewed articles and op-eds for *The Wall Street Journal.* His call to end the war on drugs in the United States, published in *The New York Times,* was widely shared. The day I met with him in his office at Stanford, he had piles of folders on his desk and he was excited because he had just recruited a new young collaborator to help him work on them. He marveled at this young fellow, Jim Timbie, who had so much energy, and that the two of them were now making such good progress. "Young" Jim Timbie was seventy-four at the time. Or, as the famous jazz drummer Art Blakey, who was constantly renewing his band the Jazz Messengers with younger players, said, "Yes sir, I'm gonna stay with the youngsters. When these get too old, I'm gonna get some younger ones. Keeps the mind active."

People age at different rates. Within the life span that you will have, the goal is to try to increase your health span and decrease your disease span (recall the illustration in Chapter 1). For most of us, some disease, including loss of mental function, is inevitable, but we can think about and deal with the negatives, putting systems in place to minimize them and the impact they have on our lives. I take a rather broader view of health span than others. To me, health span is about the health not just of your body but of your mind as well. I believe we can all stretch the health span to enjoy many more years of *mental* fitness and agility so that we can still do the things in life we care most about with intact intelligence.

The Healthy practices of the COACH principle are partly responsible for people with increased health spans: Curiosity, Openness, Associations, Conscientiousness, and Healthy practices. The people I've encountered who are still contributing to society, to arts and science, to their communities, and to their families are doing all five of these. Some examples of Healthy practices: My mother has been a vegetarian for thirty-five years. George Shultz has a Pilates instructor and works out regularly. Conscientiousness helps us to follow through on the things we start, to actually *get* a Pilates trainer and to show up. Openness to experience allowed my mother to immerse herself in the world of theater at age seventy-eight, and George Shultz to go against decades of Republican Party platform about climate change and recreational drug use. How about Associations? My mother and George Shultz both reached out to, and engaged with, others to help them achieve their visions. Their collaborations are sometimes maddening and frustrating, but they are also mentally challenging and, ultimately, fulfilling. Curiosity fueled the intellectual desire to do all these new things.

COACH allows us to maintain the intelligence we had when we were younger and to grow it at any age. Growing intellectually is one of the secrets of successful aging; it is different from intelligence, but we can't easily say how. Still, we might suspect they have something to do with each other. Let's investigate.

What Is Intelligence?

There are great disagreements about what intelligence is and how to measure it. I've come to believe that intelligence is the ability to apply knowledge in novel ways, making links between things that weren't seen as linked before. And intelligence predicts how well we are able to adapt to changing environments. For George Augspurger, the rooms he has to tune are always changing, but he applies a wondrous intelligence to each. However we measure it, more intelligence should mean that we are more likely to solve new problems. These problems could be theoretical or academic, physical, practical, aesthetic, interpersonal, or even spiritual.

Related to intelligence is the question of how we acquire information in the first place. What humans excel at, compared to other animals, is making associations: taking information, both old and new, and seeing how it interacts with other information. Whenever we encounter new information, our brains place it in a contextual frame and then seek to associate it with other things we've experienced. The brain is a giant pattern detector, applying statistical analysis to make decisions. Our brains add to that the ability to form analogies, something that (as far as we know) is uniquely human. Analogies, or analogical reasoning, have led to some of the biggest discoveries in science, from the Big Bang origins of our universe to immunotherapy for cancer.

The wisdom that we find in older adults—the most experienced members of our population—follows from these four specific things: associations, experience, pattern recognition, and the use of analogies. And this is why we gain more and more wisdom as we age. Wisdom comes from the accumulated set of things we've seen and experienced, our ability to detect patterns in those experiences, and our ability to predict future outcomes based on them. (And what is intelligence if not that?) Naturally, the more you've experienced, the more wisdom you are able to tap into. In addition, certain changes in the aging brain facilitate these kinds of comparisons. Young upstarts may be faster at playing video games and quicker to adapt to new technologies, but in the realm of wisdom they can't hold a candle to old-timers who have been witness to so many things that seem to cycle around again and again. Wisdom enables you to handle some problems more quickly and effectively than the raw firepower of youth. A young, strong person might be able carry a heavy load up a hill without breaking a sweat. An older person will think to put it on a handcart or dolly.

Making associations underpins learning. To assimilate new information we need to associate it with what we've seen before. Life experience gives us more associations to make, more patterns to recognize.

Understanding and studying intelligence have been hobbled by huge disagreements about what it is. In cognitive developmental neuroscience we can't identify the brain basis of behaviors until those behaviors are well defined. Intelligence simply isn't, and even when researchers try to define it, there are huge disagreements about whether the tests that measure it are doing a good job, or whether they're flawed or biased and miss a great many things that we would hope them to be sensitive to. We need to understand these debates about intelligence before we can see clearly how intelligence and aging interact.

Different Types of Intelligence

Starting in the early 1900s, psychometricians and cognitive psychologists—the folks who measure and study intelligence—thought of intelligence as a single, unitary thing. It varied along a single continuum and you could have more or less of it, whatever it was. Their measurement of it was called the intelligence quotient, or IQ. The idea was intuitively appealing and to some extent tracks to our normal experience. As a kid, you probably had classmates who just seemed to do better in school than others. To those kids, school came easy, but to many others, lessons were a struggle. It's easy to conclude that the people who found school easy were the more intelligent and the ones who found it more difficult were the less intelligent. That thing in the brain that led to intelligence was seen as a general factor, influencing many domains of endeavor, and so was called *g* (for general intelligence).

But if you think about your experiences, both as a student and later in life, it's apparent that this story is too simplistic. The triad of genes, culture, and opportunity plays out in how different children learn. There are surprising differences in things as basic as motor development across cultures and countries, even when you account for economic conditions. For example, infants from African countries hold up their necks and walk earlier, on average, than infants from Europe and America. (This is due to expectations by African parents that their children will acquire these milestones at earlier ages, and to them having adopted child-rearing practices that accelerate this growth, such as stretching of children's limbs during daily baths, and formalized muscle massage.) Even though humans all share basic genetics and neuroanatomy, developmental stages, and hormonal changes, each of these is shaped by the individual's particular experiences. For example, iron deficiency (affecting 9 percent of US children ages one to three), blood levels of lead, and other environmental toxins impair learning and memory. Learning doesn't happen the same way for everyone because the influence of culture, genes, and opportunity impacts everything we do from the womb to the tomb.

Variation plays out in our Western classrooms. Think back: Some of your classmates may have had difficulty in school because of a learning disability, not a lack of intelligence. They might have had dyslexia, or a short attention span, or families who didn't read, or they might have been sleep-deprived if they came from a disordered household. Some might have grown up in households or cultures that did not value education and so they lacked motivation. Stephen Stills and Joni Mitchell didn't do well in school because they found the lessons arbitrary, boring, and irrelevant to their interests. Quincy Jones got caught up with a bad crowd, occupying his mental energy with petty thefts and other criminal activities in Seattle. Many people we regard as brilliant often did poorly in school for a variety of other reasons, and their IQ scores, as established by standardized tests, might have been in the "normal" rather than "gifted" range. But you couldn't say they lacked intelligence.

So something is clearly wrong with the idea that intelligence is one thing that can be measured by a single number, IQ. As David Krakauer, president of the Santa Fe Institute and an expert in complex systems, says, "There is no topic about which we have been more stupid than intelligence."

At the other end of the continuum, we now know that students who do well in school often have advantages that other students lack, such as parents or older siblings who value education, who help them with their homework and teach them ahead of time what they'll encounter in class. That is, school becomes a place where privileged students can show off what they already learned at home. Does that mean they have more intelligence? Or does it mean they've been exposed to more knowledge? Those may not be the same thing at all. A special commission of the US National Academy of Sciences concluded in 2018 that "school failure may be partly explained by the mismatch between what students have learned in their home cultures and what is required of them in school." And the advantage of having learned a certain set of things at home doesn't just enlighten those particular things but will also give you more time to learn new things.

We need to somehow separate out the learning experiences a person has had—knowledge acquisition—from their innate ability to use whatever information they have. Scientists call the things you've already learned crystallized intelligence, and they call your potential to learn fluid intelligence. There's also a third intelligence I call acquisitional intelligence—that's the speed and ease with which you can acquire new information (if given the right opportunity). Think of it as coming before both crystallized and fluid intelligence: You can't amass a store of learned information quickly without acquisitional intelligence.

Crystallized intelligence is the knowledge you have already acquired, regardless of how easy or difficult it was for you to obtain it. It includes things such as your vocabulary, your general knowledge, your skills, and any mathematical rules or formulas you might have learned. It is heavily dependent on culture, because certain kinds of knowledge are valued more than others depending on where you live. Think *knowledge of plants* for people living in a hunter-gatherer community versus *reading* for people living in an industrialized community. Crystallized intelligence also depends on educational experience and opportunity. Crossword puzzles are an example of crystallized intelligence because you need to have amassed a big vocabulary; you need to know a lot about the world, geography, proper names, things like that—and the kinds of short words that crossword puzzle makers often have to use. How quickly and effortlessly you can acquire and retain new information, such as learning the capital of Myanmar while doing your crossword puzzle, is acquisitional intelligence.

Fluid intelligence is your ability to apply any information you have (whether it's extensive or not) to new contexts. It is your innate ability to reason, to think, to identify patterns, and to solve problems. We've all known people who have a remarkable retention for what they've learned, and can learn quickly, but lack the ability to apply that information—they would be high in crystallized but low in fluid intelligence. Some people with photographic memories are like that.

Fluid intelligence is thinking on your feet, flying by the seat of your pants; it's the kind of thinking you want to have in a pilot whose engine has just failed after takeoff as you are looking down at New York City just a few thousand feet below (Miracle on the Hudson). You need to combine that with the principles of flight and aerodynamics to right the plane (crystallized intelligence). And ideally, you can learn new information relevant to you without much effort, making you high in acquisitional intelligence. Of course the ideal situation is to have all three of these intelligences. That is, if you think intelligence is a good thing.

The terms *crystallized* and *fluid* are misleading but we're stuck with them. The word *crystallized* might seem to imply that somehow the knowledge base becomes highly structured, formed, and then doesn't change (like a crystal), but that's not what it means. Crystallized intelligence does change. Your concrete knowledge base increases with age as you learn and experience new things. Acquisitional intelligence can also change if you are highly motivated to learn something new, and not suffering from the current epidemic of information overload. The term *fluid* suggests that this type of intelligence changes over the course of a life span, but it generally doesn't (although you can learn to increase yours through systematic practice; of course, brain damage or dementia can decrease fluid intelligence).

Multiple Intelligences

The three-part distinction of crystallized, fluid, and acquisitional intelligence captures important ways to distinguish intelligence. But it misses the idea of intelligence *domains* that are vital to understanding how people differ from one another mentally. I've sat at meals with brilliant musicians or writers who did not know how to calculate the 20 percent tip on a restaurant bill. Even when given a simple trick like "ignore the last decimal place, take what's left, and double it," they go blank. They can be superior in crystallized, fluid, and acquisitional intelligence when it comes to music and literature, but they just aren't good at math. Math seems to be a special domain of ability. So does music, for that matter. Wouldn't it make sense to be able to compute a math IQ and a music IQ separately, and not have them depend on each other, or on having a large vocabulary?

Harvard professor Howard Gardner felt just that when he proposed his theory of multiple intelligences in his influential 1983 book, *Frames of Mind*. It took the cognitive neuroscience community by storm, and all the professors I knew immediately started teaching this concept in their cognitive psychology classes as a new and innovative approach to intelligence. There are several formal requirements that a skill must meet in order to be considered one of these frames of mind (a separate intelligence type), but there's no reason for us to get distracted by those requirements here. Gardner's intelligences are:

1. musical-rhythmic,
2. visual-spatial,
3. verbal-linguistic,
4. logical-mathematical,
5. bodily-kinesthetic (athleticism, dancing, acting),
6. interpersonal (or "social" intelligence),
7. intrapersonal (or self-knowledge),
8. spiritual (think Moses, Jesus, Mohammed, Buddha, for example),
9. moral (ability to solve problems within a moral and ethical frame, think King Solomon), and
10. naturalistic (knowledge of nature, plants, animals, and the sorts of things one might need to know to survive in the wilderness).

Regarding naturalistic intelligence, here's Gardner himself: "The individual who is readily able to recognize flora and fauna, to make other consequential distinctions in the natural world, and to use this ability productively (in hunting, in farming, in biological science) is exercising an important intelligence." There were clearly very smart, creative people in our preindustrial past, people who first harnessed fire, who invented the wheel, and who discovered agriculture. They might have been geniuses in this naturalistic domain and only average in others.

Intelligence expert Robert Sternberg studied naturalistic intelligence by visiting a rural village in western Kenya that is home to many parasitic infections.

He tested eighty-five villagers between the ages of twelve and fifteen. Of these, 94 percent were infected with *Schistosoma mansoni*, 54 percent with hookworm, 31 percent with whipworm, and 19 percent with roundworm. Sternberg tested their naturalistic intelligence by asking questions about their knowledge of plant-based treatments for parasites—clearly this knowledge domain has very practical significance for them. As Sternberg writes, "Children in this community use natural herbal medicines to treat themselves and others, sometimes with and sometimes without the involvement of parents or other adults." The children performed very well on these multiple-choice tests (there's an example of one of the questions in the notes on page 421), and their performance on these real-world skills was significantly better than their performance on tests of concepts they had learned in their village school, or other standard measures of intelligence, such as vocabulary. "Their knowledge of such medicines," Sternberg writes, "appears to be fairly extensive" and includes "what medicines to use for what illnesses and in what doses." What might account for this testing discrepancy? In some developing countries, the link between school success and life success is nonexistent. As Sternberg notes,

> In a village where most boys will become farmers or fishermen and most girls will become wives and mothers, success in school holds no immediate benefits. Indeed, even the time spent in school may be viewed as largely wasted in terms of the skills and resources that will lead to success in later life. . . . Someone could intelligently be spending his or her time learning the things that are most important to him or her—whether it is herbal medicines or music theory or moves on the basketball court—and thereby sacrificing points on a conventional intelligence test.

Taken more broadly, naturalistic intelligence can be seen as a type of practical intelligence, what in an urban setting we would call "street smarts." Practical intelligence (or any of the others mentioned previously) can constitute a distinct faculty from that which is measured by conventional intelligence tests.

Any of these multiple intelligences can be crystallized (you have amassed a great deal of knowledge in that domain), fluid (you have high potential in that domain), and acquisitional (you can learn things in that domain especially quickly), but what you have in one domain doesn't necessarily transfer to another.

Many cognitive scientists believe that the more expertise one obtains in a given domain, the larger the gap between that domain and others. (An exception would be polymaths, such as Leonardo da Vinci.) This is in contrast to individuals of average intelligence who tend to have low variability across the various skills subtests that are used to establish IQ. That's just a fancy way of saying that if they are moderately good in one area, like verbal ability, they tend also to be moderately good in others, like spatial and mathematical ability. This has fueled the belief in that general intelligence factor I mentioned earlier, *g*—if you're reasonably good at a whole bunch of things, there must be some common mental substrate for all of them.

But this is not true for exceptionally high-performing individuals. They tend to excel in a single domain, or perhaps two. It's not that they couldn't excel in many; it's that as these high performers start to get really good at something, they become increasingly absorbed in it and continue to develop that single area of expertise by redirecting brain resources toward it, letting other areas that are less relevant to them fall by the wayside. In the course of my work, I've met Nobel Prize winners who have such poor visual-spatial intelligence they get lost walking in their own neighborhoods. (The stories of Einstein getting lost on the Princeton campus are legendary.) It's tempting to chalk this up to absentmindedness or being preoccupied with other thoughts, but often it's not that the individual isn't paying attention; it's that they've allowed their spatial skills to atrophy because they've reallocated neural resources to the topic that consumes them. I've met mathematicians who utterly lack social intelligence and salespeople who have the uncanny ability to make everyone around them feel good but are deficient in other domains. For exceptional performers, one measure of intelligence, say, verbal, can be significantly different (several standard deviations) from other measures, such as visual-spatial. This led the great cognitive psychologist Buz Hunt to quip that *g* is not really a general intelligence factor, but a general mediocrity factor: Those who do not truly excel in any one domain are more likely to have similar scores on various subtests of intelligence. High intelligence breaks you free of the constraints of the hypothetical *g*.

Lately Gardner has been wondering if *teaching ability* should be an eleventh intelligence. He should know. Many of the most brilliant researchers at elite schools like Harvard and UC Berkeley are dreadful teachers (and maybe it's not lack of ability but lack of motivation). Many of the scholars who teach material the best—who have a gift for explaining things coupled with a real empathy for students—have not made important discoveries of their own and will never go down in the annals of great researchers. Often, poor school performance is the fault not of the student but of the teacher.

Dandelions can grow just about anywhere and do not need much maintenance in order to thrive. Orchids, on the other hand, need very specific care in order to survive. Dandelions are like the children with genetic and socioeconomic factors predisposing them to do well at school and on IQ tests—for them the environment is not as important, as they will likely do well regardless. Orchids are like the children without these genetic and socioeconomic predispositions. For them, it is critical that they receive careful attention to their education in order to succeed at school.

Gardner's theory of multiple intelligences is taught widely in universities, but the intelligence testing community has been slower to adopt it and clings to the hundred-year-old concept of a general intelligence factor, *g*. Part of the reason is that the tests they use, the WISC, Woodcock-Johnson, Ravens Matrices, and so on, have been used for decades, providing them with responses from tens of thousands of people, revealing normative data: the typical profile of responses of people on average. They have so much data that they often can predict very well how 88 percent of the population will perform. The problem is they don't know which 88 percent.

One thing that has limited the acceptance of Gardner's theory is that we don't have well-defined tests for each of these intelligences, and the tests we do have tend to correlate highly with that pesky *g*. Gardner is not a test maker, and the test makers have not jumped in to fill this gap. We can look at people like Serena Williams and Paul McCartney and agree that they exhibit exceptional, unique, and world-class abilities in their respective domains, but that's not the same as quantifying their abilities with specialized measurement tools. In psychometrics, we want a number, so that we can, for instance, say that Paul McCartney is at 212 on some scale of musical intelligence, and someone with a tin ear is down around 90. You might find it astonishing—as did I—that there aren't any good tests of musical ability. There are tests, but they don't measure anything relevant to real music in the real world. They're useless.

The Problem with Standardized Tests of Intelligence

There are a number of problems with the standardized tests of intelligence in use. Psychometricians look for two properties in a test, reliability and validity. Reliability means that if you take the same test on multiple occasions, you'll receive roughly the same score. Slight variability is to be expected—sometimes you're having a bad day, or you're hungry, you're taking the test late in the day and you're a morning person, and so on. But a reliable test is one for which your score is similar each time you take the test. Most of the standard IQ tests are like this. Validity is different—it means that the score on a test is relevant to some real-world scenario or attribute. Few of us would take seriously a general test of athletic ability if LeBron James, Tom Brady, and Serena Williams did poorly on it, while Homer Simpson (or Harry Styles) obtained high scores. The test might have high reliability, meaning that people scored more or less the same on it each time they took it, but what does it really mean if it doesn't conform to the way we perceive athletic excellence?

And that's the first problem with many psychometric intelligence tests: We aren't always sure what they are measuring. About 25 percent of the difference in school performance across students is due to IQ test scores; that leaves a whopping 75 percent unexplained. What could contribute to good school performance? Diet, exercise, socioeconomic class, family culture—and that factor that Gardner proposed, the teacher's intelligence. And even though IQ correlates moderately with school grades, there is more to life than academics. The tests are biased toward a decidedly middle-class Western conception of intelligence, learning, and values. Even a casual look at any media outlet will show that measurable intelligence has very little to do with economic success. Motivation, resilience, opportunity, and getting along with others are often even more important, contributing to that unexplained 75 percent.

Standardized IQ tests are also culturally biased. They were mostly written by white people who looked at the world a certain way, resulting in tests that are notoriously biased against African Americans. Dr. Robert Lee Williams II created a one-hundred-question black IQ test, with information relevant to blacks. Black Americans who took the test achieved higher IQ scores than on standard IQ tests, and higher scores than whites who took the test.

One component of IQ tests asks general knowledge questions, such as who was president during the US Civil War. Obviously, if you are not from the United States you are at a disadvantage. (People from the North are likely to answer Abraham Lincoln, and some people from the South might answer Jefferson Davis.)

Another problem with standardized IQ tests is that they penalize creative thinking: There is no room for creative answers or for solutions to the problem that the test writer didn't think of. For a creative person, taking a standardized IQ test requires not just solving a problem, but trying to figure out the way the white, middle-class test creator solved the problem, and that is not the same thing.

Consider this example:

> Which one does not belong: golf, tennis, squash, football, baseball?

What would you answer? Only one was considered correct, football, because it's the only sport that doesn't require an implement to hit the ball with. But you could make an equally compelling argument for golf, since it is the only game you can play alone and still get a meaningful score, or for tennis, which is the only one played with a net. I was discussing this with a friend of mine, and we were going back and forth, when his seven-year-old daughter, Jocelyn, who had overheard us, ran into the room and said, "You're both wrong! Squash doesn't belong because it's a vegetable!" She had us. Then she also pointed out that squash was the only one that is always played indoors. (By the way, that seven-year-old ended up going to MIT and is now an innovative high school math teacher. I am a very proud godfather.)

Bursts of great creativity come from somewhere, and one can't help but marvel at, and admire, the brains that produce them. When facing such moments, it seems untenable to insist that creativity isn't part of intellect.

My favorite example of this comes from the book *Conceptual Blockbusting: A Guide to Better Ideas*, by James L. Adams, emeritus professor of mechanical engineering at Stanford. At eighty-five he says, "I have been retired from paychecks for twelve years. But it isn't easy, because there are so many good things to do, and I was given neither infinite money nor infinite time at my retirement party."

Ever heard the phrase *thinking outside the box*? Jim popularized it from the solution to a problem known as the nine dot puzzle, which traces its origins at least back to 1914. You're shown three rows of three dots, and your job is to connect them all by drawing four straight, continuous lines that pass through each of the nine dots only once and never lifting the pen from the paper.

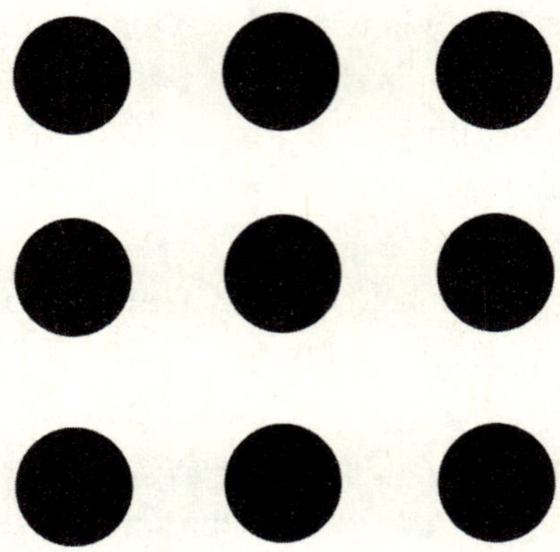

As with any puzzle, I suggest you try it yourself. There's a brain-based reason for this. It is easy to forget things that you are simply told. If you engage actively in exploring an issue—whether it's a puzzle, a thought problem, or even a question about history ("Who was president during the *Challenger* explosion?") or the arts ("In what century did Monet work?"), you're more likely to retain the answer after you've exerted some of your own effort toward finding it, using your own reasoning and problem-solving skills.

The standard solution to the nine dot puzzle is in the endnotes, on page 421. The first solution that many people attempt is to start with their pen on one of the dots (the problem doesn't say you must), and to never let their lines extend beyond those dots (the problem doesn't say that you can't extend beyond the dots either). In effect, they are imposing a frame, or box, around the dots, and they don't let their pen or their imagination go beyond the confines of this box (see following page).

Solving the problem requires thinking beyond these confines. Jim's book made a big splash in the corporate world. *Thinking outside the box* became a shorthand for not imposing constraints on a problem that didn't need to be there, whether it was designing a more fuel-efficient engine (such as Mazda did with their rotary engine) or, more recently, room sharing and ride sharing via companies such as Airbnb and Uber. (Who says that customers will only ride in a car that is painted a particular color and has a trip meter?)

After Jim's book was published, he received a flurry of letters about the nine dot puzzle from people who had managed to solve it with three lines or

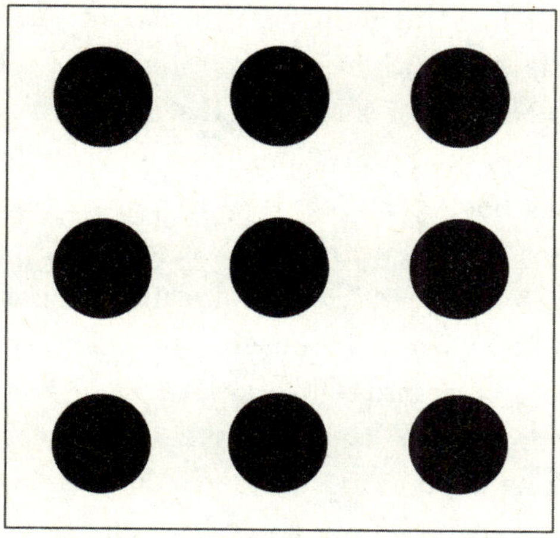

two, by folding, ripping, taping the paper—all kinds of things. Nothing in the problem says you can't. One particularly elegant solution, using only one line, involved rolling the paper into a cone shape and connecting the dots with a continuous line that goes around the cone shape in three dimensional space. My favorite comes from a ten-year-old, who wrote this letter:

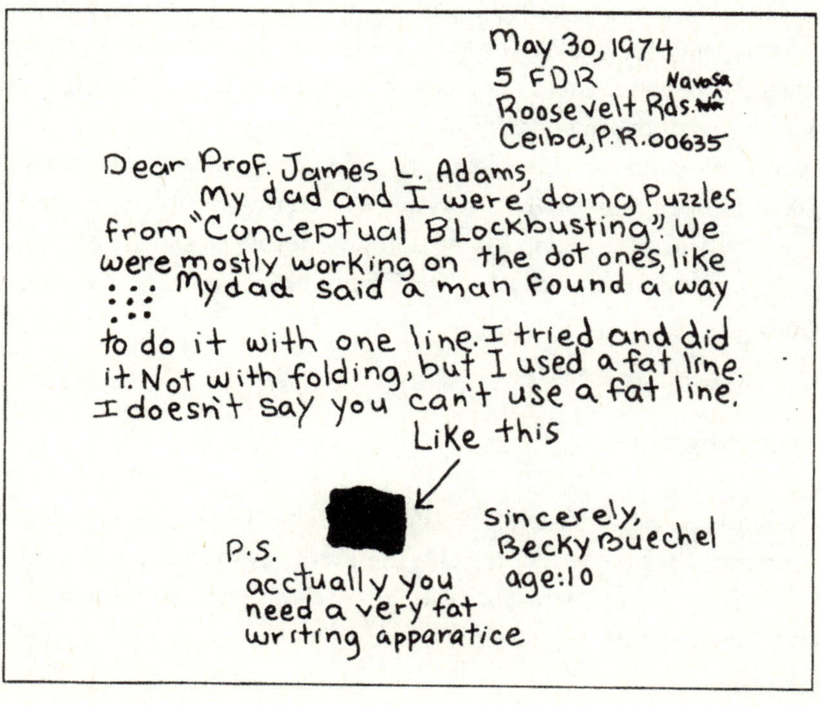

May 30, 1974
5 FDR Navasa
Roosevelt Rds. ~~Na~~
Ceiba, P.R. 00635

Dear Prof. James L. Adams,
My dad and I were doing Puzzles from "Conceptual Blockbusting". We were mostly working on the dot ones, like ⁙ My dad said a man found a way to do it with one line. I tried and did it. Not with folding, but I used a fat line. I doesn't say you can't use a fat line. Like this

Sincerely,
Becky Buechel
age: 10

P.S.
acctually you need a very fat writing apparatice

I find solutions like this tremendously exciting. The kind of open-mindedness that leads to such bursts of creativity is, I believe, a hallmark of intelligence, and I think it's something that all of us have innately. Four-year-olds incessantly ask *why* questions: Why do I have to go to bed? Why do I have to go to school? Why does it rain? We have this natural inquisitiveness trained out of us by weary teachers and parents. It's a shame. The good news is that you can rediscover and rekindle this at any age. By the way, ten-year-old Becky Buechel, who wrote this adorable letter to Jim Adams, was admitted to Stanford eight years later.

Among other things, Jim's book shows that you can prime the pump of creativity by looking underneath the hood at how some creative problem solving is done. Problem solving is a mind-set, an approach, and it can be built and improved upon just by doing it. Every sudoku or crossword puzzle you do requires some problem solving, and they get easier as you practice them. Now, if you've heard that doing these puzzles is the key to good cognitive health as we age, that's an oversimplification. The evidence is that while you will undoubtedly get better at doing sudoku and crossword puzzles, you will not necessarily get better at other things. No, the best strategy for cognitive health is to keep doing *new* things—things that require new ways of thinking. If you never did crosswords before and you start at seventy, that's great. If you've been doing crosswords since you were sixteen, there's no reason to stop now, but don't expect them to be a magic elixir that fends of dementia. Instead, find some other kind of puzzle you've never done—a Rubik's cube, logic problems, jigsaw puzzles, 3-D wooden jigsaw puzzles, brain teasers. They can be frustrating at first, so it's best to start easy. And stick with it. Maybe find a fourteen-year-old to help, which checks off another box of the COACH principle: associating with new people.

Processing Speed

Standardized tests in general, and IQ tests in particular, are typically administered using predetermined time limits; thus, processing speed is part of the conception of intelligence used by psychometricians. Someone who can solve a problem at lightning speed has more of some mental quality that certainly seems like intelligence. But what about the slow, plodding, methodical thinker who solves a huge problem but requires time to do it? It took Einstein ten years to come up with general relativity. It took Tolstoy six years to write *War and Peace* and J. R. R. Tolkien twelve years to write *The Lord of the Rings.* Are they less intelligent than Mozart, who reportedly wrote pieces as fast as he could think of them? The question, when posed like that, seems absurd. Yet the testing community has been slow to recognize that speed, while impressive, isn't everything. Neuroscientist Jeffrey Mogil at McGill University, a keen observer of the field, says, "I've always thought that processing speed, while obviously a thing, has essentially nothing to do with intelligence. It's just a party trick." The *Mona Lisa,* one of the most famous paintings in Western art, took fourteen years to paint. Nevertheless, being able to solve certain problems quickly is a skill we can lose as we age, and that can be both frustrating and worrying.

Art Shimamura has studied the aging brain and reaction times:

> The number to remember is 1/25th of a second, which is the annual decrement in reaction time that we found in participants between the ages of 30 and 71 years. This value doesn't seem very much, but after 30–40 years, such slowing can be the cause of broken hips and mental slips.

Processing speed and prefrontal cortex function are significantly correlated. The prefrontal cortex is responsible for a number of aspects of cognition that often decline as we age:

- inhibiting distracting or irrelevant information
- planning, scheduling
- analytical thinking
- executing complex, sequential motor actions
- handling novelty
- fluid intelligence

Unfortunately the prefrontal cortex is susceptible to age-related decreases in blood flow, changes in the structure of cells, and reduction of volume (shrinkage). A biological explanation is that there is no evolutionary pressure for the prefrontal cortex to stay sharp in old age, just as there is no evolutionary pressure for *anything* to stay sharp in old age. (Once we are past the age of reproducing and passing our genes to the next generation, evolution doesn't care about how we spend the rest of our lives.) And so processing speed, led by prefrontal cortex decline, slows down.

Fluid intelligence declines with age, or at least scores on tests of it do. In the Lothian Birth Cohort Study (named after the region in Scotland where the participants lived), intelligence and depressive symptoms both declined during a nine-year period between ages seventy and seventy-nine years old. But low fluid intelligence in childhood predicted greater depressive symptoms in old age. High fluid intelligence is protective against the declines of aging, not just intellectual declines but emotional ones as well.

Practical intelligence increases with age, peaking after age fifty or sixty. An example of a practical question is, "If you were traveling by car and got stranded on an interstate highway during a blizzard, what would you do?" Or it might involve social tasks such as dealing with a landlord who would not make repairs, getting a friend to visit more often, or what to do when one has been passed over for promotion. People over fifty do far better on these questions than people under fifty, and many get better after sixty or even seventy. Practical intelligence seems to grow alongside crystallized intelligence as we get older.

Analytical intelligence is preserved in old age if you can practice using it. Rather than passively taking in information, question it, relate it to other things you know, and ponder it. At the universities where I've worked, a ninety-year-old professor coming into the office every day, participating in seminars, and interacting with much younger colleagues is the norm. I haven't seen this nearly as much in boardrooms, but this vitality is not uncommon among doctors, lawyers, and judges. Take Jack Weinstein, a ninety-eight-year-old federal judge in Brooklyn who still handles a full caseload. His colleagues even hand him some of the most difficult cases they have. He and I had a delightful meeting, surrounded by piles of open cases, research briefs from his clerks, and manuscripts he was writing. That wasn't a typo—he is ninety-eight. His philosophy appears to be in accord with what I've encountered with other people in their nineties: Try not to slow down. A great deal of what goes into Judge Weinstein's work requires analysis, thoughtful probing of facts, hypotheticals, and scaffolding on a lifetime of learning and experience.

From the arts side, musician Judy Collins (age eighty, and still touring and writing) advises, "Never stop. That's the key. Never stop. Never stop growing. Never stop being curious. Never stop thinking that there's something you want to do that you haven't done. And do it!"

Jane Goodall (age eighty-five, and still holding down a rigorous program of field research in Tanzania and worldwide public lectures) adds:

> People who retire fade rather fast unless they have something really important they want to do. It's feeling that you have purpose, and that you have less and less time to make your mark. Instead of slowing down you have to speed up.

Abstract Thinking Gets Better with Age

After your brain receives inputs from the senses, the first, or lower stages of processing preserve a relatively faithful copy of sensory inputs. Abstract thinking occurs in higher brain centers; it isn't unique to humans but is most fully developed in our species, and it underlies mathematical ability, language, problem solving, and industrialization. Intelligent, adaptive behavior requires abstracting behaviorally relevant concepts and categories, an ability that gets better with age.

Neuroscientist Earl Miller from MIT found that abstraction involves a wide range of brain regions, gradually increasing as one moves up the hierarchy of the brain, reaching its peak in the prefrontal cortex. Recall that the prefrontal cortex is the last region of the brain to become fully formed as we develop, and it normally doesn't reach an adult-like state until the twenties. When we form abstract representations of objects, we go beyond their appearance and think about them in terms of categories, such as how they might be used, where one is likely to find them, how rare or common they are, or what kinds of motion they might make. These can be the kinds of abstractions that Posner and Keele studied in their random dot patterns, the abstract representations musicians have for fingerings, or that you have for using everyday objects like forks and pens.

The tendency to form abstract representations is innate, and it begins at birth, if not sooner, but takes many years to develop. This is the reason that algebra and calculus are not typically taught before ages thirteen and sixteen, respectively: because the abstract reasoning required to learn them is not present in most schoolchildren before that age. In fact, studies show that this is an overly ambitious schedule: It isn't until around sixteen or seventeen that kids begin to show an accurate ability to solve equations with letters (symbols) rather than numbers, the fundamental basis of algebra. Algebra is usually the first domain in school mathematics that encourages students' abstract reasoning. This developmental trajectory is the same reason that adult literature usually doesn't make sense to young children—it's not simply the more difficult vocabulary or adult themes; it's the abstract relations among characters and ideas. (The study of abstract thinking in other species is a cottage industry within neuroscience and biology, and an exciting new paper shows that even bees can engage in abstract thinking and can represent the number zero, something that was thought to be uniquely human.)

By age sixty, you begin to realize you can't always trust your senses and that there are more important things than appearances when considering similarities. For example, here's the kind of abstract reasoning that is handled by the prefrontal cortex: Suppose you have to prop open a door. Which of the following objects could help you do that?

- hammer
- banana
- thick book
- boot
- piece of paper
- baseball
- paperweight
- wedge

The objects have nothing in common at the level of visual appearance—it is their function that defines whether they fit in a category or not.

Relying on your visual cortex and occipital lobe won't help you here—you need that prefrontal cortex to analyze the abstract functional relation.

Much of the information that is most useful to us in the world requires abstraction and categorization. Consider foods: few of them look alike in terms of color and shape, and yet we know—learn, actually—that such disparate-looking objects as potatoes, pineapples, salmon, turmeric, and almonds are all edible. We can further subdivide into those that need to be cooked before being eaten.

Writer Diane Ackerman invented a game called Dingbats that she played with her late husband, the writer Paul West. They would start with a single object and try to generate alternative uses for it:

> What can you do with a pencil—other than write?
>
> I'd begun. "Play the drums. Conduct an orchestra. Cast spells. Ball yarn. Use as a compass hand. Play pick up sticks. Rest one eyebrow on it. Fasten a shawl. Secure hair atop the head. Use as the mast for a Lilliputian's sailboat. Play darts. Make a sundial. Spin vertically on flint to spark a fire. Combine with a thong to create a slingshot. Ignite and use as a taper. Test the depth of oil. Clean a pipe. Stir paint. Work a Ouija board. Gouge an aqueduct in the sand. Roll out dough for a pie crust. Herd balls of loose mercury. Use as the fulcrum for a spinning top. Squeegee a window. Provide a perch for your parrot. . . . Pass the pencil-baton to you . . ."
>
> "Use as a spar in a model airplane," Paul had continued. "Measure distances. Puncture a balloon. Use as a flagpole. Roll a necktie around. Tamp the gunpowder into a pint-size musket. Test bon-bons for contents. . . . Crumble, and use the lead as a poison."

Neuropsychologists use this kind of test to evaluate intelligence. And results from the tests correlate with increased cortical thickness and gray-matter volume in brain structures of the daydreaming mode. Participants might be given two minutes to generate and list as many ideas as they can, answering a question like "What can you do with a brick?" Typical answers might include build a house, break a window, use it as a penholder, prop open a door, and so on. (Weirdly, this test of divergent thinking penalizes participants for coming up with a large number of examples of the same general category without informing them ahead of time of this penalty. The sample answers above would be worth four points. But the answers "Build a house, build a factory, build a stone wall, pile them sequentially higher to make a stairway" would receive only one point. Score another blow against standardized testing.)

The developmental trend toward abstract thinking is one of the compensatory mechanisms of aging that mitigates the decline of our sensory systems. Even apart from that decline, the trend toward abstract thinking helps us to solve problems that would not be solvable otherwise. Aging is not accompanied by unavoidable cognitive decline. The aging brain changes, thanks to neuroplasticity. It changes itself, heals itself, and finds other ways to do things, some of them (such as abstract reasoning) actually better than the earlier ways of doing things; it harnesses neuroprotective and neurorestorative capabilities.

The ability to learn new things quickly reaches a peak in adolescence and the college years and declines after age forty. Fluid intelligence, the ability to use what we already know, is lower before the age of forty and picks up in each decade thereafter. Although our raw neural processing speed and reaction times may slow down (precipitously in our eighties), older adults have experienced so much more than twenty-year-olds that they have a competitive edge. This is one reason why so many Fortune 500 companies are keeping their more senior workers on as chairmen emeriti. Clive Davis, at eighty-seven, is chief creative officer of Sony Music, following a distinguished career as a record company executive and innovator. It's what makes George Augspurger so effective at what he does.

An important point should not get lost: We vary considerably in the ways that we age. Many people in their late nineties are outperforming people in their early sixties, and the opposite is also true. The rate at which our cognitive abilities decline, and the severity with which we might develop dementia, are all highly variable. Many individuals (in some reports up to 25 percent) show the biological, pathological markers for Alzheimer's disease and yet show zero impairment in thinking capacity. Cognitive reserve can insulate against the damaging effects of aging.

So how do you get cognitive reserve? High levels of education and a balanced diet help. Recall also the conclusion of the Lothian Birth Cohort Study: High fluid intelligence is protective against the declines of aging, perhaps due to cognitive reserve.

The reserve is also dependent on occupational complexity. Complex occupations require continuing education, sustained intellectual engagement, and mental effort. They feature a changing landscape of options and decisions that cannot be done on autopilot or according to simple rules. On the opposite end, epidemiological studies have established that low educational attainment and low occupational complexity increase risk factors for Alzheimer's disease.

Fluid Intelligence Training

Almost every book or article you read on intelligence says that you can't increase fluid intelligence, and certainly not over the age of sixty or seventy. While that may be true (I'm skeptical), you can certainly increase your performance scores on tests of it, which I think is just as good—it expands your brain and increases your cognitive reserve to learn new ways of approaching problems.

To a purist, fluid intelligence cannot be altered by learning. But the way we measure it is impure and imperfect, and nearly all the tests that purport to measure it are sensitive to learning effects. The tests are *not* independent of education, experience, or socioeconomic class. Very little is. Some children are taught or encouraged to embrace their mental and intellectual selves while others are taught to embrace, exclusively, their emotional, physical, or spiritual selves. This orientation early in life can have profound effects. I've visited households where the children grew up with logic problems, puzzles, and mental games as part of the day-to-day dinner conversation. I've visited others where prayer, supplication, and charity were the focus. And it's not just children. The style in which older adults live their lives, their focus, and the extent to which they engage in intellectual play affects their ability to answer the kinds of questions one sees on tests of fluid intelligence. The aging couple who share mental games are just going to be more prepared for problem-solving tests than the couple who spend all their time silently hiking and trekking together, or the couple who are immersed in community service to the exclusion of all other activities. But that doesn't make the hikers and do-gooders any less intelligent—we just don't administer tests on which they'd excel.

Karl Duncker, a great Gestalt psychologist from the twentieth century, looks at problem solving in the most general way, tieing together these various forms of intelligence:

> A problem arises when a living creature has a goal but does not know how this goal is to be reached. Whenever one cannot go from the given situation to the desired situation simply by action, then there has to be recourse to thinking. . . . Such thinking has the task of devising some action which may mediate between the existing and the desired solutions.

Duncker then proposed a problem, one that requires some thinking:

> Suppose you are a doctor who has a patient with a malignant tumor in his stomach. The tumor cannot be operated upon, but you can use a particular type of ray to destroy the tumor. If the rays reach the tumor all at once at a sufficiently high intensity, the tumor will be destroyed. Unfortunately, at this intensity, the healthy tissue that the rays pass through will also be destroyed. At a lower intensity the rays would not damage the healthy tissue but would also not destroy the tumor. What can be done to destroy the tumor and at the same time avoid destroying the healthy tissue?

This is a difficult problem for nonmedical professionals to solve—only about 10 percent come up with the solution. People who are high in fluid intelligence might ultimately attack the problem by considering stories or events that have some structural similarity. In the abstract, the problem is how to destroy a target when direct application of an intense, large force is harmful to the surrounding area. We think, "Have I ever heard of a problem like that in another domain that might be informative?"

Now consider this scenario from tactical military history:

> A general wishes to capture a fortress located in the center of a country. There are many roads radiating outward from the fortress. All have been mined so that while small groups of soldiers can pass over the roads safely, any large force will detonate the mines. A full-scale direct attack is therefore impossible. The general divides his army into small groups, sends each group to the head of a different road that leads to the fortress, and times it so that the groups converge simultaneously in the fortress.

The analogous situation in the tumor problem is to use multiple low-intensity beams all at once, aimed at the tumor from different directions. Each low-intensity beam on its own won't harm the surrounding tissue, but the sum of all the beams will destroy the tumor. The elements of both problems are similar. Where you need to make a logical or creative leap is here: In the fortress problem, there are many roads that lead outward from it; in the tumor problem there are not. But what if you could create many roads? That's what focused, dispersed beam therapy does. (If you follow medical technology, you know that brachytherapy and other surgical procedures that implant small radioactive seeds are also used these days, but they are not strictly analogous to the military fortress problem.) Resource dispersal is the abstract concept, and it comes up in a variety of different scenarios, such as illegal money laundering: Large sums of money are divided into small sums, each of which is carried into a country or deposited into a financial account in amounts that do not trigger suspicion and thus avoid detection.

In the tumor/fortress problems, an analogy is used to describe a set of particular relations among objects. When told the fortress story is a hint to the tumor problem, up to 90 percent of people solve the tumor problem. The philosopher Karl Popper has suggested that all of life is problem solving. The problem-solving strategy that works here is to think of any analogies that may apply. Analogical thinking has led to great discoveries, such as Rutherford's attempts to understand the structure of the atom and Schrödinger's cat.

The way to become good at problem solving, to get in the flow of your best fluid intelligence at any age, is to practice, to expose yourself to different kinds of problems, and to share them with friends. What people who score higher than average on fluid intelligence have going for them is that they've learned a system for attacking a particular kind of problem, and they've had lots of practice solving problems of different types. Better than doing crossword puzzles or sudoku is engaging in a variety of different kinds of problems.

Wisdom

What is wisdom? As with intelligence, there is no scientific consensus, but nine common themes emerge in the research:

1. social decision-making ability and a pragmatic knowledge of life
2. prosocial attitudes and behaviors
3. ability to maintain emotional homeostasis (with a tendency to favor positive emotions)
4. a tendency toward reflection and self-understanding
5. acknowledgment of and coping effectively with uncertainty
6. valuing of relativism and tolerance
7. spirituality
8. openness to new experience
9. a sense of humor

This is not meant to be an exhaustive list—you may disagree with some and think of others that are missing from this list—but it's a starting point. Paul Baltes defined wisdom as knowledge useful for dealing with life problems, including an awareness of the varied contexts of life and how they change over time, recognition that values and life goals differ among individuals and among groups, and acknowledgment of the uncertainties of life together with ways to manage those uncertainties.

And isn't that what we seek wisdom for? We don't climb to a high mountaintop in the Himalayas to ask a guru what to name our pet. We don't read philosophical treatises to know whether it's better to serve rice or potatoes with trout, or to deal with other small or day-to-day problems. When we seek wisdom, we seek answers to the big, *unusual* questions of life. We consult the people we consider wise, whether it's grandparents, spiritual leaders, or poets, whether it's the Dalai Lama, Shakespeare, Guinan (*Star Trek: The Next Generation*), or Vishnu, to provide a perspective we lack—an *insight* into happiness, peace, and the harmonious integration of ourselves into the world.

If you're thinking that what we call wisdom has a lot to do with the kinds of intelligence that standardized testing can miss, I agree. At the beginning of this chapter, I suggested that wisdom arises from four things: associations, experience, pattern recognition, and the use of analogies. And this is why we gain more and more wisdom as we age. Older people have more wisdom precisely because of how the brain's networks have evolved to scaffold on prior knowledge and experience, to abstract out common principles, to be able to see to the core of a matter that might elude younger (and less wise) observers, and to have more experiences on which to base analogies.

Developmental psychologist Judith Glück proposes that life challenges act as catalysts for the development of wisdom, and our internal resources influence how we appraise, deal with, and integrate these challenges. According to her model, the internal resources that predict the development of wisdom include: *mastery* (managing uncertainty and uncontrollability), *openness, reflectivity,* and *emotion regulation,* including empathy (the model is called MORE). External resources are equally important. Other people, such as friends and mentors, play a crucial role in both the short-term expression and the long-term development of wisdom. Situational contexts, including life phases, also influence the extent to which people act on their wisdom-related knowledge.

One of Gardner's multiple intelligences, interpersonal or social intelligence, is connected to what we usually think of as wisdom: helping others and mediating disagreements. In the Bible, King Solomon was called upon to mediate the dispute between two women who both claimed to be the mother of a single child. His answer has become the very archetype of wise judgment in Western culture. Older adults show higher levels of emotional regulation, experience-based decision making and conflict resolution, prosocial behaviors such as empathy and compassion, subjective emotional well-being, and self-reflection or insight, compared to younger adults. Oldsters also show a tendency toward favoring positive emotions, and greater ability to maintain positive relationships. They're more likely to say hello to strangers on the street, to wave other drivers in front of them, and to be trusting of others (this is why scammers find old people an easy mark).

The wisdom we attribute to older adults may well be neurobiologically based, born out of changes to the brain that allow the two hemispheres to communicate more freely, to combine the logical with the intuitive, the quantitative with the qualitative, the fact-based thinking with the artistic. Greater wisdom is also marked by freer connections between the frontal lobes and the much older limbic system, and by age-related changes in neurochemistry. For instance, it is known that dopamine decreases with age while norepinephrine and serotonin levels remain stable. The brain's neurochemistry is a system with complex, dynamic interactions. It is overly simplistic to say things such as "dopamine increases blah blah" or "serotonin decreases blahdedy blah." Rather, changes in even a single neurotransmitter, like dopamine, can cause the remaining chemical receptors and circuits in the brain to function differently. Some older people describe a "burning off" of previously distressing mental states. Leonard Cohen, for example, was amazed that his chronic depression, which no medication could relieve, simply disappeared in his seventies.

Yet not everyone grows wise with age. Wisdom comes from combining motivational, emotional, and cognitive experiences, having successfully overcome challenges, and having had meaningful interactions with others. Although we may think of wisdom as primarily an intellectual quality, in fact it is heavily reliant on emotional maturity and a shift in those motivations that drive us. Emotion and motivation change with age as a function of a number of different hormonal and neurotransmitter changes in the brain.

We are all flawed. Throughout the course of our lives we will likely do things that are both wise and unwise. Wisdom is perhaps reaching the point where the wise actions outnumber the unwise, and we are in a position to examine problems and decisions from a perspective that allows us to better predict a good outcome, whether it involves us or others. The good news is that wisdom can be cultivated and taught. Precursors of wisdom, such as empathy, emotion regulation, and critical thinking, can be modeled and explicitly taught from an early age. And we can strive for the higher ideal in acquiring intelligence and wisdom—to use them for the betterment of others and of the world we live in. That is what Jane Goodall says is her primary motivation, "to recruit lots of young people who will help make the world a better place."

5

FROM EMOTIONS TO MOTIVATION

Snakes, rickety bridges, *Mad Men,* and stress

Two of my favorite singers, Joni Mitchell and Stevie Wonder, do something that no one else I know does—they embrace a full range of emotions and make you feel them too, oftentimes within a single line of a song. When Stevie sings, "People hand-in-hand, have I lived to see the milk and honey land?," he is able to command both vulnerability and confidence, sorrow and hope, in the same line. When Joni sings the single word *blue* (from the song and album of the same name), she sounds as if she's crying and laughing at the same time—as if the depression is awful but she can step aside from it and see that it is only a passing phase.

Many of us turn to music for emotional support, comfort, or inspiration, or to motivate us to move. Music can trigger emotions and sometimes help us interpret our feelings when we're not sure how we feel. It can pull people with Alzheimer's out of their closed-in world and help them to re-engage with life and their surroundings.

Emotions arise inside of us and profoundly affect our moods. What are these psychological states exactly? Emotions are related to moods, but they're not the same thing. *Emotions* are an acute state of affect and arousal lasting from seconds to minutes, whereas *mood* refers to a longer-term emotional tone. Emotions occur against a background of mood. You might be in a slightly irritated mood after having had an argument with your boss. Then, when someone steps on your foot in line at a Starbucks, or your seven-year-old keeps interrupting you, well, that's when you begin to exhibit emotion.

Emotion, motivation, reinforcement, and arousal are closely related topics and often appear together in neuroscientific research. Emotions evolved because they motivate us. They are that surge of something (arousal) you feel welling up in you that makes you want to take some kind of action. They move us away from danger and toward food, dry shelter, and potential mates: key elements that positively reinforce our identities. It is no accident that the word *motion* is contained in the word *emotion*. Nor is it a coincidence that when we are feeling particularly deep emotion, we say we are *moved*. Emotions are the body's way of encouraging us to do what is best for us, and as biologist Frans de Waal says, they "focus the mind and prepare the body while leaving room for experience and judgment."

It may seem that emotions just happen in response to the environment, but that's not how neuroscientists see it. Like perception, emotions appear to be constructed out of bits and pieces of experience and inference, and the job of our brains is to tie disparate threads together and try to make sense of what's happening around us and inside of us.

In other words, emotions come about in a way that is exactly the opposite of what we usually imagine. You think that you see a snake, feel fear, and then jump back to avoid it, but snakes are fast and your conscious, analytic brain is slow. If you waited for your brain to determine that the rustling in the grass was a snake, it would be too late—you'd get bitten. Instead, a subcortical, subconscious process moves you out of the way rapidly. Only then does your brain figure out why you've jumped and signal to you, "You're afraid." This all happens so quickly that you think it's happened in the opposite order. Similarly, if you feel an ache on your arm, you rely on context. If you just got punched, your brain assigns a particular emotion—perhaps anger and a desire to retaliate, perhaps fear and a desire to run to avoid getting punched again. However, if the ache is because you just got a flu shot, you feel a different emotion—perhaps resignation, frustration, or stoicism, mixed with the optimism that it will help you avoid getting sick this winter. The same bodily feeling gives rise to two different streams of emotion.

Neuroscientist Joseph LeDoux makes a distinction between emotions that arise from survival behaviors and other emotions. Survival behaviors include things like defense, maintenance of energy and nutritional supplies, fluid balance, thermoregulation, and reproduction, and they have distinct neural circuits underlying them. Our human survival strategies go back to single-cell organisms, such as bacteria, which, despite not having a nervous system, have the capacity to close their semipermeable outer wall in the presence of harmful substances and to accept substances that have nutritional value. Our own survival circuits include chemical systems that regulate how we react to others. In humans, oxytocin and vasopressin influence our bonding and affiliations. Even a creature as lowly as the worm has an equivalent to these, a neuropeptide called nematocin that, when active, causes them to want to mate. Worms who have nematocin blocked don't particularly want to mate, and when they do try, they aren't very good at it.

Survival circuits, from worms to humans, cause specific brain and bodily responses to rise in priority, while inhibiting other circuits and actions. When the brain and body become aroused, attention becomes focused on relevant environmental and internal stimuli, motivational systems become engaged, action is taken, learning takes place, and memories are formed. What we call emotions or feelings occur when we consciously detect that a survival or motivational brain circuit is active or we detect some change in body state, and then—here's the amazing part—our consciousness appraises and labels this state.

One of my favorite experiments in psychology, the rickety bridge experiment, illustrates this. Male college students walked across one of two bridges. One bridge was chosen to be fear inducing—a rickety bridge that was high up over a deep ravine. The other was chosen to be non–fear inducing—a sturdy bridge only about ten feet above the ground. A female confederate of the experimenters was waiting at the other end of each bridge and asked the male participants if they would fill out a questionnaire about scenic environments for a psychology project she was doing. When they were done, she wrote down her phone number in case they had further thoughts. The experimenters hypothesized that the men who crossed the rickety bridge would be physiologically aroused by the time they reached the end (due to fear) but that they would construe, or misattribute, this arousal as sexual attraction to the female. Accordingly, the experimenters predicted that the rickety-bridge crossers would be more likely than the sturdy-bridge crossers to telephone the female researcher for a date. That's exactly what they found. (This experiment was the basis for one of the most memorable scenes in the television series *Mad Men*. Roger Sterling and Joan Holloway were walking at night in New York City and got mugged, causing them both to become severely frightened. Right after the mugger leaves, the two of them duck into the shadows and have passionate sex.) Other experiments showed that a whole range of emotions can easily be misattributed. All of this underscores the counterintuitive point that emotions are cognitive constructions that depend on circumstances and interpretation.

This way of looking at things causes us to reevaluate animal emotion. No one is claiming that animals don't experience emotions—they clearly do—but they probably experience them differently because they lack the cognitive analytic tools to interpret them in the complex ways that we do. It seems to many dog owners that our beloved pets experience a wide range of humanlike emotions—joy when rolling in the grass, shame after being caught peeing on the couch, jealousy when we play with another pet, sadness when we leave them alone too long. One possibility is that we are anthropomorphizing them. Another is that they experience proto-emotions that are somewhat humanlike, based on findings that they have similar neurochemistry and similar brain activations to humans in response to stimuli that would cause us to feel particular emotions. But then there are emotions that dogs and other animals appear to lack completely. For example, my dog, Madeleine, although we often think of her as human, does not experience disgust. Neither did the succession of best friends who preceded her: Winifred, Shadow, Isabella, Charlotte, Karma, or 99. Dogs will eat or roll in practically anything and show no evidence of the emotion of disgust, which appears to be uniquely human. As infants, we don't have it until we're three to seven years old, but once we get it, we hang on to it for life. In fact, the older we get, the wider our experience of disgust becomes, as we contemplate injustice, violence, and fraud in our world—not just excrement or rotten food.

Many emotions appear to be built in. Human infants don't have to be explicitly taught to avoid certain dangers. Encountering a fast-approaching, large creature with sharp teeth—even if one has never encountered it before—causes an automatic fear and avoidance reaction. Evolution has hardwired a general fear template into our brains, rather than a particularized fear of specific things, and the things we can easily become afraid of are part of that general fear template. It's easier to develop a fear of snakes, for example, than a fear of flowers.

Are there emotions that all humans have that span different time periods and cultures? A long-standing theory attributed to Paul Ekman is that there are six such basic emotions, cultural universals, meaning that they exist independent of culture: fear, anger, happiness, sadness, disgust, and surprise. According to this theory, the hundreds of other emotions we describe, such as vexation, winsomeness, regret, and hope, may be culturally dependent, or cognitive constructions. The theory is controversial and the evidence for it is mixed—even those six may not be truly universal; we just don't know yet. There may be more, including emerging evidence that we should add spite to the list. (That'll show 'em!)

On the other hand, there appear to be hundreds of emotions that are culturally specific. Words exist in disparate languages for things that your own language may not have a word for. The Dutch describe a specific emotion for the revitalizing effects of taking a walk in the wind: *uitwaaien.* If you've never had the irresistible urge to take off your clothes as you dance, you haven't experienced the Bantu emotion of *mbuki-mvuki.* If you have a crush on someone and get a jittery, fluttering feeling, you may recognize the feeling but not have a word for it unless you speak Tagalog, which calls it *kilig.* The Danish have a word for the emotion of feeling cozy, safe, comforted, and cared for, but it's more than that—it includes the feeling of pleasure that comes from chatting with a friend or bicycling in the sunshine: *hygge.* And, famously, the Germans have the word *schadenfreude*, the pleasure we take when we see others' misfortunes (especially people we don't like). These words have no equivalent in English, but they represent very precise emotions in other cultures.

One noncontroversial function of emotions is to regulate your body budget, the physiological resources that you have available at any given time, conserving or spending them as situations require. If you're breathing rapidly and sweating, what should your body's reaction be? It depends on what caused that state, your causal attribution. Is it because you've just encountered an angry tiger or because you have the flu? These situations call for different physiological reactions.

Emotions also promote social currency, the understanding of others' mental states. To do this, your brain makes emotional inferences. As emotion researcher Lisa Feldman Barrett says, "If you see a man taking quick breaths and sweating, it communicates one thing if he's wearing a jogging suit and something else entirely if he's wearing a groom's tuxedo." Making such determinations means that your brain has to be making predictions all the time. You hear that rustle in the grass, and your brain puts together a statistical inference about what it's likely to be, taking into account factors such as whether your friend is behind you, whether a wind is blowing, whether you're in an area known for snakes.

So when it comes to the emotional interpretation of events, your brain is making not predictions but superfast "postdictions," after-the-fact inferences about things that have already happened. Your brain is continually rewriting your perceptual history to conform to new incoming facts. This is a form of Bayesian inferencing: form an opinion and update that opinion as new information becomes available.

Our emotional life has to develop and mature just like anything else. Infants begin with no emotional self-consciousness and experience only a limited range of emotions: in the first month, there's not much happening other than crying (distress) and contentment. Social smiles (happiness or joy) emerge at two months. Other emotions layer onto those only after six months. Near the end of their first year, infants begin to experience fear, and in the second year, anger (the terrible twos!). Then there's a whole class of social emotions that arise in our relationship to other people, and they don't emerge until later, when the child has acquired a sense of self-consciousness and begins to worry about how others see him or her; these include guilt, shame, embarrassment, and pride. Emotion differentiation, being able to appraise and describe emotions, isn't complete until the early twenties—adolescents, for example, tend to report feeling one emotion at a time, while young adults can report mixtures of emotions and can conceptualize emotions as co-occurring.

Are Emotions Scientific?

Are emotions completely reducible to neurochemicals? In other words, would it be fair to say that your neurochemicals *are* your emotions? In theory, yes. It is an assumption of modern neuroscience that given enough information, we can map all thoughts, feelings, hopes, and desires onto specific brain states. But at the moment, and for many years to come, this is just a theoretical ideal. We are a very long way from being able to say things like "Add two microliters of progesterone to the parahippocampal gyrus and this will happen."

Why?

For one thing, there are a large number of players in the story—more than fifty hormones and neurochemicals working within a system of chemical receptors, synapses, neuronal firing rates, brain architecture, and blood flow. We don't yet have the ability to measure the momentary state of all of these factors and so we can't yet assign roles to them. In addition, they interact in complex ways. It would be like asking if ten people can cause a revolution. Maybe—it depends on the society, on the streets, the weather, and the presence of alternative political options. It's complicated.

Another practical barrier to understanding is that each of us is unique, differing from one another in uncountable ways. A dollop of dopamine in your frontal lobes may do something very different from what it does in mine, because we may have different numbers of dopamine receptors, and the circuitry they support almost certainly operates differently (that's part of what makes us different from one another). And your brain is constantly changing: That same dopamine spike may affect you differently today than tomorrow, and at age twenty versus age seventy. Our individual differences arise in part because we have different genes that influence brain development and, accordingly, behavior. Also important are gene-by-environment interactions and gene expression: You might have a genetic predisposition toward narcissistic psychopathy, but without the right environmental triggers, that gene may never become active. (Then again it might.)

Neuroscientists posit that all of our feelings, hopes, desires, beliefs, and experiences are encoded in the brain as patterns of neural firings. Just how this happens is not precisely understood, but we have made strides in understanding how neurons communicate with one another. Progress has also been made in mapping which brain systems control which kinds of operations: One system is responsible for blinking your eyes, another senses the pain when you are stung by a bee; one system helps you to solve crossword puzzles, another enjoys watching *Young Sheldon.* A new approach to studying brains and individual differences involves making maps of how neurons connect to one another. Following the term *genome,* these are called *connectomes.* Your experiences are encoded in the way your neurons connect to one another.

At some future point, when the connectome is worked out and we have better techniques for measuring brain chemistry, we may be able to talk about emotions in specific hormonal and neural terms. This medicalization of experiences may seem odd, but we're already doing it. One hundred years ago, if someone was getting cranky or sleepy before a meal, we'd just say they were hungry. Now we might say they're experiencing low blood sugar, another way of saying that the body doesn't have enough bioavailable glucose. Seventy years ago if a child acted out in school and seemed inattentive, we'd say the child was unruly. Now we might diagnose that same child with a disorder (ADD) and treat it by prescribing a dopamine agonist such as methylphenidate (Ritalin) or Adderall. (An agonist promotes the action of a particular neurochemical system; an antagonist blocks it.)

The Surprising Thing about Stress

Stress is also an emotion, one that we share with other animals and with one another across the life span, although the causes of stress can be quite variable. Chronic stress is especially harmful. Stress is also highly variable—what would stress out one person another takes in stride, and vice versa.

Stress can have a substantial impact on longevity. Consider an experiment with Pacific salmon. After swimming upstream to spawn, and releasing tons of glucocorticoids because of the stress, they die. It's not because they're exhausted, or for some other biologically preprogrammed reason—rather, they experience rapid aging because of the production of those stress hormones. When researchers removed the adrenal glands of the salmon, which release all those glucocorticoids, the salmon didn't die after spawning.

As biologist Robert Sapolsky says,

> If you catch salmon right after they spawn . . . you find they have huge adrenal glands, peptic ulcers, and kidney lesions, their immune systems have collapsed . . . [and they] have stupendously high glucocorticoid concentrations in their bloodstreams.
>
> The bizarre thing is that this sequence . . . not only occurs in five species of salmon, but also among a dozen species of

> Australian marsupial mice. . . . Pacific salmon and marsupial mice are not close relatives. At least twice in evolutionary history, completely independently, two very different sets of species have come up with the identical trick: If you want to degenerate very fast, secrete a ton of glucocorticoids.

Earlier, I mentioned my University of Montreal colleague Sonia Lupien, one of the world experts on the physiology of stress. She writes:

> A week seldom passes without hearing or reading about stress and its deleterious effects on health. . . . There is a great paradox in the field of stress research, and it relates to the fact that the popular definition of stress is very different from the scientific definition of stress.
>
> In popular terms, stress is mainly defined as time pressure. We feel stressed when we do not have the time to perform the tasks we want to perform. . . . In scientific terms, stress is not equivalent to time pressure. If this were true, every individual would feel stressed when pressured by time. However, we all know people who are extremely stressed by time pressure and others who actually seek time pressure to perform adequately (so-called procrastinators). This shows that stress is a highly individual experience.

The term *stress* dates back to Old English in 1303 as a variant of *distress* and was typically used in contexts of coercion or bribery. In modern times, stress was first used by engineers in the 1850s to describe outside forces that could put a strain on a structure—heat, cold, and pressure. In the 1930s, endocrinologist Hans Selye revived this use of the term to include physiological reactions to outside forces acting on the body, such as heat, cold, and injuries that lead to pain. It wasn't until the 1960s that we began to use the word the way we use it today, to mean the psychological tension we feel from anticipating adverse events, and the biological correlates of them.

You may be familiar with homeostasis, the idea that the body seeks to maintain consistency, say, in core temperature, or blood levels of oxygen.

In the last twenty years, though, we've recognized that levels of some of our physiological systems—such as blood sugar levels, heart rate, blood pressure, and respiration rate—require continual adjustment to function optimally. This idea of stability through change is called *allostasis*—systems fluctuating regularly in response to life's demands.

When a situation is perceived as being stressful (because it is novel, unpredictable, uncontrollable, or painful), two major classes of stress hormones are secreted, catecholamines and glucocorticoids. They are the first hormonal systems to respond to stress. The short-term secretion of these hormones in the face of a challenge serves an adaptive purpose and leads to the fight-or-flight response (allostasis). However, the same stress hormones that are essential for survival can have damaging effects on both physical and mental health if they are secreted over a longer period of time (called *allostatic load*). This happens because when these primary stress hormones are increased for long periods of time, it leads to dysregulation of other major biological pathways in the body and the brain, for example, insulin, glucose, lipids, and neurotransmitters. This in turn causes a dysregulation of various other operations, such as the immune system, the digestive system, the reproductive system, cardiac health, and mental health.

Your allostatic load is the cumulative effect of stress over time; it indexes your changes in various biomarkers of stress (blood sugar, insulin, immune markers, stress markers, etc.) in response to the events of your life. Your allostatic load can be calculated by looking at levels of certain "stress biomarkers," including C-reactive protein, insulin, blood pressure, and so on. Social support is a strong predictor of allostatic load, with those having less social support showing the highest load. This is another case of not knowing the direction of causality—does having few or no friends increase stress? Probably. Does being stressed to begin with drive friends away? Probably. Does not having friends to comfort you cause that stress to linger instead of dissipating? Again, probably.

There are many ways to reduce stress, of course. Cognitive behavioral therapy (CBT), a form of talk therapy that teaches tools to help you cope, is one of them. Exercise, meditation, listening to music, immersing yourself in nature, and sometimes just talking to friends and having social support can help to reduce stress significantly.

If emotions are constructed, like perceptions, you might think that the brain tries to fill in and predict what is going to happen next to us emotionally—and it does. For most of us, our bodies seek to maintain a kind of emotional consistency; we internally regulate our emotions so that we don't experience extremes, because they can be emotionally and physiologically overwhelming. The central nervous system learns to anticipate stressors and to make allostatic adjustments in advance. The entire process is dynamic—it is an adaptable, plastic system that responds to sensory perceptions and cognitive processing by regulating neurotransmitters and hormones to either produce or recover from stress.

Part of effective regulation is the reduction of uncertainty. Our brains try to anticipate the outcome of future events, to anticipate our needs and plan how to satisfy those needs in advance. Doing this is metabolically expensive if your life is marked by great uncertainty, and the brain can easily use up its resources, resulting in a harmful increase in allostatic load.

Because allostasis is a predictive system, it can be influenced or miscalibrated by early life stressors or extreme traumas. A stable fetal and early childhood environment can lead to a well-functioning allostatic system. But adverse childhood experiences can result in a system that either overreacts or just shuts down in response to what might otherwise be considered normal daily ups and downs, creating hypervigilance, reduced resilience, and sometimes wild mood swings—a lifetime in which normal allostatic regulation is never reached. Someone who has grown up in adverse conditions will have long-term memories that contain threatening and stressful information; their default prediction for even neutral events is that something bad could happen, and this kicks in their stress response, releasing cortisol and adrenaline in advance of a great many situations that are benign. On a systems level, we'd say that they are not regulating their HPA (hypothalamic-pituitary-adrenal) axis—the body's stress response system.

When we lack this kind of regulation, because either our lives are chaotic or our neurochemical systems are not properly calibrated, we can experience mood swings; we can act irrationally or impulsively, causing ourselves harm; and we can experience a range of illnesses, diseases, and other problems across the life span. Increased allostatic load (and the resulting loss of hormone regulation) can lead to cardiovascular disease, diabetes, compromised immune function, and cognitive decline. It has also been linked to a number of psychiatric conditions, for example, depression and anxiety disorders, and burnout and post-traumatic stress disorders.

Elevated cortisol levels in response to early life stress have been linked to accelerated hippocampal atrophy among both healthy individuals and people in the early stages of Alzheimer's disease. Thus, successful emotion regulation may protect not only older people's physical well-being but their mental capacities as well.

There are many factors that influence the stress response and the health of the allostatic system—it's not just the obvious things like a mother who took drugs during pregnancy or an early toddlerhood surrounded by domestic violence. These factors include:

- demographics, such as age, sex, socioeconomics, education;
- developmental conditions, such as poor parental attachment, chronic illness, being bullied;
- genetics, such as telomere length, cortisol insufficiency, deficiency in angiotensin converting enzyme (which regulates blood pressure);
- environment, such as culture, extreme climates, smoking behaviors, famine;
- neuroendocrine functioning; and
- psychological factors, such as locus of control, and the tools we bring to emotional regulation.

But not everyone with a stressful childhood ends up with a psychiatric disorder, or even a high allostatic load. Stressful experiences can lead to very different outcomes, depending on the interaction of the factors listed above. Some people develop resilience, grit, tenacity, and focus. Others fall apart. The prized combination that allows some people to live more positive lives, to turn lemons into lemonade, is still unknown and an active topic of research. One thing we do know is that thoughtful parenting and/or education can put people on the more positive path and give them better overall life outcomes, reducing the disadvantages caused by childhood adversity.

Because allostatic load is defined as the *cumulative* effects of stress and your body's responses to that stress, the load and associated cellular damage increase with age, no matter how well-functioning the system is. In particular, normal age-related changes in structures that regulate allostasis, the hippocampus and the prefrontal cortex, make healthy allostasis more difficult to maintain. Higher load has also been associated with reductions in the brain's gray matter. Three recent studies have also linked sleep disturbances to increases in load.

Reducing stress and increasing resilience, the ability to bounce back from adversity, can be coached and taught through specialized psychotherapy, strengthening of social networks, physical exercise, and programs that help people find meaningful and purposeful activities in their lives. But that can take some effort (and openness to new experiences).

Depression

Our emotions can certainly become crippling. Children throw tantrums. Adolescents withdraw and become pouty. As adults, we can succumb to depression, an intractable disease that affects approximately 15 percent of Americans. This number is more or less the same across continents. I say intractable because in spite of the great advances made in neuropharmacology, antidepressant drugs tend to work only 20 percent of the time.

Negative emotions can interfere with our being able to do the things we want; they can be debilitating, and the neurochemicals they release can cloud our thinking.

I went to visit the Dalai Lama at his monastery in Dharamsala, India, in order to ask his advice about successful aging. While waiting to see him, I was seated in a waiting room. He was just outside greeting a long procession of followers, one at a time. I could watch through the window where I saw him in profile, seated in a chair, with a long line stretching out through the courtyard. The people appeared to have come from all over, and from all different backgrounds and life experiences. They ranged in age from children to the very old. Some were dressed in their finest clothes; others were barefoot and in rags. As they moved slowly ahead in the procession, I could see in the lines and creases of their faces, in the set of their mouths, and in their heads leaning forward, all of the hope they attached to meeting His Holiness. It was clear they felt that he would relieve their suffering, their pain, and put their lives back on track. Some had traveled for weeks to get to this mountaintop, sixty-five hundred feet up in the Himalayas.

His Holiness spent about forty seconds with each person in the line as they filed in front of him one at a time. He spoke with them, put his hand on their foreheads, and blessed them, and they moved on. The moment was so profoundly full of emotion for so many people that there were three beefy men standing next to the Dalai Lama whose sole job was to prop up people whose legs gave out from under them when it was their turn to actually stand in front of him. They were busy that day.

At one point, I heard a woman wailing and weeping, making the most awful distressed sounds. I couldn't make out the words—it could have been Tibetan, Nepalese, or any number of languages. I went to the window and saw the woman—the Dalai Lama's attendants were holding her up by her armpits; her legs had already given out. As she was wailing, I heard her cries interrupted by the Dalai Lama, who spoke in a gruff, deep, staccato voice, a few scolding words. The woman immediately fell silent. Then he whispered to her. There was silence again for a few moments, and suddenly the two of them started laughing.

After the procession, we met in his office. I asked him about this intriguing encounter.

"She came to me and she was saying things like 'I am so miserable. I am so unhappy. I have a husband who is missing. I have a child who is malnourished. I have terrible pain in my feet . . .'

"I interrupted her," the Dalai Lama said, "and I said, 'What is this *I* that you speak of? This is not in our teaching!' And she became quiet. And I asked, 'Tell me about this *I* that is so unhappy—where is it?' She pointed to her chest. I said, 'What shape is it? A triangle? A square? A circle?' She said, 'It's a circle.' I said, 'Okay. Imagine the circle in your chest. Meditate on it. Don't let it move one centimeter to the left or to the right.' She closed her eyes and focused on it. After a few moments she whispered, 'It disappeared!' And we both laughed." The disciple awakened to the realization that she did not exist and since she did not exist there was no one to suffer.

Controlling our emotions, or at least channeling them toward positive things, is good for our health. We know this now through neuroscience, but this has been part of Buddhist teaching for centuries. The Dalai Lama is a science buff; he has attended, and spoke at, the Society for Neuroscience annual meeting, and has made his monks available for neuroimaging studies. And he notes that, "Anger, hatred, and fear are very bad for our health. . . . Passing through life, progressing to old age and eventually death, it is not sufficient to just take care of the body. We need to take care of our emotions as well."

This is not the perspective typically embraced by artists. I had the opportunity to work on an album with Stevie Wonder, who was often late, because he would be overcome by an emotion and unable to extract himself from it. One day when we were working together, news broke in the morning that a horrific fire in the United States had killed a number of people. When Stevie showed up four hours late, he was visibly shaken and said that he just couldn't stop thinking about the family. Letting your emotions carry you away might be a good thing if your job is communicating emotion to others. For the rest of us, not so much.

Depression can affect people of any age, and it often goes undiagnosed in older adults. We may notice depressive-like behaviors in ourselves or other older adults and think it is normal aging. It is not. By depression, I don't mean the occasional sadness we all feel, but persistent feelings of hopelessness, sadness, and emptiness that last for more than a couple of weeks. Depression is an illness with biological causes, not merely something you can "buck up" and will yourself out of. Signs of depression in the elderly don't always manifest themselves the way they do in younger people—they can more often show up as lethargy, lack of motivation, and lack of energy rather than sadness. So older adults may not realize that what they are suffering from is physiological depression. And some people mistakenly believe that depression is just a normal part of aging. But depression is definitely not normal and it should be treated.

The good news is that depression is less frequent among older adults than younger adults. But that's not to say that there is no risk. Eighty percent of older adults have at least one chronic medical condition, and 50 percent have two or more; the lifestyle and biological changes brought on by illness can contribute to depression, along with various bodily systems slowing down or wearing out. Some prescription medications have been associated with depression. Many older adults have trouble sleeping and so turn to prescription drugs to help them sleep—but habitual use of these drugs, including Ambien, Ativan, and Halcion, can actually cause depression after even a short period of use. The beneficial effects of a good night's sleep are completely wiped out by the depressed mood that sets in during the day. (Occasional use for periodic bouts of insomnia may be beneficial.) Other drugs associated with depression include estrogen, blood pressure medication, statins, and opioids.

Depression in old age is an independent cause of disability, and it can exacerbate existing physical problems, slowing down recovery from injury and illness by weakening our immune systems. It's also important not to underestimate the impact of the curtailment of daily activities that can accompany growing older—things that we used to derive pleasure from become physically difficult, painful, or hazardous, and that can contribute to depression.

Risk factors for depression in old age are consistent with the triad of genes, culture, and opportunity we've been looking at so far, and their interactions: genetic vulnerabilities, age-related changes in brain volume and processing speed, and stressful events. Insomnia, a hallmark of aging for many, is an often overlooked risk factor for late-life depression, affecting 25 percent of men and 40 percent of women in their eighties. Changes to the integrity of the hypothalamus, which helps regulate sleep-wake cycles, as well as age-related reductions in the production of melatonin and other neurohormones, also contribute to insomnia. If you can't get a good night's sleep, all kinds of neural and physiological systems begin to go haywire. Practicing good sleep hygiene, as detailed in Chapter 11, is almost always more effective than medication.

Blood flow to the brain decreases with age—sometimes simply due to reductions in exercise, in other cases due to normal deterioration of the circulatory system or buildup of arterial plaques. This can lead to vascular depression. White-matter hyperintensities form—regions of the brain where white matter atrophies due to lack of oxygenated blood—and these regions can be quite extensive. Depression symptoms are associated with the size of these lesions.

Some of the risk and corresponding protection factors for old-age depression are shown in the illustration on the following page, with the age at which they first emerge as factors.

Given all this, it might seem surprising that more oldsters aren't depressed. Three categories of factors appear to be most protective. First is the presence of resources that some older adults enjoy—health, cognitive function, and sufficient financial stability to get everyday needs met. Second are psychological resources—over a lifetime, and sometimes through

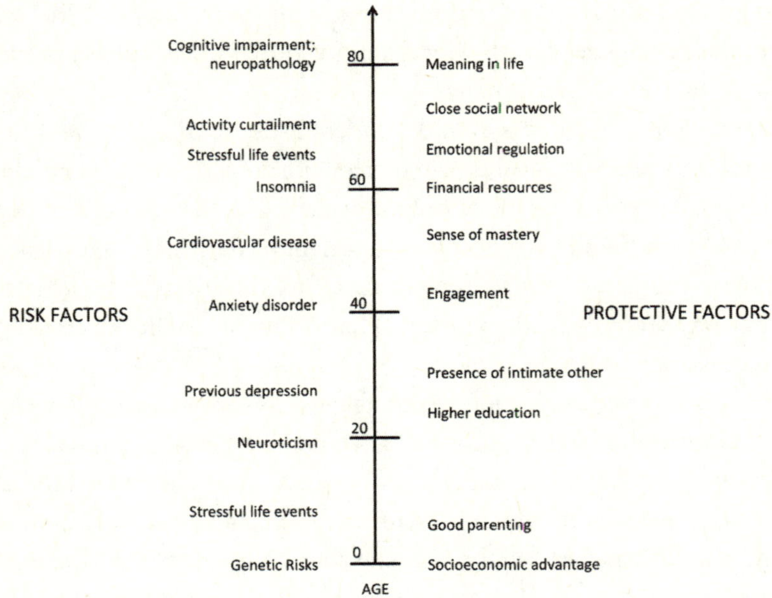

trial and error, many older adults have learned strategies and ways to use social support to manage their health-related stresses. Third is an understanding of the role of meaningful engagement with other people, through social activities, volunteer work, or congregational religion. Along these lines, the presence of intimate others in one's life significantly reduces the risk for developing depression.

People who are experiencing depression have lower levels of serotonin. So why not just give them serotonin? For two reasons—one is technical; the other is conceptual. Technically, there is no way to administer serotonin directly because a pill or injection would not be able to cross the blood-brain barrier. In the late 1980s, a new class of drugs was developed called SSRIs—selective serotonin reuptake inhibitors. SSRIs cause whatever serotonin is in the brain to linger around the synapses longer—it's as though you're giving the brain more serotonin, but you're just squeezing more mileage out of the serotonin that's already there. A fad in these drugs resulted. SSRIs such as Prozac were widely prescribed for people with depression.

David Anderson is a neurobiologist at Caltech who has been working on the neurochemistry of emotion for thirty-five years. One of the things that frustrates him about this approach is that serotonin is just one of more than a hundred neurotransmitters and neurohormones, and all of them interact in complex ways. SSRIs affect the entire brain, rather than focusing on the particular circuits that need correcting. That is the conceptual problem.

It's like spraying STP all over the engine and hoping that a little will trickle into the carburetor. As David says, your brain is not just a bag of chemicals. His TED Talk about it has more than a million views and he's become something of a hero to many of my colleagues. That list of drugs I mentioned earlier that can contribute to insomnia underscores the delicate balance that needs to be achieved in our brains for us to enjoy good mood. One well-meaning intervention, such as a heart medication, can throw everything out of whack.

I've been talking a lot about dopamine up to this point, and although it is an important neurochemical, there are many others that we shouldn't ignore. But if you read the popular press, dopamine seems to be responsible for everything! This drives neuroscientists like Jeffrey Mogil crazy. "A lot of scientists think this way, but I think that in, oh, say, twenty years from now, we're all going to look back and realize that dopamine was the drunk looking for his keys under the lamppost because there is more light there. It's just that for now, dopamine is the one we have tools for studying. But it's no more important than the one hundred other transmitters, two hundred other ion channels, or one thousand other signal transduction molecules. The actions we are most interested in are embedded in very complicated circuits." For now, it looks like much of the story of brain, behavior, emotion, and motivation is about dopamine, but that's just because it's where we can look. It's where the light is better.

David's call, an exposé of sorts, is for better biomedical and pharmaceutical research. In the meantime, however, Prozac and other SSRIs are about the best shot we've got. Indeed, the prestigious *British Medical Journal* recently concluded that SSRIs should be the first-line pharmacological treatment in older adults, including those with chronic physical illness—just like my friend and mentor John R. Pierce, who had Parkinson's, and who experienced a new lease on life within a few weeks of starting Prozac. The most effective approach to depression involves developing tools to deal with changes, through cognitive behavioral therapy or other therapeutic interventions. Other drugs, not traditionally thought of as antidepressants, can also be effective in older adults. Low doses of methylphenidate or armodafinil, either alone or in combination with antidepressants, can compensate for lost dopaminergic function and a host of signaling and transmission problems in the aging brain.

Psychotherapy can change the structure of the brain. This isn't at all surprising, given what we've seen throughout this book—that every experience changes the brain. In particular, cognitive behavioral therapy engages similar neural mechanisms as antidepressant medications, but without the side effects of withdrawal. Long dismissed by physicians who were more focused on pharmaceutical, electroshock, or other "medical" interventions, talk therapy has proven its effectiveness, and even its superiority. For depression, it is at least as effective as antidepressant drugs in the short term, and over the long term, we see less relapse—two years after intervention, people who received prior cognitive therapy are doing better than people who simply stayed on medication.

Coping

The way that we cope with setbacks and adversity is largely influenced by the combination of genes, culture, and environment. A genetic predisposition toward resilience and optimism can lead to different coping styles and outcomes than one toward fatalism and pessimism. In general, children learn to react to the world by modeling their parents. Parents who have strategies for dealing with unpleasant or traumatic events will display those to their children, and their children are likely to imitate them. (It makes you think that there should be a boot camp for parenting, doesn't it? Well, there kind of is—your own childhood.)

One of the most important findings about coping styles in depression was made by Susan Nolen-Hoeksema, who distinguished rumination from distraction and found that distraction was far more effective than rumination in coping with bad fortune, and that rumination was associated with significantly longer periods of depressed mood.

People who ruminate have a tendency to repetitively focus on what went wrong, and the causes and consequences of what went wrong, over and over and over again. They lock themselves in their rooms; they stay in bed; they catastrophize the future. All of us have a tendency to do this, to varying degrees. Withdrawal from the world after a negative experience is evolutionarily adaptive—it gives us time to heal and to reflect productively on what went wrong so that we can avoid or correct patterns of our own behavior that can lead to trouble. And to some extent, the sadness that rumination steeps us in feels good: It releases the neurochemical prolactin, which is calming and soothing—the same hormone released in mothers and their infants while nursing.

But excessive rumination increases stress hormones. It drives a downward cycle of unhappiness and can trigger one or multiple episodes of major depression. Rumination interferes with interpersonal problem solving, depletes motivation to engage in constructive behaviors, and impairs social relationships. Rumination also feeds the destructive aspects of mood-dependent memory retrieval because the hippocampus is exquisitely sensitive to emotion. When you're unhappy, the hippocampus has a far easier time accessing negative memories to the point that it can become very difficult to recall times when you *didn't* feel unhappy. This perpetuates the downward cycle of not only feeling bad in the moment, but anticipating a future that holds no promise.

The more effective strategy, according to Nolen-Hoeksema, is positive distraction—that is, immersing yourself in positive, forward-looking activities you enjoy: sports, baking, travel, music making . . . whatever it is that is engaging enough, absorbing enough, to distract you from your unhappiness, and is enjoyable and positive. Even relatively neutral activities furnish almost the same magnitude of benefits—things like looking at art, reading a book, taking a leisurely walk in natural surroundings, or spending time with pets.

Talking to others in the context of healthy supportive relationships isn't the same as rumination. It can be helpful after a negative experience and has been shown to reduce distress when it leads to greater insight and understanding about the source of one's problems. But not all social support is healthy. Talking to a friend who helps you to catastrophize, obsess, and co-ruminate increases stress hormones. (Friends like that can be worse than no friends at all.)

There are other ways to break the cycle of depressive rumination besides distraction. Meditation is one of them—it doesn't work for everyone but it does work for many. Depressed people have a magnified sense of self-consciousness. The Dalai Lama's instructions to the depressed woman I mentioned earlier cut through all that. Perseverative thought and an intense focus on yourself is bad for the brain. Meditation can cure perseverative thought because it removes the "you" from your thoughts.

One of the surest ways to get over depression is to help others—this allows you to step outside of yourself and your preoccupations. Helping others is powerful medicine.

There are countless ways to reach *bodhi,* or what Western cognitive psychologists call the *flow state.* As you might imagine, it involves that daydreaming network I wrote about earlier (see page 79), the brain's default mode. Very few people live in this state of egolessness. Some claim to, egotistically, and they say that they'll teach you to do it too for a large sum of money. If you're interested in this state, look for a reluctant guru, someone who doesn't have an inflated sense of themselves as a great teacher.

I have come to believe that this egolessness is at the heart of what draws us to the music of great improvisers like John Coltrane and Miles Davis. They become absorbed in the moment, listening to the other musicians and responding, either with playing or not playing, doing whatever will enhance the music, with no sense of self or other. Many people say they have similar experiences doing community service, working to help others in a crisis situation, or during team and individual sports . . . there are lots of ways to reach this state.

Motivation and Hormones

Much of our motivation to do things is controlled by our brains and by the hormones and neurochemicals circulating within. (Hormones are a kind of neurochemical that works both inside the central nervous system and outside of it.) We tend to think that our motivation and desire to do things are driven by our own ideas, our will. We *decide* to go out for a brisk walk and then we do it. But the hormones are the hidden strings that pull our bodies. For example, estrogen production in women follows a monthly cycle and reaches its peak around the midpoint of the menstrual cycle. Women are far more likely to walk more at this point than at any other point in the cycle. It's been speculated that this is the time of the month when women get cabin fever and want to explore the territory around them to find the most desirable mate—even if at a subconscious level. Higher estrogen is also related to increased competitiveness and possibly to reduced fearfulness.

These hidden strings pull us at all stages of life. The increased progesterone production that accompanies pregnancy causes a reduction in the body's immune-system response, and in particular a reduction in inflammation. Pregnant women who have had rheumatoid arthritis, multiple sclerosis, and migraine report reductions in their symptoms. Of course, a reduced immune-system response also makes pregnant women (and other high-progesterone women) more likely to succumb to infections, and here is where the hormones interact with thinking, the very thinking you think is under your control. High progesterone leads women to avoid situations in which germs might be transmitted and women with high progesterone levels are far more likely to wash their hands after coming into contact with germs.

Elevated progesterone is also associated with quicker reading of facial cues and body language and quicker categorization of friends versus potential enemies. Psychological scientist Martie Haselton writes, "A high-progesterone woman can potentially read the room, weed out the frenemies, and make a good call about whom to lean on and whom to avoid." Progesterone is associated with seeking out friends and spending time with them. There is also evidence that progesterone promotes calmness and diminishes suicidal tendencies.

In both women and men, testosterone appears to regulate the seeking and maintenance of social status, including sexual status and the displays that go along with seeking attractive mates. Both men and women who are high in testosterone are more likely to engage in risky activities, such as gambling and having sexual relations with multiple partners. Indeed, most people in monogamous relationships show lower levels of testosterone than those not in committed relationships. You can imagine an evolutionary basis for this, that people in a committed relationship will do a better job at staying together, and parenting, than people who are not, and this will enhance the ability of their offspring to seek a committed relationship, reproduce, and become parents themselves.

Circumstance plays a role in testosterone levels. In "the smelly T-shirt study," men were exposed to the scent of either ovulating women or nonovulating women, by smelling T-shirts that the women had recently worn. The men did not know the women involved and were not told their ovulatory status. Men's testosterone levels increased after smelling all the T-shirts, but they increased more after smelling the T-shirts of ovulating women, presumably to increase their libido and partner-seeking behaviors. Men's testosterone levels also increase after achieving public success, and decrease after public failure (possibly an evolutionary adaptation that results in high-achieving men being motivated to seek the best genetically equipped mate).

The role of testosterone in influencing behavior goes back hundreds of millions of years. In birds, song is a fundamental component of territorial defense and mate attraction, and it is typically the males that sing. When given testosterone, male finches sing more, but only in the presence of a female finch.

A feature of aging is that both sex-linked hormones, testosterone and estrogen, decline with age, and these declines have well-documented effects. First, there is a decline in interest in sexual activity. When Socrates asks sixty-eight-year-old Cephalus about his libido, Cephalus responds, "Most gladly have I escaped the thing of which you speak; I feel as if I had escaped from a mad and furious master." A sixty-eight-year-old friend of mine, H., whom I've known for forty years, was one of the most sexually active people I've ever known until a few years ago, when his libido just up and disappeared. "I can't believe how much time I have now to do other things," he notes. Indeed, we might look at our life span as occurring in three stages: childhood, before the pubertal sex hormones kick in; puberty to late adulthood, when sexual desire dominates many of our thoughts; and old age, when we are back, like children, to wanting friends to play with, but not thinking so much about sex.

Of course, there are vast individual differences. Some people maintain an active interest in sex, others lose it, and some who begin to lose it have it restored through some romantic happenstance or hormone replacement therapy (HRT). These are effective and, if properly prescribed, have few side effects and many ancillary benefits. This is because reductions in testosterone and estrogen lead to fuzzy thinking and losses in a number of areas: cognitive function, memory, motivation and mood, immune-system function, and bone density. It is wise, after age fifty, to have your hormone levels checked and possibly restored, pharmaceutically, to physiological levels if you do not have a medical condition that precludes this. Hormone replacement therapy, in both women and men, can restore quality of life and energy in a way that nothing else seems to.

Although it is commonly believed that high testosterone increases aggressive behaviors, we still aren't sure about cause and effect—it could be that aggressive behaviors increase testosterone. But I am friends with a number of men in their eighties who, according to others, were terrible people when they were younger. I know them only as sweet, kindly old men. Some of them have very few friends, having ravaged through relationships with success seeking and competitiveness—but this is a side of them I've never seen. I wonder if I, too, should be wary of them. But they are so delightful and interesting now that I am not.

Are emotions reducible to hormone levels? In other words, with more neurochemical knowledge, will we be able to say that a certain hormone balance leads to guilt and another to elation? Perhaps. But the situation is more complicated—the same hormones or neurochemicals act differently in different parts of the brain. Our emotional appraisals, as we've seen, are influenced by our cognitive appraisals of the situation. And your brain is more than a bag of chemicals.

Motivation and Learning across the Life Span

Motivation is a condition that pushes us to achieve a goal. The goal can be for survival or amusement, pleasure or a reduction of pain. If you're reading this book, there's a good chance you are motivated to learn, that you benefit from an innate or cultivated curiosity about the world. As we've seen, curiosity can be protective against aging, and a great motivator to obtain an education, which is also protective.

Tenacity and grit support staying engaged with a goal even when achieving it is difficult—and especially when achieving it turns out to be more difficult than we first thought. For many of us, those goals are intellectual—the desire to learn new skills and concepts and to apply these in pursuit of meaningful work or hobbies. The physician who attends a workshop on the newest techniques for treating Parkinson's disease is not that different from the weekend athlete taking tennis lessons or the birdwatcher going to a new locale to identify birds she's never seen before.

The compulsory education that is taught in K–12 schools is relatively well-defined and doesn't leave much room for individual choice. People have differing levels of motivation for learning school subjects and for learning more things after school is finished. Some may continue with more school, some may enter specialized vocational training, and some may go right to work. There is great variation in the degree to which people desire to learn once they are out of school, and it doesn't have a whole lot to do with the kind of work you're in. You might think that people in the professions—professors, doctors, lawyers, business leaders—are constantly pursuing self-improvement, and that people in the trades—bricklayers, pest exterminators, truck drivers—are not. But this is mistaken thinking. I'm sad to say I've encountered many doctors, lawyers, and professors who are intellectually lazy, who have grown complacent and simply don't have the motivation to keep up with changes in their fields. And I've known construction workers and truck drivers who are sponges for new technology and new information, constantly looking for ways to increase their skill level, like Pablo Casals was, in his eighties, on the cello.

What differs across these kinds of people is motivation and, to some extent, a worldview about who's in charge of your life. If you tend to think that the course your life takes is governed by other people, systems, organizations, and circumstances, you'll tend toward "accepting your fate" and not exerting yourself much to change things. In technical terms, this is called having an external locus of control (the external world is in control of you). If you tend to think otherwise, that you can change the story of your life, you have an internal locus of control and are typically more motivated, more driven, to make changes. Take Paul Simon—at one of the many peaks in his career, after his hugely successful solo album *There Goes Rhymin' Simon,* he decided that he wanted to learn more about music theory so that he wouldn't be constrained by the relatively straightforward chords and structures he already knew. So he took music lessons from Philip Glass and others. And, as great a singer as he is, he also took voice lessons for many years.

Believing you can't change your life ends up being a self-fulfilling prophecy because you bypass opportunities that *could* help you change your life.

There is an irony here, in that believing you can change your life isn't the same as being able to predict or plan how your life will go. As Linda Ronstadt said, "People always think careers are based on calculated decision-making, that your career is the outcome of how you think it's going to look. . . . The process is so different than that." Paul Simon again: "I never thought about what the public wanted to hear, or how I might write a hit. I always wrote what I wanted to hear. For a period of time, other people wanted to hear that too. Then they didn't, and then they did again. I had a career writing these songs because sometimes there was an alignment between what I wanted to hear and what the public did. But I never planned to make a hit record."

Immersing yourself fully in whatever activities you engage in—work, leisure, family, community—is protective against cognitive decline and physical illness. The rewards from doing things that please you lift your mood, and strengthen the immune system, increasing the production of cytokines, T-cells, and immunoglobulin A.

Motivation to Make Change

There is a tendency as we age to resist change, owing to a variety of factors. Depletion of dopamine and deterioration of dopamine receptors in the brain lead to a lack of novelty seeking—we're chemically less motivated to look for new experiences or to learn new things. Bodily and cognitive limitations make learning and doing new things more difficult. And memory! Our memories and perceptions are based on millions of observations of things being a certain way; our prediction circuits are basing their calculations on what happened over and over again in the past. The intact memory system becomes a competing force against our brains' quest to stay current. Add to that the hippocampal volume reductions, which make it harder to store new memories and easier to retrieve old ones, and you have a formula for conservatism.

Two knowledge domains that are of most importance to older adults are personal health and finance, and acquiring new information about them is important. Prior experience is a factor: Older adults who have a base of knowledge about health and finance are better able to retain new information on those topics, because the structure of their knowledge minimizes cognitive load. Physicians have an easier time comprehending new discoveries in medical texts than medical students, because they have memory structures and schemas within which to incorporate the new information.

Problems can arise in aging when new information contradicts prior learning or doesn't fit into the well-worn pathways of your knowledge base. Then the general slowing down of cognitive processes plus the decline in reasoning ability that accompany old age can cause difficulties that take a major surge in motivation to overcome.

If you're an older doctor, the gold standard had long been to surgically remove any cancer that was amenable to surgery (certain hard-to-get-to tumors or especially large or embedded ones were the exception). We now live in a time when some low-risk, slowly advancing cancers, such as prostate cancer, are best ignored because the treatment is more likely to cause serious harm than the cancer. Some cancers are treatable with radiation therapy, others with chemotherapy. The cutting edge is immunotherapy for cancer. I heard a talk a couple of months ago by one of the founders of immunotherapy, Nobel laureate Jim Allison, describing his work. It involves what are called checkpoint inhibitors, which cure 60 percent or more of melanomas and other cancers. Former president Jimmy Carter received a checkpoint inhibitor, Keytruda, in 2015, when melanoma had spread to his brain and liver, and as of this writing, he is cancer-free. Now, if you are an older physician who is set in your ways—and there are plenty of those—trying to integrate this new information with your old ways of thinking can be difficult. It's not a case of just taking in new information, but of tearing apart your old and entrenched ways of thinking about an entire field. How do you get the motivation and wherewithal to do that?

Consider music and films. If you're of a certain age, you lived most of your life with the idea that if you wanted to listen to music or watch a film at home, you had to buy it in a store and play it back on a suitable player. You had to put a collection together, item by item, and there were storage considerations, and ease of browsing considerations if your collection got too big, not to mention financial consequences. It can require a boost of motivation to overcome your fixed way of looking at things and embrace the new "jukebox in the sky" way of hearing music and watching TV and movies.

Or take modern security features found on web forms and apps. If you were born before 2000, there was no precedent for being asked to prove that you're not a robot when trying to accomplish basic tasks on the Internet (which itself is an entirely new and unprecedented concept if you were born before 1990). Now, before advancing to the next online page or step in what used to be a routine process carried out in person or with a telephone agent, you might be asked to "identify all the photographs that have a part of an animal in them" or "mark every photo that has a street sign in it." These work as security screens because computers can't solve these problems . . . yet. In another ten years or so, when computer vision and AI have advanced, we'll all be doing something else for authentication (possibly face or iris scans).

There are ways to jump-start your motivation in the face of these kinds of changes. First, people who are curious (the first *C* in the COACH principle) and who enjoy learning for its own sake do better in a whole big basket of life outcomes. People who focus mainly on getting recognition for their achievements are far less likely to seek challenges and less likely to persist in learning than those who focus on the learning itself. In other words, intrinsic motivation is always more powerful than extrinsic motivation.

Second, motivation takes work. As the title of a paper by psychologist Carol Dweck states, *even geniuses work hard.* Dweck describes two kinds of mind-sets we can adopt—fixed versus growth—and they relate to locus of control. As with most things, these two mind-sets refer to ends of a continuum; few people are entirely one or the other in all aspects of their life. People with a fixed mind-set believe that their qualities and abilities don't change; they say things like:

- I'm not good at math.
- I don't remember people's names.
- I don't understand technology.
- I'm not the athletic type.
- I'm too old to change.

People with a fixed mind-set generally have an external locus of control. They are low in Curiosity and Openness. They aren't interested in learning new things and don't think that the payoff of learning new things will be worth the effort.

People with a growth mind-set believe that they can change their skill sets, that they can continue to learn. They have an internal locus of control and believe that effort is sometimes its own reward and that it can yield big dividends. Hard work can be enjoyable. People with a growth mind-set are energized by learning and invigorated when they succeed at something that was previously difficult. To them, life is a journey of gathering new information, meeting new people, seeking helpful feedback from mentors or teachers, and learning new skills. People of all ages with a growth mind-set outperform students with a fixed mind-set. Often, all it takes is someone pointing out to you that you can change your brain and that you can overcome limitations you've encountered previously, not just with effort, but with focused, directed learning (this is why education works). Beyond effort, learners need to try new strategies and to seek help from others when they're stuck. Having a repertoire of approaches and perspectives to draw on enriches your mental life and can spur that much-needed motivation. Without these things, knowledge tends to stagnate.

Dweck counsels the following:

> Watch for a fixed-mindset reaction when you face challenges. Do you feel overly anxious, or does a voice in your head warn you away? . . . Do you feel incompetent or defeated? Do you look for an excuse? Watch to see whether criticism brings out your fixed mindset. Do you become defensive, angry, or crushed instead of interested in learning from the feedback? Watch what happens when you see [someone] who's better than you at something you value. Do you feel envious and threatened, or do you feel eager to learn? Accept those thoughts and feelings and work with and through them. And keep working with and through them.

As we age, our motivations to be recognized for our achievements, and to rack up more and more achievements, tend to decline—that is, older adults tend toward being more intrinsically than extrinsically motivated. Older adults show increases in their motivation to use their accumulated knowledge, to help others, to preserve their resources, and to maintain a sense of autonomy and competence.

There's a seventy-something-year-old in my neighborhood who runs up and down a steep hill every day. Twice. He's got good running shoes and knee compression, and he is staying fit. Joni Mitchell at seventy-five still swims every day and has started working with a swimming coach to improve her form and endurance. And don't forget Julia "Hurricane" Hawkins, who at 102 (in 2018) set a world record for the sixty-meter dash. My McGill colleague Jim Ramsay was a bicycling enthusiast into his seventies. When I was forty-eight and he was sixty-four we did the Tour de L'Île, a fifty-kilometer bike ride that encircles the island of Montreal and attracts thousands of cyclists every summer. I had a hard time keeping up with Jim. A few years later, at sixty-seven, he bicycled from Vancouver to Winnipeg, a twenty-four-hundred-kilometer trip that took him over the Coast Mountain Range, the Cascades, and the Canadian Rockies.

What are age-appropriate goals? They require a frank self-assessment. It was reasonable for Pablo Casals to learn to master a new cello piece. It was reasonable for my mother to stage her first play, and for Jim Ramsay to bicycle twenty-four hundred kilometers—he was in good shape and had regular checkups with his doctor. I've been a musician all my life and have played professionally, but it would probably be unrealistic for me to suddenly take up violin—an instrument I've never played before—and hope to become a world-class soloist. On the other hand, I could probably get good enough in three or four years, with focused effort and instruction, to play in a community orchestra. That's an age-appropriate goal.

With no athletic training, it might be unreasonable for an eighty-year-old to plan to become a hockey player, a sport that tends toward violence and can be harmful to brittle bones. Physical limitations are no laughing matter. A friend of mine, at sixty-two years old and a professional musician, was showing some of his twentysomething students "the proper way" to load equipment in a car without hurting your back. He saved his back but ended up rupturing two tendons in his shoulder, just like that. I severed two tendons and a nerve bundle in my right hand last year, not by engaging in an inherently risky activity, but by doing an everyday activity without inspecting the situation and environment carefully—I let my vigilance down for just thirty seconds and the consequences were severe and long-lasting.

On the other hand, it's important to fight the tendency to give up or to restrict your activities too much. Tim Laddish (age seventy-seven), former senior assistant attorney general for the state of California, writes,

> I have to not give in to age when it is not necessary. The other week, as I was walking to our mailbox, I realized that I had assumed the old man stoop—bent forward, with my chin out in front of my body. I tried telling myself, "You're not 77, you're 66." (That seemed about as far back as my imagination could

carry me.) With that, I straightened up, my stride increased (was that a slight bounce to my step?) and I truly had a better point of view because of my improved posture.

I'm not saying that you are only as old as you feel, but you can set your mind to feel not as old as you are.

That works until it doesn't. Since that day I've been diagnosed with a torn rotator cuff, arthritis in my hips, and an ailing psoas muscle that right now is causing me to walk with a stick for help. But my massage therapist is helping the psoas, I have an appointment with an orthopedist for the shoulder, and I can take Advil for the hip.

I'm convinced I'll be back—running, kayaking, playing catch with my grandson and hiking (with care) mountain trails. With luck, effort and some medical fixes, I'll get back to feeling like, well, maybe, 67.

In any event, my wife and I went to REI on Friday and bought a new camping tent.

Happiness

Happiness is an odd construct. It is highly subjective, variable, and dependent on a number of factors, such as culture and expectations. It's also fiendishly relative, context dependent, and based on social comparison theory. This is the idea that you gauge your own happiness in comparison with what those around you are doing, or—more materialistically—what they have that you don't. Few of us today would find a 1919 Model T comfortable, but if you had one in 1919, it was more comfortable than a horse, and more convenient than walking—it's relative. You might never have thought about whether a lawn would bring you happiness, but if all your neighbors have lush green lawns and yours is full of crabgrass, you might find yourself unhappy.

Happiness may also be subject to an observer distortion effect in that trying to assess it all the time may actually interfere with it. Probing happiness stops the flow of activity and pulls you out of time to inspect it. And the one constant of happy people seems to be that they don't think about happiness—they're too busy doing things and *being* happy to stop and think about it. Happiness therefore is a judgment made in retrospect.

Humans are adaptable, resilient; we bounce back. When people are asked what they think will make them most happy they often point to winning the lottery. But lottery winners tend not to be happy one year after the big win. They are besieged by people looking for money, which transforms relationships that were formerly based on the sharing of experiences and affection to transactional, monetized relationships. And if they hated their neighbor or couldn't get along with a brother-in-law, that doesn't go away just because they have money. When people are asked what they think will make them most unhappy, they often point to losing a limb. But paraplegics and quadriplegics adapt, living mostly normal lives (with some accommodation, of course) and they end up rating their lives as far happier than they would have imagined.

On happiness, the Dalai Lama says,

> I usually describe happiness in the sense of more satisfaction; happiness is not necessarily some pleasurable experience, but a neutral experience that can bring deep satisfaction.

What makes him truly happy? He says,

> Ultimately, you get the most benefit from making other people happy.

Former president Vicente Fox of the United States of Mexico agrees. "What is the key to happiness?" I asked him.

> The main thing is I was just so dedicated to this one idea all along; from kindergarten through university. I owe everything to Ignacio de Loyola, who created the largest university system and the largest number of campuses ever in the history of this world. And there is one single teaching there, which is "be for others." Being for others is the shortcut to happiness. Give as much as you can and you can get back more than you expected.

This may be why President Fox left office with the highest approval rating of any president in Mexican history.

The biggest tip of all to promote healthy emotions as we age is to find a way to help others. It is much more difficult to be depressed or feel dreary if you are working to make someone else's life better.

6

SOCIAL FACTORS

Life with people

Philosopher Jean-Paul Sartre famously wrote, "*L'enfer, c'est les autres*"—hell is other people. No. Not if you want to live long. One of the keys to a long health span and a long life is social connectedness.

Loneliness is associated with early mortality. It has been implicated in just about every medical problem you can think of, including cardiovascular incidents, personality disorders, psychoses, and cognitive decline. Loneliness can double the likelihood of developing Alzheimer's disease. It increases the production of stress hormones, which in turn lead to arthritis and diabetes, dementia, and increased suicide attempts. It leads to inflammation, increasing proinflammatory cytokines such as interleukin-6 (IL-6), and it negates the beneficial effects of exercise on neurogenesis, the growth of new neurons. Loneliness is worse for your health than smoking fifteen cigarettes a day. If you are chronically lonely, the risk that you will die in the next seven years goes up by 30 percent.

Loneliness and social isolation are not the same thing. Social isolation refers to having few interactions with people and can be evaluated objectively (for example, how many people you interact with in a week and for how long). Loneliness is entirely subjective—it's your emotional state. Social isolation can be calculated. Loneliness is felt.

People can feel lonely even when surrounded by others, such as in the middle of a party or inside a large family. Loneliness is a feeling of being detached from meaningful relationships, and that may arise from feeling unacknowledged, from feeling misunderstood, or from a lack of intimacy. Having a spouse sometimes helps, and sometimes not. There are certainly people who enjoy being alone and who do not feel lonely, just as there are people who are constantly in the presence of others, perhaps making small talk, but feeling completely alone. Being unmarried raises the risk of loneliness and a host of health-related problems, but being married doesn't help in all cases—not all marriages are happy ones.

Social isolation can lead to loneliness, of course, and both can increase in old age owing to a variety of factors. People retire and swiftly lose the social contact they had with co-workers. Friends die. Health and mobility problems make it more difficult to leave home. Ageism, present in many modern societies, leaves older adults feeling devalued, unwanted, or invisible. Younger friends and family members become caught up in their own lives and might not take time to visit older people. Government research in the UK found that two hundred thousand older adults had not had a conversation with a friend or relative in more than a month. Clearly that kind of extreme social isolation can lead to loneliness.

This seems to be a modern problem, peculiar to our times. Harvard political scientist Robert Putnam, in his book *Bowling Alone,* decries the "corrosive individualism" that has infected modern society. He documents what he sees as an unhealthy and mounting trend toward political apathy, retreat from church attendance, eroding union membership, and the decline of bridge clubs and dinner parties, volunteering and blood donation.

Sociologist Eric Klinenberg at NYU adds,

> Societies throughout the world have embraced a culture of individualism. More people are living alone, and aging alone, than ever. Neoliberal social policies have turned workers into precarious free agents, and when jobs disappear, things fall apart fast. Labor unions, civic associations, neighborhood organizations, religious groups and other traditional sources of social solidarity are in steady decline. Increasingly, we all feel that we're on our own.

Klinenberg goes on to implicate the rise of communications technology, perhaps paradoxically, as a cause of loneliness. When Facebook and other social networks began, they, along with tech companies like Apple, Microsoft, and Google, predicted that the Internet would help to create stronger and more meaningful relationships, establishing rewarding and fulfilling online communities. Instead, what we find is that the last several years have brought deepening divisions. We may have thousands of "friends" on Facebook, Instagram, Twitter, Kiwibox, Vine, Tumblr, LinkedIn, Pinterest, QZone, Sina Weibo, and MeWe, but they are rarely fulfilling. No convincing studies have been published on this yet, but I'm willing to bet that interactions in cyberspace do not trigger the release of oxytocin, prolactin, and endorphins the way that real, actual human contact does. (Although as I've written about before, getting "likes" can produce an addictive hit of dopamine.) And unfortunately, it is the unemployed, displaced, and migrant populations that suffer the worst—their lives and social spheres have been profoundly disconnected. When they get lonely, they are the least able among us to rebuild a nurturing community.

Social isolation and loneliness are associated with reductions in levels of the neurotransmitter glutamate. Glutamate is the most abundant neurotransmitter in vertebrates and is important for transmission of signals throughout the cells of the brain. If you're wondering how it relates to monosodium glutamate, the flavor enhancer known as MSG and often used in Chinese food, they are both forms of glutamic acid, one of the amino acids. Proper brain functioning depends on keeping low levels of glutamate in your extracellular fluid, and overly high levels can lead to cell death. A number of mechanisms have evolved to keep those levels low, including an intricate system of chemical scavengers with names like oxaloacetate and glutamate-pyruvate transaminase, which chase down and neutralize glutamate molecules. An unanswered question is whether dietary glutamate can impact brain levels of glutamate (which would be bad). This is where the blood-brain barrier comes in. Any molecules entering or leaving the brain must pass through two membranes, and each membrane has specific properties for keeping different molecules from passing through. These membranes prevent your brain chemistry from going haywire based on eating or drinking too much or too little of certain foods—it is, in effect, a protection that promotes homeostasis of chemical levels in the brain. So far, the weight of evidence seems to suggest that ingesting MSG does not significantly change levels of glutamate in the brain.

In addition to the harmful effects of too-high glutamate levels, too-low levels are associated with loneliness and social isolation, and so increasing glutamate levels in the brain might be helpful in these cases. Researchers have been working on identifying drugs that can help. I'm not implying that we should resort to pharmaceutical interventions for every little thing that goes wrong with us, but for some people, social isolation (and social anxiety) are debilitating, paralyzing conditions. In a finding that may delight certain members of the boomer generation, psychedelics such as LSD and psilocybin have been shown to decrease feelings of both loneliness and depression, with lasting effects, and ketamine has been shown to provide relief, although the relief seems to be only short-term.

Social isolation and loneliness can even change your genes. Social isolation, loneliness, and depression affect gene expression, causing increased inflammation in the brain and decreased production of antiviral interferon. Lonely people have increased activation of the HPA axis, causing them to be hypervigilant about social threats. They might believe that most people in the world are out to harm them, humiliate them, or behave derisively or dismissively toward them. In this respect chronically lonely people resemble people with PTSD.

Social isolation co-opts the fear and aggression circuits in the brain, causing persistent fearfulness, hypersensitivity to threatening stimuli, and increased aggressiveness toward others. For example, mice normally freeze (like deer) when they encounter a threatening stimulus, because most of their natural predators use motion cues to locate them. After the threatening stimulus is removed, normal mice stop freezing right away, whereas socially isolated mice—being hypersensitive to threat—will stay frozen for much longer.

There's a small structure deep inside the brain called the putamen (pew-TAY-men). I find it mysterious. It keeps showing up in brain imaging studies of music, of neurological disorders, speech syntax, and creativity. It also shows up in studies of emotion, particularly hate—some criminal offenders have structural anomalies in the putamen (as well as in the hippocampus, amygdala, and nucleus accumbens)—suggesting its role in antisocial behaviors. Increases in putamen size are associated with higher aggression toward others, whereas reductions in putamen size are associated with Alzheimer's disease.

It's involved in so many different things, and makes connections to so many parts of the brain, that scientists have had difficulty in assigning the putamen a specific role. It seems to me that the unifying thread has to do with reward and motivation, and the putamen's role in the brain's chemical-reward system. The putamen may also modulate social anxiety. People who try to avoid others have a low density of dopamine receptors in their putamen, which may block any pleasurable sensations from simply being with others—even people they like.

That this is neurobiological does not mean the brains of such individuals were always destined to be that way. Clearly there are genetic factors, but we also know that the formation of the system that releases dopamine is influenced substantially by environmental and social factors during childhood, including the kinds of social interactions we experience in childhood and adolescence. Together, these can lead in later adulthood to aloofness and withdrawal from others.

But recall the work of David Anderson, the Caltech neurobiologist I mentioned in the previous chapter, who gave the TED Talk on how your brain is not simply a bag of chemicals: Dopamine receptors in one part of the brain do not necessarily do the same things as dopamine receptors in other parts of the brain. In the putamen, they moderate social engagement. But in two nearby structures, the ventral striatum and globus pallidus, lower dopamine uptake leads to increased impulsiveness and hatred of monotony.

Structures such as the putamen, and neurochemicals that reward social engagement, suggest an ancient evolutionary history to our wanting to be with others. Other structures, such as the globus pallidus, suggest an evolutionary basis for managing impulse control. Our social drives and behaviors are influenced by the way our brains have responded to the triad of genes, culture, and opportunity.

Social Development

As we've seen so far, the developmental neuroscience triad of genes, culture, and opportunity influence brain development and can affect the course of your life. Social development is no different. As I've already touched on, babies need physical contact.

Harry Harlow, a psychologist, performed some of the most harrowing experiments ever conducted. He raised infant monkeys in isolation for up to twenty-four months to see what the effect would be; the young monkeys emerged profoundly disturbed and many never adjusted after the isolation ended. In another study, he put baby monkeys in a cage with two wire monkeys. One wire monkey had a milk-dispensing bottle in it. The second wire monkey had a terry-cloth blanket wrapped around it. Harlow hypothesized that the infant monkeys would want to spend more time with the wire monkey that gave milk—the nutrition they needed to satisfy their hunger. But in fact, the baby monkeys clung to the wire monkey with the soft terry-cloth blanket. The videos of the experiment are heartbreaking. (Harlow and his collaborators give all scientists a bad name even though the great majority of us would never consider such monstrous studies.) There is one video in which a baby monkey continues to cling to its terry-cloth wire mother while straining to reach over and drink some of the milk from the adjacent wire monkey. Mothering is about more than just providing food. It's about soft touch and warmth, about creature comfort.

Around the same time, a psychologist named John Bowlby was developing attachment theory, the idea that human infants need to develop a relationship with at least one primary caregiver in order to experience successful emotional and social development and to learn to regulate their emotions. The caregiver does not need to be the biological parent, or even just one or two particular people—it can involve a community of caregivers, as is often seen in non-Western cultures.

Research shows that social stress is linked to a compromised immune system. This can happen at any age. But as an early life stressor, social stress is particularly harmful because the effects are long-lasting. Michael Meaney at McGill University showed that the kind of care a mother gives to her offspring actually alters the child's physiological responses to stress throughout its life span. Rat pups who are licked more in the first ten days of life grow into adult rats who are far more secure and less likely to be destabilized by stress. Baby rats who received a great deal of licking and grooming produced fewer stress hormones when, later in life, confronted with a challenging situation, in comparison with rats who received less care. And these effects persisted well into adulthood, and persisted into the *next* generation of rats because the female offspring licked *their* offspring more. Meaney also showed that pups who were exposed to lots of licking and grooming in early life also display better memory performance in adulthood.

Early experience interacts with genetics and brain structure. The mother's health is critical. Meaney says, "The single most important factor determining the quality of mother-offspring interactions is the mental and physical health of the mother. This is equally true for rats, monkeys and humans." Parents living in poverty, suffering from mental illness, or facing great stress are much more likely to be exhausted, irritable, and anxious. These conditions are transferred in the interactions between such parents and their children.

Nurture (or lack thereof) early in life selectively affects the development of a number of brain systems, such as glucocorticoid receptors in the hippocampus—part of the feedback mechanism in the immune system that reduces inflammation. Meaney also showed that parenting affects the function of the pituitary and adrenal glands, which regulate growth and sexual function and produce cortisol and adrenaline. Although these effects can last a lifetime, they can be overcome with the right behavioral and pharmacological interventions, but it takes some work. Cuddles count, particularly in the first year of life. Think of it as a plant that has overgrown in your yard: If you prune it and shape it early in its life cycle, it becomes easy to maintain. If you ignore it for a few years until the stem is thick and woody, you can still tame it, but it takes a lot more work, and your efforts go against the shape it has adopted. As parents (and grandparents and teachers), our choices about how we raise our children in their first years will have a far greater role in what their last years look like than was previously recognized.

Don't forget that humans grow within a socioeconomic context that in turn influences development of the nervous system—particularly of the systems that underlie language and thought. Prenatal factors, parent-child interactions, and cognitive stimulation in the home environment all influence neural development. As one example, educational attainment has been associated with decreased allostatic load later in life. The direction of causality here, though, is not clear. Maybe education helps us to better manage life stressors, or maybe those who already manage life stressors effectively are able to go further in school. (Indeed in rats, environmental enrichment during early life—the rat equivalent of a good kindergarten—has been shown to increase hippocampal volume, decrease stress response, and increase memory function in adulthood.) Or maybe people with an education just earn more money and eat better food. In any case, these findings should direct us toward improving the programs and policies that are designed to reduce socioeconomic disparities in mental health services and academic support.

❖

There are currently estimated to be more than 100 million orphaned or abandoned children in the world—that's 20 million more than the entire population of Germany. In 1915, Dr. Henry Chapin, a pediatrician and professor at the New York Post-Graduate School of Medicine (now NYU) wrote in the *Journal of the American Medical Association* (*JAMA*):

> In considering the best conditions for the relief of acutely sick infants and for foundlings or abandoned babies, two important factors must always be kept in mind: (1) the unusual susceptibility of the infant to its immediate environment, and (2) its great need of individual care. The best conditions for the infant thus require a home and a mother. The further we get away from these vital necessities of beginning life, the greater will be our failure to get adequate results in trying to help the needy infant. Strange to say, these important conditions have often been overlooked, or, at least, not sufficiently emphasized, by those who are working in this field.

That was written in 1915. *More than one hundred years ago.* And yet, the problem of orphaned and abandoned children persists worldwide.

After the fall of the Ceaușescu regime in Romania in 1989, more than 170,000 children were found to have been abandoned at or shortly after birth and kept in overcrowded, poorly administered institutions all over the country. Many Americans learned of the Romanian crisis through a television segment on the ABC newsmagazine *20/20* and rushed to adopt Romanian orphans—eight thousand of them in all. But collectively, the new parents were unprepared for the psychological damage many of these children had already suffered.

Ten years later, the Bucharest Early Intervention Project (BEIP) was begun by American researchers including Charles Nelson and Nathan Fox to study the effects of foster care versus institutionalization. Sixty-eight Romanian infants and toddlers were taken out of institutions and put into foster care specifically set up for the study. The study found that all of the children who had been institutionalized had profound changes in brain development. They were severely impaired in IQ and manifested a variety of social and emotional disorders—depression, anxiety, disruptive behaviors, and ADHD. However, the earlier an institutionalized child was placed into foster care, the better the recovery, especially when placement occurred before the age of twenty months.

When the children were twelve, they were again assessed on a variety of measures including their response to stress, physical health, mental health, substance use, and academic performance. Only 40 percent of children who had ever been institutionalized were doing well at age twelve. But that 40 percent is an average, and marked differences occurred depending on whether they were eventually raised in a family situation or remained institutionalized. For the children placed with a family, roughly 55 percent were functioning well at age twelve. Of the children left in institutions, only 25 percent were functioning well. And of those placed in foster care within the first twenty months of life, 80 percent were functioning well. Early family experience is key not just to socialization, but to overall brain functioning as well. As Charles Nelson notes,

> The brain is dependent on experience to develop normally. What happens in situations of neglect, such as kids raised in institutions, is that the experiences are lacking. So the brain is sort of in a holding pattern saying, "Okay, so where's the experience? Where's the experience? Where's the experience?" And when the experience fails to occur, those circuits either fail to develop or they develop in an atypical fashion—and the result, in a sense, is the mis-wiring of circuits.
>
> The big question is, what happens 10 or 20 or 30 years down the line? The speculation would be you will progressively find yourself more and more disadvantaged or more and more handicapped.

There has been a significant increase in the number of children diagnosed with autism spectrum disorders over the last twenty years, and there are probably cultural factors at work here as well. Consider the difference between a typical Mexican childhood and a typical American one.

Mexican culture encourages social interaction, family time, and group activities. American children are often allowed to play with tablets, phones, and other electronic devices alone. Although autism has a complex etiology, one culture seems to discourage behaviors that we might characterize as autistic, while the other culture encourages them. Indeed, rates of autism among children raised in Mexico, as well as Hispanic and Latino children raised in the United States, are significantly lower than they are for "white" US children.

What You Can Do about Social Isolation

Is there a cure for loneliness? One of the first steps is to admit that you're lonely and that you want to do something about it, but this isn't so easy, according to Dhruv Khullar, an attending physician at New York–Presbyterian Hospital:

> Loneliness is an especially tricky problem because accepting and declaring our loneliness carries profound stigma. Admitting we're lonely can feel as if we're admitting we've failed in life's most fundamental domains: belonging, love, attachment. It attacks our basic instincts to save face, and makes it hard to ask for help.

And clearly the cure is not simply reducing social isolation, because we can feel lonely in a crowd. But getting out and being among people is a good start.

David Anderson has been studying social isolation in the fruit fly, *Drosophila melanogaster.* You might think of fruit flies as neurally primitive compared to humans, but they do exhibit social behaviors, and a significant number of proteins associated with mRNA translation are highly similar between fruit flies and humans (in spite of there being 780 million years of evolution between us). This suggests that fear and sociability are linked by a very ancient prehuman mechanism. Once again, we may think that we initiate our behaviors and responses to the environment and other people, but at least to some extent, the hidden strings of neurochemicals and hormones pull on us, making us dance, approach, or freeze, all while giving us the illusion that we are in control.

Anderson has also studied this mechanism in mice. Social isolation for two weeks causes an increase in the production of a particular neurochemical, neurokinin (Tac2/NkB), which engages the stress response. Blocking its production with the drug osanetant (a Tac2/NkB receptor antagonist, or blocker) neutralizes the effects of stress, causing socially isolated mice to behave like regular mice. Conversely, increasing Tac2/NkB causes socially raised mice to behave as though they were socially isolated. Interestingly, after being treated just once with osanetant, the socially isolated mice—who behaved very aggressively toward other mice prior to treatment—could be returned to cages with other mice, where they acted normally and nonaggressively. It is this same neurochemical, tachykinin, that was found to cause aggression in Anderson's fruit flies. As Anderson says, "It brings up the question whether this drug could mitigate the well-known deleterious effects of solitary confinement, such as increased violent behavior in incarcerated individuals." Or help people stuck in old age homes, who often feel agitated and disoriented.

The importance of all this goes beyond just conquering the adverse effects of social isolation, to more broadly treating a wide range of mental health disorders. The ability to regulate levels of neurochemicals like Tac2/NkB with great precision may dramatically improve mental health medicine in the coming years. Osanetant is not currently available for humans, but the field is rapidly changing and the coming years promise a number of innovative developments.

The Tac2/NkB story tells us a little about how social isolation causes aggression and fear, but not why some people find it hard to get themselves out of it. Social isolation is often self-imposed because people don't receive the normal kinds of brain-based rewards from social interactions. That is, under ordinary circumstances, we enjoy being with others—like all primates, we are a social species—and positive social interactions release opioids in the brain, especially in the brain's most important reward center, the nucleus accumbens. When people have been bullied, taunted, and humiliated by social experiences, their innate experience of pleasure with others may be hijacked by their fear system. People with an impaired reward system, because of either such negative interactions, or organic damage to the nucleus accumbens and associated limbic system, or the natural age-related shrinkage of the brain, tend to socialize less because it has stopped being rewarding. Directly stimulating the nucleus accumbens in mice leads to increased play and social motivation. But so far it is not possible to do this in humans. Indirect stimulation, however, is possible in humans, through the use of drugs that increase the reward center's activity, such as cannabinoids like marijuana, morphine, and methylphenidate, which, respectively, modulate receptors for endocannabinoids, endogenous opioids, and dopamine. Another agent that increases dopamine levels is armodafinil, which is usually used to combat jet lag or narcolepsy, but in some people it has the side effect of making them more social because it tweaks the novelty-seeking dopaminergic system.

A series of studies that I conducted in collaboration with neuroscientist Vinod Menon showed that music can activate these same reward centers. Music often occurs in social settings like parties, restaurants, and political rallies, and there is evidence that listening to music in groups releases oxytocin, the hormone that facilitates social bonding. Our studies showed that even listening to music alone, inside the sterile confines of a brain scanner, still lights up these reward centers. Without drugs, then, it's possible that social isolation and feelings of loneliness can be reduced simply by listening to music. After all, when we listen to music, we're kind of with the musicians, right?

Paxil and Zoloft, two SSRIs (selective serotonin reuptake inhibitors), although they are primarily known as antidepressants, have been shown to ease social anxiety, to help people enjoy their interactions with others. Don't give up if treatment doesn't work quickly—they are subject to what we call "therapeutic lag." Finding the right medication and dose for your situation can take some trial and error.

On the other hand, although drugs such as these are widely prescribed, there are increasing doubts about their efficacy. Patients often feel cheated if their doctors won't prescribe them something, and it's often easier for medical doctors to write a prescription than to convince patients to seek psychotherapy, something that in much of the world is still stigmatized. Cognitive behavioral therapy (CBT), which I mentioned previously, was shown in a Norwegian study to be more effective than either drug therapy or the combination of drug therapy and CBT. The problem is that drugs tend to camouflage problems by making people feel better temporarily, preventing them from learning to regulate their emotions themselves.

Regulating our emotions is fundamental to increasing health span. In particular, learning to control lifestyle elements such as sleep hygiene, diet, and physical activity has been shown to reduce feelings of loneliness, as does learning to focus on positive emotions such as gratitude. Gratitude is an important and often overlooked emotion and state of mind. Gratitude causes us to focus on what's good about our lives rather than what's bad, shifting our outlook toward the positive. Positive psychology grew out of a belief that psychology's focus on disorders and problems of adjustment was ignoring much of what makes life most worth living. Positive psychology has found that people who practice gratitude simply feel happier.

Related to this, a number of studies have shown that religious people are happier than nonreligious ones. There are a number of explanations for this but they're not what you might think: Religious people aren't happier because they believe in God or because they feel the comfort of God watching over them; these may be important to them and give them a sense of purpose, moral or ethical grounding, or simply the belief that they are doing the right thing, but those are not ingredients of happiness. The research suggests that religious people feel happier because religion promotes gratitude through prayers and gives them a social network, along with a sense of purpose and meaning—three things that benefit most of us, regardless of where they come from. Those social benefits appear also to accrue in the nonreligious who join a music listening group, volunteer in a soup kitchen, or have block parties with their neighbors. And religious people who are not part of a community do not seem to enjoy the high levels of happiness of those who are in one.

Many of us feel socially awkward, and there are programs and interventions that can help to ease those feelings. Joining book clubs, hiking groups, groups like Toastmasters or Rotary Club, and volunteer organizations, both secular and religious, can provide some help.

An innovative program begun by the Palo Alto Medical Foundation is called linkAges (a play on words that can be read as either *link ages* or *linkages*). The program functions like an exchange system that encourages young people and older adults to trade services. Members of the linkAges community post online something they want help with. Older members might seek transportation to a doctor's office or help changing light bulbs; younger members might want to take guitar lessons or learn how to prepare a balance sheet for a new business. Suppose Tiffany, age twenty-seven, helps June, age seventy-seven, to plant a vegetable garden, earning Tiffany two hours of credit. Later, Tiffany wants to take guitar lessons, which she does from Ramesh, age thirty-two; Tiffany trades in her credit, hour for hour, and Ramesh earns new credits. Ramesh wants to start an online guitar lesson company and uses his credits with June, who used to be the comptroller at a large corporation. She teaches Ramesh how to prepare a balance sheet. Tiffany and Ramesh both get to interact with June in different capacities, and June gains an increased sense of purpose and self-worth by being able to pass on her knowledge to someone who needs it. As Paul Tang, a doctor at the Palo Alto Medical Foundation, says, "You don't need a playmate every day, but knowing you're valued and a contributing member of society is incredibly reaffirming."

The Canadian Longitudinal Study on Aging found that 30 percent of women over the age of seventy-five reported being lonely. One creative way to address the problem of loneliness in seniors is intergenerational housing. Programs pair young adults, often students, with seniors, and exist in Ontario, Quebec, and Nova Scotia. Symbiosis, a program in London, Ontario, for example, has university students living alongside seniors in a retirement home. This co-housing project is run by the school of graduate studies at McMaster University and connects students in need of safe, affordable housing and local seniors in need of companionship. International students working to improve their English language skills benefit from opportunities to practice conversational English, and seniors benefit from getting help around the house. Both partners benefit from reduced social isolation and a sense of shared community.

Another new program in Britain, Befriending, matches up a volunteer with an older adult for regular one-on-one companionship. Whereas the Palo Alto program entails the older adult making a contribution to the community in their area of expertise, the Befriending program is less transactional. It is too early to say whether either program will show tangible benefits in terms of increased health span. But Befriending says that the program "often provides people with a new direction in life, opens up a range of activities and leads to increased self-esteem and self confidence.

Befriending can also reduce the burden on other services which people may use inappropriately as they seek social contact."

Losing a spouse, through late-life divorce, illness, or death, can be a time of profound difficulty. My paternal grandmother lost her husband of forty years, my grandfather, when she was only sixty-three, and she lived another sixteen years without him. She was ill prepared to be alone. When he was alive, they had an active social life, mainly with other doctors whom he worked with and had known for decades. My grandmother's own father was a tailor and an immigrant from Spain. She graduated college in 1923, majoring in philosophy. After she married, she put that philosophy degree to good use in social settings. My grandparents socialized regularly with other physicians and the level of conversation was intellectual and challenging.

But after my grandfather's death, she was adrift. The doctors who she thought were her friends stopped inviting her to parties. At first, she sought companionship by making appointments to see these doctors in their offices. Twice a week or so, she'd make the rounds of the internist, the ENT, the gynecologist, the foot and ankle surgeon, the dentist—all people she had socialized with when my grandpa was alive. She probably didn't have anything wrong with her, but this was the only way she knew how to keep in touch. It was awkward for the doctors and took them away from patients who were really ill. And I'm sure it was less than fulfilling for her. Then something clicked. She read about the Head Start program in the newspaper, and that the local San Francisco program was looking for volunteers who could go into classrooms and read to young children. As soon as she started doing that, her entire mood changed. And she stopped visiting the doctors' offices. Here was a connection that greatly benefited my grandmother and the underprivileged children she met with twice a week. As the British children's laureate Sir Michael Morpurgo writes,

> It is the need of every single one of us, child or grown-up, to feel wanted, to feel we belong and that we matter to someone else in the world. We all know, from our own experience, that feeling isolated from those around us, alienated from society, makes us sad, even angry. The deeper this isolation becomes, the more

hurtful and resentful we feel and the more this is reflected in our behavior. Such behavior only leads to greater alienation. Children who from an early age feel alone and apart from the rest of the world, and there are so many of them, who become angry and hurt, have little chance of leading fulfilled lives. They are lost from the start. Above all, they need friendship, the solid warmth of someone who cares and goes on caring. With such lasting friendship, self worth and self confidence can flourish, and a child's life can be altered forever.

Changes in Sociability among Older Adults

Laura Carstensen was a young assistant professor at Stanford when the AIDS crisis broke out in nearby San Francisco. Back then, being HIV-positive was almost an assured death sentence. As a psychological scientist interested in aging, she wondered how these predominantly young people, whose lives were about to be cut short, would deal with their impending death. In terms of how much time they had left, they resembled older adults—what, if any, psychological similarities were there?

Carstensen proposed that social goals are broadly divided into two categories, the acquisition of knowledge and the self-regulation of emotion. Further, most of us appreciate that our time is eventually going to run out; this in turn influences our goals at different points along the life span. Across our lifetimes, she says, we engage in a selection process of strategically and adaptively cultivating our social networks to help us maximize social and emotional gains while minimizing social and emotional risks. When time is perceived as open-ended—as it is for most young people—goals are most likely to be preparatory, and we spend time on things that will optimize the future—for example, gathering information, pushing ourselves to find our limits, and seeking new skills. Young adults often place great emphasis on activities that will help them later; after all, what is school if not the prime example of things that don't really help you in the moment?

In contrast, when constraints on time are perceived, goals focus more on meaningful activities that can take place in the present. As a consequence, goals shift from emphasizing future knowledge and contacts to emphasizing emotional states, seeking peace, well-being, and important friendships. When time is limited, goals related to deriving emotional meaning from life are prioritized over goals that maximize long-term payoffs in a shortened future. Of course, younger people sometimes pursue goals related to meaning, and older people sometimes pursue goals related to knowledge acquisition; it's the relative importance placed on them that is subject to change. And if knowledge or skill acquisition for its own sake is pleasurable in the moment, as it apparently was for Pablo Casals, that goal does not diminish with age.

Carstensen studied young men with symptomatic HIV infections who were approaching the end of their lives and found that their goals for how they wanted to spend their time became very similar to those of older adults near the end of their lives—they wanted to spend time with people they cared about, and whom they were close to, and placed a greater emphasis on activities that were emotionally meaningful in the moment than ones that were preparatory. Carstensen dubbed this socioemotional selectivity theory. Time perspective, not chronological age, drives these changes in social motivations. Why invest time in a new contact if you won't be there to reap the benefits? What matters, when you're running out of time, is maintaining the long-standing, deeply meaningful friendships that have nurtured your emotional life.

Another interesting age-related shift has to do with how we relate to the world. Middle-aged adults tend to direct their energy toward bringing their environment in line with their own wishes—they renovate and build houses, for example, and do other things to mold their world to their liking. Older adults typically focus on changing themselves to accord with their environment. To meet the challenges of aging, older individuals increasingly need to resort to strategies of adjusting expectations and activities in order to pursue more attainable goals when the kinds of activities that characterized their youth become more difficult to do.

Fortunately, increasing age, in many cases, is associated with better emotional balance. Part of this balance may be owing to deactivations of the amygdala—we are less likely to experience negative thoughts as we age, and less likely to be fearful. The amygdala is responsible for detecting and responding to threats, and these can result in the secretion of chemicals throughout the brain (norepinephrine, acetylcholine, dopamine, serotonin) and body (hormones such as adrenaline and cortisol). Although you may know older adults who are fearful and emotionally unbalanced, this is not the statistical trend. (It may also be due to comorbidities such as Alzheimer's or dementia, or just natural individual differences, and a few personally vivid cases don't negate the overall trend toward better emotional balance.)

Socioemotional selectivity theory states that as we age, we become increasingly aware of our shortening future time horizon. This awareness leads us to prioritize emotional meaning, emotion regulation, and well-being. There is also a developing positivity effect—older adults pay more attention to and remember more positive experiences than younger adults do. Together, these may help buffer against declines in objective well-being and lead to initial increases in subjective feelings of well-being and positivity in older adults.

Self-efficacy

The Bucharest study of orphaned children showed us the critical role of socialization on brain development in early life. But the brain is constantly changing, not just during infancy. This makes me think about how social experiences and family life impact the brain at the other end of the life span. Old age often brings retirement and (hopefully) the independence of our children, and with that comes an important psychological change: We are no longer responsible for performing a particular function within an organization or in society. That loss of a sense of responsibility can lead to a more global loss of a sense of agency—a sense that what we do in the world matters, and that we matter to other people. A belief that we can exert some control over our environment is essential for our well-being and is believed to be a psychological and biological necessity. This environmental control, and the ability to correct one's own errors, is an important principle taught to young children in the successful Montessori method. If it is important for young children, perhaps it is also important for older adults.

Think about nursing and retirement homes, what we used to call "old age homes." In many cases, the staff do everything that residents formerly did for themselves, such as cooking and cleaning. Setting aside those individuals who *can't* do things for themselves, because of mobility problems or dementia, a number of individuals who could be doing things are encouraged not to, encouraged to "relax and take it easy." The message that many older adults hear from this is "You are not capable; you no longer matter." The debilitated condition of many older adults in these facilities may result, at least in part, from being encouraged to live in a decision-free environment. Is this condition reversible?

A landmark study in the 1970s explored choice and responsibility in a nursing home. Half of the residents were given a potted plant and told that the nursing staff would water and care for it. The other half were first given a choice of whether they wanted a plant or not and, if they said yes, were told it was their responsibility to take care of it. This simple, almost trivial-sounding intervention had dramatic consequences. The residents who had even this small amount of choice and responsibility, for a houseplant, were happier and more active. They spent more time visiting with others and talking to staff. They were significantly more alert.

Albert Bandura (now ninety-four years old, and a professor at Stanford who published three major scientific articles in the past year) uses the terms *agency* and *self-efficacy* to describe the belief that one can exert control over one's environment. The higher people's sense of self-efficacy, the higher the goals they set for themselves. A sense of control is a basic necessity of psychological life. Individuals who perceive that they lack control over their environments may seek to gain control in any way possible, potentially acting out, breaking the law, lashing out at loved ones, or developing eating disorders. Remember that mysterious structure, deep inside the brain, the putamen? People who receive something desirable show great activity in the putamen when they *choose* the reward rather than having it simply given to them. Choosing, that is, exerting control over one's environment, activates the brain's reward system. That's true even when the choice occurs during a stressful situation, in a "lesser of two evils" context. The very fact that we have options that we can decide to act on seems to reduce stress responses in the brain and can lead to healthier brains as we age.

Closely related to the ideas of choice, control, self-efficacy, and agency is the idea of functional autonomy—are we really free to do what we want? As we age, by necessity we tend to increasingly rely on others as our abilities gradually fade or, in some cases, collapse. My grandfather loved doing his own handyman work around the house—he had *built* the house, acting as the general contractor, plumber, electrician, and everything else. But by age sixty-two, he found himself calling the plumber to make even minor repairs. He was tired of trying to squeeze into tight spaces or hoisting himself up into the attic. His back hurt. He didn't have the dexterity in his hands that he used to. In that moving letter to the family that he wrote shortly before he died, he bemoaned and regretted this change in his attitudes and abilities. He felt less like himself. These kinds of shifts are natural. But research shows that, as we age, our friends and family play a critical role in this unfolding story. If the people around us support and encourage our autonomy, we will tend to do better. If we are surrounded by people who discourage our autonomy and try to convince us that we shouldn't be doing things we've always done, our lives can quickly go off the rails. I helped him with the repairs, and my grandfather delighted in having skills he could impart to a future generation.

Of course, there are cases when we must intervene and discourage autonomy in our loved ones. My mother's mother, battling Alzheimer's at ninety-five, nearly set fire to her apartment several times by leaving things on the stove and forgetting about them. She forgot to clean. She could no longer live autonomously. After much deliberation and consultation, my mother brought her to a residential home for the aged. It was a good one—the staff there let her make every decision that she was capable of and boosted her autonomy rather than disparaging it. She didn't get to decide when to eat; that was programmed. And she didn't get to choose her room in the facility. But she could decide what to eat, where to go, and whom to spend time with. She died in her sleep of unrelated problems at ninety-six, but she had friends in the home and, even in her state of advanced dementia, found some enjoyment in her final year.

There is a trend in the United States toward assisted living (AL) facilities, in which adults typically have their own apartment, and the level of attention and care provided is custom-tailored to the individual, with an emphasis on autonomy. They are hospitality oriented, featuring on-site pubs, swimming pools, and gyms.

They give people socialization opportunities that wouldn't be available living at home. The problems facing ninety-year-olds are the same at home or in AL, but AL solves many of them. Someone helps them get dressed and then they go to the pub to have a beer.

Work

Walter Isaacson notes that the greatest creativity comes out of associations with others, the kinds of cross-pollination we get from talking to other people with interesting ideas. Da Vinci created his most famous works, *The Last Supper* and the *Mona Lisa,* after moving to Milan and being surrounded by people from a variety of endeavors and disciplines—1470s Milan was teeming with creativity. Benjamin Franklin created a club in Philadelphia in 1727 (when he was only twenty-one), the Leather Apron Club, that brought together people of different backgrounds and perspectives for conversation and debate. He continued to stay socially active in this same kind of way to the end of his life at eighty-four.

The emerging picture is clear. When people retire, they tend to turn in on themselves. Then cognitive decline and mood disturbances can take hold. This is not true for everyone, but it is true for a great many. And as depression seeps in, at first unnoticed, it comes on so gradually that we don't do anything about it while we still have our wits about us and our will to change. Later, someone close to us notices the change in our demeanor, our spark, and it becomes an uphill battle to try to fix it. Retirement from most jobs means a rapid shrinking of the number of people we come into contact with, and the sense that we are engaged in meaningful work.

There are exceptions. Sonny Rollins, the great jazz saxophonist, is one. At age eighty, he moved out of his home in New York City to upstate New York with his girlfriend, "where we were safe from having anybody come by and ring our bell." For people who are constituted like Sonny, social interaction can be stressful and unhappy making. And although he retired from playing the saxophone in 2013, after being diagnosed with pulmonary fibrosis, he stays active. He spends his time doing yoga, singing, and reading deeply in Eastern philosophies. After a lifetime of touring and meeting thousands and thousands of people, Sonny seems to find joy in solitude. Not everyone finds socialization exhilarating.

But for most of us, the best advice is, don't stop working. Freud said that the two most important things in life are healthy relationships and meaningful work. There are no controlled experiments on this, no studies in which older adults were randomly assigned either to keep working or to retire—all we have are anecdotes. But the anecdotes are impressive, from Ralph Hall, a Texas Democrat who served as a member of Congress until age ninety-one, to Mastanamma, a woman in India who died last year at 106 years old and whose YouTube cooking channel has more than 1.3 million subscribers.

Or Anthony Mancinelli of New York, who, until his death in September 2019 at age 108, was the world's oldest living barber, and who still came into work every day to cut hair. His manager at the barbershop had said, "He never calls in sick. I have young people with knee and back problems, but he just keeps going. He can do more haircuts than a twenty-year-old kid. They're sitting there looking at their phones, texting or whatever, and he's working." In a 2017 interview, he said that he continued to work because it helped him stay busy and upbeat after the death of his wife of seventy years, Carmella, fourteen years earlier. (He would visit her grave every day before work.) What he didn't say was that barbering is a social occupation. He was talking with customers all day, and with co-workers.

Navigating the complex mores and potential pitfalls of dealing with another human being, someone who has their own needs, opinions, and sensitivities, is about the most complex thing that we humans can do. It exercises vast neural networks, keeping them tuned up, in shape, and ready to fire. In a good conversation, we listen, we empathize. And empathy is healthful, activating networks throughout the brain, including the posterior parietal cortex and inferior frontal gyrus.

Imagine what it must be like to live a long and rich life, to feel valued and to contribute to society, and then suddenly be taken out of the loop. This is what happens to older adults all over the world in countries that have compulsory retirement, such as Brazil, China, France, Germany, and South Korea. I find this sad because in every domain of human endeavor, there is still a lot to do, and so many able-bodied and able-minded people with experience and wisdom to help us do it. Older people may be a bit slower and may have need for certain medical accommodations, but younger people are more impulsive, lack experience, and have not yet acquired the pattern-matching skill that comes from a lifetime of using their brains.

Spain, Australia, the United States, and the United Kingdom have outlawed compulsory retirement, but that doesn't mean that ageism has been eradicated. If your company downsizes or goes out of business and you're seventy years old, even in one of these countries it can be difficult to find a new job. It's even difficult after fifty.

There is no shortage of role models for people to keep working. As the number of people over sixty-five soars past 1 billion this year, and the number of people over eighty is now 125 million, we should be looking to expand the number of people who serve as role models to the point that they become the norm.

A few days ago I had a structural engineer over at the house to look at the foundation. (I live in California, in earthquake country.) He was seventy-five and no longer able to crawl around tight spaces or climb up on roofs, but my house was no problem for him. He had been to this house several times, going back long before I owned the house, and his memory for it and knowledge of the surrounding terrain was incredible. An inspector one-third his age had come by the house a year earlier and it took him twice as long to do the job, and he was not nearly as thorough.

Louise Slaughter was a Democratic member of Congress who died in 2018 while still representing her New York district at age eighty-eight. Betty White is still acting in television at age ninety-seven, with recent appearances on *Bones* and *SpongeBob SquarePants*. Brenda Milner, one of the towering figures in neuroscience, still comes to work every day at the Montreal Neurological Institute at age 101. At eighty-six, US Supreme Court justice Ruth Bader Ginsburg returned to work less than a week after breaking three ribs. Congresswoman Maxine Waters, who represents the Forty-Third Congressional District in Los Angeles, California, is serving her fifteenth term in the House at age eighty-one. She captured the attention of the entire country in 2018 and 2019 as the chair of the House Financial Services Committee. While she draws the praise of Democrats and the ire of Republicans, everyone on both sides of the aisle regards her as calm, collected, powerful, and brilliant. Love her or hate her, she is a force to be reckoned with. And she prides herself on reaching across generations. "We moan and groan all the time about a lack of involvement of young people," she said. "But they have taught me a lot about what moves them. It seems like all they are looking for is some honesty and some truth and somebody that they can believe in."

Engaging Yourself with Others

Aging has beneficial effects on our social behavior. Older adults in general (I know you can probably think of exceptions) are better at emotional regulation; they are better able to control their feelings, are less reactive to insults, and pay more attention to the positive things in their lives. Art Shimamura describes it this way:

> One explanation for this maturity is that through decades of social interactions, older adults have confronted the good, bad, and ugly of how people deal with one another. As such, they better understand that choices can be made concerning how we behave and how healthy living is best achieved by focusing on the positive side of life. This positivity bias adheres to the saying, *don't sweat the small stuff,* and is important for psychological well-being as life is too short to worry about minor annoyances.

Social engagement helps to maintain brain functions and protects against cognitive decline. Epidemiological studies find that having a large social network and more daily social contacts is significantly protective against dementia. This is true even when other factors, such as age, education, and initial health status, are controlled. Even the likelihood of dying is reduced by engaging in social activities. All this applies only to positive social engagements, however. Abusive, distressing, and otherwise bad social engagements, of course, can increase stress and be harmful.

A recent meta-analysis of seventy-six separate studies concluded that there is an urgent need to identify lifestyle activities that reduce the functional decline and dementia associated with an aging population. Volunteering appears to be one such activity. Volunteering at a local organization, community center, or hospital can have all the benefits of continuing to work: a sense of self-worth and accomplishment, and the daily interaction with others that causes the brain to light up. The data reveal that volunteering is associated with reduced symptoms of depression, better self-reported health, fewer functional limitations, and lower mortality. In the United States one-quarter of people aged sixty-five and older volunteer, and in

Canada, more than one-third do (yay Canada!). By even a conservative estimate, such volunteering worldwide contributes almost half a *trillion* dollars to local economies. Volunteering is an essentially altruistic undertaking, and altruistic acts by seniors—by all of us, really—are associated with better physical and mental health.

Volunteers in a controlled study showed improvements in the ability to switch between two task sets and in verbal learning and memory, and brain scans showed significantly increased activity in the prefrontal cortex—the seat of higher reasoning and executive function. Volunteering in management or committee roles was related to greater positive emotions, but only for women. Why? We're not sure. Maybe women developed better communication skills ten thousand years ago, keeping the campfire burning and taking care of the children while the men were out silently hunting.

Recall from Chapter 4, on the problem-solving brain, that the more complexity there was in the primary occupation you had while working, the more likely you will be protected from cognitive decline in old age. Complexity includes things like making decisions in a changing landscape of options, interacting with other people, and learning new things—basically jobs that cannot simply be done on autopilot. There is very little research on occupational complexity among volunteers, but since volunteers are essentially performing many of the same functions as paid workers, it is reasonable to infer that this relationship between complexity and benefit holds, as long as we acknowledge that there are probably optimal levels of complexity beyond which any job, even a volunteer one, just becomes annoying.

Of course, not all volunteering is beneficial. If you're stuck in a windowless room balancing a nonprofit organization's accounts and you don't get to move around or interact with anyone, there will be limited benefits, if any. Ideally, you'll find a position that matches your physical, social, and cognitive abilities, stretching them a bit, perhaps, but not to the breaking point. It can be helpful to talk with a friend or family member to make sure that the requirements of the volunteer position are a good fit with your goals and aspirations.

Surround yourself with people who are better than you at something but who don't lord it over you. When I began performing music professionally forty-five years ago, I made a promise to myself that I would never appear on a stage unless I was the worst musician on it. I'm happy to say

I've never been disappointed, and every performance has been a wonderful learning experience for me. Spend time with people who encourage you to grow, to explore new things, and who take joy in your successes. Try to find social situations that respect older adults and a role that allows you to contribute your accumulated knowledge and wisdom to a community organization whose goals you admire. And when you can, go outside. Go outside. Go outside.

7

PAIN

It hurts when I do this

One of the most common features of old age is aches and pains—it seems as though, like in an old car, parts just start to wear out. Pain accounts for 80 percent of trips to the doctor in the United States—it is the number one presenting complaint when people go to the doctor. When the doctor says, "Why are you here?" almost all doctor visits are for a patient saying, "It hurts here," or a variant, "It hurts when I do this."

My friend Michael and I have been comparing notes now for about ten years on our inventory of the physical markers of aging. They seem to make their presence known slowly, one at a time, and each one seems manageable by itself, but they add up. Some respond to treatment. Some require a change in behavior. Some you just have to live with.

Mostly what we talk about is how lucky we are. We have both known people who suffer debilitating, life-threatening pain. I met J. D. Buhl in 1984 when he was a singer-songwriter, and I was working as a record producer. By age twenty-five, he had already led two successful bands, J. D. Buhl and the Believers and the Jars. When we met he was launching a career as a solo artist. I produced some records for him, we performed together, and we became friends. I admired his talent, and I also admired his encyclopedic knowledge of records . . . he knew who wrote every song, the year that the record came out, the name of every musician who played on the session. Among my other friends, I had always been the king of this sort of trivia. But with J.D. I was a novice, and I loved him for it. In the 1990s and 2000s, we went on to do other things—we both became teachers—and we stayed in touch. In 2013, J.D. called me up and said he'd been diagnosed with terminal cancer. He wanted to write and record one last album, and he wanted me to produce it. Six months of chemotherapy had left him tired and worn-out, but the cancer was in remission and he was feeling upbeat. So we started. Slowly.

By 2016 the cancer had returned, and he asked to go back into the studio to record four new songs. The pain was now severe and there didn't seem to be anything he could do to relieve it. He'd made plans to enter a hospice. In Oakland, where he lived, the hospice workers helped him set himself up to end his life when the pain became unbearable. Anxiety has been shown to demonstrably increase pain, and knowing you can't do anything about the pain can be especially anxiety provoking. In addition, J.D. had anxiety about his dwindling finances, his loss of mobility, and his diminishing energy.

One day in the summer of 2017 at age fifty-seven, he called me and said it was time. The pain was too much. He awoke every morning from a rolling, restless half-sleep riddled with painful sensations throughout his body, inside and out, knowing that the new day held nothing but more pain with no release. He had the embarrassment of a colostomy bag and a drawn, sunken appearance. He hadn't been blessed with many romantic partners in his life, and realized he'd never have another. He lacked the energy to play music or even listen to records. "I have very little to look forward to," he said. I phoned him on the evening of August 14, 2017, to say good-bye, and the next morning he administered a special pharmaceutical cocktail to himself and was gone.

Pain is a formidable opponent and even the spectacular advances made in medical science are no match for it. We tend to think of medical science in terms of how much it can prolong life, and as a society, we pour a great deal of money and other resources into trying to cure diseases that shorten life span—such as cancer. But we haven't solved the problem of how to eradicate pain. In other words, medical science tends to focus on life span rather than disease span.

At any given time, 30 percent of the population is experiencing chronic pain—which means they've been in pain and they've had that pain for more than three months. For older adults the number is closer to 40 or 50 percent. The odds of experiencing chronic pain at some point in your life are one in two. More people are in chronic pain at this minute than have cancer, heart disease, or diabetes combined.

The Global Burden of Disease Project is a statistical, epidemiological look at the various diseases and injuries affecting people worldwide. Produced by the World Health Organization, the project provides an interactive map that allows you to look at a number of variables, including causes of death by country and state, age, and sex. An innovative feature is the reporting of YLDs—years living with (or lost to) disability—what I described as *disease span.*

Consider the two visualizations (redrawn from World Health Organization data) on the following page. The first picture shows cause of death for seventy-plus-year-olds. The second shows YLD for seventy-plus-year-olds. The point here is to show that the things that disable us are different from the things that kill us.

As the top chart shows, stroke and cancer account for 15 percent and 16 percent of deaths in people over seventy, respectively. Chronic pain accounts for that same proportion of YLDs—years within the disease span portion of your life span. (Headache accounts for around 1 percent and is grouped into "other chronic illnesses.") Note also that of people who are in chronic pain, nearly half have back pain. About one person in five has neck pain and another one in five has arthritis. And compare the magnitude of cancer as a cause of death versus a cause of disability: Cancer (at 16 percent) is a major cause of death, but in terms of disability it is a tiny 3 percent compared to, say, falls, which account for 7 percent of disability. It isn't that we shouldn't be trying to cure cancer and heart disease, but that an outsized amount of money gets spent on life span research compared to what is spent on health span research. The costs of treating chronic pain alone account for more than $635 billion in expenditures annually in the United States and can lead to catastrophic unforeseen consequences, possibly including the current opioid epidemic. Pain research receives just a tiny sliver of the funding devoted to medical research, perhaps because of the widely held belief that "pain hurts, but it doesn't kill you." But in fact, it can. Chronic pain creates a 1.57 increased mortality risk. What that means is that for every ten years you are in chronic pain, your life span is lowered by one year. Put another way, chronic pain confers on you a risk-adjusted age of six years higher than your chronological age. If you've got chronic pain at age seventy-four, you are effectively eighty.

Many people assume that pain simply gets worse as we age, but this isn't true—it peaks and then falls off. Chronic pain increases and peaks in our fifties and sixties, and then declines in our seventies and older. These

Global Causes of Death in 2017 (70+ years)

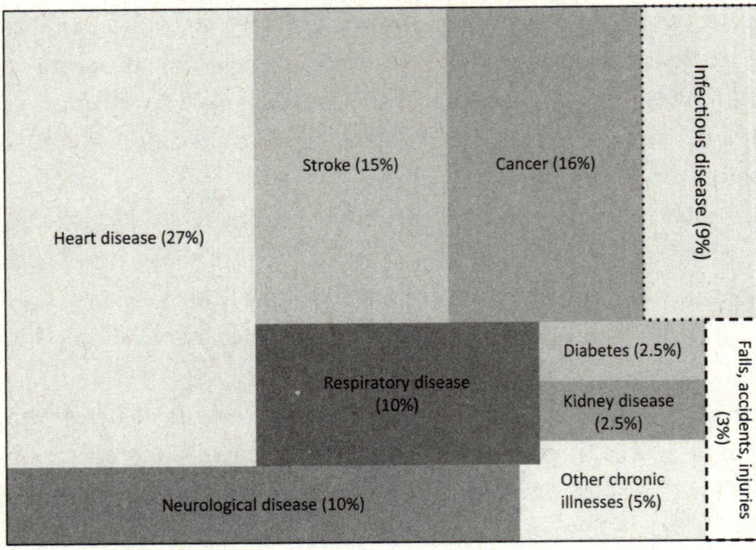

Global Years Lived with Disability in 2017 (70+ years)

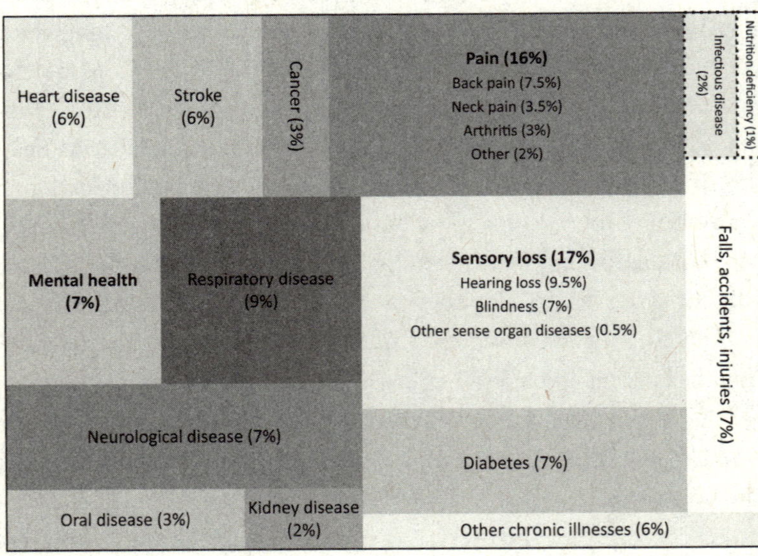

numbers could arise because older adults become more stoic and stop complaining about it, or it could be that they simply don't have it anymore.

The sensation of pain is actually generated in the brain, even though we usually experience it in a specific part of the body. In other words, your toe may hurt, but the "hurt" is occurring in the part of your brain map that represents your toe. This is why if we shut down your brain, through sleep, loss of consciousness, or certain drugs, the pain goes away. Or why, if we block the transmission of neural firings from your toe to your brain, the pain goes away. This might be done with a topical anesthetic or an intravenous nerve-blocking agent. Either way, no distress signal from the sensory receptor reaches the brain, and so no pain is felt. As we saw in the perception chapter (Chapter 3), you can experience pain even when there is no sensory input, such as with an amputee's phantom limb pain. Thus, pain is a brain-based phenomenon.

Pain isn't simply an automatic reaction you feel when you're injured. In a paper published just after World War II, Lieutenant Colonel Henry Beecher wrote, "There is a common belief that wounds are inevitably associated with pain, that the more extensive the wound, the worse the pain." He found that this is not always true after he observed a strange phenomenon: Soldiers in battle can experience a terrible injury, such as a bullet wound or severed limb, and not feel any pain until much later.

Pain also has an emotional, affective component; that is, we don't consider it pain unless we experience it as unwanted and undesirable. The same sensation of someone pressing aggressively on your neck is interpreted differently if it's from an attacker or a massage therapist. As Beecher wrote, "There was no dependable relation between the extent of a pathological wound and the pain experienced. No significant difference was found between the pain of sudden injury and that of chronic illness. The intensity of suffering is largely determined by what the pain means to the patient."

The reason that soldiers can be injured but not feel pain is due to stress-induced analgesia. Basically, the brain is telling the spinal cord, "Don't bother me now, I have more important things to worry about—I'm just trying to keep us alive."

McGill University in Montreal, where I've spent much of my career, is one of the leading centers for the study of pain. As a native Californian, I attribute this to the punishingly cold winters there. (My Canadian colleagues, who seem to *like* the cold, were quick to point out that Siberia, Alaska, Mount Everest, and the Yukon are also very cold but produce no game-changing pain research.)

One of the big contributions to pain research was made by McGill researcher Ronald Melzack in the 1960s. We tend to think that our peripheral nerves tell us when we're in pain. We stub a toe or the knife slips while chopping an onion and we cut ourselves, and voilà—pain. But Melzack showed that it is the brain that decides whether we experience pain or not. His theory, along with the British physiologist Patrick Wall's, called the gate control theory of pain, accounts for a number of real life experiences.

In particular, Melzack showed that the brain can override everything going on in the spinal cord, increasing or decreasing the sensation of pain. If the brain is sensitized or on alert to expect pain, normal run-of-the-mill sensory inputs can end up being perceived by the brain as pain signals even though the spinal cord isn't sending any. This may be what chronic pain is: You've had some injury and it's been repaired, but just touching the region causes the feeling of pain. (This is called *allodynia*.)

The neuroscientific view is that pain is an emotional-motivational condition that tells you to either do something, like rubbing or licking a wound, or refrain from doing something, like putting your hand on a hot stove. But not all experiences that tell you to do something are perceived as pain. For example, *dysesthesia,* that pins-and-needles feeling you get when your foot's asleep, may make you want to jump up and wiggle or rub the offending limb, but that's not usually considered pain. *Paresthesia* is the general term that applies to any kind of abnormal skin sensation, including numbness, tingling, chilling, or heat sensations that are not painful. When they are uncomfortable, they are called dysesthesia.

What about gut-wrenching psychological suffering, such as you experience when your boyfriend or girlfriend leaves you—is that a kind of physical pain? We talk of a broken heart as pain, metaphorically. Yet mental anguish is related to pain. Grief, for example, can be felt quite physically, and stress or sadness can lead to migraines, fatigue, gastric upset, and so on. Because all pain is ultimately brain-based, there is no scientific reason to separate mental, emotional pain from physical pain.

There are also a number of aversive, unpleasant sensory experiences that are not pain, such as eating spoiled food, hearing dripping water while you're trying to sleep, or hearing fingernails scratching on a chalkboard. Disgusting, annoying, unpleasant, perhaps, but not the same as pain.

Ronald Melzack also advanced the way that we talk about and treat pain, when he introduced the McGill Pain Questionnaire. The next time you need to see your doctor for a pain, it would be helpful to think about your pain in these descriptive terms:

0 = No pain 1 = Mild 2 = Discomforting 3 = Distressing 4 = Horrible 5 = Excruciating

Temporal	**Spatial**	**Punctate Pressure**	**Incisive Pressure**	**Constructive Pressure**
Flickering	Jumping	Pricking	Sharp	Pinching
Quivering	Flashing	Boring	Cutting	Pressing
Pulsing	Shooting	Drilling	Lacerating	Gnawing
Throbbing		Stabbing		Cramping
Beating		Lancinating		Crushing
Pounding				
Brief				
Momentary				
Transient				
Rhythmic				
Periodic				
Intermittent				
Continuous				
Steady				
Constant				

Traction Pressure	**Thermal**	**Brightness**	**Dullness**	**Misc. Sensory**
Tugging	Hot	Tingling	Dull	Tender
Pulling	Burning	Itching	Sore	Taut
Wrenching	Scalding	Smarting	Hurting	Rasping
	Searing	Stinging	Aching	Splitting
			Heavy	

Tension	Autonomic	Fear	Punishment	Misc. Affective
Tiring	Sickening	Fearful	Punishing	Wretched
Exhaustive	Suffocating	Frightful	Grueling	Blinding
		Terrifying	Cruel	
			Vicious	
			Killing	

		Misc. words		
Spreading	Tight	Cool	Nagging	Annoying
Radiating	Numb	Cold	Nauseating	Troublesome
Penetrating	Drawing	Freezing	Agonizing	Miserable
Piercing	Squeezing		Dreadful	Intense
	Tearing		Torturing	Unbearable

Note that some of the words describe sensory events (*tingling, hot*), some describe "feelings" (*fearful, wretched*), and some are cognitive-evaluative (*annoying, nagging*). The distinctions between the sensory components of pain and the feeling-related components are reflected in two different pathways that the pain signal takes through the thalamic nuclei of the brain. From there, the signals that we experience as sensory go to the somatosensory cortex, a part of the brain that contains a kind of map of your body, with different parts of the body represented in different chunks of this cortex. This neurological map shows where in your brain the sensations from different parts of your body are represented. It should be noted that different parts of the body have different amounts of brain matter assigned to them, and the relative amounts of brain matter are not related to the size of the body part. For example, a large body part like the torso is assigned a much smaller chunk of the somatosensory cortex than the thumb. This is because our evolutionary ancestors needed to develop sensitive thumbs to feel for food and use tools, while the torso was just a container for a few internal organs. This is shown in the picture below, which was originally conceived by Wilder Penfield at McGill. You're looking at a side view of the brain, with all its folds, and the sizes of the related body parts are roughly proportional to how many neurons are used to represent sensations from them.

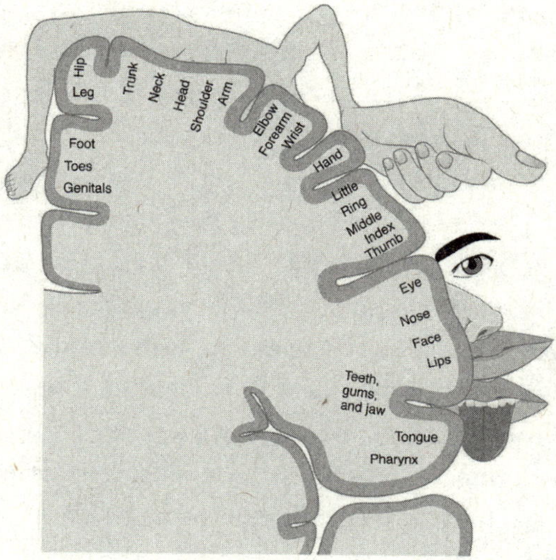

You may have noticed that you have lower resolution for distinguishing touch in different parts of your body. For instance, if you've been bitten by a mosquito near your elbow, you may feel an itch sensation but have trouble locating it, trouble knowing exactly where to scratch. This is because the number of neurons representing sensation in the elbow is relatively low, and so this area has lower sensation resolution than a bite on your face, which has a much greater number of neurons representing it.

The different types of pain in Melzack's chart—for example, stinging, burning, or aching—map to different brain regions. The pain signals that we experience as emotional (affective-motivational) travel from the thalamus to the anterior cingulate and the insula, parts of the limbic system. The pain signals we interpret cognitively are handled in different circuits of the frontal lobe, in conjunction with the limbic system. The somatosensory cortex tells you how much it hurts, where it hurts, and how long it's been hurting. The limbic system tells you how unpleasant it is and motivates you to do something about it. The cognitive system helps you to analyze, contextualize, and appraise the injury. A practical consequence of all this is that a lesion in the brain, such as due to stroke, could cause a deficit in one of these three pain systems but not the others, and we have seen patients develop indifference to pain (affective-emotional) while still noticing it (sensory) and being able to evaluate it (cognitive).

All these systems interact. For example, our perception of pain is altered through empathy—our pain sensitivity is increased when we observe a loved one in pain, compared to observing a stranger. This appears to be mediated by mirror neurons, specialized brain cells that allow us to mentally simulate the world of action. I think of them as our "monkey-see, monkey-do" neurons, because of the way they were discovered. One monkey, watching another peel a banana, started having neural activity in just the part of his brain that would move his hands to do the same thing, even though he wasn't physically making any movements at all—it was just his brain running a neural simulation. Similarly, when we see someone else get hurt, even from a scene in a movie, we wince as if we, too, are being harmed. The evolutionary basis for this may be to help us learn about aversive things without having to go through them ourselves.

Pain can have a negative effect on emotions and on cognitive function, putting us in a bad or impatient mood and impairing attention, memory, and decision making. In the other direction, a negative emotional state can lead to increased pain and a positive emotional state can reduce pain. Also, cognitive assessments of pain can increase or reduce it. The brain is wired in such a way that cognition, emotion, and pain can all interact with one another bidirectionally.

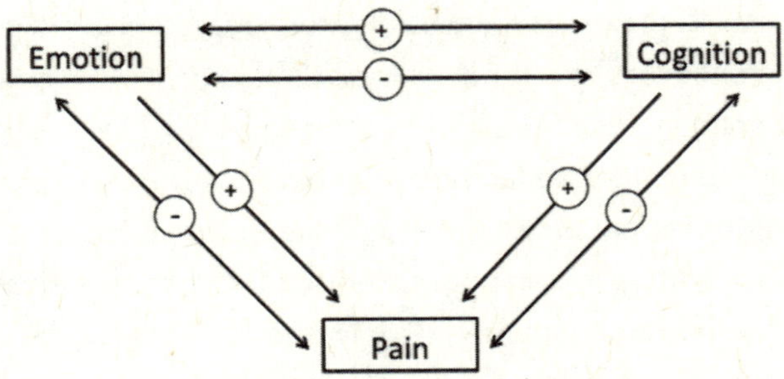

Minus signs indicate a negative effect, plus signs indicate a positive effect.

Catherine Bushnell at McGill and the National Institutes of Health has shown that cutaneous pain (on the skin, also called somatic pain) and visceral pain (internal organs—the viscera, also called epicritic pain) are experienced very differently. We tend to subjectively rate our visceral pain as being more unpleasant than our cutaneous pain. Neurologically measured, the pain intensity of a cut finger could equal that of a stomachache. But, subjectively, we would rate the stomachache as being more unpleasant. Having a dentist file or scrape your teeth may be grossly unpleasant, but it's not usually described as painful. A foot massage using acupressure or reflexology can be painful but pleasant in a weird way. So networks in our brains can separate pain from unpleasantness.

The distinction between cutaneous and visceral sensations, and between pain and unpleasantness, probably has an evolutionary origin. Sensory perception for the part of you interacting with the outside world has evolved to be very sensitive to where on your body an injury occurred. Interior pain doesn't usually require such precision. Accordingly, cutaneous pain is usually experienced as local and precise, and people are much better at discriminating different intensities of cutaneous pain. In contrast, visceral pain is more difficult to localize. Most of the nerve fibers that communicate between the internal organs and the brain are unmyelinated, and they are more sparsely distributed. This leads to a certain imprecision. For example, esophageal pain is often confused for heart trouble, and indigestion is often described as heartburn.

This evolutionary history has created distinct brain circuits for the two types of pain. Cutaneous pain activates the ventrolateral (underneath, and toward the sides) prefrontal cortex to a greater degree than visceral pain. Visceral pain in turn elicits greater activation from the somatosensory cortex, the part of the brain shown in the previous drawing, along with the anterior cingulate and the motor cortex. Why the motor cortex? The regions of the motor cortex that are activated by visceral pain control the face, tongue, and gag reflex. Researchers figured this out by inserting, and then inflating, a balloon inside the participants' esophagus. This simulated the kind of discomfort and pain experienced if we ingest harmful food or drink, and we need to prepare to close our mouths, spit out anything remaining, salivate to dilute what's left, and possibly regurgitate the harmful material. Hence the motor cortex activation of the face, tongue, and gag reflex.

The words we use to describe these two sources of pain, and the way they feel to us, are very different. We use more precise words for describing cutaneous pain and are very specific about it. Because visceral pain is not as well localized, when describing it we gesture or point. We describe it as dull or throbbing. Often we're not sure where it's coming from. Patients use more words overall, and more emotional words, to describe visceral pain.

You may remember from the previous chapter that the hallucinogenic drug ketamine can reduce social anxiety, a condition that is influenced by glutamate levels in the brain. Administration of ketamine to people in pain has differential effects on cutaneous and visceral pain, with minimal side effects. For visceral pain, ketamine reduces both pain and unpleasantness. For cutaneous pain, ketamine reduces only unpleasantness. And really, this is what anxiety is: a feeling of unpleasantness and the apprehension that it will continue in the future.

The differences in the experience of these two types of pain is especially important for older adults, and for treatment options. Older adults are more likely to experience visceral pain than younger adults, due to aging of internal organs and the systems that support them. Reductions in the effectiveness of kidneys, liver, lungs, heart, digestive tract, and gallbladder can all cause significant pain, and the coming years hold the promise of increasingly differentiated therapies for these internal pains.

The anticipation of pain lights up many of the same neural regions as actual pain, regions that are important for pain sensation, pain affect, pain modulation, and pain-associated anxiety. Similarly, the sensory cortex and the anterior cingulate are activated both during tickling and during the anticipation of tickling. (Tickling is very interesting from an evolutionary standpoint. In effect it is a simulated false threat—someone touching you in a place that is vulnerable [e.g., belly, neck]. This is why tickling only "works" if it is someone you trust doing the tickling—otherwise it is aversive. Nonhuman primates love tickles as much as human infants, and a dog's joy having a belly rub is probably related to this.)

Why We Have Pain

The most obvious reason we have pain is that for thousands of years it has given us a survival advantage—it causes us to protect that part of our bodies that has been injured, giving it a better chance to heal. The layer of skin that stretches over our bodies from the tips of our toes up to the tops of our heads serves to hold in vital fluids and organs that might otherwise come in contact with harmful things in the environment. When that skin barrier is breached, we need to know. Similarly, we have pain sensors inside our bodies to signal when something is going wrong—a stomachache, for example, after eating bad food, that discourages us from eating that food again. Pain serves as an essential warning signal.

Just consider what life is like for people with the disorder HSAD (hereditary sensory autonomic neuropathy, also called congenital insensitivity to pain, or CIPA), who don't feel any pain. Although rare (there are only fifty-six reported cases in the world), the disorder entered popular culture when Stieg Larsson wrote about it in the trilogy beginning with *The Girl with the Dragon Tattoo,* giving it to the character Ronald Niedermann. (It was also featured in an episode of the television drama *Grey's Anatomy,* and in *House,* in which a sixteen-year-old patient, Hannah, has it.) In reality, toddlers with HSAD/CIPA have trouble becoming toilet trained because they are unable to recognize the feelings associated with going to the bathroom. As children they may fall and break bones or cut themselves, or bite their cheek without knowing it. Many bite off the tip of their tongue while chewing. They may not sense that food is too hot and burn their mouth or esophagus. Foreign objects in their eyes go undetected and lead to infections and corneal damage. In one particularly horrific case, a six-month-old bit off the tips of his fingers and his thumb. Without pain perception, children with HSAD develop intractable bedsores because there is no motivation to shift positions as they sleep. The life expectancy of such people is short, around twelve years—they tend to die of hypothermia and complications from multiple bone fractures and infected sores. Twenty percent of people with this disorder die before age three, and it is uncommon to find patients over twenty-five years old. In a cruel trick of nature, they still feel emotional pain, however, just like anyone else.

One type of HSAD is caused by a random mutation in the *SCN9A* gene, which provides instructions for making sodium channels in the brain and is on the long arm of chromosome 2. Sodium channels allow positively charged sodium ions to be transported into neuronal cells, where they play a key role in the neuron's ability to transmit signals. The *SCN9A* gene encodes for one subpart of a sodium channel called NaV1.7, which governs the functioning of pain receptors in the peripheral nervous system. The reason this disorder doesn't cause a complete and total breakdown of cell signaling is that NaV1.7 isn't the only sodium channel—our physiology abounds with these kinds of redundancies, back-up systems, developed through evolution, to enhance our chance of survival.

Another type of HSAD leaves patients with an ability to feel pain, but they are entirely indifferent to it. That is, an injury that we might experience as painful isn't accompanied for them by any negative emotions, and so they have no motivation to alter their behavior.

For the rest of us, our reaction to pain typically follows a sequence: escape the painful stimulus, limit further damage (often accomplished by the site of injury becoming sensitive), seek safety and relief, and allow time for healing. So, we know why we have pain, but why does it have to be so darn unpleasant and make us so miserable? The short answer is because that unpleasantness is what motivates us to do something about the source of the pain, to learn from mistakes, to go to the doctor, to stop putting pressure on that compressed joint, to alter the repetitive movement patterns that are grinding down the cartilage in one of our hips, to rest and take it easy.

While acute, short-term pain has survival value, what about chronic pain? Chronic, disabling backaches or arthritis can last for years, even for the rest of one's life, and are not easily treated or cured. It doesn't function as a warning because there's nothing you can do about it. What could be the biological benefit of *that*? We don't know. It is one of several still-unsolved mysteries in neuroscience.

A recent study of squid and its natural predator, the black sea bass, puts us closer to an answer. Neurobiologist Robyn Crook and her colleagues wondered if in addition to the protective effects of pain, the purpose of chronic pain might also be to produce a kind of sensitization, and hypervigilance, to predators. Squid are good for this sort of study because their defensive behaviors are easy to track—they either change color (to match their environment) or squirt ink. Squid have eight arms and two tentacles. The researchers applied a minor injury to one of the arms by cutting off the tip of it. It was enough to cause pain (science can be brutal) but it didn't impair the squids' ability to swim and maneuver. They then put a group of these injured squid in a tank with some hungry black sea bass and put other, uninjured squid in a different tank with some other hungry black sea bass.

"The injured squid were really touchy," said Crook. "They responded more strongly to visual stimuli than normal squid. So an encounter that a normal squid might just want to keep an eye on caused the injured squid to start up their defense mechanisms." These injured squid paid far more attention to subtle visual cues from the black sea bass. That is, the injury made their sensory systems hypervigilant, just as Crook had hypothesized. As a control condition, the researchers anesthetized a separate group of squid before snipping the tip of one arm; these squid did not experience traumatic pain. Like the group of uninjured squid, these guys were not hypervigilant in the presence of black sea bass.

Interestingly, although the researchers couldn't discern which squid had been injured and which hadn't just by looking at their mobility and activity, the hungry fish could—they were much more likely to hunt an injured squid than a noninjured squid, regardless of whether the squid had been anesthetized or not. In this case, the experience of pain meant the difference between squid life and squid death. (Memo to squid: avoid scientists.) So although squid evolved a set of behaviors to make them more vigilant when injured, the black sea bass evolved an ability to detect squid injuries, even when squid don't know they have them and aren't feeling pain. Evolution is an arms race. (Or a tentacle race.)

What about the human experience of chronic pain? We know that humans in pain can be more attentive to their external environment, just like the squid. Think about it: If you've just been injured, it strongly suggests that the environment you're in isn't as safe as you thought it was. Cranking up sensory vigilance seems like a good idea. Any biological mechanism that is as prevalent as chronic pain probably served an important function in our ancestors, which is why it has persisted through millions of years of evolution.

The Culture, Genes, and Cognition of Pain

We don't all experience pain the same way. Pain is influenced by cultural, environmental, historical, and cognitive factors. Our culture defines what is acceptable and taboo in how we deal with pain. There are distinctive variations in how people of different ethnicities experience and communicate pain, and what their expectations are. Many cultural rituals involve what you or I might consider pain but the participants don't. Piercings, tattoos, and ornamental surgical procedures that outsiders would consider mutilation are not typically regarded as being in the same sensory-emotional category as arthritis or migraine. In many cultures, soldiers, warriors, and hunters who have survived a painful ordeal are admired.

Also the microculture of the family influences how we, as children, learn to think about, experience, and cope with pain. Parents may encourage a more stoic view (suck it up and tough it out) or a more medicalized view (wow, you seem much better after that pill and that little bit of rest). This stoicism versus medicalizing is influenced by the culture both within a family and the culture of communities. In the emergency room, medical personnel will typically ask a patient to describe their pain on a scale of one to ten, with one being no pain and ten being the worst pain imaginable. Emergency room doctors are trained to be alert to the fact that some patients will say, "Eight," and yet the doctors don't need to act right away, because as a generalization, people from some cultures tend to ascribe high numbers to relatively moderate pain levels and to make public displays of their discomfort. On the other hand, if members of other cultures report that their pain level is a "four" doctors might rush to prep the operating room because members of that group are known to be highly reserved in their public displays of pain.

The cultural backdrop in which we experience pain is one of the factors that contribute to the psychology of pain and to the attribution of that pain. The way people are injured influences their neuropsychological state, which in turn affects the way they recover. Soldiers who were shot might see their injuries as heroic and part of a noble cause. Convenience store clerks who were shot might have no such positive framing—they might see themselves as victims. The store clerks would be more likely to suffer from depression and far more likely to become addicted to opioids. Context matters. As psychological scientist Steven Linton says, "I have personally witnessed a man stick a rusty nail through his arm without the slightest complaint or flinch, while as a child I experienced a simple injection as excruciating."

For more evidence that pain is heavily influenced by psychological factors, you need look no further than the enormous success of placebos, which are nearly as successful as actual drugs. In one pain study, a placebo was effective in 35 percent of patients, and opioids in only 36 percent. Another study (funded by pharmaceutical company Eli Lilly) found that for patients with chronic knee osteoarthritis, placebo worked in 47 percent of patients—the same number that responded to Eli Lilly's Cymbalta, a nerve pain medication that is also used as an antidepressant and antianxiety drug. There are even placebo effects in acupuncture, where sham needling at nonacupuncture insertion points is as effective as actual acupuncture, with effects lasting up to one year.

Taking a placebo—an inert pill or procedure that you are unaware is inert—releases the brain's natural painkillers, endogenous opioids. One of the ways we know this is that administering naloxone, a drug that blocks the receptors for opioids, undoes the placebo effect. Neuroimaging shows that the pain-relieving aspects of placebos are recruiting brain circuits in the anterior cingulate, nucleus accumbens, and middle frontal gyrus—the same regions that generate our endogenous opioids.

There are also genetic factors to pain perception, apart from the inherited insensitivity (or indifference) to pain. Genes are complex, and a given gene can influence the development of quite different attributes or phenotypes. For decades, medical personnel noted that people with red hair were harder to anesthetize. This was well-known and even taught in medical schools, but no one could figure out why. Surely redheadedness wasn't a culture, like being from Japan or being Hindu. Who would have thought that the gene that confers red hair also yields radical increases in pain sensitivity? But it does. This was discovered by Jeffrey Mogil at McGill University, and it might, someday soon, lead to a separate line of analgesics on your drugstore shelf with the label *Specially Formulated for Redheads*. Geneticists such as Mogil don't think that having red hair causes increased pain sensitivity any more than that increased pain sensitivity causes red hair. It's just that the same DNA sequence affects both traits for reasons we don't yet understand, or just by chance. And we may never understand it. With only twenty thousand genes or so and a near-infinite number of traits, it *must* be the case that individual genes do a great many unrelated things and that a single gene usually cannot be considered a sole or deterministic cause.

As we've seen, the amount of pain we experience is related to our upbringing—family models and culture as they interact with the other two parts of the developmental triad, genes and opportunity. By opportunity I mean the particular circumstances that you're exposed to. If you grew up in an environment in which someone experienced a debilitating accident or disease, or with friends and family members coming back from military conflicts with injuries, your environment exposed you to how people in your family or culture react to pain and injury. On the other hand, if you grew up in a family with no aches and pains, you didn't have this exposure.

Another factor is that your genetic makeup can predispose you to being clumsy or fumble-fingered or to have poor balance, in which case you're more apt to experience injury. Or your genome can predispose you to having unusual pain sensitivity, such as the redheads mentioned earlier. A striking finding shows that the chemicals the body produces in response to stress and pain can be passed to infants through mother's milk, affecting the infants' own lifelong responses, even when the nursing mother is not the biological mother.

There are temporal factors to pain perception as well, and like the red hair–to–pain sensitivity link, they are counterintuitive. You would be perfectly reasonable, for example, to assume that people would rather have pain last for a shorter time period than a longer time period. Consider two different situations. (1) Pain stays constant at a level of eight (on some scale) for thirty minutes. We can graph it this way (the figure on the left). (2) Pain is constant at a level of eight for thirty minutes and then is reduced to a level of three for another twenty-five minutes (the figure on the right).

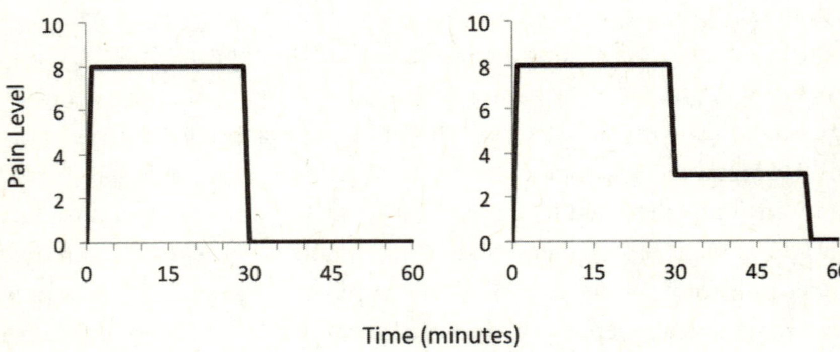

Clearly scenario 2 should be more aversive—you're experiencing pain for fifty-five minutes rather than thirty, and moreover, you're experiencing all the pain of scenario 1 and *then some.* (If you enjoy math, you could use integral calculus or plane geometry to calculate the total amount of pain experienced in each case and conclude that scenario 1 yields a total pain-time index of just under 240 and scenario 2 yields a total pain-time index of 315.) But research by Nobel Prize–winning psychologist Daniel Kahneman shows this isn't the way we react at all. When they undergo these procedures, most people rate scenario number 2 as less painful than scenario 1 and would be more likely to recommend the procedure to a friend or undergo it again themselves. This is not because all the people Kahneman studied were masochists! It's because of the nature of human memory. More pain is preferred to less pain when the most recent experience of it is lower. Rather than evaluating the total amount of time we've been in pain, the brain selectively remembers only the end of a painful episode. The duration of pain plays a very small role in our overall assessment of the pain; our discomfort is dominated by the worst and the final moments of the episode. The practical implications for this are that pain can perhaps become bearable if we can have periods of relative respite from it. A concern in medicine is that the amount of highly addictive opioids necessary to completely relieve terrible pain leads to a host of other medical problems. Perhaps alternating periods of light doses and heavier doses of such medications will prove to be more effective over the long term.

What Can We Do about It?

A central goal of modern medical practice and research is to relieve pain. Although medical science has advanced enormously in the past few decades, there have been few advances in pain technology. Opioids are still the most reliable and effective way of reducing pain, but as the recent North American opioid epidemic has revealed, pharmaceutical opioids are highly addictive and overdoses can too easily occur. Under carefully controlled conditions they may be safe, but these conditions are too often not met. Multiple pain pathways are involved in pain processing. This redundancy is important to the warning system and survival-enhancing roles of pain. But this very redundancy is one of the reasons that pain is so difficult to treat.

For inflammatory pain, such as insect bites, arthritis, sprains, and some headaches, anti-inflammatory drugs can work well. In order to increase tolerability of long-term use of anti-inflammatories in older patients, there has been a movement over the last decade to switch from oral to topical analgesics, particularly nonsteroidal anti-inflammatory agents (NSAIDs). But they remain underutilized, as physicians fall into the habit of prescribing the same things over and over again.

Fifty percent of modern NSAID prescriptions are for osteoarthritis, the most common form of arthritis, and the most prevalent pain condition in the United States, affecting around 30 million people. The most used NSAID worldwide is diclofenac and it is available as a pill, a gel, a cream, and a patch; it is currently the most effective treatment for osteoarthritis, with nearly 100 percent of patients reporting at least moderate relief from arthritic pain. The availability of a diclofenac patch has signaled a new promise for patients. The gels and creams are meant only to be absorbed by the skin, and after an hour or two, there is no more to be absorbed. The oral version of diclofenac is responsible for serious gastrointestinal problems, including stomach bleeding, in 30 percent of patients over the age of sixty, whereas the patch is associated with none. I've found the gel version to be very effective for insect bites.

Acetaminophen (aka Tylenol) has been found to be the *least* effective for arthritis, but that makes sense—it is not an anti-inflammatory and is not interchangeable with, for example, ibuprofen (e.g., Advil and Motrin). Acetaminophen is a pain reliever and reduces fever. If you have a swollen ankle, it probably won't help as much as an anti-inflammatory.

Glucosamine is commonly taken by older adults for arthritis, but the scientific results are actually inconclusive. In the United States it is considered a "dietary supplement," not a drug, and so its manufacture and use are not regulated, and it is illegal to advertise it for medical conditions. As with many supplements, its popularity is based on unsubstantiated claims infused with a lot of technical jibber-jabber that only superficially resembles scientific language and is carefully designed to persuade naive consumers. Glucosamine is a natural compound found in cartilage—the tissue that cushions joints. Some cases of osteoarthritis involve a breakdown of cartilage, so why not take cartilage in a pill? Well, there is no evidence that ingesting glucosamine actually affects its levels in joints. It might, or it might not. It's sort of like saying that if you have liver disease, you should just eat a lot of calf's liver and it will restore your own. The body doesn't work like that. Nevertheless, aggressive advertising and claims surrounding glucosamine have made it a $15-billion industry in the United States alone.

There is some early evidence that yoga can bring real and lasting pain relief. Yoga practice enlarges the insula, giving patients greater ability to tolerate pain. Mild exercise can reduce pain too—as Jeffrey Mogil says, "Exercise is the best analgesic we know of by a wide margin. The problem is that when you're in pain it hurts to exercise. But if you can get past that, it really helps."

Neuropathy affects nearly 8 percent of older adults and is among the most common complications of type 2, adult-onset diabetes. Neuropathy is kind of a catchall term for conditions in which the nerves that carry messages from the body to the brain and spinal cord are damaged—this includes nerves on the skin as well as inside the body organs and viscera. You may hear the term *peripheral neuropathy,* referring to damage to the peripheral nervous system, but it is just a fancy way of saying neuropathy. The only other nervous system is the one in your brain and spinal cord, and that's called the central nervous system. *Central neuropathy* is caused by a lesion, injury, or other damage to the brain or spinal cord. It includes things like multiple sclerosis, Parkinson's disease, and cerebral palsy.

Peripheral neuropathy is often effectively treated by amitriptyline, duloxetine, and the gabapentinoids, and some people have success with topical NSAIDs. Central neuropathy requires a different approach. If it is caused by lesions to the brain or spinal cord, surgeries are often performed, but there is no evidence such surgeries are effective. Analgesics and opioids are not typically successful for central neuropathy, but antidepressants and anticonvulsants have had some limited success, although the reason they work is not well understood.

Remember our friend neurokinin, mentioned in the context of social isolation in the previous chapter? A related neurochemical, called substance P (for *pain*), is found in sensory nerves and in the brain and is believed to be responsible for pain and inflammation. If you're thinking that blocking substance P could relieve pain, you're not alone—this was an active area of research for twenty years, until a number of clinical trials failed in 1999. The problem turned out to be that substance P also does many helpful and necessary things, such as regulating mood, anxiety, and stress, the growth of new neurons, wound healing, and the growth of new cells, so blocking it can be worse than doing nothing.

Another issue that starts to crop up in old age is pain hypersensitivity, or hyperalgesia. The skin is an organ. Pain in one part of the skin can cause pain sensitivity in another, uninjured part of the skin. Or all over the skin—part of the hypervigilance reaction we learned about from the poor squid. Imagine that you've got a nasty spider bite on your leg. It itches like crazy. So you apply Benadryl cream or cortisone cream, which eases the pain. But later, your arm starts to itch for no apparent reason. Or your back. Sensory-pain receptors in the skin (they're called nociceptors) become activated from pain or itch in one site, and—because they're all part of the same organ and are communicating electrochemically with one another—the activation spreads. Paradoxically, the chronic use of opioids to reduce pain can cause hypersensitivity. Allodynia can occur, in which you experience a painful response to something that is ordinarily not painful, such as a light touch.

Much pain comes about from nerves in the neck or spinal cord being pinched. That old neck injury from when you were in your twenties can come back to haunt you in your sixties in the form of aches and pains. There's one particularly insidious ailment that I'll mention because it is often undiagnosed and untreated, and because it sounds both comic and tragic. Picture that part of your back, between your shoulder blades, that is just out of reach. Now imagine that you get an itch there. You can't scratch it easily because, well, it's out of reach. If you manage to rub against a tree like a grizzly bear, or get one of those bamboo back-scratching tools, or a good friend to scratch it for you, you get some relief. The itch doesn't go away after several months. You try every anti-itch agent and cream you can think of, and they don't help. You try lidocaine patches, which numb the skin, but the spot continues to itch, and now, because the skin is numb, scratching provides no relief. At some point, hypersensitivity kicks in and even normally pleasurable touch experiences, like getting a back rub, having your back scratched, or holding hands with a loved one become uncomfortable. This is not a made-up disease—it is called notalgia paresthetica. It is maddening. There is no known cure; however, some patients have reported success with anti-inflammatory gels, such as diclofenac (mentioned earlier for osteoarthritis).

One case report shows some relief from notalgia paresthetica through exercise. The patient tended to work at a computer all day with her shoulders rounded and facing inward. This protracted and elevated her scapulae and flexed her head and spine, causing her spinal nerve angles to become more severe. Through exercise, she strengthened her rhomboids and latissimus dorsi muscles and stretched the pectoral muscles. This changed her posture and she experienced a decreased sensation of itch, although not 100 percent relief.

Coping Strategies

If we can manage not to think about a particular pain, it tends to bother us less; distraction is one of the most effective ways to alleviate pain. The brain is bombarded with millions of input stimulus packets every hour and we pay attention to only a small proportion of them—if we could structure things so that pain was not at the forefront of our attentional systems, we'd be more comfortable.

People who are in enriched environments—with lots of things to see, listen to, and do—experience less pain than those in simpler environments, and this sort of distraction diminshes pain signals in the insula and primary sensory cortex. Effective distraction while in pain includes exercise, hobbies, interesting conversation, practicing yoga, meditation, socializing, listening to soothing music, or immersing yourself in nature. Even when the distracting activity is forced on an individual in pain, it leads to a reduction in pain and an increase in the body's production of its own organic opioid analgesics.

The more interesting experiences we can have in the external world, the less time we focus on our internal world, which is where pain resides. Steven Linton describes the role of an enriched environment with his grandmother, which yielded an 80 percent reduction in her pain.

> My grandmother at one time lived in a sterile, gray housing unit with little to do during the day but stare at the walls. . . . Upon visiting her in the evening, she had a long list of pain-related complaints that could take between thirty to sixty minutes to describe. Fortunately she was able to move to a housing unit for the elderly where there were other people to visit with, planned social activities, and regular visits by personnel. . . . There were significantly more things happening to divert her attention to the external world. While my grandmother still had pain complaints, I was impressed that they were far fewer and took no more than five or ten minutes to describe.

Separate from distraction, if we are in a good mood, pain is less likely to get us down. If we are already in a bad mood, a bit of pain is all it takes to put us in a worse mood. Remember also that memory is mood-state dependent. If you're in a bad mood, you tend to have easier access to memories of other times you were in a bad mood or were sad, or times when things didn't go right, and it's easy to fall into a despondency cycle of "this pain is just going to get worse and worse . . . this always happens to me." If you're in a good mood, your mind tends to recall happy events, and you predict a more positive future. This good mood can lead to a virtuous cycle in which the positive-mood neurochemicals help with healing and you do actually get better more quickly. This is why mood-enhancing drugs, such as SSRIs, are often prescribed to patients in pain.

Psychological factors play a major role in pain, as mentioned previously. If you're hiking or working out and your muscles start to ache, your brain may encode this as a good thing—it means you're getting exercise and building up your muscles. That kind of framing shifts your understanding of the pain and distracts you from the discomfort, unlike, for example, getting a bee sting or having a rock in your shoe.

One common coping style is prayer or meditation. Some people pray for recovery and release from the pain, and in some forms of praying, they put responsibility for the pain in the hands of a higher power. Other fans of prayer give thanks for the opportunity to "show what they're made of." That is, if they attribute the pain they're experiencing to a test of their resolve, or an opportunity to draw on their spiritual strength, it can transform their subjective reactions to it into a positive challenge—possibly activating a completely different part of the brain.

Special Problems in Treating Pain in Old Age

Chronic Pain

Patients tend to react to short-term (acute) pain differently than they do to long-term (chronic) pain. With short-term pain, we think we can treat it with medication. We might also curtail our activities and seek help from others.

Chronic pain is much more difficult to treat. Patients with chronic pain often report that a stimulus that should seem innocuous is painful. This lowering of the general pain threshold, or increased sensitivity, occurs in many patients with chronic pain disorders, including irritable bowel syndrome, back pain, and fibromyalgia. Their brain scans show abnormal activation patterns in brain regions involved in pain regulation, especially the anterior cingulate. Structural brain changes have been observed in people with chronic pain, including loss of gray-matter and white-matter volume, not just in the anterior cingulate (which is part of the pain circuit), but also in the dorsolateral prefrontal cortex, the region of the brain responsible for decision making, working memory, cognitive flexibility, planning, inhibition, and abstract reasoning. Neurochemical systems are affected as well, including reductions in dopamine production, opioid receptor binding, and modulation of the GABA and glutamate systems. If you've ever been in pain and felt you weren't thinking clearly, these are the reasons why.

One piece of bright news in pain research in the last year is the availability of the new migraine drugs Aimovig, Emgality, and Ajovy. We still aren't sure what causes migraines, but these drugs have been life changing for migraine sufferers—they only have to be administered once a month and they act as a preventative.

On the horizon, the next biggest development is that tanezumab (who names these things?) might gain FDA approval soon; it's an antibody against nerve growth factor that treats pain and is effective against bone cancer pain, arthritis, and chronic low back pain. In phase 2 clinical trials, tanezumab was effective, but a side effect showed up: Joints began to degenerate more quickly, and so the FDA suspended further testing. Pfizer, one of the developers of the drug, looked very closely at the data and concluded that the joint degeneration was due to an interaction with the NSAIDs that people were taking at the same time. In theory, Pfizer said, if patients take only tanezumab there shouldn't be a problem. The FDA was convinced, and so they lifted the hold on further testing. Jeffrey Mogil observes, "The original Phase 2 study was actually the most impressive clinical trial data I'd ever seen. In the Phase 2 the drug was beating placebo by 40 points out of 100, which is absolutely unheard of because you can get FDA approval with 10 points. And now in the larger Phase 3 trials it's looking more like it's beating placebo by the usual 10–15. It seems to be reliably doing that. Beating placebo by 15 points doesn't sound like much, but for a subset of the population, that ends up being a big deal."

Untreated, chronic pain disrupts sleep patterns, which in turn can cause profound deficits in memory and mood. Societal attitudes about pain in older people are often at fault. Health-care providers assume (without evidence) that pain is "just a normal part of aging." Older patients often don't report pain because they are afraid of their doctors' dismissive responses, or due to the false belief that "good" patients don't complain. You don't have to be that sort of patient. It's okay to speak up.

Polypharmacy

One of the things that's important to speak up about is the drugs and supplements you're taking. The average number of prescription medications taken by older adults often exceeds ten. This situation is called polypharmacy. It results from doctors wanting to please patients by writing a quick prescription that might address a single symptom—then doing it over and over and over again. This poses huge problems, creating very complex drug interaction effects. From a scientific standpoint, we have lots of data on how drugs interact pairwise, because studies of two drugs administered at the same time are easy to do. But it's woefully difficult and impractical to study every possible interaction among a combination of ten drugs. So we simply don't have data on these complex interactions. Some drugs mask or neutralize the effects of other drugs; some drugs are dangerously incompatible with others; side effects can multiply quickly. Some drugs are contraindicated for various conditions that affect the elderly disproportionately, such as heart and circulatory problems, or organ deterioration.

As just one example, the natural course of aging can lead to decreased gastric secretions. Meanwhile the loss of vitamin D receptors leads to loss of appetite, which in turn can lead to malnutrition and decreased bone density. Drugs with the side effect of decreasing appetite are compounding an existing problem. The natural course of aging can also lead to increased thickening and rigidity of the arteries, which increases cardiovascular risk. Decreased elasticity in the lungs makes us susceptible to pulmonary disorders. Changes in the kidneys compromise filtration, increasing the body's accumulation of toxic materials. The digestive system functions less efficiently, leading to chronic constipation. Any drug with a side effect that amplifies or exacerbates these preexisting conditions can cause patients a nightmare of discomfort.

Often, these different, powerful medications have been prescribed by different doctors with no single doctor "in charge." The side effects of polypharmacy can create conditions in which you *think* that you have a disease but don't, and moreover, some drugs and drug interactions can mask early signs of illness. To add to all of this, polypharmacy persists because few doctors want to take somebody off of a drug they've been on for fear of something bad happening that they'd be blamed for. So they just keep on adding drugs without ever reevaluating the big picture.

It turns out that the primary cause of confusion, disorientation, and delirium among older adults is not Alzheimer's disease—it's adverse effects from medications or from drug interactions. There are a number of cases of older adults being shunted off to an old age home not because they have become mentally incapacitated, as well-intentioned family and friends might think, but because of polypharmaceutical complications.

An important part of successful aging is for each of us to take responsibility for our own health care by informing our doctors and pharmacists of all the different things we're taking—including over-the-counter remedies (which are often as powerful and as subject to complex interactions as prescription drugs). That's just the conscientious thing to do.

PART TWO

THE CHOICES WE MAKE

Part One presents the scientific background that motivates taking an entirely new approach to aging. This approach, combining the science of individual differences and developmental neuroscience, emphasizes strengths and compensatory mechanisms rather than the loss of abilities. We've seen how things work, from personality and intelligence to the experience of emotions and pain. In Part Two we'll look at a few specific behaviors that we can modify so that aging is as enjoyable as it can be—perhaps becoming the *best* part of your life. The modifications are not all that difficult to implement.

Ultimately, we all die. The question is, What do we want those final years to look like? In some cases, we see older adults whose minds are decaying and who live for years without being engaged in life, without an awareness of where they are, while their hearts, lungs, kidneys, and livers continue chugging along. One of my aunts, my mother's older sister, is like that—as I write this, she is ninety-two and no one has had a meaningful conversation with her in fifteen years. She's alive, her organ systems are functioning properly, but she has none of the joys or awareness that we associate with "having a life." She is firmly in the disease span part of her life, not the health span.

In other cases, older adults with active minds begin to see their *bodies* decay, and it feels like having a rug pulled out from under them. Yet this is the scenario many would prefer. In either case, your body is going to go at some point. It will fail and the big light will go out. The question is, Will your mind be intact at that moment, or will you have been consigned to the dreary mental life of my aunt?

One factor that has received relatively little attention in the popular press is the chronobiology of health, the set of internal clocks that regulate the various cycles of attention, energy, restoration, and repair that our brains and bodies go through. That's where we'll begin. The normal and synchronized functioning of these clocks plays a greater critical role in health and disease, alertness and dementia, than has been previously recognized. When they are not functioning properly, neurons degenerate; cell metabolism is compromised; the body's normal systems of cellular repair and the daily repair of DNA damage are disrupted. Faulty or misaligned internal clocks are significant contributing factors in Alzheimer's disease, Parkinson's disease, and Huntington's disease, and in depression, obesity, diabetes, heart disease, and cancer. With that as a foundation, we'll visit important practical things you can do to make the most out of three basic biological processes: diet, movement, and sleep.

8

THE INTERNAL CLOCK

It's two A.M. Why am I hungry?

Have you ever woken in the middle of the night and found yourself ravenously hungry? Or maybe you've felt hyperactive just before bedtime. Maybe you fell asleep at an inappropriate time, while at a meeting or a concert (perhaps even while reading a book about aging and the brain). If you've experienced any of these, you've experienced a deregulation of your circadian rhythms. The word *circadian* was coined by scientists in the 1950s, from the Latin words *circa* (approximately) and *diem* (day): a rhythm that operates on a cycle of around 24 hours.

Circadian rhythms are the product of biological clocks, an evolutionary adaptation in response to the earth's twenty-four-hour rotation period. They allow our bodies and minds to predict what will come next, so as to be better prepared for different situations and circumstances. For example, predicting when the sun will rise allows the brain to release wake-up chemicals (such as orexin, dopamine, and norepinephrine) and to suppress the drowsiness chemicals (such as melatonin, adenosine, and GABA) that might make us want to roll over and go back to sleep. The inner clock lets us wake up in the morning refreshed and ready to go.

Biological clocks evolved early in evolutionary history, when most cells were light-sensitive. Ultimately, these light-sensitive cells became embedded in plants, fungi, bacteria, and all multicellular animals. Clocks have also been found in a bread mold, *Neurospora crassa,* where they release spores at the appropriate time of day when spore-bearing moisture in the air is at its peak. Clocks have also been discovered in the eye of the aplysia, a marine snail (or sea slug), whose ancestors diverged from ours 500 million years ago. The aplysia's clocks modulate its memory and locomotor activity in synchrony with light-dark cycles. The clocks are wired into the genes. And across hundreds of millions of years of evolution, similar genes have been found to control cellular clocks in all these organisms, from bacteria, plants, and fruit flies to fish, birds, mammals, and humans. In the aplysia, scientists have found genes that are remarkably similar to those in humans, including those related to Parkinson's and Alzheimer's disease.

Plants use photosensitive internal cellular clocks to detect the length of days. When they sense the shorter days of autumn, the clocks activate genes that signal the plant to produce seeds and drop its leaves. When the clocks sense longer days in the spring, the plants grow back their leaves, along with flowers or fruit. Biological clocks help plants prepare for sunrise by raising their leaves, tilting them toward the sun, and preparing their internal factories to perform photosynthesis, converting sunlight into nutrients. At night, clocks orchestrate the opening and closing of leaf pores and the nighttime folding of leaves to prevent water loss. If the clocks are regulating plants, mold, and mollusks, you can imagine the complexity of the various roles they play in our functioning. They also exert a large influence on aging—so much so that when tissue from the biological clocks of young animals has been transplanted into older animals, the older animals live longer.

The Master Clock

In mammals, circadian rhythms rely on three separate processes:

1. an input system that takes in information from the environment, consisting of cues such as light-dark cycles and food consumption that are received via peripheral oscillators;
2. a central, master oscillator, or clock, that keeps track of the time of the input events and can generate a consistent rhythmic signal; and
3. output pathways that allow the master clock to influence and synchronize the various peripheral oscillators that govern physiological operations, such as digestion, sleep-wake cycles, core body temperature, hunger, and alertness.

Thus, circadian rhythms are hierarchically organized, and different parts of the clock system communicate and modify one another, using feedback and feed-forward loops. All cells in the brain and body are sensitive to time of day, and genes (such as *PER1, BMAL1, CLK1, DBT,* and most famously, *CLOCK*) activate proteins according to a more or less twenty-four-hour cycle. I say more or less because these cells function like a cheap watch—they tend to drift, to speed up and slow down. To regulate them, we evolved a master clock. In humans, this is located within the hypothalamus, in a structure called the suprachiasmatic nucleus, or SCN, a group of about twenty thousand neurons that oscillate according to an almost twenty-four-hour rhythm. The starting time or phase of that rhythm can be reset by input from light and other time givers (called zeitgebers, the German translation for the phrase *time givers*).

The SCN is like the stationmaster at a busy railroad station, keeping all the trains on schedule so that they don't run into one another, and so that people who need to get somewhere get there on time. It's less like the atomic clocks that governments set their official times to, because atomic clocks function with little or no outside interference. Our SCN, on the other hand, is sensitive to inputs from the retina and from additional photosensitive cells on the skin to distinguish daytime from nighttime. It also takes input from various metabolic processes. The SCN communicates time-of-day information to various brain regions and to peripheral organs including the heart, lungs, liver, and endocrine glands. Tissues in the liver and pancreas regulate metabolic rhythms for stable glucose levels, lipid metabolism, and the removal of foreign compounds from the body and blood (xenobiotic detoxification). So, for example, when we eat and digestive juices are released, the SCN finds out about it and uses that information to regulate digestive cycles.

The developmental science approach seeks to understand the interaction between genes, culture, and opportunity. Biological clocks are a fascinating example of this. They function by taking input from the environment—primarily light, but also your eating schedule and your own activity cycle, which are influenced by culture. Light, whether it arrives from the rising sun or that little blue light on your cell phone charger, can turn particular genes on and off, changing the timing of when they produce the proteins that influence the biological clock and our circadian rhythms. Daylight or lack of it can speed up or slow down the circadian rhythms.

All of this interacts with your own aging process in a variety of ways. Here's just one example. Light—and blue light in particular—is necessary to program the biological clock. Cataracts, which accompany aging, are yellow and so they tend to block out blue light. Consequently, cataracts can restrict the amount of blue light that reaches the retina and in turn diminish important neuronal signaling to the pineal gland and SCN. In some cases, cataract surgery has restored sleep quality to older adults by allowing more blue light in during the day and thus restoring a healthy melatonin release schedule. But blue light near bedtime, such as from a cell phone, alarm clock, or computer, can stimulate the pineal gland and make it more difficult to fall asleep. (Perhaps the engineers who designed alarm clocks should have checked with neuroscientists before they chose the LED colors they did.)

When May Be as Important as What

What you eat, how much you exercise, and how much you sleep are important, but in the past few years, neuroscientists and chronobiologists (people who study biological clocks) have come to understand that *when* you eat, *when* you exercise, and *when* you sleep may be just as important. This is particularly true of older adults.

The twelfth-century philosopher and physician Moses Maimonides understood the importance of when to eat, as well as how much. His advice for living a healthy life was to "eat like a king in the morning, a prince at noon, and a peasant at dinner." In contemporary times, the field of chrononutrition strives to synchronize our ingestion of calories with the body's circadian rhythms. The timing of meals can have profound effects on a number of physiological processes, including sleep-wake cycles, core body temperature, peak performance, and alertness. Eating at different times each day, or at times that are out of sync with your circadian rhythms, can lead to obesity, metabolic syndrome, diabetes, and other problems. Your mother was right when she told you to eat a big breakfast and to have dinner at a fixed time.

The gastrointestinal tract has a powerful circadian clock of its own and is also home to billions of microbiota, also called the microbiome.

Everyone's microbiome is unique, and the organisms that make it up have their own clocks. Research on the microbiome is still in its infancy, but early evidence points to the possibility that what and when you eat can influence the microbiomic clock (the circadian rhythms of your microbioata) and, further, that your microbiome can send information up to the master clock in your SCN to influence its timing. In addition, the SCN (suprachiasmatic nucleus in the hypothalamus) can regulate the microbiome through triggering production of cyclic glucocorticoids, insulin, and other timing- and rhythmic-altering substances.

As you probably know, people differ in terms of the time of day when they are most fresh and alert. I wake up at five thirty A.M. and I'm raring to go—I get most of my writing and research done before ten A.M. My wife, on the other hand, is most productive in the afternoon and evening—if she didn't have an eight A.M. neuroscience class to teach, she'd probably stay up all night working, and do so very efficiently. In popular parlance, I'm an early bird; my wife is a night owl. We have different chronotypes. Different chronotypes have a genetic basis, but they also interact with environment and experience. Years of staying up late, consistently, and exposure to blue light beyond sundown can cause changes in gene expression that shift your chronotype at the genetic level. But this doesn't always happen—a great many shift workers live in conflict with their inherent chronotype, and this is responsible for accidents, depression, and loss of productivity.

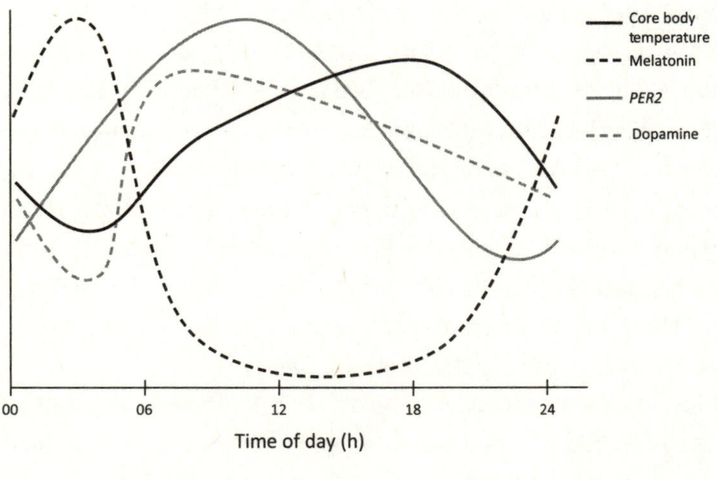

Four of the different circadian rhythms are shown on the previous page. The y-axis represents individual, scaled units for each cycle, with increasing values from bottom to top. *Dark solid line:* Core body temperature starts rising from the nighttime low of approximately 36.5°C about three hours before wakening, reaches 37.2°C by nine A.M., keeps rising slowly to a peak of 37.4°C at about eight P.M., and then falls to reach the initial level of 36.5°C at four A.M. *Dark dashed line:* Circadian rhythm of melatonin. *Gray solid line:* Temporal regulation of the *PER2* gene. *Gray dashed line:* Plasma dopamine levels throughout a twenty-four-hour period. There can be marked individual variation in the amplitude and extent of each waveform. (This graph is based on scaled averages and so the units across different systems are not identical.)

The invention of bright, artificial lights more than a century ago has caused a problem that humankind had never experienced before: the possibility of tricking the SCN into thinking it's daytime when it's not, and the possibility of allowing our circadian rhythms to become fashioned to our own will. Unfortunately, much of the time, all the lights do is disrupt our million-year-old cycles, and that can have serious health consequences. I'm not advocating a return to homes without artificial light—just a better understanding of the effects they have on us so that we can create better home environments. The use of home lighting, and most recently of computer screens, clocks, and various devices that emit blue light, has created a population of night owls. Currently only 30 percent of the population sleep best by going to bed before midnight. That means 70 percent of the population can't get to work by eight or nine A.M. without waking their body up before it is biologically ready. And teenagers experience a particular shift in their sleep schedules for reasons we don't fully understand but are related to the sudden influx of pubertal hormones. A nascent movement in the United States to delay the starting times of high schools is gaining traction. Businesses that run around the clock and employ workers outside of the normal nine-to-five workday unfortunately tend to assign workers to shifts indiscriminately, without regard to the workers' individual biological clocks. This can result in great inefficiencies and lead to sleep deprivation, work days lost to illness, and serious accidents.

As just one example, chronobiologist Till Roenneberg and his colleagues conducted an experiment at the ThyssenKrupp steel factory in Germany. ThyssenKrupp is one of the largest steel producers in the world, and its products include high-speed trains, elevators, and ships. The scientists identified those workers who were early birds versus night owls and gave them different shifts so that their work schedules aligned with their internal clocks. Once their chronotypes were aligned with their duty shifts, workers enjoyed 16 percent more sleep, almost a full night's length over the course of the week. The study did not last long enough to collect data on workplace accidents or errors, but a mountainous literature shows that sleep deprivation is responsible for some of the worst industrial disasters in modern times, including the *Exxon Valdez* oil spill, the Chernobyl nuclear accident, and the Bhopal methyl isocyanate gas leak disaster. The US National Highway Traffic Safety Administration reports that one in six traffic fatalities in the United States is caused by drowsy drivers.

Why do individuals have different chronotypes? To quote Shakespeare, "Some must watch while some must sleep." From an evolutionary standpoint, consider what life was like for our ancestors ten or twenty thousand years ago. Sleep was necessary for survival, and yet it was a time when we were especially vulnerable to attack by animal predators and violent humans, as well as the occasional hurricane or erupting volcano. The sentinel hypothesis is that when living in groups, animals share the task of nighttime vigilance, some watching over those who sleep.

Chronotype variation is found across many different species, and that's the origin of the colloquial terms that we use to describe humans: early birds and night owls. For humans, these labels represent the extremes of the distribution—most people are somewhere in the middle, with earlyish or latish tendencies. There are also sex differences, with males more likely to stay up late than females. (There isn't any research yet on why—or on the sleep patterns of trans individuals, or gender nonbinary/nonconforming individuals. Because gender identity is hormonally and biologically based, it is likely that chronotype follows gender, not biological birth sex.)

Chronotype is heritable, and a number of genes have been identified that contribute to variability across individuals. In a comprehensive new study, researchers analyzed the genomes of seven hundred thousand Britons and discovered more than 350 genes that contribute to chronotype. Additional variation comes from the fact that circadian cycles are advanced in older adults who tend to go to sleep earlier and wake earlier. Such age-related variation also may have been an evolutionary adaptation: It might have been a survival advantage for the older people, whose hunting skills had diminished, to stand on guard at night so that the younger, sharper hunters could get a good night's sleep. This has led one group of researchers to propose the "poorly sleeping grandparent hypothesis."

If the sentinel hypothesis is true, we'd predict that in ancient times, only rarely would all members of a living group be asleep at the same time. Alternatively, if all individuals were asleep at the same time, it would discredit the sentinel hypothesis.

The sentinel hypothesis was recently confirmed by anthropologists studying a contemporary group of hunger-gatherers, the Hadza of north-central Tanzania. The Hadza are a group of about twelve hundred people who live around Lake Eyasi in the central Rift Valley and in the neighboring Serengeti plateau. Anthropologists consider them an important window into the lifestyle of our Pleistocene ancestors. They have not adopted the herding or farming practices of other Tanzanians nearby, and we believe that they are living today as they did for many thousands of years.

The researchers found that, over a twenty-day period, there were only eighteen minutes in total when everyone in the group was asleep. At any given time during the night, about one-quarter of the group were awake, serving as sentinels. And they've survived.

The Aging Clock

As we age, the signaling to and from the SCN degrades. Part of this signaling deficit is due to loss or degradation of the nervous system's myelin sheath, and part due to an overall age-related depletion of neurochemicals and hormones. This is partly why older adults can have trouble getting to sleep, wake up at five in the morning, and want their dinner at four thirty in the afternoon. Lose the master clock and you're living like a ninety-year-old in Boca Raton.

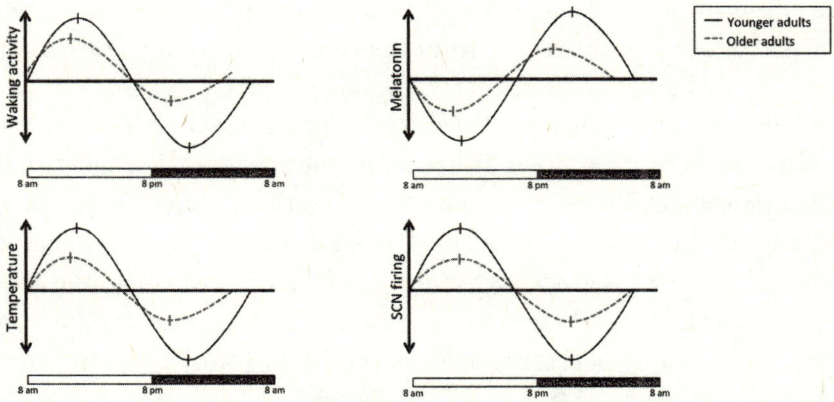

With increasing age, the amplitude of SCN signaling decreases and shifts leftward (advancing phase, the dashed lines) which accounts for changes in sleep, waking, and eating cycles among older adults. (As with the previous graph, these are based on scaled averages and so the units are not identical across graphs.)

Some evidence indicates that the problem is in fact with the integrity of neurons in the SCN itself—transplanting young tissue into the SCN of hamsters improved the clock synchrony of aging hamsters and increased their life span. This suggests that good circadian rhythm may be related to longevity. We're a long way off from being able to do such transplants in humans, but the results of these experiments help us to understand the vulnerabilities of the aging clock—and offer directions for longevity-increasing research.

Older adults tend to experience a shift in their chronobiological cycles (see figure on the previous page) called a phase advance; as they age, people are more likely to become morning types as they age. After age sixty, the rhythms of the genes *PER1* and *PER2* in the human orbitofrontal cortex are flattened and phase-advanced by approximately four to six hours, and the expression of *CRY1* becomes arrhythmic, compared to adults under forty years of age. Degradation of vasopressin signaling is responsible for increased fragmentation of the sleep-wake-activity cycle and for disruption of core body temperature rhythms, and more frequent urination—all lead to poor sleep quality and quantity, resulting in an increase in daytime drowsiness. The functioning of the biological clock is disrupted to an even greater degree in dementia. Postmortem studies of dementia patients' brains show stark degeneration of the hypothalamus's SCN.

This affects more than just eating and sleeping. There are time-of-day effects for alertness and performance that become starkly emphasized when we age. Adults after the age of sixty or so begin to show performance differences on a range of neuropsychological tests—memory, problem solving, spatial intelligence, reasoning, fine motor coordination, and athletic performance. Test them in the morning and they are normal; test them in the mid- to late afternoon and they show reduced performance, compared to forty- or fifty-year-olds (as we saw in Chapter 4, on the problem-solving brain). The differences become even more pronounced after age seventy. Give a standard memory test in the morning and they appear fine. But after noon, the decrements can be large. The take-home message is this: Make important decisions, those about finances, health, and the like, before noon. Your thinking is better. And if you're going to exercise and there might be a fall, do it earlier in the day, when you're sharper. This is why George Shultz and Vicente Fox, for example—highly productive people who are past nominal retirement age—show up at work early in the morning and tend to take the afternoons off, or at least not schedule crucial tasks for the afternoons and evenings.

The detrimental effects of disrupted cycles tend to be subtle and far less pronounced among younger adults. But at some point, it's likely that you'll begin to notice the effects. That time point is variable—it could be age fifty, sixty, seventy, or eighty, depending on the interaction of genes, culture, and environment. Disrupted circadian rhythms without a clearly identifiable external cause are an early warning sign of Parkinson's, Alzheimer's, and Huntington's diseases, chronic inflammation, and cancers.

Repetitive disturbances of the circadian rhythm, particularly from frequent time-zone shifts and irregular exposure to light, have now been implicated in a variety of diseases, including metabolic syndrome, immune deficiencies, bone and muscle weakness, cardiovascular disease, cancer, and a shortened life span. Sundowner's syndrome, the tendency for people with Alzheimer's disease to show confusion and poor memory in the early-evening hours, may well be the result of circadian rhythm disturbances—patients who can successfully restore a normal sleep-wake pattern can stay longer with their families and postpone the need to be housed in special care facilities.

Travel

One of the most well-known functions of the biological clock is to control the release of melatonin to promote sleep. When there is less light—for example, at night, or in polar latitudes in winter—your body makes less melatonin. Jet lag occurs when the ordinary zeitgebers that you are accustomed to—sunrise, intensity of light, length of the day, food intake, activity levels—are changed. This happens most typically when you cross time zones and the local time at your destination is different from the local time where you started out. The sun may come up earlier or later than your biological clock expects. The clock tries to reset itself, but this can take several days.

When we're young, the biological clock is more flexible, malleable, and it can react to environmental changes quickly. As we get older, resetting the biological clock can take longer—much longer. Phase advances—a shift to waking up earlier and going to bed earlier than usual—are more difficult for older adults to recover from; phase delays show no difference between older and younger adults. Older adults will tend to find it easier to adjust to a new time zone when traveling west, but not east, because the advanced phase shift accords with tendencies already present in their biological clocks.

Generally, it takes your body one day of recovery or planning per one hour of time-zone shift when traveling east, and half a day per one hour of time-zone shift when traveling west. This is a best case scenario. As you get older, it may well take longer. Before traveling east, start advancing your body clock as many days before your trip as the number of time zones you'll be crossing. Get into sunlight early in the day, or use a sunlight lamp. Once you're on the plane eastbound, wear eyeshades to cover your eyes two hours or so before sunset in your destination city, to acclimate yourself to the new "dark" time.

Winter months also pose a potential problem because they rob us of the most important zeitgeber, light. The cold weather can also cause us to overeat, and that can throw off the time markers associated with eating. Jet lag can also occur with north-to-south travel, even if time zones don't shift, because the length of the day can change considerably. The farther you are from the equator, the more extreme will be the difference in light between summer and winter months.

Sleep Hygiene

For most people, the sleep-wake cycle creates an energy dip between two and four A.M. (when they're asleep) and another one between about one and three P.M. (postlunch). If you're sleep-deprived—which refers not just to the amount of sleep you've gotten over the past few days but also to the quality of that sleep—you will tend to notice the postlunch dip more. And you'll notice it more as you age.

Sleep hygiene involves avoiding bright lights before bed, sleeping in a completely dark room (get blackout curtains if you need to!), and going to bed and waking at the same time every day. Now that we know about these circadian rhythms, this makes sense—your biological clock expects you to go to sleep at a certain point within the twenty-four-hour cycle. It adjusts your core body temperature, slows digestion, releases melatonin, represses dopamine, and oversees dozens of other regulations. If you go to sleep earlier or later than usual, these cycles are a little out of sync with the fact that you're sleeping. Sleep quality is impaired.

Diet is important too: Eating within two hours of bedtime can decouple the central circadian rhythms from those in the liver, stomach, and intestine. What you eat can also be a factor: Alcohol is known to disrupt sleep cycles and circadian rhythms, and high-fat diets tend to advance the clock—a practical implication of this is that if you need to stay up late, eat fatty foods like those pictured in virtually every late-night TV commercial. (Coincidence? I think not.)

Light therapy and melatonin treatments are the most effective means of resetting the circadian clock, especially in the aged. They are also effective in people with Alzheimer's-related or mild cognitive impairment. It's possible that these treatments may also prevent or delay the onset of Alzheimer's disease itself. In lab studies, melatonin interacts with beta-amyloid protein to inhibit the formation of those dangerous amyloid fibrils, and a link between disrupted circadian rhythms and Alzheimer's is well-established. In one review, melatonin use in early-stage Alzheimer's supported findings that sleep quality was improved, sundowning was reduced, and the progress of cognitive decay was slowed. In four studies of melatonin treatment, cognitive performance improved, and agitated behavior was reduced. The efficacy of therapeutic melatonin in late-stage Alzheimer's disease is likely limited by the strongly diminished number and density of melatonin receptors in the SCN.

Light-therapy lamps that simulate a gentle dawn are readily available and cost less than one hundred dollars. Increasing light intensity and optimizing the wavelength of light can compensate for some of the organic deterioration of the SCN and related chemical circuits that accompany aging. But the light therapy must be done at the correct time of day—upon waking—and it must be done consistently. Everyone is different, but by experimenting with different intensities and durations of light exposure, you can arrive at the most effective treatment. You may have heard of seasonal affective disorder (SAD), which causes mood and concentration disturbances and is triggered by the shorter, grayer days of winter. Many of the lamps sold for light therapy are branded and marketed as SAD lamps. Don't be fooled by the acronym—to my way of looking at it, the research shows that using them can make you HAPPY (healthy, asymptomatic, peppy, perceptive, and youthful).

Melatonin is available over the counter and can be used to help you entrain to a more regular sleep cycle. There are noticeable individual differences in how melatonin is processed by the body, and the best treatment would involve working with a physician who can test the dim-light melatonin-onset levels in your blood every thirty to sixty minutes throughout the late afternoon and evening and then prescribe a dose and a time to take melatonin. Sleep-medicine specialist Alfonso Padilla at UCLA recommends taking just 0.25–0.5 mg to resynchronize your biological clock. This amount mimics the psychological levels that your body naturally releases (when everything is going well). Melatonin's sleep-promoting action works as a step function, meaning that if you get enough of it, more won't help (and could be harmful). Although over-the-counter products commonly available often contain 5–10 mg (and at least one manufacturer sells 60 mg tablets), overdosing can cause extreme drowsiness the next day and disrupt your sleep cycle for a week or more. Remember: it is not a sleeping pill—it just resets your biological clock, which is not the same thing.

Melatonin levels tend to rise about fourteen hours after waking. If you get eight hours' sleep every night and wake at six A.M., that means your melatonin levels will naturally rise around eight P.M., and you'll start to get sleepy and go to bed two hours after that, around ten P.M. If it takes about an hour for a melatonin pill to be absorbed into your bloodstream, that means taking one about three hours before bedtime.

The next most effective treatment, after light therapy and melatonin, is moderate late-afternoon or early-evening exercise, like going outside for a walk. The combination of all three is the best.

Caffeine

Caffeine is one of the most widely consumed mind-altering substances in the world. For many people, it enhances wakefulness, alertness, and focus and can assist in establishing or changing circadian rhythms, particularly when crossing time zones.

The extent to which caffeine interferes with the human circadian clock, if at all, is not known yet. It has been shown to lengthen the daytime activity rhythm in fruit flies, sea snails, bread mold, and algae. The detrimental effects of caffeine on sleep are well-known, and they include delaying the onset of nighttime sleep, reducing total sleep time, impairing sleep efficiency, and worsening perceived sleep quality. Tina Burke, a young scientist at the Walter Reed Army Institute of Research in Boulder, Colorado, approached this question with converging evidence from different methods: genetics, pharmacology, and human experiments. Using cultured cells in vitro, she showed that caffeine does interfere with a number of chemical processes that contribute to circadian timekeeping and the resetting of the clock, by delaying the timing of these rhythms. Then she gave volunteers a double espresso (caffeinated or decaffeinated, unknown to the volunteers) three hours before bedtime. The caffeinated double espresso delayed the melatonin cycle by forty minutes, and she discovered further that the delay appears to be dose-dependent. Older adults may find that they have become more sensitive to the effects of caffeine on sleep than when they were younger.

Peak Performance

At the beginning of the book, I introduced the concept of health span versus disease span—the amount of time you are able to avoid declining health and live a fully productive, self-sufficient life. There's a parallel concept called productivity span that can apply not just to the arc of your life but also to the arc of a single day: There are times of day when you are at your best and other times when you are not. I mentioned this earlier in the discussion of chronotypes and the fact that older adults tend to perform better in the morning (whenever that subjective morning is—the first six hours of being awake). All of us, I think, would prefer to have longer stretches of time during the day when we are at our peak and shorter times of being in a trough. This is true regardless of how we spend our time, whether we place the most value on using our brains, our emotions, our social skills, or our physical skills. The effects of circadian rhythms on peak performance have been studied extensively in professional athletes, for obvious reasons—there is a lot of money at stake.

Top athletes often have to travel across time zones to compete, and the time of the competition can't be adjusted to suit their own particular chronobiology. Studies report conflicting findings on whether professional athletes reach their peak performance in the late afternoon/early evening or in the morning. The most obvious explanation for this is that there are individual differences among athletes and differences in the demands of various sports. The available evidence is that elite athletes tend to select, and excel in, sports that suit their chronotype. Sports that typically conduct early-morning training, such as rowing and track, tend to attract those individuals with an early-morning chronotype. Sports that are typically done in afternoons and evenings, such as water polo, volleyball, cricket, hockey, and soccer, attract late-chronotype athletes. Because chronotypes fall along a continuum, some individuals are considered neither type (neither early-morning nor late-evening), and there is evidence that these individuals can shift their chronotype simply by practicing consistently at a particular time of day.

Some studies show that peak performance in grip strength, running, jumping, oxygen uptake, and muscle function tends to occur between four P.M. and eight P.M. in the athlete's home time zone. Similar peaks have been found for football, swimming, and cycling. The differences between elite athletes' on-peak and off-peak performance, though relatively small in terms of numbers, have very large effects in the world of professional sports. An elite runner who has to perform on the other side of the world—twelve time zones away from home—could lose two seconds in the fifteen-hundred-meter race and seventy-five seconds in a marathon. For elite women hockey players traveling from Australia to Europe, crossing six time zones, full recovery time on sprinting tests took eight days. Even relatively short flights of three hours (across three time zones) have been shown to affect performance in American football, basketball, hockey, and baseball.

I've touched on the ways in which the effectiveness of eating, exercise, and sleep in maintaining optimal health and vigor is dependent on our bodies' natural rhythms. You can see that they are connected through circadian rhythms; their decoupling can cause problems, especially in old age, when our bodies are less resilient. In the next three chapters, I'll double-click on these three key components of our daily lives to reveal more of what we know about optimizing and tweaking them to give us maximum benefit.

9

DIET

Brain food, probiotics, and free radicals

After breakfast this morning, I went to YouTube to watch a new music video a friend sent me. Before it began, there was an advertisement from someone named Dr. Steven Gundry. He's sitting on a set that is made to look like a doctor's office. There's a small human skeleton model on a credenza behind him. A map of the world is hanging on the wall. (Why a map of the world?) Two prop diplomas hang in cheap frames next to the map. There are no reference books on the sparsely filled bookshelf behind him. Looking straight at the camera, he says, grim-faced, "This is a tomato. Think it's good for you? Think again." He pauses. "My name is Dr. Steven Gundry, author of the bestselling books *Dr. Gundry's Diet Evolution* and *The Plant Paradox*." Now my BS detector is kicking in. Writing bestselling books does not make you an authority. And in fact, tomatoes *are* good for you, especially when cooked, as is shown in solid, peer-reviewed studies (the lycopene they contain decreases the risk of prostate and breast cancer, heart disease, osteoporosis, and other chronic diseases).

Gundry continues, "And I'm here today to *blow your mind.*" He wags his finger at the camera emphatically on each of those last three words. "You see, over the last thirty years of research and performing over ten thousand surgeries, I've discovered some shocking things about the human body." Now my BS detector is going haywire. Performing surgeries, whether it's one or ten thousand, doesn't give you any scientific data on what people should eat. By the end of the ad, we learn that he is selling a line of supplements he created.

I noticed that Mehmet Oz endorses his work. Another red flag. Dr. Oz is widely regarded within the medical community as a charlatan, spewing a plethora of pseudoscientific nonsense and assorted quackery. The American Medical Association has admonished him as a "dangerous rogue."

Next I went to PubMed, a database of medical and scientific articles managed by the US National Library of Medicine at the National Institutes of Health. A research finding is not considered "science" until it has been subjected to peer review—validation of the paper, its methods, and its conclusions by an independent panel, typically of three expert scientists. I was not able to find any peer-reviewed studies by Dr. Steven Gundry supporting his assertions. This, and the fact that he is promoting his own brand of supplements, makes me suspicious. Is his just another in a long line of faddish diets on which people will pin their hopes, only to be disappointed?

Maybe you're fed up with science and are ready to try anything, especially when it's recommended by a freethinking renegade—just in case it works. Every ten years or so, it seems scientists have a completely different view of what we should and shouldn't eat to promote longevity and health—the meatless diet, the no-fat diet, the no-carbohydrates diet, the all-carb diet, the paleo diet. First fat was the enemy. Then sugar. Then carbs, which break down into sugars. You'd be forgiven for thinking that scientists don't know what they are talking about!

The problem here has to do with the economics and logistics of properly applying the scientific method. Most of what we know (or think we know) about foods and health comes from observational studies or samples of convenience, not proper experiments. In observational studies, as the name implies, we simply watch people who have different diets over a period of years and see how they fare. Any differences between groups of people are attributed to the difference in diets. The scientific problem is that people who eat different foods may have other differences as well that we're not keeping track of: different tendencies to exercise (or not), sleep duration, attitudes toward medicine, hydration, different daily stressors endured. Someone has just lost their job, another just had their first child, another is a heroin addict, another is a professional athlete, and so on and so on. This goes to the core theme of personal psychology and individual differences versus the generalizations neuroscience allows.

What you'd really want is to be able to take people who are identical in every lifestyle metric and then tell them exactly what to eat, putting that one variable completely under the experimenter's control. Some would get Diet A, some Diet B. This is difficult to do. The kinds of people who would volunteer for such an experiment may not be typical of the rest of the population. Unless you monitor your subjects twenty-four hours a day, many will sneak forbidden foods into their diet. And if you have any preexisting thought that one of the diets could cause harm, it would be unethical to ask anybody to follow it. Even if you could do all of this, you'd have to follow people for *years* in order to see effects.

By the way, this issue is what has hampered smoking research. You can't demand that some people smoke in a controlled experiment because it seems, from observational studies and animal models, that smoking significantly increases your chances of dying from cancer. We infer that smoking is bad, but it has not been shown in controlled experiments in humans (just rodents and monkeys). Similarly, we infer that saturated fats and sugars are bad, but we don't have controlled experiments that prove it.

So the history of dietary research has been hobbled by the lack of controlled experiments and by the very real possibility that there are individual differences (*hello!*) in the ways that people metabolize food and nutrients, their glucose metabolism, the activity of lipoprotein lipase (an enzyme that promotes fat storage versus fat oxidation), and genetic factors. On *average,* Diet A may seem no better than Diet B, but for some people, there might be big differences. What is clear is that there are no data (yet) to help clinicians match a patient's food metabolic genotype to the optimally beneficial diet. The new field of nutrigenomics promises to fill this gap. But these gaps don't mean that we know nothing. The last fifteen years of research have moved us closer to the goal of understanding how diet affects health, well-being, and longevity.

Our digestive systems today are the product of tens of thousands of years of hominid evolution. Our ancestors of the Paleolithic age, about fifty thousand years ago, subsisted by gathering plants and fishing and by hunting or scavenging wild animals. As a result, their diet was primarily lean meat, fish, fruits, vegetables, roots, eggs, and nuts. This is the so-called Paleolithic diet, or paleo diet. This diet is based on the fact that we have not evolved to eat the high amounts of sugar, salt, or saturated animal fats that are in the typical American diet; those are products of technology and industrial food production that our bodies—our genetics—have not yet caught up to.

The drive to carve out a special selection of foods to promote weight loss or health has been around as long as recorded history. In ancient

Greece (home of the Mediterranean diet), the great physician Hippocrates advised overweight citizens to follow a strict regimen of "exercise and vomiting." William the Conqueror, beginning around 1080, followed an all-alcohol diet. (He later died in a horseback riding accident.) In the early 1800s Lord Byron followed a vinegar diet. The early 1900s saw the tapeworm diet. (Yes, it is what it sounds like. The idea is that tapeworms would consume some of the food you eat and then you just expel the tapeworms—what could possibly go wrong?) The annals of diets feature grapefruit diets, cabbage soup diets, the red-pepper-lemon-juice-cleanse diet, cigarette diets, the placenta diet (celebrated by January Jones and Kim Kardashian), the cotton ball diet (stanches hunger but causes serious intestinal obstruction, and sometimes death), and the SlimFast diet. Many popular diets that seem contemporary, such as vegetarianism, veganism, and raw food, have their origins in the 1800s, and the über-faddish keto diet goes back to the 1920s. You'd think that if one was clearly superior to the others, after all this time we'd know about it.

Stanford nutrition scientist Christopher Gardner notes that "no matter how crazy a diet might be, it will work for someone if enough people try it. . . . If you give it to 100 people, it might work for only two of them, but the people promoting the diet don't test it that way; they simply focus on the two successful stories."

Maybe what's really going on is that following a diet, any diet, causes you to pay more attention to the foods you're eating—to engage in mindfulness—and that's where their effectiveness is, not in the particulars. In this respect, all diets involve some kind of lifestyle change. People on a diet typically increase their physical activity at the same time, and that is likely to be a much more important lifestyle change than the actual composition of the foods one eats. The fact is, outcomes don't differ all that much among the leading diets. The *Journal of the American Medical Association* published a research article that compared the Ornish, Atkins, Zone, and Weight Watchers diets and found no difference among them in weight loss or reduction of risk for cardiovascular disease. The researchers note that more than one thousand diet books are available, with a great many "departing substantially from mainstream medical advice," a nice way of saying that they are not evidence-based. But I don't think we should be nice about it, we should call them what they are—uninformed guesses and speculation.

Many of the bestselling diet books promote carbohydrate restriction—for example, *Dr. Atkins' New Diet Revolution, The Carbohydrate Addict's Diet,* and *The Complete Low Carb Cookbook*. As of this writing, *Simply Keto* is the thirty-third bestselling book on Amazon. This dietary advice is counter to that endorsed by governmental agencies—the US Department of Agriculture, Department of Health and Human Services, National Institutes of Health—and nongovernmental organizations—the Academy of Nutrition and Dietetics, American Heart Association, American Diabetes Association. And there is no scientific consensus that extreme carbohydrate restriction is healthful.

The most-read article of 2018 published in the *British Medical Journal* claimed that restricting dietary carbohydrates offers a metabolic advantage for keeping off lost weight, but the data may not support this conclusion. Kevin Hall, senior investigator at the National Institute of Diabetes and Digestive and Kidney Diseases, discovered that the *British Medical Journal*'s data were improperly analyzed, and when he conducted a reanalysis the effects disappeared. This sort of thing happens often in science because science is a self-correcting, self-policing process. But the corrections almost never make headlines. So the public is left with impressions created from someone's mistakes.

Many diets are innocuous. Many inspire us to pay closer attention to what (and how much) we eat. But some can be downright dangerous, such as the cotton ball diet or the cigarette diet. Or take the protocol developed by Dr. Nicholas Gonzalez, a diet purported to treat cancer. Each patient receives individualized dietary recommendations (so far, so good), and these diets range from vegetarian to diets requiring red meat two to three times a day. All the diets require the consumption of supplements, which Dr. Gonzalez's office sells. How many? Between 80 and 175 capsules a day. He himself died of a heart attack at age sixty-seven, but before he did, he persuaded a large number of people to follow a diet that has been rejected by the medical establishment and led to a stern reprimand from the New York State Medical Board. The American Cancer Society stated that there is no convincing scientific evidence that the Gonzalez treatment is effective in treating cancer and that the treatment may actually be harmful.

There are two separate dangers with these kinds of diets—the first is that the diet and supplements themselves can cause harm; the second is that people often refuse well-established medical treatments in favor of following these "alternative" protocols that have no evidence of success, and they thereby miss an important treatment window for actually being helped by legitimate medicine. (And a third danger is that you'll spend your money on them.) Gonzales lost two malpractice suits. In one, he had to pay $2.5 million to a patient who had been diagnosed with uterine cancer. He discouraged her from following the advice of her oncologist and instead recommended his own branded dietary supplements and frequent coffee enemas. After the cancer spread to her spine and blinded her, she gave up on Gonzales and went back to the oncologist.

If this story sounds familiar, it's because it has played out, in different versions, around the world, from psychic healers in Mexico to homeopathic doctors in Europe. Herbal remedies, vitamins and minerals, and dietary supplements are often marketed as "natural" products, but natural doesn't always mean safe. Cow dung is "natural." In one study, 20 percent of Indian-manufactured Ayurvedic medicines tested contained toxic levels of lead, mercury, and arsenic. The Mayo Clinic provides a helpful guide for consumers who are contemplating alternative treatments. Although terms such as *purify, detoxify,* and *energize* may sound impressive, they're generally used to cover up a lack of scientific proof. There are only a few known "toxins" (for example, lead) and these treatments do nothing to remove them. Mayo also advises consumers to beware of testimonials. Anecdotes from individuals who have used the product are no substitute for evidence from scientific research. If the product's claims were backed up with hard evidence, the purveyor would say so, pointing you to peer-reviewed scientific studies. Just remember: The plural of *anecdote* is not *data*. In other words, an anecdote is simply an observation or story that comes from uncontrolled conditions. True scientific data comes from a systematic attempt to isolate variables, document conditions, and observe trends over a large number of cases.

Scientific American went to the extraordinary measure of publishing an article titled "Why Almost Everything Dean Ornish Says about Nutrition Is Wrong." Ornish launched his foray into the diet industry with a study in 1990 that was poorly controlled and studied only forty-eight patients with heart disease—twenty-four were the control group and twenty-four were put on the Ornish diet. After a year, he reported that the Ornish diet group had a lowered incidence of arteriosclerosis. Lowering the levels of something in people who already have a disease tells you nothing about whether that same treatment will prevent the disease in the first place. But that's a minor point compared to the big flaw in the study: The diet group, but not the control group, also quit smoking, exercised more, and attended stress-management counseling. The people in the control group were told to do none of those things. As *Scientific American* reported:

> It's hardly surprising that quitting smoking, exercising, reducing stress and dieting—when done together—improves heart health. But the fact that [half] the participants were making all of these lifestyle changes means that we cannot make any inferences about the effect of the diet alone.

Antioxidants

So much for faddish diets based on pseudoscience. What is the current state of good science? I briefly mentioned antioxidants in Chapters 3 and 8. Antioxidants have become the new buzzword in nutrition, diet, and longevity circles. But few outside of the laboratory understand what they are, apart from the implication that they're good for you. You may remember from high school chemistry that electrons are negatively charged particles inside an atom, and you may also remember about electron pairing. When two atoms or molecules have electrons with opposite spins, they can become paired, and this is a stable molecular state. When an atom, molecule, or ion has an unpaired electron, it is unstable and is called a free radical. Free radicals are produced all the time as your cells convert glucose to energy. But damage to mitochondria (a subunit of the cell, found inside most cells of your body) can also lead to increased production of free radicals. And so can consuming certain substances, such as fried foods, alcohol, tobacco smoke, pesticides, and air pollutants.

Free radicals, because they're unstable, can cause damage to DNA and cell membranes by grabbing their electrons through a process called oxidation. This easily becomes a chain reaction. One molecule with a free radical grabs the electron from another, leaving it a free radical; then this one grabs the electron from another molecule, leaving it a free radical; and pretty soon the whole thing has snowballed out of control. In the meantime, all of these molecules with free radicals can't perform their cellular functions properly, and you get oxidative stress.

Fortunately, the body evolved a number of built-in antioxidant mechanisms. Antioxidants scavenge free radicals and thereby play a critical role in cellular health. They either reduce the formation of free radicals or react with and neutralize the ones that have already formed, by donating a hydrogen atom. Antioxidants often work by donating an electron to the free radical before it can damage other cell components. Once the electrons of the free radical are paired, the free radical is stabilized and becomes nontoxic.

Oxidative stress is believed to underlie a wide range of diseases, including cancer, diabetes, and neurological disorders such as Parkinson's and Alzheimer's disease, and to shorten life span. It causes high LDL levels (low density lipoprotein—the "bad" cholesterol) and the accumulation of plaques that can lead to heart disease. It even plays a role in the development of wrinkles. It's been known since the 1960s that free radicals accelerate the aging process and that the reduction of free radicals can delay aging.

The big question is whether dietary antioxidants can mitigate the damage done by the oxidation of free radicals. The matter is further confused by the fact that there is no universal agreement among scientists about which molecules are antioxidants and which aren't. Some of the well-known substances that are often mentioned as antioxidants are retinol (vitamin A), beta-carotene (a precursor of retinol), ascorbic acid (vitamin C), vitamin E, flavonoids, and some omega-3 fatty acids. Sometimes zinc can function as an antioxidant. The definition of antioxidants can be very broad, because they can act either directly or indirectly, and any substances that can detoxify free radicals might be justly called antioxidants. Selenium, for example, doesn't act directly but can deoxidize certain reactive oxygen species through indirect action. Tocoferal (vitamin E), on the other hand, acts directly by donating a hydrogen atom. At issue, in part, is whether the mere fact that a food or supplement molecule *can* donate a hydrogen atom to a free radical means that in a real, living organism it *will*, and that it's working like we think it should. We don't know.

Recall the discussion of glucosamine supplementation in Chapter 7, on pain—taking cartilage in a pill might seem that it should help with cartilage breakdowns in your body, but the body doesn't work like that. The same principle applies to substances in the foods we eat, such as antioxidants and cholesterol: They don't necessarily have the effect that you might think. There is modest research evidence that eating antioxidants in food is beneficial. The problem is that there have not been enough rigorous studies of antioxidant foods to draw any definitive conclusions. One recent meta-analysis found that "there were no randomized controlled trials. . . . All studies were judged to be at moderate to substantial risk of bias."

There is even less evidence to support taking antioxidant supplements. For example, one study followed nearly forty thousand women for ten years. Half were randomly assigned to take a vitamin E supplement and half took a placebo. After ten years, the vitamin E hadn't significantly reduced the risk of heart attack, stroke, or cancer. The results of other randomized controlled trials with a range of antioxidant supplements, including beta-carotene, vitamins A and C, and selenium, did not show reductions in cancer. For gastrointestinal cancers, the supplements actually *increased* all-cause mortality. A meta-analysis reviewed the results of studies with more than 290,000 people and found no effect of antioxidant supplements on cardiovascular disease. Antioxidant supplementation might be interfering with the immune system or with defense mechanisms responsible for the elimination of impaired cells. (For some subsets of the population with a really poor diet, or for pregnant women, supplements may be helpful, but the scientific evidence is still wanting.)

Many supplement studies fail because they study only one supplement at a time, which doesn't mimic anything like actual food. Actual foods can contain fiber, micronutrients, and beneficial gut bacteria that supplements lack. And at least some antioxidants, vitamins C and E, have been shown to block the health-promoting effects of physical exercise.

Cholesterol, Fats, and Brain Health

Most of us know of the link between cholesterol, dietary fats, and heart disease, but it is interesting, and illuminating, to learn what these mean at a molecular, biological level.

Cholesterol is a waxy substance that circulates in your blood and attaches to proteins there. Your body needs cholesterol to build healthy cells, including brain cells, but high levels of certain forms of cholesterol can increase your risk of heart disease. When cholesterol combines with proteins, the resulting molecule is called a lipoprotein. Low-density lipoprotein (LDL, the "bad" cholesterol) transports cholesterol particles throughout your body. It can build up in the walls of your arteries, making them hard and narrow and causing arteriosclerosis.

High-density lipoprotein (HDL, the "good" cholesterol) picks up excess cholesterol and takes it back to your liver, which then removes it from your body.

Unhealthy eating habits and obesity can raise your bad cholesterol levels. Lack of physical activity can lower your good cholesterol levels. Smoking does both, especially in women, by damaging the walls of blood vessels and making them more likely to accumulate LDL deposits. LDL levels naturally rise with age, making healthy lifestyle habits increasingly important, especially after age fifty. There is a genetic component as well—the rate at which bad cholesterol climbs and the ability of physical activity to increase good cholesterol are partly inherited. If adopting healthy lifestyle habits (physical activity, improved diet) doesn't optimize cholesterol levels, there are medications that can lower LDL (statins; for extreme cases, there's a procedure called lipoprotein apheresis that uses a filtering machine to remove LDLs from the blood.)

As we've seen, though, well-intentioned interventions don't always have the desired effect. It isn't entirely clear that lowering LDL through the use of statins actually lowers your risk of heart disease—the statins may simply lower a marker associated with disease, and not an actual cause. And even so, statins have a tiny effect: in some studies, three hundred people have to take a statin to delay or prevent a heart attack for one person in a given year.

Food labels in the United States and many other countries list the cholesterol content of those foods, but there is no scientific consensus about whether eating cholesterol-rich foods actually alters cholesterol levels in the blood. And many cholesterol-rich foods are high in necessary nutrients.

You do need fats in your diet: They're a major source of energy, and they're necessary for building the myelin sheath around neurons and for maintaining strong, healthy cells. But not all fats are created equal. The main types are:

- saturated fats, found in meats, eggs, and whole-fat dairy products;
- monounsaturated fats, found in olive and canola oil;
- polyunsaturated fats, found in seeds, nuts, and fish and vegetable oils;
- and trans fats, found in fried foods, microwave popcorn, and some commercially baked goods.

Saturated fats have long been considered the enemy of heart health, but a meta-analysis of seventy-two studies, tracking six hundred thousand people in eighteen countries, shows no association between the consumption of saturated fats and heart disease. None. Now, this is not a controlled experiment—it may be that the people in the study who ate saturated fat got more exercise; there may be genetic differences in the way their bodies metabolize saturated fats. But the real culprit in that analysis was trans fats, the ones found in fried foods, potato chips, and other junk food.

Diets high in soluble fibers are good because the fiber binds to the LDL cholesterol molecules in the digestive system and drags them out of the body before they get into circulation. Some good sources of soluble fiber are oats (oatmeal, Cheerios, Trader Joe's O's), barley and other whole grains, beans (including soy beans and soy milk), high-fiber fruits (apples, strawberries, citrus; the pectin they contain is a soluble fiber), eggplant, okra, fatty fish, liquid vegetable oils, and nuts (just two ounces of nuts a day can lower LDL by 5 percent). Diets high in omega-3 fatty acids, as found in fatty fish, seeds (especially chia, flaxseed, and hemp), nuts (especially walnuts), and olive and canola oils also lower LDL and reduce the risk of heart disease by 7 percent. Insoluble fibers (wheat bran, vegetables, and whole grains) are also healthy because they prevent constipation and diverticulitis.

The emerging picture is that dietary consumption of fats, even saturated ones, is not the cause of heart disease, but rather inflammatory processes that cause cholesterol to build up in arterial walls. It is the alpha-linolenic acid, polyphenols, and omega-3 fatty acids present in nuts, extra-virgin olive oil, vegetables, and oily fish that rapidly attenuate inflammation and coronary thrombosis.

Caloric Restriction

Ben Franklin advised in *Poor Richard's Almanack,* "To lengthen thy life, lessen thy meals." It's been known for more than a decade that mice and rats that have a calorie-restricted diet can live 30 to 40 percent longer. When you have easy access to food and nutrients, and your physiological stress levels are low, your genes support cellular growth and reproduction. In contrast, under harsh conditions, genetic activity shifts toward cell maintenance and protection. A number of stressors mediate this reaction, and caloric restriction is one of the most robust, working in many species, from yeast to *C. elegans,* from mice to primates. For years, it was thought that caloric restriction merely slows down an organism's metabolism and therefore slows down the rate at which cellular damage accumulates. It is now well accepted that caloric restriction triggers a change in the metabolic response, in particular, a downregulation of insulin and insulin-like growth factor (IGF-1), as well as the AMP-activated protein kinase, and sirtuins. Molecular biologist Cynthia Kenyon explains the significance of this:

> Slowing aging might seem like an overwhelming challenge, as the decline is so pervasive. So it is noteworthy that when we extend the lifespans of laboratory animals, we do not have to combat individually all the problems of age, such as the declining muscles, the wrinkled skin and the mutant mitochondria. Instead, we just tweak a regulatory gene, and the animal does the rest. In other words, animals have the latent potential to live much longer than they normally do.

In mammals, insulin levels rise in response to glucose, and this rise may ultimately shorten life span. When Kenyon modified the PI3K enzyme in the insulin/IGF-1 pathway, her worms lived *ten times* longer. There's an important story here about sugars and insulin. Insulin is a hormone produced in the pancreas. When blood sugar levels are high, pancreatic beta cells secrete insulin into the blood, and when blood sugar levels are low, insulin is inhibited. Insulin is necessary for normal metabolism; it helps glucose in your blood enter cells in your muscle, fat, and liver, where it can be used for energy. If your insulin levels rise (hyperinsulinemia) and stay that way, a host of health problems can occur, including insulin resistance (and type 2 diabetes), obesity, immune-system suppression, and cardiac arrhythmias.

Caloric restriction, because of its interaction with the insulin signaling system, appears to be good for the brain. Why might that be? Neuroscientist Mark Mattson at Johns Hopkins University says, "If you're hungry and haven't found food, you'd better find food. You don't want your brain to shut down if you're hungry." Some of the neural benefits that are found with fasting also occur with vigorous exercise. The neurochemical changes are similar: Both stimulate the production of brain-derived neurotrophic growth factors (BDNFs). Fasting stimulates the production of ketones, an energy source for neurons. Fasting can increase the number of mitochondria in neurons, which helps them produce more energy.

Kenyon speculates that it's possible that if we could inhibit insulin receptors, we could promote longevity in humans if we also eat a low-carbohydrate diet. It's also possible that we might modify the genes and signaling pathways that are affected by caloric restriction so that we can all eat whatever we want.

There's also emerging evidence that insulin may play a role in developing Alzheimer's disease. This has led some forward-thinking doctors to prescribe the diabetes medication metformin, a blood sugar–lowering drug, proactively to patients with a family history or other risk factors for Alzheimer's and dementia. Although the evidence for this is scarce, what evidence there is looks promising. A meta-analysis of three studies showed that cognitive impairment was significantly less prevalent in people who took metformin, and in six studies dementia incidence was significantly reduced. Metformin was further found to have a neuroprotective effect. Now, all of these were patients *with* diabetes. We just don't have evidence yet for the effectiveness of using the drug as a preventative. A protocol for testing the hypothesis was published in 2016, and a study was just begun in the United Kingdom.

For now the best bet for increasing longevity and the event horizon for the detrimental effects of aging appears to be just eating less, and there are many ways to do this, although we don't yet know which is going to be the most effective: reduced calories throughout the day; one fast day a week; two fast days a week; fasting every other day; fasting two weeks a year; no dinners; one month of juice fast every year; and so on. At first it can feel awful, but many people find they can build up to it and get used to it. Many researchers I know have begun to do it. Jeffrey Mogil fasts one day a week. Cynthia Kenyon gave up carbs. I don't eat if I'm not hungry and I skip dinner a couple of times a week. Mark Mattson does intermittent fasting—reducing the frequency of meals. There are, of course, dangers in following an improvised or ad hoc calorie-restrictive diet. These include malnutrition, gastrointestinal problems, and eating disorders. You shouldn't just do this on your own—it's best to discuss it with your doctor and work out a plan. And there haven't been enough longitudinal studies yet for us to know whether intermittent fasting (or other forms of fasting) could have long-lasting negative consequences beyond the initial benefits.

When you do eat, certain foods show up in study after study as being healthful. These include virgin olive oil, which is rich in monounsaturated fatty acids—the good fats. Consuming olive oil (around 3 tablespoons a day) is associated with relieving oxidative stress on cells and regulating cholesterol and anti-inflammatory activity.

Cruciferous vegetables, including Brussels sprouts, broccoli, cauliflower, kale, cabbage, and bok choy, have been shown to have protective effects against many forms of cancer and can even inhibit the progression of some cancers. They do this by initiating cellular defense mechanisms and modifying cancer-related genes. Glucosinolates and 3-carbinol are the health-promoting agents in cruciferous vegetables.

Another component of the Mediterranean diet is oily fish, such as sardines and anchovies. These contain the omega-3 fatty acids that are known to be essential in the development and maintenance of brain and retinal tissue, as well as for myelination. There have also been benefits claimed for reducing the risk of heart disease and cancer. This has led to a current fad of taking omega-3 supplements, resulting in a worldwide $33-billion industry—about the size of the global music market. As with many well-intentioned interventions begun before all the data are in, omega-3 supplements do not seem to work. A Cochrane systematic review (the gold standard for meta-analyses) in 2018 examined the results of seventy-nine separate trials involving more than twelve thousand people and found that taking omega-3 supplements makes little or no difference to the risk of cardiovascular events, coronary heart deaths, coronary heart disease events, stroke, or heart irregularities. And it may even increase the incidence of some cancers.

These negative findings apply to supplements, but what about dietary consumption of omega-3s? There is increasing evidence that omega-3 acid occurring naturally in foods helps reduce inflammation and improve insulin sensitivity, but for other health outcomes the evidence is still mixed—some studies show that it is protective against cancer and heart disease, some show that it's not. A recent report by the National Institutes of Health concludes that omega-3 *supplements* don't reduce the risk of heart disease but that people who eat seafood one to four times a week are less likely to die of heart disease. It may be that the optimal amount of omega-3s (and other antioxidants) follows what engineers call a step function: Once a certain minimum is reached, additional amounts have no effect and may actually introduce harm. The *Harvard Health* report noted:

> You should still consider eating fish and other seafood as a healthy strategy. If we could absolutely, positively say that the benefits of eating seafood comes entirely from omega-3 fats, then downing fish oil pills would be an alternative to eating fish. But it's more than likely that you need the entire orchestra of fish fats, vitamins, minerals, and supporting molecules, rather than the lone notes of EPA and DHA. The same holds true of other foods. Taking even a handful of supplements is no substitute for [the] wealth of nutrients you get from eating fruits, vegetables, and whole grains.

As with all things involving diet, don't overdo it: Too much fish can raise levels of mercury and other toxins. Also, the ocean is being hugely overfished and soon there won't be any more for your grandkids.

One of the most talked about suggestions, with origins in the Mediterranean diet, is that moderate amounts of red wine with meals promote good health. Here, it's important to disentangle the effects of red wine itself from those of its alcohol content. A systematic review found no evidence that red wine influences health outcomes differentially from the moderate, measured drinking of other alcohol products. Moderate alcohol consumption, in many studies, has been shown to lower blood pressure and thereby reduce coronary risks. But this is a complex issue. Alcohol consumption increases risks for primary tumors of the mouth, pharynx, larynx, esophagus, liver, breast, colon, and rectum. It also increases mortality in breast cancer survivors and possibly those with other cancers as well. It interferes with sleep and dream cycles and, as we saw in Chapter 8, with circadian clocks. And it can be addictive.

As with fish oil, a supplementation industry grew out of the nascent findings of red wine's potential health effects. Researchers identified a chemical in red wine that you may have read about called resveratrol. Resveratrol has antioxidant properties and in animals reduces hypertension, heart failure, and ischemic heart disease, and it improves insulin sensitivity and reduces blood glucose levels and high-fat-diet-induced obesity. However, systematic reviews conclude that there is insufficient evidence that resveratrol supplements could prevent disease or extend life in humans. That said, another comprehensive review recommended it.

Many cognitive and physical benefits are claimed for a number of diets, including the DASH, MIND, and Mediterranean diets, but there is little evidence to support them. The putative causes of cognitive decline and Alzheimer's are oxidative stress, inflammation of neural tissue, and vascular problems caused by the buildup of harmful substances in the circulatory system. Healthy diets that lower cholesterol and inflammation are a logical approach. But the history of medical science is full of treatments and advice that made sense but lacked evidence, and the evidence came in counter to the "logical" advice. The problem is that bodies (and brains) are complicated, there are multiple interacting factors, and we're really only at the very beginning of being able to understand all the implications of even the simplest interventions.

Protein

Older adults absorb protein less effectively and require 0.54 grams of protein per pound of body weight per day. If you weigh 68 kilograms (150 pounds), you need to eat 81 grams of protein, or about 3 ounces. That may not seem like a lot, but remember, if you eat a chicken drumstick

(4 ounces) it's not pure protein; in fact, it probably has less than half an ounce of protein. Consider the following:

1 cup of nonfat milk = 0.3 ounces protein
2 tablespoons of peanut butter = 0.2 ounces protein
2 medium eggs = 0.4 ounces protein
½ pound of salmon = 1.7 ounces protein

If you ate everything I've just listed, you'd still be 0.4 ounces short of your daily requirement.

The most effective proteins for older adults are ones that are rich in the amino acid leucine—milk, cheese, beef, tuna, chicken, peanuts, soybeans, and eggs. Leucine is one of nine essential amino acids (building blocks of proteins) that we need to obtain through our diet, and it is mainly found in animal proteins.

There are competing goals here—cheese and beef contain unhealthy saturated fats, tuna can contain unhealthy levels of mercury, and chicken can contain antibiotics, yet they are effective sources of protein. (A good alternative for some is 98 percent lean beef that contains less than 2 grams of fat in a 100-gram portion.) Lack of protein can cause serious problems with your brain, muscles, and immune system.

But the story of leucine is an example of the pitfalls in focusing on only one dietary component at a time and of thinking that if something is essential, more must be better. We need leucine for protein synthesis and many metabolic functions. This amino acid helps regulate blood sugar levels, the growth and repair of muscle and bone tissue, and wound healing. It enters the brain from the blood more rapidly than any other amino acid. But when levels become too high, leucine toxicity can develop and has been associated with degradation of neural circuits, delirium, cognitive impairment, reductions in serotonin levels, and excess ammonia levels in the blood, as well as blocking the absorption of *other* amino acids. You need leucine, but not too much, and so the foods just listed should be eaten in moderation. Tuna sandwiches every day at lunch are not the way to go.

Vegetable proteins are a part of that balanced diet. You may have read reports that soy products interfere with sex hormones, lowering testosterone in men and leading to estrogen problems in menopausal women. These reports were based on flawed data, and the current thinking is that soy is beneficial for all except those who are allergic to soy.

Hydration

Aristotle wrote that "living beings are moist and warm . . . however old age is dry and cold." The classical Greek physician Galen of Pergamon added that "aging is associated with a decline in innate heat and body water." Galen further lamented that dehydration is difficult to diagnose. That is still true today. It is most problematic among children and adults over seventy.

Hydration is something most of us don't think about, but it is essential for cellular and brain health. Often if you notice yourself feeling fatigued, this is the first sign of dehydration. Other symptoms include headaches and nausea. Dehydration is a medical condition—it is not thirst. Thirst is just a symptom that may or may not be present when you're dehydrated.

Dehydration is deadly. It is the second leading killer of children under four worldwide and the eighth leading cause of death among adults over seventy. It's also linked to the formation of kidney stones. Common causes are too much heat or exercise (because you lose salts through your sweat), higher altitudes, and illness. Alcohol is also a culprit: It turns off hormones that help us absorb water so we lose more fluids than normal.

Older persons have an increased risk of dehydration, even when water is readily available to them, because thirst detectors in the brain degrade. Individuals at the greatest risk for dehydration include people with fever or infections, impaired cognitive status, or impaired renal function, and those who take medications that impact fluid and electrolyte balance.

Dehydration results from an imbalance of water, salts, and electrolytes in the blood. Electrolytes include sodium, chloride, potassium, and magnesium. Rehydrating does not mean simply drinking more water, because when you're dehydrated, the body can't retain the water that you drink and water alone doesn't replace the depleted salts and electrolytes.

Rehydration requires drinking an oral rehydration salts (ORS) solution. An ORS solution is a mixture of water, salt, and sugar; it is absorbed in the small intestine and replaces the water and electrolytes lost in dehydration. If dehydration is accompanied by diarrhea, zinc supplements can reduce the duration of a diarrhea episode by 25 percent. Cases of severe dehydration require intravenous fluids.

For maintaining hydration, limit alcohol intake or drink at least one 8-ounce glass of water for every alcoholic beverage you ingest. Nutritious foods help maintain a proper balance of electrolytes and salts. Avoid bread or dried fruit if you're dehydrated—they require the body to take water from the vascular system, and that leads to further dehydration. There are several oral rehydration solutions available over the counter. You might keep some in your purse or briefcase, in your desk at work, and at home, and take it about twice a week if you're prone to dehydration. If you have a cold or flu, drink two a day. If you feel lethargic, or after a particularly hot day, intense workout, or drinking alcohol, you might take some.

Constipation

As Hippocrates noted, "It is a general rule that intestines become sluggish with age." Constipation is one of the most common and annoying problems of aging, affecting 50 percent of older adults. As we age, the intestinal muscles that help move food along weaken and the contractions are not as strong. Often, medications taken by older adults cause constipation as a side effect. Many older adults become less physically active, which also increases constipation. It disproportionately affects women, nonwhites, people from a lower socioeconomic status, and those who suffer from depression.

Why in the world is this in a book on the brain?

Clinical observations suggest that constipation interferes with cognition. Only a small number of studies have explored this, and the results, although preliminary, suggest a connection. In rats, constipation led to changes in gene expression that could in turn affect hemoglobin content and quality, the capacity of the blood to bring oxygen to neurons in the hippocampus, and alterations in the cholinergic system of the brain. In humans, an association between chronic constipation and cognitive impairment has been identified.

The noncognitive consequences can also be serious. Overstraining to produce a bowel movement can cause people to faint or blood vessels in the brain to burst. Because many people are uncomfortable or embarrassed discussing their bowel movements with their doctors and health-care providers, chronic constipation often goes untreated.

Constipation refers to two different problems: difficulty passing stools and a decreased frequency of bowel movements. Both can often be treated by increasing consumption of insoluble fibers, such as bran, whole grains and vegetables, fluids (2 liters per day), and exercise—particularly exercise that involves gently twisting or bending the abdominal region. And simply taking a good walk can get things moving. If those fail, laxatives are indicated, and there are two kinds: bulk-forming laxatives and osmotic laxatives. Before just going to the drugstore and buying something over the counter, it's important to understand the difference between the two.

Bulk-forming laxatives aren't digested; instead, the fiber they contain allows you to retain more fluid—that's why you need to be sure that if you use them, you increase your consumption of fluids. The water absorption produces a softer, bulkier stool. The bulky size stimulates the intestinal muscles to contract, causing everything to move along, leading to an easier bowel movement. It can take from twelve to thirty-six hours for bulk-forming laxatives to produce results, so they do not provide immediate relief from constipation—they are best used for ongoing digestive health. Examples include psyllium husks (Metamucil), ground flaxseed, wheat dextrin (Benefiber), methylcellulose (Citrucel), and polycarbophil (FiberCon, Prodiem).

Osmotic laxatives draw water into the bowel from the intestines, thereby softening the stool. They can deplete electrolytes and cause dehydration, and so it's also important to stay hydrated when taking them. They can work within six hours. Many are polyethylene glycol–based (Lax-A-Day, MiraLAX, PegaLAX, RestoraLAX). Unlike bulk-forming laxatives, osmotic laxatives are intended for short-term, not daily, use, they shouldn't be taken for more than seven days, and they are habit-forming. Norman Lear, a television pioneer (creator of *All in the Family, The Jeffersons, Sanford and Son*) and a political activist (People for the American Way) at ninety-seven is still active and creative. Asked how he maintains such high levels of mental agility and focus, and what keeps him going, he responded with one word: "MiraLAX."

For immediate, short-term relief, glycerin suppositories and enemas are available over the counter. If you've read about colonic irrigation in new-age health magazines or on the Web, it is ineffective and has no scientific basis.

Another thing that can help, and can reduce or eliminate the need for laxatives, is probiotics. The bacterial balance in the gut can be adversely affected by taking antibiotics, by changes in diet and exercise, by the normal process of aging, and by a host of factors we have not yet identified.

Gut Bacteria, Probiotics

Your digestive system—your gut—has its own computer, known as the enteric nervous system, with half a billion neurons, and containing about 100 trillion bacteria, both good and bad. Collectively they are known as the *gut microbiota*, a term that is often used interchangeably with *microbiome.* (Just to confuse things, they used to be called the *microflora.*)

Lining the inside walls of your large intestine is a layer of mucus that forms a biofilm and provides a moist, warm environment for the microbiome. The thousands of different species of bacteria in there perform special jobs to keep the entire intestinal community healthy. From there these bacteria regulate a number of aspects of cellular housekeeping and health throughout the body. The particular assortment of bacteria found in your gut is unique to you, as unique as a fingerprint. It is shaped by genes, culture, and opportunity, including what your parents ate, what you ate as an infant and child, and the lifetime influences of different diseases and stressors your body has experienced.

The microbiome is important for nutrition, digestion, and immune-system function. The inside of your stomach and large intestine is a highly acidic environment. The bacteria that live there had to evolve adaptations to allow them to survive there, but the reward for them is great access to food and not a lot of competition for it. The relationship is mutually beneficial to you and them.

There is an emerging body of evidence that the gut microbiome also affects cognition, behavior, and brain health. This is cutting-edge stuff and the story is still being written. We already know that serotonin is an important neuroregulator of mood, memory, and anxiety. It turns out that 90 percent of the serotonin in the body resides in the gut, and it is manufactured there by bacteria such as *Candida, Streptococcus, Escherichia,* and *Enterococcus.*

Our gut microorganisms produce other essential neurotransmitters too. *Lactobacillus* and *Bifidobacterium* create gamma-aminobutyric acid (GABA), an important inhibitory chemical, as we saw in Chapter 2. *Escherichia coli, Bacillus,* and *Saccharomyces* produce norepinephrine, which is important for alertness; *Bacillus* and *Serratia* produce dopamine. *Bifidobacterium infantis* increases levels of tryptophan, an important precursor to serotonin, melatonin, and vitamin B_3. *Lactobacillus acidophilus* increases the expression of the natural cannabinoid and opioid receptors in the brain, affecting appetite, pain, and memory.

Gut bacteria have been linked to mental well-being and depression. People who lack two particular bacteria, *Coprococcus* and *Dialister,* are more likely to be depressed, and those who have normal levels of them report a higher general quality of life. *Coprococcus* is associated with dopamine signaling, and it also produces butyrate, a fatty acid that is an important anti-inflammatory agent; increased inflammation has been linked to depressive symptoms. A third bacterium, *Faecalibacterium,* also produces butyrate and is found in people who report a higher quality of life. Neuroscientist John Cryan calls bacteria like these "melancholy microbes." (Who says science isn't fun?)

The gut microbiome can become out of balance, leading to a condition called dysbiosis. The most commonly known cause of dysbiosis is taking prescription antibiotics for an infection. These can kill not just the disease-causing bacteria but beneficial gut bacteria as well. Dysbiosis can also be brought on by unhealthy lifestyle behaviors, such as irregular eating times and high-fat diets. When we're younger, the effects are so subtle we don't notice. When we're older, the effects can be debilitating. Misbalanced microbiomes are suspected to be involved in obesity and a number of diseases including cancer and Alzheimer's.

Recall from earlier the work of Michael Meaney, showing that stressors early in life—such as infants being separated from their mothers—can have a lifelong impact on the brain's stress response. Early life stressors can also have an influence on the composition of the gut microbiome. That composition is affected by the mother's diet and stress levels and by travel through the birth canal. Children who are delivered via Caesarean section show a reduced diversity of their gut microbiome. In animals, stress caused by the separation of rhesus monkeys from their mothers changed the microbiota and decreased their *Bifidobacterium* and *Lactobacillus* levels. Rats separated from their mothers showed decreased fecal *Lactobacillus* levels.

The full extent of gut-brain interactions is still unknown, but links between these interactions and an imbalanced microbiome have been implicated in mental disorders as diverse as autism, schizophrenia, ADHD, bipolar disorder, and multiple sclerosis. A credible although still unconfirmed view is that an imbalanced microbiome during infancy and childhood can lead to these conditions and diseases later in life. But that doesn't mean the conditions are irreversible.

Probiotics as contained in foods and supplements can introduce or reintroduce beneficial bacteria into the gut. These can affect such physical functions as increasing iron absorption, protecting against pesticide absorption, and the distribution of fat around the body. They have been shown to be especially effective treatments for irritable bowel syndrome, a disease that disproportionately afflicts older adults.

But where it really gets interesting is the effects that probiotics can potentially have on cognition, emotion, and behavior. Small-scale trials have shown that a single probiotic, *Bifidobacterium infantis,* can alleviate depression and anxiety, and a cocktail of *Lactobacillus helveticus* and *Bifidobacterium longum* can reduce cortisol levels—an indicator of stress. A preliminary report finds that a probiotic mixture containing *Bifidobacterium lactis, Lactobacillus bulgaricus, Streptococcus thermophilus,* and *Lactobacillus lactis* can substantially alter brain activity in the mid- and posterior insula, regions associated with anxiety disorders and attentional focus. Kefir, yogurt, and other fermented milk products containing probiotics have been shown to have a positive effect on mood and the brain's emotional centers. And emerging evidence suggests that eating more fiber promotes gut health and microbiomic balance.

It was long believed that the microbiome of older adults, established over decades, is both stable and resistant to environmental influence. Recent studies, however, have suggested otherwise. The distinct microbiome of the elderly is accompanied by a marked reduction in the capacity to cope with a variety of stressors and by progressive inflammation throughout the body. Microbiomic balance can also be abruptly altered by short-term changes in diet.

A particular problem concerns older adults in long-term-care facilities.

The gut microbiome of such individuals shows substantially less diversity than that of older adults who continue to live in the cities, towns, and farms they always lived in. Interacting with a large and diverse number of people (and farm animals) maintains a diverse microbiome. The extremely antiseptic nature of long-term-care facilities, and the restricted pool of inhabitants (mostly older humans), may impoverish the microbiome and reduce its diversity. In a few studies so far, the loss of diverse community-associated microbiota correlates with increased frailty, inflammatory conditions, and even death. An important new frontier in gerontology is going to be modulating the individual's microbiome with dietary interventions designed to promote healthier aging. Indeed, an exciting consortium of researchers called ELDERMET has come together at University College Cork in Ireland. Their findings strongly suggest that gut microbiome interventions are necessary for older adults to maintain satisfactory levels of physical and mental health.

Research on this is just getting started. There are no clinical guidelines yet about how to do this, and medical science takes years. In the meantime, you may feel you don't want to wait. The best thing you can do is check with your doctor, preferably a gerontologist or, better yet, a gastroenterologist about gut health.

Alternatively, self-dosing with probiotics is not as crazy as it might seem, according to Harvard Medical School. Unfortunately, a broad range of products are sold in the United States, the United Kingdom, and Europe, and they vary widely in the type and amounts of bacterial cultures they include. In the United States, they are not regulated by the FDA and so quality can vary dramatically. There is a small amount of evidence showing that probiotics function best when taken in the context of actual food (or liquid suspensions) rather than in pills or capsules. The big problem is that most probiotic formulations can't survive the acidic environment of the stomach, and if they do, they don't thrive enough to colonize the gastrointestinal tract. Because different formulations and dosages can confer differential effects, no specific recommendations can be made unless a particular product has been tested. The efficacy of any probiotic product is determined by factors including the specific microbial species, the dosage, the formulation, the viability of the probiotics both on the shelf and within the intestine, the residence time in the gut, and the means of ingestion. Therefore, any scientific findings for one probiotic product or strain cannot be assumed to apply to another probiotic. It's difficult to be an informed consumer when these factors are rarely tested before a probiotic product goes to market.

The unregulated nature of the probiotic market makes it difficult to know what to do. One formulation that was tested and confirmed effective by published peer-reviewed studies, VSL#3, was sold by its inventor to a pharmaceutical company that inexplicably *changed* the formulation and rendered it ineffective. This was the subject of an $18-million jury verdict against the company. The PepsiCo-owned beverage KeVita Kombucha is advertised as containing "live probiotics," but a lawsuit filed in 2017 argued that the pasteurization process used by PepsiCo killed the live bacteria (a second lawsuit filed in 2018 argued that sugar levels in the drink tested six times higher than what was stated on the label). In 2009, the Dannon Company settled a $35-million lawsuit for false advertising claims it made about the benefits of its Activia line of probiotic yogurt, which was priced 30 percent higher than regular yogurt but in fact had no differential effects. Two probiotic products that are known to be effective as of this writing—to reestablish a healthy gut microbiome—are listed in the notes at the end of this book. Your physician or dietician may be able to provide updated information as well.

Even less is known about prebiotics, those substances that encourage the growth of healthy bacteria in the gut. Food molecules are known to protect probiotics, so it's usually suggested that probiotics be taken with a meal that contains prebiotics. Prebiotics are specialized plant fibers found in many fruits and vegetables, especially those that contain complex carbohydrates. These carbohydrates aren't digestible, so they pass through the digestive system to become food for the bacteria and other microbes. Dozens of foods act as prebiotics, including apples, asparagus, bananas, chicory root, garlic, honey, mushrooms, seaweed, wheat bran, yams, and yogurt. Your doctor or a dietician can help you to choose the best for you.

Looking at this from the other end, you may have read about fecal microbiota transplantation (bacteriotherapy), in which fecal material from a healthy person, which contains beneficial bacteria, is transplanted into the patient in order to restore the normal balance of gut bacteria. Scientists see the potential for treating a range of diseases, including cancer, diabetes, and possibly even Alzheimer's. The technique has had mixed results and is still experimental. So do not try this at home. (Or if you do, don't let it hit the fan.)

Where Do We Stand?

Taken together, cardiovascular disease, stroke, cancer, and diabetes account for approximately two-thirds of all deaths in the United States and more than $700 billion in direct and indirect costs each year. If dietary changes can reduce the incidence of these diseases, it will have a truly significant effect on world health. The professional organizations that represent the researchers and clinicians who treat these diseases, the American Heart Association, the American Cancer Society, and the American Diabetes Association, published a joint statement of dietary recommendations. They concluded, simply, that higher intake of fresh fruits and vegetables, whole grains, and fish is associated with a reduced incidence of all these diseases.

Herman Pontzer, an evolutionary anthropologist at Duke, studies health among hunter-gatherer societies whose lifestyles are similar to those of our ancestors. He found that they generally exhibit excellent health in spite of following a wide range of diets. It doesn't matter if they get 80 percent of their calories from carbohydrates, or from animal fat, or from nuts and berries—almost all eat more fiber than the average American, but that is about the only difference. (This takes a lot of wind out of the paleo diet.) Interestingly, they don't shun sugar, consuming it in the form of honey. Notably, though, they don't have access to processed foods or deep-fried foods. Kevin Hall did a short-term controlled experiment. Participants were admitted to the NIH Clinical Center (so they could not cheat) and he fed them ultra-processed foods for two weeks, and unprocessed foods such as fish and fresh vegetables for two weeks (in random order). He carefully matched the number of calories, and levels of sugar, fats, and nutrients that were presented in the meals, but participants could choose how much they wanted to eat. People scarfed down the ultra-processed foods more quickly, and they ate 500 more calories every day, gaining about a pound a week compared to when they were offered unprocessed foods.

Pontzer's research, consistent with that of many other scientists, finds that there is no one best diet and that we "can be very healthy on a wide range of diets." Pontzer notes that one reason hunter-gatherers tend not to have obesity is the lack of variety in any given individual hunter-gatherer's diet. When we have a lot of food choices, we tend to overeat because the variety of flavors is enticing. "It's the reason you always have room for dessert at a restaurant even when you're full," Pontzer says. Even though you're full "and you can't eat one more bite of steak, you're still interested in the cheesecake because it's sweet and that button hasn't been worn out in your brain yet."

There is a related movement called intuitive eating, developed by registered dietician Evelyn Tribole. It has been associated with reduced body mass index, reduced cholesterol, lowered blood pressure, and improved psychological health. Mallory Frayn, a doctoral student in my department at McGill University, studies people's experiences and frustrations with most diets. She writes:

> Why don't diets work? First off, the fact that a multi-billion-dollar diet industry still exists suggests that there's something fundamentally broken about the way we look at food and eating. We take some "expert's" advice about how we should treat our body, try it for a bit before it inevitably fails, and then move on to the next greatest thing, all the while the behind-the-scenes bigwigs are making a pretty healthy chunk of change off of our collective struggle. . . .
>
> Diets don't work because they are based on restriction. God forbid you touch carbs, our most fundamental source of energy, lest they go straight to your waistline. Restriction subsequently fosters deprivation, and ultimately, you're left craving all of the foods you've been told are off-limits. . . .
>
> It's a normal human thing to want to eat a variety of different foods that taste good.
>
> But diets don't tell you that . . . eventually, you're going to break. You're going to have a chocolate bar or order a side of fries (because both of those things are totally acceptable for a human being to eat). When it happens though, you'll feel miserable for breaking your "healthy" streak. Plus, you won't go blaming the diet for your "failure," you'll put it all on yourself for being a terrible person.

The cycle of repeatedly dieting and failing is damaging both physically and psychologically. The big idea of intuitive dieting is that your body knows what kinds of food you need—that it has an intuitive drive toward protein, carbs, and fats you can trust. Or perhaps it's the trillions of microbes in your gut that send signals to your brain to generate that intuitive drive. Maybe your body knows what it wants to eat.

The four additional principles of intuitive dieting are:

1. try to eat when you're hungry;
2. try to stop when you're no longer hungry;
3. learn to cope with emotions in alternative forms, other than eating; and
4. place no restrictions on types of food eaten unless for medical reasons.

Now, like me, you may be skeptical about your body "knowing" what foods you need. It just doesn't sound scientific. How do you distinguish intuitive eating from a decidedly maladaptive craving, such as wanting to eat a pint of ice cream every night? First, this kind of binge eating is often spurred by a desire for emotional comfort—an attempt to relieve stress and anxiety by eating traditionally forbidden foods, such as those high in fats and sugars. It results in high levels of shame and regret, not to mention weight gain and microbiome imbalance, and it feeds a vicious cycle.

In contrast, intuitive eating involves a reframing of eating for physical rather than emotional or social reasons. Thus, knowing that any food option is on the table, so to speak, makes you less likely to binge eat the forbidden foods. Proponents of intuitive eating, such as Mallory Frayn, talk about cultivating a less obsessive, healthier relationship with food and allowing the body to experience a healthy variety—in moderate amounts—of all the foods that are available to us. And all of this should be informed by good sense, and the knowledge that although you might consume them once in a while, the chocolate-cake-and-onion-rings diet is not a good long-term strategy for optimal health.

Much of the attention in the popular press about what we eat is on so-called superfoods, such as blueberries, acai, kale, and sweet potatoes. But this approach ignores what nutritionists call matrix effects, the ways in which foods in a real-life, optimal diet interact with one another. Often, you can't try to feed a particular problem without creating another one, and that's a central issue in nutrition journalism: There is often a narrow focus on only one aspect of nutrition, or one health outcome, while ignoring another.

The key to diet seems to be not what you eat, but what you don't. The American diet is too high in processed foods, sugar, salt, and red meat. Junk food is addictive—it overstimulates the brain's reward system, which evolved in an era when fats and sweets were hard to come by. Apart from that, the fact is, we just don't know enough about nutrition to say that there is a single best diet. As a report on the state of nutritional advice at Stanford University noted, "The history of nutrition science is littered with the remains of hypotheses that were once the next big thing."

At present, what does seem to be clear is that large amounts of refined sugar, deep-fried foods, and heavily processed foods are unhealthy. Apart from that, eating a variety of different foods, in moderation, and eating more vegetables than the average American currently consumes, all appear to contribute to longevity and health. Reducing the use of tobacco and alcohol is also indicated. After reviewing hundreds of papers, I find that the best dietary advice for older adults is the much-quoted phrase in Michael Pollan's 2008 book *In Defense of Food:* "Eat food. Not too much. Mostly plants."

And allow yourself to have fun now and then. Eat a little ice cream. Have some chocolate.

10

EXERCISE

Movement matters

A septuagenarian colleague of mine, visiting from San Diego, broke his hip after slipping on black ice in Montreal. He was bedridden for months. In fact, he never really recovered, and although he lived another seven years, those years were painful and frustrating for him and all who knew him. Why? You might think that something physical, like a hip injury, would have no bearing on his mental state. But we humans were not made to be sedentary. We evolved in a world that required us to explore the environment, to move. Without that stimulation the brain ceases to function at its full potential . . . and can easily go into a tailspin.

In his new book, *Physical Intelligence: The Science of How the Body and the Mind Guide Each Other Through Life,* Scott Grafton, a neuroscientist and practicing neurologist at UC Santa Barbara, proposes that the enormous complexity of the human brain is primarily there to organize movement and action. When we cease to move, to explore our environment, when we no longer use our brains to organize physical action, could it be that it slows down, atrophies, and becomes disorganized? If that were so, how can we account for people like Stephen Hawking and Jean-Dominique Bauby (the guy who dictated an entire book—*The Diving Bell and the Butterfly*—with blinks of the eye)? Are these individuals exceptions?

When I posed this question to Dr. Grafton, he explained:

> I can't speak for two geniuses who had entire staff keeping them alive for an extended period. Put enough effort into it and you can grow a rose bush in the middle of the Mojave Desert.

> Nor am I saying that *not* being physical makes you stupid or atrophy.
>
> Rather, we can ask, how to best maintain whole organismal health and well being for anyone? Step one is to eliminate the brain/body dualism. Just because some aspects of mental life and mind are intuitively separable from brain, doesn't mean the brain (or mind for that matter) is ever really free of the body.
>
> Step two. What is the single factor with the largest effect that benefits mental health, body structure (including brain structure), functioning across multiple domains, and longevity? It is physical activity (or its imprisoned corollary, "exercise"). We've now had hundreds of trials with thousands of subjects.
>
> Step three. Why is all this physicality good for us? Well, there is a long list of probable reasons. My book touches on just those that make sense from a perspective of movement science: skill, adaptation and perceptual fidelity in the natural world. But there are lots of others—problem solving, social enrichment, mind-body coordination, and fresh air.

Grafton's findings are based on the idea that at the most fundamental level, the brain is a giant problem-solving device. Furthermore, most of its problem-solving capabilities evolved to allow us to adapt to a wide range of environments. Ten thousand years ago, humans plus their pets and livestock accounted for about 0.1 percent of the terrestrial vertebrate biomass inhabiting the earth; we now account for 98 percent. Our success is owing in large part to our problem-solving, adaptive, and exploratory brains.

Our brains were built to move our bodies toward food and mates, and away from predators. Exercise is important for two reasons. The obvious one is that it oxygenates the blood. The brain runs on oxygenated glucose, carried by hemoglobin in the blood, and a fresh supply of oxygen is good. The nonobvious reason is that our brains, because they were built to navigate in unfamiliar surroundings, don't do well when they're not challenged by having to problem solve. Every step you take on a treadmill or elliptical is helping you with the first of these two imperatives—getting your blood oxygenated—but they don't help your brain to keep its navigational skills and memory systems honed. Every minute you walk on an unpaved trail, whether in a park or in the wilderness, requires you to make hundreds of microadjustments to foot pressure, angle, and pace. These adjustments stimulate the neural circuitry of your brain in the precise way that it evolved to be used. The area that is most stimulated is your hippocampus, that seahorse-shaped structure that is critical to memory formation and retrieval. This is why so many studies show that memory is enhanced by physical activity.

This way of looking at things is known as embodied cognition, the idea that physical properties of the human body, particularly the perceptual and motor systems, play an important role in cognition (thinking, problem solving, action planning, and memory). In this way of thinking, the sensation of movement is inextricably bound with knowledge. Embodied cognition is consistent with this book's developmental cognitive neuroscience approach. It sees humans as embodied, ecologically and genetically embedded social agents who shape and are shaped by their environment. The body influences the mind just as the mind influences the body. Embodied cognition puts intelligence and control out in the body. The best example of this is the spring ligament in the arch of the human foot. This dumb little spring eliminates the need for a massive feedback control circuit in the brain to give the toes a nice little push-off during walking.

If you have a cartoonish version of the different characters you went to high school with—the nerds versus the jocks—you may see them as holding down opposite lifestyle choices: The nerds, ever bookish, shun physical activity in favor of the more refined rewards of deep thoughts. The jocks, ever boisterous and active, shun the dull, nerdiferous, and slow-moving pace of reading, writing, and 'rithmetic. And although such characters surely exist, the most successful intellectuals are those who embrace the physical, and the most successful athletes are those who embrace the intellectual. Among my university colleagues, those who keep physically active are by far the most productive, from my collaborator James Ramsay—the one who rode his bicycle across the Canadian Rockies in his late sixties—to my wife, Heather, who is a distance runner and rock climber. I've recently had the opportunity to meet with top college and NFL players, including five-time Super Bowl winners (to discuss the effects of repetitive head injuries on cognition in later life), and they are as smart, inquisitive, and intellectual as anyone I've ever met in a university.

After a particularly stimulating conversation with Yauger Williams, a former Cal Bears right guard, he leaned back and said, "You know, this is great. And this is the closest I've ever been to an actual neuroscientist." I said, "It *has* been great. And this is the closest I've ever been to a football player without having my head flushed down a toilet!" (He laughed, a bit too knowingly.)

A systematic meta-analysis showed that for adults with mild cognitive impairment, exercise had a significant beneficial effect on memory. Adults with mild cognitive impairment have a considerably increased risk of progressing to dementia, and this specific risk is increased by atrophy of the hippocampus. Physical activity may be just as effective as pharmaceutical agents in improving and maintaining memory, as well as global cognition, and delaying the onset of dementia and other neurological diseases such as Alzheimer's and Parkinson's.

Aging is an irreversible and inescapable process. But the *effects* of aging are, in some cases, reversible and, if not completely escapable, at least subject to delay. There are many factors under our control—diet, gut microbiota, social networks, sleep, regular visits to the doctor. But the single most important correlate of vibrant mental and physical health is physical activity. This doesn't mean the other correlates (diet and sleep) aren't important—they are—and it doesn't mean that if you engage in more physical activity you don't need to follow other healthy practices. What it does mean is that you might want to take this seriously—particularly if, like many people, your attitude about getting active is "Yeah, yeah—I'll start tomorrow."

As Scott Grafton points out, physical activity is not the same as exercise. It's moving around, interacting with the environment. As Cicero knew, it is this kind of interaction that "supports the spirits, and keeps the mind in vigor." Running has benefits, but so does walking, even with a cane or a walker. The physical activity doesn't need to resemble the kind of workout that twenty- or thirty-five-year-olds might do. It's important to respect your body's limits and to consider age-related factors. Older adults should check with their doctors or work with a professional trainer to determine what kind of movement is right and appropriate for them. If you can run marathons like ninety-two-year-old Harriette Thompson did, that's great—but you may find that you get substantial benefits simply from lifting five-pound free weights in your bedroom and walking around the block at a slightly faster than comfortable pace.

Looking at memory, movement, and embodied cognition as being interrelated helps to explain one of the biggest mysteries of human memory: infantile and childhood amnesia. Generally speaking, we don't remember anything from our first two years of life, and only a little before age six. (People who claim to have vivid memories of early childhood are often mistaken and are reporting stories that were told to them by parents or siblings, or mistaking photographs of events for primary memories of those events.) If memory evolved to help us with spatial navigation, the reason that very young children have no memories is because they are not moving around and interacting with the environment very much. Although children, even before they can walk, are eager to explore the space around them, it appears that the onset of walking triggers neurochemical activity in the hippocampus, prompting the hippocampal place cells and grid cells to begin their internal mapping of the environment. Place cells encode particular locations, and grid cells encode the relations among those locations. Even though most children have been moving around and exploring the environment by age six, it may take time for the hippocampal place system to mature to the point that it can accurately encode spatial memory in an adult-like fashion. Hence a lack of infantile and childhood memories.

An implication here is that as older adults begin to move and explore less than, say, young or middle-aged adults, those hippocampal-based memory systems might atrophy—use it or lose it, as the professional athletes say. The central role that the hippocampus plays in general, not just in spatial memory, can additionally account for other cognitive impairments often seen in less active older adults—including decrements in reasoning, hand-eye coordination, and problem solving, as well as general cognitive slowing.

The embodied cognition view further states that our cognitive and perceptual abilities are not a static endowment but rather emerge from fruitful and active exchanges with the environment. As children, we gain a sense of agency and control over the environment through our interactions with it—playing in the sandbox, playing on a jungle gym. We can lose that sense of agency and control if we reduce our interactions with the environment, which can lead to a loss of motivation and confidence in our ability to deal with our environment, setting off a downward spiral. This is particularly a problem for older adults who are already experiencing three kinds of bodily changes that may spur them to interact with the environment less.

First is loss of dexterity, which comes from a general slowing down of nerve transmission speed, loss of nerve conductance, and reduction in eye-hand coordination. Second is a loss of motivation, which may be born of isolation and feelings of loneliness. Third is a loss of joy and pleasure at doing things for oneself, partly owing to reductions in the production and uptake of dopamine, the brain's reward-chemical signaling channels.

Taken together, these can lead people to curtail activities unnecessarily—that is, not for health or safety reasons. Abandoning a particular activity, such as walking on uneven terrain, or slicing vegetables, leads us to perceive ourselves as "someone who doesn't perform these kinds of actions anymore" and creates a growing self-image as a nonagent in the world. This can be one of the worst things about aging.

I'm not suggesting that older adults should engage in activities that are unsafe. If you or a loved one has a balance problem, or find you just can't safely handle a sharp knife anymore, those are very real considerations. But it's important to take an honest and fair assessment. Fear or trepidation about engaging in activities you've enjoyed your whole life just because you're "old" might not be a legitimate reason to abandon those activities—and may actually accelerate your entry into true "old age." Six women I know received knee replacements in the past year, and they range in age from fifty-two to eighty-four. James Adams, the "outside the box" Stanford mechanical engineering professor I mentioned in Chapter 4, is eighty-five now, and the last time I stopped by to see him, he had a fleet of antique tractors in his yard and was restoring and rebuilding their engines, a favorite pastime for him. Mick Jagger (age seventy-five) works with a personal trainer. "I train five or six days a week. . . . I alternate between gym work and dancing, then I do sprints. I'm training for stamina." Jane Fonda (age eighty-one) works out every day with long walks and weights. As Dylan Thomas advised, they are not going gently into the night.

Interacting with the world also enhances creativity. The interactions don't have to be especially complex, and they certainly don't have to be boundary pushing or dangerous. Older adults who were allowed to walk around an outdoor landscape freely, compared to those who were made to walk around a rectangular path, showed significantly higher scores in a battery of creativity tests, including a divergent thinking task—we saw these in Chapter 4, on problem solving. The researchers asked participants to generate as many uses as they could for an everyday object—in this case chopsticks. Sample answers that indicate divergent thinking included using them as drumsticks, as a conductor's baton, as a child's magic wand, as a coffee stirrer, or to toast marshmallows. You get the idea. And the researchers found that simply walking around outside enabled a person to come up with more answers.

You may have noticed that thus far in this book I have scrupulously avoided pinning down what I mean by "older adults." This is because it's all relative and subject to a large number of factors including disease history, weight, stress, and genetics. There are fifty-year-olds who are unhealthy and ninety-five-year-olds who act and feel more like sixty-year-olds. To me, "older adults" are those who are manifestly *slowing down*, physically and mentally, who can't do many of the things they used to do, and who are discovering that the things they might want to do are becoming constricted by physical and mental limitations.

A large part of the story of people who manage to stay young, in spite of their chronological age, relates to synaptic plasticity—the ability of the brain to make and form new connections. As we've seen, plasticity is influenced by your genetic makeup, your lifetime of experiences, and the culture in which you live. It is also influenced by your daily routines, especially as you get older. The act of transmitting information across synapses, and the forming of new synaptic connections, requires a dramatic increase in the amount of energy used in the brain. Astrocytes, a type of brain cell, serve as suppliers of that energy. A mounting body of evidence shows that physical activity increases the effectiveness of astrocytes and thereby enhances synaptic plasticity, memory, and overall cognition.

In addition to synaptic plasticity, cognition is maintained and enhanced by neurogenesis—the growing of new neurons. As we saw in the memory chapter, the adult hippocampus grows seven hundred new neurons per day on average, and there does not seem to be a decline with normal aging. Physical activity has been shown to increase hippocampal neurogenesis in rodents. It's not possible to observe any such changes in humans, but we have observed improvement in memory for human adults who engage in aerobic physical activity. Most effective is to engage in aerobic exercise just before learning something new. When you get your heart rate up just before a mental task, you prime the brain with increased blood flow, which creates an enriched setting for mental activity.

Different kinds of physical activity confer different benefits. Physical activity can be categorized as either aerobic or anaerobic. The American College of Sports Medicine (ACSM) defines *aerobic* activity as "any activity that uses large muscle groups, can be maintained continuously and is rhythmic in nature." It includes swimming, cycling, running, dancing, and walking. It's called aerobic because *aerobic* means "living in the presence of oxygen," and these activities leverage the body's ability to use oxygen to extract energy from carbohydrates, amino acids, and fat. The ACSM defines *anaerobic* activity as "physical activity of very short duration, fueled by the energy sources within the contracting muscles and independent of the use of inhaled oxygen as an energy source." It includes things like strength (weight) training and short-distance running. (Note that Jane Fonda's current, age eighty-one workout includes both.)

Aerobic activity is the kind that reduces risks of heart disease and promotes the kinds of cognitive functions we've discussed so far. Anaerobic activity can help to build muscles, increase your endurance and ability to withstand fatigue, and decrease body fat. It can also have a small beneficial effect on cardiovascular risk and lipid profile.

Sarcopenia is the loss of muscle tissue—similar to what osteoporosis is for bone. It is a leading contributor to functional decline and loss of independence in older adults. Fortunately, it can be reversed. In one study, twelve sedentary men aged sixty to seventy-two significantly increased their leg strength and muscle mass with a twelve-week strength-training program three times a week. In another study, eight weeks of resistance training created significant improvements in frail nursing home residents aged ninety to ninety-six. They saw a 174 percent gain in strength, and walking speed improved almost 50 percent. So it's not just about endurance or blood oxygenation—maintaining muscle strength is essential as well.

Of course, interacting with the environment isn't always possible—weather conditions in much of the world during winter make going outdoors uncomfortable and, as my colleague in Montreal who slipped on the ice found, sometimes dangerous. So we turn to indoor fitness. Although embodied cognition says that interacting with the environment is best, avoiding sedentarism is crucial. Adults aged sixty to seventy-nine years who engaged in indoor aerobic training showed increased brain volume in the frontal and temporal cortices as well as larger white-matter tracts.

These findings are significant because these formerly sedentary oldsters exhibited healthier brain measures even when aerobic exercise was first initiated later in life.

Minimal Movement; High-Intensity Interval Training

As we age, we do have a tendency to stop moving. For some people, sedentarism starts around age fifty, for others around age seventy, and some never slide into it. But as we've seen, this lack of movement can be the source of many of our problems.

Ulrik Wisløff is the head of the Cardiac Exercise Research Group at the Norwegian University of Science and Technology and a member of the American Heart Association Statistics Committee. He started something of a revolution about fifteen years ago when he published research showing that even a *little bit* of physical activity can be transformative for brain health and longevity. Wisløff has developed a high-intensity, short-interval program that confers many of the benefits of more conventional, serious workouts and can be done in just three days a week in sessions of about twenty minutes each. Even in this overcaffeinated age when all of us have so much to do, surely anyone can find an hour a week to do this. The payoff was significant, reducing the risk of heart attack or angina by up to 50 percent.

For those who don't want to do more, but really want to do less, Wisløff and others have shown that even shorter, less structured workouts are still remarkably beneficial. High-intensity interval training (HIIT) is a very short workout—thirty seconds to a minute of running, climbing stairs, or cycling—followed by a minute or two of cool-down activities, such as walking or slow pedaling. Repeat the cycle for only *ten minutes* and you've just done a HIIT. "While anything helps, a bit more is probably better," University of Michigan researcher Weiyun Chen commented.

Todd Astorino, a professor of kinesiology at California State University San Marcos, who has published more than twenty papers on HIIT, explains, "We now have more than 10 years of data showing HIIT yields pretty much the exact same health and fitness benefits as long-term aerobic exercise, and in some groups or populations, it works better than traditional aerobic exercise." The problem with most exercise programs is that the people who need them don't find them enjoyable and therefore don't stick with them. Time-efficient workouts, like HIIT, provide an alternative, one that the majority of participants find far more enjoyable, and that avoids the monotony of traditional programs. In another study, Astorino debunked the two-thousand-year-old myth that having sex before an athletic competition diminishes performance (it doesn't).

How intense does a HIIT workout need to be? You should try to achieve 90 to 95 percent of your maximum heart rate during the short, high-intensity periods. Online tools can help you figure out your maximum heart rate as a function of your age. (A well-known rule of thumb, to subtract your age from the number 220, is misleading for overweight and older populations, so it's best to talk to your doctor or find an online calculator that takes your weight into account.) If you're new to all of this, you can buy a heart rate monitor at a sporting goods store or online, and you can wear it on your wrist or across your chest. If you don't want to invest in equipment before you see if you like it, you'll know you've reached the desired intensity if you can no longer carry on a conversation while running or cycling. You can still run or bike. You just can't talk.

Wisløff's research group has also developed an online tool that allows you to enter some physical measurements and a brief lifestyle history to calculate your "fitness age." You might find that your fitness age is younger than your chronological age (keep up the good work) or older than your chronological age (time to get serious about increasing your physical activity).

Regardless of your fitness age, if you are starting from a sedentary lifestyle, you should initiate any new program gradually and with the advice of a physician or personal trainer familiar with older bodies. The risks of hurting yourself unintentionally rise with each decade after sixty—torn rotator cuffs, damaged tendons, falls, and broken bones are all too commonly the price that some older adults pay for being overexuberant. We remember back to when we were kids and would engage in any new activity without thought, moving our bodies in any way that occurred to us, usually with complete and utter impunity. In our minds we are still that limber, flexible kid. We forget that time in our thirties or forties when we got a sprained ankle or hurt back so easily. You might still be physically capable of doing a large number of things, but it's especially important for older adults to ease into it, to learn how to stretch before and after, and to stay hydrated.

Small Changes, Not Gym Memberships

The story gets better yet. Even the teensiest, tiniest, barely measurable amount of physical activity improves brain function—not as much as the HIIT mentioned previously, but it is significant and it matters. The very largest improvements we've seen for reducing risks of cardiovascular disease and diabetes, and improving memory, come not from moderately active people who engage in a more systematic and intense program, but from sedentary people who engage in the *barest minimum* of physical activity—even just getting up and walking a bit.

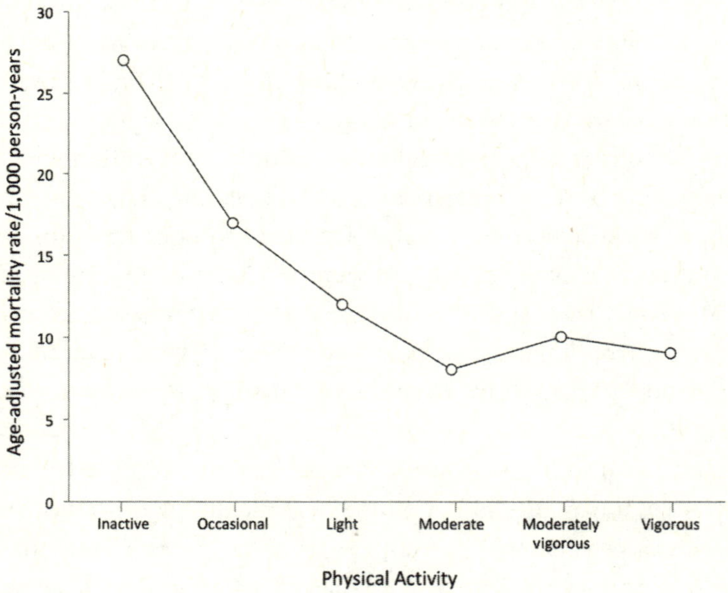

The figure above comes from a study of more than six thousand British men. The curve shows their mortality rate (death due to all causes on the y-axis) as a function of physical activity level. As you can see, the steepest drop in the curve—showing the most pronounced benefit—is between inactive men and men who had only "occasional" physical activity. And at least in this study, vigorous activity was not associated with any gains above moderate activity. The oldest adults tracked in this particular study were eighty-four.

This concept of minimal activity made a splash in 2018 with a paper published by an international research team led by Kazuya Suwabe from the University of Tsukuba in Japan and Michael Yassa at the University of California, Irvine. They had people engage in a single bout of light physical movement, just ten minutes of pedaling on a stationary bicycle so lightly that it barely raised their heart rates at all. A control group sat on the bicycles and didn't pedal. Afterward, the researchers gave everyone a standard memory test. During a study phase, participants briefly saw a series of pictures of everyday objects, say, a sofa or a tree. During a testing phase, they were then shown either the pictures they had previously seen or pictures that were different but similar. This is a difficult test because it relies on keeping subtle differences active in memory. These are the kinds of distinctions we make every day when remembering, say, that we parked our car on the second floor of a parking structure versus the third, or that the new person we just met is named Ellen and not Elaine, or that, yes, we *did* take that heart pill at lunchtime.

The participants who engaged in even this minimal physical movement outperformed the couch potatoes (er, stationary bike potatoes) by a substantial amount. The researchers performed the experiment again, but this time, they presented and tested the pictures inside a brain scanner (fMRI). They measured activity and connectivity in the hippocampus, and connectivity in other cortical areas associated with learning and memory. What they noticed was immediate enhancement of these brain regions and connections, simply as a result of this extremely light movement. The brains of the participants who pedaled lightly worked very differently from the brains of those who were stationary—there was more coordinated activity in these essential memory circuits, and the more difficult the memory task, the more coordinated activity they found. Furthermore, the neural enhancement was specific to those regions involved in learning and memory—other brain regions, such as the amygdala, perirhinal cortex, and temporal pole, showed no difference, allowing us to rule out that exercise created a globally higher state of brain arousal.

Prior to this study, it was widely thought that the benefits of exercise were dependent somehow on the body entering a stress response and releasing cortisol. But Suwabe and Yassa measured cortisol in their participants and found no differences—the improvements in both hippocampal activity and connectivity occurred even without a stress response. Further good news is that you don't have to be physically active over a long period to see benefits. Cognitive benefits show up immediately, and by twelve weeks improvements in cerebral blood flow are evident.

Movement activities are particularly helpful, indeed essential, for individuals who have a cluster of conditions called metabolic syndrome—increased blood pressure, high blood sugar, excess body fat around the waist, and abnormal cholesterol or triglyceride levels—which substantially increases the risk of heart disease, stroke, and diabetes.

One of the problems with exercise is that, like with dieting, people start out with overly ambitious plans that are difficult to maintain. The majority of people fail to follow through with these plans because they lose interest or find them boring or too difficult to integrate into their daily routines. For those who are out of shape, the thought of going to a gym may be intimidating. It is a fact of the gym industry that a large proportion of people who take out gym memberships end up not using them—this is one of the reasons that so many gyms require that you pay for a year in advance!

Walter Thompson, a kinesiology professor at Georgia State, summarizes:

> We cannot just tell people that they need to exercise more; it does not work. Our work clearly shows that we need to demonstrate lifestyle modifications that can be adopted by most of the population and get away from sending people to gyms. Small changes in behavior, like parking your car in the last row instead of the first row at the grocery store or climbing stairs instead of the elevator, are just two examples.

Richard Friedman at Weill Cornell Medical College extols the virtues of walking for neurocognitive health: "Perhaps it's the fact that you are constantly bombarded by new stimuli and inputs as you move about, which helps derail linear thinking and encourages a more associated, unfocused thought process."

Last August I visited my friends Heather and Len, who, at age sixty-nine, are both physically and mentally very active. We went for a hike in a forest near their house in the Quebec countryside, a hike they do regularly but I had never done before. Actually, calling it a hike is a bit highfalutin. It was really just a walk in nature, on dirt trails. The walk was invigorating, and all of these ideas about embodied cognition, and the words of Scott Grafton, came together for me on this walk. Look at this cell phone photo I took of the path.

A tangle of branches, roots, and rocks, it demands attention to avoid tripping. Every minute of walking requires hundreds of microdecisions about where to place my foot, how much pressure to use when setting my foot down and picking it up again, how to balance myself, how to lift off my foot to move forward to the next step. This rugged terrain wasn't the half of it. I had to be attentive to avoid getting whacked in the face by low-hanging branches. Birds and critters were all around, and although I didn't fear that any of them would attack me, I did have to brush away spiders, flies, and mosquitoes, and the occasional three-year-old running up and down the trail with a stick flaying wildly across the path. The number of variables—things that could happen to you—is infinite. You see it in the excitement of your dog. The varied terrain, the people, the vegetation, are all changing. The chance of running into people or things you haven't encountered before, or haven't encountered in exactly that way before, adds to the thrill. *This* was the kind of navigation our brains evolved to perform. *This* was the kind of embodied cognition that strengthens synapses and rejuvenates hippocampal memory systems, motor-action planning systems, and eye-body coordination. Outdoors, anything can happen. And that's the most potent way of keeping the brain flexible and active that we have so far discovered. A bustling city street can render some of these same effects, minus the hidden and ancient power of naturescapes to be mentally soothing and stimulating at the same time.

Scottish doctors have begun issuing prescriptions for "rambling and birdwatching." And as journalist Justin Housman says, these prescriptions are being used to treat a wide variety of maladies:

> For everything from high blood pressure to diabetes, anxiety, and depression . . . ailments and diseases can be treated with activities like bird watching, maybe a little kayaking, perhaps combing a beach for shells, even skipping pebbles across a slow moving stream.

Doctors in Quebec have begun prescribing free visits to the Musée des Beaux-Arts Montreal (Montreal Museum of Fine Arts) for patients suffering from a number of physical and mental health issues, to enjoy the benefits that art can have on one's health. Walking indoors through a museum (or even a mall) provides a high chance of coming across people and things you haven't seen before, and the amount of ground you cover can be surprising.

Exercising on a treadmill is good. Walking around the neighborhood is better. Walking in nature is the best. The winter after my colleague slipped on the black ice, I went out and bought crampons—traction cleats—so that I wouldn't have an excuse not to walk in the long Montreal winters. I will not go gently.

11

SLEEP

Memory consolidation, DNA repair, and sleepy hormones

When I met with His Holiness the Dalai Lama, he was eighty-three years old and had just published his 125th book. "How do you stay so mentally fit?" I asked him.

"Sleep," he said without missing a beat. "Nine hours a night."

"Every night?"

"Every night."

Sleep is restorative. While you're unconscious of what's going on around you, possibly immersed in a world of dreams and weird thoughts, your entire body and brain chemistry change. Cellular repair and cleansing mechanisms kick into overtime. Wound healing and fighting off of bacterial and viral infections increase in intensity. It's only recently that we've begun to appreciate the enormous amount of cognitive processing that occurs while we're asleep. Consolidation of memories takes place, alongside problem solving, categorization, and emotional processing.

The neural and cellular basis of the need for sleep has been called the sleep drive. Neuroscientists still don't understand where that drive comes from, but it can be conceptualized as a homeostatic pressure that builds up during the waking hours and dissipates during sleep. We do know that there are chemicals in the brain that lead us to feel sleepy—somnogenic agents such as melatonin and adenosine—and the gradual accumulation of them creates this homeostatic pressure.

Consistent with the kinds of individual differences we looked at in Chapter 1, people regard sleep differently. Some look forward to it and some see it rather neutrally, as a necessity such as brushing your teeth, and don't give it much of an affective connotation one way or another. A third group sees it as something to be avoided at any cost, for as long as possible.

In the "looking forward to sleep" camp there are some who just like it because it is pleasant—it feels good. Then there are some, like songwriter Billy Joel, who find it a great source of inspiration and creativity. His album *River of Dreams* is a nod to the fact that many of his ideas for songs came to him during sleep. "I wake up every morning, I get out of bed and I've got a song idea in my head. Not necessarily a song idea, but either a melodic idea or a symphonic idea. I dream symphonies sometimes." Paul McCartney wrote one of the Beatles' greatest hits, "Yesterday," in his sleep, and Keith Richards wrote the main riff to the Rolling Stones' "(I Can't Get No) Satisfaction" in his sleep, woke up and recorded the guitar part on tape, and then went back to sleep. Stephen Stills wrote one of his most loved songs, "Pretty Girl Why," during a dream.

In the "put sleep off as long as possible" camp, Thomas Edison viewed sleep and nightfall as annoyances, as "nuisances to be vanquished." Edison was a workaholic and his development of the incandescent light bulb allowed him to work more hours in the day. (Some say Edison "invented" the incandescent bulb—but a long list of at least twenty others preceded Edison's work on it, which largely was to refine it.) Writer David Kamp notes that the refinement of the light bulb "was as much a profound upending of the natural order as it was a huge technological advance—the first step on the path to our current age of screen addiction, overlong workdays and sleep deficits." And the first step in tricking nature's pineal gland into thinking it was daytime when it was not; the first step in messing with our chronobiological clocks; and the first step in creating several generations of artificial-light-induced insomniacs.

Joni Mitchell is also in the sleep-avoidance camp, and for most of her adult life she would drink as many as ten cups of coffee a day and smoke three packs of cigarettes in order to put off sleep. She got some of her best work done in the middle of the night when there were no distractions, no phones ringing, and no human-made noises outside her home. (On the occasions when she and I worked together, it was often between midnight and four A.M.)

Although putting off sleep may work for an occasional few nights, it is a bad long-term strategy. In his new book, *Why We Sleep,* UC Berkeley neuroscientist Matthew Walker warns that we are in the midst of a "catastrophic sleep loss epidemic" that poses "the greatest public health challenge we face in the 21st century." Many have claimed that climate change, obesity, and access to clean water are greater threats to public health, but even if sleep loss comes in at #4, it is a serious threat—and one that each of us as individuals can do something about directly.

You may have read somewhere that each individual has their own sleep requirement that can vary from only a few hours to ten or twelve a night. Although this is technically true, the proportion of people who can get along on fewer than five hours of sleep a night without showing major impairment is tiny—less than half of 1 percent. You may be one of those, but it is not at all likely that you are. The idea that older adults need less sleep is a myth. They tend to *get* less sleep, but they still need the eight hours that the rest of us need.

Today, about half of adults sleep less than seven hours a night. Why? Here's Walker:

> First, we electrified the night. Light is a profound degrader of our sleep. Second, there is the issue of work: not only the porous borders between when you start and finish, but longer commute times, too. No one wants to give up time with their family or entertainment, so they give up sleep instead. And anxiety plays a part. We're a lonelier, more depressed society. Alcohol and caffeine are more widely available. All these are the enemies of sleep.

Walker also points to one of the parts of the developmental science triune as a culprit—culture:

> We have stigmatized sleep with the label of laziness. We want to seem busy, and one way we express that is by proclaiming how little sleep we're getting. It's a badge of honor. When I give lectures, people will wait behind until there is no one around and then tell me quietly: "I seem to be one of those people who need eight or nine hours' sleep." It's embarrassing to say it in public. . . . Humans are the only species that deliberately deprive themselves of sleep for no apparent reason.

Sleep deprivation can occur in two primary ways—it can be of either insufficient duration or insufficient quality. That is, you may sleep eight hours a night, but for various reasons you may not pass through the requisite stages of sleep, or you may not stay in each of them the optimal amount of time. You may think you're asleep when you're not. Or, if you have sleep apnea, you may be waking hundreds of times during the night without realizing it.

Healthy, productive sleep allows the body to engage in cellular repair mechanisms—normal cellular housekeeping and immune-system responses—and helps us to process difficult emotions and replenish our energy levels.

The Roman poet Ovid knew something about these functions of sleep more than two thousand years ago:

> Sleep, thou repose of all things; thou gentlest of the deities; thou peace of the mind, from which care flies; who dost soothe the heart of men wearied with the toils of the day, and refittest them for labor.

One of the functions of sleep is to process the most emotionally intense experiences of the previous day, to separate the facts from our feelings so that we can reach a quasi-objective view of things. The other reason for doing so is so that the emotions themselves can be entered into and stored in memory. It is of value to be able to access a memory based not just on a particular time or a particular place (which we can all do), but also on a particular emotion. All the experiences you've had of being humiliated, for example, can be bound together through emotional memory, in order to help you extract patterns and (hopefully) modify your future behavior. Sleep-deprived people show a 60 percent greater activation in their amygdala during waking hours than those who are not sleep-deprived. Because the amygdala is part of the brain's fear circuit and is known to trigger aggression, anger, and rage, this finding highlights the relation between sleep deprivation and emotional regulation. When your mom told you that you were being crabby because you didn't get enough sleep, she was probably right.

The act of living and staying awake, going about our business, leads to a buildup of toxins in the blood and brain. Cerebrospinal fluid circulates throughout the brain and spinal cord, and it clears away toxins through a series of channels (like waterways) that expand during sleep. Almost none gets cleared away while you are awake. Why all this happens better during sleep than during wakefulness is not fully understood. Too little sleep, or—perhaps counterintuitively—too much sleep, impairs problem solving, attention to detail, memory, motivation, and reasoning.

A U-shaped distribution has been uncovered, showing that people who sleep less than seven hours a night or more than ten are at an increased risk for hypertension. Similarly, sleep duration of less than six hours or more than nine is associated with increased prevalence of diabetes and impaired glucose tolerance. Poor sleep duration or quality, as well as too much sleep, also increases stress and allostatic load—the cumulative effects of stress over time.

If I haven't frightened you into taking sleep seriously yet, sleep deprivation is now strongly associated with Alzheimer's. Alzheimer's disease occurs when a certain kind of protein, amyloid, builds up in the brain, where it forms clumps that collect between neurons, which in turn disrupt cell function. During proper, restorative sleep, these amyloid deposits get cleaned out of the brain through the action of the cerebrospinal fluid. When you're sleep-deprived—either from short duration or poor-quality sleep—these amyloid deposits don't get cleaned out, and they tend to selectively attack regions in the brain responsible for sleep, which then makes it even more difficult to sleep and, consequently, more difficult to clear out the amyloids. A vicious, sleepless, memory-killing cycle. And it doesn't happen only in chronic sleep deprivation—a study published the week I first drafted this paragraph showed evidence from PET scans that amyloid plaque deposits build up in the brain after only a single night without sleep. (Under the protocol, participants may have managed to sneak in short catnaps during the night, but nurses were vigilant, checking on them every hour throughout the night and waking them if necessary.) The areas most impacted by sleep deprivation were the hippocampus (memory) and the thalamus (control of sleep-wake cycles). It is becoming clear that a lack of sleep, particularly a chronic lack, can lead to Alzheimer's disease. If you want to lengthen your health span, better to follow Ovid than Edison.

Resetting Your Sleep Cycle

We sleep in roughly ninety-minute cycles, comprising stages that are neurochemically and electrophysiologically distinctive. You've probably heard of the two kinds of sleep, REM and non-REM. REM stands for rapid eye movement sleep, the time when we are typically dreaming. Non-REM sleep occurs first, in four stages, with increasingly deep sleep, during which the frequency of brain waves slows down.

While considering a mental hospital and its residents, Charles Dickens wondered, in his essay "Night Walks," about the feeling that dreams are a form of insanity:

> Are not the sane and the insane equal at night as the sane lie a dreaming? Are not all of us outside this hospital, who dream, more or less in the condition of those inside it, every night of our lives?

Dreams help us to work things out—to let thoughts that are too dangerous, insane, or distressing have a safe haven in our minds, while our bodies are temporarily paralyzed, preventing us from entering into dangerous real-world situations. (A small proportion of people don't experience paralysis during their dreaming. Sometimes it is drug induced: The sleep medication Ambien has been associated with sleepwalking, sleep-eating, sleep-driving, and a number of disturbing accidents and crimes, including at least two murders.)

REM sleep helps us to maintain emotional balance. And a lot of what happens during REM sleep is simply random neural firing that has no particular meaning. Non-REM sleep is when our memories of the previous day are consolidated and linked with previous experiences. If you meet someone new at a party named Mary, your brain—without your instructing it to do so, and without your conscious awareness—will recall her face and gestures and link them to the things she said and to her name. It may link to other people you know who remind you of her, and other people you know named Mary. While we enjoy non-REM sleep, our brains toss and turn over the experiences of the previous day (or two, if you stayed up all night), making connections between those and similar, past experiences.

This is especially true for procedural or motor learning. If you learn to play a musical instrument, do a Rubik's cube, or take up salsa dancing, your motor movements need to be encoded in memory. But learning wouldn't happen if in each lesson you were starting from scratch—the lessons need to build on one another. In order to do that, the fine motor and muscle movements you make today need to be integrated at a neural level with what happened on previous days. For lifelong skills, many years' and decades' worth of neural traces become linked to the new ones. Sleep does this.

Walker describes what's happening in the brain during non-REM sleep as a kind of "synchronized pattern of rhythmic chanting." He writes:

> Researchers were once fooled that this state was similar to a coma. But nothing could be further from the truth. Vast amounts of memory processing is going on. To produce these brainwaves, hundreds of thousands of cells all sing together, and then go silent, and on and on. Meanwhile, your body settles into this lovely low state of energy, the best blood-pressure medicine you could ever hope for.

Acetylcholine levels drop during non-REM sleep and then reach a peak during REM sleep, helping to prevent outside inputs from disturbing your dreaming. Acetylcholine is also an important chemical that mediates memory consolidation. If levels of it are reduced in the brain, or delayed, memory can be impaired for several days. Melatonin and acetylcholine levels trade off with norepinephrine levels during sleep—the former two reach a peak at bedtime, while norepinephrine, a neurotransmitter responsible for action and wakefulness, is decreased.

Passing through non-REM and then REM sleep adds up to a sleep cycle. A great deal gets done during such cycles, and it appears that we need five or six of them to reach full restoration. How do you know whether you're getting enough sleep? Unless you've got certain medical conditions or are taking medications that cause fatigue, a simple rule of thumb is that if you can't wake up in the morning without an alarm clock and you feel sleepy before lunch, either you are sleep-deprived or, as we saw in Chapter 8, your circadian clock is misaligned. To determine your personal amount of sleep needed, find a two-week period when you can afford to experiment, a period during which you're not under any particular stress or deadlines and when you have free evenings—no late-night dinners. Try to avoid alcohol and caffeine, or, if you must have caffeine, try to limit yourself to two or three servings a day, and none within seven hours of bedtime. Sleep in a darkened room where sunlight won't disturb you in the morning. Then just go to sleep when you're tired and wake up when you feel like waking up, without an alarm. Keep a log of your sleep and wake times. If, like most of us, you've been sleep-deprived for some time, you'll need to pay back your sleep debt. Near the end of the two weeks, however, your body should have settled into a rhythm and you should be able to wake up without the alarm, feeling refreshed.

Sleep and the Aging Brain

We've seen that aging is typically associated with a reduced ability to adapt to environmental changes, impairments in perception and normal physiological functioning, and an increased susceptibility to disease through reductions in immune-system efficacy. The time course at which all these changes become noticeable varies from person to person, but it's rare that someone over eighty hasn't noticed these changes, and many people notice them after fifty-five.

It's not surprising, then, that changes in sleep biology accompany aging as well. The causes of sleep disruptions in older adults include a decreased amplitude of the circadian rhythms generated by the SCN (the timekeeper in the brain that maintains circadian rhythms), the degradation of neural signaling in the aging brain, and impairments in melatonin production. More than 40 percent of people over sixty-five report sleep problems. Nighttime sleep is often interrupted by frequent awakenings (sleep fragmentation); these interruptions become more frequent in the early-morning hours, and it can become more and more difficult to get back to sleep.

With increasing age, the essential slow-wave sleep stage, a phase of non-REM sleep, is reduced, and early-night REM sleep increases. Restless leg syndrome, the urge to move one's legs while sleeping, is common in older adults, and this results in increased sleep fragmentation. Disordered breathing, including sleep apnea, is also common and is related to decreased lung capacity, obesity, loss of pulmonary control, and reductions in thyroid function. Sleep disturbance causes memory loss and some physical and psychiatric illnesses, including depression. And it increases the risk of neurodegeneration and mortality.

The problem is that although sleep requirements remain the same as we age, our ability to fulfill them decreases. Older adults are more likely to take naps as a way to compensate for poor nighttime sleep quality. Naps *can* compensate for poor nighttime sleep, but it's best to limit them to twenty minutes or you can suffer from sleep inertia—your body may want to stay asleep and a long nap may make you groggier than a short one. You may have read news reports showing that naps are associated with a decreased risk of cardiovascular disease, but there is conflicting evidence on this point and more research needs to be done. The problem is that most studies don't control for the duration of the naps, or for the amount of nighttime sleep that people are getting. So the studies combine different groups of behaviors, and it's hard to draw any firm conclusions.

Insomnia comes in many forms—an inability to get to sleep, an inability to stay asleep, poor and inefficient sleep quality, and their annoying cousin, daytime tiredness. As Matthew Walker notes, the past one hundred years of industrialization have interfered with sleep around the world as extended hours of artificial light, and, more recently, the blue light from computers, tablets, and phones, disrupt the melatonin-generating system in our brains. If you're going to follow the traditional folk wisdom to read a book when you have difficulty sleeping, don't read an electronic device that emits blue light—it can reduce melatonin by up to 50 percent.

Hypersomnia is the opposite of insomnia—sleeping too much. Some unfortunate people can have both at the same time, whereby they sleep too much for a day or two, then stay awake for a night or two, repeating a cycle. Such cycles are unhealthy, and often fueled by drugs, alcohol, and caffeine.

Hypersomnia can be the result of a degenerative neural disease or depression, or it can result from the more organic cause of increased sleep fragmentation among older adults: Multiple awakenings during the night can lead to poor sleep quality, which fails to restore the homeostatic balance of sleep-wake cycles, and so our bodies crave more and more sleep. Similarly, obstructive sleep apnea causes sleep fragmentation and can lead to hypersomnia. One common cause of hypersomnia is drug use, particularly benzodiazepines (such as Valium or Ativan), anxiolytic medications, antipsychotics, antihistamines, and antiepileptics.

The relationship between hypersomnia and depression is complex.

Depression leads to a modulation of brain chemistry that could cause us to want to sleep more. Yet sleeping more, even in the absence of depression, alters the balance of the wake-up chemicals, the body's own "uppers," and so can lead to depression. And antidepressants often have a paradoxical effect. Instead of motivating a get-up-and-go feeling, many people are impelled to lie down and sleep . . . and sleep and sleep. Remember David Anderson's warning: Your brain is not simply a bag of chemicals. Introducing what seems to be a desirable change in brain chemistry, such as increasing serotonin or norepinephrine availability, can have unanticipated consequences.

Treatment for hypersomnia involves slowly removing any prescription drugs that may be causing excessive sleepiness, avoiding alcohol, and resetting your sleep cycle. When that doesn't work, modafinil or armodafinil upon awakening is generally safe, is tolerated well, and helps to maintain daytime wakefulness without causing jitters, nervousness, or sleep difficulties at night.

Special Problems of Women

Menopausal symptoms last seven and a half years on average, and for some women symptoms last significantly longer. Salient among these are vasomotor symptoms, which include night sweats, hot flashes, flushes, and vaginal dryness. These vasomotor symptoms can be a direct cause of sleep disturbance, or sleep disturbances can occur independently, from any of the variety of factors already mentioned. A meta-analysis of more than fifteen thousand women showed that sleep improvements occurred with menopausal hormone therapy (MHT, also known as hormone replacement therapy, HRT or simply HT) for women who had vasomotor symptoms, but hormone therapy did *not* improve sleep quality for women who had sleep disturbances due to other reasons. Hormone therapy involves the administration of estrogen, either alone or with progesterone. There are different dosages, formulations, and routes of administration available, and their effectiveness varies.

Hormone therapy remains controversial because, on the one hand, if it helps sleep quality, it can fend off the long list of diseases associated with sleep impairments. On the other hand, there are credible—but not definitive—reports of risks associated with hormone therapy, including increased risk of breast cancer. I've found the literature to be a confusing mess, so I reached out to Sonia Lupien, a specialist in hormone replacement therapies at the University of Montreal. We went out for coffee at my favorite local coffeehouse (where they roast their own beans), and I asked her what to make of all of this.

> I would really like to give you a clear answer on this one . . . but this is exactly where we are at this point, i.e. in the middle of nowhere! On one side we have the Women's Health Initiative [WHI] study that showed increased risk of breast cancer in women using hormone therapy and on the other side, we have other studies stating that it is not that bad, we just have to start hormone therapy later in life (and not at forty years old like some did in the past) and all should be ok. Members of the public are still stuck in the middle.

A review of where we are at by Rogerio Lobo of Columbia University Medical Center, published in the *Journal of Clinical Endocrinology and Metabolism*, says that

> in the 10 years since WHI, many women have been denied hormone therapy, including those with severe symptoms, and . . . this has significantly disadvantaged a generation of women. Some reports have also suggested an increased rate of osteoporotic fractures since the WHI. Therefore, the question is posed as to whether we have now come full circle in our understanding of the use of hormone therapy in younger women.

Lobo goes on to point out some flaws in the study and in the way in which it was reported in the press. Although hormone therapy did increase the risk of breast cancer, the likelihood of getting breast cancer still remained extremely rare, and this was swept under the rug. Also not revealed in the initial reports was that women in their fifties who began hormone therapy had a 30 percent reduction in mortality. Lobo concludes,

> The current data, particularly with estrogen alone, are highly supportive for a prevention role in reducing fractures, coronary

> heart disease, and mortality in younger women who initiate therapy close to menopause. . . . We need to individualize therapy in those women with symptoms, with the view that in young healthy women, we probably have come full circle, and a role for hormone therapy in prevention may at least be entertained.

Special Problems of Men

With aging, men undergo a kind of menopause called andropause, concomitant with reductions in testosterone levels. This can lead to hot flashes, night sweats, enlarged breasts (gynecomastia), loss of strength, memory impairment, depression, cognitive decline, changes in sexual function, and disruptions in sleep. Whereas in women menopause means the end of fertility, this is not so in men, who may remain fertile into their eighties and nineties, despite reductions in androgens. Hormone replacement therapy for men consists of testosterone administration. Side effects are minimal as long as testosterone levels are kept within the normal physiological range. For men with prostate cancer, the research on hormone therapy yields contradictory results and is still in a state of confusion: Some studies show that hormone therapy feeds prostate cancer; others show that it is preventative. Add to this the conjecture that most men over the age of seventy-five are developing some form of prostate cancer, even if asymptomatic and undiagnosed, and you've got a real problem trying to figure out what to do. Some men fear cancer more than anything else; others fear that andropausal symptoms will impair their lives significantly enough that they seek to do something about it. These quality-of-life issues are very personal and difficult to sort through without professional guidance. Like the confusion with hormone therapy for women, the best advice for men is to educate yourself and consult with a doctor you trust.

What You Take before Bedtime

Caffeine can disrupt sleep, but not in everyone. My friend Max Mathews, the computer music pioneer, used to drink eight cups of strong coffee every day, and he'd have one right before bedtime. He lived to be eighty-five, which doesn't seem so old today, but for someone born in 1926 it's extraordinary. If I drink a cup of coffee before bedtime, I'll be up all night. So clearly it affects people differently, and intrepid geneticists have determined that genetics plays a role in caffeine metabolism and tolerance, and they've begun to identify some of the genes through studies of twins.

Caffeine breaks down in the body to paraxanthine (80 percent) and to theophylline and theobromine (16 percent). Theophylline is also present in tea, and theobromine is present in chocolate.

Adenosine is a somnogen—a sleep-promoting chemical in the body. The stimulant effects of caffeine and its metabolites (theophylline and theobromine) occur because they block adenosine receptors in the brain, and this blockage promotes sleeplessness. Incidentally, the principal chemical in marijuana, delta-9-THC, increases the level of adenosine in the basal forebrain, leading to sleepiness, although there are other ingredients in marijuana that can keep some people awake. It all depends on the interaction of your particular adenosine and cannabinoid receptors. In most stoners, marijuana use ultimately leads to sleep.

On average, caffeine increases sleep latency, the amount of time it takes people to fall asleep after lying down and deciding they want to sleep. It also reduces total sleep time and quality of sleep. Caffeine can reduce melatonin secretion levels by 30 percent. Caffeine also shortens stage 3 and 4 sleep, the most restorative phases, and reduces the amplitude of slow-wave delta band brain activity. Delta wave activity is a reliable indicator of how much sleep need we have. Because caffeine blocks adenosine receptors and attenuates delta waves, sleep homeostasis could be affected, meaning that the cues your body normally uses to go to sleep and stay asleep are disrupted at a molecular level.

I mentioned melatonin in Chapter 8—here's a bit more about it. Melatonin is a naturally occurring hormone in the body, secreted by the pineal gland during the dark hours of the day, typically a couple of hours before bedtime. It is also produced in other parts of the body. In the retina it is believed to have protective effects on photoreceptors. In bone marrow, it functions as a scavenger of free radicals and enhances immune function, reducing oxidative damage and protecting against iron overload and deterioration in these highly vulnerable cells. In the gastrointestinal tract, melatonin heals and protects against disorders and is being used experimentally as a treatment for gastric cancer, reflux esophagitis, peptic ulcers, ulcerative colitis, and intestinal ischemia/reperfusion.

Melatonin is also widely found in the plant kingdom, where it regulates day-night bio-cycles and acts as a scavenger of free radicals. In tomatoes, for example, it helps to protect the components of photosynthesis. In peas and red cabbage that are grown in copper-contaminated soil it enhances their tolerance and survival rates. This makes melatonin a very old chemical compound that, through evolutionary history, found expanded functionality in mammals.

The American Academy of Sleep Medicine recommends the timed use of melatonin supplements to promote adaptation to new time zones or to help individuals having trouble sleeping for other reasons (such as age-related disturbances of the sleep-wake cycle). Melatonin taken in midafternoon (in conjunction with avoiding blue light) will advance the circadian clock, causing the body to think that nighttime has come early. The effect is somewhat mild, certainly not as powerful as a sleeping pill, but for many, this gentle nudging of the clocks is enough to promote sleep. As Johns Hopkins University sleep researcher Luis Buenaver says, "Your body produces melatonin naturally. It doesn't make you sleep, but as melatonin levels rise in the evening it puts you into a state of quiet wakefulness that helps promote sleep."

Melatonin levels in the blood are highest in young people (55–75 pg/ml) and start to decline after the age of forty, with the fastest decrease found from sixty years of age onward, reaching very low levels in the elderly (18–40 pg/ml). New research suggests that melatonin may have protective effects against many cancers, which may be part of the reason that as people age—and melatonin levels go down—they are more susceptible to cancers.

Sleep Hygiene

Given the time-dependent nature of hormonal release schedules that are governed by the circadian clock, what is the most important thing about sleep? To go to bed at the same time every night and wake up at the same time every morning. Even on weekends. This may mean forgoing late parties if you're an early bird, or missing early-morning events if you're a night owl. Although few of us lived this way in our twenties and thirties, by the time you reach sixty-five or so, you may begin to notice that inconsistency has become even more punishing. Even a slight change to the schedule—staying up an hour later than usual, for instance—can affect your memory, alertness, and immune system for *days*. Adrian de Groot, the Dutch chess master and psychologist who performed some of the most famous experiments on the minds of chess players, lived to ninety-two. To maintain his mental acuity during the last twenty-five years of his life, he was fastidious about going to bed and waking up at the same time every day.

Follow these steps. They apply to people of any age, but as we get older it can become increasingly necessary to be strict about them.

1. Start getting ready for bed about two hours before sleep time. Stop watching TV, using a computer, tablet, or smartphone, or other sources of blue light (daylight wavelengths) that could act as a zeitgeber for the pineal gland and cause your brain to produce wake-up hormones. Do something that helps you relax—a warm bath, reading, music listening, whatever works for you.
2. Ensure that the room you sleep in is completely dark. If you have a clock, charger, or other device that emits blue light, cover it up. Make sure that your curtains block out both daylight and any artificial light that may come into the bedroom.
3. Sleep in a cool room if possible.
4. Help to keep your sleep and wake cycle synchronized properly by getting sunlight in the morning—even on a cloudy day, the wavelengths you need can activate the pineal gland. A simulated dawn (blue-light) lamp for fifteen to thirty minutes in the morning can help.
5. Write in a journal before bedtime. Recent research shows that it helps you to relax and can improve memory. It's especially effective if you write a quick to-do list for tomorrow. Worrying about incomplete future tasks is a significant contributor to difficulty falling asleep.

6. Don't rely on sleeping pills for more than one or two nights. The sleep they induce is less productive and less restorative than natural sleep.
7. Go to bed at the same time every night. Wake up at the same time every morning. If you have to stay up late one night, you should still get up at your fixed time the next morning—in the short run, the consistency of your cycle is more important than the amount of sleep.

PART THREE

THE NEW LONGEVITY

The applications of Part Two are relatively straightforward guides to better aging. The topics of Part Three are more complicated. Much of what we hear about longevity, quality of life, and cognitive enhancement should be confronted with skepticism. But there are many bright spots. No, we can't live forever, but we can live longer than ever before. We can stay active well into our nineties and beyond and make valuable contributions to our world. And, no, playing computer games won't save you from Alzheimer's, but . . . Read on, wise reader.

12

LIVING LONGER

Telomeres, tardigrades, insulin, and zombie cells

The longest life ever authenticated was Jeanne Calment of France, who lived to be more than 122 and died in 1997. There doesn't appear to be anything remarkable in her diet, exercise routine, or other lifestyle details, at least nothing that would suggest a life span longer than anyone else's. Jeanne enjoyed desserts. She smoked two cigarettes a day from the age of 21 to 117. (Why she quit at 117 is not clear. Of course, quitting can be difficult—maybe it just took her that long.)

What was Jeanne's secret? Maybe it's as simple as the old Groucho Marx quote: "Anyone can get old. All you have to do is live long enough." Or maybe not. When scientists talk about aging we're not talking about chronological age, because there is a wide variety of ways that people age. What we're really interested in is the accumulated effect of things that happen to our bodies that cause difficulties. Neuroscientists use the word *senescence*—just a fancy Latin-rooted word that means to grow old or to age. You can't do anything to turn back your chronological age, but you can decrease the likelihood of senescence by adopting simple practices.

It has been accepted wisdom for decades that the life span of humans is limited to around 115 years, with only a few exceptions popping up every now and then. A number of explanations for this have been offered, without proof, such as a cellular clock that preprograms our death (which begs the question of why we would be preprogrammed to die). One thing remains constant, however: People do die. As does the hope of reversing income inequality and the illusion that humans are rational. Also pets die. And houseplants. Novelist Chuck Palahniuk (*Fight Club*) writes that "on a long enough time line, the survival rate for everyone will drop to zero." Or, as economist John Maynard Keynes famously quipped, "In the long run we are all dead." The ubiquity of death suggests to some that eventual death is foreordained at the cellular, and therefore genetic, level.

But wait. In the wild, a great number of animal deaths are caused by predators. Our ancient human ancestors typically died at the claws of predators or from infections. Among modern humans, 90 percent of deaths overall are from cancer and cardiovascular disease. If you could remove injury and disease from the equation, might we live forever?

Immortal Animals

When I was eight years old my friend Barbara lived around the corner. Normally, as a self-respecting eight-year-old boy, I would not have played with girls, but Barbara had three older brothers, and she had a BB gun. She climbed trees. She loved playing in the mud in the creek behind her house, and we would spend hours there catching salamanders. She had a scout knife and one day she cut a worm in half. "You can't kill them," she said authoritatively. "Both halves will grow into a new worm." I watched in amazement as both halves squirmed and slithered and eventually found their way back into the water. (Fortunately I am not a Freudian, or I would have to confront an early female archetype during my presexual development cutting a worm in half.)

A few years later in science class we were to collect eight different butterfly species and pin them to a corkboard. I couldn't find it in me to do it and took a failing grade on the assignment. My college professors brooked no such sentimentality and I found myself working in a monkey lab during my sophomore year.

It turns out that Barbara was wrong about that earthworm. If it survived at all, the part that contained the head would have grown a new tail, but the tail would have continued to writhe and wiggle for a while before dying. But some worm species do regenerate entire new selves from just a small piece of tissue. Biologist Mansi Srivastava discovered the gene, *EGR*, that allows for worms and other animals to regenerate damaged limbs and tissues and functions as a switch turning these regeneration processes off and on. This same gene is present in other animals and humans. In an experiment Barbara would have loved, Michael Levin and Tal Shomrat of

Tufts University cut the head off of a planarian flatworm and found that the tail, in which no brain tissues remained, could regenerate a new brain. The amazing thing is that the new tail-generated worm retained the long-term memories of the old worm. How *that* works we don't know yet.

Biologists have identified several species that can theoretically live forever, if only they can avoid predators, accidents, and nosy scientists; they just don't seem to age or to die of old age. One is a species of jellyfish (*Turritopsis dohrnii*). When it encounters a life-threatening stressor, it can revert to what is essentially a younger stage of its life and start over. Another is hydras, a collection of several species of freshwater organisms that are about a third of an inch long. Instead of their cells gradually deteriorating over time, they are constantly renewing and staying young, due, we think, to the large amounts of a gene they have called *FOXO* that encodes for the protein FOXO. (But there must be more to the story than that, because artificially overexpressing *FOXO* in other animals doesn't seem to increase longevity.)

Hydra oligactus in freshwater

Lobsters are not immortal, but they don't die of aging and disease because of their ability to regenerate missing parts (it's no coincidence that the word *gene* is part of the word *regenerate*) and their ability to have continuous cell multiplication—they just keep on growing and growing. We think lobsters do this through action of the enzyme telomerase. You may recall telomeres from the perception chapter (Chapter 3), the protective caps at the end of DNA sequences that become shorter with each replication. Telomerase rebuilds these end caps. And lobsters have lots of it, in every part of their bodies. Telomerase is plentiful in human embryos, but after we're born our levels drop dramatically, leaving insufficient amounts to perform all of the telomere repair we would need to extend our lives. That's probably a good thing, because telomerase also repairs cancer cells, preferentially so over normal cells, allowing the cancer cells to replicate indefinitely. So if you were thinking that telomerase therapy might protect you from the effects of aging, as it does for lobsters, the telomerase would somehow need to be adapted to distinguish cancer cells from normal cells, and we don't know how to do that yet.

My favorite example of a long-lived and possibly immortal animal is the tardigrade, a microscopic (about half a millimeter long) eight-legged creature who looks like something from a sci-fi movie, wrapped in a burlap sack. Here's one magnified about 250 times:

Tardigrades can survive harsher conditions than any other animal we know of, including exposure to pressure extremes, radiation, lack of oxygen, dehydration, starvation, and even extreme temperatures: They can be frozen or heated past the point of boiling water. They can even survive in outer space. (NASA has tested this!) When stressed by adverse conditions, tardigrades enter a kind of superhibernation state in which their metabolism is suspended by 99 percent. They can survive thanks to an unusual type of protein (IDP) that replaces the water in their cells, causing them to transition into a glassy (vitrified) state as they dry out. Another protein, called Dsup, protects them from the effects of radiation.

Human Life Span

The study of human longevity has been marked by a great deal of controversy, and a bifurcation of efforts—focusing either on statistical studies of thousands of people at a time or on individual cells and cell assemblies. At both ends of inquiry, scientists study the interaction between genes and the environment (and, to some extent, culture). Epidemiologists and other population scientists have looked at entire groups of people (such as Mediterraneans, with their famous "diet") to identify trends in lifestyle choices and to conduct genetic studies to better understand the genetic component to longevity—no one doubts that there is one, but the question is how much of the variability in aging can be attributed to genetic differences. Cell biologists and geneticists are trying to understand cellular communication, repair processes, gene expression, and other details. The population studies have suffered from a lack of controlled experiments. Nearly all of the data come from naturalistic, opportunistic experiments. The cellular-level studies are conducted mostly in worms, flies, and other nonhuman organisms, and although these are model systems for humans—all cellular organisms kinda sorta work the same way—translating this knowledge to any practical interventions for human longevity is far from straightforward.

As an example of the first kind, the population analysis, a 2016 study published in *Nature* argued for a limit to human life span. Analyzing global demographic data, molecular geneticist Jan Vijg and his colleagues argued that improvements in survival rates with age tend to level off after age one hundred and that the age at death of the world's oldest person has not increased since the 1990s. They surmised from this that the maximum life span of humans is fixed and subject to natural constraints. I found this argument odd when I read it. Vijg did not base his conclusions on biology or genetics. Rather than demonstrating the kinds of "preprogrammed cell death" that some have speculated about, or demonstrating that regeneration processes simply become exhausted at some point when accumulated damage becomes too great, Vijg's approach used only population statistics. He looked at ages of death around the world across several decades and found that for many years, life expectancy, as well as the life span of the oldest living humans, steadily increased and then reached a plateau. If there is a plateau, he reasoned, it must be that human life is limited.

Many scientists questioned Vijg's data collection methods and his argument; neither Vijg nor his coauthors are demographers or statisticians. "They just shoveled the data into their computer like you'd shovel food into a cow," said Jim Vaupel, director of the Max Planck Institute for Demographic Research. And there's a big hole: A cornerstone of scientific reasoning is that just because you didn't find something doesn't mean that it doesn't exist. If you had looked at men's times for the one-mile run between 1850 and 1950, you would have concluded that because no one had ever run a mile in less than four minutes, no one ever would. Although the world record running times improved over this period, from 4:28 to 4:01:4, it seemed to many that four minutes represented a physical limit, a plateau. Then came Roger Bannister, and since then, eighteen new records have been set, the most recent in 1999 by Hicham El Guerrouj, at 3:43:13. We don't know if there is a limit to human longevity, but if 115- and 120-year-olds are dying of diseases, perhaps those diseases can eventually be eradicated. If they're dying of "parts wearing out," perhaps medications or technology can extend life, as it already does with artificial hearts and pacemakers. The Achilles' heel as of today is the brain—we don't know yet how to fix an aging brain. But that could change.

Two McGill biologists, Bryan Hughes and Siegfried Hekimi, challenged the *Nature* paper, showing that Vijg's mathematical assumptions were flawed. Based on their own analysis of death records, they came to the opposite conclusion, that no evidence exists for a limit on human life span, and if such a limit exists, it has not yet been reached or identified. Hekimi says he doesn't know what the age limit might be and believes that "maximum and average lifespans . . . could continue to increase far into the foreseeable future. . . . No limit to human lifespan can yet be detected." He's also quick to point out that a longer life span, say, living to 150, doesn't mean that these older adults will spend their extra years in miserable health. “The people who live a very long time,” he notes, “were *always* healthy. They didn’t have heart disease or diabetes.” Thus, a longer life span usually means a longer health span. Sociologist Jay Olshansky, at the School of Public Health at the University of Illinois, disagrees. “Hekimi needs to spend some time in a nursing home or Alzheimer’s ward,” he says, “to get a dose of reality.” (Academics can be competitive.)

Shortly after all this brouhaha, an Italian statistician at the University of Rome, Elisabetta Barbi, conducted a thorough analysis of thousands of elderly Italians who had lived to 105 or longer. Normally, the risk of dying increases with age—an 80-year-old is significantly more likely to die within the next five years than a 40-year-old. But Barbi’s team found that after 105, the risk of dying flattens out to a plateau, so after that age, your risk of dying in the upcoming year holds at fifty-fifty. Hekimi, who was not involved in the study, praised it. It suggests that there may *not* be a limit, especially if we can figure out how to control diseases that typically afflict people between the ages of 80 and 104. Statistically speaking, if you can make it to 104, it’s smooth sailing from there on. As one research group put it, “Current understanding of the biology of aging points firmly away from any idea that the end of life is itself genetically programmed.”

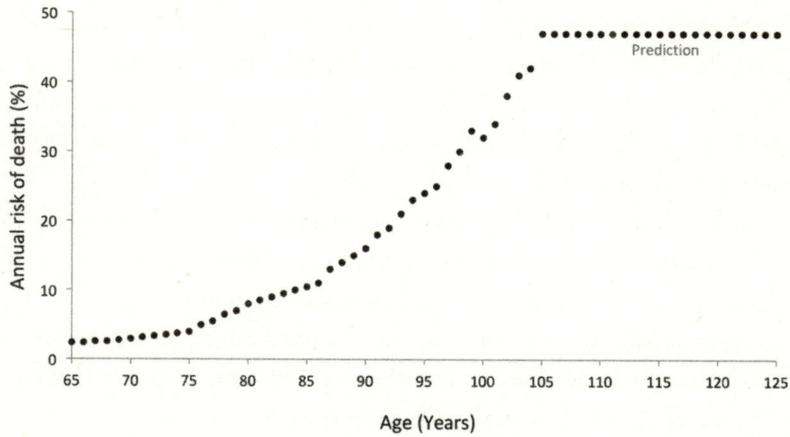

That little drop in risk of death that is visible at the one-hundred-year mark would seem to indicate that people who get close to the age of one hundred want to stay alive to see their one hundredth birthday. I know I would.

Blue Zones

So-called blue zones made headlines in 2008 when demographers discovered the four places in the world that had the highest number of people over age one hundred: Nicoya, Costa Rica; Sardinia, Italy; Ikaria, Greece; and Okinawa, Japan (some lists add Del Mar, California). Most people living in the blue zones have the following in common:

- They are physically active, not through weight and endurance training, but through chores, gardening, and walking as an integrated part of their lives—they move a lot.
- Their lives have a sense of purpose by doing things they find meaningful.
- They have lower levels of stress and a slower pace.
- They have strong family and community ties.
- They follow a varied diet with a moderate caloric intake, but mostly based on plant sources and high-quality food.

Now, all this is appealing because it's consistent with what we know about healthy lifestyles. But the blue zones are not evidence that they work, because there are a number of statistical flaws in this line of work. Few in the scientific community are taking the blue zones seriously—there are fewer than a dozen papers on the blue zones in peer-reviewed journals, and none in top-tier journals.

First, the people living in the blue zones tend to engage in these positive lifestyle factors, but still only a very, very small number of them live beyond one hundred. Doing these things does not guarantee a long life by any means. Moreover, we don't know if the particular individuals who do live beyond one hundred are among the ones that practice these behaviors, or if they practice them more or less than the average person.

Most important is the well-known statistical principle of variability and sample size. In small samples (that is, small datasets) you'll more often encounter observations that deviate from the average (the mean) than in large samples. For example, we know that there are roughly an equal number of male and female infants born. If you look at the ratio in a small hospital, say, where there were only six births, you might find four girls and two boys—67 percent girls. In a large hospital with sixty births, you might find thirty-four girls and twenty-six boys—57 percent girls. With increasing sample size you will tend to get closer to the true distribution. And so it is with aging. The number of people over one hundred years is very small compared to the population of the world—there simply aren't enough of them for the statistics to be reliable. (Another methodological brouhaha.)

Genetics versus Environment

There's an old saying that if all you have is a hammer, everything looks like a nail. Geneticists look for genes that recur in familial patterns that appear to confer certain behavioral or physical predispositions. The problem, though, is that not everything that runs in families is genetic. Consider French speaking, which does run in families. Some would say that there is a gene for speaking French. But they'd be wrong. Children of French-speaking parents are more likely to be taught French than children of non-French speakers. And a couple who speak the same language are more likely to raise children together than a couple who don't.

Graham Ruby, a bioinformatics scientist, took a hard look at the longevity data from 400 million people. It turns out that the true heritability—the influence of genes on longevity—is only around 7 percent, much less than had been previously assumed. It's true that longevity runs in families, but in Ruby's study, longevity was almost as likely to show up in nonblood relatives, like in-laws, as in blood relatives. That's because of a concept called assortative mating. When selecting a mate, most of us tend to be most comfortable with someone who is somewhat like us in terms of physical attractiveness, intellect, sociability, and other traits. That means that we're choosing people who possess some genes similar to ours, even though we are not closely related. What this all means is that culture and environment—the healthy lifestyle changes you make—are more important than genes for predicting how long you'll live. (An obvious exception is if you have a gene that strongly determines a fatal disease.) What makes it look like longevity runs in families, then, is all the things other than genes that families share—homes, neighborhoods, access to education and health care, culture, and cuisine. So it's true, for example, that a good, protective variant of the *APOE* gene keeps showing up again and again in centenarians and, yes, in blue zones and quasi-blue zones. But it seems to be telling such a minor part of the story that efforts toward living a longer life are probably better spent elsewhere.

Worms, FOXO, and Insulin

But genetics isn't just about what traits are inheritable. Your genes play a daily role in encoding the protein sequences that instruct your body in everything it does to keep you healthy and alive. Anything that can interfere with gene expression or replication can impact longevity. Earlier, I mentioned the protein FOXO, which seems to contribute to cellular renewal in hydras. When those FOXO proteins are prevented from functioning, the hydras start to age. We're just beginning to unravel the role of FOXO in humans. We all have *FOXO* genes; in fact, there are several different kinds, but the way they behave may be different across individuals and across the life span. It turns out that people who live to be ninety or one hundred have a certain form of *FOXO* that others don't.

Cynthia Kenyon was able to double the life span of the worm *C. elegans* by manipulating FOXO, which in turn activates a number of cellular repair and fortification mechanisms that normally decline with aging—it's as though the cells have some kind of clock in them that is winding down and FOXO reverses it. Kenyon explained it this way:

> You can think of FOXO as being like a building superintendent . . . maybe he's a little bit lazy, but he's there, he's taking care of the building. But it's deteriorating. And then suddenly, he learns that there's going to be a hurricane. So he doesn't actually do anything himself. He gets on the telephone—just like FOXO gets on the DNA—and he calls up the roofer, the window person, the painter, the floor person. And they all come and they fortify the house. And then the hurricane comes through, and the house is in much better condition than it

> would normally have been in. And not only that, it can also just last longer, even if there isn't a hurricane. So that's the concept here for how we think this life extension ability exists.

But get this: Under conditions of stress, FOXO sends out a signal that starts activating the mechanisms that improve the ability of the cell to protect and repair itself. Adding 2 percent glucose to the bacterial diet of *C. elegans* completely reversed this life span extension, highlighting the important role of insulin in longevity. Upon finding this, Kenyon immediately switched to a low-glycemic diet. "I tried caloric restriction," she explained, "but I didn't like being hungry all the time; I gave that up after two days!" But you have to follow a diet that's right for you, or it will be hard to stick to. After a couple of years of the low glycemic diet, Kenyon switched to intermittent fasting, which she still does today, skipping dinners a few times a week.

Kenyon also found that removing part of the worms' gonadal systems could extend their lives significantly. This parallels a finding that castrated men tend to live an average of fourteen years longer than uncastrated men who are similar on all other factors—and the younger they were when castrated, the longer the life span extension, in some cases up to twenty years. Italian castrati were also reputed to live longer. The connection between gonads and aging is not yet understood. It clearly involves something more than testosterone—probably something more fundamental—because the worms don't have testosterone (although exposing them to it can cause adverse neural changes).

The biology behind human childbirth may also hold clues to aging. By the time we have children, we are no longer children ourselves, and for many of us, the signs of aging are pretty clear. And yet, we give birth to babies—young, unwrinkled humans that show no signs of aging. How can an aged body produce an unaged one? Kenyon studied this in *C. elegans* and found that just before an egg is fertilized, there appears to be a massive burst of housecleaning in which the egg is swept clean of age-damaged, deformed proteins. Kenyon then showed that the same thing happens in frogs. Whether this happens in humans also is an open question, but if it does, the trigger that causes this housecleaning to take place may help to stanch aging.

The Hayflick Limit and Telomeres

You might be thinking that living longer only means that you're more likely to get Alzheimer's disease or cancer and have a longer but less pleasant existence. Scientists used to think that too. But we now know that many gene mutations and other interventions that increase longevity also postpone age-related diseases.

In 1961, anatomist Leonard Hayflick at the Wistar Institute in Philadelphia was having trouble getting his experiments to work. For decades, it was accepted wisdom that human cells would continue to duplicate indefinitely. But Hayflick could not get his to. He considered a number of possibilities—that the temperature or humidity in the lab was wrong, that the samples were contaminated, or maybe there was a problem in the way he had prepared the cells. In looking more carefully at his experimental logs, he discovered that it was only the oldest cells that had stopped dividing, while the younger ones continued to divide.

To rule out the possibility of contamination, he put old cells and younger ones in the same glass bottle—it was only the old ones that stopped dividing. He subsequently documented that the limit to human cell division was between forty and sixty cell divisions, or replications (the Hayflick limit is usually cited as fifty). Hayflick didn't know what caused the limit but speculated that cells had some sort of a replicometer, a kind of counter that kept track of how many replications had occurred and then stopped further replications beyond a predefined limit. One of the startling discoveries was that Hayflick could freeze the samples for up to five years, and, when thawed, they'd begin replicating as before and still stop at the forty-to-sixty limit.

Hayflick (now ninety) recalls,

> I proposed that normal human cells have an internal counting mechanism and that they are mortal. This discovery allowed me to show, for the first time, that unlike normal cells, cancer cells are immortal.
>
> I concluded also that these results were telling me something about human aging. This is the first time that evidence was found suggesting that aging might be caused by events

> occurring inside of cells. Until my discovery scientists thought that aging was caused by events outside of cells (extracellular events) like radiation, cosmic rays, stress, etc.
>
> What I clearly had shown was that the cessation of cell division is a function of the number of times the cell divides or more exactly, that the DNA in the cell copies itself. DNA copies itself only a finite number of times in normal cells and cancer cells must have a method to circumvent this mechanism.

Researchers later found that the Hayflick limit is caused by the shortening of telomeres, the disposable protective cap at the end of each chromosome. Telomeres have been likened to the plastic tips at the ends of shoelaces (aglets) that keep them from unraveling, but it's a bit more complicated than that. Imagine that your job is to record a music performance. You need to record from the first note, but you don't necessarily know when that note will be. What you need is a buffer—a count-off (1-2-3-4) or some other signal that tells you things are about to start. This is the role played by the telomeres—they let the transcription factor that copies DNA know that it is time to start transcribing. But in this case, it's as though you hear the count-off (1-2-3-4) and the band starts playing at 3. Your recording has missed one note. Later, a friend wants to record your recording off the radio, but he's not very alert, and he misses the first note you recorded, meaning his recording is missing two notes altogether. That's what happens with telomeres—the transcription factor misses a few sequences each time there is a replication, making the telomere a little shorter each time. For the first fifty replications or so it doesn't matter because telomeres contain filler DNA sequences that don't carry important information. But after fifty divisions or so, the telomeres have been completely used up, and they can no longer protect the genes. If copying were to start at that point (which it doesn't), a few strands of important genetic material would fail to be transcribed and all heck could break loose. Thus, when the telomeres get too short, cell division—and thus cellular repair and renewal—stops.

When DNA cells stop dividing, you don't die immediately—the human body has around 10 trillion cells, each carrying DNA—although it's well-established that people with short telomeres die younger than people with

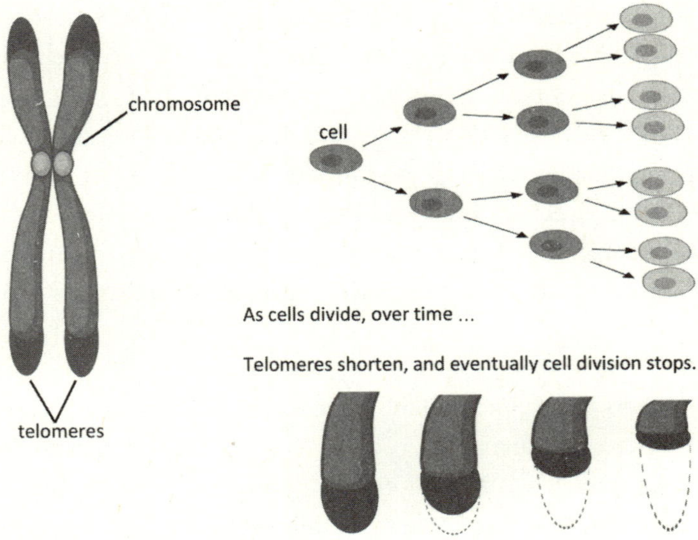

long telomeres. One leading hypothesis is that when telomeres shorten, and cells stop replicating, they enter a state of senescence and begin to gum up the works. But it is still not certain that the telomere shortening is the *cause* as opposed to simply a marker of trouble.

Telomere length is mediated by a number of factors. Remember Conscientiousness—the propensity to be planful, reliable, and industrious and to adhere to social norms and tolerate delayed gratification? It turns out that childhood Conscientiousness predicts telomere length forty years later, as shown by Sarah Hampson and her colleagues. Exercise is associated with increased telomere length and remediating the negative effects of stress. A diet of whole foods is associated with increased telomere length, whereas processed foods, especially hot dogs, smoked meats, and sweetened beverages, are associated with decreases in telomere length.

Social and cultural factors are also important: Neighborhoods with low social cohesion, where people don't know one another or trust one another, are bad for telomeres, and this is true at all income levels. It doesn't matter to the telomeres whether you're living in a sketchy part of a major city or you're in a mansion on a suburban hill—if you do not have friendly relationships with your neighbors, if you don't actually enjoy talking to them, chances are your telomeres are getting shorter by the day. Human evolution has made us a social species, and friendly human contact mitigates stress—even at the genetic level.

Not all kinds of stress shorten telomeres. Short-term, manageable stressors are actually good for you because they keep you challenged and give you a repertoire of coping skills, strengthening cells through a process called hormesis—this describes anything that in a low dose is helpful but in a high dose is toxic. Other examples of hormesis are ultraviolet light (you need some to stimulate the pineal gland and synthesize vitamin D, but too much causes skin cancers and cataracts) and vitamin A (you need a small amount for normal development and eye function, but too much leads to anorexia, headaches, drowsiness, and altered mental states). The kind of stress that shortens telomeres is long-term, chronic stress. In particular, long-term caregiving for a family member, job burnout, and serious traumas such as rape, abuse, domestic violence, and bullying are damaging to telomeres. And in general, it takes a long period of stress before your telomeres are damaged—a monthlong crisis at work probably isn't enough. But when stress is an enduring, defining feature of your life, that's when your telomeres will get shorter.

As we've seen as a theme throughout *Successful Aging*, an important moderating factor in the relationship between stress and telomere length is your response to stress. If you've developed good methods of coping and you can stay calm, and find reasons to be happy, your telomeres may not take a hit at all. Some people approach difficult events with a "can-do" attitude, a "bring it on" mentality, seeing these events as a challenge and an opportunity to learn; other people cave in to despair. The physiological response to a sudden stressor is that your adrenal gland releases cortisol. In short bursts that is a good thing, a hormetic response that increases your energy. Athletes who have this kind of healthful challenge response during competitions win more often; Olympic athletes and successful people in many domains tend to see life's problems as challenges to be overcome.

Mindfulness meditation (the kind favored by the Dalai Lama) increases the activity of telomerase and lengthens telomeres. Whether this will eventually lead to increased or decreased cancer risk is not yet known. And, as with the distinction between dietary supplements and food sources of helpful molecules, such as antioxidants, it may turn out that injecting yourself with telomerase has a completely different physiological effect than organically increasing telomerase through healthful activities, such as meditation and exercise.

Chronic pain is a stressor, and stress decreases telomere length. Jeffrey Mogil has just collected new data indicating that the relationship between pain and telomeres might be bidirectional—that telomere dysfunction can cause pain. "We think the reason that telomere dysfunction turns into pain is because after four months—but not before—we start to see cellular senescence in the spinal cord correlating robustly with the amount of pain the mice were in."

I've heard a lot of patients say that they "can live with" the pain they are in, and I wonder if this is some effort to display toughness and hardiness. If they knew that living in pain could shorten their lives, would they still eschew the physical therapy and medications that might relieve their pain?

Telomerase—a Goldilocks Zone?

Surprisingly, it turns out that excessively *long* telomeres are also bad for you. In one large study of more than twenty-six thousand people, overall cancer risk increased by 37 percent with doubled telomere length. And some cancers were more impacted than others. For people with the longest telomeres, lung cancer risk increased by 90 percent, breast cancer by 48 percent, prostate cancer by 32 percent, and colorectal cancer by 35 percent. The most troubling effect was a more than doubling of the risk for pancreatic cancer. But just to show how complicated the relationship is between telomere length and cancer, those who had the *shortest* telomeres also had increased risk for certain cancers: 63 percent greater for stomach cancer and 41 percent greater for liver cancer. In a study of 9,127 patients and thirty-one cancer types, telomeres were found to be shorter in tumors and longer in sarcomas and gliomas. (Sarcomas are cancers of connective tissues such as bones, tendons, cartilage, muscle, and fat; gliomas are tumors that start in glial cells of the brain or spine.) The relationship between telomere length and telomerase activity in this study remains unclear.

In their book *The Telomere Effect*, psychiatrist Elissa Epel and molecular biologist Elizabeth Blackburn describe the situation this way (Blackburn won the Nobel Prize for discovering telomerase):

> We need our good Dr. Jekyll telomerase to stay healthy, but if you get too much of it in the wrong cells at the wrong time, telomerase takes on its Mr. Hyde persona to fuel the kind of uncontrolled cell growth that is a hallmark of cancer. Cancer is, basically, cells that won't stop dividing; it's often defined as "cell renewal run amok."
>
> You don't want to bomb your cells with artificial telomerase that may goad them into taking the road toward becoming cancerous. Unless the telomerase supplement field comes up with more thorough demonstrations of safety in large—and *long-term*—clinical trials, in our view it's sensible to skip any pills, cream, or injection that claims it will increase your telomerase.

Siegfried Hekimi concurs, and adds that we would do well to avoid "anything else that is claimed to increase your longevity as clearly no experiment could yet have shown that it does." The research is just too recent for us to have seen long-term effects of any of the potions, tinctures, oils, essences, and supplements that are being marketed to gullible consumers.

Elizabeth Parrish, the CEO of a biotechnology company called BioViva, must not have read Epel and Blackburn's book or talked to Hekimi. Using herself as an experimental subject, she found a doctor in Colombia who was willing to inject telomerase into her intravenously (this is illegal in the United States). So far, four years later, she reports that her telomere length has increased. But telomere length measurements are notoriously imprecise—the change that she reports is well within the margin of error of measurement. The telomerase injections could well fuel cancer and actually shorten her life span and we wouldn't know it yet because she's still young at forty-eight. It's been speculated that telomere shortening evolved as an *anticancer* adaptation. Scientists have labeled Parrish's self-experimentation pseudoscience and unethical. A pathology professor who was on the board of Parrish's company resigned when he heard what she had done. The *MIT Technology Review* called it "a new low in medical quackery."

Maybe Parrish should have read the paper coauthored by Leonard

Hayflick, Jay Olshansky, and Bruce Carnes in which they stated, unequivocally:

> Disturbingly large numbers of entrepreneurs are luring gullible and frequently desperate customers of all ages to "longevity" clinics, claiming a scientific basis for the antiaging products they recommend and, often, sell. At the same time, the Internet has enabled those who seek lucre from supposed antiaging products to reach new consumers with ease.
>
> Alarmed by these trends, scientists who study aging, including the three of us, have issued a position statement containing this warning: No currently marketed intervention—none—has yet been proved to slow, stop or reverse human aging, and some can be downright dangerous.

People are living longer and longer on average, and this is owing to a number of positive environmental factors such as medical advances, access to clean water, and so on—not to longevity products. Olshansky doubles down on this view in a 2017 paper in which he notes that the best we can hope for now is essentially to increase health span, but that extending life span artificially is still out of reach.

That doesn't stop a lot of people from trying, nor does it look like it will slow the multibillion-dollar antiaging industry. I remember reading about the death of Robert Atkins, the physician who popularized the low-carb, high-fat, and high-protein diet bearing his name. He did not live particularly long, dying at age seventy-two after slipping on some ice in New York City and hitting his head. A running, dark joke in my lab was that while the Atkins diet did great things for your heart, it caused people to slip on ice. In fact, at least in Atkins' own case, it wasn't so great for his heart, either, as medical records released posthumously revealed that he had hypertension, a heart attack, and congestive heart failure—all the reasons we were told *not* to eat diets high in animal fat. (If you've got to choose, it looks like you're better off getting your calories from fat than from sugar.) Roy Walford, who pioneered and practiced caloric restriction himself, died of ALS at age seventy-nine—that's pretty old, but not an advertisement for longevity.

Journalist Pagan Kennedy tracked down a number of people who famously tried to live forever, using various for-profit schemes, diets, concoctions, and routines, to see how long they actually lived and what they died of. None of them lived especially long and most died young—not of causes directly related to the self-experimentation they were doing, but who really knows? The irony award goes to Jerome Rodale, the founder of *Prevention* magazine. Taping an episode of *The Dick Cavett Show* in 1971 at age seventy-two, he boasted, "I've decided to live to be a hundred . . . I never felt better in my life!" He died onstage, right there in the interview chair.

We don't know how long these people would have lived if they hadn't practiced their favorite longevity regimens, and we don't have enough people practicing the same regimens under controlled conditions to really track what's going on. All we have so far are intuitions about what *might* work.

The Cellular Garbage Problem

Shortened telomeres cause otherwise healthy cells to go senescent. Senescent cells are a double-edged sword. On the one hand, they can't divide, meaning they don't go cancerous; cellular senescence is a way to prevent tumors from forming. On the other hand they produce SASP (senescence-associated secretory phenotype)—toxins and inflammatory mediators that do most of the damage that we associate with aging and mortality. You might be thinking, "Why can't I just take ibuprofen or naproxen sodium, NSAIDs, to cure this?" The reason is that this kind of inflammation doesn't respond to them. It's what some people are calling *stealth inflammation.* (When you examine the tissue under a microscope, you don't see the standard markers of inflammation, and yet cytokines and chemokines and toxic inflammatory chemicals are being released anyway.)

Normally, when cells die, they are cleaned out by cellular housekeeping processes. But these cells, like zombies in a horror movie, won't die. So basically, unless the uncontrolled cellular reproduction of cancer gets us, we die in a pile of senescent cellular garbage of our own making. (Memo to self: Lighten up. Enjoy life.)

Biochemist Jan van Deursen and his colleagues found a chemical marker that distinguishes certain senescent cells from healthy ones and then administered a drug called AP20187 that causes those cells to die. Drugs like this are called senolytics (combining the first part of the word *senescence* with *lytic*, which means *destroying*) and the proposed treatment is called senotherapy. Van Deursen found that clearance of these zombie cells in young mice delayed aging. In already aged mice, it slowed the progression of age-related disorders. Removing the senescent cells appears to jump-start some of the tissues' natural repair mechanisms. Subsequent work in mice has shown that removing the zombie cells in this way can repair damage from lung disease and damaged cartilage, and it can extend life span by 25 percent. It can also prevent memory loss.

So far, fourteen different senolytics have been identified and tested, but each one works on a different type of senescent cell. "There is no doubt that for different indications, different types of drug will need to be developed," says molecular biologist Nathaniel David. "In a perfect world, you wouldn't have to. But sadly, biology did not get that memo." As I write this, David's company, Unity, is in the middle of a clinical trial to inject senolytics directly into damaged tissue, such as arthritic joints. The drug they're using acts specifically on the kinds of senescent cells that accumulate in the knee.

Now, the complicated part of all this is that cellular senescence is a good thing—if a cell becomes damaged it could start to divide uncontrollably and cause cancer. One of the risks of using senolytics is that they could interfere with the processes that normally inhibit cancer growth if they target presenescent cells that could go either way—toward zombies or cancer. There are other problems. In rats, senolytics slow down the wound-healing process. None of the known senolytics are yet safe in humans. As one researcher says, "Everything looks good in mice and when you get to people that is where things go wrong." But if they prove otherwise safe in humans, we still run the risk that senolytics could promote cancer. If only there was a way to somehow check the progression of cancer before it takes over.

Two immunologists, Jim Allison and Tasuku Honjo, received the 2018 Nobel Prize for their work on immunotherapy cures for cancer. (Again, cancer is uncontrolled cell division.) Allison has been working on what he calls immune checkpoint blockades. (I mentioned his work in Chapter 5, on emotion.) The goal was to use your own body's immune system to attack cancers as they form, something our immune system does all the time without our knowing it. Allison says:

> The immune system doesn't know what kind of cancer you have, it just knows there are cells that shouldn't be there. I thought, we can ignore the specific cancer and just create a blockade to the factors that are inhibiting the body's natural immune response.
>
> T-Cells circulate throughout your system, looking for foreign objects. In 1982, I worked out the structure of the T-Cell, the TCR receptor. Unfortunately a tumor cell doesn't turn T-Cells on, it requires a second signal, which comes from antigen presenting cells. Specifically the protein CD28 sends the signals that generate the army of immune responses. Now the molecule CTLA-4 turns it off—it's an inhibitory system. Without CTLA-4 you die, because the immune system attacks everything, nondiscriminately, willy-nilly, including healthy cells and tissue. Another T-Cell off switch is PD-1.
>
> Cancer cells don't send out the 2nd signal that the immune system needs, the antigen presenting cells, so they get a head start. There is a window during which you can turn off the inhibitory action of CTLA-4 or PD-1 (putting on the brakes) for a few weeks to kill the cancer. This checkpoint blockade should work with any cancer, theoretically.

The US FDA approved the drugs ipilimumab (for CTLA-4) and nivolumab (for PD-1) based on Allison's work for the treatment of melanoma; the two drugs are sometimes given together. A course of treatment typically involves four intravenous administrations of the drug on separate occasions separated by about three weeks (some melanomas require additional treatments). These are among the first of many immunotherapies on the market, and as such, they are of limited value due to the potential for serious side effects. For ipilimumab alone, the adverse effects include colitis, hepatitis, or severe inflammation of the pituitary gland in 60 percent of patients; 1 percent of patients develop diabetes. It hasn't been tested on pregnant women, but scientists speculate that it is probably toxic to the fetus. "Unleashing the immune system can have very bad consequences," Allison says in a wry understatement, "so it needs to be done carefully."

According to one analysis, within the first three years after treatment, 80 percent of patients die. But for the 20 percent who get past those first three years, the ten-year survival rate is very close to 100 percent. It's important to put these numbers in perspective. Survival outcomes for patients with advanced melanoma have, historically, been very poor, with a median overall survival around eight months and a five-year survival rate only around 10 percent. Immunotherapy doubles the five-year survival rate. And these drugs, as well as others like them, have now been approved for use in a range of cancers, including melanoma; renal cell carcinoma; Hodgkin's lymphoma; bladder, head, and neck cancer; Merkel cell carcinoma; and colorectal, gastric, and hepatocellular cancer. For some forms of prostate cancer, a checkpoint inhibitor, Keytruda, that I mentioned earlier in connection with Jimmy Carter, was just announced in 2019 to have received FDA approval. One patient had his PSA levels reduced from over one hundred to less than one within just a few weeks of therapy, and his cancer was eradicated.

Earlier I mentioned prions, misfolded versions of a protein that can spread like an infection by forcing normal copies of that protein into the same misfolded shape. Stan Prusiner won a Nobel Prize for discovering them; it was the first time anyone had shown that a disease could be transmitted not just by an infestation (for example, through bacteria or a virus) but through an infectious protein. Prusiner had long thought that prions were involved in Alzheimer's disease, but few took him seriously. Recall that Alzheimer's disease is defined based on the presence of amyloid plaques and tau tangles in the brain, accompanied by cognitive decline.

In 2019, Prusiner and his colleagues at UCSF, Bill DeGrado, Carlo Condello, and others, published an exciting new study based on a postmortem analysis of seventy-five Alzheimer's patients, in which they found a self-propagating prion form of the proteins amyloid beta and tau. Higher levels of these prions in their patients were highly associated with earlier onset forms of Alzheimer's and a younger age of death. This new finding could lead scientists to explore new therapies that focus on prions directly. "This shows, beyond the shadow of a doubt," Prusiner told me, "that amyloid beta and tau are both prions, and that Alzheimer's is a double-prion disorder in which these two rogue proteins destroy the brain." DeGrado adds, "We now know that prion activity correlates with the disease, rather than the amount of plaques and tangles at autopsy." For years, scientists worked on drugs that might clear out the plaques and tangles and made no progress. Now, they can focus on therapies that will target the active prion forms.

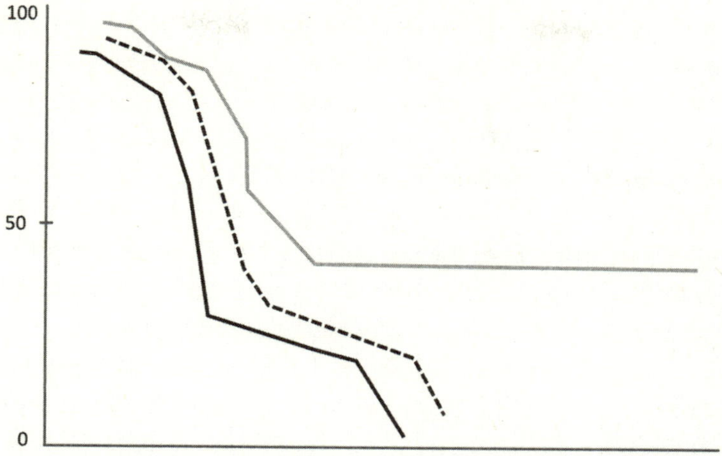

Solid black line: Survival curve for control group. Dashed line: Conventional cancer therapies. Gray line: Immunotherapy.

The challenge in the coming decade will be to find ways of mitigating side effects, perhaps by targeting the on-off switch to cancer cells and not allowing the drugs to affect other systems. And interactions with other systems need to be studied more closely. If the microbiome in your gut is underdeveloped, perhaps damaged by antibiotics or chemotherapies that cancer patients often use, these therapies don't work at all. The more diverse your gut biome, the more effective the immunotherapies are. But we don't know why that is.

Immunotherapeutic approaches to cancer are getting a lot of laboratory attention. As the techniques become more refined over the coming five to ten years, I predict that they will become increasingly important for longevity, wiping out one of the biggest killers that prevent us from living longer. As the curves above show, conventional therapies have a survival rate of close to zero. Immunotherapy allows for the curve to level off.

All of this is great news, but it's not the end-all answer to longevity; it's been calculated that even if cancer were eradicated, it would only extend average life span by seven years—that's because if you survive cancer, you'll die of other things, like cardiovascular disease or neurodegeneration. I began this chapter with a hypothetical question: If we could remove all disease, might we live forever? Maybe, but that's a long way off. Most diseases are caused by the basic biological process of aging. Removing diseases present today would permit a new set of diseases to get you—like a game of Whac-A-Mole. And we probably wouldn't like those diseases very much either.

Living Forever (Senescence, Revisited)

Aubrey de Grey is the chief science officer of the SENS Research Foundation (Strategies for Engineered Negligible Senescence). De Grey raised eyebrows when he told the *Financial Times* that in theory, humans could live to be one thousand. De Grey believes he has identified seven types of molecular and cellular damage that he thinks can potentially be repaired: cell loss, cell death resistance, cell overproliferation, intracellular and extracellular "junk," tissue stiffening, and mitochondrial defects. If true, this repair would not just slow down the effects of aging but could actually reverse them. Ethicists and sociologists have already begun speculating what this will mean for things like marriage vows. (Will we stay married to the same person for eight hundred years, or will it be acceptable to change partners every, say, two hundred years?) Or age differences in couples. (Will society consider it scandalous for a five-hundred-year-old man to date a three-hundred-fifty-year-old woman?) If I live to one thousand and have more than ten generations of offspring, I'm going to need to get a bigger table for Thanksgiving dinners.

De Grey's ideas fall apart when you apply what we actually know about science to them. I'm reminded of the time when the inventor of the PalmPilot, Jeff Hawkins, came to give an address at the Montreal Neurological Institute on how he was going to use technology to improve memory. After taking the podium, he said that he had carefully avoided reading any of the research literature on memory and the brain so as not to be constrained by what other people were doing or had thought about it. This is a typical brash Silicon Valley or start-up approach. Disrupters want to disrupt the status quo. The problem is that every single thing Hawkins suggested stood in direct contradiction to hundreds or thousands of papers about how memory actually works in the brain. To purposefully avoid finding out what are known facts is to waste time pursuing things that either can't work or are so unlikely to work as to be foolhardy.

So it is with de Grey, according to a great many biologists, immunologists, gerontologists, and neuroscientists. If you are an outsider it all sounds very impressive. To solve the various problems of aging, you employ "senescence marker-tagged toxins . . . total telomerase deletion plus cell therapy . . . IL-7 mediated thymopoiesis . . . allotopic [mitochondrial]-coded proteins . . . stem cell therapy and growth factors . . . genetically engineered muscle . . . periodic exposure to phenacyldimethylthiazolium chloride." Those are impressive-sounding words and it's easy to be dazzled by them. We may not know what they mean, but it sounds like he knows what he's doing. A red flag is that among these ideas, he does not propose a testable hypothesis or a specific experiment that will move his research agenda forward.

I get emails like this: "We could teach people to be better musicians just by rewiring their brains surgically. I don't understand why no one is doing this."

First of all, we don't know how to "rewire" the brain—you don't just connect things up differently, the way you might rewire the electrical outlets in a house. Even if we *do* figure out a way to move connections between one pair of neurons to another, you'd have to do this to tens or hundreds of thousands of neurons to make a difference. And even if you could do this—automating, for example, with nanorobotic technology we don't yet possess—how would you know *which* neurons to rewire? I'm not even mentioning the fact that brain surgery is dangerous and that recovery times are many months. Of the infinity of ideas that are out there, part of the scientist's job is to select those that are consistent with demonstrable facts and that are actually doable. This is one of the most difficult things to teach graduate students, and many never learn. Those who run successful laboratories choose experiments and research directions that they have theory-based reasons to believe will pan out, and even then, it is typical that 50 to 75 percent of things that we try in our laboratories don't work for one reason or another.

A 2011 paper pointed out that one of de Grey's ideas is wholly inconsistent with what we know about mitochondria, the providers of energy in cells (and nothing we've learned since then changes that conclusion). Another paper in 2014 took issue with his repair-based approach as oblivious to the plethora of unknown variables embedded in the world of cells.

Other papers have found flaws in de Grey's ideas. But the real nail in the coffin is something that I've hardly ever seen happen in science. A consortium of twenty-eight scientists from different universities and research centers from around the world took it upon themselves to publish a joint, sweeping article debunking his claims. They began by quoting H. L. Mencken: "For every complex problem, there is a simple solution, and it is wrong." Many of the things de Grey has proposed as solutions have already been tested and have never been shown to work in animals, let alone in humans. Other proposed solutions, based on what we know about human physiology, are likely to have harmful side effects that would prevent their use. Those "senescent marker-tagged toxins" de Grey mentions don't exist. The consortium points out, soberly, what all of us in science know but what journalists and the public often fail to appreciate—that "most therapeutic ideas, even the most plausible, come to nothing—in preclinical studies or clinical research, the proposed interventions are found to be toxic or induce unwelcome side effects . . . or, most often, simply fail to work." And the development time for these ideas is *decades,* not mere years. The twenty-eight scientists conclude quite solemnly—perhaps to counteract the media frenzy that surrounds de Grey's SENS Research Foundation:

> The idea that a research programme organized around the SENS agenda will not only retard ageing, but also reverse it—creating young people from old ones—and do so within our lifetime, is so far from plausible that it commands no respect at all within the informed scientific community.

They continue to say that none of them believe that de Grey's plans to prevent aging indefinitely, or to "turn old people young again," have even the remotest chance of success.

> We can and must insist that speculation based on evidence be discriminated from speculation based on wish fulfillment alone. . . . Presenting buzzwords as substitutes for carefully selected and testable hypotheses about ageing . . . might be clever marketing, but it is a poor substitute for scientific thought.

Aubrey de Grey's work is a textbook example of pseudoscience, a kind of quackery. Fortunately, there is a lot of evidence-based work that offers hope.

On the Horizon

Drugs like resveratrol and Chloromycetin may mimic the effects of caloric restriction without your actually having to fast. Two big studies were conducted with monkeys starting in the eighties, but they had contradictory results. That might be because the control conditions differed; we don't really know.

A new use for a drug that prevents coronary transplant rejections, rapamycin, may also mimic the effects of caloric restriction. It's an immunosuppressant, so potentially full of side effects in humans, but in mice it can extend life by 25 percent. It's been tested in other mammals; in dogs it's too early to tell if it will extend their lives, but it does improve cardiac function, and in human and mouse cell cultures, it appears to have antitumor properties. A study by the drug company Novartis found, counterintuitively (because it's an immunosuppressant), that weekly doses of rapamycin *increased* immune function in elderly adults.

Another experimental treatment is using the diabetes medication metformin—the drug I mentioned in Chapter 9, on diet—to combat aging. Researchers aren't sure why it works, but in mice and humans without diabetes, it appears to mimic caloric restriction and reduce inflammation and oxidative stress, and its use leads to lower risks of getting diabetes, heart disease, cognitive decline, and possibly cancer. The US FDA just approved a study to test it (TAME—Targeting Aging with MEtformin), and we'll just have to wait a few years to see if it improves health span as hoped. One idea about why it might have antiaging effects is that it enhances an enzyme called AMPK (adenosine monophosphate-activated protein kinase). AMPK helps mimic the beneficial effects of calorie restriction and it can also reduce insulin-like growth factor, or IGF-1, a protein that promotes tumor formation. And if that weren't enough, it appears to reduce those toxic inflammatory products of senescent cells. Because metformin is one of the oldest and most widely prescribed drugs (it was discovered in the 1950s), many doctors feel safe prescribing it for the off-label use of retarding aging.

Perhaps the most famous new antiaging product on the market is NAD+ (nicotinamide adenine dinucleotide). NAD+ is produced in the brain, and our levels of it decline with age, although fasting increases naturally produced levels. NAD+ supplements may be able to mimic the effects of caloric restriction and have been made famous by articles in *Time* magazine, *Men's Journal, Good Housekeeping,* and others. NAD+ regulates cellular metabolism, cellular signaling, DNA repair, and circadian rhythms and maintains normal mitochondrial function. There are several different compounds that raise NAD+ levels in the blood, including nicotinamide riboside (NR), pterostilbene (PT), and nicotinamide mononucleotide (NMN).

It's no coincidence that the first three syllables of NAD+, *nicotin*amide, sound like nicotine. NAD+ is a form of vitamin B_3 and was one of the first vitamins ever discovered. Nicotine, the addictive substance found in tobacco, interferes with absorption of nicotinamide and B_3 in the body because of the similarity between the two molecules. If you've heard that smoking compromises the immune system, this is one of the reasons why.

Geneticist David Sinclair from Harvard is one of the leading players in this field. His work has shown in a number of studies with mice that NAD+ has antiaging properties. After just a week of supplementation, his team could no longer tell the difference between a twenty-four-month-old mouse and a two-month-old mouse—that's like saying a sixty-year-old human looks like a twenty-year-old. (This caused Siegfried Hekimi to quip, "Apparently working too much with NAD makes you unaware that you need glasses.")

A randomized controlled trial led by MIT biologist Leonard Guarente studied the effects on people who took a combination of two NAD+ precursors, NR and PT. Participants were divided into three groups randomly and given either a placebo or a single dose or a double dose of the supplement for eight weeks. The supplement significantly increased levels of NAD+ by 40 percent in the single-dose group and 90 percent in the double-dose group. No serious adverse events were reported. (The study considered a standard dose to be 250 mg of NR and 50 mg of PT per day, and some participants took double that.)

An important complication is that Guarente is the co-founder of a company called Elysium Health that is selling the very compound he tested. This certainly has the appearance of bias. Few scientists will take this finding seriously until it has been replicated by someone who does not have a profit motive. A small study was performed by University of Delaware physiologist Christopher Martens, who used 1,000 mg per day of NR and also found significantly increased levels of NAD+, by 60 percent. But this was a very small, exploratory study with only fifteen participants in each experimental group—not nearly enough to make any generalizations.

Another complication is this: All that these two studies showed is that the supplement increases NAD+ levels in the blood—we don't know whether the risk for cardiovascular events, diabetes, or cancer will be reduced or whether wrinkles will magically disappear and hair become more lustrous. Jeffrey Flier, former dean of Harvard Medical School, has come out against the company for hawking these NAD+ boosters: "Elysium is selling pills [without] evidence that they actually work in humans at all," a charge that would seem to apply equally to all of the companies selling NAD+ supplements (or antioxidant supplements, for that matter). Animal studies on NAD+ have not been easy to replicate, and hundreds of drugs that work in mice never make it to humans. Felipe Sierra of the US National Institute on Aging (NIA), and who of course wants to live a long and healthy life, says:

> None of this is ready for prime time. The bottom line is I don't try any of these things. Why don't I? Because I'm not a mouse.

David Sinclair doesn't have anything good to say about *any* of the companies selling boosters. "I have tested the NMN or NR that's for sale in the market place and I stay clear of those products," he told me. Sinclair has doubts about the purity and contents of the commercially available products, but unlike Felipe Sierra does not harbor doubts about the benefits of boosting NAD+ levels. In fact, the research has persuaded Sinclair to take an NAD+ supplement daily, 1,000 mg of an NMN formulation that is not yet commercially available. He also takes metformin, by the way, 1,000 mg per evening, and 500 mg of resveratrol (pterosilbene) every morning. My advice, based on what I've learned from the literature and from Sinclair himself, is to wait for the dust to settle on this whole NAD+ thing. If it becomes approved by the FDA as a drug, rather than a supplement, the purity will be tightly regulated, which it is not now—and it will have been shown to work in humans, not just mice.

Another idea being studied is the possibility of harnessing the power of regeneration that some amphibians possess. The Mexican axolotl, a type of salamander, is about nine inches long and has astonishing abilities to regenerate severed limbs, damaged brain tissue, and even a crushed spinal cord. Its genome was just recently sequenced, and you can be sure that researchers on aging will be looking for clues about how genetic therapies might help to regenerate aging human tissue. Interestingly, axolotls do not live particularly long, unlike, say, hydras, but their ability to avoid dying after accidents that would be fatal for most species is a promising direction for future research.

The Mexican axolotl

A large number of other drugs are being tested for antiaging properties. One that received a great deal of attention is thioflavin T, a chemical that extended life dramatically in a number of different species of worms, which, perhaps counterintuitively to nonscientists, differ from one another genetically more than mice and humans do. In one species, it doubled life span. But of course (to echo Felipe Sierra), humans are not worms.

One of the pernicious difficulties, as you may have gathered from the preceding pages, is that not everything that has a theoretical basis works in practice, and even when it does, not everything that works in a laboratory setting works in the real world. As Richard Klausner, CEO of Lyell Immunopharma, says:

> 70–80 percent of findings in science that industry tries to translate to drugs or therapies just don't work. They worked in one

particular cell line in the lab, or one particular set of people. We've seen a history of faulty translation. For example, "low fat!" That was a boon for the food industry; less fat, less calories, you can eat more. The current obesity epidemic is a direct result of that faulty translation.

Where Do We Stand?

An octogenarian today can count on living another eight years, four years longer than eighty-year-olds had in 1990. Centenarians live longer than ever before after they have reached one hundred. And the number of people over eighty who are making meaningful contributions, to their families, to their communities, and to the world, is increasing as we find health spans increasing dramatically. We are living in a time during which being old means more health and more opportunities than at any point in recorded history. Sixty-year-olds are doing the things that forty-year-olds used to do. It is no longer surprising to hear about people in their eighties who still work. In the United States, eight out of one hundred senators are in their eighties. In the House of Representatives, generally a younger group, nine members are in their eighties. Among Fortune 500 CEOs, five are over seventy-seven. Jane Fonda, eighty-one, is starring in the hit TV show I mentioned earlier, *Grace and Frankie*, Jiro Ono, aged ninety-four, is considered the world's greatest sushi chef and still works in his world-class Tokyo restaurants, and Rita Moreno, eighty-eight, just finished a three-year run in another hit TV show (*One Day at a Time*).

We really don't know how to extend health span or life span with any certainty. You could avoid smoking, and war, and getting repeatedly hit in the head. You can be conscientious about vaccination, hygiene, exercise, not working too hard, being warm in the winter and cool in the summer, and eating noncontaminated fresh produce all year long . . .

Or you could be like Jeanne Calment and smoke until you're 117. Or like Richard Overton, the oldest surviving World War II veteran (at the time of his death), who lived to be 112 and whose secret to a long life was cigars (twelve a day), whiskey, and coffee (with three teaspoons of sugar). Fate is capricious.

13

LIVING SMARTER

Cognitive enhancement

Get rich without working! Lose weight by eating anything you want!! Get smarter by doing crossword puzzles or sudoku four times a week!!! (The companies that advertise these promises seem to be in cahoots with the companies that manufacture exclamation points.) We all like the sound of these promises, and Americans are especially drawn to these kinds of claims. We are a paradoxical culture of do-it-yourselfers, self-made millionaires, and people who still think they can get something for nothing.

There has been much media attention paid to the idea of "brain games for better aging." Added to the old standbys like crosswords, KenKen, and sudoku are new Internet- or computer-based brain-training games. The important questions about these puzzles and games, both old and new, are: If I play brain games, will it make me less likely to lose my glasses? Will I drive more safely? Will my memory improve? In other words, will the skills and practice I gain transfer from one activity to others? Unfortunately, the answer for most of these is no. If you spend time doing sudoku, there is little evidence that you'll get better at other things—all that happens is that you get better at doing sudoku. Several systematic reviews and meta-analyses have concluded that there is no convincing evidence that brain-training games enhance cognition beyond the realm of the game, nor do they fend off dementia.

Why do we think these games will lead to cognitive enhancement? In part because of aggressive advertising by Lumos Labs, the company that makes a brain-training game called Lumosity, which was found guilty of false advertising and fined $50 million. But they're not the only culprits.

A competing company, Neurocore, backed by US education secretary Betsy DeVos, was admonished by the National Advertising Review Board for making unsupported claims in their advertising. Collectively, these "brain-training" games may actually set you back because if you spend time doing them, that's time you're not doing the things that we *know* make a difference, such as outdoor exercise or spending time with others. (In addition, the phrase adopted by the manufacturers of these games, *brain training*, is misleading because very few studies have looked at actual brain changes in response to the training.)

The Association for Psychological Science (APS) published a paper in 2016 by a team of experts led by Daniel Simons, an experimental psychologist at the University of Illinois. The team analyzed 132 papers cited by these for-profit brain-training companies. The paper is very carefully prepared and documented. It reads something like an indictment from a federal prosecutor. Of the 132 papers, 21 were review papers that did not report any new data and therefore were redundant; 15 reported on data from only a single study; 36 lacked an adequate control group; 6 papers with a control group lacked random assignment; 5 other papers had similar reasons not to include them. Of the remaining 49 papers, 25 were reporting on the same six experiments. Many of those 49 were authored or co-authored by employees of the company whose products they were testing, and so they are not independent assessments of the products. If you are not an expert, it is easy to be bowled over by the sheer number of papers cited by these companies. But you know better now. Simons' team found, as many others had, that brain-training games develop a particular, narrow set of skills and lead to improvement in those skills but not others, even others that would seem to be related. Simons and his colleagues concluded,

> We found little compelling evidence that practicing cognitive tasks in brain-training products produces lasting cognitive benefits for real-world cognition. . . . If your hope is to stave off the cognitive losses that sometimes accompany aging or to enhance your performance at school or in your profession, you should be skeptical.
>
> Consumers should also consider the comparative costs and benefits of engaging in a brain-training regimen. Time spent using brain-training software could be allocated to other

> activities or even other forms of "brain training" (e.g., physical exercise) that might have broader benefits for health and well-being.

These brain-training activities are fun. They present us with challenges and an opportunity to get better at something. I do crosswords and Ken-Ken every day, but they don't make me better at writing books or calculating a tip on a restaurant check—they are their own world, a world I enjoy and consider to be among my rewarding hobbies. I do them because they give me pleasure and challenge me mentally, not because I think they'll make me better at other things.

Art Shimamura counsels:

> You may be better off engaging in things that more closely resemble the kind of mental activities you enjoy or want to improve. Do you want to learn more from reading? Join a book club and discuss your thoughts with others. Do you want to be more attentive in daily activities? Practice the specific kinds of activities that demand such mental processes. Do you want to be creative? Learn a new musical piece, dance step, or dinner recipe. Explore new locations around your neighborhood.

Ethical Issues

Imagine a time, say, twenty-five years in the future, when bioengineers and genetic engineers have developed ways of enhancing our lungs and muscles, allowing more of us to run marathons, and to do so more easily. That would not have been their primary goal, at least not at first. These intrepid researchers, some of whom are probably at their lab benches right now, would be trying to find cures for lung cancer or sarcopenia (recall from Chapter 10, on movement and exercise, that sarcopenia is for muscle what osteoporosis is for bone). Somewhere along the line someone would realize that the technology they've developed can be used to enhance normal function, creating greater capacity than a person would typically have.

If an athlete with lung cancer received a treatment that eradicated it and brought them back to their own normal, would you allow them to compete in the Olympics? Why not? That seems no different than letting them take aspirin for a headache, having a bunion taken off their foot, or training in high-altitude thin air, all of which the International Olympic Committee allows. But what if that same lung treatment conferred an advantage when given to someone without cancer? That strikes many of us as unethical, tantamount to the use of steroids. We allow athletes to take steroids if it is a medical necessity, but not if it is purely for enhancement. Many of us share the feeling that sports competitions should follow well-defined rules that ensure fairness. The idiom *level the playing field* is, of course, a sports metaphor.

Now imagine also that in this near future, neurochemists have developed various ways of modifying our brains to enhance cognition. Collectively, these are called pharmaceutical cognitive enhancers, or PCEs. The initial motivation might be to restore lost function in people with cognitive impairment brought on by disease or injury. But then, the medicinal cat would be out of the bag. Would it be fair for otherwise healthy people to take them? This strikes many people as unfair. Okay. But if people who you are competing with are taking drugs—people within your own company vying for a promotion, workers at other companies plotting to overtake your market position—should you take the drugs also just to keep pace? Now, to up the ethical ante: What if cognitive enhancement taken by scientists could speed up finding a cure for cancer, or if taken by negotiators could solve the Palestinian-Israeli conflict—would that change the ethical calculus?

If you're still feeling uncomfortable about cognitive enhancement, consider that we already alter our neurochemistry through caffeine and alcohol (not to mention Prozac). A neural implant may more efficiently stimulate the prefrontal cortex and brain stem the way that these drugs do, but with greater precision. A PCE or implant that can improve memory could allow you to remember crucial details such as whom to call for help, how to use the phone, and where you live. Will we accept an implanted memory restorer for people with Alzheimer's? What about schoolchildren? Neuroscientist Michael Gazzaniga imagines one such possible conversation: "Honey, I know that we were saving this money for a vacation, but maybe we should get the twins neural chips instead. It is hard for them in school when so many of the other kids have them." If this feels fundamentally different from previous generations buying glasses or hearing aids or paying for Ritalin, the difference is that glasses, hearing aids, and Ritalin (at least for those diagnosed with ADHD or related conditions) are treating something. Healthy students and corporate execs who take Ritalin, on the other hand, might be construed as cheats, trying to game the system.

And yet, why should we draw an artificially defined line between socially sanctioned drugs, such as caffeine, and pharmaceuticals, such as Ritalin? It is difficult to say, and ethicists disagree about where to draw the line.

In the case of aging adults, drawing the line requires subtlety and medical knowledge we don't yet possess. Roughly one out of six adults over age sixty has mild cognitive impairment, a legitimate medical condition. We treat a whole range of maladies for individuals in this age group, from blood pressure to elevated cholesterol and arthritis. Why not treat mild cognitive impairment? Should diseases of the brain be so stigmatized that we don't treat them? That attitude thrusts us backward a hundred years to when people with schizophrenia, Down syndrome, and autism were locked away in sanitariums. And then, as a step further, what about the other five in six adults who have *not* been diagnosed with mild cognitive impairment but might be developing cases of it, or have cases that are as yet undetected? Suppose you just feel like you're losing it, only a little. Your memory and energy aren't what they once were. Why can't *you* have this enhancement, too?

Ethicists have begun to grapple with all of these issues, and some of the considerations raised so far include (1) unknown long-term effects and side effects of cognitive enhancement drugs and implants, (2) inequality of access to these technologies, (3) the possibility that some military or business organizations might force individuals to use them, and (4) whether the use of them constitutes cheating in competitive contexts (academics, business, military operations, diplomatic negotiations, sports).

The US Bioethics Commission issued a report in which they delineate these different uses as a way to frame the ethical discussion.

> Neural modification can serve at least three purposes, to (1) maintain or improve neural health and cognitive function within typical or statistically normal ranges; (2) treat disease, deficiency, injury, impairment, or disorder (referred to as "neurological disorders") to achieve or restore typical or statistically

> normal functioning; and (3) expand or augment function above typical or statistically normal ranges. In delineating these neural modification objectives, the Bioethics Commission is mindful that they are not always sharply distinguishable.

Point 1 is relevant to the discussion of older adults and mild cognitive impairment: Older adults may seek simply to *maintain* their neural health and cognitive function as it was when they were younger, to the best of their abilities. Whether that is deemed an ethical use or not isn't clear-cut. The commission fell short of taking a position, but they were firm on one point: If such enhancements are available to some, they should be equally available to all. "We urged that policymakers ensure equitable access to beneficial neural enhancers. In our society, access to existing services and opportunities, such as education and nutrition, is not equal across individuals or groups." The commission argues that these various enhancers should not be the exclusive province of those who are already the wealthiest and most successful, because this would serve only to enlarge the gaps in opportunity, a trans-societal problem. The wealthy already have better access to health care, legal representation, and social mobility.

Stimulants—Adderall, Modafinil, Pitolisant, Ritalin, Nicotine

Members of the US Bioethics Commission write:

> Adderall and other stimulants are used off-label by individuals who desire to increase their competitive advantage by working longer hours with greater attentiveness while sleeping less. At every turn, we see headlines announcing "epidemic" amphetamine use by high-achieving students seeking top grades and standardized test scores.

There is no evidence that this condition has changed in the years since the commission issued this statement. Adults who are experiencing the effects of aging may find that stimulants, carefully used (and preferably under a doctor's supervision), can make them feel younger, more energetic, and more alert. What we don't know for sure is whether such medications have lasting, damaging effects.

Adderall is one of a group of amphetamines, which are often taken "off label" (that is, in a nonapproved application) for cognitive enhancement. There are mixed results as to whether Adderall and other amphetamines actually enhance cognition; however, they are known to increase motivation, which is no small thing. On the flip side, there are a few reports that they impair creativity.

I've mentioned modafinil, a drug that is prescribed for jet lag or shifting your circadian rhythm. It does not stimulate the production of dopamine, but it binds to dopamine receptors in the brain and inhibits dopamine reuptake, causing whatever dopamine is already in the system to stay around longer, and it is also an adenosine receptor antagonist, like coffee, tea, and caffeine. Like Adderall, modafinil (originally sold under the brand names Provigil and Alertec) can increase motivation and promote wakefulness. Some healthy individuals who are not chronobiologically shifted have turned to it for cognitive enhancement. One systematic review found that modafinil consistently enhanced attention, executive functions, and learning, with few side effects. However, other reviews show mixed results including impairments, such as a reduction in creativity, and in another, it led to cognitive slowing with no increase in performance accuracy. Some use it when they have repetitive, boring work to do that doesn't require creativity. Others report that it allows them to focus on a task but that the focus can be so narrow that it makes them inattentive to other things, causing them to be absentminded, misplace things, or not properly shift attention when an attentional shift is required. (A newer formulation of the drug is called armodafinil and is sold under the brand name Nuvigil; they have essentially the same effects.)

Pitolisant, currently available only in the United Kingdom and Europe (but scheduled for FDA approval in the United States), is a wakefulness- and alertness-promoting agent that acts as an H3 (histamine) receptor antagonist. Developed for narcoleptics, it has also been used off label for cognitive enhancement and alleviating depression.

Ritalin (generic name methylphenidate) is one of several available dopamine promoters, and it also enhances levels of norepinephrine. As we've seen, aging is typically accompanied by loss of dopamine receptor neurons in the brain, and it is believed that this is partly responsible for the cognitive decline we observe, including the finding that older adults are especially disadvantaged when fast and efficient processing in novel situations is required. College students have been taking Ritalin for fifty years to help them study and for general cognitive enhancement—in surveys, between 5 and 35 percent report having used it within the past year. This is not to say that changes in other neurotransmitters, such as serotonin, acetylcholine, or noradrenaline, don't affect cognition, just that dopamine appears to, and dopamine promoters such as Ritalin serve as effective neuroenhancers.

To a neuroscientist, nicotine is in many ways the perfect drug for cognitive enhancement. It increases vigilance, attention, focus, memory, and creativity, and it refines motor skills, all without causing the jitters or stress that usually accompany stimulants—in fact, it tends to reduce stress. In particular, nicotine enhances attention by deactivating areas of the default mode, such as the posterior cingulate. It is being considered as a treatment for late-life depression and Parkinson's disease and Alzheimer's disease, where it is believed to have neuroprotective effects. *Scientific American* touted nicotine as the next smart drug.

The problem with nicotine is that the most common delivery systems, smoking and chewing, cause cancer. Even with other delivery systems, such as gum, patches, and the new mouth sprays, it is highly addictive. It can increase heart rate, blood pressure, and inflammation, it can cause nausea, and in rodents it promotes cancer growth. In large doses nicotine is a poison, an evolutionary adaptation in the leaves of the tobacco plants to prevent insects from eating it. Humans can tolerate it in small doses, however, and if you get the dose right, you might get the benefits without the drawbacks. To minimize the possibility of addiction, it's best to use it occasionally, for focus and energy, and not for more than a few days in a row. And it's important to use a low dose. If you want to experiment, try the gum or the mouth spray, and start out with the smallest dose possible. But caveat emptor. As of this writing, vaping tobacco is no better than smoking and may in fact be much worse.

There are dozens of other drugs linked to cognitive enhancement. One is tolcapone, a nonstimulant dopamine promoter that in a small number of studies has been shown to significantly improve information processing, attention, and memory. The problem is that it is highly toxic to the liver; after three patients in Europe died from liver injury attributed to tolcapone, it was withdrawn from the market. A drug that is chemically similar, entacapone, is easier on the liver but doesn't cross the blood-brain barrier as well, and so doesn't confer equivalent cognitive benefits. Then there's pramipexole (Mirapex, Mirapexin, Sifrol), another dopamine promoter that researchers thought would enhance cognition but instead induced sleepiness and impaired learning in healthy people. I mention all these as cautionary tales of how a drug that can enhance one physiological system can wreak havoc on another. I've reported in this section those drugs that are relatively safe (at least for short- and medium-term use), compared to the dozens that have either been withdrawn from the market or are risky to other systems.

Dave Hamilton, co-founder of *The Mac Observer,* attended a "Cannabis and Parenting" meet-up at the SXSW festival recently. One woman spoke and shared the story of a teenage girl whose doctor put her on cannabis to deal with a medical condition. The doctor's instructions to the girl were the salient point and apply to any medication or treatment: Watch yourself.

> If your grades (or work) start to slip, we need to find a different treatment plan. Similarly, you need to stay socially engaged. If you find yourself withdrawing from the company of others and holing up in your room, your treatment plan needs to change.

Dave notes that "such smart, enlightened advice is for any of us on any treatment plan with any medication. Just because our doctors and WebMD say something is 'right,' we need to maintain that self-awareness of any residual effects on our lives as a whole."

Memory and Attention Enhancement

Rivastigmine and Memantine

There is early and incomplete evidence that rivastigmine (brand name Exelon) can ease some of the symptoms of cognitive decline, including memory difficulties and disorientation. Rivastigmine enhances acetylcholine in the brain (it is a cholinergic agonist), but we still don't understand its precise mechanism of action or why it has the therapeutic effects that it does. You may recall that acetylcholine is involved in sleep, and so rivastigmine may simply help patients to achieve a better night's sleep, and that's a big deal. But as we've seen, neurotransmitters are typically involved in a great number of activities, and acetylcholine is also associated with transmission among brain regions involved in attention, memory, and cognitive control. Rivastigmine has a long list of side effects, suffered by about two-thirds of users, and many discontinue its use. But the side effects appear to be reversible, and if you are suffering and high on Factor V (Openness to Experience) you might ask your doctor to let you try it and decide for yourself.

Similarly, there is early and incomplete evidence that memantine (brand name Namenda) might ease and reverse symptoms of mild cognitive impairment and mild neurocognitive disorders. Memantine blocks glutamate (it is a glutamatergic antagonist), and glutamate is associated with excitation of neural signaling. As with rivastigmine, we still don't understand the mechanisms of action. Part of what might be going on is related to hyperexcitability that can occur in the hippocampus if too much glutamate is released, or if it is not absorbed quickly enough; either of these things could happen due to general age-related wearing out of cellular assemblies in the brain. When the hippocampus gets too much glutamate, a condition called glutamate-induced excitotoxicity, we have observed decreased neuronal regeneration and dendritic branching, and impairments to memory and learning.

In terms of the difference between rivastigmine and memantine, Carlos Quintana, a board-certified neurologist in San Francisco, uses the analogy of tuning in a car radio station. "Rivastigmine is like tuning in the frequency more precisely, and memantine is like turning up the gain. The two drugs work together very well and are often co-prescribed." Indeed, a recent meta-analysis concluded that there is moderate evidence that combination therapy using the two drugs yields small improvements in cognition, mood, and behavior. The thing to keep in mind is that this small improvement represents a statistical average of people who see large improvements, people who see none, and people who get worse. You may very well experience greater than "small" improvements (but you may very well not). As before, if you're feeling adventuresome, and your doctor has not diagnosed you with a condition that contraindicates it, you might try it as an experiment.

Hormones, Revisited

I've mentioned the role of hormones in physical and mental health, and in particular, how hormone replacement therapy can help with restoring sleep cycles. Some individuals are very sensitive to the hormonal balance in their bodies, and age-related declines of even a small amount of testosterone, estrogen, or progesterone can cause cognitive difficulties, particularly in memory and attention.

You'll recall that senescence is the cumulative effect of things that happen to our bodies over time that may be harmful or cause difficulties for us. Cellular senescence is the specific case of our cells losing the ability to repair themselves and replicate. Much of what we recognize as the undesirable effects of aging is caused by cellular senescence—wrinkles, memory loss, and a lowered immune-system response. This is paralleled by a progressive decline in the ability of most organs to repair and recover from injury and disease. Many—perhaps most—older adults are living with chronic low-grade inflammation and decreased immune-system function. The majority of studies suggest that this inflammation is due to hormone deprivation (estrogen and testosterone).

Why some people age more successfully than others is clearly not a simple question. If the effects of aging are simply due to low-grade inflammation, everyone who took anti-inflammatories would stop aging. If it were just lack of hormones, hormone replacement therapy would solve the problem—but it doesn't. Many driven, successful people I know in their seventies and beyond are taking prescription hormonal supplements, but many are not. There are, as with everything else, great individual differences. But for many, testosterone for men and estrogen for women can lead to increased mental clarity, ability to focus, and improved memory.

Cognitive Stimulation Therapy

Among nondrug treatments, cognitive stimulation therapy (CST) has the highest record of efficacy. Administered by a therapist or facilitator, CST strives to reorient individuals to their memories and current lives, as well as promote physical and social activity. The data on this are not particularly strong, because of a lack of rigorously controlled studies, but the preliminary picture is that cognitive stimulation therapy is responsible for significant improvements in cognitive function and self-reported quality of life, although it had no significant effect on self-sufficiency.

Other Treatments

The studies I'm about to review in this section are only preliminary. By a rigorous definition, none of them qualify as "medicine" because the evidence is still being gathered. Many of the findings are based on animal models and have yet to be verified in humans. To my knowledge, none of these treatments has been shown to be harmful; they should all be regarded as works in progress. The list of supplements for which manufacturers declare age-defying properties could take up more than a hundred pages. If it is not listed here, I know of no reliable evidence that it works. This includes things like DHEA, beta-carotene, vitamin E, selenium, ginseng, creatine, ginkgo, ginseng, and piracetam.

Vitamin B_{12}

Vitamin B_{12} (cobalamin), found in meat, poultry, eggs, milk, and fish, is necessary for the production of myelin in the brain and is involved in the metabolism of every cell in the body. Vegans are prone to B_{12} deficiency and are advised to take supplements. As we age, our stomachs produce less gastric acid, reducing the body's ability to absorb vitamin B_{12} that's found in food, and so B_{12} deficiency is more common among older adults.

Much B_{12} research has been driven by the homocysteine hypothesis. Homocysteine is a potentially toxic amino acid, and elevated levels of it are associated with cognitive impairment, Alzheimer's disease, dementia, and cardiovascular disease. We believe that it increases oxidative stress and increases damage to DNA and that its neurotoxicity leads to cell death. B_{12} (along with B_6 and folate) is responsible for recycling homocysteine, thereby keeping its levels in check; insufficient amounts of B_{12} are therefore believed responsible for a toxic buildup of homocysteine.

Vitamin B_{12} deficiency is associated with cognitive decline, and older individuals with higher B_{12} levels generally perform better on cognitive tests. Of course, the mere fact that deficient levels of B_{12} are correlated with cognitive deficits does not mean that B_{12} supplementation will correct that. Indeed, a 2003 Cochrane review showed no association between B_{12} supplementation and improvements in cognitive function. Although a 2017 review demonstrated that B_{12} was indeed effective at lowering homocysteine levels, that alone did not translate to measurable cognitive improvements.

On the other hand, a different meta-analysis found B_{12} supplementation led to significant memory improvement, and another found that it slowed the rate of brain atrophy associated with dementia and mild cognitive impairment, with the strongest effect being in those with higher homocysteine levels to begin with.

Anecdotally, many doctors and patients claim that B_{12} supplementation increases energy and lifts depressed mood. Taking B_{12} supplementation does not cause any harm as far as we know, provided that your blood plasma levels don't exceed recommended maximums, and there is a possibility that it may be neuroprotective as we age by promoting myelination.

Neuroshroom

Bob Weir, a founding member of the Grateful Dead (age seventy-two), has been taking a commercially available formulation of dried mushroom extracts called Neuroshroom. He started, he says, because "a medical doctor friend of mine who lives near me in Mill Valley, who is also a shaman, suggested I try them. They contain a neurotrophic growth factor. The effect is subtle but I feel like it makes my day a little bit lighter and my focus a little bit better."

Mushrooms are a mixture of proteins, unsaturated fatty acids, carbohydrates, and a variety of trace elements. One of the active ingredients in the Neuroshroom mix is *Hericium erinaceus* polysaccharides (HEP). It increases levels of acetylcholine in the brain (the same system that rivastigmine affects), which is normally secreted in great quantities during stage 4 sleep (as we saw in Chapter 11, on sleep). The dreamy quality we associate with sleep, or being in certain altered states, is mediated by this neurochemical. HEP rapidly increases gene expression of neural growth factor in the hippocampus, the seat of memory. This could simultaneously improve the storage of new memories and the retrieval of old ones—even old memories that you thought were long gone.

HEP also has neuroprotective and neuroregenerative qualities, allowing for the repair of damaged nerves and the growth of new ones. In one study it improved overall cognitive performance and was even effective in people up to age eighty who are suffering from mild cognitive impairment. There's also some evidence that it improves immune-system function and can form a natural immunological resistance to cancer. Some studies have shown that it reduces depression and anxiety.

Another ingredient in the mushrooms Weir takes is *Cordyceps militaris,* which has been shown to eradicate fatigue and boost energy levels. A third ingredient is *Ganoderma lucidum,* which has been shown to reduce fatigue in breast cancer patients. It appears to have neuroprotective effects on the hippocampus and promotes cognitive function in mouse models of Alzheimer's disease. It also has anti-inflammatory properties and reduces oxidative stress. A 2019 study examined nearly seven hundred adults aged sixty and over in Singapore and found that participants who consumed more than two portions of mushrooms a week reduced their odds of having mild cognitive impairment by 50 percent, and this was independent of age, gender, education, cigarette smoking, alcohol consumption, hypertension, diabetes, heart disease, stroke, physical activities, and social activities.

Bacopa

Bacopa monnieri, water hyssop, is a plant native to southern and eastern India, Australia, Europe, Africa, Asia, and South and North America, including parts of the southeastern United States. There is emerging evidence that it can improve higher-order cognitive processes such as learning and memory and, in particular, has a significant effect on retaining new information, even among older adults. It appears that it does this by regulating tryptophan hydroxylase and serotonin transporter expression. Capsule formulations of the extract are available, and traditional Indian cooking uses it as an ingredient in food. It is fat soluble so should be taken with a meal. It takes time to work—don't expect a noticeable effect before twelve weeks.

The treatments mentioned in this section, such as Neuroshrooms and bacopa, and the omega-3 fatty acids mentioned in Chapter 9, on diet, are foods, of course, not "medication." What exactly is the distinction between diets and medicine, given that the food we consume can also affect our health in a similar way to pills or medication? It isn't clear. To some degree, diet and food choices are a form of medicine. (Perhaps my grandmother was right about the chicken soup.)

Revisiting the 1960s

Recreational Drugs

Many members of the Woodstock generation took drugs in an effort to expand their consciousness, for spiritual enlightenment, to feel closer to nature, or just for fun. The hallucinogenics (aka psychedelics), such as peyote, mescaline, LSD, and psilocybin, were most closely associated with these uses, whereas cocaine, amphetamines, barbiturates, and quaaludes were associated less with mind expansion and more with mood modification, energy-state manipulation, or just experimentation ("Hey, man—try this"). The problem is that all of these get lumped into a single category of "drugs" and yet they are very different substances with dramatically different effects, both biologically and psychologically.

For current members of the Woodstock generation, now in their sixties and seventies, judicious ingestion of hallucinogenics can, for some, be cognitively and emotionally enhancing. Physicist Leonard Mlodinow reports that experiences with cannabis can enhance an ability he calls "elastic thinking."

> There are certain talents that can help us, qualities of thought. . . . For example, the capacity to let go of comfortable ideas and become accustomed to ambiguity and contradiction; the capability to rise above conventional mind-sets and to reframe the questions we ask . . . to overcome the neural and psychological barriers that can impede us.

And the effects of cannabis are most pronounced on those who are less creative to begin with. In other words, it acts as a perception, creativity, and insight equalizer.

Psilocybin users report having "mystical experiences" and terminal cancer patients have found it helpful in reducing the anxiety about their impending deaths. A single dose of the drug in older adults caused a lasting, positive change in Factor V of personality—Openness to Experience. Science writer Michael Pollan's book *How to Change Your Mind: What the New Science of Psychedelics Teaches Us About Consciousness, Dying, Addiction, Depression, and Transcendence* explores a kind of resonant echo of some of the more idealistic goals for the use of psychedelics that drew many to them in the 1960s.

> I got intensely curious about the experiences of people I was interviewing—stone-cold atheists telling me they'd had a profound spiritual journey, and people who'd been terrified of death completely losing their fear. It was clear there was so much more to learn about these extraordinary molecules—at the level of neuroscience, but also at the level of personal experience.

This led Pollan to experiment with them himself, and in the book, he describes these recent experiences as a sixty-year-old taking hallucinogenics for the first time, which he says improved his life. He emphasizes the importance of having a guide to help you prepare for the experiences, and an integrator to help you process them—in Pollan's case, the integrator was his wife. Pollan summarizes:

> The journeys have shown me what the Buddhists try to tell us but I have never really understood: that there is more to consciousness than the ego, as we would see if it would just shut up.

Psychedelics also helped him feel more open, more patient, and more connected to nature. In effect, it seems to me, they helped him to hit the reset button, to stop taking mundane things in his life for granted, and to approach the world and his life in it more like a younger person would. If you are interested in learning more about these, Pollan's book is a good place to start, and there is a nonprofit informational website, Erowid.org, that provides information about plant-based psychoactives.

I want to be careful here and point out that these are powerful drugs and they are not without risks, especially for people who may have psychiatric problems. (Then again, everything we take has risks.) David Nutt, a neuropsychopharmacologist at Imperial College London, calls hallucinogenics "among the safest drugs we know of." Nevertheless, if you have latent tendencies toward mental disorders, drugs can put you over the edge, sometimes to the point of no return. This is what may have happened to Brian Wilson, the creative genius behind the Beach Boys, who ended up with schizoaffective disorder. In another case, an artist who took powerful drugs for many years (who shall remain unnamed due to privacy considerations) suffers from paranoid delusions, thinking that CIA agents are living in the basement of their home, and delusional parasitosis, thinking that thousands of microscopic bugs are under their skin, and that snakes inhabit every bed in the house. In the latter case, these delusions have not interfered with creativity or productivity, and the artist refuses to acknowledge that these delusions are products of the mind.

My own observations of people who have taken LSD multiple times have caused me to believe that there is a more or less fixed number of times that you can take it with no ill effects, and that this number is unique to each person and their own psychological makeup. The problem is that you don't have any way of knowing what that number is. For some people it may be only a handful of times; for others it could be one hundred. I know many people who took multiple LSD trips and were fine, until one day, suddenly, they weren't. By the time you're sixty or seventy, though, you probably know yourself pretty well. You know if you've heard voices in your head or had manic-depressive episodes, paralyzing self-doubt, or suicidal thoughts. If you have had any of these, drug experimentation is probably not for you.

Microdosing

I have been spending time in Silicon Valley since I first attended Stanford there as a student in 1974. I still go back regularly to give talks, meet with colleagues at Google, or visit friends. It has always been odd, but recently it has gotten weirder. There was a casual, laid-back quality to it in the 1970s that has morphed into an intense desire everyone seems to have to outperform everyone around them in every domain possible. You see it in the frenetic way people drive, or in the tech workers eating in restaurants while manipulating two or three smartphones at once. Silicon Valley these days is full of people in their twenties and thirties who are looking for anything they can do to gain a competitive edge.

So it was no surprise to me when *Forbes* published an article in 2015 (following a report in *Rolling Stone*) that twentysomethings in Silicon Valley had started taking psychedelics in microdoses to enhance creativity and productivity. (In *The Good Fight,* Diane Lockhart, played by Christine Baranski, experiments with microdosing psilocybin.)

Microdosing is just taking small amounts of substances, such as LSD, that are believed to be below the threshold of any noticeable effect, typically 5 to 10 percent of a normal dose. An ideal dose is "when you feel good, you're working effectively, and you've forgotten that you've taken anything." Many of the reported beneficial effects associated with regular doses of hallucinogens are reported for microdoses of them but, understandably, in more controllable and less spectacular form. Users report enhancements of creativity, reductions in fear and anxiety, and lifting of mood. Microdosers scored lower on measures of dysfunctional attitudes and negative emotionality and higher on measures of wisdom, open-mindedness, and creativity, as well as a reduced incidence of suicide. Regular low doses of THC, the active ingredient in cannabis, were found to reverse memory deficits and restore cognitive function in old mice, a promising avenue for future human experiments.

Devices

Earlier, I mentioned neural implants. As futuristic and crazy as they sound, they already exist. Cochlear implants are surgically implanted in people who are born deaf and whose hearing deficit is due to problems in the inner ear, inside a snail-shaped structure called the cochlea. When you hear any kind of sound, your eardrum wiggles in and out with the frequency of the sound. The cochlea translates this in-and-out motion into electrical signals that it transmits to the auditory cortex. They have been in use since the first one was implanted at Stanford University in 1964, and today there are an estimated six hundred thousand people who have them worldwide.

Other forms of neural implants have been in use to control epilepsy, treat Parkinson's, and lift clinical depression. The downside to them is that they are invasive—they require surgically opening the skull and implanting something in your brain (and really, is there anything more invasive than that?). But as robotic surgery becomes more refined, and more commonplace, we may soon see the sorts of implants that seemed fanciful in the past—memory enhancement by stimulating hippocampal pathways (or more intriguingly, by stimulating selectively those emotional pathways that facilitate memory storage and retrieval), or attentional networks in the prefrontal cortex, insular cortex, and anterior cingulate.

As I am writing this, a paper was just published in *Nature Communications* by a team at the University of Pennsylvania led by Michael Kahana. They developed a neural implant that increased memory encoding and recall of newly presented information, a possible first step toward alleviating the most devastating symptoms of Alzheimer's disease and dementia. An innovative feature of their implant is that it doesn't fire all the time—it studies neural firing patterns in the brains of implantees and sends electrical signals only when the brain appears to be having trouble encoding new information, and it remains dormant the rest of the time. (In this way it resembles a pacemaker for the heart.)

"We all have good days and bad days, times when we're foggy, or when we're sharp," said Kahana. "We found that jostling the system when it's in a low-functioning state can jump it to a high-functioning one." Kahana thinks that future research could preferentially target the retrieval of old, forgotten memories as well.

Bionics

Bionic products can enhance our sensory receptors, delivering information to us that we might not otherwise receive. They can allow us to do things with our bodies that we couldn't do before, and through embodied cognition, this could enhance our mental lives. Bionics are becoming increasingly sophisticated and people's attitudes toward them are changing. The technology, driven in part by the need to serve war veterans with amputations, has allowed us to provide functionality. We've now seen Olympic runners using prosthetic legs. One recipient of a prosthetic hand skydives, chops vegetables, and can even use chopsticks, and an experimental "sensory" hand is allowing another amputee to feel the shape and composition of objects for the first time since his amputation.

Samantha Payne, COO of Open Bionics, a prosthetics company, says that the commercialization of this technology is just around the corner. "All we need is smaller motors, better batteries; once the components advance, the products will come to market. . . . I feel there has been a huge cultural shift. We've found a very distinct gap between younger amputees and those aged forty and older. The older ones wanted a bionic hand as close to real skin as possible. The younger generation all want highly personalized hands. We've moved from a society that valued conformity to one that celebrates individuality. People are more willing to experiment with their body. It's wide open."

Brain implants are being used to help quadriplegics type or move paralyzed limbs with their minds. One twenty-four-year-old broke his neck in an accident and hadn't been able to move for six years. A neural implant now lets him move his previously paralyzed right arm enough that he can play video games. Imagine a neurosurgeon whose hands are too shaky to operate but who can think about what he wants to do while a robot does it.

Zoltan Istvan is a controversial figure who self-identifies as part of the transhumanist movement, a group of individuals who seek to augment the human body and mind with implants as a way to greatly enhance human intellect, achievement, and physiology; some see it as a road to immortality. So far followers have not done much beyond radio-frequency chip implants that allow them to unlock doors and start cars, a skull implant to allow listening to music wirelessly (the neurojack, the writer Sandy Pearlman once called it), and magnetic implants that allow people a sixth sense to know when metal is nearby. Another enthusiast, Neil Harbisson, had an antenna installed in his head that allows him to hear color waves, sensing colors he wouldn't normally experience, such as infrared and ultraviolet. He also has a Bluetooth implant in his head. "I can either connect to devices that are near me," he says, "or I can connect to the internet. So I can actually connect to anywhere in the world."

But before any of these far-out-sounding devices become commonplace, a real revolution is under way for diagnostics. Many of us already carry around or wear devices that track our movements and heart rate, and these communicate with smartphones to create an exercise record. In the coming five years, other wearables—patches, sensor-lined shirts, bracelets, and, yes, tiny implants, will be able to collect data that signal whether your blood sugar levels are off, whether you're dehydrated, or whether you're about to experience a seizure or migraine. The technology exists for these already. Serena Williams has been seen in ads wearing a patch manufactured by Gatorade that reads levels of chloride in sweat to indicate total electrolyte loss, an indicator of dehydration.

Meditation

A great number of claims have been made for meditation, and if you don't meditate yourself, its adherents can seem annoyingly zealous about it. Meditation is not going to cure cancer or reverse Alzheimer's disease or Parkinson's disease. It's not going to bring you fame beyond your wildest dreams. But as part of a healthy lifestyle, it can help to make your brain more effective and more efficient.

I asked the Dalai Lama, "In the future, suppose that you're eighty-five years old, ninety years old, and you feel that your memory is getting bad. It could happen. Would you take a drug from a doctor that would help your memory improve?"

He replied, "I don't know. I feel the training of mind through meditation is really what helps the sharpening of mind. And that is also helpful, you see, for keeping memory strong." It also helps him to stay mindful of what is most important to him and to tame his own impulses. He continues . . .

> I love to talk. I usually tell people one of my weaknesses is once my mouth opens *blah blah blah blah blah,* like that. So the time gets always from me. I think the main source of my strength is that I'm a Buddhist monk. Every day is filled with praying and thinking; my body, speech, and mind are dedicated to the well-being of others. Not just in this life, but as long as space remains, as long as sentient beings remain, I will remain to serve. So that really gives me inner strength, and I dedicate that strength. A mental life so full of enthusiasm also has a beneficial effect on the body.

He has worked closely with neuroscientists to better understand the brain basis of this. Meditation involves maintaining attention on your immediate experience in the moment and in the world, and away from distractions such as self-referential thinking and mind wandering. It helps to train you to avoid thinking about something other than what you're currently doing, taming the default mode network that I mentioned earlier. Meditation reduces activity within the default mode network and increases connectivity between it and regions of the brain that are implicated in cognitive control—that is, controlling our thoughts: the dorsal anterior cingulate and dorsolateral prefrontal cortices. The result is that meditation simultaneously turns down the default mode's pull on our attention, while streamlining and honing the network. Increased connectivity between the prefrontal region and the default areas also has an anti-inflammatory effect by reducing cytokines.

Neuroscientist Richard Davidson from the University of Wisconsin–Madison has found that monks show greater gamma waves during compassion meditation. Gammas are the signature of neuronal activity that knits together far-flung brain circuits. They underlie higher-level mental activity, such as consciousness. The mechanism is that gamma waves cause synchronization of neurons, and the resulting unity of firing leads to a unity of consciousness. Imagine the beautiful, mystical symmetry: An activity that can make us feel one with the universe is that which makes our billions of neurons fire as one.

Long-term meditators show structural changes in the brain as well, including increases in cortical thickness, hippocampal gray-matter density, and the size of the hippocampus. Additional changes are enlargement of the insula, somatomotor areas, orbitofrontal cortex, parts of the prefrontal cortex that help in paying attention and in self-awareness, and regions of the cingulate cortex instrumental in self-regulation and staying focused.

Even brief meditation reduces fatigue and anxiety and increases visuospatial processing, working memory, and executive functioning, and in many cases these benefits persist even after meditation practice is stopped. Meditators show lower levels of cortisol following a stressful task and decreased inflammation, not just during meditation, but day-to-day, and the benefits show up after as little as four weeks (or thirty hours) of mindfulness practice.

Davidson also showed that meditation may drive benefits at the level of genes. After an eight-hour day of practice, a group of long-term meditators (with about six thousand lifetime hours of practice) showed a significant downregulation of inflammatory genes. This decrease, if sustained over a lifetime, might help fight diseases with onsets marked by chronic low-grade inflammation—cardiovascular disorders, arthritis, diabetes, Alzheimer's disease, and cancer. A handful of other pilot studies support the finding that meditation seems to have epigenetic effects. Loneliness triggers higher levels of pro-inflammatory genes; meditation can both lower those levels and decrease feelings of loneliness, as the Dalai Lama found when he meditates on how he is just one of 7 billion people on the planet (recall his remarks about this in Chapter 1, on individual differences). Mindfulness meditation is also associated with increased telomerase. In people with mild cognitive impairment and early-stage Alzheimer's, meditation has been shown to slow or reverse cognitive decline, reduce stress, and increase quality of life, along with the neuroplastic changes I just described.

❖

I've come to see a future in which we can plan ahead to fend off some of the adverse effects of aging; a future in which we can harness what we know about neuroplasticity to write our own upcoming chapters the way we want them to unfold; a future in which a combination of medical developments and healthy lifestyle choices can temper or reverse the effects of cognitive decline, depression, and loss of energy that we have for too long assumed were a nonnegotiable part of the aging process. That future is to a large degree already here for those who are willing to harness it.

14

LIVING BETTER

The greatest days of our lives

If I had known I was going to live so long, I would have taken better care of myself.

—Psychological scientist Eleanor Maccoby, on turning one hundred

At my age, the most embarrassing thing I'll ever do is probably something I've already done.

—David Bradley, actor (*Harry Potter, Game of Thrones*), age seventy-seven

There is an ancient story about the tension between longevity and quality of life. According to Greek mythology, Eos was the goddess of the dawn. Every morning she rode on a purple chariot drawn by two horses, wearing a saffron-colored robe, to bring in the day. She fell deeply in love with the mortal Tithonos, the prince of Troy. As a goddess she was immortal and couldn't stand the thought that Tithonos would eventually die and she'd have to spend eternity without him. She implored Zeus to grant immortality to Tithonos, and Zeus agreed. But Eos didn't think to also ask for the gift of youth that she and the other gods and goddesses enjoyed. While Eos stayed eternally young, Tithonos became an old man, decrepit, lacking even enough strength to move his legs. He continued to age until he eventually lost his mind. She moved him out of her home and put him in a chamber by himself, where he continued to live mindlessly and infirm. Immortality and youth are not the same thing.

Philosopher David Velleman suggests that we consider two hypothetical lives that represent possible extremes.

> One life begins in the depths but takes an upward trend: a childhood of deprivation, a troubled youth, struggles and setbacks in early adulthood, followed finally by success and satisfaction in middle age and a peaceful retirement. Another life begins at the heights but slides downhill: a blissful childhood and youth, precocious triumphs and rewards in early adulthood, followed by a midlife strewn with disasters that lead to misery in old age.

Now imagine that we could somehow manage to quantify what we mean by deprivation, trouble, struggles, triumphs, rewards, success, and satisfaction. We'd simply assign numbers to these different experiences and tally them up. (You could choose how fine a resolution you want: Was this a good year? A good week? A good day or even a good minute?) Next, imagine that we did this across the life span and compared two lifetimes of exactly the same duration, but with the good times and the bad times distributed differently, as in the story Velleman tells. Numerically, the lives might be identical—that is, the number of bad episodes or moments in each are equal, and so are the number of good episodes or moments in each. If a good life is one in which the good outweighs the bad by a certain amount, and if well-being were simply additive, then these two lives should be seen as equally desirable. But that is not how most people look at it. Given a choice, most people would prefer the life that takes the upward trend and we'd consider the person with that life the more fortunate.

What Daniel Kahneman found about pleasure and pain—that people were willing to endure pain longer if the ending was relatively pleasant—was found in the narrow context of painful medical procedures, such as colonoscopies. Does this same principle apply to life itself? Psychological scientist Ed Diener found that it does. Diener started with the following straightforward question: Do additional years of lower quality among elderly people enhance or detract from their perceived overall quality of life? In other words, he investigated whether people judge it better to have a shorter life that ends on a high note versus a longer life with an end that is marked by misery and discomfort. He also considered that how close a person is to the end of their own life might influence their judgments.

A happy life that ended abruptly was considered more desirable than a happy one with five extra years tacked on at the end that were merely pleasant but not as happy as before. In contrast, a terrible life was considered more desirable if it was longer, provided the last five years—although still unpleasant—weren't as terrible as life had been before. The same results were obtained from older adults and younger adults, indicating that as the end is near, people still don't see longevity as the only goal. The study confirms the "end point" effect found by Kahneman. (From a strictly statistical view, these findings are irrational. In a real, numerical sense, the people with good lives who lived longer lives actually experienced more pleasure in their lives than the people who lived shorter lives.) Diener called this the James Dean effect, after the actor who died suddenly at age twenty-four at the height of stardom.

Velleman's explanation about why we prefer an improving life to a declining one isn't because we place greater weight on what happens at the end, but because later events can alter the meaning of earlier events. This may derive from our yearning to instill life with meaning. We are drawn to the story of someone who sees the error of their youthful ways and grows, someone who becomes a better person. This makes for a more satisfying trajectory, a more inspirational and aspirational theme, than someone who goes in the opposite direction. *When* we have the good times and the bad times actually matters. We're sensitive to the timing of events because we seek patterns in the world around us—including our lives within it. A particular success can mean that one's frustrations are finally over, or it can foreshadow a slump we didn't see coming, depending on when it happens in our timeline. And that event's perceived meaning depends very much on the events that happened before and after it.

Taken together, these studies suggest that quality of life is important to consider, not just longevity, and that it may even deserve some of the resources that are being put into longevity research. I raised this idea with the Global Burden of Disease charts, showing that the things people die from (heart disease, cancer) tend not to be the things that impact quality of life (disability, pain, hearing loss, vision loss). Add to that the fact that the medical profession tends to focus on saving lives and cures, with relatively less attention paid to the sequelae of disease—the "What next?" question. This has become such an issue that the journal *Nature* published an editorial urging researchers to study the long-term effects of therapies that are taken for granted. As one example, they tell the story of Gregory Aune, who was treated for Hodgkin's lymphoma at age sixteen with a combination of drugs and radiation. He saw many of the patients in his ward die. Now forty-six, he has had to deal with hypothyroidism, diabetes, skin cancer, infertility, open-heart surgery, and a stroke, all tied to the treatments he received. Now a pediatric oncologist, he is pushing for more awareness of the aftermath. "The toxicity of the treatment has hung with me," he says.

Moving in this direction, the World Health Organization has introduced a measure called healthy life expectancy (HALE) that tracks how many years a person lives without significant impairment, defined by objective criteria such as the ability to work, walk, dress, converse, and remember.

Not everyone agrees with me about the value of balancing longevity and quality of life—some just want to stay alive no matter what. But I think that life endings should be surrounded by positive events and memories and should be as free as possible of physical and psychological pain. Three of my grandparents experienced this gift—they went quickly, enjoying life, and without knowing what hit them. One of them died in a hospital and couldn't wait to leave this mortal coil. "I feel like a pin cushion in here," she said, of all the times that nurses came and poked her with needles. Her days were bleak, as she no longer enjoyed her mealtime and didn't have the energy to enjoy visits from her grandchildren. I am not sure that medicine served her well. And yet I am grateful for the extra months I got to spend with her and know her better, but my happiness is not the issue—hers is.

Well-Being and Happiness

We can change the conversation, throughout society, about what it means to be an older adult. We often look at old age as a time of limitations, infirmities, and sadness. Of course, it's true that as we get older there are a number of things we don't do as well as when we were younger. But that doesn't necessarily mean that all older adults are sad or depressed. Some certainly are, but as a group, they are actually happier than younger people. Happiness tends to decrease beginning in the late thirties (midlife crisis, anyone?) and then begins to increase sharply after age fifty-four. This holds true across seventy-two countries, from Albania to Zimbabwe.

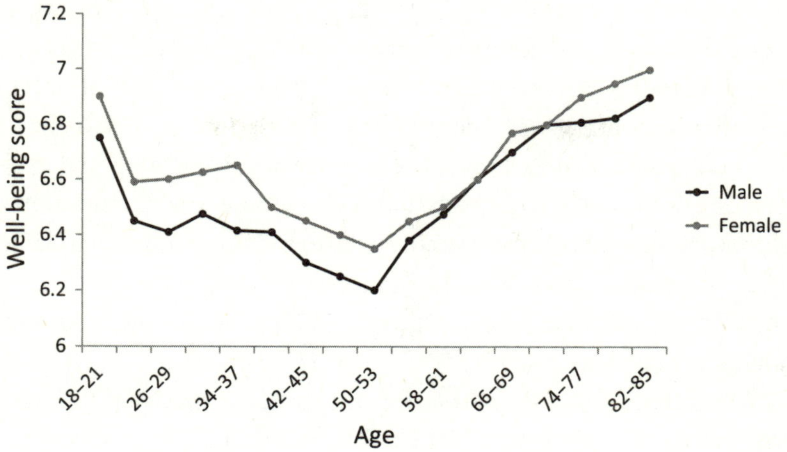

You might spin a story about this happening because of social factors. As Daniel Pink says about the middle-aged dip:

> One possibility is the disappointment of unrealized expectations. In our naïve twenties and thirties, our hopes are high, our scenarios rosy. Then reality trickled in like a slow leak in the roof. Only one person gets to be CEO—and it's not going to be you. Some marriages crumble—and yours, sadly, is one of them. . . . Yet we don't remain in the emotional basement for long, because over time we adjust our aspirations and later realize that life is pretty good. In short, we dip in the middle because we're lousy forecasters. In youth, our expectations are too high.

Or maybe it's Velleman's explanation again: As a species, we are driven to make sense of our lives. Looking back, we find happiness in seeing that whatever inevitable struggles we had brought us to where we are now. Even if things have taken a downturn, we are happy to be alive and to have had whatever good experiences we had. Yes, we would prefer to have things get better, but we recontextualize and recast our lives in a positive way. This is consistent with and predicted by Carstensen's socioemotional selectivity theory (as we saw in Chapter 6, on life with people): Older adults show a positivity bias. They live differently than younger adults, spending more of their available time doing things they like. No wonder they're happier than forty-year-olds who are doing things they don't like in order to get ahead in life so that they can eventually (they hope) enjoy the fruits of unhappy labor. In addition to this, older adults show a positivity bias—they are much more likely to attend to and remember positive stimuli and experiences. The positivity bias has been found in a number of different contexts, including short-term memory, autobiographical memory, attention to positive emotional faces, recall of positive facial expressions, memory for health information, and the positive interpretation of emotionally ambiguous situations.

What might be the brain basis for the positivity bias? Carstensen believes that it is caused by top-down (volitional) changes in motivated cognition that shift priorities toward emotionally satisfying goals. Indeed, two areas associated with selective attention and these kinds of motivated cognition are the ventral-medial region of the prefrontal cortex and the adjacent anterior cingulate cortex. These areas have been shown to be especially active in older adults, and this may be contributing to older adults' positivity and well-being.

I mentioned Sonny Rollins, one of the greatest living jazz musicians, in Chapter 6, on life with people. He lost his ability to play his instrument a few years ago due to pulmonary fibrosis. In a career spanning seven decades, he has played with the greats—Miles Davis, Dizzy Gillespie, Thelonious Monk, Bud Powell, and Max Roach—and he has recorded more than sixty albums as an acclaimed bandleader. Now that he is eighty-nine, you might expect that his health problems have caused him sadness or frustration, but when we visited, I found him to be remarkably content, philosophical, and upbeat, and focused on quality of life rather than length of life. According to Sonny Rollins:

> The purpose of life according to Buddhists and other people that think like that is we live and we learn. We keep learning. It doesn't mean anything to me, if I lived 144 years. It's not about 144 years. If I learned everything that I need to advance in Buddhahood or anything like that, where you're really becoming a more enlightened person . . . that's what we're here for . . . enlightened soul. We go through who knows how many lives? I

> don't know. I don't try to contemplate that. That's not my business. People tell me oh Sonny you think about these things a lot—what's heaven like? And I tell them look, don't waste my time. That's not my business what heaven is like. My business is right here on earth. Trying to be a better person, trying to do things which would make other people happy, which as I've said makes me happy by making other people happy. That's what it's about. This other stuff it doesn't mean anything. At least that's my way of thinking. That's what Eastern philosophy is about. I think I'm happier now than I . . . I have much more understanding.

Social Comparisons Influence Satisfaction

One of my students, a refugee from Romania who settled in Canada, shared this story with me:

> My first encounter with the topic of quality of life was early in my childhood. I was playing with a group of local children in a small Romanian village when a team of North American missionaries approached us and pulled me aside to ask me about what they assumed to be the miserable, poverty-stricken lives of me and my friends. They looked at us dirty, barefoot children with pity, and my friends and I looked back at them with confusion—we couldn't understand why these foreigners looked so concerned. We didn't think anything was wrong. One could argue then, that *perceived* quality of life is more important to an individual's well-being than *objective* measures of quality of life.

Social comparison theory states that our life satisfaction tends to be influenced not so much by what we have but by what we have in relation to others. That is, we look to see how others are living, such as whether they have shoes or have fewer aches and pains—and we judge ourselves in comparison. We are a social species, and we are attuned to fairness. If we see others who have things we don't, like shoes or good health, we feel cheated. If no one we know has shoes or good health, we just think to ourselves, "That's life." At eighty-nine, Sonny Rollins is doing well compared to almost any of his jazz contemporaries. Most are dead and suffered from more debilitating health problems than Sonny.

Measuring Quality of Life and Happiness

Happiness is a personal perception, and its determinants differ vastly across cultures. Most quality of life indexes combine objective measures, such as health, independence, standard of living, and security (e.g., freedom from crime), with subjective measures, such as a person's own self-assessment of their satisfaction about a number of key components of their lives—freedom of choice, social relationships, romantic relationships, meaningful work, and mood.

You might assume that everyone aspires to more happiness—that is, given the choice, people would want to have the maximum amount possible of something good. But that view is a biased one, held by people who live in individualist societies such as Europe and North America. For people from collectivist and holistic societies—where contradiction, change, and context are emphasized—ideal states of being for the self are more moderate than in other cultures. This approach might be called the moderation principle, under which people impose mindful ceilings on how much of a good thing they aspire to in a perfect world. Although he is living in New York, this is the view taken by Sonny Rollins and, in fact, by followers of Eastern philosophies and religions, such as Buddhism, Confucianism, Hinduism, Jainism, and Taoism. You may recognize the similarities with Aristotle's principle of the golden mean (neither too much nor too little of a thing).

Westerners tend to see happiness and misery as opposites, and life as a challenge to minimize the negative and accentuate the positive. Easterners tend to see happiness and misery as interrelated and mutually necessary, like the yin and yang in Chinese philosophy. Indeed, studies of thousands of people have found that members of holistic cultures aspire to less happiness, pleasure, freedom, health, self-esteem, and longevity than members of individualistic cultures, although their goals for society at large are the same. Russia—which has a sociological history of being somewhat between an individualistic and collectivist culture—fell on the side of the Eastern cultures when included in this study.

Americans have been falling in the world happiness rankings over the past several years, according to *The World Happiness Report.* In their 2019 ranking of 156 countries, the United States dropped one rank to number 19 for its worst rank since the report began. "We finished nineteenth on the list behind Belgium," comedian Jimmy Kimmel quipped. "The people who feel the need to put mayonnaise on their french fries are happier than we are. Cheer up, everybody!"

The report looks at six variables: GDP, social support, health span (not life span!), freedom to make life choices, generosity, and freedom from corruption. "By most accounts, Americans should be happier now than ever," said Jean Twenge, one of the report's authors. "The violent crime rate is low, as is the unemployment rate." The authors speculate that the US ranking has dropped due to a spate of addictions—opioids, gambling, social media, and risky sexual behaviors—as well as the rise in obesity and major depression.

The authors also blame overuse of digital devices. By 2017, the average seventeen- or eighteen-year-old spent more than six hours a day of leisure time—in addition to any time spent on schoolwork—on the Internet, social media, and texting, activities that have been linked to increases in depression. With increasing screen time, people became less likely to engage in face-to-face interactions, such as getting together with their friends or going to parties. There was also a decline in other non-screen-related solitary activities, such as reading and sleeping. Although we talk about how social media is bringing us closer to others and making the world smaller, digital devices weaken actual social contact in favor of some kind of amorphous and sporadic virtual contact.

Another part of this nationwide drop in happiness may be the rash of corruption convictions in the United States of people in high-level positions in corporations and in government in 2018 and 2019—freedom from corruption is one of the indexes in quality of life.

The longest study on health and happiness ever conducted is the Harvard Grant Study (now part of the Study of Adult Development). Begun in 1938, it tracked 268 male Harvard students and 456 controls from Boston for more than seventy-five years, without knowing how their life stories were going to turn out. (One of the study members was President John F. Kennedy.) Around 59 of them, mostly in their nineties, are still in the study, and researchers are studying their children and grandchildren and in the early 2000s began collecting data from the participants' wives also. Psychiatrist Robert Waldinger, who now leads the study, summarized the findings this way:

> The clearest message we get from this 75 year study is this: good relationships keep us happy and healthier, period . . . social connections are really good for us . . . loneliness kills. People who are more socially connected to family, to friends and community, are happier, healthier, and they live longer. And loneliness turns out to be toxic. . . . High conflict marriages without much affection are very bad for our health—worse than getting divorced.

A bigger predictor than cholesterol level at age fifty for health at age eighty is the quality of your relationships. Good relationships protect your brain. Especially in their eighties, a person who feels they are in an attached relationship, where they can count on the other person in times of need, will retain sharper memories for longer and better overall health. The Beatles were right about this (and so many other things): Love is the most important thing. A second important pillar of happiness is finding a way of coping with life that does not push love away.

The study's most important finding is the enormous impact of relationships, far larger than we ever realized before. A person could have a successful career, money, and good physical health, but without supportive, loving relationships, they won't be happy. Men's relationships at age forty-seven, the researchers found, predicted late-life adjustment better than any other variable, except ability to cope with setbacks (what he called defense mechanisms). Good sibling relationships loomed especially powerful: 93 percent of the men who were thriving at age sixty-five had been close to a brother or sister when younger. "It is social aptitude," wrote George Vaillant, who directed the study for three decades, "not intellectual brilliance or parental social class, that leads to successful aging." Asked what he had learned after thirty years of studying the cohort, Vaillant was clear: "That the only thing that really matters in life are your relationships to other people."

At age eighty-five, one man in the study described the pleasure of his three-decades-long second marriage as "really just being together. Share each other's lives and our children's lives. Snuggle on cold nights." One woman, after fifty years of marriage, said the secret was that they were best friends. "There's a physical relationship. It's not quite what it was when we were young, but the main thing is, I *adore* him. More than I ever did. We laugh a lot, we laugh at ourselves, and we don't take ourselves too seriously. I don't know how we got here, but it's wonderful. Equally important, we hold each other loosely." (If you love somebody, set them free.)

One interesting finding from the study is that those who married a second time were often just as happy as those who stayed in their first marriage. That is, people who divorce are not, as a group, malcontents who can't work things out. In the 1960s and '70s, many researchers thought that divorce was caused by personality disorders, poor coping style, passive aggression, acting out, aggression, and alcohol abuse. But that has not been borne out by research. Marriages fail for a variety of reasons, and often the simplest explanation is the most accurate: The couple were merely mismatched and didn't realize it until later. And for many, their marriages just get better and better in old age. As Vaillant notes, "In time, hormones can feminize the men and masculinize the women, making the playing field more level." Politics appears to correlate with late-life happiness as well, at least insofar as sex is concerned: Aging liberals have more sex, according to the Harvard study. The most conservative men ceased sexual relations at an average age of sixty-eight, while the most liberal men had active sex lives into their eighties.

Part of the Harvard Grant Study was a control group of inner-city men from Boston—the Glueck Study. Parental social class, IQ, and income did not predict longevity and happiness for either the Glueck or Harvard men. But education mattered a lot, and it didn't have to be an elite education—at age seventy, the inner-city men who graduated from non-elite colleges were just as healthy as the Harvard men. Interestingly, while the Glueck men were 50 percent more likely to become dependent on alcohol than the Harvard men, the ones who did were more than twice as likely to eventually get sober. "The difference has nothing to do with treatment, intelligence, self-care, or having something to lose," Vaillant says. "It does have to do with hitting bottom. Someone sleeping under the elevated-train tracks can at some point recognize that he's an alcoholic, but the guy getting stewed every night at a private club may not." Another interesting fact about alcohol use: Divorced people often say that they drink because their spouses left them. But this is self-deception: In the great majority of cases, the spouse left them because of the drinking.

It's not just social connections late in life that determine happiness and other measures of life satisfaction. Although they're crucial, they occur in a context of a lifetime of social connections. Men who had "warm" childhood relationships with their mothers earned an average of $87,000 more a year than men whose mothers were uncaring. (Wow! Thanks, Mom!) Men who had poor childhood relationships with their mothers were much more likely to develop dementia when old. Late in their professional lives, the men's boyhood relationships with their mothers—but not with their fathers—were associated with effectiveness at work. On the other hand, warm childhood relations with fathers correlated with lower rates of adult anxiety, greater enjoyment of vacations, and increased "life satisfaction" at age seventy-five—whereas the warmth of childhood relationships with mothers had no significant bearing on life satisfaction at seventy-five.

Older couples often find the solution to loneliness in each other, after careers and children are a smaller part of their lives. It can require some effort to get to know each other again. Without that effort, old gripes or a "grass is greener" attitude can cause older couples to feel distant from each other and even seek divorce. In fact, according to the US Census, the divorce rate for couples over sixty-five has tripled in the last twenty-five years. But for those who make it work, the benefits are measurable: Couples who are more satisfied with their spouses have increased longevity—up to 25 percent. So there you go—the right romantic relationship wins you the double payout of increased longevity and increased quality of life. Science says so. Love the one you're with. Making your spouse happy will help you live better.

Work versus Retirement

What is the ideal age to retire? Never. Even if you're physically impaired, it's best to keep working, either in a job or as a volunteer. Quincy Jones is in a wheelchair, but at age eighty-six he is still involved in producing music, discovering talent, giving speeches, and being a public spokesperson for the importance of the arts in society. Lamont Dozier, the co-writer of such iconic songs as "Heat Wave," "Stop! In the Name of Love," and "Reach Out, I'll Be There" (and with fourteen number one *Billboard* hits), is seventy-eight and still writing. "I get up every morning and write for an hour or two," he says. "It's why the good Lord put me here." Too much time spent with no purpose is associated with unhappiness. Stay busy! Not with busy-work or trivial pursuits, but with meaningful activities.

Economists have coined the term *unretirement* to describe the hordes of people who retire, find they don't like it, and go back to work. Between 25 and 40 percent of people who retire reenter the workforce. Harvard economist Nicole Maestas says, "You hear certain themes: a sense of purpose. Using your brain. And another key component is social engagement." Recall Sigmund Freud's words that the two most important things in life are to have love and meaningful work. (He was wrong about a great number of things, but he seems to have gotten that right.)

I interviewed a number of people for this book between the ages of seventy and ninety-eight in order to better understand what contributes to life satisfaction. Every single one of them has continued working. Some, like musicians Donald Fagen of Steely Dan (age seventy-one) and Judy Collins (age eighty), have increased their workload. Others, like George Shultz (age ninety-nine) and the Dalai Lama (age eighty-four), have modified their work schedules to accommodate age-related slowing, but in the partial days they work, they accomplish more than most of their younger counterparts.

Staying busy with meaningful activities requires some strategies and reshifting of priorities. Author Barbara Ehrenreich (age seventy-eight) rejects the many tests that her doctor orders because she doesn't want to waste time in a doctor's office for something that might only add three weeks to her life. Why?

> Because I have other things to do. Partly this seems to start for me with the kind of trade-off decision: Do I want to go sit in a windowless doctor's office waiting room, or meet my deadline, or go for a walk? It always came down to the latter.

Many employers will allow older adult workers to modify their schedules in order to continue working. In the United States, employers are required to make reasonable accommodations, such as start and end times, break rooms, even a cot to lie down on for a nap, and age discrimination is illegal. Age discrimination is similarly illegal in Canada, Mexico, and Finland. The laws around the world vary. Generally, the European Union permits termination at the pension retirement age (in Germany, for example, that's currently age sixty-five and is being extended to sixty-seven). In South Korea the mandatory retirement age is sixty. In other countries, such as Australia, the laws and interpretations of those laws are evolving. (Courts in Australia, for example, found in favor of Qantas Airways, which terminated a pilot at age sixty. Although this was in violation of the country's Age Discrimination Act of 2004, the high court ruled that because it was a requirement of the Convention on International Civil Aviation that captains aged sixty or over be barred from flying over certain routes, termination of pilots over sixty was lawful.)

Most important, I think we need to work together to fight for changes in the way our societies see older adults, particularly how they see them in the workforce. Corporate culture in the United States has tended toward ageism. It is difficult for older adults to get a job or get promoted. Two-thirds of American workers said they had witnessed or experienced age discrimination at work. Employers should recognize that offering opportunities to older workers is smart business, not just a feel-good, charitable act. Multigenerational teams with older members tend to be more productive; older adults boost the productivity of those around them, and such teams outperform single-generational ones. Deutsche Bank has been at the forefront of this kind of approach, and they report fewer mistakes as well as increased positive feedback between young and old.

Many countries have passed laws prohibiting discrimination in employment against people with disabilities, including Alzheimer's disease (e.g., in the United States the Americans with Disabilities Act of 1990, and in the United Kingdom the Equality Act of 2010). The BrightFocus Foundation, a nonprofit, lists the following accommodations among those that might be helpful for workers with Alzheimer's:

- Incorporating reminders into their day—written or verbal
- Dividing large tasks into many smaller tasks

- Providing additional training when there are workplace changes
- Keeping the workspace clutter-free
- Reducing the number of hours worked per day or week
- Changing the time of day worked

In recognition of this, Heathrow Airport in London became the world's first "dementia-friendly" airport, with one thousand employees dedicated to serving the special needs of those with cognitive impairment, and special training for all seventy-six thousand airport employees. Researchers at John Carroll University, a private Jesuit university in University Heights, Ohio, created an intergenerational choir, bringing together young people and older adults with dementia. It changed the attitudes of the students, who talked about the closeness they felt in the choir and the development of intergenerational friendships. Through singing together, the adults with dementia felt included, welcomed, valued, and respected.

The late Tennessee women's basketball coach Pat Summitt, who was also a silver medalist from the 1976 Summer Olympics, was diagnosed with Alzheimer's in August 2011 and continued working, finishing out the athletic season through 2012. "There's not going to be any pity party," she said, "and I'll make sure of that."

If continuing to work in your job isn't possible after a certain age, and if new employers aren't willing to hire older workers, there are still many ways to stay actively engaged in meaningful work. I mentioned the Head Start program earlier—the organization that allowed my grandmother to come in and read to underprivileged children. The AARP Foundation has a program called Experience Corps, which matches older adults as tutors in public schools for economically disadvantaged children. The program has had a positive impact on the children in the ways you might imagine—improved literacy, increased test scores, and improved classroom and social behavior. It also has a positive impact on the volunteers. In one study, volunteers felt a greater sense of accomplishment than a group of control participants and had increases in brain volume for the hippocampus and cortex, compared to the controls, who had brain volume reductions. This was particularly true of male volunteers, who showed a *reversal* of three years of aging over two years of volunteering. As Anaïs Nin observed, "Life shrinks or expands in proportion to one's courage." It's true of brain volume as well.

That courage, that expansion of life, can come about in a variety of ways for different people: taking classes online, such as from Coursera or Khan Academy (but be sure you interact with real, live people to discuss what you've learned; learning in isolation can only go so far in keeping your mind active); joining (or hosting) a book club or current events discussion group; volunteering in a hospital or church; asking your local YMCA or church what they need; working in a soup kitchen. There is a transformative effect in helping others. In his novel *Disgrace,* the Nobel Prize–winning South African writer J. M. Coetzee wrote:

> He continues to teach because . . . it teaches him humility, brings it home to him who he is in the world. The irony does not escape him: that the one who comes to teach learns the keenest of lessons, while those who come to learn learn nothing.

I have observed this firsthand in my own life, although I like to think that my students avoided learning nothing. And I am perhaps not so cynical as Coetzee (or at least his character in the novel). I think that the right teacher, the right *believer* in a child or an older adult, can tip the balance for that person's life and help them to overcome life's obstacles, to get on a track toward happiness and success that will lead them into successful aging. My teachers did that for me.

Continuity of Care and Quality of Life

As medicine becomes more automated, and as diagnostic technology has become more sophisticated and impersonal, there have been calls for reducing the personal relationship that doctors and their patients have enjoyed for centuries, in favor of patients seeing whomever is available and for short periods of time. In fact, the *New England Journal of Medicine* suggested that nonpersonal care should become the default option in medicine. This system has already been adopted, if not by plan, then by necessity, in many locations, including Montreal, where, until 2016, there was a severe shortage of doctors. In nearly twenty years of living there, I never had a family doctor because none were taking any new patients. I rarely saw the same doctor twice—not even specialists, and appointments rarely exceeded twelve minutes.

The alternative is the system that I have known the rest of my life, in which I develop a good working relationship with my doctors over time. A systematic review in the *British Medical Journal* confirms the superiority of this approach, finding that increased continuity of care leads to greater longevity, in studies spanning a variety of cultures and countries.

A good example of this is the relationship I had with my ear, nose, and throat specialist, Dr. Meyer Schindler. My *grandfather* had seen him, and so had my father, meaning that he knew our family history firsthand, an important predictor of a range of possible conditions and diseases. When I first saw him, he was already old, but his two children had joined his practice and they would sometimes sit in on my examinations. Meyer continued working until he died, and then his sons, David and Brian, took over my care. I got a new family doctor about six years ago, and he is the most attentive physician I've ever had. He encourages me to phone him (on his cell) or to email him when questions come up. For the first time in my life I have a doctor who is younger than me, and so I am hopeful that he'll be with me for a long time. As we get to know each other, I believe the quality of care I get will increase. If I'm hospitalized, or facing a major illness, he will coordinate the care with the specialists, serving as the conductor of the orchestra of care.

Dr. Eduardo Dolhun, a Mayo Clinic–trained physician and the head of the Dolhun Clinic in San Francisco, describes the ideal doctor-patient relationship this way:

> You want to have a doctor who knows you and your family, who knows not just your history but your personality, your habits, and hobbies—who knows how you live and how you spend your time. All of this informs medical decision making and making differential diagnoses. A physician who has to treat without this context is very much handicapped.
>
> Context matters. If the environment can modify gene expression-epigenetics, then it stands to reason that the context within which a person lives is not only important, but critical to understand. The patient-doctor dyad is a dialectic that grows

> over time, and allows the doctor to more fully appreciate the subtle nuances of behavior and physiology that can signal disease or lack of health. The ability of the doctor to tap into this relationship allows him or her to potentially discover pathology and make early interventions to redirect or steer the patient out of disease and towards health. This is especially important in diseases like cardiovascular disease that generally take years or decades to manifest into a heart attack or stroke.

Increasingly, affluent patients are choosing to see specialists and forgoing a primary care or family physician. Yet, specialization tends to divide the patient into parts. It not only increases the cost of treatment but can result in different specialists working at cross-purposes with one another.

"I can't overestimate the importance of the relationship between the patient and their primary care doc," said Dr. David Brill, a family medicine physician at the Cleveland Clinic. "What we are rediscovering in the U.S. is that the best and most cost-effective medicine is what they practiced from 1910 to 1970: Patients had a relationship with their family doc."

A movement is building to provide more customized care from family doctors, through what is called a patient-centered medical home. The concept is to provide

- a single centralized source of medical care and medical records;
- a patient-centered approach that emphasizes the whole person; and
- a team of caregivers in addition to the physician, including a nursing team, physician assistants, and office staff, who all contribute to continuity of care.

The patient-centered medical home might typically provide access to clinicians outside of normal practice hours, such as evenings and weekends; provide consistent nurses and care managers to follow up with patients after an office visit, to make sure they've gotten their medications and know how to take them, for example; keep track of when patients need to schedule appointments and when they need prescription refills; and monitor them if they've been hospitalized.

Doctoring is a difficult job and it's easy for physicians to suffer from information overload, especially as they try to care for a new patient who is in distress. Here's where the advantage of having a doctor who knows you and your history is made clear. Consider Dr. Gordon Caldwell, a consulting physician in Oban, Scotland (home of great single malt Scotch). During hospital rounds every morning, physicians have a short time to figure out what is going on with patients. He shared the inner dialogue going on in his head one morning for a ward-round review of a lady who seemed to have pneumonia and diabetes with very high glucose levels.

> This is the sort of stuff going on in my brain whilst I consult with the patient. "Wow, she looks very thin and has clubbed tar-stained fingers, I wonder if she has lung cancer as well? Have I introduced myself clearly and got a good rapport going? This could turn into a tricky consultation. Oh, she's mentioned a headache, maybe she has metastases to the brain or temporal arteritis, have we measured the ESR [erythrocyte sedimentation rate], and did we even look at the chest X-ray? Now she says she hasn't been outdoors for six months, so she could be vitamin D deficient. Will we measure the vitamin D level or just prescribe some? Maybe she was already on vitamin D, she was on a long list of meds. Why is the student looking bored, I'll ask him to look at the meds list and the F2 [second-year postgraduate student in training] can look for an ESR.
>
> Now should I go on to the high-glucose problem or the pneumonia next? Oh her husband has arrived and he looks angry, where has the nurse gone to? I need her to hear the whole conversation so she can calm the patient and her husband down after I leave, if this all turns difficult. Oh, and I must remember the Medical Director said we are doing poorly on VTE [venous thromboembolism] and Dementia forms and looking for pressure risks, and the 4th target is going badly, could I discharge this lady and do all her investigations as an outpatient and

> damn there goes Henry the Hoover and the F2 has left to answer her bleep and PACS [picture archiving and communication system] has gone down so we can't review the chest X-ray, now "how many years have you smoked for?"
>
> Well that's what it is like for me no matter how calm I look from the outside. This doesn't leave any residual reasoning capacity for "Could her weight loss be from an overactive thyroid or from badly fitting false teeth or depression or only drinking alcohol and eating no food?"

This kind of thought process is typical, as doctors have to play detective a great deal of the time, and there are an enormous number of variables. You can help cut through the noise by preparing a piece of paper with all your medications—even supplements and nonprescription drugs such as antihistamines and pain relievers. Recall that just because something is available over the counter doesn't mean that it can't have a negative interaction with other drugs you're taking. Turmeric and ginkgo, for example, are anticoagulants. If you're taking a prescription anticoagulant too, the effects can be amplified, leading to serious situations if you cut yourself or get an ulcer or any kind of internal bleed . . . or if the doctor needs to perform an emergency surgery or biopsy.

Difficult Conversations

At some point, if you live long enough, you or someone you love is going to experience a marked reduction in some ability, physical or mental, of the sort that may necessitate a lifestyle change. I'm not talking about needing a little longer to leave the house, or having to use a pill-sorting box to avoid double dosing or missing medications—I'm talking about an inability to drive, do housework, prepare meals, or remember important appointments and people. I've heard from parents who resent their children telling them what they can and cannot do, and from children who are terrified of their parents driving or keeping the firearms they've kept safely for decades. These are difficult conversations to have. Many older adults do lose some abilities and functions and need help. Some are more comfortable asking for help than others, who see the very act of asking as an admission of decline. And no one wants to think of themselves as incompetent or cognitively impaired.

Part of conscientious planning for old age includes having these kinds of conversations ahead of when you actually need to have them. Having these conversations early means that they won't seem abrupt or sudden when the time comes. It means considering options and making plans in advance, when you're clearheaded and less emotional. Involve your doctor in these conversations too. Basically, plan ahead. When did Noah build the ark? *Before* the flood.

Joseph F. Coughlin, director of the MIT AgeLab, poses three questions we should all ask ourselves and our older family members as a way to think about what our quality of life will be as we age. Although the particular questions may seem shallow or even whimsical, they are effective stand-ins for our quality of life.

1. Who'll change my light bulbs?

This is a proxy question for who will do the chores around the house that most of us did when we were younger. Do you really want your ninety-year-old spouse climbing a ladder to replace a recessed bulb in the ceiling? Who will take out the garbage cans on pickup day or lug around the heavy vacuum cleaner? Who'll chop vegetables when your eyesight is failing and your hands may have developed a tremor? Think ahead not only to who you can call for help, but whether or not you'll need to pay them, and how much money you need to set aside for it. Find out what social services are available in your area.

2. What if I want an ice cream cone?

The ability to be spontaneous is key to feeling as though you are an author of the script of your own life. If you want to go out for an ice cream cone, who will take you there? Have you situated yourself so that you're in walking distance? What if the weather is dangerously hot? Is there someone who can drive you? More broadly, Coughlin asks, "Will I age in a community where there are ample activities and people to keep me engaged, active, and having fun?" Quality of life is about being able to easily and routinely access those little experiences that bring a smile.

3. Who will I have lunch with?

As we've seen, social isolation is one of the biggest risk factors for older adults. A vital social community—someone nearby you can call up and go to lunch with once in a while—can make all the difference. "Planning where, and with whom to retire may be as important as how much it will cost," Coughlin says. "For example, a home in the mountains may be alluring as you approach retirement, but it may lead to an inadequate network of friends, or complete isolation during old age. The baby boomers are facing a different retirement than their parents. They're more likely to live alone, to have fewer children, and to live in suburban and rural locations that may not provide easy access to active and livable communities."

There are more options now than ever before for how to live out later years when you feel you might need a bit of assistance with day-to-day tasks. Intergenerational families are on the rise, either older parents moving in with their children or the children bringing their own families in to live with their parents in the homes they grew up in.

Although the dark, dank nursing homes of 1950s movies still exist, there is a worldwide trend toward facilities that promote independence. I mentioned assisted living (also called memory care) in Chapter 6 on living with people, as one part of this trend. As Argentum, one of the leading advocacy groups, describes it,

> Assisted Living is a home- and community-based setting for older adults combining housing, supportive services, and health care as needed. Individuals who choose assisted living enjoy an independent lifestyle with assistance customized to meet each resident's needs and benefits that enrich their lives. Assisted Living promotes independence, purpose and dignity for each resident and encourages the involvement of a resident's family and friends. Staff is available to meet both scheduled and unscheduled needs. Communities typically offer dining, social and wellness activities, and personal care services. There are currently 28,585 communities in the United States with more than 835,200 residents calling assisted living home.

As comfortable and convenient as many assisted living communities have become, many older adults want to stay in their own homes as long as they can. There are some things we can do to help make staying at home an option.

Putting Systems in Place: Alzheimer's, mild cognitive impairment preparedness

One of the greatest difficulties that people with Alzheimer's and mild cognitive impairment have is getting used to something new. Start planning now so that new systems seem familiar. The idea here is that by the time you need them, all these things will be old hat. Don't wait until you or your loved one has symptoms—it's too late then. Introduce these changes early. Make them easy and routine.

Write your address on your cell phone and on a card in your wallet. Add to that card the phone number of your doctor, your spouse, and a family member or friend who can help out if you need it. If you're in an accident, emergency personnel may need to call these people if you're unable to respond.

If you take medications, start using a pill-sorting box so that you're used to using it later when you really need it. CVS and other pharmacies will actually prepare a daily pill pack for you at no additional expense, and they'll deliver it to your home. If you take pills in the morning, noon, and evening, for example, there will be a separate pack for each, clearly marked.

Keep your keys and wallet in a designated place. Consider purchasing a sensing refrigerator that orders food automatically and has it delivered. Or find a local or online grocer that delivers food and place a standing order for certain staples. Put all your bills on autopay. Have a system for keeping track of account passwords, and someone else who knows or could access this information. Work with local police officers or someone close to you to learn how to protect yourself from scammers.

What we can all do now is to be more intentional and mindful of how we live in the world. Remain *Curious* and mentally engaged. Be *Open* to new experiences. Keep up your social *Associations*. Try to be *Conscientious*. Follow the *Healthy* lifestyle practices I've described regarding diet, exercise, and good sleep hygiene.

Choose the Right Hospital—before You Need It

As with anything, there are good hospitals and bad. Some are good for certain things but not others. Some hospitals are dreadful all around. Medicare's Hospital Compare website shows rates of surgical complications and infections for hospitals, and which hospitals have lower-than-average mortality rates for six medical conditions—heart attacks, heart failure, pneumonia, stroke, coronary bypass surgery, and chronic obstructive pulmonary disease. It also shows which hospitals have higher-than-average readmission rates—patients having to go *back* because the problem wasn't solved. Then there is HospitalInspections.org, which is like a city's restaurant inspector, showing you which hospitals have serious problems. Several websites allow you to find the nearest hospital or emergency room and their average wait times. Learn *now* where the good hospitals are, and where the closest ERs are and their wait times. Update your list once a year. Write down this information near the telephone in your home, and if you have a smartphone, put it in there as well.

(When choosing an ER in an urban setting, by the way, you're better off going to one in a quiet neighborhood, rather than a county hospital in the middle of a major urban center—the latter could be filled with stabbing or gunshot victims, especially on a Friday or Saturday night, and unless you've been stabbed or shot, you'll wait a long time to be seen.)

Advance Medical Directives

In what is perhaps a macabre way to look at things, we've reached an awkward point in history in which you get to choose (more or less) what you want to die from. Some interventions we've looked at reduce the chance of heart attack but increase the chance of cancer. Some treatments reduce the risk of cancer death but increase the risk of dying from an infection. Particularly if you're over age eighty-five or so, some surgeries have a less than 50 percent chance of success and don't extend life for much more than the recovery time.

Science has done a great deal to reduce the risk of dying from heart disease, and all the more so for people who exercise regularly, eat well, don't smoke, and limit alcohol. If you don't die of heart disease, you'll live longer, and then the highest risks are to die from cancer, stroke, and dementia, all comparatively unpleasant things to die from. Physician Alex Lickerman notes this uncomfortable paradox:

> Decreasing the risk of dying from one disease has increased our risk from dying from other, arguably more horrible ones.

It's helpful to consider these issues when you're younger and before you're confronted with having to make a choice—and to share your feelings with your loved ones. In a moment of crisis, your feelings may certainly change, and that's all right. The point is to be practiced in thinking about these things, in considering the various issues and ramifications. Some questions to consider (I know that these are uncomfortable, but it might be better for *you* to have a say in these decisions than to have a team of doctors make them for you if you're unconscious):

- Where do I want to be if I am no longer aware of my surroundings? At home, with loved ones, or in a rest home or assisted care facility?
- Where do I draw the line regarding quality of life versus longevity? Do I want to stay alive no matter what—even if I'm being kept alive by machines and I'm only conscious for thirty minutes a day? What if I'm in a coma with no reasonable chance of waking?
- If doctors need to provide emergency, lifesaving procedures, how far should they go? What am I willing to put up with in terms of collateral damage? What if the procedures damage my voice permanently? What if they can save me but I'll have permanent memory impairment, or paralysis?
- Where do I want to be when I die? At home? In a hospital?
- If I'm unable to make a decision, or if something comes up I didn't anticipate, is there someone I would like to designate whom I trust to make decisions for me?

And don't be rash in your thought process about this. As psychological scientist Dan Gilbert at Harvard has shown, we tend to underestimate our resilience. We tend to think that certain setbacks will make us *miserable*, and we are often surprised to find, if they happen, that we got through them and it wasn't that bad. Studies with amputees and quadraplegics, for example, have shown that they are not *nearly* as unhappy as you might think they'd be, or even as they themselves thought they'd be. Life is amazing and beautiful, and yes, challenging and *annoying* sometimes, even downright depressing; but after adapting to a downward turn, many of us find we still love being alive.

An advance medical directive, also called an advance health directive or living will, is a formal document that allows you to answer questions like these and to specify what you'd like done in various scenarios in which you are unable to respond to health-care workers yourself. They have legal status in some countries, such as the US and the UK, and in other countries they serve as non-legally-binding guidelines. You can find forms online, or—if you want to be extra careful—you can get the help of an attorney. Once you have one of these, you should make sure that family members and your authorized decision maker know where the original document is, and you should provide copies for them, as well as for all your doctors. (In some jurisdictions, copies are not accepted by medical or governmental authorities, and so people should know where you keep the original.)

Dr. Barak Gaster, a professor at the University of Washington Medical School, has designed an advance medical directive for dementia. Gaster underscores the uniqueness of dementia in an advance directive context, in an article he wrote for the *Journal of the American Medical Association:*

> Standard advance directives are often not helpful for patients who develop dementia. Dementia is a unique disease from the standpoint of advance directives. It usually progresses slowly over many years and leaves people with a long time frame of diminishing cognitive function and loss of ability to guide their own care. Advance directives typically address scenarios such as an imminently terminal condition or a permanent coma, but they generally do not address the more common scenario of gradually progressive dementia.

Gaster's dementia directive presents four health-care goals for three different contexts: mild, moderate, or severe dementia. You choose which goals suit you. Of course, if you change your mind, you can withdraw an earlier directive and replace it with a newer one. The body of the directive looks like this:

> If I had [mild/moderate/severe] dementia then I would want the goal for my care to be:
>
> - To live for as long as I could. I would want full efforts to prolong my life, including efforts to restart my heart if it stops beating.
> - To receive treatments to prolong my life, but if my heart stops beating or I can't breathe on my own then do not shock my heart to restart it (DNR) and do not place me on a breathing machine. Instead, if either of these happens, allow me to die peacefully. Reason why: if I took such a sudden turn for the worse then my dementia would likely be worse if I survived, and this would not be an acceptable quality of life for me.
> - To only receive care in the place where I am living. I would not want to go to the hospital even if I were very ill, and I would not want to be resuscitated (DNR). If a treatment, such as antibiotics, might keep me alive longer and could be given in the place where I was living, then I would want such care. But if I continued to get worse, I would not want to go to an emergency room or a hospital. Instead, I would want to be allowed to die peacefully. Reason why: I would not want the possible risks and trauma which can come from being in the hospital.
> - To receive comfort-oriented care only, focused on relieving my suffering such as pain, anxiety, or breathlessness. I would not want any care that would keep me alive longer.

As with any preformatted advance directive, these are just guidelines. You can reword it or fashion it to reflect your own feelings.

End of Life

Like any part of life itself, the end of life is less stressful and potentially more peaceful if we take the time to learn about it. We may decide to not go gently into that good night, but if the night overtakes us, we are better off knowing what to expect of it, and to put ourselves in situations that are of our own choosing, rather than someone else's. "Death, when it approaches, ought not to take one by surprise," says Gloria Steinem.

I want to die at home, surrounded by familiar sights and sounds, preferably with loved ones nearby, and the sounds of nature trickling in through the window, whether it's songbirds during the day or crickets and owls at night. Other people want to be in the hospital to have every chance of claiming an extra hour or day or two—possibly a few extra months. Some don't want to burden their families and prefer to be in a rest home of one kind or another.

Much of what happens to us when we are terminally ill—shots, tests, various diagnostic and treatment procedures—is painful and anxiety provoking. Aversive experiences such as these can undermine patients' willingness to undergo or continue treatment but can be counteracted by immersion in nature. Virtual reality (VR) environments have become increasingly available in health-care contexts and have been found effective for acute pain management. (If you're unfamiliar, this is essentially like watching a three-dimensional movie; in some versions, you can control the views you see to simulate walking through or interacting with the environment.) Patients who experienced VR scenes of nature reported less pain during a procedure and in their recollections of it one week later than patients who experienced VR urban scenes or no VR, suggesting that it is not just the distracting effects of VR, but the immersion in nature itself. Other studies have found that natural sounds, such as birdsong and ocean waves, can even speed up recovery times and reduce stress.

With this as a background, hospitals and end-of-life care facilities are coming to realize the restorative qualities of nature and are looking at ways to provide their patients with increased access to natural scenes. Seen as peripheral to medical care for most of the twentieth century, gardens are back in style now and are integrated into the design of most new hospitals, according to the American Society of Landscape Architects.

The TriPoint Medical Center in Concord, Ohio, is one example. The center is surrounded by mature forest, wetlands, and a pristine freshwater stream. To enter the medical center, you cross a landscaped pond and pass by a waterfall. The natural theme permeates the entire site and sets the tone of serenity and healing, which is reinforced with paintings of natural scenes by local artists. Henry Ford West Bloomfield Hospital in Michigan is surrounded by eighty acres of natural landscape, and the interior spaces are richly filled with trees and shrubs; a fifteen-hundred-square-foot greenhouse is on the property. The Matilda International Hospital in Hong Kong sits high atop the historic Victoria Peak with sweeping views of the South China Sea. The Glotterbad Clinic is in the middle of the Black Forest in Germany.

Rachel Clarke, a physician with Britain's National Health Service, has seen firsthand that nature can provide intense solace for many who are terminally ill. She tells the story of one patient, in his eighties, who had cancer of the tongue and so couldn't speak—at least not well enough to make himself understood by the hospital staff. Sitting in his chair, he grew increasingly agitated—thrashing around, flailing his arms, grimacing, flinging his head from side to side. No one could figure out what he wanted except for one younger doctor, who simply turned the patient's chair outward to face the garden. "He sat calmly, transfixed by the trees and sky," Clarke says. "All he had wanted was that view."

Another patient, suffering from metastatic breast cancer at fifty-one, was moved to hospice. "My first thought," the patient said, "my urge, was to get up and find an open space. I needed to breathe fresh air, to hear natural noises away from the hospital and its treatment rooms. . . . Somehow, when I listened to the song of a blackbird in the garden, I found it incredibly calming. It seemed to allay that fear that everything was going to disappear." About her patient, Clarke recalls, "Whenever she was able to sit outside in her garden or be somewhere where there were trees and wildlife it gave her this peace, it took her away from all of the fear and loss that accompanied her diagnosis of terminal cancer."

In the end, in the battle to hang on to life, nature always wins. The playwright Dennis Potter described the profound effects of immersing himself in nature during his final days suffering from pancreatic cancer, and the refocusing of his attention on immediate, sensory experiences, a Zen-like state:

The only thing you know for sure is the present tense.

That nowness becomes so vivid to me now, that in a perverse sort of way, I'm almost serene, I can celebrate life. Below my window, for example, the blossom is out in full. It's a plum tree. It looks like apple blossom, but it's white. And instead of saying, "Oh, that's a nice blossom," looking at it through the window when I'm writing, it is the whitest, frothiest, blossomiest blossom that there ever could be.

Things are both more trivial than they ever were, and more important than they ever were, and the difference between the trivial and the important doesn't seem to matter—but the nowness of everything is absolutely wondrous.

And if people could see that—there's no way of telling you, you have to experience it—the glory of it, if you like, the comfort of it, the reassurance. . . . Not that I'm interested in reassuring people, you know. The fact is that if you see the present tense, boy, do you see it, and boy, can you celebrate it!

Putting It All Together

The single most important factor in determining successful aging is the personality trait of Conscientiousness. Conscientiousness is associated with a great number of positive outcomes in life. As I wrote in the first chapter, the fields of psychiatry and clinical psychology are predicated on the premise that you can change; you can will yourself or train yourself to be more conscientious, even later in life, and the benefits will still accrue to you. The latest science seems to confirm what has been argued, for millennia, by various forms of religion—that personality is malleable and one can learn to interact with the world in new ways, even well into one's eighties and beyond.

No one said that it's easy to change, and this is especially true later in life as we become set in our ways—which is just a colloquial way of describing the kind of biological fixedness that is going on in older brains. Adopting new lifestyle choices is difficult. But if you remember *why* the lifestyle change is important, you're more likely to stay with it, even when your motivation flags a little bit.

Three additional factors that determine how well we age are more important than the rest. The first is childhood experiences, in particular of parental attachment and of head injury. It's too late for you to do anything about these now, but you can protect and nurture the young people in your life, and you can predict your own outcomes by thinking about these. Children who are poorly attached, whose parents provide on-again, off-again care and attention, grow into adults who find it difficult to establish long-term intimate relationships.

If you had a concussion as a child, your chances of developing dementia in old age are increased by a factor of two to four. If you had multiple concussions, the increased risk is not additive—that is, each additional concussion doesn't increase the risk by the same amount, but rather accelerates the chances of a bad outcome in old age. Sports in which a child's head is used as a battering ram, or other kinds of contact with an object or another person, are dangerous to mental health.

The second most important factor in retaining mental vitality later in life is to exercise in varied, natural environments. You don't need to run marathons. Power walking in a park or forest, fast enough to get your heart rate up and your brain full of rich, oxygenated blood, is the goal. The varied environment will stimulate your brain and in particular the hippocampus, the seat of memory. And the thousands of little microadjustments you need to make to your gait, the angle of your feet, and maintaining your balance and pace will exercise the circuits in your brain that evolved to adapt to the environment. Adapting to new things, especially in the physical world, strengthening the visual-motor-kinesthetic circuits in your brain, can make an enormous difference in fending off cognitive decline. Even just ten minutes of slow walking every day has long-term benefits for your body and mind. And if that's not possible, do what you can. "I have a two-story house and a very bad memory," says Betty White (age ninety-seven), "so I'm up and down those stairs all the time. That's my exercise."

The third most important factor is social interaction. Interacting with others is among the most complex things we can do with our brains. It could be through playing music with them, playing bridge or golf, acting in community theater, reminiscing, or discussing literature in a book group. Nearly every part of our brains is activated by interacting with others, live, face-to-face, in real time. (Sorry, Skype.) Doing so requires us to read their body language, the emotions in their faces, and the contours of their speech. We have to follow along with what they're saying and try to figure out a way that we can contribute to the conversation without derailing it. In conversation, we need to employ empathy, compassion, logic, and turn taking—all relatively advanced cognitive operations. Isolation and lack of connectedness are strong predictors of disease and mortality. A study from the Karolinska Institute showed that people with strong social networks were 60 percent less likely to develop dementia. "Your brain was built for the very purpose of social engagement," notes Art Shimamura. One block to that social engagement is the many angers we have collected throughout our lives, sometimes directed at individuals, sometimes only directed toward a political party, group, or class they are members of. The Dalai Lama doesn't have a monopoly on the view that practicing compassion is healthful. We've seen evidence of this from neuroscience as well. A good strategy for life, at any age, is to let go of grievances, both petty and large. Don't spend your life hating and being angry. As former U.S. senator Alan Simpson (age eighty-eight) says, "Hatred corrodes the container in which it is carried."

Children have an innate need for physical and emotional connections to their parents, even those children who appear not to need it. For centuries we thought that individuals on the autism spectrum were socially phobic loners—they don't look people in the eye and seem to enjoy solitary activities. We now know that this masks a deep social anxiety and that most of them desperately want to connect. (Scientists are often perceived as socially awkward, and indeed, many of us in science are on the spectrum. How do you recognize an extraverted mathematician at a party? He's the one staring at *your* shoes.)

When it comes to aging, we tend to think that as we get older, our brains slow down. While this is true in some ways, abstract reasoning and practical intelligence increase with age. The more we've experienced, the better equipped we are to notice patterns and predict future outcomes. While it may be difficult for older adults to pick up a new skill, they will excel in their area of expertise more than ever before, as George Augspurger and Maxine Waters demonstrate.

Remember that the world is changing, and those changes are at odds with your accumulated experience. Force yourself to update, to keep current with changes in the world. That involves getting out of your cocoon, doing things you wouldn't normally do, like learn to use a new cell phone app, or preorder and prepay for a coffee at your local café. These things can be annoying, but they will help prevent the mental rigidity that can accompany aging.

Remember also that pain is physical and informed by our senses, yet it is also influenced by emotional and cultural factors. A negative emotional state can lead to increased pain, and an otherwise painful sensation can be interpreted as positive, such as soreness after exercise. Just in the way that we may misattribute an increased heart rate to physical attraction, as I wrote about in Chapter 5 on emotions, so, too, can we misattribute pain to false sources. Our bodies can misinform us, presenting a false reality.

Practice gratitude for what you have. This is motivating, alters brain chemistry toward more positive emotions, and oils the pleasure circuits of the brain. It can be as simple as appreciating the taste of your morning coffee or the sunlight peeking through the window. Gratitude is a powerful mind-set. As Walt Whitman wrote,

> Happiness . . . not in another place . . . but this place, not for another hour but this hour.

Keep Milking the Cows

In 2018, Placido Domingo (then age seventy-seven) sang his 150th role, an extraordinary milestone in opera. "If you look at the history of singers in opera, he stands by himself," said the former general manager of the Metropolitan Opera. And that's not all. Domingo has recorded more than one hundred albums and CDs and performed nearly four thousand times. When Maria Callas told him that he was singing too much, back when he was forty-one, he didn't listen. In 2018, he told *The New York Times,* "When I rest, I rust." As Neil Young sang, "It's better to burn out than it is to rust . . . rust never sleeps." Although Young wrote that when he was thirty-four, at age seventy-three he is still singing it. At age eighty-six, T. Boone Pickens, chairman of BP Capital Management and an alternative energy activist, said, "I'm going to retire in a box being carried out of my office." He continued to work until his death five years later.

A friend told me the story of how her grandmother lived to 113. She died while milking a cow. Every day she walked to the barn, used her eye-hand coordination and hand and wrist muscles to do the actual milking. It gave her a sense of responsibility and purpose. Individual strivings for accomplishment, persistent dedication to one's career or to community or, yes, domestic animals, are associated with sizable health benefits.

By 2030 there will be more individuals in the United States over sixty-five than under fifteen years of age. It's been estimated that two-thirds of the people over sixty-five who have ever lived are alive today, and three-quarters of the people over seventy-five who have ever lived are alive today. We need to change the way our society thinks about the aged. A relationship of mutual respect between older and younger people is one of the greatest enhancers of anyone's quality of life.

I began this book with a question for us to ask ourselves, one that gets to the heart of how we see the future of aging. What would it mean for all of us to think of the elderly as resource rather than burden and of aging as culmination rather than denouement? I have tried to show here that it would mean harnessing a human resource that is being underutilized. It would mean restoring dignity to a marginalized group of human beings just when they need it most. It would promote stronger family bonds and stronger bonds of friendship among us all. It would mean that important decisions in every domain, from personal matters to international agreements between nations, would be informed by experience and reason, along with the perspective that old age brings. And it might even mean a more compassionate world.

We can have that future if we want it. We need to educate ourselves and our families about the *advantages* of aging—the wisdom, the bias toward positivity, the compassion that older adults exhibit. As individuals, as community members, as a society, it is in all of our best interests to help construct a culture that embraces the gifts of the elderly, weaving cross-generational interactions into the fabric of everyday experience. By learning from the science of the brain we can create a transformative understanding of the aging process, its human story, and in the process create a richer quality of life. This is the new truth about aging.

In 2018, eighty-four-year-old Gloria Steinem was asked, "Who are you passing the torch to?" "Nobody," she said, laughing. "I'm holding on to my torch. I'll let other people light theirs from mine." Hold on to your torch. Do not go gently. And don't forget to laugh. Whatever's going on around you, remember to laugh.

APPENDIX
REJUVENATING YOUR BRAIN

1. Don't retire. Don't stop being engaged with meaningful work.
2. Look forward. Don't look back. (Reminiscing doesn't promote health.)
3. Exercise. Get your heart rate going. Preferably in nature.
4. Embrace a moderated lifestyle with healthy practices.
5. Keep your social circle exciting and new.
6. Spend time with people younger than you.
7. See your doctor regularly, but not obsessively.
8. Don't think of yourself as old (other than taking prudent precautions).
9. Appreciate your cognitive strengths—pattern recognition, crystallized intelligence, wisdom, accumulated knowledge.
10. Promote cognitive health through experiential learning: traveling, spending time with grandchildren, and immersing yourself in new activities and situations. Do new things.

NOTES

I reviewed somewhere around four thousand papers from the peer-reviewed scientific literature to gather material for this book. If this were itself a scientific paper, most would be cited within the text as they are mentioned, and then keyed to a references section. But my experience as a reader of nonfiction books is that all those parentheses with researcher names in the text are distracting and take me out of the story that the author has woven together. My aim in compiling these notes is to provide backup support for factual assertions (for example, statistics on the prevalence of a certain disease) and for descriptions of experiments (such as the inverting prism goggles) so that interested readers can follow up. In each case, I tried to cite something that was representative of the issue, often a meta-analysis or review that itself covers hundreds of articles, rather than the string of empirical papers that led up to that review.

For a more complete story, a full bibliography (in APA format) is available on my website at DanielLevitin.org, and the references listed here contain many more references themselves.

INTRODUCTION

xvi **It has been tied to diabetes in pregnancy:** N. Bakalar, "Lack of Sleep Tied to Diabetes in Pregnancy," *The New York Times,* October 18, 2017, http://www.nytimes.com.

xvi **postpartum depression in new fathers:** D. Quenqua, "Can Fathers Have Postpartum Depression?," *The New York Times,* October 17, 2017, http://www.nytimes.com.

xvii **Alzheimer's disease (AD) is now the third leading cause of death:** B. James et al., "Contribution of Alzheimer Disease to Mortality in the United States," *Neurology* 82, no. 12 (2014): 1045–1050.

xvii **two-thirds of the overall risk that you'll get Alzheimer's:** This may be a confusing way to look at it, but standing at the beginning of your life, as a newborn, that's how the risk ratios work out. Obviously if you experience a number of environmental factors—toxins, repeated blows to the head—that end up causing Alzheimer's, your personal risk of environmental causes rises to 100 percent; Klodian Dhana, Denis A. Evans, Kumar B. Rajan, David Bennett, and Martha Clare Morns, *Impact of Healthy Lifestyle Factors on the Risk of Alzheimer's Dementia: Findings from Two Prospective Cohort Studies*, Alzheimer's Association International Conference, Los Angeles, July 14, 2019; I. E. Jansen et al., "Genome-wide Meta-analysis Identifies

New Loci and Functional Pathways Influencing Alzheimer's Disease Risk," *Nature Genetics* 5, no. 3 (2019): 404–413.

xviii **chronic inflammatory process precedes the onset of Alzheimer's:** P. Eikelenboom et al., "Whether, When and How Chronic Inflammation Increases the Risk of Developing Late-Onset Alzheimer's Disease," *Alzheimer's Research and Therapy* 4, no. 3 (2012): 15, http://dx.doi.org/10.1186/alzrt118.

xviii **Another cutting-edge treatment being investigated:** Eikelenboom et al., "Whether, When and How Chronic Inflammation"; D. J. Marciani, "Development of an Effective Alzheimer's Vaccine," in *Immunology,* vol. 1, *Immunotoxicology, Immunopathology, and Immunotherapy,* ed. M. A. Hayat, pp. 149–169 (London: Elsevier, 2018).

xix **baby rats that received a great deal of licking:** M. J. Meaney and M. Szyf, "Environmental Programming of Stress Responses through DNA Methylation: Life at the Interface between a Dynamic Environment and a Fixed Genome," *Dialogues in Clinical Neuroscience* 7, no. 2 (2005): 103–123.

xix **"Women's health is critical":** Direct or near direct quotes from L. Warwick, "Dr. Michael Meaney: More Cuddles, Less Stress!," *Bulletin of the Centre of Excellence for Early Childhood Development,* October 2005, http://www.excellence-earlychildhood.ca/documents/Page2Vol4No2Oct05ANG.pdf.

CHAPTER 1

4 **If they survived these increased risks:** S. E. Hampson, "Personality Development and Health," in *The Handbook of Personality Development,* ed. D. McAdams, R. Shiner, and J. Tackett, pp. 489–502 (New York: Guilford Press, 2019).

4 **"Lack of self-control may result in behaviors":** Hampson, "Personality Development and Health."

4 **Childhood personality traits:** S. E. Hampson et al., "Lifetime Trauma, Personality Traits, and Health: A Pathway to Midlife Health Status," *Psychological Trauma: Theory, Research, Practice, and Policy* 8, no. 4 (2016): 447–454, http://dx.doi.org/10.1037/tra0000137.

4 **The same childhood traits even predict life span:** H. S. Friedman et al., "Does Childhood Personality Predict Longevity?," *Journal of Personality and Social Psychology* 65, no. 1 (1993): 176–185, http://dx.doi.org/10.1037/0022-3514.65.1.176.

4 **people, even older adults, can meaningfully change:** W. Bleidorn, "What Accounts for Personality Maturation in Early Adulthood?," *Current Directions in Psychological Science* 24, no. 3 (2015): 245–252; G. W. Edmonds et al., "Personality Stability from Childhood to Midlife: Relating Teachers' Assessments in Elementary School to Observer- and Self-Ratings 40 Years Later," *Journal of Research in Personality* 47, no. 5 (2013): 505–513; N. W. Hudson and R. C. Fraley, "Volitional Personality Trait Change: Can People Choose to Change Their Personality Traits?," *Journal of Personality and Social Psychology* 109, no. 3 (2015): 490–507.

4 **people retain the capacity to change throughout their life span:** N. Bayley, "The Life Span as a Frame of Reference in Psychological Research," *Vita Humana* 6, no. 3 (1963): 125–139.

5 **"Most developmental researchers":** P. B. Baltes and K. W. Schaie, "On Life-Span Developmental Research Paradigms: Retrospects and Prospects," in *Life-Span Developmental Psychology* (Cambridge, MA: Academic Press, 1973), pp. 365–395.

5 **the idea that people can change is the entire basis of modern psychotherapy:** B. P. Chapman, S. Hampson, and J. Clarkin, "Personality-Informed Interventions for Healthy Aging: Conclusions from a National Institute on Aging Workgroup," *Developmental Psychology* 50, no. 5 (2014): 1426–1441.

6 **Someone who is described as high on one trait:** C. DeYoung, "Personality Neuroscience and the Biology of Traits," *Social and Personality Psychology Compass* 4, no. 12 (2010): 1165–1180, http://dx.doi.org/10.1111/j.1751-9004.2010.00327.

7 **One way to think about gene expression:** "A Super Brief and Basic Explanation of Epigenetics for Total Beginners," WhatIsEpigenetics, July 30, 2018, www.whatisepigenetics.com/what-is-epigenetics/.

7 **Jason Alexander:** R. Gajewski, "Jason Alexander: 'Seinfeld' Killed Off Susan Because Actress Was 'F—ing Impossible' to Work With," *Hollywood Reporter*, June 4, 2015, https://www.hollywoodreporter.com/live-feed/jason-alexander-seinfeld-killed-susan-800031.

9 **Skin color, weight, and attractiveness:** L. A. Zebrowitz and J. M. Montepare, "Social Psychological Face Perception: Why Appearance Matters," *Social and Personality Psychology Compass* 2, no. 3 (2008): 1497–1517; P. Belluck, "Yes, Looks Do Matter," *The New York Times*, April 24, 2009, p. ST1.

9 **male, nonwhite, poor, and younger suspects:** W. Terrill and S. D. Mastrofski, "Situational and Officer-Based Determinants of Police Coercion," *Justice Quarterly* 19, no. 2 (2002): 215–248.

9 **actress Kristen Stewart:** C. Gibson, "Scientists Have Discovered What Causes Resting Bitch Face," *The Washington Post*, February 2, 2016, https://www.washingtonpost.com.

12 **"individual differences that are of the most significance":** L. R. Goldberg, personal communication, 1994; see also L. R. Goldberg, "Language and Individual Differences: The Search for Universals in Personality Lexicons," *Review of Personality and Social Psychology* 2, no. 1 (1981): 141–165.

13 **"The more important an individual difference is":** Goldberg, "Language and Individual Differences."

13 **very little that is distinctive culturally:** J. M. Murphy, "Psychiatric Labeling in Cross-Cultural Perspective," *Science* 191, no. 4231 (1976): 1019–1028.

13 **in English, there are 4,500 of them:** G. W. Allport and H. S. Odbert, "Trait-Names: A Psycho-Lexical Study," *Psychological Monographs* 47, no. 1 (1936): 1–171; J. S. Wiggins, *Paradigms of Personality Assessment* (New York: Guilford Press, 2003); L. R. Goldberg, personal communication, August 8, 2018.

15 **One prominent scientist argued for twenty:** L. R. Goldberg, "What the Hell Took So Long? Donald Fiske and the Big-Five Factor Structure," in *Personality Research, Methods, and Theory: A Festschrift Honoring Donald W. Fiske*, ed. P. E. Shrout and S. K. Fiske, pp. 29–43 (Hillsdale, NJ: Erlbaum, 1995).

15 **several others for two:** L. R Goldberg, "The Structure of Phenotypic Personality Traits," *American Psychologist* 48, no. 1 (1993): 26–34.

16 **Openness to Experience + Intellect:** G. Saucier, "Openness versus Intellect: Much Ado about Nothing?," *European Journal of Personality* 6 (1992): 381–386.

16 **EXTRAVERSION includes:** L. R. Goldberg, "The Development of Markers for the Big-Five Factor Structure," *Psychological Assessment* 4, no. 1 (1992): 26.

16 **People who score high on the Extraversion dimension:** L. R. Goldberg, "A Broad-Bandwidth, Public Domain, Personality Inventory Measuring the Lower-Level Facets of Several Five-Factor Models," in *Personality Psychology in Europe*, vol. 7, ed. I. Mervielde et al., pp. 7–28 (Tilburg, The Netherlands: Tilburg University Press, 1999); L. R. Goldberg et al., "The International Personality Item Pool and the Future of Public-Domain Personality Measures," *Journal of Research in Personality* 40 (2006): 84–96.

16 **People who score high on this dimension are quick to understand:** Lew Goldberg notes that few if any large-scale lexical studies have found an "Openness" factor.

Indeed, personality psychologist Robert McCrae wrote a classic article asserting that there were very few "openness" terms in the English lexicon. However, it is the case that many personality scientists prefer the label "openness" to "intellect," on the grounds that the former seems more a personality trait, while the latter seems more like intelligence as measured by an intelligence test.

17 **If you want to sound like a personality researcher:** You may have seen these in other books presented as the OCEAN or CANOE model, which simply put the factors in a different order and renamed Emotional Stability as its opposite, Neuroticism.

18 **all personality differences are biological:** DeYoung, "Personality Neuroscience."

18 **Higher levels lead us toward aggressive behaviors:** DeYoung, "Personality Neuroscience."

18 **such as a successful hunt:** B. C. Trumble et al., "Successful Hunting Increases Testosterone and Cortisol in a Subsistence Population," *Proceedings of the Royal Society of London B: Biological Sciences* 281, no. 1776 (2014): 20132876.

18 **driving a fast car:** G. Saad and J. G. Vongas, "The Effect of Conspicuous Consumption on Men's Testosterone Levels," *Organizational Behavior and Human Decision Processes* 110, no. 2 (2009): 80–92.

18 **being in charge of a large number of people:** S. M. Van Anders, J. Steiger, and K. L. Goldey, "Effects of Gendered Behavior on Testosterone in Women and Men," *Proceedings of the National Academy of Sciences* 112, no. 45 (2015): 13805–13810.

18 **Low levels of serotonin are associated with:** DeYoung, "Personality Neuroscience."

18 **Alterations to the gene known as *SLC6A4*:** X. Gonda et al., "Association of the S Allele of the 5-HTTLPR with Neuroticism-Related Traits and Temperaments in a Psychiatrically Healthy Population," *European Archives of Psychiatry and Clinical Neuroscience* 259, no. 2 (2009): 106–113.

19 **Babies are born with certain predispositions:** J. T. Nigg, "Temperament and Developmental Psychopathology," *Journal of Child Psychology and Psychiatry* 47, nos. 3–4 (2006): 395–422.

19 **Temperament and the young child's early life experiences:** M. K. Rothbart, "Temperament, Development, and Personality," *Psychological Science* 16, no. 4 (2007): 20–26.

19 **it is biologically based:** M. I. Posner, M. K. Rothbart, and B. E. Sheese, "Attention Genes," *Developmental Science* 10 (2007): 24–29.

19 **Temperament is typically measured:** H. E. Fisher et al., "Four Broad Temperament Dimensions: Description, Convergent Validation Correlations, and Comparison with the Big Five," *Frontiers in Psychology* 6 (2015): 1098.

19 **meta-analysis of ninety-two research papers:** B. W. Roberts, K. E. Walton, and W. Viechtbauer, "Patterns of Mean-Level Change in Personality Traits across the Life Course: A Meta-Analysis of Longitudinal Studies," *Psychological Bulletin* 132, no. 1 (2006): 1–25; Sarah Hampson adds this caveat after reading Chapter 1: "I like the upbeat message that personality changes and we can change. I believe this, but I also have to acknowledge that our findings on the Hawaii project (childhood personality influences health outcomes 40 years later, independent of adult personality influences) are a challenge for this position. What can we do as adults if we were poorly controlled, unconscientious kids? Our long-term health may have been damaged by these early influences. At least, as adults, we can strive to be more conscientious and use this trait to take steps to address the health issues that may have originated in childhood (e.g., compensate by living a healthier

lifestyle). . . . The Hawaii project's current phase is looking at personality and cognitive impairment, and past research indicates that personality is an important influence on cognitive resilience. We are hoping to predict mild cognitive decline from prior personality and perhaps from prior personality change."

20 **Older adults tend to be better at controlling impulses:** B. W. Roberts and D. Mroczek, "Personality Trait Change in Adulthood," *Current Directions in Psychological Science* 17, no. 1 (2008): 31–35.

20 **men typically show increased emotional sensitivity:** R. Helson, C. Jones, and V. S. Kwan, "Personality Change over 40 Years of Adulthood: Hierarchical Linear Modeling Analyses of Two Longitudinal Samples," *Journal of Personality and Social Psychology* 83, no. 3 (2002): 752.

20 **Openness increases around adolescence:** Roberts, Walton, and Viechtbauer, "Patterns of Mean-Level Change."

20 **Agreeableness increases substantially:** Helson, Jones, and Kwan, "Personality Change over 40 Years"; Roberts, Walton, and Viechtbauer, "Patterns of Mean-Level Change."

20 **They show increased Emotional Stability:** Roberts and Mroczek, "Personality Trait Change in Adulthood"; W. Bleidorn, "What Accounts for Personality Maturation?"

20 **a study of nearly 1 million individuals:** Bleidorn, "What Accounts for Personality Maturation?"

20 **Individuals appear to become more self-content in old age:** Roberts, Walton, and Viechtbauer, "Patterns of Mean-Level Change in Personality Traits."

21 **Older adults are less likely to engage in risky:** R. R. McCrae et al., "Age Differences in Personality across the Adult Life Span: Parallels in Five Cultures," *Developmental Psychology* 35, no. 2 (1999): 466.

22 **we can become our own autobiographers:** D. P. McAdams, "The Psychological Self as Actor, Agent, and Author," *Perspectives on Psychological Science* 8, no. 3 (2013): 272–295.

22 **Julia "Hurricane" Hawkins:** K. Peveto, "101-Year-Old Baton Rouge Runner Earns World Record, and a New Nickname, at National Senior Games," *The Advocate,* July 2, 2017, https://www.theadvocate.com.

23 **"Keep in good shape":** J. McCoy, "Meet Julia Hawkins, the 101-Year-Old Who Has Recently Taken Up Competitive Running," *Runner's World,* March 24, 2017, https://www.runnersworld.com/runners-stories/a20851266/meet-julia-hawkins-the-101-year-old-who-has-recently-taken-up-competitive-running/.

23 **"What Lily and I hear very often":** L. Bonos, "Jane Fonda and Lily Tomlin on 'Grace and Frankie,' Aging in Hollywood and Female Sexuality," *The Washington Post,* March 28, 2017, https://www.washingtonpost.com/news/soloish/wp/2017/03/28/jane-fonda-and-lily-tomlin-on-grace-and-frankie-aging-in-hollywood-and-female-sexuality/?utm_term=.77d6c3821fc8.

25 **a man who was born poor in Indiana in 1890:** David Emery, "The Life of Colonel Sanders," Snopes, December 2, 2016, https://www.snopes.com/fact-check/colonel-sanders/.

25 **At age eighty-nine, Colonel Sanders was asked:** "Jim Bakker PTL Club with Colonel Sanders 1979," posted by PTL Club TV, November 20, 2011, https://www.youtube.com/watch?v=ttdTGPQer-o.

26 **Conscientiousness has been linked to lower all-cause mortality:** S. E. Hampson et al., "Childhood Conscientiousness Relates to Objectively Measured Adult Physical Health Four Decades Later," *Health Psychology* 32, no. 8 (2013): 925.

26 **To become more conscientious:** Chapman, Hampson, and Clarkin, "Personality-Informed Interventions."

26 **Charles Koch, CEO:** C. Koch, personal communication, July 22, 2017.

27 **Overdiagnosis is common:** H. G. Welch and W. C. Black, "Overdiagnosis in Cancer," *Journal of the National Cancer Institute* 102 (2010): 605–613; H. G. Welch, L. Schwartz, and S. Woloshin, *Overdiagnosed: Making People Sick in the Pursuit of Health* (Boston: Beacon, 2011).

28 **people who forced a smile:** F. Strack, L. L. Martin, and S. Stepper, "Inhibiting and Facilitating Conditions of the Human Smile: A Nonobtrusive Test of the Facial Feedback Hypothesis," *Journal of Personality and Social Psychology* 54 (1988): 768–777; T. L. Kraft and S. D. Pressman, "Grin and Bear It: The Influence of Manipulated Facial Expression on the Stress Response," *Psychological Science* 23, no. 11 (2012): 1372–1378.

28 **"Compassion is the key to happiness":** Thupten Jinpa Langri, personal communication, April 2, 2018.

28 **He tries to avoid feeling anger, suspicion, and distrust:** J. Oliver, "Tibetan Sovereignty Debate and Human Rights in Tibet," *Last Week Tonight with John Oliver*, produced by J. Oliver, aired March 5, 2017, HBO.

28 **he avoids thinking of himself as privileged:** "Dalai Lama's Guide to Happiness," posted by A Million Smiles, October 8, 2013, https://www.youtube.com/watch?v=IUEkDc_LfKQ.

29 **studies since Bayley and Baltes:** R. Helson, C. Jones, and V. S. Kwan, "Personality Change over 40 Years."

29 **Exposure to high levels of glucocorticoids:** S. J. Lupien et al., "Increased Cortisol Levels and Impaired Cognition in Human Aging: Implication for Depression and Dementia in Later Life," *Reviews in the Neurosciences* 10, no. 2 (1999): 117–140.

CHAPTER 2

33 **George Martin, the Beatles' producer:** G. Martin, personal communication, September 17, 1993.

38 **The recognition that memory is not one thing:** A. J. O. Dede and C. N. Smith, "The Functional and Structural Neuroanatomy of Systems Consolidation for Autobiographical and Semantic Memory," in *Behavioral Neuroscience of Learning and Memory, Current Topics in Behavioral Neurosciences*, vol. 37, ed. R. E. Clark and S. Martin (Cham, Switzerland: Springer, 2016); M. Moscovitch et al., "Functional Neuroanatomy of Remote Episodic, Semantic and Spatial Memory: A Unified Account Based on Multiple Trace Theory," *Journal of Anatomy* 207, no. 1 (2005): 35–66; B. Milner, S. Corkin, and H. L. Teuber, "Further Analysis of the Hippocampal Amnesic Syndrome: 14-Year Follow-Up Study of HM," *Neuropsychologia* 6, no. 3 (1968): 215–234.

41 **different parts of the brain hold semantic memories versus episodic ones:** Dede and Smith, "Functional and Structural Neuroanatomy"; Moscovitch et al., "Functional Neuroanatomy."

46 **television images of an airplane crashing into the first tower:** I wrote about this previously in D. J. Levitin, *The Organized Mind* (New York: Dutton, 2014).

47 **Gazzaniga tells the story of a patient:** M. S. Gazzaniga, *Who's in Charge: Free Will and the Science of the Brain* (New York: Ecco, 2012).

49 **conducted an experiment in 1991:** D. J. Levitin, "Absolute Memory for Musical Pitch: Evidence from the Production of Learned Melodies," *Perception & Psychophysics* 56, no. 4 (1994): 414–23.

53 **contemporary version of the residue theory—multiple-trace theory:** See, for example, D. L. Hintzman and R. A. Block, "Repetition and Memory: Evidence for a Multiple-Trace Hypothesis," *Journal of Experimental Psychology* 88, no. 3 (1971): 297; D. L. Hintzman, "Judgments of Frequency and Recognition Memory in a Multiple-Trace Memory Model," *Psychological Review* 95, no. 4 (1988): 528; S. D. Goldinger, "Echoes of Echoes? An Episodic Theory of Lexical Access," *Psychological Review* 105, no. 2 (1998): 251.

54 **The creation of multiple, related traces facilitates:** D. L. Hintzman, "'Schema Abstraction' in a Multiple-Trace Memory Model," *Psychological Review* 93, no. 4 (1986): 411.

54 **this occurs in brain cells without having to involve the hippocampus:** Moscovitch et al., "Functional Neuroanatomy"; B. R. Postle, "The Hippocampus, Memory, and Consciousness," in *The Neurology of Consciousness,* 2nd ed., ed. S. Laureys, O. Gosseries, and G. Tononi (San Diego, CA: Elsevier, 2016).

57 **if we need to remember something, we should draw it:** J. D. Wammes, M. E. Meade, and M. A. Fernandes, "The Drawing Effect: Evidence for Reliable and Robust Memory Benefits in Free Recall," *Quarterly Journal of Experimental Psychology* 69, no. 9 (2016): 1752–1776.

57 **"I keep thinking of Dr. Spock":** J. Weinstein, personal communication, Brooklyn, NY, April 25, 2018.

57 **cognitive prostheses:** S. Kosslyn, personal communication, September 8, 2018.

58 **"I remember in *Dr. Zhivago*":** J. Mitchell, personal communication, September 9, 2012.

58 **"You have a routine":** G. Shultz, personal communication, Stanford, CA, March 21, 2018.

58 **mental checklist of five things:** J. Kimball, personal communication, Los Angeles, CA, March 3, 2018.

59 **Neuroscientist Sonia Lupien:** S. Lupien, personal communication, Montreal, QC, March 13, 2019.

60 **traditional form of memory testing:** S. Sindi et al., "When We Test, Do We Stress? Impact of the Testing Environment on Cortisol Secretion and Memory Performance in Older Adults," *Psychoneuroendocrinology* 38, no. 8 (2013): 1388–1396; S. Sindi et al., "Now You See It, Now You Don't: Testing Environments Modulate the Association between Hippocampal Volume and Cortisol Levels in Young and Older Adults," *Hippocampus* 24, no. 12 (2014): 1623–1632; in a more naturalistic memory context, younger and older adults did not differ in overall accuracy: D. Davis, N. Alea, and S. Bluck, "The Difference between Right and Wrong: Accuracy of Older and Younger Adults' Story Recall," *International Journal of Environmental Research and Public Health* 12, no. 9 (2015): 10861–10885; one study concluded that older adults were not more stressed by laboratory testing than younger, but they did not measure stress directly and did not collect cortisol levels: A. Ihle et al., "Adult Age Differences in Prospective Memory in the Laboratory: Are They Related to Higher Stress Levels in the Elderly?," *Frontiers in Human Neuroscience* 8 (2014): 1021.

60 **Uncorrected losses to vision and hearing:** B. M. Ben-David, G. Malkin, and H. Erel, "Ageism and Neuropsychological Tests," in *Contemporary Perspectives on Ageism,* ed. Liat Ayalon and Clemens Tesch-Römer, pp. 277–297 (Cham, Switzerland: Springer, 2018).

60 **retrieval of words . . . can decline with age:** M. A. Shafto et al., "On the Tip-of-the-Tongue: Neural Correlates of Increased Word-Finding Failures in Normal Aging," *Journal of Cognitive Neuroscience* 19, no. 12 (2007): 2060–2070.

CHAPTER 2.5

62 **the Bible taught us the centrality of ethics:** S. Innes, "Review of *The Cambridge Introduction to Emmanuel Levinas* by Michael Morgan," *Religious Studies* 48, no. 4 (2012): 552–557, http://www.jstor.org/stable/23351460.

63 **Neural growth in the womb:** L. K. Jones, "Neurophysiological Development across the Lifespan," in *Neurocounseling: Brain-Based Clinical Approaches,* ed. T. A. Field, L. K. Jones, and L. A. Russell-Chapin (Alexandria, VA: John Wiley & Sons, 2017).

64 **Why are humans at the top of the food chain?:** I thank "Darpa" Dan Kaufman for this formulation. D. Kaufman, personal communication, July 14, 2018.

65 **more than 1 million per minute at birth:** Center on the Developing Child, "Five Numbers to Remember about Early Childhood Development," brief, 2009, www.developingchild.harvard.edu.

65 **by six months, up to 2 million new connections a minute:** E. Santos and C. A. Noggle, "Synaptic Pruning," in *Encyclopedia of Child Behavior and Development,* ed. S. Goldstein and J. A. Naglieri (Boston: Springer, 2011).

65 **Humans have roughly twenty:** https://ghr.nlm.nih.gov/primer/basics/gene.

66 **Humans have 99 percent of our DNA in common with chimps:** K. Wong, "Tiny Genetic Differences between Humans and Other Primates Pervade the Genome," *Scientific American,* September 1, 2014, https://www.scientificamerican.com/article/tiny-genetic-differences-between-humans-and-other-primates-pervade-the-genome/.

66 **Some understandings appear to be hardwired:** I've been careful to use the terms *statistical inferencing* and *statistical analysis.* Just how the brain learns complex things like language is a contentious issue. There are some who believe that the brain has a modular structure and that some of these modules are "hardwired," a term you may see both in scientific articles and in popular books. Others believe that the brain has biological predispositions but that experience shapes those, and that "hardwired" is too strong a claim. Reasonable scientists are disagreeing. We'll just have to wait until more experiments are conducted and more data come in.

67 **Evan Balaban describes the fetal brain:** "Entrevista a Evan Balaban. CASEIB 2010" (Interview with Evan Balaban), posted by UC3M, December 21, 2010, https://www.youtube.com/watch?v=sIqD98W9k64.

67 **blooming, buzzing confusion:** W. James, *The Principles of Psychology* (London: MacMillan, 1890).

68 **a condition called synesthesia:** B. Brogaard, "Serotonergic Hyperactivity as a Potential Factor in Developmental, Acquired and Drug-Induced Synesthesia," *Frontiers in Human Neuroscience* 7 (2013): 657.

68 **the infant brain overwires:** L. K. Low and H. J. Cheng, "Axon Pruning: An Essential Step Underlying the Developmental Plasticity of Neuronal Connections," *Philosophical Transactions of the Royal Society of London. Series B, Biological Sciences* 361 (2006): 1531–1544.

68 **axons and dendrites extend to more targets:** Low and Cheng, "Axon Pruning."

68 **Some adult, late-onset mental disorders:** Z. Petanjek et al., "Extraordinary Neoteny of Synaptic Spines in the Human Prefrontal Cortex," *Proceedings of the National Academy of Sciences* 108, no. 32 (2011): 13281–13286.

69 **twenty kilometers across:** I thank Michael Gazzaniga for this calculation.

69 **pruning forces the brain to specialize:** M. Gazzaniga, personal communication, July 15, 2018.

70 **learn any of the thousand or so sounds:** I. Maddieson and K. Precoda, UCLA Phonological Segment Inventory Database (UPSID), n.d., http://web.phonetik.uni-frankfurt.de/upsid_info.html; S. Shih, personal communication, August 7, 2018.

71 **This skill is a precursor to mathematical ability:** O. T. Giles et al., "Hitting the Target: Mathematical Attainment in Children Is Related to Interceptive-Timing Ability," *Psychological Science* 29, no. 8 (2018): 1334–1345.

73 **Cochlear implants:** J. K. Niparko et al., "Spoken Language Development in Children following Cochlear Implantation," *Journal of the American Medical Association* 303 (2010): 1498–1506; J. G. Nicholas and A. E. Geers, "Sensitivity of Expressive Linguistic Domains to Surgery Age and Audibility of Speech in Preschoolers with Cochlear Implants," *Cochlear Implants International* 19, no. 1 (2018): 26–37.

73 **it's not *sound* that the brain needs to acquire the statistical underpinnings of language:** M. L. Hall et al., "Auditory Access, Language Access, and Implicit Sequence Learning in Deaf Children," *Developmental Science* 21, no. 3 (2018): e12575.

73 **The term *sensitive period* refers to:** A. K. Bhatara, E. M. Quintin, and D. J. Levitin, "Musical Ability and Developmental Disorders," *The Oxford Handbook of Intellectual Disability and Development* (New York: Oxford University Press, 2012), 138.

74 **having an alcoholic father:** H. J. Lee et al., "Transgenerational Effects of Paternal Alcohol Exposure in Mouse Offspring," *Animal Cells and Systems* 17, no. 6 (2013): 429–434; J. Day et al., "Influence of Paternal Preconception Exposures on Their Offspring: Through Epigenetics to Phenotype," *American Journal of Stem Cells* 5, no. 1 (2016): 11.

74 **This applies across species:** To see a giant tortoise who wants to cuddle, go to the Animal Lovers Only Facebook page, https://www.facebook.com/AnimalLoversOnly1/videos/242545276572254/.

75 **sensory receptors in the fetus's developing tongue:** Neurons from the retina grow along a path until they find the visual cortex at the back of the brain, stopping first at a relay station, the lateral geniculate nucleus. Neurons also terminate in the superior colliculus, for the control of eye movements; at the pretectum, to control the dilation and constriction of the pupils; and at the suprachiasmatic nucleus, to help control diurnal rhythms and to regulate hormones in response to time of day, as indicated by sunlight. They are guided in part by genetic instructions.

75 **Neuroplasticity provides this compensatory mechanism:** M. Bedny, H. Richardson, and R. Saxe, "'Visual' Cortex Responds to Spoken Language in Blind Children," *Journal of Neuroscience* 35, no. 33 (2015): 11674–11681; B. Röder et al., "Speech Processing Activates Visual Cortex in Congenitally Blind Humans," *European Journal of Neuroscience* 16, no. 5 (2002): 930–936.

76 **blocked the path from the retina to the visual cortex:** M. Sur, P. E. Garraghty, and A. W. Roe, "Experimentally Induced Visual Projections into Auditory Thalamus and Cortex," *Science* 242, no. 4884 (1988): 1437–1441; S. L. Pallas, A. W. Roe, and M. Sur, "Visual Projections Induced into the Auditory Pathway of Ferrets. I. Novel Inputs to Primary Auditory Cortex (AI) from the LP/Pulvinar Complex and the Topography of the MGN-AI Projection," *Journal of Comparative Neurology* 298, no. 1 (1990): 50–68.

76 **sensory integration can begin to fail:** A. L. de Dieuleveult et al., "Effects of Aging in Multisensory Integration: A Systematic Review," *Frontiers in Aging Neuroscience* 9 (2017): 80, http://dx.doi.org/10.3389/fnagi.2017.00080.

76 **A reduction in the ability to produce neurochemicals:** A. Shimamura, *Get SMART! Five Steps toward a Healthy Brain* (Scotts Valley, CA: CreateSpace, 2017).

76 **Dopamine levels fall about 10 percent:** R. Peters, "Ageing and the Brain," *Postgraduate Medical Journal* 82, no. 964 (2006): 84–88; R. Rutledge et al., "Risk Taking for Potential Reward Decreases across the Lifespan," *Current Biology* 26, no. 12 (2016): 1634–1639.

76 **alcohol consumption can lead to neuronal death:** M. Kubota et al., "Alcohol Consumption and Frontal Lobe Shrinkage: Study of 1432 Non-Alcoholic Subjects," *Journal of Neurology, Neurosurgery and Psychiatry* 71, no. 1 (2001): 104–106; X. Yang et al., "Cortical and Subcortical Gray Matter Shrinkage in Alcohol-Use Disorders: A Voxel-Based Meta-Analysis," *Neuroscience and Biobehavioral Reviews* 66 (2016): 92–103.

77 **5 percent per decade through age sixty:** A. M. Hedman et al., "Human Brain Changes across the Life Span: A Review of 56 Longitudinal Magnetic Resonance Imaging Studies," *Human Brain Mapping* 33, no. 8 (2012): 1987–2002.

77 **decline speeding up after age seventy:** Peters, "Ageing and the Brain."

77 **"one of the most significant problems in older adults":** Shimamura, *Get SMART!*.

78 **White-matter tracts . . . decay with age:** M. Balter, "The Incredible Shrinking Human Brain," *Science,* July 25, 2011, http://www.sciencemag.org/news/2011/07/incredible-shrinking-human-brain; C. C. Sherwood et al., "Aging of the Cerebral Cortex Differs between Humans and Chimpanzees," *Proceedings of the National Academy of Sciences* 108, no. 32 (2011): 13029–13034.

80 **Disruptions of this daydreaming mode:** R. Buckner, J. Andrews-Hanna, D. Schacter, "The Brain's Default Network: Anatomy, Function, and Relevance to Disease," *Annals of the New York Academy of Sciences* 1124, no. 1 (2008): 1–38.

80 **Mild cognitive impairment:** S. Gauthier et al., "Mild Cognitive Impairment," *Lancet* 367, no. 9518 (2006): 1262–1270.

80 **leads to Alzheimer's disease:** Gauthier et al., "Mild Cognitive Impairment."

80 **other times it exists independently:** R. C. Petersen, "Mild Cognitive Impairment," *Continuum: Lifelong Learning in Neurology* 22, no. 2, Dementia (2016): 404.

80 **systematic changes in the brain:** B. C. M. Stephan et al., "The Neuropathological Profile of Mild Cognitive Impairment (MCI): A Systematic Review," *Molecular Psychiatry* 17, no. 11 (2012): 1056.

80 **no single neurophysiological profile:** R. C. Petersen et al., "Mild Cognitive Impairment: A Concept in Evolution," *Journal of Internal Medicine* 275, no. 3 (2014): 214–228.

80 **able to classify individuals:** L. Qian et al., "Intrinsic Frequency Specific Brain Networks for Identification of MCI Individuals Using Resting-State fMRI," *Neuroscience Letters* 664 (2018): 7–14.

80 **the concept of cognitive reserve:** Y. Stern, "Cognitive Reserve in Ageing and Alzheimer's Disease," *Lancet Neurology* 11, no. 11 (2012): 1006–1012; Y. Stern, "Cognitive Reserve: Implications for Assessment and Intervention," *Folia Phoniatrica et Logopaedica* 65, no. 2 (2013): 49–54; H. Amieva et al., "Compensatory Mechanisms in Higher-Educated Subjects with Alzheimer's Disease: A Study of 20 Years of Cognitive Decline," *Brain* 137, no. 4 (2014): 1167–1175.

81 **One particular protein, called beta-amyloid:** Shimamura, *Get SMART!*.

81 **drugs that reduce amyloid buildup:** P. Belluck, "Will We Ever Cure AD?," *The New York Times,* November 19, 2018, p. D6.

82 **chronic inflammatory processes:** P. Eikelenboom and R. Veerhuis, "The Importance of Inflammatory Mechanisms for the Development of Alzheimer's Disease," *Experimental Gerontology* 34, no. 3 (1999): 453–461.

82 **taking NSAIDs . . . before the expected onset of Alzheimer's:** P. L. McGeer, J. Rogers, and E. G. McGeer, "Inflammation, Antiinflammatory Agents, and Alzheimer's Disease: The Last 22 Years," *Journal of Alzheimer's Disease* 54, no. 3 (2016): 853–857.

82 **The *APOE* gene:** N. Brouwers, K. Sleegers, and C. Van Broeckhoven, "Molecular Genetics of Alzheimer's Disease: An Update," *Annals of Medicine* 40, no. 8 (2008): 562–583; A. Pink et al., "Neuropsychiatric Symptoms, APOE ε4, and the Risk of Incident Dementia: A Population-Based Study," *Neurology* 84, no. 9 (2015): 935–943.

82 **the presence of the gene is protective:** Y. Y. Lim, E. C. Mormino, and Alzheimer's Disease Neuroimaging Initiative, "APOE Genotype and Early β-Amyloid Accumulation in Older Adults without Dementia," *Neurology* 89, no. 10 (2017): 1028–1034.

82 **John Zeisel:** "Dr John Zeisel: Looking at Dementia with Hope," posted by Jewish Home Life Communities, June 20, 2018, https://www.youtube.com/watch?v=Ze1WyCh_5zQ.

82 **The *Lancet*'s expert panel:** G. Livingston et al., "Dementia Prevention, Intervention, and Care," *Lancet* 390, no. 10113 (2017): 2673–2734.

83 **baby aspirin:** Associated Press, "Low-Dose Aspirin Too Risky for Most People, Studies Find," NBC News, August 27, 2018, https://www.nbcnews.com/health/heart-health/low-dose-aspirin-too-risky-most-people-studies-find-n904281.

83 **a study of twelve thousand Europeans:** European Society of Cardiology, "Jury Still Out on Aspirin a Day to Prevent Heart Attack and Stroke," *ScienceDaily,* August 26, 2018, www.sciencedaily.com/releases/2018/08/180826120759.htm.

84 **For decades, physicians and scientists assumed:** J. Rée, "The Brain's Way of Healing: Stories of Remarkable Recoveries and Discoveries by Norman Doidge—Review," *The Guardian,* January 23, 2015, https://www.theguardian.com/books/2015/jan/23/the-brains-way-healing-stories-remarkable-recoveries-norman-doidge-review; N. Doidge, *The Brain's Way of Healing: Stories of Remarkable Recoveries and Discoveries* (London: Penguin UK, 2015).

84 **As explained by physician Abigail Zuger:** A. Zuger, "The Brain: Malleable, Capable, Vulnerable," *The New York Times,* May 29, 2007, https://www.nytimes.com/2007/05/29/health/29book.html.

84 **seven hundred new neurons per day:** S. M. Ryan and Y. M. Nolan, "Neuroinflammation Negatively Affects Adult Hippocampal Neurogenesis and Cognition: Can Exercise Compensate?," *Neuroscience and Biobehavioral Reviews* 61 (2016): 121–131.

84 **hippocampus is estimated to have around 47 million neurons:** O. Bergmann, K. L. Spalding, and J. Frisén, "Adult Neurogenesis in Humans," *Cold Spring Harbor Perspectives in Biology* 7, no. 7 (2015): a018994.

84 **hippocampal neurogenesis drops to undetectable levels in childhood:** S. F. Sorrells et al., "Human Hippocampal Neurogenesis Drops Sharply in Children to Undetectable Levels in Adults," *Nature* 555, no. 7696 (2018): 377.

84 **preserved neurogenesis:** M. Boldrini et al., "Human Hippocampal Neurogenesis Persists throughout Aging," *Cell Stem Cell* 22, no. 4 (2018): 589–599.

84 **resolve the contradiction:** S. C. Danzer, "Adult Neurogenesis in the Human Brain: Paradise Lost?," *Epilepsy Currents* 18, no. 5 (2018): 329–331; G. Kempermann et al., "Human Adult Neurogenesis: Evidence and Remaining Questions," *Cell Stem Cell* 23, no. 1 (2018): 25–30.

86 **Mari Kodama:** M. Kodama, personal communication, December 25, 2016.

87 **older adults can learn how to use computers:** R. W. Berkowsky, J. Sharit, and S. J. Czaja, "Factors Predicting Decisions about Technology Adoption among Older Adults," *Innovation in Aging* 1, no. 3 (2018): igy002; T. L. Mitzner et al., "Technology Adoption by Older Adults: Findings from the PRISM Trial," *Gerontologist* 59, no. 1 (2018): 34–44.

87 **90 percent of people over the age of fifty-five wear glasses:** Vision Council Research, "U.S. Optical Overview and Outlook," December 2015, https://www.thevisioncouncil.org/sites/default/files/Q415-Topline-Overview-Presentation-Stats-with-Notes-FINAL.PDF.

87 **one in six Americans with hearing loss wears hearing aids:** W. Chien and F. R. Lin, "Prevalence of Hearing Aid Use among Older Adults in the United States," *Archives of Internal Medicine* 172, no. 3 (2012): 292–293.

87 ***not* wearing hearing aids is associated:** L. Rapoport, "Hearing Aids Tied to Less Hospitalization for Older U.S. Adults," Reuters, May 9, 2018, https://www.reuters.com/article/us-health-hearing/hearing-aids-tied-to-less-hospitalization-for-older-u-s-adults-idUSKBN1IA2ZR.

CHAPTER 3

90 **The lens of the eye is shaped:** I. Kohler, "Experiments with Goggles," *Scientific American* 206, no. 5 (1962): 62–73.

93 **Perceptual completion emerges in infancy:** S. P. Johnson and E. E. Hannon, "Perceptual Development," *Handbook of Child Psychology and Developmental Science* 2 (2015): 63–112; L. G. Craton, "The Development of Perceptual Completion Abilities: Infants' Perception of Stationary, Partially Occluded Objects," *Child Development* 67, no. 3 (1996): 890–904; B. S. Hadad and R. Kimchi, "Perceptual Completion of Partly Occluded Contours during Childhood," *Journal of Experimental Child Psychology* 167 (2018): 49–61.

94 **he studied this using distorting glasses:** H. E. F. von Helmholtz, *Treatise on Physiological Optics,* ed. and trans. J. P. C. Southall (1909; repr., New York: Dover, 1962).

94 **adaptations produce changes in the brain:** J. Luauté et al., "Dynamic Changes in Brain Activity during Prism Adaptation," *Journal of Neuroscience* 29, no. 1 (2009): 169–178; Y. Rossetti et al., "Testing Cognition and Rehabilitation in Unilateral Neglect with Wedge Prism Adaptation: Multiple Interplays between Sensorimotor Adaptation and Spatial Cognition," in *Clinical Systems Neuroscience,* ed. K. Kansaku, L. G. Cohen, and N. Birbaumer, pp. 359–381 (Tokyo: Springer, 2015).

94 **the hippocampus, the seat of spatial maps:** J. Luauté et al., "Functional Anatomy of the Therapeutic Effects of Prism Adaptation on Left Neglect," *Neurology* 66, no. 12 (2006): 1859–1867; M. Lunven et al., "Anatomical Predictors of Successful Prism Adaptation in Chronic Visual Neglect," *Cortex* (2018).

95 **interactions between the visual and motor system:** R. Held, "Plasticity in Sensory-Motor Systems," *Scientific American* 213, no. 5 (1965): 84–97; J. Fernández-Ruiz and R. Díaz, "Prism Adaptation and Aftereffect: Specifying the Properties of a Procedural Memory System," *Learning and Memory* 6, no. 1 (1999): 47–53.

95 **But as few as three interactions can bootstrap:** The system is sensitive to two separate parameters: the angle of displacement and the number of times that a motor adaptation must be made.

95 **the Innsbruck experiments included a pair of inverting goggles:** A video of the experiment can be seen here: "Erismann and Kohler inversion 'upside-down' goggles—Film 2," posted by Perceiving Acting, April 10, 2013, https://www.youtube.com/watch?v=z1HYcN7f9N4.

95 **took the goggles off:** P. Sachse et al., "'The World Is Upside Down'—The Innsbruck Goggle Experiments of Theodor Erismann (1883–1961) and Ivo Kohler (1915–1985)," *Cortex* 92 (2017): 222–232.

96 **Consider strokes:** Heart and Stroke Foundation of Canada, "One Quarter of Seniors over 70 Have Had Silent Strokes," *ScienceDaily*, October 5, 2011, www.sciencedaily.com/releases/2011/10/111004113739.htm.

96 **hemispatial neglect:** A. R. Riestra and A. M. Barrett, "Rehabilitation of Spatial Neglect," in *Handbook of Clinical Neurology*, vol. 110, ed. M. P. Barnes and D. C. Good, pp. 347–355 (Amsterdam: Elsevier, 2013).

96 **A reliable way to treat hemispatial neglect:** Y. Rossetti et al., "Prism Adaptation to a Rightward Optical Deviation Rehabilitates Left Hemispatial Neglect," *Nature* 395, no. 6698 (1998): 166; F. Frassinetti et al., "Long-Lasting Amelioration of Visuospatial Neglect by Prism Adaptation," *Brain* 125, no. 3 (2002): 608–623; N. Vaes et al., "Rehabilitation of Visuospatial Neglect by Prism Adaptation: Effects of a Mild Treatment Regime. A Randomised Controlled Trial," *Neuropsychological Rehabilitation* 28, no. 6 (2018): 899–918.

97 **"rubber hand illusion":** M. Botvinick and J. Cohen, "Rubber Hands 'Feel' Touch That Eyes See," *Nature* 391 (1998): 756, http://dx.doi.org/10.1038/35784; A. Kalckert and H. H. Ehrsson, "The Onset Time of the Ownership Sensation in the Moving Rubber Hand Illusion," *Frontiers in Psychology* 8 (2017): 344; M. Tsakiris, "My Body in the Brain: A Neurocognitive Model of Body-Ownership," *Neuropsychologia* 48 (2010): 703–712, http://dx.doi.org/10.1016/j.neuropsychologia.2009.09.034; M. Tsakiris and P. Haggard, "The Rubber Hand Illusion Revisited: Visuotactile Integration and Self-Attribution," *Journal of Experimental Psychology: Human Perception and Performance* 31 (2005): 80–91, http://dx.doi.org/10.1037/0096-1523.31.1.80; you can see videos of this at "The Rubber Hand Illusion—Horizon: Is Seeing Believing?—BBC Two," posted by BBC, October 15, 2010, https://www.youtube.com/watch?v=sxwn1w7MJvk, and "Is That My Real Hand? Breakthrough," posted by National Geographic, November 4, 2015, https://www.youtube.com/watch?v=DphlhmtGRqI.

98 **In the enfacement illusion:** M. Tsakiris, "Looking for Myself: Current Multisensory Input Alters Self-Face Recognition," *PLoS One* 3 (2008): e4040, http://dx.doi.org/10.1371/journal.pone.0004040; M. Tsakiris, "The Multisensory Basis of the Self: From Body to Identity to Others," *Quarterly Journal of Experimental Psychology* 70, no. 4 (2017): 597–609; M. P. Paladino et al., "Synchronous Multisensory Stimulation Blurs Self-Other Boundaries," *Psychological Science* 21 (2010): 1202–1207, http://dx.doi.org/10.1177/0956797610379234; you can see a video of this at "Demo Enfacement Illusion Tsakiris October 2011," posted by "manostsak," February 13, 2018, https://www.youtube.com/watch?v=WO1MrUX0K3c.

98 **your very sense of self is constructed:** G. Porciello et al., "The 'Enfacement' Illusion: A Window on the Plasticity of the Self," *Cortex* 104 (2018): 261–275.

98 **This is what happened to John F. Kennedy Jr.:** National Transportation Safety Board, NTSB ID: NYC99MA178: Accident occurred July 16, 1999, in Vineyard Haven, MA (Washington, DC: NTSB, 1999). The official report on the accident, by the National Transportation Safety Board, emphasizes that "illusions or false impressions occur when information provided by sensory organs is misinterpreted or inadequate . . . some illusions might lead to spatial disorientation or the inability to determine accurately the attitude or motion of the aircraft in relation to the earth's surface." For more information, see R. Gibb, B. Ercoline, and L. Scharff, "Spatial Disorientation: Decades of Pilot Fatalities," *Aviation, Space, and Environmental Medicine* 82, no. 7 (2011): 717–724.

100 **After pain is experienced in a localized part:** W. Magerl and R. D. Treede, "Secondary Tactile Hypoesthesia: A Novel Type of Pain-Induced Somatosensory Plasticity in Human Subjects," *Neuroscience Letters* 361, nos. 1–3 (2004): 136–139; T. Weiss, "Plasticity and Cortical Reorganization Associated with Pain," *Zeitschrift für Psychologie* (2016).

100 **phantom limb pain:** S. Aglioti, A. Bonazzi, and F. Cortese, "Phantom Lower Limb as a Perceptual Marker of Neural Plasticity in the Mature Human Brain," *Proceedings of the Royal Society of London. Series B: Biological Sciences* 255, no. 1344 (1994): 273–278; L. Nikolajsen and K. F. Christensen, "Phantom Limb Pain," in *Nerves and Nerve Injuries,* ed. R. Tubbs et al., pp. 23–34 (New York: Elsevier, 2015).

100 **A different approach to phantom limb pain:** E. L. Altschuler et al., "Rehabilitation of Hemiparesis after Stroke with a Mirror," *Lancet* 353, no. 9169 (1999): 2035–2036; V. S. Ramachandran and D. Rogers-Ramachandran, "Phantom Limbs and Neural Plasticity," *Archives of Neurology* 57, no. 3 (2000): 317–320; J. Barbin et al., "The Effects of Mirror Therapy on Pain and Motor Control of Phantom Limb in Amputees: A Systematic Review," *Annals of Physical and Rehabilitation Medicine* 59, no. 4 (2016): 270–275.

101 **surgical correction of presbyopia:** R. S. Davidson et al., "Surgical Correction of Presbyopia," *Journal of Cataract & Refractive Surgery* 42, no. 6 (2016): 920–930.

103 **this kind of automatic categorization:** D. E. Levari et al., "Prevalence-Induced Concept Change in Human Judgment," *Science* 360, no. 6396 (2018): 1465–1467.

103 **abstract judgments:** Levari et al., "Prevalence-Induced Concept Change."

104 **Another common visual problem is cataracts:** National Eye Institute, "Facts about Cataracts," September 2015, https://nei.nih.gov/health/cataract/cataract_facts.

104 **Cataract surgery:** National Eye Institute, "Facts about Cataracts."

105 **age-related deterioration in mitochondrial DNA:** J. O. Pickles, "Mutation in Mitochondrial DNA as a Cause of Presbycusis," *Audiology and Neurotology* 9, no. 1 (2004): 23–33; Y. Shen et al., "Cognitive Decline, Dementia, Alzheimer's Disease and Presbycusis: Examination of the Possible Molecular Mechanism," *Frontiers in Neuroscience* 12 (2018): 394.

105 **This imbalance can lead to problems:** V. Lobo et al., "Free Radicals, Antioxidants and Functional Foods: Impact on Human Health," *Pharmacognosy Reviews* 4, no. 8 (2010): 118; A. Santo, H. Zhu, and Y. R. Li, "Free Radicals: From Health to Disease," *Reactive Oxygen Species* 2, no. 4 (2016): 245–263.

105 **Foods that are high in antioxidants:** Lobo et al., "Free Radicals"; M. Serafini and I. Peluso, "Functional Foods for Health: The Interrelated Antioxidant and Anti-Inflammatory Role of Fruits, Vegetables, Herbs, Spices and Cocoa in Humans," *Current Pharmaceutical Design* 22, no. 44 (2016): 6701–6715.

105 **evidence for the effectiveness of antioxidant foods:** E. A. Decker et al., "Hurdles in Predicting Antioxidant Efficacy in Oil-in-Water Emulsions," *Trends in Food Science and Technology* 67 (2017): 183–194.

105 **the Mayo Clinic and other experts recommend:** The Mayo Clinic, "Antioxidants," February 7, 2017, https://www.mayoclinic.org/healthy-lifestyle/nutrition-and-healthy-eating/multimedia/antioxidants/sls-20076428.

105 **Hearing loss affects one-third of people:** National Institute on Deafness and Other Communication Disorders, "Age-Related Hearing Loss," March 2016, https://www.nidcd.nih.gov/health/age-related-hearing-loss.

105 **auditory hallucinations:** T. G. Sanchez et al., "Musical Hallucination Associated with Hearing Loss," *Arquivos de Neuro-psiquiatria* 69, no. 2B (2011): 395–400; M. M. J. Linszen et al., "Auditory Hallucinations in Adults with Hearing Impairment: A Large Prevalence Study," *Psychological Medicine* 49, no. 1 (2019): 132–139.

105 **tinnitus, a ringing in the ears:** The Mayo Clinic, "Tinnitus," https://www.mayoclinic.org/diseases-conditions/tinnitus/symptoms-causes/syc-20350156.

106 **Many experience emotional distress:** J. Henry, K. Dennis, and M. Schechter, "Theoretical/Review Article—General Review of Tinnitus: Prevalence, Mechanisms, Effects, and Management," *Journal of Speech, Language, and Hearing Research* 48, no. 5 (2005): 1204–1234; A. McCormack et al., "A Systematic Review of the Reporting of Tinnitus Prevalence and Severity," *Hearing Research* 337 (2016): 70–79.

106 **"The notion of peace and quiet":** Henry et al., "Theoretical/Review Article—General Review of Tinnitus," p. 1207.

106 **Tinnitus does appear to be occurring in the brain:** A. L. Giraud et al., "A Selective Imaging of Tinnitus," *Neuroreport* 10, no. 1 (1999): 1–5; N. Weisz et al., "Tinnitus Perception and Distress Is Related to Abnormal Spontaneous Brain Activity as Measured by Magnetoencephalography," *PLoS Medicine* 2, no. 6 (2005): e153; A. B. Elgoyhen et al., "Tinnitus: Perspectives from Human Neuroimaging," *Nature Reviews Neuroscience* 16, no. 10 (2015): 632.

106 **results from homeostatic neural plasticity:** M. Dominguez et al., "A Spiking Neuron Model of Cortical Correlates of Sensorineural Hearing Loss: Spontaneous Firing, Synchrony, and Tinnitus," *Neural Computation* 18, no. 12 (2006): 2942–2958; R. Schaette and R. Kempter, "Development of Tinnitus-Related Neuronal Hyperactivity through Homeostatic Plasticity after Hearing Loss: A Computational Model," *European Journal of Neuroscience* 23 (2006): 3124–3138; S. E. Shore, L. E. Roberts, and B. Langguth, "Maladaptive Plasticity in Tinnitus—Triggers, Mechanisms and Treatment," *Nature Reviews Neurology* 12, no. 3 (2016): 150.

106 **An experimental therapy for tinnitus:** R. Schaette et al., "Acoustic Stimulation Treatments against Tinnitus Could Be Most Effective When Tinnitus Pitch Is within the Stimulated Frequency Range," *Hearing Research* 269, nos. 1–2 (2010): 95–101; R. Schaette, "Mechanisms of Tinnitus," in *Annual Tinnitus Research Review,* ed. D. Baguley and N. Wray, pp. 10–15 (Sheffield, UK: British Tinnitus Association, 2016).

107 **As Atul Gawande writes:** A. Gawande, *Being Mortal: Medicine and What Matters in the End* (New York: Metropolitan Books, 2014), p. 31.

108 **Decreased sense of smell:** R. L. Doty and V. Kamath, "The Influences of Age on Olfaction: A Review," *Frontiers in Psychology* 5 (2014): 20; J. Seubert et al., "Prevalence and Correlates of Olfactory Dysfunction in Old Age: A Population-Based Study," *Journals of Gerontology Series A: Biomedical Sciences and Medical Sciences* 72, no. 8 (2017): 1072–1079.

109 **detect a trillion different smells:** C. Bushdid et al., "Humans Can Discriminate More Than 1 Trillion Olfactory Stimuli," *Science* 343, no. 6177 (2014): 1370–1372; S. C. P. Williams, "Human Nose Can Detect a Trillion Smells," *Science,* March 20, 2014, https://www.sciencemag.org/news/2014/03/human-nose-can-detect-trillion-smells.

110 **taste helps us prepare the body:** S. S. Schiffman, "Taste and Smell Losses in Normal Aging and Disease," *Journal of the American Medical Association* 278, no. 16 (1997): 1357–1362; E. McGinley, "Supporting Older Patients with Nutrition and Hydration," *Journal of Community Nursing* 31, no. 4 (2017).

110 **a fifth taste, umami:** Y. Zhang et al., "Coding of Sweet, Bitter, and Umami Tastes: Different Receptor Cells Sharing Similar Signaling Pathways," *Cell* 112, no. 3 (2003): 293–301; K. Kurihara, "Umami the Fifth Basic Taste: History of Studies on Receptor Mechanisms and Role as a Food Flavor," *BioMed Research International* (2015): article ID 189402.

110 **Many older adults complain that food lacks flavor:** J. L. Garrison and Z. A. Knight, "Linking Smell to Metabolism and Aging," *Science* 358, no. 6364

(2017): 718–719; S. Nordin, "Sensory Perception of Food and Aging," in *Food for the Aging Population,* ed. M. Raats, L. De Groot, and D. van Asselt, pp. 57–82 (New York: Elsevier, 2017); G. Sergi et al., "Taste Loss in the Elderly: Possible Implications for Dietary Habits," *Critical Reviews in Food Science and Nutrition* 57, no. 17 (2017): 3684–3689; S. Schiffman and M. Pasternak, "Decreased Discrimination of Food Odors in the Elderly," *Journal of Gerontology* 34 (1979): 73–79, http://dx.doi.org/10.1093/geronj/34.1.73; S. S. Schiffman, "Taste and Smell Losses with Age," *Boletín de la Asociación Médica de Puerto Rico* 83 (1991): 411–414; S. S. Schiffman, J. Moss, and R. P. Erickson, "Thresholds of Food Odors in the Elderly," *Experimental Aging Research* (1976): 389–398, http://dx.doi.org/10.1080/03610737608257997; S. S. Schiffman and J. Zervakis, "Taste and Smell Perception in the Elderly: Effect of Medication and Disease," *Advances in Food and Nutrition Research* 44 (2002): 247–346, http://dx.doi.org/10.1016/S1043-4526(02)44006-5.

110 **The loss of flavor:** J. M. Boyce and G. R. Shone, "Effects of Ageing on Smell and Taste," *Postgraduate Medical Journal* 82, no. 966 (2006): 239–241; L. E. Spotten et al., "Subjective and Objective Taste and Smell Changes in Cancer," *Annals of Oncology* 28, no. 5 (2017): 969–984; B. N. Landis, C. G. Konnerth, and T. Hummel, "A Study on the Frequency of Olfactory Dysfunction," *Laryngoscope* 114, no. 10 (2004): 1764–1769.

112 **reduced ability of older adults to identify foods:** S. Schiffman, "Changes in Taste and Smell with Age: Psychophysical Aspects," in *Sensory Systems and Communication in the Elderly: Aging,* vol. 10, ed. J. M. Ordy and K. Brizzee, pp. 227–246 (New York: Raven Press, 1979).

113 **healing power of the outdoors:** S. Grafton, personal communication, March 29, 2018.

CHAPTER 4

117 **Art Blakey:** A. Blakey, quoted in the liner notes for Art Blakey Quintet, *A Night at Birdland,* vol. 3, Blue Note Records, compact disc / 10-inch LP, 1954.

120 **infants from African countries:** L. B. Karasik et al., "WEIRD Walking: Cross-Cultural Research on Motor Development," *Behavioral and Brain Sciences* 33, nos. 2–3 (2010): 95–96. WEIRD stands for Western, educated, industrialized, rich, and democratic because, ironically, that subpopulation accounts for about 80 percent of what behavioral scientists know about human behavior, even though the subpopulation comprises less than 12 percent of the world population.

121 **environmental toxins impair learning:** R. D. Baker and F. R. Greer, "Diagnosis and Prevention of Iron Deficiency and Iron-Deficiency Anemia in Infants and Young Children (0–3 Years of Age)," *Pediatrics* 126, no. 5 (2010): 1040–1050; P. M. Gupta et al., "Iron, Anemia, and Iron Deficiency Anemia among Young Children in the United States," *Nutrients* 8, no. 6 (2016): 330, http://dx.doi.org/10.3390/nu8060330.

121 **Learning doesn't happen the same way:** Committee on How People Learn II, *How People Learn II: Learners, Contexts and Cultures* (Washington, DC: National Academies Press, 2018), p. 21, free download at http://nap.edu/24783.

121 **David Krakauer:** D. Krakauer, personal communication, July 19, 2019.

121 **"school failure may be partly explained":** Committee on How People Learn II, *How People Learn II.*

122 **acquisitional intelligence:** Robert Sternberg wrote about the importance of knowledge acquisition in his triarchic theory of intelligence, although he did not consider it a separate type of intelligence as I do here; R. J. Sternberg, *Beyond IQ: A Triarchic Theory of Intelligence* (Cambridge: Cambridge University Press, 1985).

123 **information overload:** I wrote about information overload in a previous book: D. J. Levitin, *The Organized Mind: Thinking Straight in the Age of Information Overload* (New York: Dutton, 2014).

124 **or "social" intelligence:** E. L. Thorndike, "The Measurement of Intelligence: Present Status," *Psychological Review* 31 (1924): 219–252.

124 **naturalistic (knowledge of nature):** H. Gardner, "Reflections on Multiple Intelligences: Myths and Messages," *Phi Delta Kappan* 77 (1995): 200–209.

124 **Sternberg studied naturalistic intelligence:** R. J. Sternberg et al., "The Relationship between Academic and Practical Intelligence: A Case Study in Kenya," *Intelligence* 29, no. 5 (2001): 408.

125 **The children performed very well:** A typical question was as follows:

> A small child in your family has homa. She has a sore throat, headache, and fever. She has been sick for 3 days. Which of the following five Yadh nyaluo (Luo herbal medicines) can treat homa?

i. Chamama. Take the leaf and fito (sniff medicine up the nose to sneeze out illness).
ii. Kaladali. Take the leaves, drink, and fito.
iii. Obuo. Take the leaves and fito.
iv. Ogaka. Take the roots, pound, and drink.
v. Ahundo. Take the leaves and fito.

In this item, Options 1 and 2 represent common treatments for homa, Option 3 represents a rare treatment, Option 4 represents a treatment that is not used for homa, and Option 5 represents an imaginary (nonexistent) herb. Thus Options 1–3 were scored as correct answers. If Option 5 was chosen, a penalty of 3 points was applied.

To avoid ethnocentric bias, scoring was based on healers' knowledge, not on what Westerners might believe to be the correct answers.

125 **As Sternberg notes:** Sternberg et al., "The Relationship between Academic and Practical Intelligence," p. 414.

127 **Dandelions can grow:** M. Gazzaniga et al., *Psychological Science,* 3rd Canadian ed. (New York: W. W. Norton, 2010).

129 **My favorite example of this:** J. L. Adams, *Conceptual Blockbusting: A Guide to Better Ideas* (New York: W. W. Norton, 1980).

130 **The standard solution to the nine dot puzzle:**

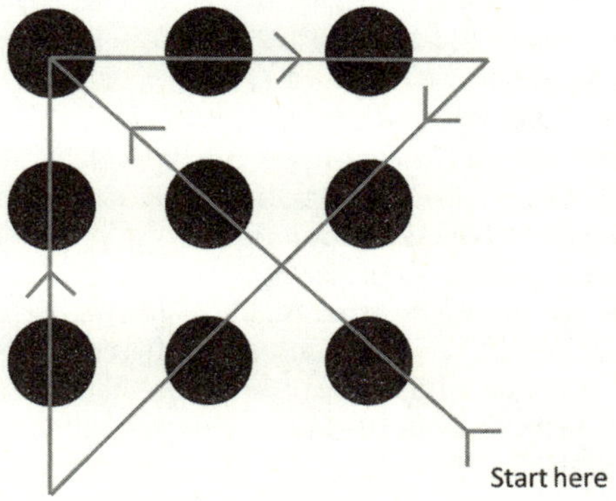

For the more mathematically inclined, my former professor George Polya wrote a book called *How to Solve It,* a great little book that has expanded the problem-solving skills of generations of students—and because of his infectious and easy writing style, he reaches even those who are math-phobic. G. Polya, *How to Solve It: A New Aspect of Mathematical Method* (Princeton, NJ: Princeton University Press, 2004).

133 **"It's just a party trick":** J. Mogil, personal communication, July 15, 2019.

133 **The *Mona Lisa*:** M. Lankford, *Becoming Leonardo: An Exploded View of the Life of Leonardo da Vinci* (Brooklyn, NY: Melville House, 2017).

133 **the aging brain and reaction times:** A. P. Shimamura et al., "Memory and Cognitive Abilities in Academic Professors: Evidence for Successful Aging," *Psychological Science* 6 (1995): 271–277; A. P. Shimamura, *Get SMART! Five Steps toward a Healthy Brain* (Scotts Valley, CA: CreateSpace, 2017).

133 **age-related decreases in blood flow:** R. C. Gur et al., "Age and Regional Cerebral Blood Flow at Rest and during Cognitive Activity," *Archives of General Psychiatry* 44 (1987): 617–621.

133 **changes in the structure of cells:** R. L. Buckner, "Memory and Executive Function in Aging and AD: Multiple Factors That Cause Decline and Reserve Factors That Compensate," *Neuron* 44 (2004): 195–208.

134 **low fluid intelligence in childhood:** S. Aichele et al., "Fluid Intelligence Predicts Change in Depressive Symptoms in Later Life: The Lothian Birth Cohort 1936," *Psychological Science* (2018): 1–12, http://dx.doi.org/10.1177/0956797618804501.

134 **Practical intelligence increases with age:** Sternberg et al., "The Relationship between Academic and Practical Intelligence."

135 **Intelligent, adaptive behavior requires abstracting:** S. L. Brincat et al., "Gradual Progression from Sensory to Task-Related Processing in Cerebral Cortex," *Proceedings of the National Academy of Sciences* 115, no. 30 (2018): E7202—E7211.

135 **abstraction involves a wide range of brain regions:** Brincat et al., "Gradual Progression from Sensory to Task-Related Processing in Cerebral Cortex," *Proceedings of the National Academy of Sciences* 115, no. 30 (2018): E7202–E7211.

136 **tendency to form abstract representations:** A. Susac et al., "Development of Abstract Mathematical Reasoning: The Case of Algebra," *Frontiers in Human Neuroscience* 8 (2014): 679.

136 **It isn't until around sixteen or seventeen:** Susac et al., "Development of Abstract Mathematical Reasoning."

136 **abstract thinking in other species:** S. R. Howard et al., "Numerical Ordering of Zero in Honey Bees," *Science* 360, no. 6393 (2018): 1124–1126; A. Nieder, "Honey Bees Zero In on the Empty Set," *Science* 360, no. 6393 (2018): 1069–1070.

137 **Diane Ackerman invented a game called Dingbats:** D. Ackerman, *One Hundred Names for Love* (New York: W. W. Norton, 2011), pp. 82–83.

137 **increased cortical thickness and gray-matter volume:** S. Kühn et al., "The Importance of the Default Mode Network in Creativity—a Structural MRI Study," *Journal of Creative Behavior* 48, no. 2 (2014): 152–163; R. E. Beaty et al., "Creativity and the Default Network: A Functional Connectivity Analysis of the Creative Brain at Rest," *Neuropsychologia* 64 (2014): 92–98.

138 **Aging is not accompanied by unavoidable cognitive decline:** T. A. Salthouse, "The Processing-Speed Theory of Adult Age Differences in Cognition," *Psychological Review* 103, no. 3 (1996): 403; T. A. Salthouse, T. M. Atkinson, and D. E. Berish, "Executive Functioning as a Potential Mediator of Age-Related

Cognitive Decline in Normal Adults," *Journal of Experimental Psychology: General* 132, no. 4 (2003): 566; L. J. Whalley et al., "Cognitive Reserve and the Neurobiology of Cognitive Aging," *Ageing Research Reviews* 3, no. 4 (2004): 369–382.

138 **neuroprotective and neurorestorative capabilities:** Whalley et al., "Cognitive Reserve."

138 **biological, pathological markers for Alzheimer's disease:** P. G. Ince, "Pathological Correlates of Late-Onset Dementia in a Multicenter Community-Based Population in England and Wales," *Lancet* 357, no. 9251 (2001): 169–175.

138 **Cognitive reserve can insulate against:** Whalley et al., "Cognitive Reserve."

139 **occupational complexity:** Whalley et al., "Cognitive Reserve"; K. Fujishiro et al., "The Role of Occupation in Explaining Cognitive Functioning in Later Life: Education and Occupational Complexity in a US National Sample of Black and White Men and Women," *Journals of Gerontology: Series B* (2017): gbx112, https://doi.org/10.1093/geronb/gbx112.

139 **low educational attainment and low occupational complexity:** S. Cullum et al., "Decline across Different Domains of Cognitive Function in Normal Ageing: Results of a Longitudinal Population-Based Study Using CAMCOG," *International Journal of Geriatric Psychiatry* 15 (2000): 853–862; M. Zhang et al., "The Prevalence of Dementia and Alzheimer's Disease in Shanghai, China: Impact of Age, Gender, and Education," *Annals of Neurology: Official Journal of the American Neurological Association and the Child Neurology Society* 27, no. 4 (1990): 428–437; Y. Stern, "Cognitive Reserve in Ageing and Alzheimer's Disease," *Lancet Neurology* 11, no. 11 (2012): 1006–1012; E. A. Boots et al., "Occupational Complexity and Cognitive Reserve in a Middle-Aged Cohort at Risk for Alzheimer's Disease," *Archives of Clinical Neuropsychology* 30, no. 7 (2015): 634–642.

140 **Karl Duncker:** K. Duncker and L. S. Lees, "On Problem-Solving," *Psychological Monographs* 58, no. 5 (1945): 1.

140 **Duncker then proposed a problem:** This problem has been used in several different versions and wordings, from Duncker's original conception, to papers by Gick and Holyoak and entries in cognitive psychology texts. This formulation is my own amalgamation of those. Duncker and Lees, "On Problem-Solving"; M. L. Gick and K. J. Holyoak, "Schema Induction and Analogical Transfer," *Cognitive Psychology* 15, no. 1 (1983): 1–38; M. L. Gick and K. J. Holyoak, "Analogical Problem Solving," *Cognitive Psychology* 12, no. 3 (1980): 306–355.

142 **What is wisdom?:** E. E. Lee and D. V. Jeste, "Neurobiology of Wisdom," in *The Cambridge Handbook of Wisdom,* ed. R. J. Sternberg and J. Glück (Cambridge, UK: Cambridge University Press, 2019).

142 **Paul Baltes defined wisdom as:** P. B. Baltes and J. Smith, "The Fascination of Wisdom: Its Nature, Ontogeny, and Function," *Perspectives on Psychological Science* 3, no. 1 (2008): 56–64.

143 **the development of wisdom:** J. Glück, S. Bluck, and N. M. Weststrate, "More on the MORE Life Experience Model: What We Have Learned (So Far)," *Journal of Value Inquiry* (2018): 1–22.

143 **King Solomon:** In the biblical account, two women present themselves to the king, who acted as judge for the kingdom, both claiming to be the mother of a small baby. Solomon proposes that the baby be cut in half. One of the women agreed to the solution and the other begged him not to, and to instead give the baby to her rival. Solomon knew that the real mother's love for the child would be borne out by his proposal and that only the real mother would object to the proposal.

143 **Older adults show higher levels of emotional regulation:** S. Brassen et al., "Don't Look Back in Anger! Responsiveness to Missed Chances in Successful and Nonsuccessful Aging," *Science* 336, no. 6081 (2012): 612–614.

143 **experience-based decision making and conflict resolution:** I. Grossmann et al., "Reasoning about Social Conflicts Improves into Old Age," *Proceedings of the National Academy of Sciences* 107, no. 16 (2010): 7246–7250; D. A. Worthy et al., "With Age Comes Wisdom," *Psychological Science* 22, no. 11 (2011): 1375–1380.

143 **prosocial behaviors:** J. N. Beadle et al., "Aging, Empathy, and Prosociality," *Journals of Gerontology, Series B: Psychological Sciences and Social Sciences* 70, no. 2 (2015): 215–224.

143 **subjective emotional well-being:** L. L. Carstensen et al., "Emotional Experience Improves with Age: Evidence Based on over 10 Years of Experience Sampling," *Psychology and Aging* 26, no. 1 (2011): 21–33.

143 **self-reflection or insight:** Brassen et al., "Don't Look Back in Anger!"

144 **favoring positive emotions:** L. L. Carstensen and M. DeLiema, "The Positivity Effect: A Negativity Bias in Youth Fades with Age," *Current Opinion in Behavioral Sciences* 19 (2018): 7–12.

144 **greater ability to maintain positive relationships:** K. S. Birditt, L. M. Jackey, and T. C. Antonucci, "Longitudinal Patterns of Negative Relationship Quality across Adulthood," *Journals of Gerontology, Series B: Psychological Sciences and Social Sciences* 64, no. 1 (2009): 55–64.

144 **Greater wisdom is also marked by:** T. W. Meeks and D. V. Jeste, "Neurobiology of Wisdom," *Archives of General Psychiatry* 66, no. 4 (2009): 355–365.

144 **dopamine decreases with age:** P. S. Goldman-Rakic and R. M. Brown, "Regional Changes of Monoamines in Cerebral Cortex and Subcortical Structures of Aging Rhesus Monkeys," *Neuroscience* 6, no. 2 (1981): 177–187; L. Bäckman et al., "The Correlative Triad among Aging, Dopamine, and Cognition: Current Status and Future Prospects," *Neuroscience and Biobehavioral Reviews* 30, no. 6 (2006): 791–807; V. Kaasinen et al., "Age-Related Dopamine D2/D3 Receptor Loss in Extrastriatal Regions of the Human Brain," *Neurobiology of Aging* 21, no. 5 (2000): 683–688.

144 **Precursors of wisdom:** R. J. Sternberg, "Why Schools Should Teach for Wisdom: The Balance Theory of Wisdom in Educational Settings," *Educational Psychologist* 36, no. 4 (2001): 227–245.

CHAPTER 5

146 **When Stevie sings:** S. Wonder, *Visions*, from *Inner Visions*, Tamla, T326L.

146 **When Joni sings the single word *blue*:** I wrote about this previously in D. J. Levitin, "Inside the Theater of the Mind. Review of *How Emotions Are Made* by Lisa Feldman Barrett," *The Wall Street Journal*, March 4, 2017, p. B5.

146 **Emotions occur against:** R. J. Davidson, "On Emotion, Mood, and Related Affective Constructs," in *The Nature of Emotion: Fundamental Questions*, ed. P. Ekman and R. J. Davidson, pp. 51–55 (New York: Oxford University Press, 1994).

146 **Emotion, motivation, reinforcement, and arousal:** J. LeDoux, "Rethinking the Emotional Brain," *Neuron* 73 (2002): 653–676.

147 **biologist Frans de Waal:** F. de Waal, *Mama's Last Hug* (New York: W. W. Norton, 2019).

147 **Our human survival strategies go back:** R. M. Macnab and D. E. Koshland, "The Gradient-Sensing Mechanism in Bacterial Chemotaxis," *Proceedings of the National Academy of Sciences* 69, no. 9 (1972): 2509–2512.

148 **a neuropeptide called nematocin:** S. W. Emmons, "The Mood of a Worm," *Science* 338, no. 6106 (2012): 475–476; J. L. Garrison et al., "Oxytocin/Vasopressin-Related

Peptides Have an Ancient Role in Reproductive Behavior," *Science* 338, no. 6106 (2012): 540–543.

148 **Survival circuits, from worms to humans:** LeDoux, "Rethinking the Emotional Brain."

148 **What we call emotions or feelings:** LeDoux, "Rethinking the Emotional Brain."

148 **the rickety bridge experiment:** D. G. Dutton and A. P. Aron, "Some Evidence for Heightened Sexual Attraction under Conditions of High Anxiety," *Journal of Personality and Social Psychology* 30, no. 4 (1974): 510.

149 **emotions can easily be misattributed:** S. Schachter and J. Singer, "Cognitive, Social, and Physiological Determinants of Emotional State," *Psychological Review* 69, no. 5 (1962): 379; G. L. White, S. Fishbein, and J. Rutsein, "Passionate Love and the Misattribution of Arousal," *Journal of Personality and Social Psychology* 41, no. 1 (1981): 56.

149 **there are emotions that dogs:** I wrote about this previously in D. J. Levitin, "Brain Candy. Review of *Human: The Science behind What Makes Us Unique,* by M. Gazzaniga," *The New York Times Sunday Book Review,* August 24, 2008, 5.

150 **we should add spite to the list:** K. Jensen, J. Call, and M. Tomasello, "Chimpanzees Are Vengeful but Not Spiteful," *Proceedings of the National Academy of Sciences* 104, no. 32 (2007): 13046–13050.

150 **Tagalog, which calls it *kilig*:** T. Lomas, "Towards a Positive Cross-Cultural Lexicography: Enriching Our Emotional Landscape through 216 'Untranslatable' Words Pertaining to Well-Being," *Journal of Positive Psychology* 11, no. 5 (2016): 546–558, http://dx.doi.org/10.1080/17439760.2015.1127993; T. Lomas, "The Magic of Untranslatable Words," *Scientific American,* July 12, 2016, https://www.scientificamerican.com/article/the-magic-of-untranslatable-words/?print=true.

150 **As emotion researcher Lisa Feldman Barrett says:** L. F. Barrett, *How Emotions Are Made: The Secret Life of the Brain* (Boston: Houghton Mifflin Harcourt, 2017).

151 **Emotion differentiation:** E. C. Nook et al., "The Nonlinear Development of Emotion Differentiation: Granular Emotional Experience Is Low in Adolescence," *Psychological Science* 29, no. 8 (2018): 1346–1357.

152 **gene-by-environment interactions:** I've written about some of this previously in D. J. Levitin, "The Ultimate Brain Quest. Review of *Connectome: How the Brain's Wiring Makes Us Who We Are* by Sebastian Seung," *The Wall Street Journal,* February 4, 2012, C5–C6.

154 **University of Montreal colleague Sonia Lupien:** S. J. Lupien et al., "Beyond the Stress Concept: Allostatic Load—A Developmental Biological and Cognitive Perspective," in *Developmental Psychopathology,* vol. 2, *Developmental Neuroscience,* ed. D. Cicchetti and D. J. Cohen, pp. 578–628 (Hoboken, NJ: John Wiley and Sons, 2015).

154 **The term *stress*:** OED Online, s. v. "stress," accessed February 25, 2019, www.oed.com/view/Entry/191511.

155 **some of our physiological systems . . . require continual adjustment:** P. Sterling, "Allostasis: A Model of Predictive Regulation," *Physiology and Behavior* 106 (2012): 5–15; G. H. Ice and G. D. James, *Measuring Stress in Humans: A Practical Guide for the Field* (Cambridge: Cambridge University Press, 2007), p. 284.

155 **stability through change is called *allostasis*:** P. Sterling and J. Eyer, "Allostasis: A New Paradigm to Explain Arousal Pathology," in *Handbook of Life Stress, Cognition and Health,* ed. S. Fisher and J. Reason, pp. 629–649 (Oxford, UK: John Wiley and Sons, 1988).

155 **This in turn causes a dysregulation:** I thank Sonia Lupien for her help with the previous two paragraphs.

155 **Your allostatic load can be calculated:** A. Edes and D. E. Crews, "Allostatic Load and Biological Anthropology," *American Journal of Physical Anthropology* 162 (2017): 44–70.

155 **ways to reduce stress:** H. Frumkin et al., "Nature Contact and Human Health: A Research Agenda," *Environmental Health Perspectives* 125, no. 7 (2017): 075001; C. E. Hostinar and M. R. Gunnar, "Social Support Can Buffer against Stress and Shape Brain Activity," *AJOB Neuroscience* 6, no. 3 (2015): 34–42; A. Linnemann et al., "Music Listening as a Means of Stress Reduction in Daily Life," *Psychoneuroendocrinology* 60 (2015): 82–90.

156 **Doing this is metabolically expensive:** A. Danese and B. S. McEwen, "Adverse Childhood Experiences, Allostasis, Allostatic Load, and Age-Related Disease," *Physiology and Behavior* 106, no. 1 (2012): 29–39; B. S. McEwen, "Allostasis and Allostatic Load: Implications for Neuropsychopharmacology," *Neuropsychopharmacology* 22, no. 2 (2000): 108–124.

156 **A stable fetal and early childhood:** D. J. Barker, "Developmental Origins of Chronic Disease," *Public Health* 126, no. 3 (2012): 185–189.

156 **Increased allostatic load:** T. Booth et al., "Association of Allostatic Load with Brain Structure and Cognitive Ability in Later Life," *Neurobiology of Aging* 36 (2015): 1390–1399.

157 **linked to a number of psychiatric conditions:** G. Bizik et al., "Allostatic Load as a Tool for Monitoring Physiological Dysregulations and Comorbidities in Patients with Severe Mental Illnesses," *Harvard Review of Psychiatry* 21 (2012): 296–313; R. W. Kobrosly et al., "Depressive Symptoms Are Associated with Allostatic Load among Community-Dwelling Older Adults," *Physiology and Behavior* 123 (2014): 223–230; J. A. Stewart, "The Detrimental Effects of Allostasis: Allostatic Load as a Measure of Cumulative Stress," *Journal of Physiological Anthropology* 25 (2006): 133–145.

158 **normal age-related changes in structures that regulate allostasis:** E. Zsoldos et al., "Allostatic Load as a Predictor of Grey Matter Volume and White Matter Integrity in Old Age: The Whitehall II MRI Study," *Scientific Reports* 8, no. 1 (2018): 6411.

158 **sleep disturbances to increases in load:** R. P. Juster and B. S. McEwen, "Sleep and Chronic Stress: New Directions for Allostatic Load Research," *Sleep Medicine* 16, no. 1 (2015): 7–8.

158 **Reducing stress and increasing resilience:** B. L. Ganzel, P. A. Morris, and E. Wethington, "Allostasis and the Human Brain: Integrating Models of Stress from the Social and Life Sciences," *Psychological Review* 117, no. 1 (2010): 134; B. S. McEwen and P. J. Gianaros, "Stress- and Allostasis-Induced Brain Plasticity," *Annual Review of Medicine* 62 (2011): 431–445; G. Tabibnia and D. Radecki, "Resilience Training That Can Change the Brain," *Consulting Psychology Journal: Practice and Research* 70, no. 1 (2018): 59–88.

158 **the same across continents:** G. Y. Lim et al., "Prevalence of Depression in the Community from 30 Countries between 1994 and 2014," *Scientific Reports* 8, no. 1 (2018): 2861; J. Wang et al., "Prevalence of Depression and Depressive Symptoms among Outpatients: A Systematic Review and Meta-analysis," *BMJ Open* 7, no. 8 (2017): e017173, http://dx.doi.org/10.1136/BMJopen-2017-017173; D. J. Brody, L. A. Pratt, and J. P. Hughes, "Prevalence of Depression among Adults Aged 20 and Over: United States, 2013–2016" (Hyattsville, MD: NCHS Data Brief 303, National Center for Health Statistics, 2018), pp. 1–8.

158 **antidepressant drugs tend to work only 20 percent:** Institute for Quality and Efficiency in Health Care, "Depression: How Effective Are Antidepressants?," Informed Health Online, updated January 12, 2017, https://www.ncbi.nlm.nih.gov/books/NBK361016/; A. Cipriani et al., "Antidepressants Might Work for People with Major Depression: Where Do We Go from Here?," *Lancet Psychiatry* 5, no. 6 (2018): 461–463.

159 **After the procession, we met in his office:** His Holiness the Dalai Lama, personal communication, Dharamsala, India, August 30, 2018.

160 **"Anger, hatred, and fear":** "Dalai Lama: 'Anger, hatred, fear, is very bad for our health,'" posted by CBS News, October 2013, https://www.dailymotion.com/video/x16a709.

160 **"Passing through life, progressing to old age":** "No Regrets: Dalai Lama's Advice for Living and Dying," posted by Karuna Hospice Service, August 6, 2015, https://www.youtube.com/watch?v=k3eJ4ezYXDI.

160 **depression is less frequent among older adults:** Centers for Disease Control and Prevention, "Depression Is Not a Normal Part of Growing Older," https://www.cdc.gov/aging/mentalhealth/depression.htm.

161 **Depression in old age is:** U. Padayachey, S. Ramlall, and J. Chipps, "Depression in Older Adults: Prevalence and Risk Factors in a Primary Health Care Sample," *South African Family Practice* 59, no. 2 (2017): 61–66.

161 **the impact of the curtailment of daily activities:** A. Fiske, J. L. Wetherell, and M. Gatz, "Depression in Older Adults," *Annual Review of Clinical Psychology* 5 (2009): 363–389.

161 **Insomnia, a hallmark of aging:** K. L. Lichstein et al., "Insomnia in the Elderly," *Sleep Medicine Clinics* 1, no. 2 (2006): 221–229.

162 **understanding of the role of meaningful engagement:** H. C. Hendrie et al., "The NIH Cognitive and Emotional Health Project: Report of the Critical Evaluation Study Committee," *Alzheimer's and Dementia* 2, no. 1 (2006): 12–32.

162 **the presence of intimate others:** R. J. Davidson et al., "Neural and Behavioral Substrates of Mood and Mood Regulation," *Biological Psychiatry* 52, no. 6 (2002): 478–502; G. Gariepy, H. Honkaniemi, and A. Quesnel-Vallee, "Social Support and Protection from Depression: Systematic Review of Current Findings in Western Countries," *British Journal of Psychiatry* 209, no. 4 (2016): 284–293.

163 **"dopamine was the drunk":** J. Mogil, personal communication, July 16, 2019.

163 **SSRIs should be the first-line pharmacological:** J. Rodda, Z. Walker, and J. Carter, "Depression in Older Adults," *British Medical Journal* 343, no. 8 (2011): d5219.

163 **Low doses of methylphenidate:** H. Lavretsky et al., "Combined Citalopram and Methylphenidate Improved Treatment Response Compared to Either Drug Alone in Geriatric Depression: A Randomized Double-Blind, Placebo-Controlled Trial," *American Journal of Psychiatry* 172, no. 6 (2015): 561; T. A. Ketter et al., "Long-Term Safety and Efficacy of Armodafinil in Bipolar Depression: A 6-Month Open-Label Extension Study," *Journal of Affective Disorders* 197 (2016): 51–57.

164 **Psychotherapy can change the structure of the brain:** K. N. Månsson et al., "Neuroplasticity in Response to Cognitive Behavior Therapy for Social Anxiety Disorder," *Translational Psychiatry* 6, no. 2 (2016): e727; D. Collerton, "Psychotherapy and Brain Plasticity," *Frontiers in Psychology* 4 (2013): 548.

164 **talk therapy has proven its effectiveness:** R. D. Lane et al., "Memory Reconsolidation, Emotional Arousal, and the Process of Change in Psychotherapy: New Insights from Brain Science," *Behavioral and Brain Sciences* 38 (2015).

164 **as effective as antidepressant drugs:** R. J. DeRubeis, G. J. Siegle, and S. D. Hollon, "Cognitive Therapy versus Medication for Depression: Treatment Outcomes and Neural Mechanisms," *Nature Reviews Neuroscience* 9, no. 10 (2008): 788.

164 **coping styles in depression:** Davidson et al., "Neural and Behavioral Substrates."

165 **rumination . . . feels good:** W. H. Frey II, *Crying: The Mystery of Tears* (Minneapolis, MN: Winston Press, 1985); R. Turner et al., "Effects of Emotion on Oxytocin, Prolactin, and ACTH in Women," *Stress* 5, no. 4 (2002): 269–276.

165 **The more effective strategy:** S. Nolen-Hoeksema, "Responses to Depression and Their Effects on the Duration of the Depressive Episode," *Journal of Abnormal Psychology* 100, no. 4 (1991): 569–582; S. Nolen-Hoeksema and J. Morrow, "Effects of Rumination and Distraction on Naturally Occurring Depressed Mood," *Cognition and Emotion* 7, no. 6 (1993): 561–570.

166 **the time of the month when women get cabin fever:** N. M. Morris and J. R. Udry, "Variations in Pedometer Activity during the Menstrual Cycle," *Obstetrics and Gynecology* 35, no. 2 (1970): 199–201; M. Haselton, *Hormonal: The Hidden Intelligence of Hormones—How They Drive Desire, Shape Relationships, Influence Our Choices, and Make Us Wiser* (Boston: Little, Brown, 2018).

167 **Higher estrogen is:** S. J. Stanton and O. C. Schultheiss, "Basal and Dynamic Relationships between Implicit Power Motivation and Estradiol in Women," *Hormones and Behavior* 52, no. 5 (2007): 571–580; K. Lebron-Milad, B. M. Graham, and M. R. Milad, "Low Estradiol Levels: A Vulnerability Factor for the Development of Posttraumatic Stress Disorder," *Biological Psychiatry* 72, no. 1 (2012): 6–7, http://dx.doi.org/10.1016/j.biopsych.2012.04.029.

167 **The increased progesterone production:** M. Østensen, P. M. Villiger, and F. Förger, "Interaction of Pregnancy and Autoimmune Rheumatic Disease," *Autoimmunity Reviews* 11, nos. 6–7 (2012): A437–A446.

167 **Pregnant women who have had rheumatoid arthritis:** J. Greenspan et al., "Studying Sex and Gender Differences in Pain and Analgesia: A Consensus Report," *Pain* 132 (2007): S26–S45.

167 **High progesterone leads women:** M. L. Smith et al., "Facial Appearance Is a Cue to Oestrogen Levels in Women," *Proceedings of the Royal Society of London B: Biological Sciences* 273, no. 1583 (2006): 135–140; D. S. Fleischman and D. M. Fessler, "Progesterone's Effects on the Psychology of Disease Avoidance: Support for the Compensatory Behavioral Prophylaxis Hypothesis," *Hormones and Behavior* 59, no. 2 (2011): 271–275.

167 **Psychological scientist Martie Haselton writes:** Haselton, *Hormonal,* p. 76.

167 **Progesterone is associated with:** O. C. Schultheiss, A. Dargel, and W. Rohde, "Implicit Motives and Gonadal Steroid Hormones: Effects of Menstrual Cycle Phase, Oral Contraceptive Use, and Relationship Status," *Hormones and Behavior* 43, no. 2 (2003): 293–301.

167 **progesterone promotes calmness:** E. Timby et al., "Pharmacokinetic and Behavioral Effects of Allopregnanolone in Healthy Women," *Psychopharmacology* 186, no. 3 (2006): 414; A. Smith et al., "Cycles of Risk: Associations between Menstrual Cycle and Suicidal Ideation among Women," *Personality and Individual Differences* 74 (2015): 35–40.

167 **testosterone appears to regulate:** C. Eisenegger, J. Haushofer, and E. Fehr, "The Role of Testosterone in Social Interaction," *Trends in Cognitive Sciences* 15, no. 6 (2011): 263–271.

167 **risky activities, such as gambling:** S. J. Stanton, S. H. Liening, and O. C. Schultheiss, "Testosterone Is Positively Associated with Risk Taking in the Iowa

Gambling Task," *Hormones and Behavior* 59, no. 2 (2011): 252–256; see also J. M. Coates and J. Herbert, "Endogenous Steroids and Financial Risk Taking on a London Trading Floor," *Proceedings of the National Academy of Sciences* 105, no. 16 (2008): 6167–6172.

167 **having sexual relations with multiple partners:** S. M. van Anders, L. D. Hamilton, and N. V. Watson, "Multiple Partners Are Associated with Higher Testosterone in North American Men and Women," *Hormones and Behavior* 51, no. 3 (2007): 454–459.

167 **In "the smelly T-shirt study":** S. L. Miller, and J. K. Maner, "Scent of a Woman: Men's Testosterone Responses to Olfactory Ovulation Cues," *Psychological Science* 21, no. 2 (2010): 276–283.

168 **increase after achieving public success:** O. C. Schultheiss, K. L. Campbell, and D. C. McClelland, "Implicit Power Motivation Moderates Men's Testosterone Responses to Imagined and Real Dominance Success," *Hormones and Behavior* 36, no. 3 (1999): 234–241.

168 **male finches sing more:** M. Ritschard et al., "Enhanced Testosterone Levels Affect Singing Motivation but Not Song Structure and Amplitude in Bengalese Finches," *Physiology and Behavior* 102, no. 1 (2011): 30–35.

169 **aggressive behaviors increase testosterone:** Eisenegger et al., "The Role of Testosterone in Social Interaction."

169 **The compulsory education:** Committee on How People Learn II, *How People Learn II: Learners, Contexts and Cultures* (Washington, DC: National Academies Press, 2018), p. 21, free download at http://nap.edu/24783.

170 **Take Paul Simon:** P. Simon, personal communication, New York, September 19, 2013.

170 **As Linda Ronstadt said:** R. Lewis, "No Longer Singing, Linda Ronstadt's Latest Tour Is a Conversation with the Audience," *Los Angeles Times,* October 3, 2018, http://www.latimes.com/entertainment/music/la-et-ms-linda-ronstadt-conversation-20181003-story.html.

171 **Paul Simon again:** P. Simon, personal communication, New York, March 4, 2009.

171 **Two knowledge domains that are:** Committee on How People Learn II, *How People Learn II,* p. 21.

171 **Prior experience is a factor:** P. L. Ackerman and M. E. Beier, "Determinants of Domain Knowledge and Independent Study Learning in an Adult Sample," *Journal of Educational Psychology* 98, no. 2 (2006): 366–381; M. E. Beier and P. L. Ackerman, "Determinants of Health Knowledge: An Investigation of Age, Gender, Abilities, Personality, and Interests," *Journal of Personality and Social Psychology* 84, no. 2 (2003): 439–448; M. E. Beier and P. L. Ackerman, "Age, Ability, and the Role of Prior Knowledge on the Acquisition of New Domain Knowledge: Promising Results in a Real-World Learning Environment," *Psychology and Aging* 20, no. 2 (2005): 341–355, http://dx.doi.org/10.1037/0882-7974.20.2.341; M. E. Beier, C. K. Young, and A. J. Villado, "Job Knowledge: Its Definition, Development and Measurement," in *The Handbook of Industrial, Work, and Organization Psychology,* ed. D. Ones et al. (Los Angeles, CA: Sage, 2018).

171 **Physicians have an easier time comprehending:** V. L. Patel, G. J. Groen, and C. H. Frederiksen, "Differences between Medical Students and Doctors in Memory for Clinical Cases," *Medical Education* 20, no. 1 (1986): 3–9; see also B. L. Anderson-Montoya et al., "Running Memory for Clinical Handoffs: A Look at Active and Passive Processing," *Human Factors* 59, no. 3 (2017): 393–406.

173 **People who focus mainly on getting recognition:** E. L. Deci and R. M. Ryan, *Intrinsic Motivation and Self-Determination in Human Behavior* (New York: Plenum

Press, 1985); E. L. Deci and R. M. Ryan, "The 'What' and 'Why' of Goal Pursuits: Human Needs and the Self-Determination of Behavior," *Psychological Inquiry* 11 (2000): 227–268; R. M. Ryan and E. L. Deci, *Self-Determination Theory: Basic Psychological Needs in Motivation, Development, and Wellness* (New York: Guilford Publications, 2017).

173 ***even geniuses work hard*:** C. S. Dweck, "Even Geniuses Work Hard," *Educational Leadership* 68, no. 1 (2010): 16–20.

173 **Dweck describes two kinds of mind-sets:** C. S. Dweck, *Mindset: The New Psychology of Success* (New York: Penguin Random House, 2008).

173 **People with a fixed mind-set:** Some of these bullet points are from S. Levitin, *Heart and Sell* (Wayne, NJ: Career Press, 2017), p. 31.

174 **Dweck counsels the following:** C. Dweck, "Carol Dweck Revisits the Growth Mindset," *Education Week* 35, no. 5 (2015): 20–24.

174 **Older adults show increases in their motivation:** Committee on How People Learn II, *How People Learn II,* p. 21; L. L. Carstensen, D. M. Isaacowitz, and S. T. Charles, "Taking Time Seriously: A Theory of Socioemotional Selectivity," *American Psychologist* 54, no. 3 (1999): 165–181.

175 **I let my vigilance down for just thirty seconds:** D. J. Levitin, "Severed," *The New Yorker,* October 10, 2018, https://www.newyorker.com/culture/personal-history/severed.

175 **Tim Laddish (age seventy-seven), former senior assistant attorney general:** T. Laddish, email communication, October 29, 2018.

177 **But lottery winners tend not to be happy:** P. Brickman, D. Coates, and R. Janoff-Bulman, "Lottery Winners and Accident Victims: Is Happiness Relative?," *Journal of Personality and Social Psychology* 36, no. 8 (1978): 917.

177 **But paraplegics and quadriplegics adapt:** See also D. A. Schkade and D. Kahneman, "Does Living in California Make People Happy? A Focusing Illusion in Judgments of Life Satisfaction," *Psychological Science* 9, no. 5 (1998): 340–346; D. Gilbert, *Stumbling on Happiness* (Toronto: Vintage Canada, 2009); S. Lyubomirsky, *The Myths of Happiness: What Should Make You Happy, but Doesn't, What Shouldn't Make You Happy, but Does* (New York: Penguin, 2014).

177 **Vicente Fox:** V. Fox, personal communication, Léon, Mexico, May 18, 2018.

CHAPTER 6

179 **"*L'enfer, c'est les autres*":** I open with this quote because it is so well-known and rings true to many of us; we understand the desire to be free of the demands and irritating nature of others. But this is a misinterpretation of Sartre's line. He did not actually mean that one is happier hiding in isolation. What he meant is that we cannot escape the judgments of others, their watchful eyes, the shame we feel in our flaws being revealed to them. The full quote, from the play *No Exit,* is:

> All those eyes intent on me. Devouring me. What? Only two of you? I thought there were more; many more. So this is hell. I'd never have believed it. You remember all we were told about the torture-chambers, the fire and brimstone, the "burning marl." Old wives' tales! There's no need for red-hot pokers. HELL IS OTHER PEOPLE!

P. Caws, "To Hell and Back: Sartre on (and in) Analysis with Freud," *Sartre Studies International* 11, no. 1 (2005): 166–176. And Sartre himself said,

> "Hell is other people" has always been misunderstood. It has been thought that what I meant by that was that our relations with other people are always

poisoned, that they are invariably hellish relations. But what I really mean is something totally different. I mean that if relations with someone else are twisted, vitiated, then that other person can only be hell. Why? Because . . . when we think about ourselves, when we try to know ourselves, . . . we use the knowledge of us which other people already have. We judge ourselves with the means other people have and have given us for judging ourselves. Into whatever I say about myself someone else's judgment always enters. Into whatever I feel within myself someone else's judgment enters. . . . But that does not at all mean that one cannot have relations with other people. It simply brings out the capital importance of all other people for each one of us.

179 **Loneliness is associated with early mortality:** L. C. Hawkley and J. T. Cacioppo, "Loneliness Matters: A Theoretical and Empirical Review of Consequences and Mechanisms," *Annals of Behavioral Medicine* 40, no. 2 (2010): 218–227.

179 **It leads to inflammation:** L. M. Jaremka et al., "Loneliness Promotes Inflammation during Acute Stress," *Psychological Science* 24, no. 7 (2013): 1089–1097.

179 **it negates the beneficial effects of exercise:** A. M. Stranahan, D. Khalil, and E. Gould, "Social Isolation Delays the Positive Effects of Running on Adult Neurogenesis," *Nature Neuroscience* 9, no. 4 (2006): 526.

179 **worse for your health than smoking:** J. McGregor, "This Former Surgeon General Says There's a Loneliness Epidemic and Work Is Partly to Blame," *The Washington Post,* October 4, 2017, https://www.washingtonpost.com/news/on-leadership/wp/2017/10/04/this-former-surgeon-general-says-theres-a-loneliness-epidemic-and-work-is-partly-to-blame/.

179 **If you are chronically lonely:** J. Holt-Lunstad et al., "Loneliness and Social Isolation as Risk Factors for Mortality: A Meta-Analytic Review," *Perspectives on Psychological Science* 10, no. 2 (2015): 227–237.

180 **Government research in the UK:** Holt-Lunstad et al., "Loneliness and Social Isolation."

180 **Harvard political scientist Robert Putnam:** R. D. Putnam, "Bowling Alone: America's Declining Social Capital," in *Culture and Politics,* ed. L. Crothers and C. Lockhart, pp. 223–234 (New York: Palgrave Macmillan, 2000).

180 **Sociologist Eric Klinenberg:** E. Klinenberg, "Is Loneliness a Health Epidemic?," *The New York Times,* February 9, 2018, https://www.nytimes.com/2018/02/09/opinion/sunday/loneliness-health.html.

181 **(getting "likes" can produce an addictive hit of dopamine):** I previously wrote about this in D. J. Levitin, *The Organized Mind* (New York: Dutton, 2014).

181 **Proper brain functioning depends on:** M. Ankarcrona et al., "Glutamate-Induced Neuronal Death: A Succession of Necrosis or Apoptosis Depending on Mitochondrial Function," *Neuron* 15, no. 4 (1995): 961–973; R. Sattler and M. Tymianski, "Molecular Mechanisms of Glutamate Receptor-Mediated Excitotoxic Neuronal Cell Death," *Molecular Neurobiology* 24, nos. 1–3 (2001): 107–129.

181 **MSG does not significantly change levels of glutamate:** R. A. Hawkins, "The Blood-Brain Barrier and Glutamate," *American Journal of Clinical Nutrition* 90, no. 3 (2009): 867S–874S; M. B. Bogdanov and R. J. Wurtman, "Effects of Systemic or Oral Ad Libitum Monosodium Glutamate Administration on Striatal Glutamate Release, as Measured Using Microdialysis in Freely Moving Rats," *Brain Research* 660, no. 2 (1994): 337–340.

182 **psychedelics such as LSD and psilocybin:** F. X. Vollenweider and M. Kometer, "The Neurobiology of Psychedelic Drugs: Implications for the Treatment of Mood Disorders," *Nature Reviews Neuroscience* 11, no. 9 (2010): 642.

182 **and depression affect gene expression:** S. W. Cole et al., "Myeloid Differentiation Architecture of Leukocyte Transcriptome Dynamics in Perceived Social Isolation," *Proceedings of the National Academy of Sciences* 112, no. 49 (2015): 15142–15147.

182 **Social isolation co-opts the fear:** J. Rodriguez-Romaguera and G. D. Stuber, "Social Isolation Co-opts Fear and Aggression Circuits," *Cell* 173, no. 5 (2018): 1071–1072.

182 **After the threatening stimulus is removed:** K. Asahina et al., "Tachykinin-Expressing Neurons Control Male-Specific Aggressive Arousal in Drosophila," *Cell* 156, no. 1 (2014): 221–235.

182 **It also shows up in studies of emotion:** Y. Yang et al., "Neural Correlates of Proactive and Reactive Aggression in Adolescent Twins," *Aggressive Behavior* 43, no. 3 (2017): 230–240.

182 **Increases in putamen size are associated with higher aggression:** Yang et al., "Neural Correlates."

182 **reductions in putamen size:** L. W. De Jong et al., "Strongly Reduced Volumes of Putamen and Thalamus in Alzheimer's Disease: An MRI Study," *Brain* 131, no. 12 (2008): 3277–3285.

182 **The putamen may also modulate social anxiety:** F. Caravaggio et al., "Exploring Personality Traits Related to Dopamine D⅔ Receptor Availability in Striatal Subregions of Humans," *European Neuropsychopharmacology* 26, no. 4 (2016): 644–652; A. Laakso et al., "Prediction of Detached Personality in Healthy Subjects by Low Dopamine Transporter Binding," *American Journal of Psychiatry* 157, no. 2 (2000): 290–292.

183 **He raised infant monkeys in isolation:** H. F. Harlow and S. J. Suomi, "Social Recovery by Isolation-Reared Monkeys," *Proceedings of the National Academy of Sciences* 68, no. 7 (1971): 1534–1538.

185 **educational attainment has been associated with decreased allostatic load:** Å. M. Hansen et al., "School Education, Physical Performance in Late Midlife and Allostatic Load: A Retrospective Cohort Study," *Journal of Epidemiology and Community Health* 70 (2016): 748–754.

186 **In 1915, Dr. Henry Chapin:** H. D. Chapin, "Are Institutions for Infants Necessary?," *Journal of the American Medical Association* 64, no. 1 (1915): 1–3.

186 **Many Americans . . . rushed to adopt Romanian orphans:** T. Bahrampour, "A Lost Boy Finds His Calling," *The Washington Post,* January 30, 2014, https://www.washingtonpost.com/sf/style/2014/01/30/a-lost-boy-finds-his-calling/?utm_term=.cc5a7ffce49d.

187 **Early family experience is key not just to socialization:** K. L. Humphreys et al., "Foster Care Promotes Adaptive Functioning in Early Adolescence among Children Who Experienced Severe, Early Deprivation," *Journal of Child Psychology and Psychiatry* 59, no. 7 (2018): 811–821.

187 **As Charles Nelson notes:** T. Bahrampour, "Romanian Orphans Subjected to Deprivation Must Now Deal with Dysfunction," *The Washington Post,* January 30, 2014, https://www.washingtonpost.com/local/romanian-orphans-subjected-to-deprivation-must-now-deal-with-disfunction/2014/01/30/a9dbea6c-5d13-11e3-be07-006c776266ed_story.html?utm_term=.478da5126060.

188 **rates of autism among children raised in Mexico:** E. Fombonne et al., "Prevalence of Autism Spectrum Disorders in Guanajuato, Mexico: The Leon Survey," *Journal of Autism and Developmental Disorders* 46, no. 5 (2016): 1669–1685.

188 **"Loneliness is an especially tricky problem":** D. Khullar, "How Social Isolation Is Killing Us," *The New York Times,* December 22, 2016, https://www.nytimes.com/2016/12/22/upshot/how-social-isolation-is-killing-us.html.

188 **social isolation in the fruit fly:** K. Asahina et al., "Tachykinin-Expressing Neurons Control Male-Specific Aggressive Arousal in Drosophila," *Cell* 156, no. 1 (2014): 221–235.

188 **mRNA translation are highly similar:** J. Shih, R. Hodge, and M. A. Andrade-Navarro, "Comparison of Inter- and Intraspecies Variation in Humans and Fruit Flies," *Genomics Data* 3 (2015): 49–54.

189 **Social isolation for two weeks:** M. Zelikowsky et al., "The Neuropeptide Tac2 Controls a Distributed Brain State Induced by Chronic Social Isolation Stress," *Cell* 173, no. 5 (2018): 1265–1279.

189 **As Anderson says:** Cell Press, "One Way Social Isolation Changes the Mouse Brain," EurekAlert!, May 17, 2018, https://www.eurekalert.org/pub_releases/2018-05/cp-ows051018.php; see also Zelikowsky et al., "The Neuropeptide Tac2."

190 **Directly stimulating the nucleus accumbens:** V. Trezza et al., "Nucleus Accumbens μ-Opioid Receptors Mediate Social Reward," *Journal of Neuroscience* 31, no. 17 (2011): 6362–6370.

190 **Indirect stimulation, however, is possible in humans:** Trezza et al., "Nucleus Accumbens μ-Opioid Receptors."

190 **loneliness can be reduced simply by listening to music:** M. L. Chanda and D. J. Levitin, "The Neurochemistry of Music," *Trends in Cognitive Sciences* 17, no. 4 (2013): 179–193; V. Menon and D. J. Levitin, "The Rewards of Music Listening: Response and Physiological Connectivity of the Mesolimbic System," *Neuroimage* 28, no. 1 (2005): 175–184.

190 **"therapeutic lag":** S. M. Wang et al., "Five Potential Therapeutic Agents as Antidepressants: A Brief Review and Future Directions," *Expert Review of Neurotherapeutics* 15, no. 9 (2015): 1015–1029.

190 **Cognitive behavioral therapy . . . was shown in a Norwegian study:** H. M. Nordahl et al., "Paroxetine, Cognitive Therapy or Their Combination in the Treatment of Social Anxiety Disorder with and without Avoidant Personality Disorder: A Randomized Clinical Trial," *Psychotherapy and Psychosomatics* 85, no. 6 (2016): 346–356.

191 **learning to control lifestyle elements:** L. C. Hawkley and J. T. Cacioppo, "Loneliness Matters: A Theoretical and Empirical Review of Consequences and Mechanisms," *Annals of Behavioral Medicine* 40, no. 2 (2010): 218–227; S. Ni et al., "Effect of Gratitude on Loneliness of Chinese College Students: Social Support as a Mediator," *Social Behavior and Personality* 43, no. 4 (2015): 559–566.

191 **Those social benefits appear also to accrue:** C. Lim and R. D. Putnam, "Religion, Social Networks, and Life Satisfaction," *American Sociological Review* 75, no. 6 (2010): 914–933.

192 **Paul Tang:** Khullar, "How Social Isolation Is Killing Us."

192 **The Canadian Longitudinal Study on Aging:** Canadian Longitudinal Study on Aging, "Canadian Longitudinal Study on Aging Releases First Report on Health and Aging in Canada," May 22, 2018, https://www.clsa-elcv.ca/stay-informed/new-clsa/2018/canadian-longitudinal-study-aging-releases-first-report-health-and-aging.

192 **Befriending, matches up a volunteer with an older adult:** Befriending Networks, "What Is Befriending?," https://www.befriending.co.uk/aboutbefriending.php.

193 **British children's laureate Sir Michael Morpurgo writes:** https://www.broomhousecentre.org.uk/our-projects/youth-befriending/befriender-quotes-and-case-studies/.

194 **strategically and adaptively cultivating our social networks:** K. T. K. Lim and R. Yu, "Aging and Wisdom: Age-Related Changes in Economic and Social Decision Making," *Frontiers in Aging Neuroscience* 7 (2015): 120.

194 **In contrast, when constraints on time are perceived:** The structure and ideas of this paragraph were influenced by Lim and Yu, "Aging and Wisdom."

195 **socioemotional selectivity theory:** L. L. Carstensen and B. L. Fredrickson, "Influence of HIV Status and Age on Cognitive Representations of Others," *Health Psychology* 17, no. 6 (1998): 494; L. L. Carstensen, D. M. Isaacowitz, and S. T. Charles, "Taking Time Seriously: A Theory of Socioemotional Selectivity," *American Psychologist* 54, no. 3 (1999): 165; L. L. Carstensen, H. H. Fung, and S. T. Charles, "Socioemotional Selectivity Theory and the Regulation of Emotion in the Second Half of Life," *Motivation and Emotion* 27, no. 2 (2003): 103–123; C. E. Löckenhoff and L. L. Carstensen, "Socioemotional Selectivity Theory, Aging, and Health: The Increasingly Delicate Balance between Regulating Emotions and Making Tough Choices," *Journal of Personality* 72, no. 6 (2004): 1395–1424; L. L. Carstensen, "The Influence of a Sense of Time on Human Development," *Science* 312, no. 5782 (2006): 1913–1915.

195 **how we relate to the world:** J. Heckhausen, C. Wrosch, and R. Schulz, "A Motivational Theory of Life-Span Development," *Psychological Review* 117, no. 1 (2010): 32.

195 **better emotional balance:** Löckenhoff and Carstensen, "Socioemotional Selectivity Theory."

195 **less likely to experience negative thoughts as we age:** T. Hedden and J. D. Gabrieli, "Insights into the Ageing Mind: A View from Cognitive Neuroscience," *Nature Reviews Neuroscience* 5, no. 2 (2004): 87.

196 **exert some control over our environment:** L. A. Leotti, S. S. Iyengar, and K. N. Ochsner, "Born to Choose: The Origins and Value of the Need for Control," *Trends in Cognitive Sciences* 14, no. 10 (2010): 457–463.

197 **choice and responsibility in a nursing home:** E. J. Langer and J. Rodin, "The Effects of Choice and Enhanced Personal Responsibility for the Aged: A Field Experiment in an Institutional Setting," *Journal of Personality and Social Psychology* 34, no. 2 (1976): 191.

197 **Albert Bandura . . . uses the terms *agency* and *self-efficacy*:** A. Bandura and R. Wood, "Effect of Perceived Controllability and Performance Standards on Self-Regulation of Complex Decision Making," *Journal of Personality and Social Psychology* 56, no. 5 (1989): 805.

197 **great activity in the putamen when they *choose*:** E. M. Tricomi, M. R. Delgado, and J. A. Fiez, "Modulation of Caudate Activity by Action Contingency," *Neuron* 41, no. 2 (2004): 281–292; G. Coricelli et al., "Regret and Its Avoidance: A Neuroimaging Study of Choice Behavior," *Nature Neuroscience* 8, no. 9 (2005): 1255.

197 **Choosing . . . activates the brain's reward system:** Leotti, Iyengar, and Ochsner, "Born to Choose."

198 **friends and family play a critical role:** R. M. Ryan et al., "The Significance of Autonomy and Autonomy Support in Psychological Development and Psychopathology," in *Developmental Psychopathology,* vol. 1, *Theory and Method,* ed. D. Cicchetti and D. J. Cohen, pp. 795–849 (Hoboken, NJ: John Wiley and Sons, 2015).

200 **Anthony Mancinelli of New York:** C. Kilgannon, "The World's Oldest Barber Is 107 and Still Cutting Hair Full Time," *The New York Times,* October 7, 2018, https://www.nytimes.com/2018/10/07/nyregion/worlds-oldest-barber-anthony-mancinelli.html.

201 **Maxine Waters . . . "We moan and groan":** Y. Hayashi and R. Tracy, "Partisan or Deal Maker? Maxine Waters Rises as Banking Industry's Overseer," *The Wall Street Journal*, November 20, 2018, https://www.wsj.com/articles/partisan-or-deal-maker-maxine-waters-rises-as-banking-industrys-overseer-1542717000.

202 **pay more attention to the positive things in their lives:** A. P. Shimamura, *Get SMART! Five Steps toward a Healthy Brain* (Scotts Valley, CA: CreateSpace, 2017).

202 **Art Shimamura describes it this way:** Shimamura, *Get SMART!*.

202 **having a large social network:** Shimamura, *Get SMART!*.

202 **urgent need to identify lifestyle activities:** N. D. Anderson et al., "The Benefits Associated with Volunteering among Seniors: A Critical Review and Recommendations for Future Research," *Psychological Bulletin* 140, no. 6 (2014): 1505.

202 **volunteering is associated with reduced symptoms of depression:** Anderson et al., "The Benefits Associated with Volunteering."

203 **volunteering worldwide contributes:** International Labour Organization, *Manual on the Measurement of Volunteer Work* (Geneva, Switzerland: International Labour Organization, 2011).

203 **Volunteers in a controlled study showed improvements:** M. C. Carlson et al., "Exploring the Effects of an 'Everyday' Activity Program on Executive Function and Memory in Older Adults: Experience Corps," *Gerontologist* 48 (2008): 793–801.

203 **Volunteering in management or committee roles:** T. D. Windsor, K. J. Anstey, and B. Rodgers, "Volunteering and Psychological Well-Being among Young-Old Adults: How Much Is Too Much?," *Gerontologist* 48, no. 1 (2008): 59–70.

CHAPTER 7

205 **It hurts when I do this:** The subtitle of this chapter is from an old vaudeville joke. A man goes to his doctor, and, jerking his elbow hard and to the side, he says, "It hurts when I do this." The doctor replies, "Don't do that!"

205 **Pain accounts for 80 percent of trips to the doctor in the United States:** R. J. Gatchel et al., "The Biopsychosocial Approach to Chronic Pain: Scientific Advances and Future Directions," *Psychological Bulletin* 133, no. 4 (2007): 581.

206 **Anxiety has been shown to demonstrably increase pain:** C. S. Lin, S. Y. Wu, and C. A. Yi, "Association between Anxiety and Pain in Dental Treatment: A Systematic Review and Meta-analysis," *Journal of Dental Research* 96, no. 2 (2017): 153–162; M. Zhuo, "Neural Mechanisms Underlying Anxiety—Chronic Pain Interactions," *Trends in Neurosciences* 39, no. 3 (2016): 136–145.

206 **30 percent of the population is experiencing chronic pain:** N. D. Volkow and A. T. McLellan, "Opioid Abuse in Chronic Pain—Misconceptions and Mitigation Strategies," *New England Journal of Medicine* 374, no. 13 (2016): 1253–1263.

206 **The Global Burden of Disease Project:** World Health Organization, "About the Global Burden of Disease (GBD) Project," https://www.who.int/healthinfo/global_burden_disease/about/en/; http://www.healthdata.org/data-visualization/gbd-compare; R. Lozano et al., "Global and Regional Mortality from 235 Causes of Death for 20 Age Groups in 1990 and 2010: A Systematic Analysis for the Global Burden of Disease Study 2010," *Lancet* 380, no. 9859 (2012): 2095–2128.

207 **the project provides an interactive map:** http://www.healthdata.org/data-visualization/gbd-compare.

207 **The costs of treating chronic pain:** D. J. Gaskin and P. Richard, "The Economic Costs of Pain in the United States," *Journal of Pain* 13, no. 8 (2012): 715–724.

207 **the current opioid epidemic:** N. D. Volkow and A. T. McLellan, "Opioid Abuse in Chronic Pain—Misconceptions and Mitigation Strategies," *New England Journal of Medicine* 374, no. 13 (2016): 1253–1263.

209 **paper published just after World War II:** H. K. Beecher, "Pain in Men Wounded in Battle," *Annals of Surgery* 123, no. 1 (1946): 96.

209 **Pain also has an emotional, affective component:** The observation that sensory and affective components of pain are distinguishable was the basis for Melzack and Wall's (1965) paper, which launched the modern study of pain; R. Melzack and P. D. Wall, "Pain Mechanisms: A New Theory," *Science* 150 (1965): 971–979; see also J. Katz and B. N. Rosenbloom, "The Golden Anniversary of Melzack and Wall's Gate Control Theory of Pain: Celebrating 50 Years of Pain Research and Management," *Pain Research and Management* 20, no. 6 (2015): 285–286.

209 **"There was no dependable relation":** H. K. Beecher, "Relationship of Significance of Wound to Pain Experienced," *Journal of the American Medical Association* 161, no. 17 (1956): 1609–1613.

210 **the brain can override everything:** Melzack and Wall, "Pain Mechanisms."

211 **McGill Pain Questionnaire:** R. Melzack, "The McGill Pain Questionnaire from Description to Measurement," *Anesthesiology* 103, no. 1 (2005): 199–202.

211 **"the sensory components of pain and the feeling-related components":** R. D. Treede et al., "The Cortical Representation of Pain," *Pain* 79, nos. 2–3 (1999): 105–111.

213 **lower resolution for distinguishing touch in different parts of your body:** There's a separate cortical representation map for motor movements, also derived by Penfield, with a linear map of how muscles from head to toe are represented in the brain. The muscles of the face and pharynx take up about 40 percent of all your motor cortex, and the hands take up another 30 percent. That means that controlling the entire rest of your body gets only 30 percent of the cortex. That 70 percent allows us to speak, to gesture while we speak, and to play musical instruments. The 30 percent dedicated to the hands is what allows watchmakers and painters and other highly skilled professionals to pursue their work, and research shows that those areas become enlarged with more training and experience.

213 **The different types of pain . . . map to different brain regions:** M. C. Bushnell, M. Čeko, and L. A. Low, "Cognitive and Emotional Control of Pain and Its Disruption in Chronic Pain," *Nature Reviews Neuroscience* 14, no. 7 (2013): 502.

214 **cutaneous pain . . . and visceral pain . . . are experienced very differently:** I. A. Strigo et al., "Psychophysical Analysis of Visceral and Cutaneous Pain in Human Subjects," *Pain* 97, no. 3 (2002): 235–246. Subjects were subjected to heat pain on their chest, or a balloon was inflated in their esophagus. The esophageal balloon creates a discomfort similar to the endorectal balloon sometimes used in endoscopy. The cutaneous heat used was up to 46 degrees Celsius (115 degrees Fahrenheit), and the visceral pressure was up to 40 mmHg.

215 **visceral pain is more difficult to localize:** Strigo et al., "Psychophysical Analysis."

215 **This leads to a certain imprecision:** F. Cervero and L. A. Connell, "Distribution of Somatic and Visceral Primary Afferent Fibres within the Thoracic Spinal Cord

of the Cat," *Journal of Comparative Neurology* 230, no. 1 (1984): 88–98; F. Cervero and L. A. Connell, "Fine Afferent Fibers from Viscera Do Not Terminate in the Substantia Gelatinosa of the Thoracic Spinal Cord," *Brain Research* 294, no. 2 (1984): 370–374.

215 **Visceral pain in turn elicits greater activation:** I. A. Strigo et al., "Differentiation of Visceral and Cutaneous Pain in the Human Brain," *Journal of Neurophysiology* 89 (2003): 3294–3303.

216 **Administration of ketamine:** I. A. Strigo et al., "The Effects of Racemic Ketamine on Painful Stimulation of Skin and Viscera in Human Subjects," *Pain* 113, no. 3 (2005): 255–264.

216 **The anticipation of pain lights up:** P. Raineville, "Brain Mechanisms of Pain Affect and Pain Modulation," *Current Opinion in Neurobiology* 12 (2002): 195–204.

217 **toddlers with HSAD/CIPA:** L. Sztriha et al., "Congenital Insensitivity to Pain with Anhidrosis," *Pediatric Neurology* 25, no. 1 (2001): 63–66.

217 **Twenty percent of people with this disorder:** S. Mardy et al., "Congenital Insensitivity to Pain with Anhidrosis (CIPA): Effect of TRKA (NTRK1) Missense Mutations on Autophosphorylation of the Receptor Tyrosine Kinase for Nerve Growth Factor," *Human Molecular Genetics* 10, no. 3 (2001): 179–188.

217 **The *SCN9A* gene encodes for:** NIH, US National Library of Medicine, Genetics Home Reference, "SCN9A Gene," https://ghr.nlm.nih.gov/gene/SCN9A#location.

218 **Another type of HSAD:** E. M. Nagasako, A. L. Oaklander, and R. H. Dworkin, "Congenital Insensitivity to Pain: An Update," *Pain* 101, no. 3 (2003): 213–219.

218 **reaction to pain typically follows a sequence:** P. D. Wall, *Pain: The Science of Suffering* (New York: Columbia University Press, 2000).

218 **acute, short-term pain has survival value:** R. Y. Hwang et al., "Nociceptive Neurons Protect Drosophila Larvae from Parasitoid Wasps," *Current Biology* 17, no. 24 (2007): 2105–2116; Nagasako et al., "Congenital Insensitivity to Pain."

218 **purpose of chronic pain:** R. J. Crook et al., "Nociceptive Sensitization Reduces Predation Risk," *Current Biology* 24, no. 10 (2014): 1121–1125.

218 **"They responded more strongly to visual stimuli":** D. Netburn, "What Injured Squid Can Teach Us about Irritability and Pain," *Los Angeles Times*, May 8, 2014.

219 **humans in pain can be more attentive:** L. Tiemann et al., "Behavioral and Neuronal Investigations of Hypervigilance in Patients with Fibromyalgia Syndrome," *PLoS One* 7, no. 4 (2012): e35068.

219 **culture defines what is acceptable:** S. Linton, *Understanding Pain for Better Clinical Practice: A Psychological Perspective*, vol. 16 (New York: Elsevier Health Sciences, 2005), p. 15.

219 **people of different ethnicities experience and communicate pain:** R. Moore and I. Brodsgaard, "Cross-Cultural Investigations of Pain," *Epidemiology of Pain* (1999): 53–80.

220 **Parents may encourage a more stoic view:** Linton, *Understanding Pain*, p. 14.

220 **As psychological scientist Steven Linton says:** Linton, *Understanding Pain*, p. 3.

220 **the enormous success of placebos:** D. D. Price, D. G. Finniss, and F. Benedetti, "A Comprehensive Review of the Placebo Effect: Recent Advances and Current Thought," *Annual Review of Psychology* 59 (2008): 565–590.

220 **a placebo was effective in 35 percent of patients:** R. Dobrila-Dintinjana and A. Načinović-Duletić, "Placebo in the Treatment of Pain," *Collegium Antropologicum* 35, no. 2 (2011): 319–323.

220 **chronic knee osteoarthritis:** P. Tétreault et al., "Brain Connectivity Predicts Placebo Response across Chronic Pain Clinical Trials," *PLoS Biology* 14, no. 10 (2016): e1002570.

221 **placebo effects in acupuncture:** M. Cummings, "Modellvorhaben Akupunktur—a Summary of the ART, ARC and GERAC Trials," *Acupuncture in Medicine* 27, no. 1 (2009): 26–30; K. Linde et al., "The Impact of Patient Expectations on Outcomes in Four Randomized Controlled Trials of Acupuncture in Patients with Chronic Pain," *Pain* 128, no. 3 (2007): 264–271; D. C. Cherkin et al., "A Randomized Trial Comparing Acupuncture, Simulated Acupuncture, and Usual Care for Chronic Low Back Pain," *Archives of Internal Medicine* 169, no. 9 (2009): 858–866.

221 **the gene that confers red hair:** J. S. Mogil et al., "Melanocortin-1 Receptor Gene Variants Affect Pain and μ-opioid Analgesia in Mice and Humans," *Journal of Medical Genetics* 42, no. 7 (2005): 583–587.

222 **response to stress and pain can be passed to infants:** D. Francis et al., "Nongenomic Transmission across Generations of Maternal Behavior and Stress Responses in the Rat," *Science* 286, no. 5442 (1999): 1155–1158.

222 **Nobel Prize–winning psychologist Daniel Kahneman:** D. Kahneman et al., "When More Pain Is Preferred to Less: Adding a Better End," *Psychological Science* 4, no. 6 (1993): 401–405.

223 **A central goal of modern medical practice:** Linton, *Understanding Pain,* p. 14.

223 **the recent North American opioid epidemic:** US Department of Health and Human Services, "What Is the U.S. Opioid Epidemic?," January 22, 2019, https://www.hhs.gov/opioids/about-the-epidemic/index.html; National Institute on Drug Abuse, "Opioid Overdose Crisis," January 2019, https://www.drugabuse.gov/drugs-abuse/opioids/opioid-overdose-crisis.

223 **switch from oral to topical analgesics:** T. J. Atkinson et al., "Medication Pain Management in the Elderly: Unique and Underutilized Analgesic Treatment Options," *Clinical Therapeutics* 35, no. 11 (2013): 1669–1689.

224 **The most used NSAID worldwide is diclofenac:** B. R. Da Costa et al., "Effectiveness of Non-Steroidal Anti-Inflammatory Drugs for the Treatment of Pain in Knee and Hip Osteoarthritis: A Network Meta-Analysis," *Lancet* 390, no. 10090 (2017): e21–e33.

224 **The oral version of diclofenac:** C. A. Heyneman, C. Lawless-Liday, and G. C. Wall, "Oral versus Topical NSAIDs in Rheumatic Diseases," *Drugs* 60, no. 3 (2000): 555–574.

224 **Yoga practice enlarges the insula:** C. Villemure et al., "Insular Cortex Mediates Increased Pain Tolerance in Yoga Practitioners," *Cerebral Cortex* 24, no. 10 (2013): 2732–2740. Several styles of yoga were studied: the practice of physical postures (*asana* in Sanskrit), breathing exercises (*pranayama*), concentration exercises that focus and stabilize attention (*dharana*), and meditation (*dhyana*).

224 **Mild exercise can reduce pain:** M. H. Pitcher et al., "Modest Amounts of Voluntary Exercise Reduce Pain- and Stress-Related Outcomes in a Rat Model of Persistent Hind Limb Inflammation," *Journal of Pain* 18, no. 6 (2017): 687–701.

224 **"Exercise is the best analgesic":** J. Mogil, personal communication, July 20, 2019.

225 **Neuropathy affects nearly 8 percent of older adults:** R. W. Shields, "Peripheral Neuropathy," August 2010, www.clevelandclinicmeded.com/medicalpubs/diseasemanagement/neurology/peripheral-neuropathy/.

225 **blocking substance P could relieve pain:** R. Hill, "NK1 (Substance P) Receptor Antagonists—Why Are They Not Analgesic in Humans?," *Trends in Pharmacological Sciences* 21, no. 7 (2000): 244–246.

225 **regulating mood, anxiety, and stress:** K. Ebner and N. Singewald, "The Role of Substance P in Stress and Anxiety Responses," *Amino Acids* 31, no. 3 (2006): 251–272.

225 **the growth of new neurons:** S. W. Park et al., "Substance P Is a Promoter of Adult Neural Progenitor Cell Proliferation under Normal and Ischemic Conditions," *Journal of Neurosurgery* 107, no. 3 (2007): 593–599.

225 **wound healing, and the growth of new cells:** T. W. Reid et al., "Stimulation of Epithelial Cell Growth by the Neuropeptide Substance P," *Journal of Cellular Biochemistry* 52, no. 4 (1993): 476–485; S. M. Brown et al., "Neurotrophic and Anhidrotic Keratopathy Treated with Substance P and Insulinlike Growth Factor 1," *Archives of Ophthalmology* 115, no. 7 (1997): 926–927.

225 **Pain in one part of the skin can cause:** V. Gangadharan and R. Kuner, "Pain Hypersensitivity Mechanisms at a Glance," *Disease Models and Mechanisms* 6, no. 4 (2013): 889–895.

226 **Allodynia can occur:** A. Latremoliere and C. J. Woolf, "Central Sensitization: A Generator of Pain Hypersensitivity by Central Neural Plasticity," *Journal of Pain* 10, no. 9 (2009): 895–926.

226 **relief from notalgia paresthetica through exercise:** A. B. Fleischer, T. J. Meade, and A. B. Fleischer, "Notalgia Paresthetica: Successful Treatment with Exercises," *Acta Dermato-venereologica* 91, no. 3 (2011): 356–357.

227 **distraction diminishes pain signals in the insula:** M. C. Bushnell, M. Čeko, and L. A. Low, "Cognitive and Emotional Control of Pain and Its Disruption in Chronic Pain," *Nature Reviews Neuroscience* 14, no. 7 (2013): 502.

227 **Effective distraction while in pain:** N. J. Stagg et al., "Regular Exercise Reverses Sensory Hypersensitivity in a Rat Neuropathic Pain Model: Role of Endogenous Opioids," *Anesthesiology* 114, no. 4 (2011): 940–948.

227 **Steven Linton describes the role of an enriched environment:** Linton, *Understanding Pain*, p. 28.

228 **This lowering of the general pain threshold:** K. B. Jensen et al., "Evidence of Dysfunctional Pain Inhibition in Fibromyalgia Reflected in rACC during Provoked Pain," *Pain* 144, nos. 1–2 (2009): 95–100; M. N. Baliki et al., "Chronic Pain and the Emotional Brain: Specific Brain Activity Associated with Spontaneous Fluctuations of Intensity of Chronic Back Pain," *Journal of Neuroscience* 26, no. 47 (2006): 12165–12173.

229 **Structural brain changes have been observed:** K. D. Davis and M. Moayedi, "Central Mechanisms of Pain Revealed through Functional and Structural MRI," *Journal of Neuroimmune Pharmacology* 8, no. 3 (2013): 518–534.

229 **"The original Phase 2 study":** J. Mogil, personal communication, June 5, 2018.

231 **The side effects of polypharmacy:** M. C. S. Rodrigues and C. D. Oliveira, "Drug-Drug Interactions and Adverse Drug Reactions in Polypharmacy among Older Adults: An Integrative Review," *Revista Latino-Americana de Enfermagem* (2016): 24.

231 **primary cause of confusion:** O. C. Gleason, "Delirium," *American Family Physician* 67, no. 5 (2003): 1027–1034.

PART TWO

234 **Faulty or misaligned internal clocks:** A. A. Kondratova and R. V. Kondratov, "The Circadian Clock and Pathology of the Ageing Brain," *Nature Reviews Neuroscience* 13, no. 5 (2012): 325.

CHAPTER 8

235 **Have you ever woken in the middle:** This opening gambit was inspired by that used by U. Schibler and P. Sassone-Corsi, "A Web of Circadian Pacemakers," *Cell* 111, no. 7 (2002): 919–922.

235 **Circadian rhythms are:** T. Roenneberg and M. Merrow, "The Circadian Clock and Human Health," *Current Biology* 26, no. 10 (2016): R432–R443.

235 **Biological clocks evolved early in evolutionary history:** J. C. Dunlap and J. J. Loros, "Making Time: Conservation of Biological Clocks from Fungi to Animals," *Microbiology Spectrum* 5, no. 3 (2017).

235 **Clocks have also been found in a bread mold:** R. Lehmann et al., "Morning and Evening Peaking Rhythmic Genes Are Regulated by Distinct Transcription Factors in *Neurospora crassa,*" in *Information and Communication Theory in Molecular Biology,* ed. M. Bossert, Lecture Notes in Bioengineering (Cham, Switzerland: Springer, 2018).

236 **In the aplysia, scientists have found:** L. L. Moroz et al., "Neuronal Transcriptome of Aplysia: Neuronal Compartments and Circuitry," *Cell* 127, no. 7 (2006): 1453–1467.

236 **clocks orchestrate the opening and closing of leaf:** Genetic Science Learning Center, "The Time of Our Lives," March 1, 2016, https://learn.genetics.utah.edu/content/basics/clockgenes/.

236 **They also exert a large influence on aging:** O. Froy, "Circadian Rhythms, Aging, and Life Span in Mammals," *Physiology* 26, no. 4 (2011): 225–235; H. Li and E. Satinoff, "Fetal Tissue Containing the Suprachiasmatic Nucleus Restores Multiple Circadian Rhythms in Old Rats," *American Journal of Physiology—Regulatory, Integrative and Comparative Physiology* 275, no. 6 (1998): R1735–R1744.

237 **All cells in the brain and body:** In humans, clocks are presumed to exist in every cell; they have been found in the adrenal glands, esophagus, lungs, liver, pancreas, spleen, thymus, skin, and brain.

237 **Our SCN . . . is sensitive to inputs from the retina:** S. B. S. Khalsa et al., "A Phase Response Curve to Single Bright Light Pulses in Human Subjects," *Journal of Physiology* 549, no. 3 (2003): 945–952; K. N. Paul, T. B. Saafir, and G. Tosini, "The Role of Retinal Photoreceptors in the Regulation of Circadian Rhythms," *Reviews in Endocrine and Metabolic Disorders* 10, no. 4 (2009): 271–278; J. M. Zeitzer et al., "Response of the Human Circadian System to Millisecond Flashes of Light," *PLoS One* 6, no. 7 (2011): e22078; P. C. Zee and P. Manthena, "The Brain's Master Circadian Clock: Implications and Opportunities for Therapy of Sleep Disorders," *Sleep Medicine Reviews* 11, no. 1 (2007): 59–70.

237 **The SCN communicates time-of-day information:** C. Dibner and U. Schibler, "Circadian Timing of Metabolism in Animal Models and Humans," *Journal of Internal Medicine* 277, no. 5 (2015): 513–527.

237 **Tissues in the liver and pancreas regulate:** S. Hood and S. Amir, "The Aging Clock: Circadian Rhythms and Later Life," *Journal of Clinical Investigation* 127, no. 2 (2017): 437–446.

238 **The timing of meals:** G. Asher and P. Sassone-Corsi, "Time for Food: The Intimate Interplay between Nutrition, Metabolism, and the Circadian Clock," *Cell* 161 (2015): 84–93.

239 **SCN can regulate the microbiome:** Asher and Sassone-Corsi, "Time for Food."

239 **Different chronotypes have a genetic:** T. Roenneberg, "What Is Chronotype?," *Sleep and Biological Rhythms* 10, no. 2 (2012): 75–76; T. Roenneberg, A. Wirz-Justice, and M. Merrow, "Life between Clocks: Daily Temporal Patterns of Human Chronotypes," *Journal of Biological Rhythms* 18, no. 1 (2003): 80–90.

240 **waking their body up before it is biologically ready:** E. Laber-Warren, "Up for the Job? Check the Clock," *The New York Times,* December 25, 2018, p. D1.

240 **an experiment at the ThyssenKrupp steel factory:** C. Vetter et al., "Aligning Work and Circadian Time in Shift Workers Improves Sleep and Reduces Circadian Disruption," *Current Biology* 25, no. 7 (2015): 907–911.

241 **Once their chronotypes were aligned:** Laber-Warren, "Up for the Job?"

241 **sleep deprivation is responsible for some of the worst industrial disasters:** S. Horstmann et al., "Sleepiness-Related Accidents in Sleep Apnea Patients," *Sleep* 23, no. 3 (2000): 383–392.

241 **"Some must watch while some must sleep":** W. Shakespeare, *The Tragedy of Hamlet,* act 3, scene 2.

241 **The sentinel hypothesis is:** D. R. Samson et al., "Chronotype Variation Drives Night-Time Sentinel-like Behaviour in Hunter-Gatherers," *Proceedings of the Royal Society B: Biological Sciences* 284, no. 1858 (2017): 20170967.

241 **Chronotype is heritable:** D. A. Kalmbach et al., "Genetic Basis of Chronotype in Humans: Insights from Three Landmark GWAS," *Sleep* 40, no. 2 (2017).

241 **researchers analyzed the genomes of seven hundred thousand Britons:** S. E. Jones et al., "Genome-wide Association Analyses of Chronotype in 697,828 Individuals Provides Insights into Circadian Rhythms," *Nature Communications* 10, no. 1 (2019): 343.

242 **"poorly sleeping grandparent hypothesis":** Samson et al., "Chronotype Variation."

242 **The Hadza are a group of about twelve hundred people:** F. Marlowe, *The Hadza: Hunter-Gatherers of Tanzania* (Berkeley: University of California Press, 2010).

243 **signaling deficit is due to loss:** S. Michel, G. D. Block, and J. H. Meijer, "The Aging Clock," in *Circadian Medicine,* 1st ed., ed. C. S. Colwell, pp. 321–335 (Hoboken, NJ: John Wiley and Sons, 2015).

243 **transplanting young tissue into the SCN of hamsters:** M. W. Hurd and M. R. Ralph, "The Significance of Circadian Organization for Longevity in the Golden Hamster," *Journal of Biological Rhythms* 13, no. 5 (1998): 430–436; H. Li and E. Satinoff, "Fetal Tissue Containing the Suprachiasmatic Nucleus Restores Multiple Circadian Rhythms in Old Rats," *American Journal of Physiology—Regulatory, Integrative and Comparative Physiology* 275, no. 6 (1998): R1735–R1744.

244 **rhythms of the genes *PER1* and *PER2*:** Hood and Amir, "The Aging Clock."

244 **Postmortem studies of dementia patients' brains:** D. G. Harper et al., "Dorsomedial SCN Neuronal Subpopulations Subserve Different Functions in Human Dementia," *Brain* 131, no. 6 (2008): 1609–1617; Michel et al., "The Aging Clock."

245 **Repetitive disturbances of the circadian rhythm:** M. H. Smolensky et al., "Circadian Disruption: New Clinical Perspective of Disease Pathology and Basis for Chronotherapeutic Intervention," *Chronobiology International* 33, no. 8 (2016): 1101–1119.

245 **Sundowner's syndrome:** Michel et al., "The Aging Clock."

246 **time-zone shift:** S. Forbes-Robertson et al., "Circadian Disruption and Remedial Interventions," *Sports Medicine* 42, no. 3 (2012): 185–208.

246 **Eating within two hours of bedtime:** M. P. Mattson et al., "Meal Frequency and Timing in Health and Disease," *Proceedings of the National Academy of Sciences* 111, no. 47 (2014): 16647–16653.

246 **Alcohol is known to disrupt sleep cycles:** C. B. Forsyth et al., "Circadian Rhythms, Alcohol and Gut Interactions," *Alcohol* 49, no. 4 (2015): 389–398; G. R. Swanson et al., "Decreased Melatonin Secretion Is Associated with Increased Intestinal Permeability and Marker of Endotoxemia in Alcoholics," *American Journal*

of Physiology—Gastrointestinal and Liver Physiology 308, no. 12 (2015): G1004–G1011.

247 **high-fat diets tend to advance the clock:** K. Eckel-Mahan and P. Sassone-Corsi, "Metabolism and the Circadian Clock Converge," *Physiological Reviews* 93, no. 1 (2013): 107–135; V. Leone et al., "Effects of Diurnal Variation of Gut Microbes and High-Fat Feeding on Host Circadian Clock Function and Metabolism," *Cell Host and Microbe* 17, no. 5 (2015): 681–689; A. Zarrinpar et al., "Diet and Feeding Pattern Affect the Diurnal Dynamics of the Gut Microbiome," *Cell Metabolism* 20, no. 6 (2014): 1006–1017.

247 **Light therapy and melatonin treatments:** Kondratova and Kondratov, "The Circadian Clock"; R. F. Riemersma-Van Der Lek et al., "Effect of Bright Light and Melatonin on Cognitive and Noncognitive Function in Elderly Residents of Group Care Facilities: A Randomized Controlled Trial," *Journal of the American Medical Association* 299, no. 22 (2008): 2642–2655.

247 **effective in people with Alzheimer's:** D. P. Cardinali, A. M. Furio, and L. I. Brusco, "Clinical Aspects of Melatonin Intervention in Alzheimer's Disease Progression," *Current Neuropharmacology* 8, no. 3 (2010): 218–227.

247 **In lab studies, melatonin interacts with beta-amyloid protein:** R. Hornedo-Ortega et al., "In Vitro Effects of Serotonin, Melatonin, and Other Related Indole Compounds on Amyloid-β Kinetics and Neuroprotection," *Molecular Nutrition and Food Research* 62, no. 3 (2018): 1700383; M. Shukla et al., "Mechanisms of Melatonin in Alleviating Alzheimer's Disease," *Current Neuropharmacology* 15, no. 7 (2017): 1010–1031.

247 **melatonin use in early-stage Alzheimer's:** A. de Jonghe et al., "Effectiveness of Melatonin Treatment on Circadian Rhythm Disturbances in Dementia. Are There Implications for Delirium? A Systematic Review," *International Journal of Geriatric Psychiatry* 25, no. 12 (2010): 1201–1208.

247 **noticeable individual differences in how melatonin:** A. J. Lewy, "Circadian Misalignment in Mood Disturbances," *Current Psychiatry Reports* 11, no. 6 (2009): 459; A. J. Lewy, "Clinical Implications of the Melatonin Phase Response Curve," *Journal of Clinical Endocrinology and Metabolism* 95, no. 7 (2010): 3158–3160.

248 **Sleep-medicine specialist Alfonso Padilla:** A. Padilla, personal communication, August 26, 2019.

248 **next most effective treatment:** A. M. Schroeder et al., "Voluntary Scheduled Exercise Alters Diurnal Rhythms of Behaviour, Physiology and Gene Expression in Wild-Type and Vasoactive Intestinal Peptide-Deficient Mice," *Journal of Physiology* 590, no. 23 (2012): 6213–6226; Y. Yamanaka et al., "Physical Exercise Accelerates Reentrainment of Human Sleep-Wake Cycle but Not of Plasma Melatonin Rhythm to 8-H Phase-Advanced Sleep Schedule," *American Journal of Physiology—Regulatory, Integrative and Comparative Physiology* 298, nos. 3 (2009): R681–R691.

248 **Caffeine is one of the most:** J. W. Daly, J. Holmen, and B. B. Fredholm, "Is Caffeine Addictive? The Most Widely Used Psychoactive Substance in the World Affects Same Parts of the Brain as Cocaine," *Lakartidningen* 95, nos. 51–52 (1998): 5878–5883.

248 **caffeine interferes with the human circadian clock:** M. Lazarus et al., "Adenosine and Sleep," in *Handbook of Experimental Pharmacology*, ed. J. Barret (Berlin: Springer, 2017).

248 **lengthen the daytime activity rhythm in fruit flies:** T. M. Burke et al., "Effects of Caffeine on the Human Circadian Clock In Vivo and In Vitro," *Science Translational Medicine* 7, no. 305 (2015): 305ra146.

248 **The detrimental effects of caffeine on sleep:** Clark and Landolt, "Coffee, Caffeine, and Sleep."

249 **Using cultured cells in vitro:** Burke et al., "Effects of Caffeine."

249 **elite athletes . . . chronotype:** M. Lastella et al., "The Chronotype of Elite Athletes," *Journal of Human Kinetics* 54, no. 1 (2016): 219–225.

250 **Because chronotypes fall along a continuum:** L. C. Roden, T. D. Rudner, and D. E. Rae, "Impact of Chronotype on Athletic Performance: Current Perspectives," *ChronoPhysiology and Therapy* 7 (2017): 1–6; J. A. Vitale and A. Weydahl, "Chronotype, Physical Activity, and Sport Performance: A Systematic Review," *Sports Medicine* 47, no. 9 (2017): 1859–1868.

250 **An elite runner who:** S. Forbes-Robertson et al., "Circadian Disruption and Remedial Interventions," *Sports Medicine* 42, no. 3 (2012): 185–208.

250 **affect performance in American football:** J. Roy and G. Forest, "Greater Circadian Disadvantage during Evening Games for the National Basketball Association (NBA), National Hockey League (NHL) and National Football League (NFL) Teams Travelling Westward," *Journal of Sleep Research* 27, no. 1 (2017): 86–89; A. Song, T. Severini, and R. Allada, "How Jet Lag Impairs Major League Baseball Performance," *Proceedings of the National Academy of Sciences* 114, no. 6 (2017): 1407–1412.

250 **decoupling can cause problems:** Kondratova and Kondratov, "The Circadian Clock."

CHAPTER 9

251 **tomatoes *are* good for you:** S. Agarwal and A. V. Rao, "Tomato Lycopene and Its Role in Human Health and Chronic Diseases," *Canadian Medical Association Journal* 163, no. 6 (2000): 739–744; A. V. Rao and L. G. Rao, "Carotenoids and Human Health," *Pharmacological Research* 55, no. 3 (2007): 207–216.

252 **The American Medical Association has admonished:** J. C. Tilburt, M. Allyse, and F. W. Hafferty, "The Case of Dr. Oz: Ethics, Evidence, and Does Professional Self-Regulation Work?," *AMA Journal of Ethics* 19, no. 2 (2017): 199–206.

253 **their glucose metabolism:** A. Astrup and M. F. Hjorth, "Low-Fat or Low Carb for Weight Loss? It Depends on Your Glucose Metabolism," *EBioMedicine* 22 (2017): 20–21.

253 **the activity of lipoprotein lipase:** R. H. Eckel, ed., *Obesity: Mechanisms and Clinical Management* (Philadelphia: Lippincott Williams and Wilkins, 2003).

253 **genetic factors:** E. Topol, "The A.I. Diet," *The New York Times,* March 3, 2019, p. SR1.

253 **nutrigenomics promises to fill this gap:** M. Müller and S. Kersten, "Nutrigenomics: Goals and Strategies," *Nature Reviews Genetics* 4, no. 4 (2003): 315.

254 **Stanford nutrition scientist Christopher Gardner:** S. Ipaktchian, "Read This and Lose 50 Pounds," *Stanford Medicine Magazine,* Fall 2007, http://sm.stanford.edu/archive/stanmed/2007fall/diet.html; see also C. D. Gardner et al., "Comparison of the Atkins, Zone, Ornish, and LEARN Diets for Change in Weight and Related Risk Factors among Overweight Premenopausal Women: The A to Z Weight Loss Study: A Randomized Trial," *Journal of the American Medical Association* 297, no. 9 (2007): 969–977.

254 **People on a diet typically:** R. H. Eckel, "The Dietary Approach to Obesity: Is It the Diet or the Disorder?," *Journal of the American Medical Association* 293, no. 1 (2005): 96–97.

254 **a research article that compared:** M. L. Dansinger et al., "Comparison of the Atkins, Ornish, Weight Watchers, and Zone Diets for Weight Loss and Heart Disease Risk Reduction: A Randomized Trial," *Journal of the American Medical Association* 293, no. 1 (2005): 43–53.

255 **restricting dietary carbohydrates offers:** C. B. Ebbeling et al., "Effects of a Low Carbohydrate Diet on Energy Expenditure during Weight Loss Maintenance: Randomized Trial," *British Medical Journal* 363 (2018): k4583.

255 **Kevin Hall, senior investigator:** K. D. Hall and J. Guo, "Carbs versus Fat: Does It Really Matter for Maintaining Lost Weight?," *bioRxiv* (2019): 476655.

255 **a diet purported to treat cancer:** N. Gonzalez, "The Gonzalez Protocol," n.d., https://www.dr-gonzalez.com/case-reports/.

256 **he had to pay $2.5 million:** S. Lerner, "When Medicine Is Murder," *The Village Voice,* March 26, 2002.

256 **20 percent of Indian-manufactured Ayurvedic:** R. B. Phillips et al., "Lead, Mercury, and Arsenic in US- and Indian-manufactured Ayurvedic Medicines Sold via the Internet," *Journal of the American Medical Association* 300, no. 8 (2008): 915–923; Centers for Disease Control and Prevention, "Lead Poisoning Associated with Ayurvedic Medications—Five States, 2000–2003," *Morbidity and Mortality Weekly Report* 53, no. 26 (2004): 582–584.

256 **consumers who are contemplating alternative:** Mayo Clinic Staff, "Integrative Medicine: Evaluate CAM Claims," 2018, https://www.mayoclinic.org/healthy-lifestyle/consumer-health/in-depth/alternative-medicine/art-20046087.

256 ***Scientific American* went to:** M. Wenner Moyer, "Why Almost Everything Dean Ornish Says about Nutrition Is Wrong," *Scientific American,* 2015, https://www.scientificamerican.com/article/why-almost-everything-dean-ornish-says-about-nutrition-is-wrong/.

257 **increased production of free radicals:** S. Liou, "About Free Radical Damage," Huntington's Outreach Project for Education at Stanford, June 29, 2011, https://hopes.stanford.edu/about-free-radical-damage/.

258 **a number of built-in antioxidant mechanisms:** T. A. Polk, *The Aging Brain* (Chantilly, VA: The Great Courses, 2016); Khan Academy, "Introduction to Cellular Respiration and Redox," n.d., https://www.khanacademy.org/science/biology/cellular-respiration-and-fermentation/intro-to-cellular-respiration/a/intro-to-cellular-respiration-and-redox; R. Boumis, "What Is Being Oxidized and What Is Being Reduced in Cell Respiration?," *Sciencing,* May 29, 2019, https://sciencing.com/being-oxidized-being-reduced-cell-respiration-17081.html. This excerpt from an article by Lobo et al. fills in some more detail:

> The term [oxidative stress] is used to describe the condition of oxidative damage resulting when the critical balance between free radical generation and antioxidant defenses is unfavorable. Oxidative stress, arising as a result of an imbalance between free radical production and antioxidant defenses, is associated with damage to a wide range of molecular species including lipids, proteins, and nucleic acids. Short-term oxidative stress may occur in tissues injured by trauma, infection, heat injury, hypertoxia, toxins, and excessive exercise. These injured tissues produce increased radical generating enzymes (e.g., xanthine oxidase, lipogenase, cyclooxygenase), activation of phagocytes, release of free iron, copper ions, or a disruption of the electron transport chains of oxidative phosphorylation, producing excess ROS. The initiation, promotion, and progression of cancer, as well as the side-effects of radiation and chemotherapy, have been linked to the imbalance between ROS and the antioxidant defense system. ROS have been implicated in the

induction and complications of diabetes mellitus, age-related eye disease, and neurodegenerative diseases such as Parkinson's disease.

V. Lobo et al., "Free Radicals, Antioxidants and Functional Foods: Impact on Human Health," *Pharmacognosy Reviews* 4, no. 8 (2010): 118.

258 **free radicals accelerate the aging process:** B. T. Ashok and R. Ali, "The Aging Paradox: Free Radical Theory of Aging," *Experimental Gerontology* 34, no. 3 (1999): 293–303.

258 **reduction of free radicals can delay aging:** A lot of transgenic work shows that downregulating antioxidant enzymes doesn't necessarily shorten life span. This is controversial, however.

258 **no universal agreement among scientists:** D. Han (associate professor of biopharmaceutical sciences at KGI), email communication, January 22, 2019.

258 **substances that are often mentioned as antioxidants:** J. King (Professor Emerita, University of California at Berkeley), email communication, January 21, 2019.

259 **One recent meta-analysis found:** U. Nurmatov, G. Devereux, and A. Sheikh, "Nutrients and Foods for the Primary Prevention of Asthma and Allergy: Systematic Review and Meta-Analysis," *Journal of Allergy and Clinical Immunology* 127, no. 3 (2011): 724–733.

259 **randomized controlled trials with a range of antioxidant supplements:** A. M. Pisoschi and A. Pop, "The Role of Antioxidants in the Chemistry of Oxidative Stress: A Review," *European Journal of Medicinal Chemistry* 97 (2015): 55–74.

259 **no effect of antioxidant supplements on cardiovascular disease:** S. K. Myung et al., "Efficacy of Vitamin and Antioxidant Supplements in Prevention of Cardiovascular Disease: Systematic Review and Meta-Analysis of Randomised Controlled Trials," *British Medical Journal* 346 (2013): f10.

259 **might be interfering with the immune system:** Pisoschi and Pop, "The Role of Antioxidants."

259 **(For some subsets of the population with a really poor diet):** D. Han, personal communication, February 25, 2019.

259 **vitamins C and E:** M. Ristow et al., "Antioxidants Prevent Health-Promoting Effects of Physical Exercise in Humans," *Proceedings of the National Academy of Sciences* 106, no. 21 (2009): 8665–8670.

260 **Cholesterol is a waxy substance:** Mayo Clinic, "High Cholesterol," n.d., https://www.mayoclinic.org/diseases-conditions/high-blood-cholesterol/symptoms-causes/syc-20350800; US National Library of Medicine, "Cholesterol," n.d., https://medlineplus.gov/cholesterol.html.

260 **three hundred people have to take a statin:** R. Chou et al., "Statins for Prevention of Cardiovascular Disease in Adults: Evidence Report and Systematic Review for the US Preventive Services Task Force," *Journal of the American Medical Association* 316, no. 19 (2016): 2008–2024; A. Thompson and N. J. Temple, "The Case for Statins: Has It Really Been Made?," *Journal of the Royal Society of Medicine* 97, no. 10 (2004): 461–464.

261 **not all fats are created equal:** Mayo Clinic Staff, "High Cholesterol."

261 **no association between the consumption of saturated fats and heart disease:** R. Chowdhury et al., "Association of Dietary, Circulating, and Supplement Fatty Acids with Coronary Risk: A Systematic Review and Meta-Analysis," *Annals of Internal Medicine* 160, no. 6 (2014): 398–406.

261 **Diets high in soluble fibers are good:** Harvard Medical School Staff, "11 Foods That Lower Cholesterol," Harvard Health Publishing, https://www.health.harvard.edu/heart-health/11-foods-that-lower-cholesterol.

261 **Diets high in omega-3 . . . reduce the risk of heart disease by 7 percent:** Chowdhury et al., "Association of Dietary, Circulating, and Supplement Fatty Acids."

261 **consumption of fats . . . is not the cause of heart disease:** A. Malhotra, R. F. Redberg, and P. Meier, "Saturated Fat Does Not Clog the Arteries: Coronary Heart Disease Is a Chronic Inflammatory Condition, the Risk of Which Can Be Effectively Reduced from Healthy Lifestyle Interventions," *British Journal of Sports Medicine* 51, no. 15 (2017): 1111–1112; M. M. Pinheiro and T. Wilson, "Dietary Fat: The Good, the Bad, and the Ugly," in *Nutrition Guide for Physicians and Related Healthcare Professionals,* ed. N. J. Temple, T. Wilson, and G. A. Bray, pp. 241–247 (Cham: Humana Press, 2017).

262 **mice and rats that have a calorie-restricted diet:** M. Mattson, "Why Fasting Bolsters Brain Power," TEDx Talks, March 18, 2014, https://www.youtube.com/watch?v=4UkZAwKoCP8.

262 **A number of stressors mediate this reaction:** R. J. Colman et al., "Dietary Restriction Delays Disease Onset and Mortality in Rhesus Monkeys," *Science* 325 (2009): 201–204; W. Mair et al., "Demography of Dietary Restriction and Death in Drosophila," *Science* 301 (2003): 1731–1733.

262 **caloric restriction triggers a change in the metabolic response:** C. Lee and V. Longo, "Dietary Restriction with and without Caloric Restriction for Healthy Aging," *F1000Research* 5 (2016).

262 **Molecular biologist Cynthia Kenyon explains:** C. Kenyon, "The Genetics of Ageing," *Nature* 464 (2010): 504–512.

263 **(hyperinsulinemia) . . . obesity:** N. M. Templeman et al., "A Causal Role for Hyperinsulinemia in Obesity," *Journal of Endocrinology* 232, no. 3 (2017): R173–R183.

263 **(hyperinsulinemia) . . . immune-system suppression:** R. Marín-Juez et al., "Hyperinsulinemia Induces Insulin Resistance and Immune Suppression via Ptpn6/Shp1 in Zebrafish," *Journal of Endocrinology* 222, no. 2 (2014): 229–241.

263 **(hyperinsulinemia) . . . cardiac arrhythmias:** L. Drimba et al., "The Role of Acute Hyperinsulinemia in the Development of Cardiac Arrhythmias," *Naunyn-Schmiedeberg's Archives of Pharmacology* 386, no. 5 (2013): 435–444.

263 **Neuroscientist Mark Mattson:** Mattson, "Why Fasting Bolsters Brain Power."

263 **insulin may play a role in developing:** G. Bedse et al., "Aberrant Insulin Signaling in Alzheimer's Disease: Current Knowledge," *Frontiers in Neuroscience* 9 (2015): 204.

263 **Metformin was further found to have a neuroprotective effect:** J. M. Campbell et al., "Metformin Use Associated with Reduced Risk of Dementia in Patients with Diabetes: A Systematic Review and Meta-Analysis," *Journal of Alzheimer's Disease* 65, no. 4 (2018): 1225–1236.

263 **A protocol for testing the hypothesis:** V. M. Walker et al., "Can Commonly Prescribed Drugs Be Repurposed for the Prevention or Treatment of Alzheimer's and Other Neurodegenerative Diseases? Protocol for an Observational Cohort Study in the UK Clinical Practice Research Datalink," *BMJ Open* 6, no. 12 (2016): e012044; see also A. Gupta, B. Bisht, and C. S. Dey, "Peripheral Insulin-Sensitizer Drug Metformin Ameliorates Neuronal Insulin Resistance and Alzheimer's-like Changes," *Neuropharmacology* 60, no. 6 (2011): 910–920.

264 **Mark Mattson does intermittent fasting:** Mattson, "Why Fasting Bolsters Brain Power."

264 **Consuming olive oil:** F. R. Pérez-López et al., "Effects of the Mediterranean Diet on Longevity and Age-Related Morbid Conditions," *Maturitas* 64, no. 2 (2009): 67–79.

264 **Cruciferous vegetables:** As of this writing, the Wikipedia entry on glucosinolates states that there is no clinical evidence that they are effective against cancer. Wikipedia articles can change at any time and, in general, are only as accurate as the last person who decided to edit them. This conclusion is at odds with my reading of the literature and that of the many professional scientists who vetted this book. Here is a sample of the literature that supports my view:

G. Tse and G. D. Eslick, "Cruciferous Vegetables and Risk of Colorectal Neoplasms: A Systematic Review and Meta-Analysis," *Nutrition and Cancer* 66, no. 1 (2014): 128–139.

R. W.-L. Ma and K. Chapman, "A Systematic Review of the Effect of Diet in Prostate Cancer Prevention and Treatment," *Journal of Human Nutrition and Dietetics* 22, no. 3 (2009): 187–199.

M. Loef and H. Walach, "Fruit, Vegetables and Prevention of Cognitive Decline or Dementia: A Systematic Review of Cohort Studies," *Journal of Nutrition, Health and Aging* 16, no. 7 (2012): 626–630.

J. D. Potter and K. Steinmetz, "Vegetables, Fruit and Phytoestrogens as Preventive Agents," *IARC Scientific Publications* 139 (1996): 61–90.

H. Steinkellner et al., "Effects of Cruciferous Vegetables and Their Constituents on Drug Metabolizing Enzymes Involved in the Bioactivation of DNA-Reactive Dietary Carcinogens," *Mutation Research/Fundamental and Molecular Mechanisms of Mutagenesis* 480 (2001): 285–297.

H. H. Nguyen et al., "The Dietary Phytochemical Indole-3-Carbinol Is a Natural Elastase Enzymatic Inhibitor That Disrupts Cyclin E Protein Processing," *Proceedings of the National Academy of Sciences* 105, no. 50 (2008): 19750–19755.

F. Fuentes, X. Paredes-Gonzalez, and A. N. T. Kong, "Dietary Glucosinolates Sulforaphane, Phenethyl Isothiocyanate, Indole-3-Carbinol/3, 3′-Diindolylmethane: Antioxidative Stress/Inflammation, Nrf2, Epigenetics/Epigenomics and in Vivo Cancer Chemopreventive Efficacy," *Current Pharmacology Reports* 1, no. 3 (2015): 179–196.

K. J. Royston and T. O. Tollefsbol, "The Epigenetic Impact of Cruciferous Vegetables on Cancer Prevention," *Current Pharmacology Reports* 1, no. 1 (2015): 46–51.

264 **a current fad of taking omega-3 supplements:** Grand View Research, "Omega 3 Supplement Market Analysis by Source (Fish Oil, Krill Oil), by Application (Infant Formula, Food and Beverages, Nutritional Supplements, Pharmaceutical, Animal Feed, Clinical Nutrition), and Segment Forecasts, 2018–2025," May 2017, https://www.grandviewresearch.com/industry-analysis/omega-3-supplement-market; Statista, "Global Omega-3 Supplement Market Size in 2016 and 2025 (in Billion US Dollars)," 2016, https://www.statista.com/statistics/758383/omega-3-supplement-market-size-worldwide/.

264 **A Cochrane systematic review:** A. S. Abdelhamid et al., "Omega-3 Fatty Acids for the Primary and Secondary Prevention of Cardiovascular Disease," *Cochrane Database of Systematic Reviews* 11 (2018).

265 **report by the National Institutes of Health:** NIH National Center for Complementary and Integrative Health, "Omega-3 Supplements: In Depth," 2018, https://nccih.nih.gov/health/omega3/introduction.htm.

265 **The *Harvard Health* report noted:** H. LeWine, "Fish Oil: Friend or Foe?," Harvard Health Publishing, 2019, https://www.health.harvard.edu/blog/fish-oil-friend-or-foe-201307126467.

265 **no evidence that red wine influences:** S. E. Brien et al., "Effect of Alcohol Consumption on Biological Markers Associated with Risk of Coronary Heart Disease: Systematic Review and Meta-Analysis of Interventional Studies," *British Medical Journal* 342 (2011): d636.

265 **Moderate alcohol consumption:** A. Artero et al., "The Impact of Moderate Wine Consumption on Health," *Maturitas* 80, no. 1 (2015): 3–13.

266 **Alcohol consumption increases risks:** World Cancer Research Fund and American Institute for Cancer Research, *Food, Nutrition, Physical Activity, and the Prevention of Cancer: A Global Perspective,* vol. 1 (Washington, DC: American Institute for Cancer Research, 2007).

266 **increases mortality in breast cancer survivors:** L. Schwingshackl and G. Hoffmann, "Adherence to Mediterranean Diet and Risk of Cancer: An Updated Systematic Review and Meta-Analysis of Observational Studies," *Cancer Medicine* 4, no. 12 (2015): 1933–1947.

266 **insufficient evidence that resveratrol supplements:** Pérez-López et al., "Effects of the Mediterranean Diet"; O. Vang et al., "What Is New for an Old Molecule? Systematic Review and Recommendations on the Use of Resveratrol," *PLoS One* 6, no. 6 (2011): e19881.

266 **another comprehensive review recommended it:** J. M. Smoliga, J. A. Baur, and H. A. Hausenblas, "Resveratrol and Health—a Comprehensive Review of Human Clinical Trials," *Molecular Nutrition and Food Research* 55, no. 8 (2011): 1129–1141.

266 **Many cognitive and physical benefits are claimed:** D. G. Loughrey et al., "The Impact of the Mediterranean Diet on the Cognitive Functioning of Healthy Older Adults: A Systematic Review and Meta-Analysis," *Advances in Nutrition* 8, no. 4 (2017): 571–586.

266 **Healthy diets that lower cholesterol:** O. van de Rest et al., "Dietary Patterns, Cognitive Decline, and Dementia: A Systematic Review," *Advances in Nutrition* 6, no. 2 (2015): 154–168.

266 **Older adults absorb protein less effectively:** J. Brody, "Muscle Loss in Aging Can Be Reversed," *The New York Times,* September 4, 2018, p. D5.

267 **Consider the following:** United States Department of Agriculture, Agricultural Research Service, USDA Food Composition Databases, n.d., https://ndb.nal.usda.gov/ndb/nutrients/index.

267 **The most effective proteins for older adults:** Brody, "Muscle Loss in Aging."

267 **Leucine:** US National Library of Medicine, National Center for Biotechnology Information, PubChem Database, Leucine, CID 6106, 2019, https://pubchem.ncbi.nlm.nih.gov/compound/6106.

267 **leucine toxicity:** R. Elango et al., "Determination of the Tolerable Upper Intake Level of Leucine in Acute Dietary Studies in Young Men," *American Journal of Clinical Nutrition* 96, no. 4 (2012): 759–767; A. G. Wessels et al., "High Leucine Diets Stimulate Cerebral Branched-Chain Amino Acid Degradation and Modify Serotonin and Ketone Body Concentrations in a Pig Model," *PLoS One* 11, no. 3 (2016): e0150376; M. Yudkoff et al., "Brain Amino Acid Requirements and Toxicity: The Example of Leucine," *Journal of Nutrition* 135, no. 6 (2005): 1531S–1538S.

268 **current thinking is that soy is beneficial:** M. Messina, "Soy and Health Update: Evaluation of the Clinical and Epidemiologic Literature," *Nutrients* 8, no. 12 (2016): 754.

268 **second leading killer of children under four:** E. Dolhun, "Aftermath of Typhoon Haiyan: The Imminent Epidemic of Waterborne Illnesses in Leyte, Philippines," *Disaster Medicine and Public Health Preparedness* 7, no. 6 (2013): 547–548.

268 **eighth leading cause of death:** C. Troeger et al., "Estimates of the Global, Regional, and National Morbidity, Mortality, and Aetiologies of Diarrhoea in 195 Countries: A Systematic Analysis for the Global Burden of Disease Study 2016," *Lancet Infectious Diseases* 18, no. 11 (2018): 1211–1228; C. Trinh and K. Prabhakar, "Diarrheal Diseases in the Elderly," *Clinics in Geriatric Medicine* 23, no. 4 (2007): 833–856.

268 **Alcohol is also a culprit:** E. P. Dolhun (MD), personal communication, February 21, 2017.

268 **the greatest risk for dehydration:** D. R. Thomas et al., "Understanding Clinical Dehydration and Its Treatment," *Journal of the American Medical Directors Association* 9, no. 5 (2008): 292–301.

269 **Cases of severe dehydration require:** World Health Organization, "Diarrhoeal Disease," 2017, https://www.who.int/news-room/fact-sheets/detail/diarrhoeal-disease.

269 **Avoid bread or dried fruit:** Dolhun, personal communication.

269 **oral rehydration solutions:** Unfortunately, many of the ORS products have a bad taste, which causes the people who need them not to drink them; others are loaded with refined sugar to improve the taste, which is counterproductive. I recommend DripDrop, developed by a colleague of mine, Eduardo Dolhun, a Mayo Clinic–trained doctor who regularly performs humanitarian missions to Third World countries and treats dehydration using his product. I have no financial interest in the company, nor do I benefit from your purchasing of this product. See a list of references here: Eduardo P. Dolhun, Oral rehydration composition, US Patent 8,557,301, filed July 1, 2011, and issued October 15, 2013, https://patentimages.storage.googleapis.com/bd/54/5b/cd03de0b6f973c/US8557301.pdf.

269 **Constipation is one of the most common:** D. Gandell et al., "Treatment of Constipation in Older People," *CMAJ* 185, no. 8 (2013): 663–670.

269 **constipation led to changes in gene expression:** Y. Li et al., "Hippocampal Gene Expression Profiling in a Rat Model of Functional Constipation Reveals Abnormal Expression Genes Associated with Cognitive Function," *Neuroscience Letters* 675 (2018): 103–109.

269 **chronic constipation and cognitive impairment:** Y. M. I. Kazem et al., "Constipation, Oxidative Stress in Obese Patients and Their Impact on Cognitive Functions and Mood, the Role of Diet Modification and *Foeniculum vulgare* Supplementation," *Journal of Biological Sciences* 17, no. 7 (2017): 312–319; R. T. Wang and Y. Li, "Analysis of Cognitive Function of Old People with Functional Constipation," *Journal of Harbin Medical University* 6 (2011): 603–605.

270 **Bulk-forming laxatives aren't digested:** A. Low, "Treating Constipation with Laxatives," 2010, GI Society: Canadian Society of Intestinal Research, https://www.badgut.org/information-centre/a-z-digestive-topics/treating-constipation-with-laxatives/.

271 **SCN (suprachiasmatic nucleus in the hypothalamus) can regulate the microbiome:** G. Asher and P. Sassone-Corsi, "Time for Food: The Intimate Interplay between Nutrition, Metabolism, and the Circadian Clock," *Cell* 161 (2015): 84–93.

271 **90 percent of the serotonin in the body resides in the gut:** A. Evrensel and M. E. Ceylan, "The Gut-Brain Axis: The Missing Link in Depression," *Clinical Psychopharmacology and Neuroscience* 13, no. 3 (2015): 239; Y. E. Borre et al., "Microbiota

and Neurodevelopmental Windows: Implications for Brain Disorders," *Trends in Molecular Medicine* 20, no. 9 (2014): 509–518.

272 ***Lactobacillus acidophilus* increases the expression of the natural cannabinoid:** C. Rousseaux et al., "*Lactobacillus acidophilus* Modulates Intestinal Pain and Induces Opioid and Cannabinoid Receptors," *Nature Medicine* 13, no. 1 (2007): 35.

272 **Gut bacteria have been linked to mental well-being:** M. Valles-Colomer et al., "The Neuroactive Potential of the Human Gut Microbiota in Quality of Life and Depression," *Nature Microbiology* 1 (2019).

272 **John Cryan calls bacteria:** T. G. Dinan and J. F. Cryan, "Melancholy Microbes: A Link between Gut Microbiota and Depression?," *Neurogastroenterology and Motility*, no. 25 (2013): 713–19.

272 **composition of the gut microbiome:** Borre et al., "Microbiota and Neurodevelopmental Windows."

273 **Rats separated from their mothers:** Evrensel and Ceylan, "The Gut-Brain Axis"; J. F. Cryan and T. G. Dinan, "Mind-Altering Microorganisms: The Impact of the Gut Microbiota on Brain and Behaviour," *Nature Reviews Neuroscience* 13, no. 10 (2012): 701.

273 **The full extent of gut-brain interactions:** Cryan and Dinan, "Mind-Altering Microorganisms"; E. G. Severance et al., "Discordant Patterns of Bacterial Translocation Markers and Implications for Innate Immune Imbalances in Schizophrenia," *Schizophrenia Research* 148, nos. 1–3 (2013): 130–137; A. I. Petra et al., "Gut-Microbiota-Brain Axis and Its Effect on Neuropsychiatric Disorders with Suspected Immune Dysregulation," *Clinical Therapeutics* 37, no. 5 (2015): 984–995; F. Dickerson, E. Severance, and R. Yolken, "The Microbiome, Immunity, and Schizophrenia and Bipolar Disorder," *Brain, Behavior, and Immunity* 62 (2017): 46–52.

273 **an imbalanced microbiome:** Borre et al., "Microbiota and Neurodevelopmental Windows."

273 **increasing iron absorption:** M. Hoppe et al., "Probiotic Strain *Lactobacillus plantarum* 299v Increases Iron Absorption from an Iron-Supplemented Fruit Drink: A Double-Isotope Cross-Over Single-Blind Study in Women of Reproductive Age," *British Journal of Nutrition* 114, no. 8 (2015): 1195–1202.

273 **protecting against pesticide absorption:** M. Trinder et al., "Probiotic Lactobacilli: A Potential Prophylactic Treatment for Reducing Pesticide Absorption in Humans and Wildlife," *Beneficial Microbes* 6, no. 6 (2015): 841–847.

273 **distribution of fat around the body:** M. Zarrati et al., "Effects of Probiotic Yogurt on Fat Distribution and Gene Expression of Proinflammatory Factors in Peripheral Blood Mononuclear Cells in Overweight and Obese People with or without Weight-Loss Diet," *Journal of the American College of Nutrition* 33, no. 6 (2014): 417–425.

273 **treatments for irritable bowel syndrome:** Y. Zhang et al., "Effects of Probiotic Type, Dose and Treatment Duration on Irritable Bowel Syndrome Diagnosed by Rome III Criteria: A Meta-analysis," *BMC Gastroenterology* 16, no. 1 (2016): 62.

273 ***Bifidobacterium infantis*, can alleviate depression:** M. Messaoudi et al., "Assessment of Psychotropic-like Properties of a Probiotic Formulation (*Lactobacillus helveticus* R0052 and *Bifidobacterium longum* R0175) in Rats and Human Subjects," *British Journal of Nutrition* 105, no. 5 (2011): 755–764.

273 ***Lactobacillus helveticus* and *Bifidobacterium longum* can reduce cortisol levels:** Cryan and Dinan, "Mind-Altering Microorganisms."

273 **a probiotic mixture containing *Bifidobacterium lactis*:** Cryan and Dinan, "Mind-Altering Microorganisms"; T. Chen et al., "Role of the Anterior Insular Cortex in Integrative Causal Signaling during Multisensory Auditory-Visual Attention," *European Journal of Neuroscience* 41, no. 2 (2015): 264–274.

273 **Kefir, yogurt, and other fermented milk:** K. Tillisch et al., "Consumption of Fermented Milk Product with Probiotic Modulates Brain Activity," *Gastroenterology* 144, no. 7 (2013): 1394–1401.

273 **eating more fiber promotes gut health:** A. Reynolds et al., "Carbohydrate Quality and Human Health: A Series of Systematic Reviews and Meta-Analyses," *Lancet* 393, no. 10170 (2019): 434–445.

273 **The distinct microbiome of the elderly:** M. J. Claesson et al., "Gut Microbiota Composition Correlates with Diet and Health in the Elderly," *Nature* 488, no. 7410 (2012): 178; Cryan and Dinan, "Mind-Altering Microorganisms."

273 **Microbiomic balance:** Borre et al., "Microbiota and Neurodevelopmental Windows."

274 **loss of diverse community-associated microbiota:** Claesson et al., "Gut Microbiota Composition Correlates with Diet and Health in the Elderly."

274 **Research on this is just getting started:** Harvard Medical School Staff, "Health Benefits of Taking Probiotics," Harvard Health Publishing, August 22, 2018, https://www.health.harvard.edu/vitamins-and-supplements/health-benefits-of-taking-probiotics.

274 **probiotics function best:** C. C. Dodoo et al., "Use of a Water-Based Probiotic to Treat Common Gut Pathogens," *International Journal of Pharmaceutics* 556 (2019): 136–141; M. Fredua-Agyeman and S. Gaisford, "Comparative Survival of Commercial Probiotic Formulations: Tests in Biorelevant Gastric Fluids and Real-Time Measurements using Microcalorimetry," *Beneficial Microbes* 6, no. 1 (2014): 141–151.

275 **It's difficult to be an informed consumer:** Y. Ringel, E. M. Quigley, and H. C. Lin, "Using Probiotics in Gastrointestinal Disorders," *American Journal of Gastroenterology Supplements* 1, no. 1 (2012): 34.

275 **$18-million jury verdict:** Prosauker Rose LLP, "$15 Million False Ad Verdict Boosts Damages in Probiotic IP Dispute," Lexology, December 21, 2018, https://www.lexology.com/library/detail.aspx?g=fac1ef1c-2e1e-4108-b0da-d998aaf70ed2.

275 **KeVita Kombucha:** E. Watson, "'Confusing' False Ad Lawsuit over KeVita Kombucha Reflects Split in Industry over Production Methods, Say Attorneys," Food Navigator USA, October 25, 2017, https://www.foodnavigator-usa.com/Article/2017/10/26/Confusing-false-ad-lawsuit-over-KeVita-kombucha-reflects-split-in-industry-over-production-methods-say-attorneys.

275 **the Dannon Company settled:** GI Society: Canadian Society of Intestinal Research, "Lawsuit Settled: Dannon Yogurt Didn't Measure Up to Its Claims," November 16, 2016, https://www.badgut.org/information-centre/a-z-digestive-topics/dannon-lawsuit-settled/. An additional class-action suit not mentioned in the text settled for $8.25 million in 2017 against GT's Kombucha found the brand had up to 2.5 percent alcohol, similar to low-alcohol beers. The suit also charged that GT's Kombucha contained more than the 2 grams of sugar per 8-ounce serving noted on the nutrition label. M. Caballero, "Judge Approves $8.25 Million Settlement in GT's Kombucha and Whole Foods Suit," BevNet News, February 3, 2017, https://www.bevnet.com/news/2017/judge-approves-8-25-million-settlement-gts-kombucha-whole-foods-suit.

275 **products that are known to be effective:** Two probiotic products that are supported by evidence are Symprove, available from https://www.symprove.com/, and Visbiome, available from https://www.visbiome.com/. I have no financial stake in these companies and I do not benefit from your buying these products.

275 **Even less is known about prebiotics:** D. Charalampopoulos and R. A. Rastall, "Prebiotics in Foods," *Current Opinion in Biotechnology* 23, no. 2 (2012): 187–191.

275 **Food molecules are known to protect probiotics:** B. M. Corcoran et al., "Survival of Probiotic Lactobacilli in Acidic Environments Is Enhanced in the Presence of Metabolizable Sugars," *Applied and Environmental Microbiology* 71, no. 6 (2005): 3060–3067.

275 **Dozens of foods act as prebiotics:** M. Lyte et al., "Resistant Starch Alters the Microbiota-Gut Brain Axis: Implications for Dietary Modulation of Behavior," *PLoS One* 11, no. 1 (2016): e0146406; A. Gunenc, C. Alswiti, and F. Hosseinian, "Wheat Bran Dietary Fiber: Promising Source of Prebiotics with Antioxidant Potential," *Journal of Food Research* 6, no. 2 (2017): 1; F. M. N. A. Aida et al., "Mushroom as a Potential Source of Prebiotics: A Review," *Trends in Food Science and Technology* 20, nos. 11–12 (2009): 567–575; M. de Jesus Raposo, A. de Morais, and R. de Morais, "Emergent Sources of Prebiotics: Seaweeds and Microalgae," *Marine Drugs* 14, no. 2 (2016): 27.

275 **fecal microbiota transplantation . . . for treating a range of diseases:** G. J. Bakker and M. Nieuwdorp, "Fecal Microbiota Transplantation: Therapeutic Potential for a Multitude of Diseases beyond *Clostridium difficile*," *Microbiology Spectrum* 5, no. 4 (2017); J. F. Petrosino, "The Microbiome in Precision Medicine: The Way Forward," *Genome Medicine* 10, no. 1 (2018): 12.

275 **The technique has had mixed results:** S. Paramsothy et al., "Faecal Microbiota Transplantation for Inflammatory Bowel Disease: A Systematic Review and Meta-Analysis," *Journal of Crohn's and Colitis* 11, no. 10 (2017): 1180–1199.

276 **cardiovascular disease, stroke, cancer, and diabetes:** H. Eyre et al., "Preventing Cancer, Cardiovascular Disease, and Diabetes: A Common Agenda for the American Cancer Society, the American Diabetes Association, and the American Heart Association," *Circulation* 109, no. 25 (2004): 3244–3255.

276 **health among hunter-gatherer societies:** A. O'Connor, "The Hunt for an Optimal Diet," *The New York Times,* December 25, 2018, D4; H. Pontzer, B. M. Wood, and D. A. Raichlen, "Hunter-Gatherers as Models in Public Health," *Obesity Reviews* 19 (2018): 24–35.

276 **he fed them ultra-processed foods:** K. Hall et al., "Ultra-Processed Diets Cause Excess Calorie Intake and Weight Gain: An Independent Randomized Controlled Trial of Ad Libitum Food Intake," *Cell Metabolism* 30 (2019): 67–77.

277 **intuitive eating:** N. Van Dyke and E. J. Drinkwater, "Relationships between Intuitive Eating and Health Indicators: Literature Review," *Public Health Nutrition* 17, no. 8 (2014): 1757–1766.

277 **people's experiences and frustrations with most diets:** M. Frayn, "Doing Away with Diets Once and for All," Eat North, January 9, 2019, https://eatnorth.com/mallory-frayn/doing-away-diets-once-and-all.

277 **The cycle of repeatedly dieting and failing:** K. Buchanan and J. Sheffield, "Why Do Diets Fail? An Exploration of Dieters' Experiences Using Thematic Analysis," *Journal of Health Psychology* 22, no. 7 (2017): 906–915.

278 **four additional principles of intuitive dieting:** Van Dyke and Drinkwater, "Relationships between Intuitive Eating."

278 **binge eating:** M. Frayn and B. Knäuper, "Emotional Eating and Weight in Adults: A Review," *Current Psychology* 37, no. 4 (2018): 924–933.

279 **state of nutritional advice:** N. Johnson, "Food Confusion," *Stanford Magazine,* July–August 2013, https://stanfordmag.org/contents/food-confusion.

CHAPTER 10

280 **"I can't speak for two geniuses":** S. Grafton, email communication, December 21, 2018.

281 **the brain is a giant problem-solving device:** I previously wrote about this in D. J. Levitin, *The Organized Mind* (New York: Dutton, 2014); see also D. C. Dennett, "The Cultural Evolution of Words and Other Thinking Tools," in *Evolution: The Molecular Landscape,* ed. B. Stillman, D. Stewart, and J. Witkowski, *Cold Spring Harbor Symposia on Quantitative Biology,* vol. 74, pp. 435–441 (Cold Spring Harbor, NY: Cold Spring Harbor Laboratory Press, 2009); and P. MacCready, "An Ambivalent Luddite at a Technological Feast," Designfax, August 1999, http://maccready.library.caltech.edu/islandora/object/pbm%3A27832#page/1/mode/2up.

282 **memory is enhanced by physical activity:** P. D. Loprinzi, M. K. Edwards, and E. Frith, "Potential Avenues for Exercise to Activate Episodic Memory-Related Pathways: A Narrative Review," *European Journal of Neuroscience* 46, no. 5 (2017): 2067–2077.

282 **embodied cognition:** A. Setti and A. M. Borghi, "Embodied Cognition over the Lifespan: Theoretical Issues and Implications for Applied Settings," *Frontiers in Psychology* 9 (2018): 550. Scott Grafton advises, "We need to be careful and explicit about what we mean by embodied cognition. It has been hijacked by some psychologists into a kind of woo woo explanandum for cosmic oneness with the senses, like J. J. Gibson on acid.

> The term arises from Rodney Brooks, a roboticist who made the case that it is really stupid from an engineering perspective to put all the control elements of a sense and respond system in a central CPU. You want some stuff to get done out in the periphery to free up the central control unit (i.e., the brain). Another clear example with nerves is the Sherrington reflex (knee jerk reflex), which involves just the spinal cord. These are layered loops, each adding function. The first two don't need a cortex at all. In other words, embodied cognition is putting intelligence and control out in the body. (Grafton, email communication.)

282 **movement is inextricably bound with knowledge:** D. Krakauer, personal communication, July 19, 2019.

282 **embodied, ecologically and genetically embedded social agents:** A. Linson et al., "The Active Inference Approach to Ecological Perception: General Information Dynamics for Natural and Artificial Embodied Cognition," *Frontiers in Robotics and AI* 5 (2018): 21.

282 **The body influences the mind:** C. R. Madan and A. Singhal, "Using Actions to Enhance Memory: Effects of Enactment, Gestures, and Exercise on Human Memory," *Frontiers in Psychology* 3 (2012): 507.

283 **exercise had a significant beneficial effect on memory:** P. D. Loprinzi et al., "Experimental Effects of Exercise on Memory Function among Mild Cognitive Impairment: Systematic Review and Meta-Analysis," *Physician and Sportsmedicine* (2018): 1–6.

283 **risk is increased by atrophy of the hippocampus:** Loprinzi et al., "Experimental Effects."

283 **Aging is an irreversible:** S. F. Tsai et al., "Exercise Counteracts Aging-Related Memory Impairment: A Potential Role for the Astrocytic Metabolic Shuttle," *Frontiers in Aging Neuroscience* 8 (2016): 57.

284 **onset of walking triggers neurochemical activity:** A. M. Glenberg and J. Hayes, "Contribution of Embodiment to Solving the Riddle of Infantile Amnesia," *Frontiers in Psychology* 7 (2016): 10.

284 **The central role that the hippocampus:** M. C. Costello and E. K. Bloesch, "Are Older Adults Less Embodied? A Review of Age Effects through the Lens of Embodied Cognition," *Frontiers in Psychology* 8 (2017): 267.

284 **cognitive and perceptual abilities are not a static:** B. Hommel and A. Kibele, "Down with Retirement: Implications of Embodied Cognition for Healthy Aging," *Frontiers in Psychology* 7 (2016): 1184.

284 **three kinds of bodily changes:** Hommel and Kibele, "Down with Retirement."

285 **Mick Jagger (age seventy-five) works with a personal trainer:** L. Valenti, "At 75, Mick Jagger Shares His Incredible Post-Heart Surgery Dance Moves," *Vogue*, May 15, 2019, https://www.vogue.com/article/mick-jagger-post-heart-surgery-dance-workout-moves-fitness.

285 **Jane Fonda (age eighty-one) works out every day:** J. Sitzes, "How Jane Fonda Looks So Young at 80," *Prevention*, May 18, 2018, https://www.prevention.com/fitness/a20686775/jane-fonda-age.

285 **Interacting with the world also enhances creativity:** C. Y. Kuo and Y. Y. Yeh, "Sensorimotor-Conceptual Integration in Free Walking Enhances Divergent Thinking for Young and Older Adults," *Frontiers in Psychology* 7 (2016): 1580.

286 **physical activity increases the effectiveness of astrocytes:** Tsai et al., "Exercise Counteracts Aging-Related Memory Impairment."

286 **hippocampus grows seven hundred new neurons per day:** S. M. Ryan and Y. M. Nolan, "Neuroinflammation Negatively Affects Adult Hippocampal Neurogenesis and Cognition: Can Exercise Compensate?," *Neuroscience and Biobehavioral Reviews* 61 (2016): 121–131.

286 **increase hippocampal neurogenesis:** Ryan and Nolan, "Neuroinflammation Negatively Affects."

286 **"improvement in memory for human adults":** Ryan and Nolan, "Neuroinflammation Negatively Affects."

286 **prime the brain with increased blood flow:** A. Shimamura, *Get SMART! Five Steps toward a Healthy Brain* (Scotts Valley, CA: CreateSpace, 2017).

287 ***aerobic* activity:** American College of Sports Medicine, *ACSM's Guidelines for Exercise Testing and Prescription* (Philadelphia: Lippincott Williams and Wilkins, 2013).

287 **Anaerobic activity can help to build:** H. Patel et al., "Aerobic vs Anaerobic Exercise Training Effects on the Cardiovascular System," *World Journal of Cardiology* 9, no. 2 (2017): 134.

287 **Sarcopenia is the loss of muscle tissue:** J. Brody, "Muscle Loss in Aging Can Be Reversed," *The New York Times*, September 4, 2018, p. D5.

287 **significantly increased their leg strength and muscle mass:** W. R. Frontera et al., "Strength Conditioning in Older Men: Skeletal Muscle Hypertrophy and Improved Function," *Journal of Applied Physiology* 64, no. 3 (1988): 1038–1044.

287 **significant improvements in frail nursing home residents:** M. A. Fiatarone et al., "High-Intensity Strength Training in Nonagenarians: Effects on Skeletal Muscle," *Journal of the American Medical Association* 263, no. 22 (1990): 3029–3034.

287 **Adults aged sixty to seventy-nine years who engaged in indoor aerobic:** S. J. Colcombe et al., "Aerobic Exercise Training Increases Brain Volume in Aging

Humans," *Journals of Gerontology Series A: Biological Sciences and Medical Sciences* 61, no. 11 (2006): 1166–1170.

288 **Wisløff has developed a high-intensity:** Cardiac Exercise Research Group, "7 Week Fitness Program," https://www.ntnu.edu/cerg/regimen.

288 **reducing the risk of heart attack:** J. M. Letnes et al., "Peak Oxygen Uptake and Incident Coronary Heart Disease in a Healthy Population: The HUNT Fitness Study," *European Heart Journal* (2018).

288 **"a bit more is probably better":** "Making 2019 Happier," *The Week*, January 11, 2019, p. 16.

289 **Time-efficient workouts:** J. S. Thum et al., "High-Intensity Interval Training Elicits Higher Enjoyment Than Moderate Intensity Continuous Exercise," *PLoS One* 12, no. 1 (2017): e0166299.

289 **having sex before an athletic competition:** L. M. Valenti et al., "Effect of Sexual Intercourse on Lower Extremity Muscle Force in Strength-Trained Men," *Journal of Sexual Medicine* 15, no. 6 (2018): 888–893.

289 **"fitness age":** World Fitness Level, "How Fit Are You, Really?," https://www.worldfitnesslevel.org/#/.

290 **barely measurable amount of physical activity:** K. Suwabe et al., "Rapid Stimulation of Human Dentate Gyrus Function with Acute Mild Exercise," *Proceedings of the National Academy of Sciences* 115, no. 41 (2018): 10487–10492; A. Wahid et al., "Quantifying the Association between Physical Activity and Cardiovascular Disease and Diabetes: A Systematic Review and Meta-Analysis," *Journal of the American Heart Association* 5, no. 9 (2016): e002495; see also P. Siddarth et al., "Sedentary Behavior Associated with Reduced Medial Temporal Lobe Thickness in Middle-Aged and Older Adults," *PLoS One* 13, no. 4 (2018): e0195549.

291 **single bout of light physical movement:** Suwabe et al., "Rapid Stimulation."

292 **benefits show up immediately:** S. B. Chapman et al., "Shorter Term Aerobic Exercise Improves Brain, Cognition, and Cardiovascular Fitness in Aging," *Frontiers in Aging Neuroscience* 5 (2013): 75.

292 **Walter Thompson, a kinesiology professor:** S. Scutti, "'Pandemic' of Inactivity Increases Disease Risk Worldwide, WHO Study Says," CNN, September 5, 2018, https://www.cnn.com/2018/09/04/health/exercise-physical-activity-who-study/index.html.

292 **virtues of walking for neurocognitive health:** R. A. Friedman, "Standing Can Make You Smarter," *The New York Times*, April 19, 2018, p. A31.

294 **"rambling and birdwatching":** S. Carrell, "Scottish GPs to Begin Prescribing Rambling and Birdwatching," *The Guardian*, October 4, 2018, https://www.theguardian.com/uk-news/2018/oct/05/scottish-gps-nhs-begin-prescribing-rambling-birdwatching.

294 **"For everything from high blood pressure":** J. Housman, "Scottish Doctors Are Now Issuing Prescriptions to Go Hiking," *Adventure Journal*, October 22, 2018, https://www.adventure-journal.com/2018/10/scottish-doctors-are-now-issuing-prescriptions-to-go-hiking/.

CHAPTER 11

295 **chemicals in the brain that lead us to feel sleepy:** M. Lazarus et al., "Adenosine and Sleep," in *Handbook of Experimental Pharmacology*, J. Barrett, ed. (Berlin: Springer, 2017).

296 **ideas for songs came to him during sleep:** P. Doyle, "The Last Word: Billy Joel on Self-Doubt, Trump and Finally Becoming Cool," *Rolling Stone*, June 14, 2017.

296 **Thomas Edison viewed sleep:** D. Kamp, "Nighty Night," *The New York Times Sunday Book Review,* October 15, 2017, p. BR16.

296 **twenty others preceded Edison's:** R. Friedel and P. Israel, *Edison's Electric Light: The Art of Invention,* rev. ed. (Baltimore, MD: Johns Hopkins University Press, 2010), pp. 29–31.

296 **putting off sleep:** M. Walker, *Why We Sleep: Unlocking the Power of Sleep and Dreams* (New York: Scribner, 2017). And this line summarizing the book comes from Kamp, "Nighty Night."

297 **fewer than five hours of sleep:** R. Cooke, "'Sleep Should Be Prescribed': What Those Late Nights Out Could Be Costing You," *The Guardian,* September 24, 2017.

297 **They tend to *get* less sleep:** Walker, *Why We Sleep.*

297 **adults sleep less than seven hours:** Cooke, "'Sleep Should Be Prescribed.'"

298 **The Roman poet Ovid:** Ovid, *Metamorphoseon libri* (*Metamorphoses*) (AD 8).

298 **Sleep-deprived people:** S. S. Yoo et al., "The Human Emotional Brain without Sleep—a Prefrontal Amygdala Disconnect," *Current Biology* 17, no. 20 (2007): R877–R878.

299 **Cerebrospinal fluid circulates:** L. Xie et al., "Sleep Drives Metabolite Clearance from the Adult Brain," *Science* 342, no. 6156 (2013): 373–377.

299 **A U-shaped distribution:** J. Fang et al., "Association of Sleep Duration and Hypertension among US Adults Varies by Age and Sex," *American Journal of Hypertension* 25, no. 3 (2012): 335–341.

299 **sleep duration of less than six hours:** D. J. Gottlieb et al., "Association of Sleep Time with Diabetes Mellitus and Impaired Glucose Tolerance," *Archives of Internal Medicine* 165, no. 8 (2005): 863–867.

299 **Poor sleep duration or quality:** A. J. Clark et al., "Impaired Sleep and Allostatic Load: Cross-Sectional Results from the Danish Copenhagen Aging and Midlife Biobank," *Sleep Medicine* 15, no. 12 (2014): 1571–1578; R. P. Juster and B. S. McEwen, "Sleep and Chronic Stress: New Directions for Allostatic Load Research," *Sleep Medicine* 16, no. 1 (2015): 7–8.

299 **areas most impacted by sleep deprivation:** E. Shokri-Kojori et al., "β-Amyloid Accumulation in the Human Brain after One Night of Sleep Deprivation," *Proceedings of the National Academy of Sciences* 115, no. 17 (2018): 4483–4488.

300 **We sleep in roughly ninety-minute cycles:** E. van Der Helm and M. P. Walker, "Overnight Therapy? The Role of Sleep in Emotional Brain Processing," *Psychological Bulletin* 135, no. 5 (2009): 731.

300 **Charles Dickens wondered:** C. Dickens, *Night Walks* (New York: Penguin Classics, 1860).

300 **The sleep medication Ambien:** C. M. Paradis, L. A. Siegel, and S. B. Kleinman, "Two Cases of Zolpidem-Associated Homicide," *Primary Care Companion for CNS Disorders* 14, no. 4 (2012).

301 **brain during non-REM sleep:** Cooke, "'Sleep Should Be Prescribed.'"

301 **Acetylcholine levels drop during non-REM:** This paragraph is from D. J. Levitin, *The Organized Mind: Thinking Straight in the Age of Information Overload* (New York: Dutton, 2014); M. Sarter and J. P. Bruno, "Cortical Cholinergic Inputs Mediating Arousal, Attentional Processing and Dreaming: Differential Afferent Regulation of the Basal Forebrain by Telencephalic and Brainstem Afferents," *Neuroscience* 95, no. 4 (1999): 933–952.

301 **memory can be impaired for several days:** X. De Jaeger et al., "Decreased Acetylcholine Release Delays the Consolidation of Object Recognition Memory,"

Behavioural Brain Research 238 (2013): 62–68; J. Micheau and A. Marighetto, "Acetylcholine and Memory: A Long, Complex and Chaotic but Still Living Relationship," *Behavioural Brain Research* 221, no. 2 (2011): 424–429; E. J. Wamsley et al., "Dreaming of a Learning Task Is Associated with Enhanced Sleep-Dependent Memory Consolidation," *Current Biology* 20, no. 9 (2010): 850–855.

302 **More than 40 percent of people over sixty-five:** S. Drechsler et al., "With Mouse Age Comes Wisdom: A Review and Suggestions of Relevant Mouse Models for Age-Related Conditions," *Mechanisms of Ageing and Development* 160 (2016): 54–68.

302 **the essential slow-wave sleep stage:** S. Farajnia et al., "Aging of the Suprachiasmatic Clock," *Neuroscientist* 20, no. 1 (2014): 44–55.

302 **Sleep disturbance causes memory loss:** Drechsler et al., "With Mouse Age Comes Wisdom."

303 **sleep requirements remain the same as we age:** M. A. Lluch, T. Lloret, and P. V. Llorca, "Aging and Sleep, and Vice Versa," *Approaches to Aging Control* 16 (2012): 17–21.

303 **naps are associated with a decreased:** See, for example, A. Naska et al., "Siesta in Healthy Adults and Coronary Mortality in the General Population," *Archives of Internal Medicine* 167, no. 3 (2007): 296–301.

303 **the past one hundred years of industrialization:** Walker, *Why We Sleep.*

303 **obstructive sleep apnea:** L. Barateau et al., "Hypersomnolence, Hypersomnia, and Mood Disorders," *Current Psychiatry Reports* 19, no. 2 (2017): 13.

303 **hypersomnia and depression:** Barateau et al., "Hypersomnolence."

304 **Treatment for hypersomnia:** K. Gleason and W. V. McCall, "Current Concepts in the Diagnosis and Treatment of Sleep Disorders in the Elderly," *Current Psychiatry Reports* 17, no. 6 (2015): 45.

304 **Menopausal symptoms last seven and a half years:** N. E. Avis et al., "Duration of Menopausal Vasomotor Symptoms over the Menopause Transition," *JAMA Internal Medicine* 175, no. 4 (2015): 531–539.

304 **vasomotor symptoms can be a direct cause of sleep disturbance:** M. Bruyneel, "Sleep Disturbances in Menopausal Women: Aetiology and Practical Aspects," *Maturitas* 81, no. 3 (2015): 406–409; L. Lampio et al., "Predictors of Sleep Disturbance in Menopausal Transition," *Maturitas* 94 (2016): 137–142.

304 **A meta-analysis of more than fifteen thousand women:** D. Cintron et al., "Efficacy of Menopausal Hormone Therapy on Sleep Quality: Systematic Review and Meta-Analysis," *Endocrine* 55, no. 3 (2017): 702–711.

305 **Sonia Lupien:** S. Lupien, email communication, December 5, 2018.

305 **"Women's Health Initiative [WHI] study":** Writing Group for the Women's Health Initiative Investigators, "Risks and Benefits of Estrogen plus Progestin in Healthy Postmenopausal Women: Principal Results from the Women's Health Initiative Randomized Controlled Trial," *Journal of the American Medical Association* 288, no. 3 (2002): 321–333.

305 **A review of where we are at:** R. A. Lobo, "Where Are We 10 Years after the Women's Health Initiative?," *Journal of Clinical Endocrinology and Metabolism* 98, no. 5 (2013): 1771–1780.

306 **reductions in androgens:** A. Vermeulen, "Andropause," *Maturitas* 34, no. 1 (2000): 5–15; A. M. Matsumoto, "Andropause: Clinical Implications of the Decline in Serum Testosterone Levels with Aging in Men," *Journals of Gerontology Series A: Biological Sciences and Medical Sciences* 57, no. 2 (2002): M76–M99.

306 **testosterone administration:** Vermeulen, "Andropause."

306 **most men over the age of seventy-five:** H. B. Carter, S. Piantadosi, and J. T. Isaacs, "Clinical Evidence for and Implications of the Multistep Development of Prostate Cancer," *Journal of Urology* 143, no. 4 (1990): 742–746.

307 **genetics plays a role in caffeine metabolism:** A. Yang, A. A. Palmer, and H. de Wit, "Genetics of Caffeine Consumption and Responses to Caffeine," *Psychopharmacology* 211, no. 3 (2010): 245–257.

307 **Caffeine breaks down in the body:** T. Roehrs and T. Roth, "Caffeine: Sleep and Daytime Sleepiness," *Sleep Medicine Reviews* 12, no. 2 (2008): 153–162.

307 **adenosine receptors in the brain:** E. Murillo-Rodriguez et al., "Anandamide Enhances Extracellular Levels of Adenosine and Induces Sleep: An In Vivo Microdialysis Study," *Sleep* 26, no. 8 (2003): 943–947.

307 **reduces total sleep time and quality:** I. Clark and H. P. Landolt, "Coffee, Caffeine, and Sleep: A Systematic Review of Epidemiological Studies and Randomized Controlled Trials," *Sleep Medicine Reviews* 31 (2017): 70–78.

307 **reduce melatonin secretion:** L. Shilo et al., "The Effects of Coffee Consumption on Sleep and Melatonin Secretion," *Sleep Medicine* 3, no. 3 (2002): 271–273.

307 **Caffeine also shortens stage 3 and 4:** Roehrs and Roth, "Caffeine."

307 **caffeine blocks adenosine receptors and attenuates delta waves:** H. P. Landolt, "Caffeine, the Circadian Clock, and Sleep," *Science* 349, no. 6254 (2015): 1289–1289.

307 **cues your body normally uses:** J. Snel and M. M. Lorist, "Effects of Caffeine on Sleep and Cognition," in *Human Sleep and Cognition Part II: Clinical and Applied Research, Progress in Brain Research*, vol. 190, ed. H. P. A. Van Dongen and G. A., Kerkhof, pp. 105–117 (Amsterdam: Elsevier, 2011).

307 **In the retina:** T. Jiang et al., "Protective Effects of Melatonin on Retinal Inflammation and Oxidative Stress in Experimental Diabetic Retinopathy," *Oxidative Medicine and Cellular Longevity* (2016).

307 **In bone marrow:** F. Yang et al., "Melatonin Protects Bone Marrow Mesenchymal Stem Cells against Iron Overload–Induced Aberrant Differentiation and Senescence," *Journal of Pineal Research* 63, no. 3 (2017): e12422.

307 **In the gastrointestinal tract:** Z. Xin et al., "Melatonin as a Treatment for Gastrointestinal Cancer: A Review," *Journal of Pineal Research* 58, no. 4 (2015): 375–387.

308 **reflux esophagitis, peptic ulcers:** N. T. de Talamoni et al., "Melatonin, Gastrointestinal Protection, and Oxidative Stress," in *Gastrointestinal Tissue,* ed. J. Gracia-Sancho and J. Salvadó, pp. 317–325 (Cambridge, MA: Academic Press, 2017).

308 **components of photosynthesis:** V. Martinez et al., "Tolerance to Stress Combination in Tomato Plants: New Insights in the Protective Role of Melatonin," *Molecules* 23, no. 3 (2018): 535.

308 **timed use of melatonin supplements:** T. I. Morgenthaler et al., "Practice Parameters for the Clinical Evaluation and Treatment of Circadian Rhythm Sleep Disorders," *Sleep* 30, no. 11 (2007): 1445–1459.

308 **sleep researcher Luis Buenaver:** Hopkins Medicine Staff, "Melatonin for Sleep: Does It Work?," n.d., https://www.hopkinsmedicine.org/health/healthy-sleep/sleep-science/melatonin-for-sleep-does-it-work.

308 **Melatonin levels in the blood are highest:** G. Chechile, "Melatonin and Cancer," *Approaches to Aging Control* 17 (2012): 33–47.

308 **protective effects against many cancers:** Chechile, "Melatonin and Cancer."

309 **write a quick to-do list:** M. K. Scullin et al., "The Effects of Bedtime Writing on Difficulty Falling Asleep: A Polysomnographic Study Comparing To-Do Lists and Completed Activity Lists," *Journal of Experimental Psychology: General* 147, no. 1 (2018): 139.

CHAPTER 12

313 **Jeanne Calment of France:** Recently there have been challenges to the claim of 122 years, but I don't think this changes our understanding of longevity in humans. There are other cases of people who lived nearly as long, such as 119-year-old Sarah Knauss. See N. Zak, "Evidence That Jeanne Calment Died in 1934—Not 1997," *Rejuvenation Research* 22, no. 1 (2019): 3–12; J. Daly, "Was the World's Oldest Person Ever Actually Her 99-Year-Old Daughter?," *Smithsonian*, January 2, 2019, https://www.smithsonianmag.com/smart-news/study-questions-age-worlds-oldest-woman-180971153/.

314 **some worm species do regenerate:** G. Quirós, "These Flatworms Can Regrow a Body from a Fragment. How Do They Do It and Could We?," Shots—Health News from NPR, November 6, 2018, https://www.npr.org/sections/health-shots/2018/11/06/663612981/these-flatworms-can-regrow-a-body-from-a-fragment-how-do-they-do-it-and-could-we.

314 **the gene, *EGR*:** A. R. Gehrke et al., "Acoel Genome Reveals the Regulatory Landscape of Whole-Body Regeneration," *Science* 363, no. 6432 (2019): eaau6173.

315 **the tail . . . could regenerate a new brain:** T. Shomrat and M. Levin, "An Automated Training Paradigm Reveals Long-Term Memory in Planarians and Its Persistence through Head Regeneration," *Journal of Experimental Biology* 216, no. 20 (2013): 3799–3810. Their work was based on earlier work by K. Agata and Y. Umesono: "Brain Regeneration from Pluripotent Stem Cells in Planarian," *Philosophical Transactions of the Royal Society B: Biological Sciences* 363, no. 1500 (2008): 2071–2078, and others.

316 **telomerase also repairs cancer cells:** W. C. Hahn et al., "Inhibition of Telomerase Limits the Growth of Human Cancer Cells," *Nature Medicine* 5, no. 10 (1999): 1164.

316 **Tardigrades can survive:** S. J. McInnes and P. J. A. Pugh, "Tardigrade Biogeography," in *Water Bears: The Biology of Tardigrades*, ed. R. O. Schill, pp. 115–129 (Cham, Switzerland: Springer, 2018).

317 **unusual type of protein (IDP):** T. C. Boothby et al., "Tardigrades Use Intrinsically Disordered Proteins to Survive Desiccation," *Molecular Cell* 65, no. 6 (2017): 975–984; Boothby made an educational video about the tardigrade: R. Cans, director, "Meet the Tardigrade, the Toughest Animal on Earth," TEDEd, March 21, 2017, http://ed.ted.com/lessons/meet-the-tardigrade-the-toughest-animal-on-earth-thomas-boothby.

317 **maximum life span of humans is fixed:** X. Dong, B. Milholland, and J. Vijg, "Evidence for a Limit to Human Lifespan," *Nature* 538, no. 7624 (2016): 257.

318 **"shoveled the data into their computer":** Quoted in R. Mandelbaum, "Scientists Push Back against Controversial Paper Claiming a Limit to Human Lifespans," Gizmodo, June 28, 2017, https://gizmodo.com/scientists-push-back-against-controversial-paper-claimi-1796483675.

318 **Hicham El Guerrouj, at 3:43:13:** Wikipedia, s.v. "Mile Run World Record Progression," updated July 13, 2019, https://en.wikipedia.org/wiki/Mile_run_world_record_progression#cite_note-iaaf-5.

318 **Two McGill biologists, Bryan Hughes and Siegfried Hekimi:** B. G. Hughes, and S. Hekimi, "Many Possible Lifespan Trajectories," *Nature* 546, no. 7660 (2017): E8.

318 **Hekimi says:** Quoted in S. Kirkey, "Forever Young: No Detectable Limit to Human Lifespan, McGill Biologists Say," *The National Post*, June 28, 2017, https://nationalpost.com/news/canada/no-detectable-limit-to-human-lifespan.

319 **Olshansky . . . disagrees:** J. Olshansky, personal communication, March 21, 2019.

319 **analysis of thousands of elderly Italians:** E. Barbi et al., "The Plateau of Human Mortality: Demography of Longevity Pioneers," *Science* 360, no. 6396 (2018): 1459–1461.

319 **Hekimi, who was not involved in the study:** C. Zimmer, "What Is the Limit of Our Life Span?," *The New York Times*, July 3, 2018, p. D3.

319 **"Current understanding of the biology of aging":** M. P. Rozing, T. B. Kirkwood, and R. G. Westendorp, "Is There Evidence for a Limit to Human Lifespan?," *Nature* 546, no. 7660 (2017): E11.

320 **Most people living in the blue zones:** D. Buettner and S. Skemp, "Blue Zones: Lessons from the World's Longest Lived," *American Journal of Lifestyle Medicine* 10, no. 5 (2016): 318–321; M. Poulain, A. Herm, and G. Pes, "The Blue Zones: Areas of Exceptional Longevity around the World," *Vienna Yearbook of Population Research* 11, no. 1 (2013): 87.

321 **longevity data from 400 million people:** J. G. Ruby et al., "Estimates of the Heritability of Human Longevity Are Substantially Inflated Due to Assortative Mating," *Genetics* 210, no. 3 (2018): 1109–1124.

321 **What makes it look like longevity runs in families:** M. Molteni, "The Key to Long Life Has Little to Do with 'Good Genes,'" *Wired*, November 6, 2018.

322 **variant of the *APOE* gene:** S. Ryu et al., "Genetic Landscape of APOE in Human Longevity Revealed by High-Throughput Sequencing," *Mechanisms of Ageing and Development* 155 (2016): 7–9.

322 **FOXO in humans:** R. Martins, G. J. Lithgow, and W. Link, "Long Live FOXO: Unraveling the Role of FOXO Proteins in Aging and Longevity," *Aging Cell* 15, no. 2 (2016): 196–207.

322 **double the life span of the worm:** Kenyon did this indirectly, by manipulating insulin-like signaling upstream of FOXO.

322 **Kenyon explained it this way:** C. Kenyon, "Experiments That Hint of Longer Lives," TEDGlobal, November 17, 2011, https://www.ted.com/talks/cynthia_kenyon_experiments_that_hint_of_longer_lives/transcript#t-157928.

323 **"I tried caloric restriction":** C. Kenyon, personal communication, February 28, 2016.

323 **removing part of the worms' gonadal systems:** H. Hsin and C. Kenyon, "Signals from the Reproductive System Regulate the Lifespan of *C. elegans*," *Nature* 399, no. 6734 (1999): 362.

323 **castrated men tend to live an average of fourteen years longer:** J. B. Hamilton and G. E. Mestler, "Mortality and Survival: Comparison of Eunuchs with Intact Men and Women in a Mentally Retarded Population," *Journal of Gerontology* 24, no. 4 (1969): 395–411.

323 **involves something more than testosterone:** M. Gámez-del-Estal et al., "Epigenetic Effect of Testosterone in the Behavior of *C. elegans*. A Clue to Explain Androgen-Dependent Autistic Traits?," *Frontiers in Cellular Neuroscience* 8 (2014): 69.

323 **egg is swept clean of age-damaged, deformed proteins:** K. A. Bohnert and C. Kenyon, "A Lysosomal Switch Triggers Proteostasis Renewal in the Immortal *C. elegans* Germ Lineage," *Nature* 551, no. 7682 (2017): 629; C. Zimmer, "Young Again: How Mating Turns Back Time," *The New York Times*, November 22, 2017, p. D3.

324 **gene mutations and other interventions that increase longevity:** C. Kenyon, "The Genetics of Ageing," *Nature* (2010): 464, 504–512.

324 **(the Hayflick limit):** L. Hayflick, "Human Cells and Aging," *Scientific American* 218, no. 3 (1968): 32–37.

324 **Hayflick (now ninety) recalls:** J. Cepelewicz, "Ingenious: Leonard Hayflick," *Nautilus,* November 24, 2016, http://nautil.us/issue/42/fakes/ingenious-leonard-hayflick.

325 **role played by the telomeres:** Alexey Olovnikov, a Russian biologist, came up with an analogy having to do with a subway train and a tunnel, but I have never been able to follow the logic of it, nor to visualize what he was talking about. A. M. Olovnikov, "Telomeres, Telomerase, and Aging: Origin of the Theory," *Experimental Gerontology* 31, no. 4 (1996): 443–448.

325 **people with short telomeres die younger:** M. Armanios and E. H. Blackburn, "The Telomere Syndromes," *Nature Reviews Genetics* 13, no. 10 (2012): 693.

326 **childhood Conscientiousness predicts telomere length:** G. W. Edmonds, H. C. Côté, and S. E. Hampson, "Childhood Conscientiousness and Leukocyte Telomere Length 40 Years Later in Adult Women—Preliminary Findings of a Prospective Association," *PLoS One* 10, no. 7 (2015): e0134077.

326 **Exercise is associated with increased telomere length:** N. C. Arsenis et al., "Physical Activity and Telomere Length: Impact of Aging and Potential Mechanisms of Action," *Oncotarget* 8, no. 27 (2017): 45008; E. Puterman et al., "The Power of Exercise: Buffering the Effect of Chronic Stress on Telomere Length," *PLoS One* 5, no. 5 (2010): e10837; J. H. Kim et al., "Habitual Physical Exercise Has Beneficial Effects on Telomere Length in Postmenopausal Women," *Menopause* 19, no. 10 (2012): 1109–1115.

326 **A diet of whole foods:** J. Y. Lee et al., "Association between Dietary Patterns in the Remote Past and Telomere Length," *European Journal of Clinical Nutrition* 69, no. 9 (2015): 1048; N. Rafie et al., "Dietary Patterns, Food Groups and Telomere Length: A Systematic Review of Current Studies," *European Journal of Clinical Nutrition* 71, no. 2 (2017): 151; A. M. Fretts et al., "Processed Meat, but Not Unprocessed Red Meat, Is Inversely Associated with Leukocyte Telomere Length in the Strong Heart Family Study," *Journal of Nutrition* 146, no. 10 (2016): 2013–2018.

326 **Neighborhoods with low social cohesion:** S. Y. Gebreab et al., "Perceived Neighborhood Problems Are Associated with Shorter Telomere Length in African American Women," *Psychoneuroendocrinology* 69 (2016): 90–97; B. L. Needham et al., "Neighborhood Characteristics and Leukocyte Telomere Length: The Multi-Ethnic Study of Atherosclerosis," *Health and Place* 28 (2014): 167–172.

327 **hormesis:** T. G. Son, S. Camandola, and M. P. Mattson, "Hormetic Dietary Phytochemicals," *Neuromolecular Medicine* 10, no. 4 (2008): 236.

327 **long-term, chronic stress:** E. Blackburn and E. Epel, *The Telomere Effect: A Revolutionary Approach to Living Younger, Healthier, Longer* (New York: Hachette, 2017).

327 **healthful challenge response:** Blackburn and Epel, *The Telomere Effect.*

327 **Mindfulness meditation:** N. S. Schutte and J. M. Malouff, "A Meta-Analytic Review of the Effects of Mindfulness Meditation on Telomerase Activity," *Psychoneuroendocrinology* 42 (2014): 45–48; M. Alda et al., "Zen Meditation, Length of Telomeres, and the Role of Experiential Avoidance and Compassion," *Mindfulness* 7, no. 3 (2016): 651–659; E. A. Hoge et al., "Loving-Kindness Meditation Practice Associated with Longer Telomeres in Women," *Brain, Behavior, and Immunity* 32 (2013): 159–163.

328 **"telomere dysfunction turns into pain":** J. Mogil, "What's Wrong with Animal Models of Pain?," The Opioid Crisis and the Future of Addiction and Pain Therapeutics: Opportunities, Tools, and Technologies Symposium, Washington, DC, February 2019, video, at 30:35: https://videocast.nih.gov/summary.asp?Live=31408&bhcp=1.

328 **study of more than twenty-six thousand people:** University of Pittsburgh Schools of the Health Sciences, "Telomere Length Predicts Cancer Risk," *ScienceDaily,* April 3, 2017, www.sciencedaily.com/releases/2017/04/170403083123.htm; J. M. Yuan et al., "A Prospective Assessment for Telomere Length in Relation to Risk of Cancer in the Singapore Chinese Health Study," AACR Annual Meeting, Washington, DC, April 2017.

328 **study of 9,127 patients and thirty-one cancer types:** F. P. Barthel et al., "Systematic Analysis of Telomere Length and Somatic Alterations in 31 Cancer Types," *Nature Genetics* 49, no. 3 (2017): 349. See also P. C. Haycock et al., "Association between Telomere Length and Risk of Cancer and Non-Neoplastic Diseases: A Mendelian Randomization Study," *JAMA Oncology* 3, no. 5 (2017): 636–651.

328 **In their book *The Telomere Effect*:** Blackburn and Epel, *The Telomere Effect.*

329 **Siegfried Hekimi concurs:** S. Hekimi, personal communication, March 26, 2019.

329 **Elizabeth Parrish, the CEO of . . . BioVia:** D. Warmflash, "Liz Parrish Is Patient Zero in Her Own Anti-Aging Experiment," *The Crux,* April 29, 2016, http://blogs.discovermagazine.com/crux/2016/04/29/liz-parrish-is-an-ceo-and-patient-zero/#.XLdySpNKjox.

329 **telomere shortening evolved as an *anticancer* adaptation:** J. W. Shay, "Role of Telomeres and Telomerase in Aging and Cancer," *Cancer Discovery* 6, no. 6 (2016): 584–593.

329 **"a new low in medical quackery":** A. Regalado, "A Tale of Do-It-Yourself Gene Therapy," *MIT Technology Review,* October 14, 2015, https://www.technologyreview.com/s/542371/a-tale-of-do-it-yourself-gene-therapy/.

329 **paper coauthored by Leonard Hayflick:** S. J. Olshansky, L. Hayflick, and B. A. Carnes, "No Truth to the Fountain of Youth," *Scientific American* 286, no. 6 (2002): 92–95.

330 **extending life span artificially is still out of reach:** S. J. Olshansky, "Is Life Extension Today a Faustian Bargain?," *Frontiers in Medicine* 4 (2017): 215.

330 **in Atkins' own case:** K. McLaughlin and R. Winslow, "Report Details Dr. Atkins's Health Problems," *The Wall Street Journal,* February 10, 2004, https://www.wsj.com/articles/SB107637899384525268.

330 **people who famously tried to live forever:** P. Kennedy, "No Magic Pill Will Get You to 100," *The New York Times,* March 9, 2018, p. SR1.

331 **Jerome Rodale:** D. Cavett, "When That Guy Died on My Show," *The New York Times,* May 3, 2007, https://opinionator.blogs.nytimes.com/2007/05/03/when-that-guy-died-on-my-show/.

332 **clearance of these zombie cells:** D. J. Baker et al., "Clearance of p16 Ink4a-Positive Senescent Cells Delays Ageing-Associated Disorders," *Nature* 479, no. 7372 (2011): 232.

332 **Removing the senescent cells:** M. Scudellari, "To Stay Young, Kill Zombie Cells," *Nature* 550, no. 7677 (2017): 448–450.

332 **Subsequent work in mice:** M. J. Schafer et al., "Cellular Senescence Mediates Fibrotic Pulmonary Disease," *Nature Communications* 8 (2017): 14532; O. H. Jeon et al., "Local Clearance of Senescent Cells Attenuates the Development of Post-Traumatic Osteoarthritis and Creates a Pro-Regenerative Environment," *Nature Medicine* 23, no. 6 (2017): 775; D. J. Baker et al., "Naturally Occurring p16 Ink4a-Positive Cells Shorten Healthy Lifespan," *Nature* 530, no. 7589 (2016): 184.

332 **It can also prevent memory loss:** T. J. Bussian et al., "Clearance of Senescent Glial Cells Prevents Tau-Dependent Pathology and Cognitive Decline," *Nature* 562, no. 7728 (2018): 578.

332 **fourteen different senolytics:** Scudellari, "To Stay Young, Kill Zombie Cells."

332 **molecular biologist Nathaniel David:** Scudellari, "To Stay Young, Kill Zombie Cells."

332 **senescent cells that accumulate in the knee:** Z. Corbyn, "Want to Live for Ever? Flush Out Your Zombie Cells," *The Guardian*, October 6, 2018, https://www.theguardian.com/science/2018/oct/06/race-to-kill-killer-zombie-cells-senescent-damaged-ageing-eliminate-research-mice-aubrey-de-grey.

332 **"Everything looks good in mice":** Quoted in Corbyn, "Want to Live for Ever?"

333 **"The immune system doesn't know":** J. Allison, personal communication, July 28, 2018.

333 **"Unleashing the immune system":** Allison, personal communication.

333 **80 percent of patients die:** F. S. Hodi et al., "Two-Year Overall Survival Rates from a Randomised Phase 2 Trial Evaluating the Combination of Nivolumab and Ipilimumab versus Ipilimumab Alone in Patients with Advanced Melanoma," *Lancet Oncology* 17, no. 11 (2016): 1558.

334 **self-propagating prion form:** A. Aoyagi et al., "Aβ and Tau Prion-Like Activities Decline with Longevity in the Alzheimer's Disease Human Brain," *Science Translational Medicine* 11, no. 490 (2019): eaat8462.

334 **Prusiner told me:** S. Prusiner, personal communication, September 12, 2019.

334 **DeGrado adds:** B. DeGrado, personal communication, September 11, 2019.

336 **humans could live to be one thousand:** H. Cox, "Aubrey de Grey: Scientist Who Says Humans Can Live for 1,000 Years," *Financial Times*, February 18, 2017, https://www.ft.com/content/238cc916-e935-11e6-967b-c88452263daf.

336 **seven types of molecular and cellular damage:** A. D. N. J. de Grey, "Undoing Aging with Molecular and Cellular Damage Repair," *MIT Technology Review*, 2017, https://www.technologyreview.com/s/609576/undoing-aging-with-molecular-and-cellular-damage-repair/.

337 **To solve the various problems of aging:** H. Warner et al., "Science Fact and the SENS Agenda: What Can We Reasonably Expect from Ageing Research?," *EMBO Reports* 6, no. 11 (2005): 1006–1008.

337 **inconsistent with what we know about mitochondria:** A. Kowald and T. B. Kirkwood, "Evolution of the Mitochondrial Fusion-Fission Cycle and Its Role in Aging," *Proceedings of the National Academy of Sciences* 108, no. 25 (2011): 10237–10242.

337 **plethora of unknown variables:** M. Kyriazis, "The Impracticality of Biomedical Rejuvenation Therapies: Translational and Pharmacological Barriers," *Rejuvenation Research* 17, no. 4 (2014): 390–396.

337 **A consortium of twenty-eight scientists:** Warner et al., "Science Fact and the SENS Agenda.

339 **On the Horizon:** N. Barzilai, "An Update on Anti-Aging Drug Trials," *Innovation in Aging* 2, suppl. 1 (2018): 544.

339 **rapamycin . . . in mice . . . can extend life by 25 percent:** D. E. Harrison et al., "Rapamycin Fed Late in Life Extends Lifespan in Genetically Heterogeneous Mice," *Nature* 460, no. 7253 (2009): 392.

339 **weekly doses of rapamycin *increased* immune function:** J. B. Mannick et al., "mTOR Inhibition Improves Immune Function in the Elderly," *Science Translational Medicine* 6, no. 268 (2014): 268ra179.

339 **metformin . . . to combat aging:** G. Garg et al., "Antiaging Effect of Metformin on Brain in Naturally Aged and Accelerated Senescence Model of Rat," *Rejuvenation Research* 20, no. 3 (2017): 173–182; M. G. Novelle et al., "Metformin: A Hopeful Promise in Aging Research," *Cold Spring Harbor Perspectives in Medicine* 6, no. 3 (2016): a025932.

339 **(TAME—Targeting Aging with MEtformin):** PR Newswire, "Anti-Aging Human Study on Metformin Wins FDA Approval," December 16, 2015, https://www.prnewswire.com/news-releases/anti-aging-human-study-on-metformin-wins-fda-approval-300193724.html.

340 **NAD+ regulates cellular metabolism:** Y. Aman et al., "Therapeutic Potential of Boosting NAD+ in Aging and Age-Related Diseases," *Translational Medicine of Aging* (2018); S. I. Imai and L. Guarente, "NAD+ and Sirtuins in Aging and Disease," *Trends in Cell Biology* 24, no. 8 (2014): 464–471.

340 **interferes with absorption of nicotinamide and B_3:** S. Loui, "Nicotinamide," Huntington's Outreach Project for Education at Stanford, June 29, 2010, https://hopes.stanford.edu/nicotinamide/#relationship-between-nicotinamide-and-nicotine.

340 **After just a week of supplementation:** J. Li et al., "A Conserved NAD+ Binding Pocket That Regulates Protein-Protein Interactions During Aging," *Science* 355, no. 6331 (2017): 1312–1317.

340 **a sixty-year-old human looks like a twenty-year-old:** S. Dutta and P. Sengupta, "Men and Mice: Relating Their Ages," *Life Sciences* 152 (2016): 244–248.

340 **combination of two NAD+ precursors, NR and PT:** R. W. Dellinger et al., "Repeat Dose NRPT (Nicotinamide Riboside and Pterostilbene) Increases NAD+ Levels in Humans Safely and Sustainably: A Randomized, Double-Blind, Placebo-Controlled Study," *NPJ Aging and Mechanisms of Disease* 3, no. 1 (2017): 17.

340 **1,000 mg per day of NR:** C. R. Martens et al., "Chronic Nicotinamide Riboside Supplementation Is Well-Tolerated and Elevates NAD+ in Healthy Middle-Aged and Older Adults," *Nature Communications* 9, no. 1 (2018): 1286.

341 **"Elysium is selling pills":** Quoted in M. Bolotnikova, "Anti-Aging Approaches," *Harvard Magazine,* September–October 2017, https://harvardmagazine.com/2017/09/anti-aging-breakthrough.

341 **"None of this is ready for prime time":** Quoted in M. Taylor, "A 'Fountain of Youth' Pill? Sure, If You're a Mouse," *Kaiser Health News,* February 11, 2019, https://khn.org/news/a-fountain-of-youth-pill-sure-if-youre-a-mouse/.

341 **"I have tested the NMN":** D. Sinclair, personal communication, March 19, 2019.

341 **The Mexican axolotl:** S. Nowoshilow et al., "The Axolotl Genome and the Evolution of Key Tissue Formation Regulators," *Nature* 554, no. 7690 (2018): 50.

342 **In one species, it doubled life span:** M. Lucanic et al., "Impact of Genetic Background and Experimental Reproducibility on Identifying Chemical Compounds with Robust Longevity Effects," *Nature Communications* 8 (2017): 14256.

342 **As Richard Klausner, CEO of Lyell Immunopharma, says:** R. Klausner, *In Favor of Science: The Importance and Impact of Scientific Research*, Minerva Schools at KGI (San Francisco: Consequent, 2019).

343 **Centenarians live longer than ever:** P. B. Baltes and J. Smith, "New Frontiers in the Future of Aging: From Successful Aging of the Young Old to the Dilemmas of the Fourth Age," *Gerontology* 49, no. 2 (2003): 123–135.

343 **Richard Overton:** S. Sault, "If You Ask Richard Overton the Secret to Longevity, He'll Tell You God and Cigars Are the Answer," *Texas Hill Country,* June 15, 2017, https://texashillcountry.com/richard-overton-the-secret-to-longevity/; B. Meyer, "At 112, America's Oldest Man Has the Secret to a Long Life: 'Just Keep

Living. Don't Die,'" *Dallas News,* May 10, 2017, https://www.dallasnews.com/life/better-living/2018/05/10/americas-oldest-man-still-kicking-smoking-nears-112-secret-dont-die.

CHAPTER 13

344 **spend time doing sudoku:** M. Melby-Lervåg and C. Hulme, "Is Working Memory Training Effective? A Meta-Analytic Review," *Developmental Psychology* 49, no. 2 (2013): 270.

344 **no convincing evidence that brain-training games:** A. Bahar-Fuchs, L. Clare, and B. Woods, "Cognitive Training and Cognitive Rehabilitation for Mild to Moderate Alzheimer's Disease and Vascular Dementia," *Cochrane Database of Systematic Reviews* 6 (2013); Stanford Center on Longevity, "A Consensus on the Brain Training Industry from the Scientific Community," October 20, 2014, http://longevity3.stanford.edu/blog/2014/10/15/the-consensus-on-the-brain-training-industry-from-the-scientific-community-2/.

344 **found guilty of false advertising and fined $50 million:** The settlement was later reduced to $2 million. Federal Trade Commission, "Lumosity to Pay $2 Million to Settle FTC Deceptive Advertising Charges for Its 'Brain Training' Program," January 5, 2016, https://www.ftc.gov/news-events/press-releases/2016/01/lumosity-pay-2-million-settle-ftc-deceptive-advertising-charges.

345 **Neurocore, backed by US education secretary Betsy DeVos:** E. L. Green, "Brain-Function Firm Backed by DeVos Misled in Ads," *The New York Times,* June 27, 2018, p. B3.

345 **(brain changes in response to the training):** D. J. Simons et al., "Do 'Brain-Training' Programs Work?," *Psychological Science in the Public Interest* 17, no. 3 (2016): 103–186.

345 **analyzed 132 papers cited by . . . brain-training companies:** Simons et al., "Do 'Brain-Training' Programs Work?"

345 **Simons and his colleagues concluded:** Simons et al., "Do 'Brain-Training' Programs Work?"

346 **Art Shimamura counsels:** A. Shimamura, *Get SMART! Five Steps toward a Healthy Brain* (Scotts Valley, CA: CreateSpace, 2017).

347 **A PCE or implant that can improve memory:** B. Carey, "A Memory Jolt Raises Hopes," *The New York Times,* February 13, 2018, p. D1.

347 **Neuroscientist Michael Gazzaniga imagines:** M. S. Gazzaniga, *Human: The Science behind What Makes Your Brain Unique* (New York: Harper Perennial, 2008). I wrote about this previously in D. J. Levitin, "Brain Candy," *The New York Times,* August 22, 2008, p. BR9.

348 **Ethicists have begun to grapple:** A. D. Mohamed, "Neuroethical Issues in Pharmacological Cognitive Enhancement," *Wiley Interdisciplinary Reviews: Cognitive Science* 5, no. 5 (2014): 533–549; H. Maslen, N. Faulmüller, and J. Savulescu, "Pharmacological Cognitive Enhancement—How Neuroscientific Research Could Advance Ethical Debate," *Frontiers in Systems Neuroscience* 8 (2014): 107.

348 **The US Bioethics Commission issued a report:** Presidential Committee for the Study of Bioethical Issues, "Gray Matters: Topics at the Intersection of Neuroscience, Ethics, and Society," March 2015, https://bioethicsarchive.georgetown.edu/pcsbi/sites/default/files/GrayMatter_V2_508.pdf.

349 **Members of the US Bioethics Commission write:** A. L. Allen and N. K. Strand, "Cognitive Enhancement and Beyond: Recommendations from the Bioethics Commission," *Trends in Cognitive Sciences* 19, no. 10 (2015): 549–551.

350 **mixed results as to whether Adderall:** K. L. Cropsey et al., "Mixed-Amphetamine Salts Expectancies among College Students: Is Stimulant Induced Cognitive Enhancement a Placebo Effect?," *Drug and Alcohol Dependence* 178 (2017): 302–309.

350 **impair creativity:** M. J. Farah et al., "When We Enhance Cognition with Adderall, Do We Sacrifice Creativity? A Preliminary Study," *Psychopharmacology* 202, nos. 1–3 (2009): 541–547.

350 **modafinil . . . adenosine receptor antagonist:** P. Gerrard and R. Malcolm, "Mechanisms of Modafinil: A Review of Current Research," *Neuropsychiatric Disease and Treatment* 3, no. 3 (2007): 349.

350 **increase motivation and promote wakefulness:** M. J. Farah, "The Unknowns of Cognitive Enhancement," *Science* 350, no. 6259 (2015): 379–380.

350 **modafinil consistently enhanced attention:** R. M. Battleday and A.-K. Brem, "Modafinil for Cognitive Neuroenhancement in Healthy Non-Sleep-Deprived Subjects: A Systematic Review," *European Neuropsychopharmacology* 25 (2015): 1865–1881.

350 **a reduction in creativity:** A. D. Mohamed, "The Effects of Modafinil on Convergent and Divergent Thinking of Creativity: A Randomized Controlled Trial," *Journal of Creative Behavior* 50, no. 4 (2014): 252–267.

350 **modafinil . . . led to cognitive slowing:** A. D. Mohamed and C. R. Lewis, "Modafinil Increases the Latency of Response in the Hayling Sentence Completion Test in Healthy Volunteers: A Randomised Controlled Trial," *PLoS One* 9, no. 11 (2014): e110639.

350 **loss of dopamine receptor neurons:** L. Bäckman et al., "The Correlative Triad among Aging, Dopamine, and Cognition: Current Status and Future Prospects," *Neuroscience and Biobehavioral Reviews* 30, no. 6 (2006): 791–807.

351 **5 and 35 percent report having used it:** T. E. Wilens et al., "Misuse and Diversion of Stimulants Prescribed for ADHD: A Systematic Review of the Literature," *Journal of the American Academy of Child and Adolescent Psychiatry* 47, no. 1 (2008): 21–31.

351 **nicotine . . . tends to reduce stress:** I. Smith, "Psychostimulants and Artistic, Musical, and Literary Creativity," in *The Neuropsychiatric Complications of Stimulant Abuse,* International Review of Neurobiology, vol. 120, ed. P. Taba, A. Lees, and K. Sikk, pp. 301–326 (Waltham, MA: Academic Press, 2015); S. J. Heishman, B. A. Kleykamp, and E. G. Singleton, "Meta-Analysis of the Acute Effects of Nicotine and Smoking on Human Performance," *Psychopharmacology* 210, no. 4 (2010): 453–469.

351 **deactivating areas of the default mode:** B. Hahn et al., "Nicotine Enhances Visuospatial Attention by Deactivating Areas of the Resting Brain Default Network," *Journal of Neuroscience* 27, no. 13 (2007): 3477–3489.

351 **treatment for late-life depression:** J. A. Gandelman, P. Newhouse, and W. D. Taylor, "Nicotine and Networks: Potential for Enhancement of Mood and Cognition in Late-Life Depression," *Neuroscience and Biobehavioral Reviews* 84 (2018): 289–298.

351 **neuroprotective effects:** G. E. Barreto, A. Iarkov, and V. E. Moran, "Beneficial Effects of Nicotine, Cotinine and Its Metabolites as Potential Agents for Parkinson's Disease," *Frontiers in Aging Neuroscience* 6 (2015): 340; M. Kolahdouzan and M. J. Hamadeh, "The Neuroprotective Effects of Caffeine in Neurodegenerative Diseases," *CNS Neuroscience and Therapeutics* 23, no. 4 (2017): 272–290.

351 **nicotine as the next smart drug:** D. Hurley, "Will a Nicotine Patch Make You Smarter?," *Scientific American,* February 9, 2014, https://www.scientificamerican.com/article/will-a-nicotine-patch-make-you-smarter-excerpt/.

351 **tolcapone, a nonstimulant dopamine promoter:** J. A. Apud et al., "Tolcapone Improves Cognition and Cortical Information Processing in Normal Human Subjects," *Neuropsychopharmacology* 32, no. 5 (2007): 1011.

351 **liver injury attributed to tolcapone:** N. Borges, "Tolcapone-Related Liver Dysfunction," *Drug Safety* 26, no. 11 (2003): 743–747.

352 **pramipexole (Mirapex, Mirapexin, Sifrol):** J. Micallef et al., "Antiparkinsonian Drug-Induced Sleepiness: A Double-Blind Placebo-Controlled Study of L-Dopa, Bromocriptine and Pramipexole in Healthy Subjects," *British Journal of Clinical Pharmacology* 67, no. 3 (2009): 333–340; D. A. Pizzagalli et al., "Single Dose of a Dopamine Agonist Impairs Reinforcement Learning in Humans: Behavioral Evidence from a Laboratory-Based Measure of Reward Responsiveness," *Psychopharmacology* 196, no. 2 (2008): 221–232.

352 **doctor's instructions to the girl:** D. Hamilton, personal communication, June 8, 2019.

352 **early and incomplete evidence that rivastigmine:** A. Ströhle et al., "Drug and Exercise Treatment of Alzheimer Disease and Mild Cognitive Impairment: A Systematic Review and Meta-Analysis of Effects on Cognition in Randomized Controlled Trials," *American Journal of Geriatric Psychiatry* 23, no. 12 (2015): 1234–1249; J. T. O'Brien et al., "Clinical Practice with Anti-Dementia Drugs: A Revised (Third) Consensus Statement from the British Association for Psychopharmacology," *Journal of Psychopharmacology* 31, no. 2 (2017): 147–168.

353 **glutamate-induced excitotoxicity:** B. M. Altevogt, M. Davis, and D. E. Pankevich, eds., *Glutamate-Related Biomarkers in Drug Development for Disorders of the Nervous System: Workshop Summary* (Washington, DC: National Academies Press, 2011).

353 **difference between rivastigmine and memantine:** C. Quintana, personal communication, May 21, 2018.

353 **combination therapy using the two drugs:** P. L. Santaguida, T. A. Shamliyan, and D. R. Goldmann, "Cholinesterase Inhibitors and Memantine in Adults with Alzheimer Disease," *American Journal of Medicine* 129, no. 10 (2016): 1044–1047.

354 **inflammation is due to hormone deprivation:** C. M. Gameiro, F. Romão, and C. Castelo-Branco, "Menopause and Aging: Changes in the Immune System—A Review," *Maturitas* 67, no. 4 (2010): 316–320; C. Castelo-Branco and I. Soveral, "The Immune System and Aging: A Review," *Gynecological Endocrinology* 30, no. 1 (2014): 16–22.

354 **cognitive stimulation therapy:** A. Spector et al., "Efficacy of an Evidence-Based Cognitive Stimulation Therapy Programme for People with Dementia: Randomised Controlled Trial," *British Journal of Psychiatry* 183, no. 3 (2003): 248–254; J. D. Huntley et al., "Do Cognitive Interventions Improve General Cognition in Dementia? A Meta-Analysis and Meta-Regression," *BMJ Open* 5, no. 4 (2015): e005247.

355 **supplements for which manufacturers declare age-defying:** J. Birks and J. G. Evans, "Ginkgo Biloba for Cognitive Impairment and Dementia," *Cochrane Database of Systematic Reviews* 1 (2009); J. Geng et al., "Ginseng for Cognition," *Cochrane Database of Systematic Reviews* 12 (2010); P. E. Gold, L. Cahill, and G. L. Wenk, "Ginkgo Biloba: A Cognitive Enhancer?," *Psychological Science in the Public Interest* 3, no. 1 (2002): 2–11; A. W. Rutjes et al., "Vitamin and Mineral Supplementation for Maintaining Cognitive Function in Cognitively Healthy People in Mid and Late Life," *Cochrane Database of Systematic Reviews* 12 (2018); Q. Yuan et al., "Effects of Ginkgo Biloba on Dementia: An Overview of Systematic Reviews," *Journal of Ethnopharmacology* 195 (2017): 1–9.

355 **Vitamin B_{12} (cobalamin):** NIH Office of Dietary Supplements, "Vitamin B12," November 29, 2018, https://ods.od.nih.gov/factsheets/VitaminB12-HealthProfessional/.

355 **necessary for the production of myelin:** G. Scalabrino, "The Multi-Faceted Basis of Vitamin B12 (Cobalamin) Neurotrophism in Adult Central Nervous System: Lessons Learned from Its Deficiency," *Progress in Neurobiology* 88, no. 3 (2009): 203–220.

355 **homocysteine hypothesis:** D. Kennedy, "B Vitamins and the Brain: Mechanisms, Dose and Efficacy—A Review," *Nutrients* 8, no. 2 (2016): 68.

355 **Vitamin B_{12} deficiency:** J. L. Reay, M. A. Smith, and L. M. Riby, "B Vitamins and Cognitive Performance in Older Adults," *ISRN Nutrition* 2013 (2013).

356 **no association between B_{12} supplementation:** R. Malouf and A. A. Sastre, "Vitamin B12 for Cognition," *Cochrane Database of Systematic Reviews* 3 (2003).

356 **B_{12} was indeed effective at lowering homocysteine:** D. M. Zhang et al., "Efficacy of Vitamin B Supplementation on Cognition in Elderly Patients with Cognitive-Related Diseases: A Systematic Review and Meta-Analysis," *Journal of Geriatric Psychiatry and Neurology* 30, no. 1 (2017): 50–59.

356 **B_{12} supplementation led to significant memory improvement:** R. L. Kane et al., "Interventions to Prevent Age-Related Cognitive Decline, Mild Cognitive Impairment, and Clinical Alzheimer's-Type Dementia," *Comparative Effectiveness Reviews* 188 (2017).

356 **strongest effect being in those with higher homocysteine levels:** G. Douaud et al., "Preventing Alzheimer's Disease-Related Gray Matter Atrophy by B-Vitamin Treatment," *Proceedings of the National Academy of Sciences* 110, no. 23 (2013): 9523–9528.

356 **Taking B_{12} supplementation does not cause any harm:** B. Bistrian, "Should I Stop Taking These Vitamins?," *Harvard Health Letter,* May 2010.

356 **Neuroshroom:** PrimalHerb, https://primalherb.com/product/neuro-shroom/?rfsn=2393934.d10479. I wrote about this previously in D. J. Levitin, "What It Was Like Doing Mushrooms with Grateful Dead's Bob Weir," *High Times,* March 22, 2019.

356 **Mushrooms are a mixture of proteins:** E. Ulziijargal and J. L. Mau, "Nutrient Compositions of Culinary-Medicinal Mushroom Fruiting Bodies and Mycelia," *International Journal of Medicinal Mushrooms* 13, no. 4 (2011).

356 ***Hericium erinaceus* polysaccharides . . . increases levels of acetylcholine:** K. Mori et al., "Effects of *Hericium erinaceus* on Amyloid β (25-35) Peptide-Induced Learning and Memory Deficits in Mice," *Biomedical Research* 32, no. 1 (2011): 67–72.

357 **HEP also has neuroprotective and neuroregenerative qualities:** K. Mori et al., "Improving Effects of the Mushroom Yamabushitake (*Hericium erinaceus*) on Mild Cognitive Impairment: A Double-Blind Placebo-Controlled Clinical Trial," *Phytotherapy Research* 23, no. 3 (2009): 367–372.

357 **it reduces depression and anxiety:** M. Nagano et al., "Reduction of Depression and Anxiety by 4 Weeks *Hericium erinaceus* Intake," *Biomedical Research* 31, no. 4 (2010): 231–237.

357 ***Ganoderma lucidum*:** H. Zhao et al., "Spore Powder of *Ganoderma lucidum* Improves Cancer-Related Fatigue in Breast Cancer Patients Undergoing Endocrine Therapy: A Pilot Clinical Trial," *Evidence-Based Complementary and Alternative Medicine* 2012 (2012).

357 **neuroprotective effects on the hippocampus:** Y. Zhou et al., "Neuroprotective Effect of Preadministration with *Ganoderma lucidum* Spore on Rat Hippocampus," *Experimental and Toxicologic Pathology* 64, nos. 7–8 (2012): 673–680.

357 **promotes cognitive function in mouse models of AD:** S. Huang et al., "Polysaccharides from *Ganoderma lucidum* Promote Cognitive Function and Neural Progenitor Proliferation in Mouse Model of Alzheimer's Disease," *Stem Cell Reports* 8, no. 1 (2017): 84–94.

357 **anti-inflammatory properties:** W. B. Stavinoha, "Status of *Ganoderma lucidum* in United States: *Ganoderma lucidum* as an Anti-Inflammatory Agent," in *Proceedings of the 1st International Symposium on Ganoderma Lucidum in Japan*, pp. 17–18 (2008).

357 **reduces oxidative stress:** W. J. Li et al., "*Ganoderma atrum* Polysaccharide Attenuates Oxidative Stress Induced by D-Galactose in Mouse Brain," *Life Sciences* 88, nos. 15–16 (2011): 713–718.

357 **seven hundred adults aged sixty and over in Singapore:** L. Feng et al., "The Association between Mushroom Consumption and Mild Cognitive Impairment: A Community-Based Cross-Sectional Study in Singapore," *Journal of Alzheimer's Disease* 68 (2019): 197–203.

357 ***Bacopa monnieri*:** S. C. Pierce et al., "Hydrology and Species-Specific Effects of *Bacopa monnieri* and *Leersia oryzoides* on Soil and Water Chemistry," *Ecohydrology: Ecosystems, Land and Water Process Interactions, Ecohydrogeomorphology* 2, no. 3 (2009): 279–286.

357 **improve higher-order cognitive processes:** C. Stough et al., "The Chronic Effects of an Extract of *Bacopa monniera* (Brahmi) on Cognitive Function in Healthy Human Subjects," *Psychopharmacology* 156, no. 4 (2001): 481–484.

357 **significant effect on retaining new information:** S. Roodenrys et al., "Chronic Effects of Brahmi (*Bacopa monnieri*) on Human Memory," *Neuropsychopharmacology* 27, no. 2 (2002): 279.

357 **regulating tryptophan hydroxylase and serotonin transporter expression:** P. D. Charles et al., "*Bacopa monniera* Leaf Extract Up-Regulates Tryptophan Hydroxylase (TPH2) and Serotonin Transporter (SERT) Expression: Implications in Memory Formation," *Journal of Ethnopharmacology* 134, no. 1 (2011): 55–61.

358 **"elastic thinking":** L. Mlodinow, *Elastic: Flexible Thinking in a Time of Change* (New York: Pantheon, 2018).

358 **A single dose of the drug in older adults:** Hopkins Medicine Staff, "Single Dose of Hallucinogen May Create Lasting Personality Change," September 29, 2011, https://www.hopkinsmedicine.org/news/media/releases/single_dose_of_hallucinogen_may_create_lasting_personality_change.

359 **Science writer Michael Pollan's book:** J. Zack, "Michael Pollan Takes a Trip in His Latest Book, 'How to Change Your Mind,'" *San Francisco Chronicle,* May 21, 2018, https://www.sfchronicle.com/books/article/Michael-Pollan-gets-stoned-in-his-latest-book-12932010.php.

359 **"among the safest drugs we know of":** D. Nutt, *Drugs without the Hot Air: Minimising the Harms of Legal and Illegal Drugs* (Cambridge: UIT Cambridge, 2012), p. 254.

360 **Brian Wilson:** S. Belli, "A Psychobiographical Analysis of Brian Douglas Wilson: Creativity, Drugs, and Models of Schizophrenic and Affective Disorders," *Personality and Individual Differences* 46, no. 8 (2009): 809–819. See also D. H. Linszen, P. M. Dingemans, and M. E. Lenior, "Cannabis Abuse and the Course of Recent-Onset Schizophrenic Disorders," *Archives of General Psychiatry* 51, no. 4 (1994): 273–279.

361 **psychedelics in microdoses:** R. Glatter, "LSD Microdosing: The New Job Enhancer in Silicon Valley and Beyond?," *Forbes,* November 27, 2015, https://www.forbes

.com/sites/robertglatter/2015/11/27/lsd-microdosing-the-new-job-enhancer-in-silicon-valley-and-beyond/#36bbc7e2188a.

361 **An ideal dose:** J. Fadiman and S. Korb, "Microdosing Psychedelics," in *Advances in Psychedelic Medicine: State-of-the-Art Therapeutic Applications,* ed. M. J. Winkelman and B. Sessa, p. 323 (Westport, CT: Praeger, 2019).

361 **Microdosers scored lower:** T. Anderson et al., "Microdosing Psychedelics: Personality, Mental Health, and Creativity Differences in Microdosers," *Psychopharmacology* (2018): 1–10; P. S. Hendricks et al., "Classic Psychedelic Use Is Associated with Reduced Psychological Distress and Suicidality in the United States Adult Population," *Journal of Psychopharmacology* 29, no. 3 (2015): 280–288.

361 **Regular low doses of THC:** A. Bilkei-Gorzo et al., "A Chronic Low Dose of Δ 9-Tetrahydrocannabinol (THC) Restores Cognitive Function in Old Mice," *Nature Medicine* 23, no. 6 (2017): 782.

361 **Cochlear implants:** J. Saliba et al., "Functional Near-Infrared Spectroscopy for Neuroimaging in Cochlear Implant Recipients," *Hearing Research* 338 (2016): 64–75.

361 **Cochlear implants . . . six hundred thousand people:** A. P. Sanderson et al., "Exploiting Routine Clinical Measures to Inform Strategies for Better Hearing Performance in Cochlear Implant Users," *Frontiers in Neuroscience* 12 (2019).

361 **neural implants . . . Parkinson's:** J. M. Bronstein et al., "Deep Brain Stimulation for Parkinson Disease: An Expert Consensus and Review of Key Issues," *Archives of Neurology* 68, no. 2 (2011): 165.

361 **neural implants . . . depression:** A. M. Lozano et al., "Subcallosal Cingulate Gyrus Deep Brain Stimulation for Treatment-Resistant Depression," *Biological Psychiatry* 64, no. 6 (2008): 461–467.

362 **neural implant that increased memory encoding:** Y. Ezzyat et al., "Closed-Loop Stimulation of Temporal Cortex Rescues Functional Networks and Improves Memory," *Nature Communications* 9, no. 1 (2018): 365.

362 **"jostling the system":** Quoted in B. Carey, "'Pacemaker' for the Brain Can Help Memory, Study Finds," *The New York Times,* April 21, 2017, p. A19.

362 **Kahana thinks that future research:** B. Carey, "A Brain Implant Improved Memory, Scientists Report," *The New York Times,* February 7, 2018, p. A17.

362 **an experimental "sensory" hand:** E. Landau, "Artificial Hand Lets Amputee Feel Object," CNN, February 6, 2014, https://www.cnn.com/2014/02/05/health/bionic-hand/index.html.

362 **Samantha Payne, COO of OpenBionics:** Quoted in R. Godwin, "We Will Get Regular Body Upgrades: What Will Humans Look Like in 100 Years?," *The Guardian,* September 22, 2018.

363 **A neural implant . . . paralyzed right arm:** C. E. Bouton et al., "Restoring Cortical Control of Functional Movement in a Human with Quadriplegia," *Nature* 533, no. 7602 (2016): 247.

363 **Imagine a neurosurgeon:** I thank Google's Dan Kaufman for this idea.

363 **Zoltan Istvan is a controversial figure:** Z. Istvan, "I Just Got a Computer Chip Implanted in My Hand—and the Rest of the World Won't Be Far Behind," *Business Insider,* September 25, 2015.

363 **Neil Harbisson, had an antenna installed:** S. Jeffries, "Neil Harbisson: The World's First Cyborg Artist," *The Guardian,* May 6, 2014. To be clear, Harbisson is not able to browse the Internet with his brain or to receive video images displayed on some sort of mind-screen. People with Bluetooth can send and receive auditory

signals through an implant in their tooth that transmits sound into their brain through bone conduction; M. Franco, "Antenna Implanted in Cyborg's Skull Gets Wi-Fi, Color as Sound," CNET, April 14, 2014, https://www.cnet.com/news/cyborg-interview-hear-colors-with-antenna-in-your-skull/.

364 **The technology exists for these:** A. Mandavilli, "A Patch Uses Sweat to Get a Read on Your Body's Toil," *The New York Times,* January 21, 2019, p. B3.

364 **Serena Williams has been seen in ads:** A. Stych, "Serena Williams Rocks Wearable Tech in Gatorade Ad," *The Business Journals,* December 27, 2018, https://www.bizjournals.com/bizwomen/news/latest-news/2018/12/serena-williams-rocks-wearable-tech-in-gatorade-ad.html?page=all.

365 **Meditation reduces activity within the default mode network:** J. A. Brewer et al., "Meditation Experience Is Associated with Differences in Default Mode Network Activity and Connectivity," *Proceedings of the National Academy of Sciences* 108, no. 50 (2011): 20254–20259; K. A. Garrison et al., "Meditation Leads to Reduced Default Mode Network Activity beyond an Active Task," *Cognitive, Affective, and Behavioral Neuroscience* 15, no. 3 (2015): 712–720.

365 **anti-inflammatory effect by reducing cytokines:** J. D. Creswell et al., "Alterations in Resting-State Functional Connectivity Link Mindfulness Meditation with Reduced Interleukin-6: A Randomized Controlled Trial," *Biological Psychiatry* 80, no. 1 (2016): 53–61.

365 **Long-term meditators show structural changes:** J. H. Jang et al., "Increased Default Mode Network Connectivity Associated with Meditation," *Neuroscience Letters* 487, no. 3 (2011): 358–362; S. W. Lazar et al., "Meditation Experience Is Associated with Increased Cortical Thickness," *Neuroreport* 16, no. 17 (2005): 1893; R. E. Wells et al., "Meditation's Impact on Default Mode Network and Hippocampus in Mild Cognitive Impairment: A Pilot Study," *Neuroscience Letters* 556 (2013): 15–19; K. C. Fox et al., "Is Meditation Associated with Altered Brain Structure? A Systematic Review and Meta-Analysis of Morphometric Neuroimaging in Meditation Practitioners," *Neuroscience and Biobehavioral Reviews* 43 (2014): 48–73.

365 **Even brief meditation reduces fatigue:** F. Zeidan et al., "Mindfulness Meditation Improves Cognition: Evidence of Brief Mental Training," *Consciousness and Cognition* 19, no. 2 (2010): 597–605.

365 **benefits persist even after meditation:** M. A. Cohn and B. L. Fredrickson, "In Search of Durable Positive Psychology Interventions: Predictors and Consequences of Long-Term Positive Behavior Change," *Journal of Positive Psychology* 5, no. 5 (2010): 355–366.

365 **lower levels of cortisol:** M. A. Rosenkranz et al., "Reduced Stress and Inflammatory Responsiveness in Experienced Meditators Compared to a Matched Healthy Control Group," *Psychoneuroendocrinology* 68 (2016): 117–125.

365 **benefits show up after as little as four weeks:** E. Walsh, T. Eisenlohr-Moul, and R. Baer, "Brief Mindfulness Training Reduces Salivary IL-6 and TNF-α in Young Women with Depressive Symptomatology," *Journal of Consulting and Clinical Psychology* 84, no. 10 (2016): 887.

366 **downregulation of inflammatory genes:** P. Kaliman et al., "Rapid Changes in Histone Deacetylases and Inflammatory Gene Expression in Expert Meditators," *Psychoneuroendocrinology* 40 (2014): 96–107.

366 **meditation seems to have epigenetic effects:** J. A. Dusek et al., "Genomic Counter-Stress Changes Induced by the Relaxation Response," *PLoS One* 3, no. 7 (2008): e2576; H. Lavretsky et al., "A Pilot Study of Yogic Meditation for Family Dementia Caregivers with Depressive Symptoms: Effects on Mental Health, Cognition, and

Telomerase Activity," *International Journal of Geriatric Psychiatry* 28, no. 1 (2013): 57–65; E. Luders et al., "The Unique Brain Anatomy of Meditation Practitioners: Alterations in Cortical Gyrification," *Frontiers in Human Neuroscience* 6, (2012): 34.

366 **lower those levels and decrease feelings of loneliness:** J. D. Creswell et al., "Mindfulness-Based Stress Reduction Training Reduces Loneliness and Pro-Inflammatory Gene Expression in Older Adults: A Small Randomized Controlled Trial," *Brain, Behavior, and Immunity* 26, no. 7 (2012): 1095–1101.

366 **associated with increased telomerase:** N. S. Schutte and J. M. Malouff, "A Meta-Analytic Review of the Effects of Mindfulness Meditation on Telomerase Activity," *Psychoneuroendocrinology* 42 (2014): 45–48; T. L. Jacobs et al., "Intensive Meditation Training, Immune Cell Telomerase Activity, and Psychological Mediators," *Psychoneuroendocrinology* 36, no. 5 (2011): 664–681.

366 **mild cognitive impairment and early-stage Alzheimer's, meditation:** J. Russell-Williams et al., "Mindfulness and Meditation: Treating Cognitive Impairment and Reducing Stress in Dementia," *Reviews in the Neurosciences* 29, no. 7 (2018): 791–804.

CHAPTER 14

367 **David Bradley:** Quoted in N. Narboe, ed., *Aging: An Apprenticeship* (Portland, OR: Red Notebook Press), p. 80.

368 **Philosopher David Velleman suggests:** D. Velleman, "Well-Being and Time," *Pacific Philosophical Quarterly* 72, no. 1 (1991): 48–77.

368 **prefer the life that takes the upward trend:** M. Slote, *Goods and Virtues* (New York: Oxford University Press, 1983).

368 **additional years of lower quality:** E. Diener, D. Wirtz, and S. Oishi, "End Effects of Rated Life Quality: The James Dean Effect," *Psychological Science* 12, no. 2 (2001): 124–131.

369 **We're sensitive to the timing of events:** See also J. Glasgow, "The Shape of a Life and the Value of Loss and Gain," *Philosophical Studies* 162, no. 3 (2013): 665–682.

369 **the journal *Nature* . . . therapies that are taken for granted:** Nature Editorial Staff, "Study the Survivors," *Nature* 568 (2019): 143; R. Garza, "Children's Cancer Research to Expand, with Help from Local Oncologist, Survivor," *Rivard Report,* June 11, 2018, https://therivardreport.com/childrens-cancer-research-to-expand-with-help-from-local-oncologist-survivor/.

370 **healthy life expectancy (HALE):** H. S. Friedman and M. L. Kern, "Personality, Well-Being and Health," *Annual Reviews of Psychology* 65 (2014): 719–742.

370 **This holds true across seventy-two countries:** D. G. Blanchflower and A. J. Oswald, "Is Well-Being U-Shaped over the Life Cycle?," *Social Science and Medicine* 66, no. 8 (2008): 1733–1749.

371 **the middle-aged dip:** Pink is summarizing an argument made by social scientist Hannes Schwandt. D. H. Pink, *When: The Scientific Secrets of Perfect Timing* (New York: Penguin Press, 2019).

372 **The positivity bias:** L. L. Carstensen and M. DeLiema, "The Positivity Effect: A Negativity Bias in Youth Fades with Age," *Current Opinion in Behavioral Sciences* 19 (2018): 7–12.

372 **two areas associated with selective attention:** M. Mather, "The Affective Neuroscience of Aging," *Annual Review of Psychology* 67 (2016): 213–238; L. K. Sasse et al., "Selective Control of Attention Supports the Positivity Effect in Aging," *PLoS One* 9, no. 8 (2014): e104180.

372 **Sonny Rollins:** S. Rollins, personal communication, June 2018.

374 **Most quaily of life indexes:** See, for example, Economist Intelligence Unit, "The Economist Intelligence Unit's Quality-of-Life Index," 2005, http://www.economist.com/media/pdf/QUALITY_OF_LIFE.pdf; European Union European Commission, "Quality of Life Indicators," 2013, https://ec.europa.eu/eurostat/statistics-explained/index.php/Quality_of_life_indicators; P. Haslam, J. Schafer, and P. Beaudet, eds., *Introduction to International Development: Approaches, Actors, and Issues,* 2nd ed. (Don Mills: Oxford University Press, 2012); D. Kahneman and A. B. Krueger, "Developments in the Measurement of Subjective Well-Being," *Journal of Economic Perspectives* 20, no. 1 (2006): 3–24; United Nations Development Program, *Human Development Report,* 2013, http://hdr.undp.org/en/statistics/hdi/. I thank my McGill honors students Lauren Guttman, Jane Stocks, and Noa Yaakoba-Zohar for bringing these issues and papers to my attention.

374 **For people from collectivist and holistic societies:** M. J. Hornsey et al., "How Much Is Enough in a Perfect World? Cultural Variation in Ideal Levels of Happiness, Pleasure, Freedom, Health, Self-Esteem, Longevity, and Intelligence," *Psychological Science* 29, no. 9 (2018): 1393–1404. See also Y. Uchida and S. Kitayama, "Happiness and Unhappiness in East and West: Themes and Variations," *Emotion* 9 (2009): 441–456.

375 ***The World Happiness Report*:** A. Chiu, "Americans Are the Unhappiest They've Ever Been, U.N. Report Finds. An 'Epidemic of Addictions' Could Be to Blame," *The Washington Post,* March 21, 2019.

375 **comedian Jimmy Kimmel:** Quoted in Chiu, "Americans Are the Unhappiest."

375 **Jean Twenge:** Quoted in Chiu, "Americans Are the Unhappiest."

375 **spate of addictions:** J. M. Twenge and W. K. Campbell, "Associations between Screen Time and Lower Psychological Well-Being among Children and Adolescents: Evidence from a Population-Based Study," *Preventive Medicine Reports* 12, no. 271 (2018).

375 **blame overuse of digital devices:** Chiu, "Americans Are the Unhappiest."

376 **Psychiatrist Robert Waldinger:** R. Waldinger, "What Makes a Good Life? Lessons from the Longest Study on Happiness," TEDx Beacon Street, 2016, https://www.youtube.com/watch?v=8KkKuTCFvzI.

376 **A bigger predictor than cholesterol:** Waldinger, "What Makes a Good Life?"

376 **Love is the most important thing:** C. Gregoire, "The 75-Year Study That Found the Secrets to a Fulfilling Life," *Huffington Post,* August 11, 2013, http://www.huffingtonpost.com/2013/08/11/how-this-harvard-psycholo_n_3727229.html.

376 **without supportive, loving relationships:** J. W. Shenk, "What Makes Us Happy?," *The Atlantic,* June 2009, https://www.theatlantic.com/magazine/archive/2009/06/what-makes-us-happy/307439/.

376 **George Vaillant, who directed the study for three decades:** Quoted in Shenk, "What Makes Us Happy?"

377 **one man in the study described:** G. Vaillant, "The Importance of Relationships to Health, Resilience, and Ageing," Edith Dominian Memorial Lecture, London, UK, June 2014, https://www.youtube.com/watch?v=XHnuReGjkws.

377 **As Vaillant notes:** Vaillant, "The Importance of Relationships."

377 **Glueck men were 50 percent more likely:** C. Lambert, "Deep Cravings," *Harvard Magazine,* March 1, 2000, http://harvardmagazine.com/2000/03/deep-cravings.html.

378 **satisfied with their spouses have increased longevity:** An increase of one standard deviation in spousal satisfaction was correlated with a 13 percent reduction in

mortality; an increase in two standard deviations of spousal satisfaction would be correlated with a 25 percent reduction in mortality; O. Stavrova, "Having a Happy Spouse Is Associated with Lowered Risk of Mortality," *Psychological Science* (2019): 0956797619835147.

379 **Lamont Dozier:** L. Dozier, personal communication, July 26, 2018.

379 **Too much time spent with no purpose:** M. A. Killingsworth and D. T. Gilbert, "A Wandering Mind Is an Unhappy Mind," *Science* 330, no. 6006 (2010): 932.

379 **25 and 40 percent of people who retire reenter:** N. Maestas, "Back to Work Expectations and Realizations of Work after Retirement," *Journal of Human Resources* 45, no. 3 (2010): 718–748; A. Mergenthaler et al., "The Changing Nature of (Un-)Retirement in Germany: Living Conditions, Activities and Life Phases of Older Adults in Transition" (working paper); L. G. Platts et al., "Returns to Work after Retirement: A Prospective Study of Unretirement in the United Kingdom," *Ageing and Society* 39, no. 3 (2019): 439–464; R. Kanabar, "Unretirement in England: An Empirical Perspective" (discussion paper, Department of Economics and Related Studies, University of York, 2012).

379 **Harvard economist Nicole Maestas says:** Quoted in P. Span, "When Retirement Doesn't Quite Work Out," *The New York Times,* April 3, 2018, p. D5.

379 **Author Barbara Ehrenreich:** I. Chotiner, "Barbara Ehrenreich Doesn't Have Time for Self-Care," *Slate,* April 13, 2018, https://slate.com/news-and-politics/2018/04/barbara-ehrenreich-says-smoking-bans-are-a-war-on-the-working-class.html.

380 **age discrimination:** A summary of age discrimination laws in forty countries is available at AgeDiscrimination.info, http://www.agediscrimination.info/international-age-discrimination/.

380 **Deutsche Bank:** "The Joys of Living to 100," *The Economist,* July 6, 2017, https://www.economist.com/special-report/2017/07/06/the-joys-of-living-to-100.

380 **accommodations . . . workers with Alzheimer's:** K. Allen, "Alzheimer's and Employment," BrightFocus, October 24, 2017, https://www.brightfocus.org/alzheimers/article/alzheimers-and-employment.

381 **Heathrow . . . the world's first "dementia-friendly" airport:** A. Shaw, "London Heathrow Set to Become World's First 'Dementia-Friendly' Airport," *The Sunday Post,* September 2, 2018, https://www.sundaypost.com/fp/positive-progress-for-heathrow-with-dementia-friends/#r3z-addoor.

381 **intergenerational choir:** P. B. Harris and C. A. Caporella, "Making a University Community More Dementia Friendly through Participation in an Intergenerational Choir," *Dementia* (2018): 1471301217752209.

381 **Pat Summitt:** Wikipedia, s.v. Pat Summitt, updated July 14, 2019, https://en.wikipedia.org/wiki/Pat_Summitt.

381 **volunteers felt a greater sense of accomplishment:** M. C. Carlson et al., "Impact of the Baltimore Experience Corps Trial on Cortical and Hippocampal Volumes," *Alzheimer's and Dementia* 11, no. 11 (2015): 1340–1348.

381 **As Anaïs Nin observed:** C. A. Dingle, *Memorable Quotations: French Writers of the Past* (iUniverse, 2000), p. 126.

382 **South African writer J. M. Coetzee:** J. M. Coetzee, *Disgrace* (New York: Viking, 1999).

382 **nonpersonal care:** S. Duffy and T. H. Lee, "In-Person Health Care as Option B," *New England Journal of Medicine* 378, no. 2 (2018): 104–106.

383 **increased continuity of care:** D. J. P. Gray et al., "Continuity of Care with Doctors—A Matter of Life and Death? A Systematic Review of Continuity of Care and Mortality," *BMJ Open* 8, no. 6 (2018): e021161.

383 **Dr. Meyer Schindler:** "The History of San Francisco Otolaryngology," n.d., http://www.sfotomed.com/history.html.

383 **Dr. Eduardo Dolhun . . . ideal doctor-patient relationship:** E. Dolhun, personal communication, July 9, 2013.

384 **specialization tends to divide:** R. Yeravdekar, V. R. Yeravdekar, and M. A. Tutakne, "Family Physicians: Importance and Relevance," *Journal of the Indian Medical Association* 110, no. 7 (2012): 490–493.

384 **Dr. David Brill:** "Why Keeping the Same Doctor Can Help You Live Longer," HealthLine, https://www.healthline.com/health-news/same-doctor-help-you-live-longer#1.

384 **patient-centered medical home:** G. L. Jackson et al., "The Patient-Centered Medical Home: A Systematic Review," *Annals of Internal Medicine* 158, no. 3 (2013): 169–178; Patient-Centered Primary Care Collaborative, "Defining the Medical Home," https://www.pcpcc.org/about/medical-home; K. C. Stange et al., "Defining and Measuring the Patient-Centered Medical Home," *Journal of General Internal Medicine* 25, no. 6 (2010): 601–612; The Commonwealth Fund, "Primary Care: Our First Line of Defense," June 12, 2013, https://www.commonwealthfund.org/publications/publication/2013/jun/primary-care-our-first-line-defense.

385 **Dr. Gordon Caldwell:** G. Caldwell, personal communication, March 27, 2019.

387 **three questions we should all ask:** J. F. Coughlin, "Three Questions That Can Predict Future Quality of Life," MIT AgeLab, n.d., http://agelab.mit.edu/system/files/2018-12/three_questions_that_can_predict_future_quality_of_life_0.pdf.

388 **Argentum . . . "Assisted Living":** Argentum, "Senior Living Innovation Series: Memory Care" (white paper, 2016). Full disclosure: Argentum paid me to speak at their annual meeting, but I wrote this section before they invited me, and the invitation did not influence my decision to include them in this book.

389 **daily pill pack:** CVS, "Multi-Dose Packs," https://www.cvs.com/content/multidose; Pill Pack, https://www.pillpack.com/.

390 **Medicare's Hospital Compare website:** https://www.medicare.gov/hospitalcompare.

390 **HospitalInspections.org:** A. Frakt, "Why It's Crucial to Choose the Right Hospital," *The New York Times,* August 22, 2016, p. A3.

390 **Several websites allow you to find the nearest hospital:** See, for example, "ER Wait Watcher," ProPublica, https://projects.propublica.org/emergency/.

391 **Physician Alex Lickerman notes:** A. Lickerman, "The Best Disease from Which to Die," *Psychology Today,* September 9, 2012, https://www.psychologytoday.com/us/blog/happiness-in-world/201209/the-best-disease-which-die.

392 **an advance medical directive for dementia:** P. Span, "One Day Your Mind May Fade. But You Can Plan Ahead," *The New York Times,* January 23, 2018, p. D5; Dr. Gaster's advance directive is available here: Advance Directive for Dementia, https://dementia-directive.org/.

392 **Gaster underscores the uniqueness of dementia:** B. Gaster, E. B. Larson, and J. R. Curtis, "Advance Directives for Dementia: Meeting a Unique Challenge," *Journal of the American Medical Association* 318, no. 22 (2017): 2175–2176.

394 **says Gloria Steinem:** G. Steinem, "Into the Seventies," in *Aging: An Apprenticeship,* ed. N. Narboe, p. 177 (Portland, OR: Red Notebook Press, 2017).

394 **"want to die at home":** Singer-songwriter Conor Oberst has a song called "I Don't Want to Die (in the Hospital)": https://www.youtube.com/watch?v=-JoCQhh3_pE.

394 **when we are terminally ill:** R. Sinatra, "Causes and Consequences of Inadequate Management of Acute Pain," *Pain Medicine* 11 (2010): 1859–1871, http://dx.doi.org/10.1111/j.1526-4637.2010.00983.x.

394 **Aversive experiences . . . nature:** K. Tanja-Dijkstra et al., "The Soothing Sea: A Virtual Coastal Walk Can Reduce Experienced and Recollected Pain," *Environment and Behavior* 50, no. 6 (2018): 599–625.

394 **Patients who experienced VR scenes of nature:** Tanja-Dijkstra et al., "The Soothing Sea."

394 **natural sounds:** T. O. Iyendo, "Exploring the Effect of Sound and Music on Health in Hospital Settings: A Narrative Review," *International Journal of Nursing Studies* 63 (2016): 82–100.

394 **increased access to natural scenes:** See M. Jonwiak, "Nature Scenes and Hospital Recovery," September 15, 2016, Association of Nature and Forest Therapy, https://www.anft.blog/blog/nature-scenes-and-hospital-recovery.

394 **gardens are back in style now:** D. Franklin, "How Hospital Gardens Help Patients Heal," *Scientific American,* March 1, 2012, https://www.scientificamerican.com/article/nature-that-nurtures/.

395 **The TriPoint Medical Center:** J. Ference, "Nature's Calming Influence," *Health Facilities Management* 23, no. 7 (2010): 44.

395 **Rachel Clarke:** R. Clarke, "In Life's Last Moments, Open a Window," *The New York Times,* September 9, 2018, p. SR7.

395 **Clarke recalls:** Quoted in L. Hawkins, "The Uplifting Power of Nature at the End of Life," e-hospice, November 23, 2018, https://ehospice.com/uk_posts/the-uplifting-power-of-nature-at-the-end-of-life/.

395 **The playwright Dennis Potter:** Quoted in J. Rockwell, "Dennis Potter's Last Interview, on 'Nowness' and His Work," *The New York Times,* June 12, 1994, p. 2002030.

397 **says Betty White:** As told to Camille Sweeney in L. H. Lapham, "Old Masters," *The New York Times Magazine,* October 23, 2014, https://www.nytimes.com/interactive/2014/10/23/magazine/old-masters-at-top-of-their-game.

398 **A study from the Karolinska Institute:** L. Fratiglioni et al., "Influence of Social Network on Occurrence of Dementia: A Community-Based Longitudinal Study," *Lancet* 355, no. 9212 (2000): 1315–1319.

399 **Gratitude:** S. Ni et al., "Effect of Gratitude on Loneliness of Chinese College Students: Social Support as a Mediator," *Social Behavior and Personality* 43, no. 4 (2015): 559–566.

399 **Placido Domingo:** Quoted in J. Barone, "Placido Domingo Nears the Unthinkable," *The New York Times,* August 23, 2018, p. C1.

399 **T. Boone Pickens:** As told to Camille Sweeney in Lapham, "Old Masters."

400 **Individual strivings for accomplishment:** H. S. Friedman and M. L. Kern, "Personality, Well-Being, and Health," *Annual Reviews of Psychology* 65 (2014): 719–742.

400 **two-thirds of the people over sixty-five:** K. Dychtwald, "Will the 'Age Wave' Make or Break America? The Questions That Trump, Clinton and Sanders Must Answer," *Huffington Post,* May 19, 2017, http://agewave.com/media_files/05%2018%2016%20HP_Questions.pdf.

400 **three-quarters of the people over seventy-five:** G. Vradenburg, personal communication, March 28, 2019. Vradenburg is the CEO of USAgainstAlzheimer's.

400 **Gloria Steinem:** G. Steinem, *Boston Speaker Series: Gloria Steinem,* Boston Speakers Series, Boston, MA, January 9, 2019.

ACKNOWLEDGMENTS

I am grateful to the following for reading and improving previous drafts of all or part of this book: Heather Bortfeld, Howard Gardner, Michael Gazzaniga, Lew Goldberg, Sarah Hampson, Siegfried Hekimi, Mike Lankford, Sonia Lupien, Jay Olshansky, and Robert Sternberg, and to the following for answering questions as they arose: Neil Charness, Daniel Dennett, Eduardo Dolhun, Mallory Frayn, Derek Han, Janet King, Stan Kubow, Joe LeDoux, Jasper Rine, Stephanie Shih, Daniel Simons, and David Sinclair.

Stephen Morrow, Jeffrey Mogil, Lindsay Fleming, Sarah Chalfant, and Rebecca Nagel read everything very closely and brought great insight and clarity with their notes and suggestions to me. Lindsay functioned as research assistant and editor and drew most of the figures appearing in the book. Len Blum brought his sense of humor and masterful editing pen to the entire book, vastly improving it. Hannah Feeney oversaw hundreds of details in the editing and production of the book with great efficiency and skill.

I'm so grateful to the many individuals who shared their own experiences of being over seventy with me: Judy Collins, His Holiness the Dalai Lama, Lamont Dozier, Donald Fagen, Jane Fonda, President Vicente Fox, Charles Koch, Tim Laddish, my mother and father, Sonia and Lloyd Levitin, Joni Mitchell, Sonny Rollins, Secretary George Shultz, Paul Simon, Jack Weinstein, and Bob Weir.

Around the time I was starting my training, a well-known cognitive neuroscientist, Michael Posner, began a fruitful collaboration with a well-known developmental psychologist, Mary Rothbart. (This doesn't happen as often as you might think.) Mike became my doctoral advisor and I learned to embrace these two different fields. Always looking out for me, Mike suggested that developmental cognitive neuroscientist Helen Neville serve on my doctoral committee, along with the biologist Terry Takahashi. While all this was going on, I had an office at the Oregon Research Institute and was a member of the research group headed by Lewis R. Goldberg, a psychometrician (measurement of psychological factors) and the father of modern-day personality psychology. Jack Digman and Sarah Hampson were a big part of my education there. Along the way, I also had the great fortune to have learned from a number of leading thinkers outside my field, such as Susan Nolen-Hoeksema (who died tragically in her early fifties), Lee Ross, Ellen Markman, Susan Carey, and Laura Carstensen. I am grateful for this education and mentorship.

ART CREDITS

24 [top]: Photo used under Creative Commons license.

24 [bottom]: Photo used under Creative Commons license.

35: Figure drawn by Dan Piraro, based on S. L. Armstrong, L. R. Gleitman, and H. Gleitman, "What Some Concepts Might Not Be," *Cognition* 13, no. 3 (1983): 263–208.

131 [bottom]: Image courtesy of James Adams.

162: Figure adapted from A. Fiske, J. L. Wetherell, and M. Gatz, "Depression in Older Adults," *Annual Review of Clinical Psychology* 5 (2009): 363–389.

213: Photos used under Creative Commons license.

214: Figure redrawn by Lindsay Fleming, from M. C. Bushnell, M. Čeko, and L. A. Low, "Cognitive and Emotional Control of Pain and Its Disruption in Chronic Pain," *Nature Reviews Neuroscience* 14, no. 7 (2013): 502.

242: Photos used under Creative Commons license.

243: Figure drawn by Lindsay Fleming, based on S. Hood and S. Amir, "The Aging Clock: Circadian Rhythms and Later Life," *Journal of Clinical Investigation* 127, no. 2 (2017): 437–446.

290: Figure redrawn by Lindsay Fleming, from S. G. Wannamethee, A. G. Shaper, and M. Walker, "Changes in Physical Activity, Mortality, and Incidence of Coronary Heart Disease in Older Men," *Lancet* 351, no. 9116 (1998): 1603–1608.

319: Figure redrawn by Lindsay Fleming, from E. Dolgin, "There's No Limit to Longevity, Says Study That Revives Human Lifespan Debate," *Nature* (2018), https://www.nature.com/articles/d41586-018-055823.

371: Figure redrawn by Lindsay Fleming, from A. A. Stone et al., "A Snapshot of the Age Distribution of Psychological Well-Being in the United States," *Proceedings of the National Academy of Sciences* 107, no. 22 (2010): 9985–9990.

All other images and figures are either in the public domain or were drawn by Dan Levitin and Lindsay Fleming, © 2020 by Daniel J. Levitin.

INDEX

Note: Page numbers in *italics* refer to illustrations.

abstract thinking, 71, 135–39, 398
acetaminophen (Tylenol), 224
acetylcholine, 51, 109, 301, 352–53, 356
Ackerman, Diane, 137
activity and exercise, 280–94
  aerobic and anaerobic, 287
  age-appropriate goals for, 175
  and Alzheimer's defense, xvii
  benefits of, 263, 282–83, *290*, 290–92
  and blood flow to brain, 161
  and cognitive function, 281–82, 284, 286, 287, 289, 291–92
  and constipation, 270
  curtailment of, 161, 175–76, 285
  and embodied cognition, 282, 283
  high-intensity, interval training (HIIT), 288–89
  importance of, 281, 283
  and injury risks, 288
  and longevity, 320
  and memory, 286, 291
  minimal levels of, 290–91
  motivation to stay fit, 174–75
  and neurogenesis, 286
  and neuroplasticity, 286
  in outdoor settings, 113–14, 204, 227, 281–82, 285–86, 292–94, 396–97
  and pain management, 224–25, 226, 227
  and sedentary lifestyles, 280–81
  and sense of agency, 284, 285
  of Shultz, 118
  and sleep hygiene, 248
  and social isolation and loneliness, 191
  and telomere length, 326
  and walking, 292–94
Adams, James L., 129–30, 132, 285
adaptability, 20, 119
Adderall, 349–50
addictions, 375
Adelson, Edward, 91–92
adrenaline, xx, 156
advance medical directives, 390–93
affirmations, personal, 28
age discrimination, 380, 472n380
agency, sense of, 196–99, 284, 285
aggression, 18, 169, 182, 189
agreeableness, 10, 15, 16, 18, 20, 21, *21*
alcohol consumption, 76, 246–47, 265–66, 268, 269, 377–78
Alexander, Jason, 7
all-cause mortality, 26, 202, 207, *208*
Allen, David, 26
Allison, Jim, 172, 332–33
allostasis and allostatic load, 155–58, 185
Allport, Gordon, xxiii
ALS (amyotrophic lateral sclerosis), 109
alternative medicine, 255–56
Alzheimer's disease (AD)
  about, 81
  and age-related changes in personalities, 20
  and amyloids, xvii, xviii, 81, 247, 299, 334

Alzheimer's disease (AD) *(cont.)*
and Bredesen Protocol, xvii–xviii
causes of, 81–82, 266
and chronic inflammation, 82
and circadian rhythm disruption, 245
and cortisol levels, 157
and daydreaming mode, 80
environmental component of, xvii
genetic component of, xvii, 81, 82, 405n
and hippocampus, xvii, 41
and insulin levels, 263
light therapy and melatonin treatments for, 247
and loneliness, 179
and meditation, 366
and memory, 41, 42, 61, 81
and microbiome, 272
and mild cognitive impairment, 80
and music, 146
and neural implants, 362
and neuroinflammation, xviii
and olfactory deficits, 109
preparedness for, 389
and prions, xviii, 334
and putamen, 182
risk factors for, xvii, 389, 403n
and sleep deprivation, xvii, 299
and sundowner's syndrome, 245, 247
symptoms of, 81
as third leading cause of death, xvii
treatment strategies being researched, xvii–xviii
without cognitive impairment, 138
women's risk of, xvii
and work accommodations, 380–81
amnesia, infantile and childhood, 283
amphetamines, 349–52, 358
amygdala, 195, 298
amyloids, xvii, xviii, 81, 247, 299, 334
analogical reasoning, 119, 140–41
Anderson, David, 162–63, 183, 188–89, 304
andropause, 306
anger, 150, 398
animals, 88–89, 149
antibiotics, 272
antidepressants, xvi, 74, 158, 162–64, 190
anti-inflammatory drugs, xviii
antioxidants, 105, 257–59, 442n258
anxiety, 13, 18, 21, 206, 273, 361, 365
APOE gene, 82
appetite loss, 230
apps, security features on, 172–73
arteriosclerosis, 76
arthritis, 207, 223–24, 366
artists and artistic endeavors, 24, 25, 135, 160
aspirin, 83
assertiveness, 18
assisted living (AL), 198–99, 388
associations, making, 119. *See also* sociability
Astorino, Todd, 288–89
athleticism, 22–23, 249–50
Atkins, Robert, 330
attachment theory, 184, 397
attention, 79, 81, 273, 352–53, 365
attitudes toward elderly, xiii, xxi–xxii
auditory memory circuits in the brain, 7
auditory system, 63, 73, 75, 105
Augspurger, George, 115–16, 119, 138
Aune, Gregory, 370
autism spectrum disorders, 41, 80, 187–88, 398–99
autobiographical memories, 39, 40, 45–46, 49
autonomy, functional, 197–98

babies and infancy
adverse experiences in, 272–73
amnesia in, 284
brains of, 62–65, 66–68
critical periods for, 72–74, 75
deaf, 75
egocentric psychopathy of, 19
emotional needs of, 74
emotions of, 149, 151
and language acquisition/fluency, 69, 70, 71–72, 75
neurons and neural growth in, 64–65, 68, 69, 70, 71
and nurturing in early life, 184–85
old age compared to, 76
and parental attachment, 184, 397
predispositions (temperament), 19
prenatal influences on development, xx, 185
senses of, 66–68
statistical inferencing of, 70–71
Bacopa monnieri (water hyssop), 357
Balaban, Evan, 67
balance, retaining sense of, 99

Baltes, Paul, 5, 29, 142
Bandura, Albert, 197
Barbi, Elisabetta, 319
Barrett, Lisa Feldman, 150
Bartlett, Frederic, 55
Bayley, Nancy, 5, 29
Beatles, 33, 49
Beecher, Henry, 209
Befriending program, 192–93
Bellugi, Ursula, xxii
Bermuda Triangle, 99
Bible, references to brain in, 62
Big Five personality model, 15–17, 19, 21
biological clocks, 235–50
  age-related changes in, 241–42, *243*, 243–45
  and alcohol consumption, 266
  and artificial light, 240, 296, 303
  and caffeine intake, 248–49
  and chronotypes, *239*, 239–42, 249–50
  disruptions in, 244–45
  evolution of, 235
  genetic component of, 236, 237, 239, 241–42
  and hunger, 235, 243
  and master clock, 236–38, 239, 243
  and melatonin, 238, *239*, 240, 245, 246–48, 308
  and peak performance, 249–50
  and sentinel hypothesis, 241, 242
  and sleep requirements, 301
  and travel, 245–46, 250
  and winter months, 246
  and work/school schedules, 240–41
bionics, 362–64
birds, testosterone in, 168
birth order, 8–9
Blackburn, Elizabeth, 328–29
Blakey, Art, 117
blind individuals, 75–76
blood glucose, 4, 237, 262–63
blood pressure, 83, 105
blueberries, 105
blue light exposure, 238, 303, 308
blue zones, 320–21
bodily-kinesthetic intelligence, 124
Bogues, Muggsy, 7
bone density, 168
Bowlby, John, 184
Bowling Alone (Putnam), 180
Bradley, David, 367
brains
  of babies, 62–65, 66–68
  blood flow to, 161
  brain/body dualism, 281
  brain-derived neurotrophic factor, 76
  brain injuries, 47
  compensatory mechanisms of, xi–xii, 75, 90, 94
  continual changes in, xxiii
  critical periods of development in, 72–74
  of embryos and fetuses, 67, 74
  evolutionary blueprint of, 66
  and language acquisition/fluency, 69, 70, 73, 74
  meditation's effect on, 365
  mirror neurons of, 214
  and myelin coating, 65, 77, 78, 79
  and neural pruning, 67, 68–69, 70
  neurogenesis in, 84–85, 179
  and neurological turn inward, 31
  neurons and neural growth in, 64–65, 71, 84–85
  normal aging in, 31
  and nurturing in early life, 185, 187
  and pain perception, 208–10, 212–15, *213*
  processing speed of, 132–35, 138
  and putamen, 182–83, 197
  reduction in volume of, 77
  remapping in, 75–76
  "rewiring," 337
  spatial maps of, 94–95
  specific effects of aging on, 76–80
  white matter declines in, 78, 161
  See also cognitive health/function; intelligence; neuroplasticity; strokes
"brain training games," 132, 344–46
Bredesen, Dale, xvii
Bredesen Protocol, xvii–xviii
brightness, perception of, *91*, 91–92, *92*
Brill, David, 384
Buddhism, 29, 159, 372–73, 374
Buenaver, Luis, 308
Buhl, J. D., 205–6
Burke, Deborah, 60
Burke, Tina, 248–49
Bush, George W., 46, 63
Bushnell, Catherine, 214–15
business enterprises, late-life, 25

caffeine intake, xxi, 248–49, 306–7
Caldwell, Gordon, 385–86
Calment, Jeanne, 313, 343, 457n313
calmness (personality trait), 10
caloric restriction, 262–66, 330, 339–40
Campbell, Glen, 87
Canadian Longitudinal Study on Aging (CLSA), 192
cancer
as cause of death, 207, *208*
and cellular senescence, 331, 332
changes in treatments for, 172
and chemotherapy, 58, 105
and circadian rhythm disruption, 245
and diet, 264, 265
and immortality of cancer cells, 324
immunotherapies for, 172, 332–34, 335, *335*
and meditation, 366
and melatonin, 308
and microbiome, 272
overdiagnosis in screenings for, 27
and sleep deprivation, xvii
and telomere length, 327, 328, 329
cannabis/cannabinoids, 190, 352, 358, 361
carbohydrate restriction, 255
Carey, Susan, xxii
Carnes, Bruce, 330
Carstensen, Laura, 194–95, 371, 372
Carter, Jimmy, 172, 334
Casals, Pablo, 115, 170, 175
castration and longevity, 323
cataracts, 104, 238
catecholamines, 155
categorization and category members, 103
cell-division, 324–26, *326*
central executive mode of attention, 79
change, motivation/capacity for, 4–5, 9, 171–76
Chapin, Henry, 186
character, 6. *See also* personalities
Charles Bonnet syndrome, 105
Chen, Weiyun, 288
childhood socioeconomic status (SES), xx
children and childhood
adverse experiences in, 156, 272–73
amnesia in, 284
on autism spectrum, 398–99
concussions during, 397
coping styles of, 164
and health outcomes in adulthood, 3–4
individual differences in, 3–4, 5
and language acquisition/fluency, 69, 70, 71–72, 73, 74, 75
and long-term effects of parental relationships, 184, 378, 397
and mental/physical health of mother, xix–xx
orphaned or abandoned, 186
and parental attachment, 184, 397
predispositions (temperament), 19
social development of, 74
socioeconomic context of, xx
cholesterol, 259–62, 266
chronic disease and conditions, rates of, 160
chronobiology. *See* activity and exercise; biological clocks
chronotypes, *239*, 239–42, 249–50
circadian rhythms, 235, 236–37, 238, 247, 301, 308. *See also* chronobiology
Clarke, Rachel, 395
COACH principle, xxiv, 29, 118
cochlear implants, 73, 75, 107, 361
Coetzee, J. M., 382
cognitive behavioral therapy (CBT), 155–56, 163, 164, 190
cognitive enhancement
ethics of, 346–49
memory/attention enhancement, 352–53
and recreational drugs, 358–61
and stimulants, 349–52
cognitive health/function, 344–66
and activity/exercise, 284, 287, 289, 291–92, 398
and *Bacopa monnieri* (water hyssop), 357
and biological clocks of aging adults, 244
and "brain training games," 132, 344–46
and challenges associated with aging, 76
cognitive prostheses, 57
and cognitive reserve, 80–81, 138–39
and cognitive stimulation therapy, 354–55
and constipation, 269
decline in, xvii, 77, 78, 199, 202, 266, 355–56
and declining hormones, 168

filling in missing information (perceptional completion), 93–94, 102–3
and hormone replacement therapy, 354
and meditation, 364–66
and microdosing, 361
and neural implants, 361–62
and Neuroshrooms, 356–57
pain's impact on, 214, *214*, 229
and relationships, 376
and relationships, meaningful, 376
sleep's impact on, xvii, 309
and social engagement, 26, 202, 203–4, 398
and time outdoors, 113–14, 281–82, 292–94, *293*, 398
and vitamin B_{12}, 355–56
cognitive stimulation therapy (CST), 354–55
Cohen, Leonard, 144
Collins, Judy, 135, 379
color constancy, 92
Coltrane, John, 166
compassion, xxii, 6, 28–29, 398, 400
competitive sports, 22–23, 25
complex/enriched environments, 113–14, 203, 227, 281–82
Conceptual Blockbusting (Adams), 129, 132
concussions, 20, 397
Condello, Carlo, 334
conditioning, behavioral, 39
confabulations, 47
confusion, 231
connectomes, 152–53
conscientiousness, 26–27
age-related changes in, 20, *21*, 21
and COACH principle, xxiv, 29, 118
and family values, 8
and health outcomes, 22, 26
importance of, 396–97
improving levels of, 26
intelligence without, 26
Koch on hiring people with, 26
and physical traits, 10
and serotonin, 18
and telomere length, 326
traits included in, 16
unhealthy levels of, 27
conservatism in older adults, xxii, 87
constipation, 269–71
continuity of care, 382–86
control, sense of, 196–99
coping styles, 164–66
corporations, senior workers in, 138
cortisol
and activity/exercise, 291
and adverse childhood experiences, 156
effects of, xiv, 29, 157
meditation's effect on, 365
and memory testing, 59
parenting's impact on, xx
and probiotics, 273
Coughlin, Joseph F., 387–88
creative arts, 85–86
creativity, 129–32, *130*, *131*, 199, 285–86, 296, 361
Creutzfeldt-Jakob disease, xviii
critical periods of development, 72–74, 75
Crook, Robyn, 218–19
crosswords, 132
cruciferous vegetables, 264, 445n264
Cryan, John, 272
culture, 6, 8, 10, 12–13
curiosity
benefits of, 25–26, 173
in children's temperament, 19
and COACH principle, xxiv, 29, 118
curiosity quotient (CQ), 27
and internal vs. external locus of control, 173
and jump-starting motivation, 173
Koch on hiring people with, 26
unhealthy levels of, 27

Dalai Lama
on compassion, 28–30
counseling followers, 158–59
on emotional regulation, 159–60
on happiness, 28, 177
humility practiced by, 28–29
on intense self focus, 159, 165–66
on meditation, 364, 366
on sleep, 295
work schedule of, 379
Daltrey, Roger, xiii
David, Nathaniel, 332
Davidson, Richard, 365
da Vinci, Leonardo, 125, 199
Davis, Clive, 138
Davis, Miles, 166
daydreaming mode, 79–80, 137, 166
deaf individuals, 73, 75, 76, 105

death
acceptance of, xii
and advance medical directives, 390–93
annual risk of, 319, *319*
and end-of-life care, 394–96
inevitability of, 313–14
and psilocybin, 358
DeGrado, Bill, 334
De Grey, Aubrey, 336–38
De Groot, Adrian, 309
delirium, 231
dementia
and activity/exercise, 283
advance medical directive for, 391–93
and autonomy of older people, 198
and biological clocks of aging adults, 244
and "brain training games," 344
and childhood concussions, 397
genetic factors related to, 82
and insulin levels, 263
and loneliness, 179
and memory, 42, 61
and mild cognitive impairment, 80
misperception on inevitability of, 82–83
and neural implants, 362
prevention of, 86
and social engagement, 202, 398
and synesthesia, 67
term, 81
variety of brain conditions leading to, 80
and vitamin B_{12}, 356
and work accommodations, 381
See also Alzheimer's disease
depression, 158–64
and Alzheimer's defense, xviii
and coping styles, 164–66
and digital devices, 375
and drug therapies, xvi, 74, 158, 162–64, 190
factors contributing to, 160–61
and genetics, 18, 182
and hypersomnia, 303–4
and intelligence, 134
and lifestyle choices, xvi
and microbiome, 272
prevalence of, 158, 160
and probiotics, 273
and protective factors, 161–62, *162*
and psychedelics, 182
risk factors for, 161, *162*
and rumination, 164–66
and serotonin, 18, 162–63
and sleep quality, 303
symptoms of, 160
and talk therapies, 163, 164
upon retirement, 199
vascular, 161
and volunteerism, 202
and world happiness rankings, 375
developmental neuroscience, xxii–xxiii
De Waal, Frans , 147
dexterity, losses in, 107–8, 285
diabetes, 104, 105, 238, 263, 366
diagnostics, implants for, 363–64
diarrhea, 268–69
Dickens, Charles, 300
Diener, Ed, 368, 369
diet and nutrition, 251–79
and alcohol consumption, 265–66, 268, 269
and antioxidants, 105, 257–59
bland, 112–13
and caloric restriction, 262–66, 330, 339–40
and charlatans in diet industry, 251–52
and cholesterol, 259–62, 266
and cognitive reserve, 139
and constipation, 269–71
and dietary fats, 260–62, 264
and fiber, 261, 270, 273, 275, 276
and fish/fish oils, 79, 264, 265, 276
and fruits and vegetables, xvii, 261, 264, 265, 270, 276
history of research in, 252–53, 279
and hydration, 268–69
and inflammation, 266
and intuitive eating, 277–78
and longevity, 320
and microbiome, 238–39, 271–75, 278
and nuts/seeds, 261
and omega-3 fatty acids, 79, 261, 264–65
popular and alternative diets, 254, 255–57, 266, 277
and prebiotics, 275
and probiotics, 271, 273, 274–75, 452
and processed foods, 276, 279, 326
and protein, 266–68
and sleep hygiene, 246–47
and social isolation and loneliness, 191
and soy, 267–68

standard American diet, 279
and superfoods, 278
and supplements, 258–59, 264–65, 266
and telomere length, 326
and timing of meals, 238, 243, 246
and variety of foods, 276–77
and whole grains, 261, 265, 270, 276
difficult conversations, 386–89
digestive cycles, 237
digital devices, 375
disability, living with, 207–8, *208*
disease span, 207, *208*, 233
Disgrace (Coetzee), 382
disgust, 113, 149, 150
disorientation, 41, 231
distractions
and aging, 57, 78
as coping style, 164, 165
and memory disruption, 42–43, 59
and pain management, 227, 394–95
divorce, 193, 376, 377, 378
doctors, 171–72, 382–86
Doidge, Norman, 85
Dolhun, Eduardo, 383
dominance, 18
Domingo, Placido, 399
dopamine
and circadian rhythm, 246
and depression, 163, 164
and individual differences, 152
influence on personality traits, 18
and "likes" in cyberspace, 181
and microbiome, 272
and novelty seeking, 171
and putamen, 183
reductions in production/uptake of, 76, 171, 285, 350–51
and social anxiety, 183
and social isolation, 190
and wisdom, 144
Down syndrome, 65, 109
Dozier, Lamont, 379
drawing as memory aid, 56–57
dreaming, 51, 300
drive and productivity, 21
Duncker, Karl, 140, 421n140
Dweck, Carol, 173–74

Eastern cultural attitudes, xv, 374–75
Edison, Thomas, 296
education, 139, 185, 377
EGR gene, 314
Ehrenreich, Barbara, 379
Einstein, Albert, 126, 133
Ekman, Paul, 150
embodied cognition, 282, 283, 293, 362, 451n282
emotional stability
age-related changes in, 20, 21, *21*
as Big Five dimension, 16
and physical traits, 10
and serotonin, 18
traits included in, 16
and wisdom, 143, 144
emotions, 146–78
about, 146
of animals, 149
and bodily regulation, 150
categorization of, 103
culturally specific/universal, 150
development and maturation of, 151
differentiation of, 151
disgust, 113, 149, 150
and emotional eating, 278
evolutionary function of, 147, 149
fear, 149
gratitude, 6, 191, 399
grief, 210
hardwired, 149
and hormones, 169
and memories, 40, 46, 298
misattribution of, 148–49
in musical performances, 146
neurochemical basis of, 151–53
and pain of mental anguish, 210
pain's interaction with, 214, *214*, 399
regulation of, 159–60, 184, 191, 194, 202
as related to moods, 146
sleep's role in processing, 298
survival related, 147–49
understanding others,' 150–51
See also depression; happiness; stress and stress response
empathy, 144, 200, 214
energy, loss of, xviii
environment/genes, interactions of, 7, 152
Eos and Tithonos, myth of, 367
Epel, Elissa, 328–29
episodic memory (particular knowledge store), 39, 40–41, 51, 54
estrogen, 166–67, 168, 304, 354
ethical behaviors, 103

executive function, xx, 365
exercise. *See* activity and exercise
experience as related to wisdom, 119
Experience Corps, 381
expertise in older adults, 115–16, 119, 398
explicit memory, 39, 41, 54
extraversion, 10, 15, 16, 18, 20, 21
Eysenck, Hans, xxiii

Facebook, xxv, 180
facial recognition, 38
Fagen, Donald, 379
families
  family bonds, xxii
  intergenerational, 388
  and longevity, 320
  as microcultures, 8
  and pain attitudes, 220
  roles adopted in (birth order), 8–9
  See also parents
fasting, 263–64, 323
fats, dietary, xvii, 260–62, 264
Fazah, Ziad, 69
fear, 149, 150, 188, 189
fecal transplants, 275
fiber, 261, 270, 273, 275, 276
films, collecting, 172
finances, personal, 26, 171–72
fish and fish oils, 79, 264, 265
flavors, detection of, 110–13
flexibility, 20
Flier, Jeffrey, 341
flow state, 166
Fonda, Jane, 22, 23, 285, 343
forgiveness, xxii
Fox, Nathan, 186–87
Fox, Vicente, 177–78, 244
FOXO proteins and *FOXO* genes, 315, 322–23
Frames of Mind (Gardner), 123–24
Franklin, Benjamin, 199, 262
Frayn, Mallory, 277, 278
free radicals, 105, 257–58, 442n257
Freud, Sigmund, 199–200, 379
Friedman, Richard, 292
friends. *See* relationships
fruits and vegetables, xvii, 261, 264, 265, 270, 276

Gall, Franz Joseph, xxiii
Galton, Sir Francis, xxiii, 12
Gardner, Christopher, 254
Gardner, Howard, 123–24, 126–27, 128
gas detection devices, 113
gassiness, xxi
Gaster, Barak, 392–93
gate control theory of pain, 210
Gawande, Atul, 107–8
Gazzaniga, Michael, 47, 347
generalization principle, 34–38
general knowledge, 39
genes and genetics
  and biological clock, 236, 237, 239, 241–42
  and breakdown of DNA, 79
  in common with other organisms, 66
  and cultural context, 8
  and dementia risks, 82
  environment's interaction with, 7, 152
  and gene expression, 7–8, 152, 182
  influence on mental and personality traits, 6–7, 18
  and loneliness and social isolation, 182
  and longevity, 321
  meditation's effect on, 365–66
  and pain perception, 221–22
  and telomeres, 316, 325
Gestalt psychologists, 52–53
Getting Things Done (Allen), 26
Gilbert, Dan, 392
ginkgo, 386
Ginsburg, Ruth Bader, 201
glasses, 87, 96, 101
Global Burden of Disease Project, 206–7
Glück, Judith, 143
glucocorticoids, xx, 29, 153–54, 155, 185
glucosamine, 224
Glueck Study, 377–78
glutamate, 181–82, 215
goals, 175, 197
Goldberg, Lewis R.
  author's relationship with, xxii, 10–11
  and individual differences in manufactured objects, 37
  on "openness" factor, 405n16
  personality research of, xxiii–xxiv, 12, 13, 15
Goleman, Daniel, 26
Gonzalez, Nicholas, 255–56
Goodall, Jane, 135, 145
good-naturedness (personality trait), 10
Grace and Frankie (television series), 23

Grafton, Scott, 113, 280–81, 283, 293, 451n282
gratitude, 6, 191, 399
Greeks, ancient, 62
grief, 210
grit, 6, 169
growth mind-sets, 173–74
Guarente, Leonard, 340
guilt, 18
Gundry, Steven, 251–52
gustatory deficits, 108–13
gym memberships, 292

Hadza people, *242*, 242
Hafter, Erv, 52
Hall, Kevin, 255, 276
Hall, Ralph, 200
hallucinogenics, 358–61
Hamilton, Dave, 352
Hampson, Sarah, xxii, 4, 10–11, 22, 326, 406n19
happiness, 176–78
  and compassion, 28
  and conscientiousness, 26
  as culturally universal emotion, 150
  Dalai Lama on, 28, 177
  effect of smiling on, 28
  and gratitude, 191
  and happiest time of life, xxv
  and helping others, 177–78
  and love, 376
  measuring, 374–78
  and observer distortion effect, 176
  and positivity in older adults, 196, 202, 371–73
  relationships' impact on, 376–78
  relativism of, 176
  and religious affiliation, 191
  trends in, 370–71, *371*
  world rankings of, 375
Harbisson, Neil, 363, 468n363
Harlow, Harry, 183–84
Harvard Grant Study, 375–77
Haselton, Martie, 167
hatreds, letting go of, 398
Hawkins, Jeff, 336
Hawkins, Julia "Hurricane," 22–23, 174
Hayflick, Leonard, 324–25, 329–30
Hayflick limit, 324–26
health spans, 118, 191, 207, 319, 343, 375
healthy life expectancy (HALE), 370
healthy practices, xxiv, 29, 118
hearing
  age-related changes in, 104–7
  and cochlear implants, 73, 75, 107, 361
  and deafness, 73, 75–76, 105
  and hearing aids, 87, 104, 106–7
  rates of hearing loss, 87, 105
  and tinnitus, 105–6
heart disease, xvii, 261–62, 264, 265, 287
Hekimi, Siegfried, 318–19, 329
Helmholtz, Hermann von, 94, 95
helping others, 166, 177–78, 381–82
high-intensity, interval training (HIIT), 288–89
Hintzman, Doug, 52, 53
hippocampus
  and activity/exercise, 282, 283, 284, 291, 397
  and adverse childhood experiences, 157
  and Alzheimer's disease, xvii, 41
  and childhood amnesia, 284
  and consolidation of memories, 51
  glucocorticoid receptors in, xx
  meditation's effect on, 365
  and memory, 52, 54, 77, 78, 165, 171
  and neurogenesis, 84–85, 286
  and nurturing in early life, 185
  research on function of, 52
  sensitivity to emotion, 165
  shrinking of, with age, xvii, 41, 59, 77
  and sleep deprivation, 299
  and stress, 29
  and time outdoors, 397
hobbies, 227
Hofstadter, Douglas, 69
honesty, 26
Honjo, Tasuku, 332
hopelessness, 18
hormone replacement therapy (HRT), 168–69, 304–6, 354
hormones, 166–69, 354, 377
hospitals, choosing, 390
hostility, 18
housing, intergenerational, 192
Housman, Justin, 294
How to Change Your Mind (Pollan), 359
HPA (hypothalamic-pituitary-adrenal) axis, 29
HSAD (hereditary sensory autonomic neuropathy), 217–18
Hughes, Bryan, 318

humor, 142
hunger, 235, 243
Hunt, Buz, 126
Huntington's diseases, 245
hydration, 268–69
hypermnesia, 38
hypothalamus, 160–61

ibuprofen, xviii
identity, role of memory in, 32, 61
imagination, traits included in, 16–17
immune systems
  and circadian rhythm disruption, 245
  and hormone reductions, 168
  and immunotherapies, 332–34, *335*, 335
  and insulin levels, 263
  and social stress, 184
implicit memory, 39, 41, 54
impulse control, 18, 20, 26, 57, 77
In Defense of Food (Pollan), 279
individual differences, xxii–xxiv, 3–30, 152
individualism, 180
inferior frontal gyrus, 200
inflammation
  and Alzheimer's, xviii, 82, 266
  and cellular senescence, 331
  and circadian rhythm disruption, 245
  and diet, 261–62, 266
  and experimental treatments, 339
  and hormone replacement therapy, 354
  and loneliness, 179
  meditation's effect on, 365, 366
  and microbiome, 272
  and omega-3 fatty acids, 265
  and pain treatments, 223–25
Innsbruck, Austria, sensory adaptation experiments in, 95–96
insomnia, 161, 163, 303
insulin, 262–63, 323
intellect, 10, 16–17, 405n16. *See also* openness to experience
intelligence, 115–45
  about, 118–20
  and abstract thinking, 135–39, 399
  and analogical reasoning, 119, 140–41, 421n140
  and COACH principle, 118
  and cognitive reserve, 80–81
  and conscientiousness, 26
  and creativity, 129–32, *130*, *131*, 419n130
  and depression, 134
  and expertise in older adults, 115–17, 119, 398
  fluid, 122–23, 133, 134, 138, 139–42
  measuring, 118
  multiple domains of, 123–27
  and processing speed, 132–35, 138
  and Romanian orphan crisis, 187
  and school performance, 120–21, 128
  tests evaluating, 127–32, 137–38, 139–40
  types of, 120–23, 134
  and wisdom, 119, 142–45
interceptive timing, 71–72
intergenerational living options, 192, 388
inter-/intrapersonal intelligence, 124
internal monologues, 27
Internet, 172–73, 180–81
inter-rater agreement, 9–10
intuitive eating, 277–78
irritable bowel syndrome, 229, 273
Isaacson, Walter, 199
isolation. *See* loneliness and social isolation
Istvan, Zoltan, 363
itching, 108, 226

Jagger, Mick, 285
James, William, 4, 67, 79
JND (just noticeable difference), 111–12
Jobs, Steve, 27
Joel, Billy, 296
Jones, Quincy, 121, 378
jury trials, 48

Kahana, Michael, 362
Kahneman, Daniel, 222–23, 368, 369
Kamp, David, 296
Keele, Steve, 34–35, 54, 135
Kendrick, Anna, 9
Kennedy, John F., Jr., 98–99, 415n98
Kennedy, Pagan, 330–31
Kentucky Fried Chicken (KFC), 25
Kenyon, Cynthia, 262, 263, 264, 322–23
ketamine, 182, 215
Keynes, John Maynard, 314
Khullar, Dhruv, 188
Kimball, Jeffrey, 58
Klausner, Richard, 342–43
Klinenber, Eric, 180
knowledge, general and episodic, 39
Koch, Charles, 26
Kodama, Mari, 86

Korsakoff's syndrome, 109
Kosslyn, Stephen, 57
Krakauer, David, 121

lactose intolerance, xxi
Laddish, Tim, 175–76
La Dolce Vita effect, 20–21
language, 69–75, 81, 105
Larsson, Stieg, 217
Lashley, Karl, 84
laughter, value of, 400
laxatives, 270
Lear, Norman, 270
learning
  active vs. passive, 55–56
  and Alzheimer's, 81
  and cognitive reserve, 139
  influence of genes, culture, and opportunity on, 120, 121
  and intelligence, 120
  and making associations, 119
  manual skills, 87
  motivation for, 169–71
  and new experiences, 132
  new things in old age, 87
  and quality of life, 382
  and sleep, 301
  statistical inferencing in, 70–71
LeDoux, Joseph, 147
Lennon, John, 27
leucine, 267–68
Levin, Michael, 314–15
Lewisohn, Mark, 33
lexical hypothesis, 12–13
libido, 167–68
Lickerman, Alex, 391
life spans of humans
  and annual risk of death, *319*, 319
  and antiaging industry, 330
  and disease span, xviii–xix, *xix*, 324
  expectations for, 343
  and health span, xviii–xix, *xix*, 319, 324, 330, 343
  and oldest living human, 313, 459n315
  and population over sixty-five, 400
  search for limits of, 317–19
  and telomere length, 325–26
lifestyle choices
  and COACH principle, xxiv, 29, 118
  committing to, 118
  understanding the *why* in, 397
light, artificial, 238, 240, 296, 303
linkAges community program, 191–92
Linton, Steven, 220, 227
lipid levels, as predicted by childhood personality traits, 4, 26
lists, making, 56
living wills (advance medical directives), 390–93
Lobo, Rogerio, 305–6
Locke, John, 88
locus of control, external vs. internal, 170, 173
logical-mathematical intelligence, 124
Logic of Perception, The (Rock), 90
loneliness and social isolation
  about, 179–80
  and couplehood, 378
  effects of, 181–82, 189, 366, 376
  factors contributing to, 180–81
  and meditation, 366
  and motivation loss, 285
  pervasiveness of, 180
  as predictors of disease and mortality, 398
  reducing, 188–94
longevity
  in animal species, 315–17, *316*
  and antiaging industry, 330
  and blue zones, 320–21
  and caloric restriction, 339
  and cellular senescence, 313, 331–32
  and circadian rhythms, 243
  and conscientiousness, 26
  and couplehood, 378
  and disease span, 324
  failed attempts at, 330–31
  genes' impact on, 321–22
  and Hayflick limit, 324–26
  and health/disease spans, 330
  and human life span, 317–19, *319*
  and immunotherapies, 332–34, *335*, 335
  and oldest living human, 313, 457n313
  openness as related to, 25–26
  and pseudoscience of de Grey, 336–38
  and quality of life, 367–70
  role of insulin in, 323
  and stress, 153
  and telomere length, 325–29
  therapies on the horizon, 339–43
long-term care facilities, 196–97, 273–74, 388

Lothian Birth Cohort Study, 134, 139
lottery winners, 177
Louis-Dreyfus, Julia, 7
love, importance of, 376, 377, 378, 379
LSD, 182, 360
Lupien, Sonia, 59–60, 154, 305
Luria, Alexander, 38

Maccoby, Eleanor, 367
Mad Men (series), 148–49
Maestas, Nicole, 379
Maimonides, Moses, 238
Mancinelli, Anthony, 200
manual skills, 87
marriages and couplehood, 193, 376, 377, 378, 471n378
Martens, Christopher, 340–41
Martin, George, 33, 43, 49
Mastanamma, 200
math and abstract thinking, 136
Mathews, Max, 306–7
Mattson, Mark, 263, 264
McCartney, Paul, 33, 49, 127, 296
McCrae, Robert, 408n16
McGill Pain Questionnaire, 211
McGill University, Montreal, Canada, 209–10
meals, timing of, 238
Meaney, Michael, xix–xx, 184–85, 272
medial temporal lobe, 41, 59, 77–78, 81
medical care, 382–86
medications
  associated with depression, 160–61
  and future-impairment preparedness, 389
  and hypersomnia, 303–4
  and polypharmacy, 230–31
  sharing list of, with doctors, 386
meditation, 165–66, 327–28, 364–66
melatonin
  about, 245, 307–8
  and blue light exposure, 303
  and caffeine intake, 307
  and cancer, 308
  and cataract surgery, 238
  and circadian rhythms, 235, *239*, 240, 246, 248, 301
  and resetting sleep cycle, 247–48
  timing administration of, 308
Melzack, Ronald, 210, 211, 213, 434n209
memantine (Namenda), 353
Memento (film), 32
memory/memories, 31–61
  accuracy of, 49
  and active vs. passive learning, 55–56
  and activity/exercise, 282, 286, 291
  age-related lapses in, 39
  and Alzheimer's, 41, 42, 61, 81
  autobiographical, 39, 40, 45–46, 49
  and biological clocks of aging adults, 244
  and childhood amnesia, 284
  decline in, 59–60
  and depth of processing, 56–57
  disruption of, 42–43
  and distractions, 42–43, 57, 59
  drugs' enhancement of, 352–53
  and emotions, 40, 46, 298
  episodic memory (particular knowledge store), 39, 40–41, 51, 54
  evolution of, 34, 39, 44–45
  explicit and implicit memory systems, 39, 41, 54
  and facial recognition, 38
  fundamental importance of, 31–32
  and generalization principle, 34–38
  hierarchy in systems of, 39
  and hormone reductions, 168
  and identity, 32, 61
  inferences and confabulations in, 47–49
  location of, in brain, 50–51, 85
  long-term, 43
  and medial temporal lobe, 77–78
  meditation's effect on, 365
  memory systems, 38–56
  misrememberings, 33, 43–44
  and multiple-trace theory (MTT), 53–55
  of music, 49, 61
  negative, 165
  and neural implants, 362
  and normal aging of brain, 31
  organization and retrieval of, 49–50, 52, 53–55, 78
  and pain perception, 223
  and pattern matching and abstraction, 34–37
  procedural memory, 39, 43, 54
  and resistance to change, 171
  rewriting/editing of, 43–47
  semantic memory (general knowledge store), 39–41, 51, 54
  and sensory decline, 60

and sentimentality, 37–38
short-term, 39, 42, 55, 56
sleep's function in consolidating, 295, 300, 301
spatial memory, 39, 41
storage of, 50–51, 52, 54–55, 78
strategies for improving and managing, 56–58
and test performance of older adults, 59–60, 409n60
and wisdom, 37
worries about failures in, 31–32
men, emotional sensitivity of, 20
Mencken, H. L., 338
Menon, Vinod, 190
menopausal symptoms, 304–6
mental agility, 26. *See also* cognitive health/function
mental health, 13, 202–3, 272, 273. *See also* depression
mental stimulation, 203–4, 227
metabolic syndrome, 238, 245, 292
metformin, 263, 339, 341
Mexican axolotl, 341–42, *342*
microbiome, 238–39, 271–75, 278, 335
microdosing, 360–61
migraines, 229
mild cognitive impairment, 80–83, 247, 283, 348, 356, 357, 389
Miller, Earl, 135
Milner, Brenda, 201
Milton, John, 69
mindfulness, 56, 254
mind-sets, fixed vs. growth, 173–74
mirror neurons, 214
Mitchell, Joni, 58, 113, 121, 146, 174, 296
Mlodinow, Leonard, 358
modafinil, 304, 350
moderation principle, 374
Mogil, Jeffrey, 133, 163, 221, 224–25, 229, 264, 328
Mona Lisa (da Vinci), 133, 199
monogamy, 167
mood disorders/disturbances, 21, 199
moods, 146, 156, 168, 227–28, 361. *See also* emotions
morality, 21, 124
Moreno, Rita, 343
Morpurgo, Sir Michael, 193–94
Moses, Grandma, 24, *24*
mothers, mental and physical health of, xix–xx
motivation
about, 169
decline in, 285
emotions' function in, 146–47
and external vs. internal locus of control, 170, 173
and fixed vs. growth mind-sets, 173–74
and hormones, 166–69
intrinsic vs. extrinsic, 173
and learning across the life span, 169–71
to make change, 171–76
motor skills and movements, 78, 87, 94, 120
"Mouse Wreckers" Warner Bros. cartoon, 98
movie theater screens, rendering blacks on, 91, *91*
Mozart, Wolfgang, 133
multiple-trace theory (MTT), 53–54
multitasking, 56
muscles, 43, 287
mushrooms, 182, 356–57, 358–59
music and musicians
and abstract thinking, 136
adapting to changing mediums in, 172
and Alzheimer's, 146
and emotion, 146
improvisation in, 166
learning to play, 74
motivation of, 170–71
musical memories, 49, 61
and musical-rhythmic intelligence, 124
and neuroplasticity, 86
and pain management strategies, 227
and reward centers of brain, 190
tests evaluating ability in, 127
myelin
decline in, 77, 78, 108
and dietary fats, 261
function of, 65
and neural health, 79
and omega-3 fatty acids, 264
repairing damaged, 79
and vitamin B_{12}, 356

NAD+ (nicotinamide adenine dinucleotide), 339–41
names, remembering, 55

napping, 303
naturalistic intelligence, 124–25, 419n125
natural remedies, 256
nature and end-of-life care, 395–96. *See also* outdoors, spending time
Nelson, Charles, 186–87
nervous system, 62, 66
neural implants, 361–62, 363
neural pruning, 67, 68–69, 70
neurogenesis, 84–85, 286
neuroinflammation, xviii
neuropathy, 225
neuroplasticity
  about, 73
  across a lifespan, 84–87, 99–100
  and activity/exercise, 286
  compensatory mechanisms of, 75
  and interceptive timing, 72
  in older adults, 85
  and perceptional completion, 94
  and prism adaptation experiments, 94, 97
  and remapping process, 75–76
  sensitive period for, 73–74
  and tinnitus, 106
Neuroshrooms, 356–57
neuroticism, 10, 18
Neurotrack, 56
Newton, Sir Isaac, 89
nicotine, 351
NK (natural killer), xiv
Nolan, Christopher, 32
Nolan, Jonathan, 32
Nolen-Hoeksema, Susan, 164–65
norepinephrine, 144, 301
nose, 63–64
notalgia paresthetica, 108, 226
novelty seeking, 18, 132, 171
NSAIDs (nonsteroidal anti-inflammatory drugs), 82, 223–24, 225, 229
numbness, 108
nursing homes. *See* long-term care facilities
nuts and seeds, 261
Nutt, David, 359

obesity, 26, 238, 260, 263, 272, 375
observer distortion effect, 176
obsessive compulsive disorder behaviors, 27
"older adults," defining, 286
oldest living human, 313, 457n313
olfactory system, declines in, 108–13
olive oil, 264
Olshansky, Jay, 319, 330
omega-3 fatty acids, 79, 261, 264–65, 357
Ono, Jiro, 343
openness to experience, 27–28
  age-related changes in, 20, 21
  and alternative "intellect"/"imagination" terms, 16, 407n16
  and COACH principle, xxiv, 29, 118
  correlated with health and longevity, 25–26
  and internal vs. external locus of control, 173
  and microdosing, 361
  and psilocybin, 359
  and serotonin, 18
  traits included in, 16–17
  unhealthy levels of, 27
  and wisdom, 142, 143
opportunity, 8–9
optimism, 22
Organized Mind, The (Levitin), 82
Ornish, Dean, 256–57
osteoarthritis, 223–24
outdoors, spending time
  and cognitive function, 113–14, 281–82, 292–94, *293*, 398
  and creativity, 285–86
  importance of, 204, 397–98
  and pain management, 227
Overton, Richard, 343
oxidative stress, 105, 258, 264, 266, 339, 355, 357, 442n258
oxytocin, 190
Oz, Mehmet, 251–52

Padilla, Alfonso, 248
pain, 205–31
  age-related problems with, 228–31
  anticipation of, 216
  and cause of injury, 220
  chronic, 206, 207, 210, 218–19, 228–30, 328
  and cognitive function, 214, *214*, 229
  and coping strategies, 227–28
  costs of treating, 207
  and culture considerations, 219–20, 398
  cutaneous, 214–16, 434n214

emotions' interactions with, 214, *214*, 398
and empathy, 214
environmental exposure to, 221–22
function of, 210, 216–19
gate control theory of, 210
genetic factors of, 221–22
hypersensitivity to, 225–26
insensitivity/indifference to, 217–18
managing, 223–26
and mental anguish, 210
misattribution of, 399
misperception on inevitability of, 230
neurological basis of, 208–10, 212–15, *213*, 221
and opioids, 48, 207, 220, 223, 225, 226, 375
peaks and declines over time, 207–8
perception of, 209, 214–16
phantom limb effect, 100, 209
and placebo effects, 220–21
and polypharmacy, 230–31
psychological factors in, 220–21, 222–23, 228
and risk-adjusted age, 207
and telomere length, 328
temporal aspects, *222*, 222–23
tool for describing, *211–12*
and virtual reality environments, 394–95
visceral, 215–16, 434n215
Palahniuk, Chuck, 313
paleo diets, 253, 276
Palmer, Steve, 52
Palo Alto Medical Foundation, 191–92
parents
and attachment theory, 184, 397
and children's stress responses, 184–85
coping styles modeled by, 164
and Harlow's baby monkey experiments, 183–84
long-term effects of relationships with, 184, 378, 397
and mental/physical health of mother, xix–xx, 185
and prenatal influences on development, xx, 185
Parkinson's disease, xviii, 109, 245
Parrish, Elizabeth, 329
Parrott, Matthew, 49
patient-centered medical home, 384
patient-doctor relationships, 382–86
pattern matching and abstraction, 34–37, 102, 119
Paxil, 74, 190
Payne, Samantha, 362–63
Peabody, Dean, 15
peak performance, 249–50
Penfield, Wilder, 212, 434n213
perceptional completion, 102–3
personal affirmations, 28
personalities
age-related changes in, 19–22
Big Five model of, 15–17
biological basis of, 18
in childhood, 3–4, 5
and culture, 6, 8, 12–13
dark shifts in, xiii
and genetics, 6–7, 18, 152
health-related changes in, 21–22
individual differences in, 152
malleability of, xiii, 4–5, 27–28, 29, 397, 406n19
and opportunity, 8–9
organizing traits, 14–15
and physical traits, 9–10
and role models, 22–26
scientific measurement of, 10–17
temperament versus, 19
traits in, 5–6, 8, 13–17
See also specific traits, including conscientiousness
phantom limb effect, 100, 209
pharmaceutical cognitive enhancers (PCEs), 347–49
Physical Intelligence (Grafton), 280
physical traits, 9–10
Pickens, T. Boone, 399
Pick's disease, 20
Pierce, John R., xv–xvi, 163
pilots, sensory perception of, 98–99, 417n98
Pink, Daniel, 371
pitolisant, 350
pituitary glands, xx
placebo effects, 220–21
police, biases in, 9
Pollan, Michael, 279, 359
Polya, George, 420n130
polyglots, 69
polypharmacy, 230–31
Pontzer, Herman, 276–77

Popper, Karl, 141
positive psychology, 191
positivity bias in older adults, xi, 142, 144, 196, 202, 371–73, 400
Posner, Michael, xxii, 34–35, 54, 135
Potter, Dennis, 395
prebiotics, 275
predispositions, 19, 152, 164
prefrontal cortex
  and abstract thinking, 135–38
  age-related changes in, 133–34
  declining efficacy of, 78
  functions of, 57, 133
  and GABA receptors, 57
  and impulse control, 77
  meditation's effect on, 365
  and neural pruning, 69
  and pain perception, 215
  and processing speed, 133
  role of, in successful aging, 77
  and self-control, 20
  shrinking of, with age, 77
  and volunteerism, 203
prenatal influences on development, xx, 185
presbyopia, 101, 104
prions, xviii, 334
prisoners, aggressive behavior of, 189
probiotics, 271, 273, 274–75, 449–50
problem solving
  and abstract thinking, 138
  and analogical reasoning, 140–41, 421n140
  and creativity, 132, 285–86
  practicing, 132, 141–42
  and sleep deprivation, 299
  and wisdom, 119
procedural memory, 39, 43, 54
processed foods, 276, 279, 326
processing speed, 132–35, 138
procrastination, 154
productivity span, 249
progesterone, 167, 304
prosocial attitudes/behaviors, 142
prostate cancer screening, 27
protein, 266–68
Prozac, xvi, 74, 162–63, 347
Prusiner, Stan, xvii, xviii, 334
psilocybin, 182, 358–59
psychedelics, 182, 358–61
psychotherapy, 5, 29, 164, 190
putamen, 182–83, 197
Putnam, Robert, 180
puzzles, solving, 132

quality of life
  and advance medical directives, 390–93
  and couplehood, 378
  and difficult conversations, 386–89
  and doctor-patient relationships, 382–86
  effects of new endeavors on, 25
  and end-of-life care, 394–96
  and future-impairment preparedness, 389
  and healthy life expectancy (HALE), 370
  and hormone replacement therapy, 169
  and hospitals, 390
  and longevity, 367–70
  and meaningful work, 378–82
  measuring, 374–78
  and positivity in older adults, 371–73
  and social comparisons, 373–74
  and three questions to consider, 387–89
  and volunteerism, 381
Quintana, Carlos, 353

Ramachandran, Vilayanur, 100
Ramsay, Jim, 175, 282
realism, 22
recreational drugs, 358–61
reflectivity, 142, 143
regeneration, 314–15, 341–42, *342*
rejection, feelings of, xiv
relationships
  bonds of, xxii
  and cognitive function, 376
  exercising compassion in, 28–29
  and happiness, 376–78
  importance of meaningful, 200, 376–78
  lack of, 155
  marriages and couplehood, 193, 376, 377, 378, 471n378
  with parents, 184, 378, 397
  positive, 144
  and progesterone production, 167
  rumination's effect on, 165
  and sex hormones, 167
  social media's effects on, 180–81
  and telomere length, 326–27
relativism, valuing, 142

reliability, 21
religious practices, 191
Remembering (Bartlett), 55
reproduction, 323
resentments, letting go of, 398
resilience, 6, 158
resource, treating the elderly as a, xxii
respect, loss of, xiv
responsibility (personality trait), 10
"resting bitch face," 9
resting-state mode of attention, 79
restless leg syndrome, 302
resveratrol, 266, 339, 341
retirement
  and acceleration of end of life, xiv, 135
  forced, xiv, xv, 200–201, 380
  and loss of sense of agency, 196–97
  and quality of life, 378–82
  Sanders on, 25
  and tendency to turn inward, 199
  and unretirement, 379
Richards, Keith, 296
Richards, Michael, 7
rickety-bridge experiment, 148–49
rigidity, 27
risk taking behaviors, 18, 21, 167
Ritalin, 348, 350–51
rivastigmine (Exelon), 352–53
Robertson, Anna Mary (Grandma Moses), 24, *24*
Rock, Irv, 52, 53, 90, 92–93, 94, 112
Rodale, Jerome, 331
Roenneberg, Till, 240–41
role models, 22–26, 199–201
roles of older adults, transitions in, 21
Rollins, Sonny, 199, 372–73, 374
Romanian orphan crisis, 186–87, 196
Ronstadt, Linda, 170–71
Ruby, Graham, 321
rules, following, 8, 20
rumination, 164–66

sadness, 150
salmon, 153–54
Sanders, Harland, 25
Sapolsky, Robert, 153–54
Sartre, Jean-Paul, 179, 428n179
satisfaction in life, 373–74
Schiffman, Susan, 112
Schindler, Meyer, 383
schizophrenia, 68–69
school performance, 120–21, 128
SCN (suprachiasmatic nucleus), 237–38, 239, 240, 243–44, 247, 302
seasonal affective disorder (SAD), 247
sedentary lifestyles, 280–81, 287–88
Segovia, Andrés, 23
Seinfeld, Jerry, 7
self-discipline, 20
self-efficacy, 196–99
self-reflection, 142
self-regulation, 4, 19, 20, 26, 365
Selye, Hans, 154
semantic memory (general knowledge store), 39–41, 51, 54
senescence, 313, 331–32, 354
sensory perception, 88–114
  adaptations in, 94–98, 99–100
  of animals, 88–89
  of babies, 66–68
  of brightness, *91*, 91–92, *92*
  and complex environments, 113–14
  decline in, 60, 87
  illusions in, 93
  logic of, 90–94, *91*
  and "Mouse Wreckers" WB cartoon, 98
  and perceptional completion, 102–3
  and phantom limb effect, 100
  and physical interaction with environment, 99
  of pilots, 98–99, 415n98
  and prism adaptation experiments, 94–95, 96–97
  and rubber hand illusion, 97–98
  and sense of self, 98
  sense of touch, 107–8
  senses of taste and smell, 108–13
  and sensory receptors, 89
  See also hearing; vision and visual system
sentimentality, 37–38
sentinel hypothesis, 241, 242
September 11, 2001, terrorist attacks, 46
serotonin, xvi, 18, 76, 144, 162, 271–72
sexual activity, 168, 377
Shepard, Roger, xxii, 34
Shereshevsky, Solomon, 38
Shimamura, Art, 55–56, 77, 133, 202, 346, 398
Shomrat, Tal, 314–15
short-term memory, 39, 42, 55, 56
Shultz, George, 58, 117, 118, 244, 379

Sierra, Felipe, 341
sign language, 73, 75
Simon, Paul, 170, 171
Simons, Daniel, 345–46
Simpson, Alan, 398
Sinclair, David, 340, 341
Slaughter, Louis, 201
SLC6A4 (gene), 18
sleep, 295–310
  age-related changes in, 302–4
  and alcohol consumption, 266
  and Alzheimer's disease, xvii
  and blue light exposure, 238, 303, 308
  and Bredesen Protocol, xvii
  and caffeine intake, 248–49, 306–7
  and cataract surgery, 238
  and cognitive function, 309
  and diet, 246–47
  difficulties with, 160–61
  disturbances in, 302–3
  and dreaming, 51, 300
  and hypersomnia, 303–4
  and insomnia, 161, 163, 303
  and memory consolidation, 51
  and napping, 303
  need for (sleep drive), 295
  and pain, 230
  and prescription sleep aids, 160–61
  resetting sleep cycle, 300–302
  and restless leg syndrome, 302
  restorative function of, 295, 298, 299
  sleep hygiene, xvii, 161, 191, 246–48, 308–10
  and social isolation and loneliness, 191
  special problems of men, 306
  special problems of women, 304–6
  time required for, 297, 299, 301–2
  and work/school schedules, 240–41
  See also melatonin
sleep deprivation
  and Alzheimer's, xvii, 299
  and amygdala activation, 298
  cognitive penalties of, xvii, 299
  epidemic levels of, 297
  and post-lunch energy dips, 246
  risks associated with, xvi–xvii, 241, 299
  social factors contributing to, 297
  and work/school schedules, 240–41
smell, sense of, 108–13
smiling, emotional effects of, 28
smoking, 104, 253, 340, 351
sociability
  age-related changes in, 194–96
  in children's temperament, 19
  and COACH principle, xxiv, 29, 118
  fear's ancient link to, 188
  and physical traits, 10
  time perspective in, 194–96
  See also social engagement
social anxiety, 182–83, 190, 216
social cohesion, low levels of, 326
social comparisons, 373–74
social engagement, 179–204
  and attachment theory, 184
  and autism spectrum, 398–99
  barriers to, 398
  benefits of, 398
  and brain development, 196
  and cognitive function, 26, 202, 203–4, 398
  and coping styles, 165
  and digital devices, 375
  and easing social awkwardness, 191
  evolutionary basis of, 183
  importance of, 179, 376, 398
  and internal reward system, 189–90
  and longevity, 320
  negative, 202
  and pain management strategies, 227
  and preference for solitude, 199
  and religious affiliation, 191
  and retirement planning, 387–89
  and social development, 183–88
  and social media, 180–81
  and social stress, 184
  and telomere length, 326–27
  and volunteerism, 193–94, 202–3
  and work, 199–201
social media, xxv, 180–81, 375
social psychology, 28
socioeconomic influences, xx
socioemotional selectivity theory, 194–96
soldiers, injured, 209
Solomon (biblical), 143, 421n143
soy, 267–68
spatial memory and skills, 39, 41, 81, 94–95, 126
spirituality, 124, 142, 191
spite, 150
spontaneity, 8
sports, competing in, 22–23

spouses, losing, 193. *See also* marriages and couplehood
Srivastava, Mansi, 314
standard American diet, 279
statistical inferencing, 70–71
Steinem, Gloria, 394, 401
stem cells, 63
Sternberg, Robert, 124–25, 418n122
Stewart, Kristen, 9
Stills, Stephen, 121, 296
stimulants, 349–52
stress and stress response, 153–58
  and allostasis/allostatic load, 155–58
  biomarkers of, 155
  chronic, 327
  compassion's effect on, 29
  and emotional eating, 278
  factors influencing, 157
  and glucocorticoid receptors in the hippocampus, xx
  and longevity, 320
  and memory testing, 59, 409n60
  and microbiome, 272–73
  optimal levels of, 29
  and parents' impact children's stress responses, 184
  reducing levels of, 155–56, 158
  of salmon, 153–54
  and self-efficacy, 197
  and social isolation, 189
  and stress hormones, 29, 155, 165, 179
  and telomere length, 326–27, 328
strokes, 83–84
  aftereffects of, 83–84
  as cause of death, 207, *208*
  causes of, 83
  and confabulations/inferences, 47, 48–49
  hemispatial neglect following, 96
  and personality changes, 20
  prevention of, 83
  types of, 83
substance P (neurochemical), 225
success, 26, 27
sugar, refined, xxi
Summitt, Pat, 381
sundowner's syndrome, 245
superfoods, 278
supplements, xvii, xviii, 258–59, 264–65, 266, 386
Sur, Mriganka, 76
surgency, 19
surprise, 150
survival, emotions related to, 147–49
Suwabe, Kazuya, 291
Swedberg, Heidi, 7
synesthesia, 67

Tac2/NkB (neurokinin), 189, 225
tanezumab, 229
Tang, Paul, 192
tardigrades, *316*, 316–17
taste, sense of, 108–13
teaching ability, 126–27, 128
technology, 56, 58, 78, 87, 108, 303
telomerase, 316, 327–29, 366
Telomere Effect, The (Epel), 328–29
telomeres, 109, 316, 325–29, *326*, 331
temperament, 19
temporal lobes, 51, 52
tenacity, 169
testing oneself, 23
testosterone, 18, 167–68, 169, 306, 354
thalamus, 299
thalidomide, 74
thinking outside the box, 129–30, *130*, *131*, 421n130
thioflavin T, 342
Thomas, Alma, 24
Thomas, Dylan, xi, 285
Thompson, Harriette, 283
Thompson, Walter, 292
thrill-seeking behaviors, 21
ThyssenKrupp steel factory, 240–41
tickling, 216
tinnitus, 105–6
tolerance, xxii, 142
Tolkien, J. R. R., 133
Tolstoy, Lev, 133
Tomlin, Lily, 23
touch, sense of, 61, 100, 107–8
traffic fatalities, 241
trans fats, 261
transhumanist movement, 363, 471n365
travel, 114, 245–46, 250
Tribole, Evelyn, 277
trust, difficulties with, 74
turmeric, 386
Turner syndrome, 65
Tversky, Amos, xxiii

Twenge, Jean, 375
twins, 9

uncertainty, coping with, 142, 143, 156

Vaillant, George, 376, 377
Van Deursen, Jan, 331–32
Vaupel, Jim, 318
Velleman, David, 368, 371
verbal-linguistic intelligence, 124
Vijg, Jan, 317–18
virtual reality environments for pain management, 394–95
vision and visual system
  age-related dysfunction in, 87, 101–4
  and cataracts, 104
  and glasses, 87, 96, 101
  and perceptional completion, 102–3
  and presbyopia, 101, 104
  and prism adaptation experiments, 94–95, 96–97
  and remapping to auditory cortex, 75–76
  and rubber hand illusion, 97–98
  and visual hallucinations, 105
  at week four of gestation, 62
visual-spatial intelligence, 124
vitamin B_{12}, 79, 355–56
volunteerism, 193–94, 202–3, 381, 382

waist size, as predicted by childhood personality traits, 4
Waldinger, Robert, 376
Walford, Roy, 330
Walker, Matthew, xvi–xvii, 296–97, 301, 303
Wall, Patrick, 210, 434n209
Waters, Maxine, 201
Webb, Spud, 7
Weinstein, Jack, 57, 134–35
Weir, Bob, 356, 357
West, Kanye, 9
West, Paul, 137
Westworld (series), 32
White, Betty, 201, 398
Whitman, Walt, 399
whole grains, 261, 265, 270, 276
Why We Sleep (Walker), 296–97
Williams, Robert Lee, II, 128
Williams, Serena, 127, 364
Williams, Yauger, 282–83
Wilson, Brian, 360
Winehouse, Amy, 27
winter months and biological clocks, 246
wisdom, 142–45
  as advantage of aging, 400
  four factors contributing to, 119, 143
  Glück's MORE model of, 143
  and microdosing, 361
  neurobiological basis of, 144
  neurocognitive perspective on, 37
  nine themes of, 142
  precursors of, 144–45
  and problem solving, 119
Wisløff, Ulrik, 288
withdrawal, periods of, 164–65
women, emotional vulnerability of, 20
Wonder, Stevie, 146, 160
Woodstock generation, xiii, xxi, 358
work, xv, 199–201, 240–41, 378–82. *See also* retirement
World Trade Center attacks of 2001, 46

Yassa, Michael, 291
yoga, 224–25, 227
Young, Neil, 399

Zeisel, John, 82
Zika virus, 74
Zoloft, 190
Zuger, Abigail, 84